■ **Improved Integrated Case** provides students with theoretical and practical experience

The Hobbit's Choice Restaurant is an integrated case that makes learning more efficient and enables students to understand the interrelationships in the steps of the research process. We've retained and improved by offering additional versions of the dataset to allow instructors to keep their course material new. Please visit **www.prenhall.com/burnsbush** to view the new datasets. *The Hobbit's Choice Restaurant* offers students a chance to experience the research process by staying with the same material as they:

1. Define the problem and research objectives

2. Select a data collection method

3. Apply measurement concepts

4. Develop a questionnaire

5. Make sampling decisions

6. Analyze the data

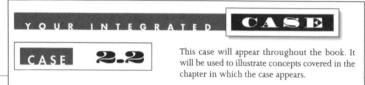

YOUR INTEGRATED **CASE**

CASE **2.2**

This case will appear throughout the book. It will be used to illustrate concepts covered in the chapter in which the case appears.

THE HOBBIT'S CHOICE: A RESTAURANT

Jeff Dean is a restaurant supply sales representative. He works in a large metropolitan area and calls on many of the restaurant owners in the city. His dream is to one day own his own restaurant. He had saved a substantial amount of his earnings during his 15 years in

■ **NEW Certification Program for the Industry.**

We are pleased to be the first text in marketing research to provide information on the new certification program which was adopted by the Marketing Research Association in February, 2005. Marketing Researchers will now be able to be certified similar to CPA's or CFA's. The adoption of a certification program by the Marketing Research Association represents a significant event in the marketing industry.

Fifth Edition

Marketing Research

ALVIN C. BURNS

Louisiana State University

RONALD F. BUSH

University of West Florida

PEARSON

Prentice
Hall

Upper Saddle River, New Jersey 07458

Library of Congress Cataloging-in-Publication Data
Burns, Alvin C.
    Marketing research / Alvin C. Burns, Ronald F. Bush—5th ed.
        p. cm.
    "SPSS integration"—Pref.
    Includes bibliographical references and index.
    ISBN 0-13-147732-3
    1. Marketing research 2. SPSS for Windows. I. Bush, Ronald F. II. Title.
HF5415.2.B779 2006
658.8'3—dc22

                                    2005053464

Acquisitions Editor: Katie Stevens
VP/Editorial Director: Jeff Shelstad
Project Manager: Melissa Pellerano
Editorial Assistant: Christine Ietto
Media Project Manager: Peter Snell
Marketing Manager: Ashaki Charles
Marketing Assistant: Joanna Sabella
Associate Director Production Editorial: Judy Leale
Managing Editor (Production): Renata Butera
Production Editor: Mary Ellen Morrell
Permissions Supervisor: Charles Morris
Associate Director, Manufacturing: Vincent Scelta
Production Manager: Arnold Vila
Manufacturing Buyer: Michelle Klein
Design Manager: Maria Lange
Art Director: Kevin Kall
Interior Design: QT Design
Cover Design: Kevin Kall
Illustrator (Interior): GGS Book Services
Director, Image Resource Center: Melinda Reo
Manager, Rights and Permissions: Zina Arabia
Manager, Visual Research: Beth Brenzel
Manager, Cover Visual Research and Permissions: Karen Sanatar
Image Permission Coordinator: Richard Rodrigues
Manager, Print Production: Christy Mahon
Composition/Full-Service Project Management: GGS Book Services
Printer/Binder: Courier-Kendallville

Credits and acknowledgments borrowed from other sources and reproduced, with permission, in this textbook appear on appropriate page within text. Photo credits appear on page 647.

Microsoft® and Windows® are registered trademarks of the Microsoft Corporation in the U.S.A. and other countries. Screen shots and icons reprinted with permission from the Microsoft Corporation. This book is not sponsored or endorsed by or affiliated with the Microsoft Corporation.

Pearson Education LTD.
Pearson Education Singapore, Pte. Ltd
Pearson Education, Canada, Ltd
Pearson Education—Japan

Pearson Education Australia PTY, Limited
Pearson Education North Asia Ltd
Pearson Educación de Mexico, S.A. de C.V.
Pearson Education Malaysia, Pte. Ltd

Brief Contents

Contents

THE MARKETING RESEARCH PROCESS 22

THE MARKETING RESEARCH INDUSTRY 40

DEFINING THE PROBLEM AND DETERMINING RESEARCH OBJECTIVES 84

6

USING SECONDARY DATA AND ONLINE INFORMATION DATABASES 144

STANDARDIZED INFORMATION SOURCES 176

OBSERVATION, FOCUS GROUPS, AND OTHER QUALITATIVE METHODS 200

SURVEY DATA–COLLECTION METHODS 232

Advantages of Surveys 235

Surveys Provide for Standardization 235
Surveys Are Easy to Administer 235
Surveys Get "Beneath the Surface" 235
Surveys Are Easy to Analyze 236
Surveys Reveal Subgroup Differences 236

Four Alternative Types of Data Collection 236

Person-Administered Surveys (without Computer
　Assistance) 238
Computer-Administered Surveys 239
Self-Administered Surveys (without Computer
　Assistance) 241
Mixed-Mode Surveys 242

Descriptions of Data–Collection Modes 243

Person-Administered Interviews 245
Computer-Administered Interviews 250
Self-Administered Surveys 255

Choice of the Survey Method 258

How Much Time Is There for Data Collection? 260
How Much Money Is There for Data Collection? 260
What Is the Incidence Rate? 260
Are There Cultural and/or Infrastructure
　Considerations? 261
What Type of Respondent Interaction Is Required? 261

◾ **Summary 261**
◾ **Key Terms 262**
◾ **Review Questions/Applications 263**

10 MEASUREMENT IN MARKETING RESEARCH 268

DESIGNING THE QUESTIONNAIRE 298

DETERMINING HOW TO SELECT THE SAMPLE 328

DETERMINING THE SIZE OF A SAMPLE 362

DATA COLLECTION IN THE FIELD, NONRESPONSE ERROR, AND QUESTIONNAIRE SCREENING 390

17

TESTING FOR DIFFERENCES BETWEEN TWO GROUPS OR AMONG MORE THAN TWO GROUPS 484

20

THE MARKETING RESEARCH REPORT: PREPARATION AND PRESENTATION 596

Marketing Research was created with the undergraduate student of marketing research explicitly in mind. Accordingly, we have not included techniques that are more appropriate for advanced classes of marketing research. Our many years of teaching experience led us to understand that most undergraduate students do not get excited about the theoretical rationale for statistical formulas. We set out to write a book that demonstrates how to use statistical tools for marketing research. We leave the explanation of theoretical underpinnings of those tools to our colleagues who teach statistics to our students. Our approach of providing a conceptual understanding and a hands-on, practical what-and-how-to-do-it presentation has been successful since our first edition. Our adopters confirm this approach by telling us that their students give the book high marks on course evaluations: they understand the book and find it interesting to read. We believe an understandable book in the hands of a capable instructor enhances the chances of student learning, and that is the goal of all of us who teach marketing research.

SPSS Integration. Our goal has always been to help students use SPSS software without having techniques and details get in the way of interpretation. Our philosophy is to demonstrate when a statistical tool is needed, to teach students which statistical tool to run, how to run it, and how to interpret the output. Accordingly, we have integrated the software into the text and provided output screens that help students see what to look for in analyzing data. Furthermore, we have developed a Student Assistant tutorial that walks students through the SPSS software (**www.prenhall.com/burnsbush**).

HOW THE FIFTH EDITION IS IMPROVED

In writing the fifth edition, we have continued to "hear the voice of the market" by listening carefully to comments made by students, adopters of the book, and reviewers. For each new edition we get critiques from both adopters and nonadopters. We have gathered this data in a number of ways including unsolicited e-mail and other comments from our adopters, formal reviews conducted by our publisher, suggestions and recommendations of our students, and our own experiences using the text.

New Certification Program for the Industry and Other Current Information from Industry Practitioners.
The field of marketing research is truly a moving target, and the velocity of change in the industry has increased dramatically over the life of our fourth edition. The industry adopted a certification program in February, 2005. This represents a significant event in the industry as different organizations worked together for a certification program sponsored by the Marketing Research Association. We are pleased to be the first text in marketing research to provide information on the certification program.

Computer-based and online marketing research practices have proliferated in the last few years, and major parts of the research industry have transitioned rapidly into high-tech status. We have observed this transition, and we have noticed that academic reports, while insightful, lag behind these changes. Consequently, in order to do justice to our treatment of online marketing research in our fifth edition, we have relied on input from our colleagues in the marketing research industry.

Online Survey Research and Spam. The practice of sending spam threatens online survey research. Potential respondents, flooded with unwanted e-mails, will come to regard all but the most personal messages as trash. Marketing research organizations fight to reduce spam. Though the "Can Spam Act" was passed in 2003, two years later it was estimated that 60% of all e-mail that enters in-boxes everyday is spam![62] A **"Do Not Spam"** registry, allowing citizens to register their e-mail addresses to avoid spamming, similar to the "Do Not Call" registry, has been considered by the FTC. However, in June 2004 the FTC recommended not to establish such a register. The FTC cited as their primary reason lack of an effective authentication system and the inability to enforce the registry. In fact, the report stated that there was a high likelihood that such a list would be obtained by spammers and those registering would receive more spam![63] Marketing research firms have not been included in the definitions of spam abusers and have not, thus far, been included in any anti-spam legislation. In addition to marketing research organizations there are consumer organizations to fight it such as CAUCE, Coalition Against Unsolicited Commercial Email (**http://www.cauce.org/**) and MAPS, Mail Abuse Prevention System (**www.mail.abuse.org**).

New Online Research Applications Are Highlighted.
A few years ago we correctly identified the significance of online research applications in the industry. In fact, we felt so strongly about the potential of online research at the time that we subtitled the fourth edition, *"Online Research Applications."* True to our predictions, online research is firmly entrenched today as standard operating procedure in the vast majority of marketing research firms. Still, new online innovations are being developed daily and we highlight these new innovations throughout the 5th edition.

New SPSS Student Version Software Integrated in the 5th Edition.
We keep current with the latest SPSS Student Version software editions and integrate the SPSS improved software with each edition of *Marketing Research.* A major factor for the success of our earlier editions has been the SPSS Student Version software that accompanies the textbook. In fact, if "imitation is the sincerest form of flattery," we are indeed thrilled that practically all of our competitors have followed our lead and have SPSS Student Version CDs bundled with their texts.

STRENGTHS OF MARKETING RESEARCH, FIFTH EDITION

Marketing Research, Fifth Edition, builds on the strengths of earlier editions, and it has some unique features that are new strengths. The key strengths are described as follows:

Active Learning Exercises. A new feature developed for the fifth edition, responds to The Association to Advance Collegiate Schools of Business-International (AACSB)'s recommendations to assess the student learning. Embedded in each chapter, are exercises that require immediate use of the knowledge that the student just acquired. That is, the exercises are assigned while the learning is "fresh" and are directly related to the text content. The active learning exercises include website visitations so students can experience marketing research examples, mental exercises for students to test their knowledge, computations where students make use of data analysis concepts to ensure that they can apply them properly, and SPSS analyses and interpretations using the integrated dataset to further familiarize students with this learning resource.

Almost everyone has heard of the "Nielsen TV ratings," yet few people know much about them. Where can you find ratings? How are ratings collected? Are the ratings accurate measurements of TV audiences? What is a rating and what is a share? Does Nielsen Media Research cancel TV programs? Here is your opportunity to learn about a well-known, though little understood, firm in the marketing research industry. To answer these and other questions, go to: **http://www.nielsenmedia.com/index.html.** As a suggestion, go to FAQ. Also take a look at the options under Quick Links.

Nielsen
Media Research

Updated Industry Examples Integrated Throughout the Textbook.
With each new edition we spend a considerable amount of time talking with our friends in the marketing research industry. Our goal is to bring to you the latest techniques, analyses, and trends happening in the industry. As we noted earlier, many of these new innovations have been in the area of online research. These examples, and others, we cite throughout the text. In several cases we also illustrate the applications of these new techniques with actual client firms. We think keeping our readers current with the world of the marketing research practitioner is essential to understanding the research industry today.

SPSS™ Student Version 13.0.
SPSS Student Version is state of the art statistical software and SPSS is the most popular statistical software in the marketing research industry. It has been a proven program in colleges and universities for many years. This student copy of SPSS will last for one year from the time it is first loaded on a student's computer. For schools having SPSS available in an on-campus computer lab, instructors may order this text without the SPSS Student Version 13.0 CD at a price discount. (0-13-147730-7).

Annotated SPSS Menus and Output.
An improvement in our fifth edition is the inclusion of easy-to-use, annotated screen captures that show SPSS menu click-streams as well as SPSS output. These screen captures are faithful to what students will see when they run SPSS, and the annotations are in the form of simulated post-it notes, arrows, circles, colored highlights, and clip art. The

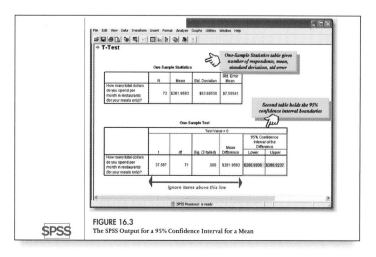

FIGURE 16.3
The SPSS Output for a 95% Confidence Interval for a Mean

fifth edition screen captures are cleaner and less cluttered than those in the fourth edition, so by looking at the annotated SPSS menu clickstreams, students will learn what menus to use, how to make them appear, and how to use them. With the annotated SPSS output, students' attention will be directed to the precise parts of the output that are relevant, and the annotations show them how to interpret the SPSS output.

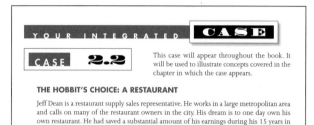

YOUR INTEGRATED CASE

CASE 2.2

This case will appear throughout the book. It will be used to illustrate concepts covered in the chapter in which the case appears.

THE HOBBIT'S CHOICE: A RESTAURANT

Jeff Dean is a restaurant supply sales representative. He works in a large metropolitan area and calls on many of the restaurant owners in the city. His dream is to one day own his own restaurant. He had saved a substantial amount of his earnings during his 15 years in

Improved Integrated Case. As a result of feedback we received to our first three editions, we introduced an integrated case, *The Hobbit's Choice*, in the fourth edition. Based on positive feedback, we have retained the integrated case in the fifth edition, but, we have added a significant improvement. We offer the instructor additional versions of the dataset to allow them to keep their course material new. The SPSS dataset for this survey is provided on our Prentice Hall Textbook Web site (**www.prenhall.com/burnsbush**), and all data analysis topic SPSS examples in the book use this dataset.

User-friendly Descriptions of Difficult Concepts. Some of our adopters have voiced a desire for less emphasis on statistical formulas and more on interpretation of SPSS output. The more complex statistical analyses, such as t-tests, ANOVA, and regression, are more conceptual in description, and more emphasis is placed on how to interpret the SPSS output for these analyses. In our sample size chapter, we have not eliminated formulas, but we have based the idea of sample size around nine tenets so that students will focus on the basic concepts, rather than memorize formulas. Again, adopters have commented that this approach is appropriate and should be continued.

Defining Problems Correctly Is Needed to Solve the Problems

Where We Are:
1 Establish the need for marketing research
2 Define the problem
3 Establish research objectives
4 Determine research design
5 Identify information types and sources
6 Determine methods of accessing data
7 Design data collection forms
8 Determine sample plan and size
9 Collect data
10 Analyze data

Golfers the world over golf industry, *Golf Dige* lishes three other highly ferent markets of golf readers; *Golf World, Golf fc Golf World Business.* Publishers often conduct m need information to help them evaluate readershi levels in cover stories, and so on. They also condu make better promotional decisions. While most g very few know that Golf Digest Companies is al Their Corporate Marketing and Research Departm service research/marketing consulting firm. Not o four magazines with information, they also solve facturers of golf equipment, travel destination reso cals, and apparel.

To help potential advertisers make dec Corporate Marketing and Research Department information such as how much time readers sp how "involved" readers are with the magazine zines, and, of course, number of sales of magaz

An 11-step Process Approach to Marketing Research. Because we believe it aids learning marketing research, we kept our process approach by using the 11-step marketing research process that we used in the first four editions. Beginning in Chapter 3, we discuss marketing research as a step-by-step process, and we refer to this process continually as the student makes his or her way through the text. With each new chapter, we highlight the appropriate section of the research process so that the students always know where they are in terms of the overall research process. They are reminded that each section of the research process is linked to some previous section.

New End-of-Chapter Cases. *Marketing Research, Fifth Edition*, contains many new cases designed to teach students to apply the knowledge they have learned in the chapter material. In an effort to keep students' interest high, we strive to find current examples that are relevant to learning marketing research. As an example, we open Chapter 1 with a case about the Apple iPod™. Other cases feature current "hot topics" such as hybrid automobiles and actual online panel data. Cases feature many industries including electronics, tourism, consumer packaged goods (CPGs) and, of course, the marketing research industry.

Management Perspective Throughout. Our textbook is written using a manager's perspective. Chapter 4 emphasizes the role of management being involved to define the research problem properly. We present marketing research as a useful source of information, but one that has its own costs. Students are taught that managers must weigh the benefits of more information with the costs of obtaining that information. Throughout the text, a decision-making approach is used. Students are also taught the many trade-offs involved in research that managers constantly make, the use of a probability sample versus a non probability sample, the effects of undersampling, and so on.

Global Applications. Marketing research today is very different than it was just a few years ago. Research firms work all over the globe. As we note in Chapter 3, revenue from international operations of research firms continues to grow, and online research applications make global research practical and affordable. We highlight our examples of doing marketing research internationally by using the globe icon throughout the book.

Creating Awareness of the Ethically Sensitive Issues Confronting the Industry. In Chapter 3 we present the major ethical issues confronting the marketing research industry. We have cases devoted to ethics in the industry and we refer students to several industry association sources to examine codes of ethics used in the industry. We also provide examples of ethical problems throughout our chapters, and we use our ethics icon to point out ethical examples to students. We hope, by doing this, students will be more aware of the areas that are "ethically sensitive" whether they are in the research industry or acting as clients in the industry.

Review Questions and Applications. At the end of each chapter we provide review questions and applications. These materials are provided to aid students' learning of marketing research. Some of the questions require answers that may be taken directly from the test material. Such questions serve the purpose of organizing and reinforcing what the student has just read. Other questions or applications require the students to synthesize the chapter material with other business course material. Finally, there are applications that require extensive work outside of class—for instance—talking with local business firms, looking up additional library material, or working with SPSS. Professors can assign different questions/applications to suit their particular course objectives. Adopters who are not using a class project will find adequate supplementary material by focusing on some of the application questions, if desired.

Marginal Notes and Icons. Students will find comments in the margins. We do this to repeat important points and to serve as effective study guides. The icons are readily identifiable visual aids that signal text material that deals with ethical considerations, online research, global applications, or SPSS-related topics.

Datasets, Including Different Versions of the Integrated Case Dataset. Datasets are available to be downloaded from our textbook Web site (**www.prenhall.com/burnsbush**). In addition to our integrated case, "The Hobbit's Choice Restaurant" dataset, there is a dataset based on an online survey conducted by an online automobile dealer. These datasets are provided to aid the students in learning and running various analyses using SPSS. In addition to the "standard" version that is integrated into the textbook examples and end-of-chapter cases, we have developed additional versions that yield results quite differently from those in the standard version. Instructors have a choice as to how to assign the dataset versions to students to challenge them to interpret a completely different set of findings for the Hobbit's Choice Restaurant survey.

In conclusion, we have studied recent trends and discussed marketing research issues and practices with individuals who work daily in the marketing research industry, and listened to our students, adopters, reviewers, and the professionals at Prentice Hall and SPSS. We have contemplated the various ways to bring practice and conceptual understanding together and we have created *Marketing Research, Fifth Edition*. We have also endeavored to retain the winning features of our previous editions, so we emphasize that we have improved the textbook, rather than change it for the sake of change. We hope you'll enjoy learning or teaching from the fifth edition as much as we enjoyed writing it.

RESOURCES

Based upon our own years of experience in teaching, we know that teaching marketing research can be a challenge. The subject matter of marketing research ranges from plain descriptions of research company services to explanations of complicated statistical analysis with many different topics in between. Teaching across all of these topics requires a multifaceted approach. Consequently, we have developed a variety of teaching and learning aids, and adopters of this textbook will receive the following ancillary materials to help them prepare their course and teach it effectively.

WebSurveyor. WebSurveyor Corporation is the leading provider of online survey software that empowers people with real-time feedback to drive their businesses. Through its Academic Grant Program, WebSurveyor provides students with the practical experience of conducting online surveys. Websurveyor can be used for hands-on market research projects, social and political studies, or any other information gathering assignments deemed appropriate by the instructor. Through the grant program, students are getting the same software that is used by industry practitioners worldwide to collect and analyze vital data.

Instructors at universities, colleges, community colleges, business and trade schools applying for the grant are requested to fill out a brief online form at: **www.web-surveyor.com/prenhall**. WebSurveyor evaluation committee will make a decision within five business days.

Companion Web Site (www.prenhall.com/burnsbush). Resources for students and instructors may be found at our Web site. Students may view chapter outlines, chapter objectives, case study hints and take sample tests for each chapter.

Instructor's Manual. There is a comprehensive instructor's manual prepared by Al Burns. The manual has chapter outlines, key terms, teaching pointers, answers to end-of-chapter questions, answers to active learning exercises as needed, and case solutions.

PowerPoint Slides. We have greatly improved our PowerPoint presentation slides with the fifth edition. The presentations are now animated and dynamic, rather than static. The file(s) may be downloaded by students or instructors from the textbook Web site.

Test Bank. There is a test bank of objective questions prepared by Ron Bush. We do not outsource our test questions. This test bank is available from Prentice Hall and can be loaded into Prentice Hall's TestGen software. TestGen allows random selection of test questions, modification of individual questions, or insertion of new questions into a test. A printed version of the test bank is also available.

Instructor's Resource Center (IRC). One source for all your supplement needs. The IRC is available online at **www.prenhall.com/marketing**, where instructors can access our complete array of teaching materials. Simply go to the catalog page for this text and click on the Instructor link to download the Instructor's Manual, Test Item File, TestGen, and PowerPoint slides. Note: Faculty registration is required. The IRC is also available on CD-ROM for your convenience.

SPSS Student Assistant. With previous editions, we created the SPSS Student Assistant, a stand-alone tutorial that teaches students how to use and interpret SPSS. With the fifth edition, the SPSS Student Assistant may be downloaded from the Prentice Hall textbook Web site. Upon downloading the software, installation on one's personal computer is simple, and the SPSS Student Assistant will reside there for easy, immediate access. The videos show cursor movements and resulting SPSS operations and output. There is a test for each Student Assistant session so students may assess their learning of the material.

ACKNOWLEDGMENTS

Many people are involved in writing and producing a book. We are fortunate to have so many friends and colleagues who provide support to us with each edition of *Marketing Research*. First, we want to thank the professional staff at Prentice Hall, especially our editor, Katie Stevens. We have worked with Katie for several years now, and we have found her to be a superb editor in every respect. She is very knowledgeable of the publishing industry, has many insightful ideas, and she is an excellent manager of the multiple resources she must handle in order to produce successful textbooks. We appreciate the professional support and positive attitude of Prentice Hall's Marketing Manager, Ashaki Charles. Those not associated with the publishing business do not understand the detailed effort it takes to produce a book. We wish to thank Prentice Hall's patient and fastidious staff: Melissa Pellerano, Mary Ellen Morrell, Judy Leale, and Kevin Kall. We are proud to be associated with the professionals at Prentice Hall.

We are thankful for our colleagues at our universities. They provide us with support, comment, and constructive criticism. We thank our deans, Dean Robert Sumichrast of LSU and Dean Ed Ranelli of UWF, for providing us with an environment conducive to pursuing knowledge in our discipline. We thank the members of our support staff who help us with the myriad of detail necessary to write a book. Thank you, Mary McBride, Phyllis Detrick, Pat Cravat, and Rachel Luecht of UWF. Jane DeBellis is the business reference librarian at the University of West Florida. Ms. DeBellis updated secondary information sources for Chapter 6.

There are always a few people who make special contributions to a book-writing project. Working with outside organizations, setting up schedules, discussing contributions of other individuals, and acquiring permissions to reprint information are but a few of the unseen tasks. We have been fortunate to have someone who not only is very knowledgeable of research and has taught the course but who has excellent time management skills. Dr. Heather H. Donofrio serves as the authors' "managing editor." As always, Dr. Donofrio did an outstanding job.

We could not write a book about the marketing research industry without a great deal of input from those who practice marketing research daily. We are fortunate to have developed many friendships and relations in the industry. We call on these people, ranging from CEO's to highly specialized technicians, to provide our readers with current practice in the industry. Often these individuals share their knowledge of new techniques they are developing as well as evaluations of their use based upon experiences with clients. Often, we ask them to read our manuscripts and give us their reactions. Time and again, our friends spend hours reading our manuscript and penning new information based on their special insights. Many of the contributions made to the fifth edition came from David Nelems, ActiveGroup; Allison Groom, American Heart Association; Yin Chang, Arbitron; Diane Bowers, CASRO; Ronald Tatham and Nancy Bunn, Burke, Inc.; Stephen F. Moore of Claritas, Inc.; Jerry Thomas and Cristi Allen of Decision Analyst; Brent Roderick and David Huffman, ESRI Business Information Solutions; Keith Price and Janice Caston of Greenfield Online; Nancy Wong of Harris Interactive; Lee Smith, Insight Express; Lawrence D. Gibson, Eric Marder, and Associates; Holly Ford, MRSI; Jack Honomichl, Marketing Aid Center; Marilyn Ramond and Penny Wamback, New Product Works, A Division of Arbor Strategy Group; Erica Demme, Knowledge Networks; Dan Quirk, Quirk's Marketing Research Review; B. Venkatesh and Anthony Zahorik, The Burke Institute; William D. Neal, SDR Consulting; Christopher DeAngelis, Terrence Coen, and Dian Urso, Survey Sampling, Inc.; Howard Gershowitz, Mktg., Inc.; Alan Grabowsky, ABACO Research; Stoney A. Scales, ACNielsen Market Decisions; Amy Jacobsen, SPINS; Matt Bell and Mary Ellen Ryan, ACNielsen; Matt Tatham, Nielsen Media Research; Joe Ottaviani, Burke, Inc., and MRA; President Thomas Trebon and Shirley Baker, Carroll College; Robert Smith and Jeff Williams, The Listener Group; Dr. Stephen McDaniel, Texas A&M University; Brian Dautch, CMOR; Don E. Schultz, AGORA, Inc.; Larry Hills, Microtab; Larry Hadcock and Linda Schoenborn, MRA; Megan Burdick, C&R Research; Holly McLennan, 1-800-GOT-JUNK?; Jim Flannery, Synovate; Mathew E. Seward, MarketResearch.com; Christi Allen, Decision Analyst; Carrie Hollenberg, SRI Consulting-Business Intelligence; Jon Last, The Golf Digest Companies; Julie Malkin, TNS-NFO; Michelle McCann, WebSurveyor; David Disher, The Opinion Suites; Benjamin Rietti, E-Tabs; David A. Kay, Research Dimensions; and Jeff Drake, Kimberly-Clark. All of these dedicated professionals in the research industry gave us their time, opinions, and much valuable information.

We wish to thank the many individuals who served as reviewers for this book. Reviewers for the *Fifth Edition* were:

Manoj Agarwal, *Binghamton University*

Anthony R. Fruzzetti, *Johnson & Wales University*

Ben Judd, *University of New Haven*

Aron Levin, *Northern Kentucky University*

James A. Roberts, *Baylor University*

Angelia M. Russell, *West Virginia University Institute of Technology*

Srivatsa Seshadri, *University of Nebraska at Kearney*

Birud Sindhav, *University of Nebraska at Omaha*

Paul Thornton, *Wesley College*

Heiko de B. Wijnholds, *Virginia Commonwealth University*

Bonghee Yoo, *Hofstra University*

Xin Zhao, *University of Utah*

We also thank those who reviewed the first, second, third, and fourth editions, as many of their suggestions and insights are incorporated in these earlier editions:

Linda Anglin, *Mankato State University*

Silva Balasubramanian, *Southern Illinois University*

Ron Beall, *San Francisco State University*

Jacqueline J. Brown, *University of Nevada, Las Vegas*

Joseph D. Brown, *Ball State University*

E. Wayne Chandler, *Eastern Illinois University*

Thomas Cossee, *University of Richmond*

B. Andrew Cudmore, *Florida Institute of Technology*

Eric Freeman, *Concordia University*

Corbett Gaulden Jr., *University of Texas of the Permian Basin*

Ashok Gupta, *Ohio University*

Douglas Hausknecht, *The University of Akron*

M. Huneke, *University of Iowa*

James Leigh, *Texas A&M University*

Bryan Lilly, *University of Wisconsin*

Joann Lindrud, *Mankato State University*

Subhash Lonial, *University of Louisville*

Gary McCain, *Boise State University*

Sumaria Mohan-Neill, *Roosevelt University*

V. Padmanabhan, *Stanford University*

Diane Parente, *State University of New York, Fredonia*

Don Sciglimpaglia, *San Diego State University*

Terri Shaffer, *Southeastern Louisiana University*

Bruce L. Stern, *Portland State University*

John H. Summey, *Southern Illinois University*

Nicolaos E. Synodinos, *University of Hawaii*

Peter K. Tat, *The University of Memphis*

Dr. William Thomas, *University of South Carolina*

Jeff W. Totten, *Southeastern Louisiana State University*

Dr. R. Keith Tudor, *Kennesaw State University*

Steve Vitucci, *University of Central Texas*

Charles J. Yoos II, *Fort Lewis College*

Once again, only we know how much our wives, Jeanne and Libbo, have sacrificed during the times we have been devoted to this book. We are fortunate in that, for both of us, our wives are our best friends and smiling supporters.

Al Burns,
Louisiana State University

Ron Bush,
University of West Florida

1

Introduction to Marketing Research

Welcome to the World of Marketing Research!

Marketing Research Association

You will find marketing research to be a very interesting subject. In this book you will learn about the role marketing research plays in providing decision makers with timely and objective information to help them make informed decisions in many areas. At Burke, Inc., we assist our clients' decision making by conducting the following types of research: brand equity measurement and management, concept testing, price and value research, product testing, choice modeling and analysis, customer loyalty and relationship management, and linkage and integrated services. You will also learn about the marketing research process that Al Burns and Ron Bush conceptualize in an 11-step approach. By using this approach you will have a basic understanding of what it takes to conduct a marketing research project.

Marketing research is a viable, growing industry supported by some outstanding professional associations, including the Marketing Research Association (MRA), CASRO (Council of American Survey Research Organizations), CMOR (Council for Marketing & Opinion Research), QRCA (Qualitative Research Consultants Association), and the American Marketing Association. The Marketing Research Association is dedicated to advancing the practical application, use, and understanding of the opinion and marketing research profession. It promotes excellence by providing members with

a variety of opportunities for advancing and expanding their marketing research and related business skills. The association also acts as an advocate with appropriate governmental entities, other associations, and the public to protect the interests of the marketing research profession. You will learn more about the MRA and the exciting new certification program they have created in Chapter 3.

As you study this book, remember that although very few of you will likely end up being marketing researchers, most of you will be seeking information to help you make business decisions you will face during your careers. This course is your opportunity to learn about the process of generating objective, high-quality information you will rely on to make those important decisions. Finally, for some of you, this book will be your introduction to your career choice. Now, let's get started learning about marketing research!

Joe Ottaviani, President, Marketing Research Association and Managing Director, Burke, Inc.

We wanted to start this new, fifth edition of *Marketing Research* with a welcoming statement to you from Joe Ottaviani. Mr. Ottaviani has many successful years as a marketing research practitioner with one of the industry's leading firms, Burke, Inc. In addition he is the President of the Marketing Research Association, which launched the first ever certification program for marketing researchers.[1] You will learn more about this certification program in Chapter 3.

In this book you will learn about the types of studies conducted by Burke, Inc. and the many other firms in the world of marketing research. We have also included coverage of many of the latest developments in the industry, including the exciting new MRA certification program and several new, innovative services now being offered by industry firms. In this fifth edition, you will also see many examples of the role of marketing research, which is to provide decision makers with information to help them make better decisions. In this book you will learn the process and the procedures marketing researchers use to provide decision makers with clear, objective, and unbiased information. Decision makers at Wrangler, Ford, Kimberly-Clark, Apple,

For the first time, Marketing Researchers may now be certified. Researchers fulfilling certain requirements may earn their Professional Researchers Certification, PRC. By permission, Marketing Research Association.

Kodak, Nike, Sony, and a host of other companies have produced highly successful products and services using marketing research.

We will start your journey into marketing research by learning why marketing research is a part of marketing and why marketing research is necessary for the practice of marketing, especially for managers who have adopted the philosophy known as the marketing concept. You should learn a definition of marketing research, and we introduce you to the official definition of the American Marketing Association as well as our shorter definition. We also want you to know the purpose and uses of marketing research and the types of marketing research studies being conducted in the industry. In this chapter you will learn the role marketing research plays in the total marketing information systems (MIS) and how to distinguish marketing research from the other MIS components. Finally, we will introduce you to some hot topics in the industry.

We will start your journey into marketing research by learning why marketing research is a part of marketing and why marketing research is necessary for the practice of marketing, especially for managers who have adopted the philosophy known as the marketing concept.

MARKETING RESEARCH IS PART OF MARKETING

This is marketing research and you've already taken at least one course in marketing. If this is a book about marketing research, why do we need to first discuss marketing? The answer is that because marketing research is part of marketing and you cannot fully appreciate marketing research and the role it plays in the marketing process unless you know how it fits into the marketing process. What is **marketing**?

What is marketing? The American Marketing Association has defined marketing as an organizational function and a set of processes for creating, communicating and delivering value to customers and for managing customer relationships in ways that benefit the organization and its stakeholders.

The American Marketing Association has defined marketing as an organizational function and a set of processes for creating, communicating and delivering value to customers and for managing customer relationships in ways that benefit the organization and its stakeholders.[2]

Marketing is an organizational function, not a group of persons or separate entity within the firm. It is also a set of processes and not a single tactic such as creating an end-aisle display. The processes create, communicate, and deliver value to customers. Marketing is not trying to sell customers something; rather, it is providing customers with something they value. Finally, our definition of marketing emphasizes that the objective of marketing is to create and manage customer relationships for the benefit of the organization and its stakeholders. This means marketing is not just attempting to create an exchange, it also attempts to develop long-term customer relationships. And, if marketers do create long-term customer relationships, they will likely satisfy their organization's objectives, such as sales volume, profits, ROI and shareholder wealth.[3] Companies that keep customers over the long run usually perform very well in terms of financial objectives.

Now that we have a better appreciation of what marketing is, let's think about what marketers must do in order to practice marketing. Marketers must determine what consumers value and create, communicate, and deliver that value to customers. Marketers at

Ford determined that customers would value a fuel-efficient SUV and are delivering their fuel-efficient Escape SUV in record numbers. Louis Vuitton creates and delivers such value in their handbags that customers pay as much as $1,200 for them. China's Chery car manufacturer is producing a highly fuel-efficient mini-car that provides customers a value in transportation at a price of $3,600. ABC creates entertainment value in its TV production *Good Morning America!* and has enjoyed high viewer ratings among its customers for many years. The American Red Cross creates value in the sense that it provides donors with "peace of mind for helping others." Winning political parties communicate value to voters with their ideas to provide a better world of employment opportunities, affordable health care, a solvent social security system, and protection from terrorism. In order to create, communicate, and deliver these values, marketers must "hear the voice of the consumer." Marketers must know the wants and needs of consumers. They must know how to effectively communicate to consumers, and they must know how to best deliver goods and services. When marketers do all these processes well, they establish long-term relationships with their customers.

Certainly, not all organizations and companies "hear the voice of the consumer." They do not conceive of products or services that meet the needs and wants of the market. They do not provide value, and their sales come from short-term exchanges, not enduring customer relationships. These companies produce the wrong products or services. They have the wrong price, poor advertising, or poor distribution. Then they become part of the many firms that experience product failure. Our Marketing Research Insight 1.1, illustrates some examples of product failure.

But, fortunately, not all companies and/or their products fail. Peter Drucker wrote that successful companies are those that know and understand the customer so well that the product conceived, priced, promoted, and distributed by the company is ready to be bought as soon as it is available.[4] Drucker, as usual, is right on target with his statement but how can a marketer know and understand how to deliver value to the customer so well? The answer is by having information about consumers. So to practice marketing correctly, managers must have information, and this is the purpose of marketing research. This is why we say that marketing research is a part of marketing; it provides the necessary information to enable managers to market ideas, goods, and services *properly*. But how do you market ideas, goods, and services *properly*? You have probably already learned in your studies that you must begin by having the right philosophy, followed by proper marketing strategy. We call that philosophy the "marketing concept."

> Marketers understand how to deliver value to their consumers by having information about consumers. To practice marketing correctly, managers must have information, and this is the purpose of marketing research.

The Importance of Philosophies and the Philosophy We Call "The Marketing Concept"

Have you ever thought why your philosophies are so important? A philosophy may be thought of as a system of values, or principles, by which you live. Your values, or principles, are important because they dictate what you do each day. This is why philosophies are so important; your philosophy affects your day-to-day decisions. For example, you likely have a philosophy similar to this: "I believe that higher education is important because it will provide the knowledge and understanding I will need in the world to enable me to enjoy the standard of living I desire." Assuming this does reflect your philosophy regarding higher education, consider what you do from day to day. You are going to class, listening to your professors, taking notes, reading this book. If you did not share the philosophy we just described, you would likely be doing something entirely different. Well, the same is true for business managers. A manager's philosophy will affect how he or she will make day-to-day decisions in the business. There are many different philosophies that managers may use to guide them in their decision making. "We are in the locomotive business; we make and run trains." Or "To be successful we must set high sales quotas and sell, sell, sell!"[5] The managers

> Your values, or principles, are important because they dictate what you do each day.

1.1 Marketers Need the Right Information to Properly Market Ideas, Goods, and Services

Unfortunately, we have many examples in which marketers did not have the proper information to help them understand consumers' wants and needs. Adams, a division of Pfizer, Inc., introduced "Body Smarts" in the summer of 2001. "Body Smarts" were nutritional crunch bars and assorted fruit chews. The product was positioned as a healthy alternative to candy, but Adams announced it was taking the product off the shelf in 2002. It could have been that when consumers want candy, they want products that *taste* like candy. Some other examples of product failures include the *IncrEdibles* "push-up," eat-on-the-go scrambled eggs and *Hey! There's a Monster in My Room* spray.

A marketing research firm that helps company's avoid these types of mistakes is New Product Works, a Division of The Arbor Strategy Group. This firm provides a team of highly qualified consultants to help companies make new product development faster, more efficient, and more effective. The company has over 80,000 new and once-new products, which they use to teach marketers how to market their products successfully.

IncrEdibles Breakaway Foods, L.L.P launched IncrEdibles in late 1999, touting its "Push n' Eat" self serving unit as fast, easy, and convenient. The breakfast fast food alternative was available in three scrambled egg flavors including cheese, cheese and sausage, and cheese and bacon. However, because of some operational problems the product was pulled, with the hope that it would be retooled and relaunched, but to no avail. It was an interesting concept, but the execution was riddled with problems. It was frozen, and according to reports, when you started eating it on the run, it fell over onto your lap.

Hey! There's A Monster In My Room-Spray: In 1993, OUT! International, Inc. introduced this monster-buster spray to rid scary creatures from the rooms of children. The spray came in a bubble gum fragrance. The idea was cute, but the name was not, and set up a fright for the kids.

Courtesy: New Product Works, A Division of the Arbor Strategy Group.

---

who guided their companies by these philosophies guided those companies right out of business. A much better philosophy is called the "marketing concept." A prominent marketing professor, Philip Kotler, has defined the marketing concept as follows:

> The **marketing concept** is a business philosophy that holds that the key to achieving organizational goals consists of the company being more effective than competitors in creating, delivering, and communicating customer value to its chosen target markets.[6]

For many years, business leaders have recognized that this is the "right philosophy." And although the marketing concept is often used interchangeably with other terms, such as "customer-oriented" or "market-driven," the key point is that this philosophy puts the consumer first! Recently, scholars have added the concept of *holistic marketing*, which includes four components: relationship marketing, integrated marketing, internal marketing, and social responsibility marketing.[7] Time has proven that a philosophy that focuses on the consumer is superior to one in which company management focuses on production, the product itself, or high-pressure selling. If you satisfy consumers, they will seek to do business with your company.

New Product Works, a division of the Arbor Strategy group, is a new product development consulting organization. Explore what they offer their clients at www.newproductworks.com

A manager's philosophy will affect how he or she will make day-to-day decisions in the business. A well-accepted philosophy managers should adopt is known as "The Marketing Concept."

What does all this mean? It means that having the "right philosophy" is an important first step in being successful. But, just appreciating the importance of satisfying consumer wants and needs is not enough. Firms must put together the "right strategy."

The "Right Marketing Strategy"

A strategy is nothing more than a plan. The term *strategy* was borrowed from military jargon that stressed developing plans of attack that would minimize the enemy's ability to respond. Firms may also have strategies in many different areas, such as financial strategy, production strategy, technology strategy, and so on. How do we define marketing strategy?

A **marketing strategy** consists of selecting a segment of the market as the company's target market and designing the proper "mix" of product/service, price, promotion, and distribution system to meet the wants and needs of the consumers within the target market.

This definition of strategy assumes that we have *already* adopted the marketing concept. A manager who did not have the marketing concept, for example, would not be concerned whether or not his or her plan addressed any particular market segment and certainly would not be concerned with consumers' wants and needs. So, to continue, we are thinking like *enlightened* managers; we have adopted the marketing concept. Now, as we shall see, because we have adopted the marketing concept, we cannot come up with just any strategy. We have to develop the "right" strategy—the strategy that allows our firm to truly meet the wants and needs of the consumers within the market segment we have chosen. Think of the many questions we now must answer: What is the market, and how do we segment it? What are the wants and needs of each segment, and what is the size of each segment? Who are our competitors, and how are they already meeting the wants and needs of consumers? Which segment(s) should we target? Which model of a proposed product will best suit the target market? What is the best price? Which promotional method will be the most efficient? How should we distribute the product/service?

From the above we see that many decisions must be made in order to develop the "right" strategy for the purpose of succeeding in business. In order to make the right decisions, managers must have objective, accurate, and timely *information*.

Having the right information to implement a strategy at a *point in time* is not enough. As environments change, business decisions must be revised again and again to produce the right strategy for the new environment. Automobile manufactuer's know, for example, that they need to develop more fuel-efficient models when petroleum prices skyrocket. Many restaurants found that their best-selling menu items were no longer selling when the "low-carb" diets became widespread. They had to react by introducing new menu items. The bottom line of this entire discussion: To make the right decisions, managers continuously need information. As we shall learn next, marketing research supplies much of this information.

WHAT IS MARKETING RESEARCH?

We have established that managers need information in order to carry out the marketing process. Now you are ready to learn exactly what marketing research is.

Marketing research is the process of designing, gathering, analyzing, and reporting information that may be used to solve a specific marketing problem.

This definition tells us that marketing research is a process that reports information that can be used to solve a marketing problem, such as determining price, how to advertise, and so on. The focus then is on a process that results in information that will be used to make decisions. (We introduce you to this 11-step process in Chapter 2). Notice also that our

---

The marketing concept is a business philosophy that holds that the key to achieving organizational goals consists of the company being more effective than competitors in creating, delivering, and communicating customer value to its chosen target markets. This philosophy puts the consumer first!

Managers must have not only the right philosophy, the marketing concept, they must also put together the "right strategy."

A marketing strategy consists of selecting a segment of the market as the company's target market and designing the proper "mix" of product/service, price, promotion, and distribution to meet the wants and needs of the consumers within the target market.

Many decisions must be made in order to develop the "right" strategy.

Marketing research is the process of designing, gathering, analyzing, and reporting information that may be used to solve a specific marketing problem.

definition refers to information that may be used to solve a *specific* marketing problem. We are going to explain the importance of this later in this chapter. Ours is not the only definition of marketing research. The American Marketing Association (AMA) formed a committee several years ago to establish a definition of marketing research. The AMA definition is:

> Marketing research is the function that links the consumer, customer, and public to the marketer through information—information used to identify and define marketing opportunities and problems; generate, refine, and evaluate marketing actions; monitor marketing performance; and improve the understanding of marketing as a process.[8]

Each of these definitions is correct. Our definition is shorter and illustrates the process of marketing research. The AMA's definition is longer because it elaborates on the function (we call it the *purpose*) as well as the *uses* of marketing research. Note that market research, a part of marketing research, refers to applying marketing research to a specific market area. One definition of **market research** is: The systematic gathering, recording, and analyzing of data with respect to a particular market, where *market* refers to a specific customer group in a specific geographic area.[9] In the next two sections, we will talk more about the purpose and uses of marketing research.

WHAT IS THE PURPOSE OF MARKETING RESEARCH?

By now you have probably guessed that the purpose of marketing research has to do with providing information to make decisions. That is essentially correct, but the AMA definition includes a reference to the consumer: The **purpose of marketing research** is to link the consumer to the marketer by providing information that can be used in making marketing decisions. Some believe that having the link to the consumer by marketing research is more important today than ever. Competition for the consumer has become fierce as globalization has taken hold. Consumers expect greater value in the marketplace. It is more important today than ever to learn insights from the customer in order to keep them loyal.[10] Our Marketing Research Insight 1.2 illustrates how, by using marketing research, Kimberly-Clark Corporation markets successful products.

The AMA definition expands on our definition by telling us that the information provided by marketing research for decision making should represent the consumer. In fact, by mentioning the consumer, this implies that marketing research is consistent with the marketing concept because it "links the consumer . . . to the marketer." The AMA definition is normative. That is, it tells us how marketing research should be used to ensure the firm is consumer-oriented. We certainly agree with this but what should be done is not always followed. Clancy and Krieg, in their book *Counterintuitive Marketing: Achieve Great Results Using Uncommon Sense*, argue that many failures can be attributed to managers just making "intuitive" decisions.[11] They implore managers to use research in order to make better decisions. These well-known authors make a good argument for studying marketing research. While the AMA definition makes the point that marketing research links the firm to the consumer, we want to point out that marketing research information is also collected on entities other than the consumer. Information is routinely gathered on members of distribution channels, employees, and all the environments, including competitors.[12] Of course, one could argue that the point of all this research is to do a better job of satisfying consumers.

Sometimes marketing research studies lead to the wrong decisions. We should point out here that just because a manager uses marketing research does not mean that the decisions based on the research are infallible. In fact, marketing research studies are not always accurate. There are plenty of examples in which marketing research said a product would fail, yet if the product made it to market in spite of the research prognosis, the product turned out to be a resounding success.

Sidebar notes:

The AMA has defined *marketing research* as the function that links the consumer, customer, and public to the marketer through information—information used to identify and define marketing opportunities and problems; generate, refine, and evaluate marketing actions; monitor marketing performance; and improve the understanding of marketing as a process.

Sometimes managers say *market research* when they mean *marketing research*. *Market research* is the appropriate term when *marketing research* is being conducted on a specific customer group in a specific geographic area.

The purpose of marketing research is to link the consumer to the marketer by providing information that can be used in making marketing decisions.

Marketing research should be used to ensure the firm is consumer-oriented, but some firms do not use marketing research.

Sometimes marketing research predicts failure, yet the product or service is a success.

1.2 Understanding the Consumer Leads to Better Product Innovations

Kimberly-Clark's Child Care team focuses on "understanding the consumer" says Steve Kalmanson, group president of North Atlantic Personal Care. This philosophy has led to several successful new products.

Extensive consumer research with kids and moms helped Kimberly-Clark better understand how a product could help the bedwetting condition. Kimberly-Clark used the research to design absorbent underpants for boys and another model for girls that would provide customized protection against leaks. The studies also led to incorporating colorful pant graphics on GoodNites® Disposable Underpants to provide a more underwear-like look than diapers. GoodNites has driven segment dollar growth to upwards of +20% since the introduciton of these gender-specific pants in July 2004.

Kimberly-Clarks's strong commitment to consumer research also produced HUGGIES® LITTLE SWIMMERS® Disposable Swimmers. The innovative swimpants protect in the water without swelling like diapers and feature tear-away sides that make changing easier. In 2004, the Good Housekeeping Institute selected LITTLE SWIMMERS® Disposable Swimmers as one of the four most outstanding "Good Buys" of the past decade, an award only achieved after 20,000 new consumer products were reviewed. LITTLE SWIMMERS® Disposable Swimmers are currently sold in 60 countries and sales are fast approaching $100 million worldwide.

Copyright Kimberly-Clark Worldwide, Inc. Reprinted with Permission.

Stella Artois beer appealed primarily to people in urban areas. The company's ad agency developed an ad showing a peasant selling flowers in a rural setting. The ad was 60 seconds long, and marketing research results showed the ad to be a failure, citing below-average brand awareness and the fact that the ad positioned the beer away from the group to which it primarily appealed. Management at Stella Artois, however, believed that the ad was good and the marketing research was flawed. The ad was so successful it is credited with helping to turn the company's product from a niche beer to one of the top-selling grocery-store beer brands in the United Kingdom.[13]

One of the classic examples of a success that marketing research predicted to be a failure is Jerry Seinfeld's popular TV program, *Seinfeld*. The marketing research that was

Marketing research studies indicated that Jerry Seinfeld's very popular TV show, *Seinfeld*, would be a failure.

conducted on the pilot for the Jerry Seinfeld TV show stated the show was so bad that executives gave up on the idea. It was six months before another manager questioned the accuracy of the research and resurrected the show, which became one of the most successful shows in television history.[14] Likewise, marketing research studies also predicted that hair styling mousse and answering machines would fail if brought to market.[15]

There are also plenty of failures in cases for which marketing research predicted success. Most of these failures are removed from the shelves with as little fanfare as possible. Sainsbury's, the U.K. grocery chain, had an ad prepared by their ad agency that tested favorably in marketing research testing. However, the company received negative reactions from customers and staff alike when the ad ran. Sainsbury switched ad agencies.[16]

Many upstart retailers go out of business because of "flawed" research. GrandKids, a toy store targeting grandparents, failed. The owner relied on local school data and statistics from a company soliciting advertising for her marketing research. Had she conducted better research, such as examining the most recent census data, she would have discovered that there were only 3219 families in the whole town and those 50 and over made up only 31% of town residents. There simply were not enough grandparents to support her store.[17]

Another classic example of a failure when research predicted success was Beecham's cold-water-wash product, *Delicare*. The new product failed even though marketing research predicted it would unseat the category leader, Woolite. When this happened, there was a great deal of publicity because Beecham sued the research company that predicted success.[18]

These examples illustrate that marketing research is not infallible, but this does not mean that marketing research is not useful. Remember, most marketing research studies are trying to understand and predict consumer behavior, and that is a difficult task. The fact that the marketing research industry has been around for many years and is growing means that it has passed the toughest of all tests to prove its worth—the test of the marketplace. If the industry did not provide value, it would cease to exist. And for each of the examples cited above, there are tens of thousands of success stories supporting the use of marketing research.

Sometimes marketing research predicts success, yet the product or service is a dismal failure.

The fact that the marketing research industry has been around for many years and is growing means that it has passed the toughest of all tests to prove its worth—the test of the marketplace.

WHAT ARE THE USES OF MARKETING RESEARCH?

Identifying Market Opportunities and Problems

Now that you understand the purpose of marketing research, let's take a closer look at the *uses* of marketing research. In our short definition we simply refer to the use of marketing research to provide information to solve a specific marketing problem; the AMA definition spells out what some of these problems may be.

The identification of market opportunities and problems is a use of marketing research.

For example, the *identification of market opportunities and problems* is certainly a use of marketing research. Mintel, a British consumer market research firm, looks for opportunities for new products. Some of its interests include baby milk sold in disposable bottles, tea and coffee that heat themselves, and a spray that temporarily whitens teeth.[19] Many research studies are being conducted today to determine health and wellness effects of omega-3s, lutein, choline, lecithin, lycopene, soy and how best to offer these ingredients in new foods.[20] Marketing Research Services, Inc. (MRSI), a research firm in the United States also helps client firms identify market opportunities.

Visit MRSI at www.mrsi.com.

Generate, Refine, and Evaluate Potential Marketing Actions

Marketing research can also be used to generate, refine, and evaluate a potential marketing action. When the marketing "action" was evaluating proposed ads, Wrangler conducted research that allowed them to determine which of several magazine ads was best.

MRSI is a marketing research firm that specializes in helping firms identify opportunities in the marketplace. By permission, MRSI.

When the marketing "action" was designing a better product, Kimberly-Clark researchers found that the most important criterion for women in feminine napkins is comfort. They designed a new product based on this information.[21]

Another use of marketing research is to generate, refine, and evaluate a potential marketing action.

Monitor Marketing Performance

The AMA definition also states that marketing research may be used to monitor marketing performance. After companies have implemented their marketing strategies, they want to monitor the effectiveness of their ads, salesforce, in-store promotions, dealer effectiveness, and competitors. Of course, companies also wish to monitor their sales and market shares. This monitoring is often done through what is called "tracking research." Tracking research is used to monitor how well products of companies such as Hershey's, Campbell's Soup, Kellogg's, and Heinz are performing in the supermarkets. These "consumer packaged goods" firms want to monitor the sales of their brands and sales of their competitor's brands as well. Research firms such as ACNielsen and Information Resources, Inc., are two of several firms monitoring the performance of products in supermarkets and other retail outlets. They monitor how many units of these products are being sold, through which chains, at what retail price, and so on. You will learn more about tracking studies later on in this book.

MARKETERS MONITOR CUSTOMER SATISFACTION THROUGH THE USE OF MARKETING RESEARCH

Active

As more companies have adopted the marketing concept they have become very interested in monitoring customer satisfaction. As a result, marketing research firms have devised methods for measuring customer satisfaction that not only tell a client firm to what extent

Another use of marketing research is to monitor marketing performance.

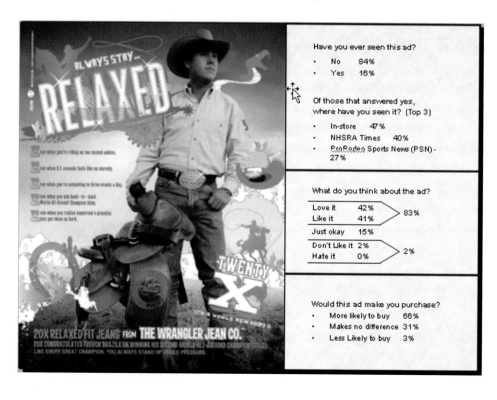

Would this ad make you purchase?
- More likely to buy 66%
- Makes no difference 31%
- Less Likely to buy 3%

Wrangler executives use marketing research to help them make better decisions regarding their design and evaluation of proposed advertisements. WebSurveyor, an online surveying software, was used by Wrangler to test different promotional messages. By permission, WebSurveyor.

Burke, Inc., monitors customer satisfaction for firms such as Hewlett-Packard, Roche Diagnostics, Eastman Kodak, and many others. By permission, Burke, Inc.

their customers are satisfied/dissatisfied (diagnostic information) but the research also gives clients information on what they should do to improve customer satisfaction (prescriptive information). As an example, go to Burke, Inc.'s website at **www.burke.com** and click on the "Customer Loyalty and Relationship Management" link. Read about how Burke provides the expertise to monitor a company's customer satisfaction.

Improve Marketing as a Process

Finally, a use of marketing research is to improve marketing as a process. To improve our understanding of the marketing process means that some marketing research is conducted to expand our basic knowledge of marketing.

Finally, our AMA definition says that a use of marketing research is to improve marketing as a process. To improve our understanding of the marketing process means that some marketing research is conducted to expand our basic knowledge of marketing. Typical of such research would be attempts to define and classify marketing phenomena and to develop theories that describe, explain, and predict marketing phenomena. Such knowledge is often published in journals such as the *Journal of Marketing Research* or *Marketing Research*. Much of this research is conducted by marketing professors at colleges and universities and by other organizations, such as the *Marketing Science Institute*. The latter use could be described as the only part of marketing research that is basic research. **Basic research** is conducted to expand our knowledge rather than to solve a specific problem. Research conducted to solve specific problems is called "**applied research**," and this represents the vast majority of marketing research studies. We will revisit the idea that marketing research solves specific problems a little later in this chapter.

Basic research is conducted to expand our knowledge rather than to solve a specific problem. Research conducted to solve specific problems is called "applied research," and this represents the vast majority of marketing research studies.

CLASSIFYING MARKETING RESEARCH STUDIES

Another way to introduce you to marketing research is to look at a classification of the different types of marketing research studies being conducted in the industry. In Table 1.1 we organize the major types of studies under the usage categories from the AMA definition. Under each of these four categories we provide example studies.

THE MARKETING INFORMATION SYSTEM

Marketing research is not the *only* source of information.

In order to stay abreast of competitive markets, firms must attempt to have the right information at the right time in the right format in the hands of those who must make decisions. We have learned that this is not an easy task. In fact, one author suggests that more than 25% of critical data within Fortune 1000 companies is inaccurate or incomplete.[22] To manage information properly companies develop information systems. So far, we have presented marketing research as if it were the only source of information. This is not the case, as you will understand by reading this section on marketing information systems.

An MIS is a structure consisting of people, equipment, and procedures to gather, sort, analyze, evaluate, and distribute needed, timely, and accurate information to marketing decision makers.

Marketing decision makers have a number of sources of information available to them. We can understand these different information sources by examining the components of the **marketing information system (MIS)**. An MIS is a structure consisting of people, equipment, and procedures to gather, sort, analyze, evaluate, and distribute needed, timely, and accurate information to marketing decision makers.[23] The role of

TABLE 1.1 — A Classification of Marketing Research Studies

A. Identifying Market Opportunities and Problems

As the title implies, the goal of these studies is to find opportunities or to identify problems with an existing strategy. Examples of such studies include the following:

Market-demand determination
Market segments identification
Marketing audits SWOT analysis
Product/service-use studies
Environmental analysis studies
Competitive analysis

B. Generating, Refining, and Evaluating Potential Marketing Actions

Marketing research studies may be used to generate, refine, and then evaluate potential marketing actions. Marketing actions could be as broad as a proposed marketing strategy or as narrow as a tactic (a specific action taken to carry out a strategy). Typically these studies deal with one or more of the marketing-mix variables (product, price, distribution, and promotion). Examples include the following:

Proposed marketing-mix evaluation testing
Concept tests of proposed new products or services
New-product prototype testing
Reformulating existing product testing
Pricing tests
Advertising pretesting
In-store promotion effectiveness studies
Distribution effectiveness studies

C. Monitoring Marketing Performance

These studies are control studies. They allow a firm that already has a marketing mix placed in the market to evaluate how well that mix is performing. Examples include the following:

Image analysis
Tracking studies
Customer-satisfaction studies
Employee-satisfaction studies
Distributor-satisfaction studies
Web site evaluations

D. Improving Marketing as a Process[a]

A small portion of marketing research is conducted to expand our knowledge of marketing as a process rather than to solve a specific problem facing a company. By having the knowledge generated from these studies, managers may be in a much better position to solve a specific problem within their firms. This type of research is often conducted by institutes, such as the Marketing Science Institute, or universities. Examples include the following:

How managers learn about the market
Consumer behavior differences in e-business transactions
Determining the optimal amount that should be spent on e-business and measuring success in e-business
Predictors of new-product success
The impact of long-term advertising on consumer choice
Measuring the advantage to being the first product in the market
Marketing-mix variable differences over the Internet

[a]These study topics were taken from the Marketing Science Institute's research priorities list and former award-winning research papers. See **www.MSI.org** for additional studies designed to improve marketing as a process.

the MIS is to determine decision makers' information needs, acquire the needed information, and distribute that information to the decision makers in a form and at a time when they can use it for decision making. However, this sounds very much like marketing research—providing information to aid in decision making. We can understand the distinction by understanding the components of an MIS.

Components of an MIS

The four subsystems of an MIS are the internal reports system, marketing intelligence system, marketing decision support system (DSS), and marketing research system.

As noted previously, the MIS is designed to assess managers' information needs, to gather this information, and to distribute the information to the marketing managers who need to make decisions. Information is gathered and analyzed by the four subsystems of the MIS: internal reports, marketing intelligence, marketing decision support, and marketing research. We discuss each of these subsystems next.

The internal reports system gathers information generated by internal reports, which includes orders, billing, receivables, inventory levels, stockouts, and so on.

▶ **Internal Reports System.** The **internal reports system** gathers information generated by internal reports, which includes orders, billing, receivables, inventory levels, stockouts, and so on. In many cases, the internal reports system is called the "accounting information system." Although this system produces financial statements (balance sheets and income statements, etc.) that generally contain insufficient detail for many marketing decisions, the internal reports system also contains extreme detail on both revenues and costs that can be invaluable in making decisions. Other information is also collected, such as inventory records, sales calls records, and orders. A good internal reports system can tell a manager a great deal of information about what has happened within the firm in the past. When information is needed from sources *outside* the firm, other MIS components must be called on.

The marketing intelligence system is a set of procedures and sources used by managers to obtain everyday information about pertinent developments in the environment.

▶ **Marketing Intelligence System.** A second component of an MIS is the **marketing intelligence system**, defined as a set of procedures and sources used by managers to obtain everyday information about pertinent developments in the environment. Such systems include both informal and formal information-gathering procedures. Informal information-gathering procedures involve activities such as scanning newspapers, magazines, and trade publications. Formal information-gathering activities may be conducted by staff members who are assigned the specific task of looking for anything that seems pertinent to the company or industry. They then edit and disseminate this information to the appropriate members or company departments. Formerly known as "clipping bureaus" (because they clipped relevant newspaper articles for clients), several online information service companies, such as Lexis-Nexis, provide marketing intelligence. To use its service a firm would enter key terms into search forms provided online by Lexis-Nexis. Information containing the search terms appears on the subscriber's computer screen as often as several times a day. By clicking on an article title, subscribers can view a full-text version of the article. In this way, marketing intelligence goes on continuously and searches a broad range of information sources in order to bring pertinent information to decision makers.

A marketing decision support system (DSS) is defined as collected data that may be accessed and analyzed using tools and techniques that assist managers in decision making.

▶ **Marketing Decision Support System (DSS).** The third component of an MIS is the decision support system. A **marketing decision support system (DSS)** is defined as collected data that may be accessed and analyzed using tools and techniques that assist managers in decision making. Once companies collect large amounts of information, they store this information in huge databases that, when accessed with decision-making tools and techniques (such as break-even analysis, regression models, and linear programming), allow companies to ask "what if" questions. Answers to these questions are then immediately available for decision making.

▶ **Marketing Research System.** Marketing research, which we have already discussed and defined, is the fourth component of an MIS. Now that you understand the three other components of an MIS, we are ready to discuss the question we raised at the beginning of this section—that is, if marketing research and an MIS both are designed to provide information for decision makers, how are the two different? In answering this question we must see how marketing research differs from the other three MIS components.

First, the **marketing research system** gathers information not gathered by the other MIS component subsystems: Marketing research studies are conducted for a *specific* situation facing the company. It is unlikely that other components of an MIS have generated the particular information needed for the specific situation. When *People* magazine wants to know which of three cover stories it should use, can its managers obtain that information from internal reports? No. From the intelligence system or the DSS? No. This then is how marketing research plays a unique role in the total information system of the firm. By providing information for a specific problem at hand, marketing research provides information not provided by other components of the MIS. This is why persons in the industry sometimes refer to marketing research studies as "ad hoc studies." *Ad hoc* is Latin meaning "with respect to a specific purpose." (Recall that earlier in the chapter when we defined marketing research, we told you we would revisit the word *specific*. Now you see why we used that word in our definition.)

There is another characteristic of marketing research that differentiates it from the other MIS components. Marketing research projects, unlike the previous components, are not continuous—they have a beginning and an end. This is why marketing research studies are sometimes referred to as "projects." The other components are available for use on an ongoing basis. However, marketing research projects are launched only when there is a justifiable need for information that is not available from internal reports, intelligence, or the DSS.

HOT TOPICS IN MARKETING RESEARCH

As we end this chapter, which introduces you to marketing research, it is appropriate to identify the "hot topics" occurring in the industry. We have identified hot topics as online research, declining respondent cooperation, and globalization.

Online Marketing Research

Online research has dramatically changed the research industry.[24] However, while the phrase is often used, there are different interpretations of the exact meaning of "online research." We offer the following definition of **online research** as:

> The use of computer networks, including the Internet, to assist in any phase of the marketing research process, including development of the problem, research design, data gathering, analysis, and report writing and distribution.

Computer networks, particularly the Internet, have brought about many changes not only in terms of how people shop, learn, and communicate but also in how businesses operate. Not only have computer networks had an impact on how businesses market to one another (B2B) and how businesses market to consumers (B2C), they have also affected how marketing research is conducted. This impact has been so dramatic that the authors of *Online Marketing Research* state: "The advent of the Web has led to a revolution in the research community."[25] What are some of the applications of online research in marketing research? Today RFPs (requests for proposals to do research), sample design and ordering, data collection (we have a separate definition for online *survey* research), data analysis and report writing and distribution are carried out through online tools and services. You will learn more about these throughout this book, and we will note them using our online research icon that you see at the beginning of this section. Before we move to

Web-based research is research conducted *on* Web applications. This type of research, sometimes confused with online research, may use traditional research methods as well as online research methods.

the next hot topic, you should know that some other terms are often confused with online research. First, by **Web-based research**, we mean research that is conducted *on* Web applications. This type of research, sometimes confused with online research, may use traditional methods as well as online research methods in conducting research on Web-based applications. Some Web-based applications would include research on the popularity of the Web pages themselves, such as "site hit counts," effectiveness studies of pop-up ads on Web sites, or research measuring consumers' reactions to various components of Web sites. Any of these Web-based projects could be researched using either online research or traditional research. Because online research refers to using computer networks in conducting the research process, it may be used regardless of the application.

"Online survey research" refers to the collection of data using computer networks. It is a subset of online research.

Second, another type of research, online *survey* research, may be confused with online research. Online survey research has experienced rapid growth in the past several years, and many erroneously think that this is the same as online research. "**Online survey research**" refers to the collection of data using computer networks. Collecting employee satisfaction data using a company's intranet would constitute online survey research. Many research firms, such as Greenfield Online and InsightExpress®, were created for the purpose of using the Internet to gather survey data. Because online survey research uses computer networks to collect data (part of the research process), we would consider it to be a subset of online research.

Online survey research has become a significant part of firms' research budgets.[26] Benefits attributed to online survey research include the ability to examine data as they are collected, speed, low cost per respondent, no interviewer bias, and a reduction in the total cost of doing research.[27] The potential and growth of online research makes it a hot topic in the marketing research industry.

Weary from telemarketers and other direct marketers, consumers resent invasions of privacy more and more, including requests for information from legitimate marketing researchers.

Growing Consumer/Respondent Resentment

Another hot topic in marketing research is that of growing consumer resentment to invasions of privacy. Marketing research, because it often seeks information from consumers, is "invasive." Weary from abuse from telemarketers and other direct marketers, potential respondents have grown resentful of any attempt by others to gather information from them. Finally, consumer rights groups have grown so powerful that the government, acting through the Federal Trade Commission (FTC), introduced a national "Do Not Call" registry in the summer of 2003, to curb calls made by telemarketers to anyone requesting that the calls be stopped (**www.donotcall.gov**). The registry has been effective. Fortunately, the marketing research industry is excluded from the ban placed on telemarketers in the Do Not Call regulations. However, the industry is very concerned about this trend. The Council of American Survey Research Organizations (CASRO) reported research showing that 97% of consumers felt that telemarketers should be excluded through Do Not Call legislation but, alarmingly, CASRO found that 64% of consumers felt the legislation should also apply to marketing researchers.[28] Marketing researchers have also been watching anti-spam legislation and encourage the reduction of spam. The "Can Spam" Act became effective on January 1, 2004, but it has done little to reduce spam. (We cover this in greater detail in Chapter 3.) Increases in spam make respondents even more wary of their loss of privacy, which adversely affects legitimate requests for research information. Consumers have responded to their sense of loss of privacy by refusing to participate in research studies. The Council for Marketing and Opinion Research (CMOR) tracks refusal rates, which have shown a steady increase year after year. The research industry realizes that gaining consumer confidence to participate in research is an important hot topic facing the research industry. Some firms are battling the rising nonresponse rates by investing in panels of consumers who are recruited to be available for several research requests. Still, the cost of recruiting such panel members is increasing yearly. The industry must devote

A hot topic in marketing research is determining how to combat growing consumer resentment and increasing refusal rates to marketing research requests. Ethical treatment of respondents is necessary.

considerable time and effort to maintaining trusted relationships with consumer respondents. Respondents are the "lifeblood" of the marketing research industry. Ethical treatment of respondents is necessary if marketing research firms are to stop the growing resentment by consumers. We will discuss this topic throughout this book and will identify those sections with the ethical icon you see at the beginning of this section.

Globalizaton

As marketing firms spread globally during the 1990s marketing research firms followed them to their distant markets. In his annual report on research spending, Jack Honomichl reported that the top 50 largest U.S. marketing research firms reported that about 48% of their revenues were generated from outside the United States.[29] Honomichl also reports that the top 25 marketing research firms in the world earn 67% of their revenues from operations outside their own country. The largest firm is VNU, a Dutch-based publisher that owns ACNielsen and Nielsen Media Research. They earned only 1% of their revenues in their home country. The rest of their revenues came from operations in 80 countries around the world.[30] To illustrate the influence of global marketing research, a research firm, Opinion Access Corp., advertised that they do business in 10 languages![31] You will see many global applications as you learn about marketing research in this book. We will highlight them for you by using the global icon you see at the beginning of this section.

Marketing research firms followed their globe-trotting clients by locating and operating in markets around the world. Likewise, marketing research companies located in other countries moved into the United States.

THE ORGANIZATION OF THIS TEXTBOOK: WHAT TO EXPECT IN FUTURE CHAPTERS

At this point you understand how marketing research is a part of the marketing process, the role marketing research plays in providing managers with information to help them make more informed decisions. You also understand the unique role marketing research plays in a firm's marketing information system, MIS. You are ready to continue learning about marketing research. In the next chapter we will introduce you to the 11-step marketing research process. You will have a better understanding of the marketing research process as we introduce you to each of these steps. You will see how marketing research begins and where it ends. The remainder of this book will give you an in-depth analysis of each one of the 11 steps. But, before we take you through each of these steps, we pause in Chapter 3 to give you a look at the industry of marketing research. You will learn about the industry structure (the types and sizes of firms) and the major issues facing the industry, including the ethical challenges. You will also learn much more about the Marketing Research Association's new certification program.

SUMMARY

It is important to understand the role of marketing research by appreciating that marketing research is part of marketing. The American Marketing Association has defined marketing as an organizational function and a set of processes for creating, communicating, and delivering value to customers and for managing customer relationships in ways that benefit the organization and its stakeholders. In order to practice marketing properly, managers must "hear the voice of the consumer" to determine how to create, communicate, and deliver value that will result in long-lasting relationships with customers. Some firms "hear" the voice and have success, others do not and experience product and service failures.

Marketers should follow the philosophy known as the marketing concept. Also known as being "customer-oriented" or "market-driven," the marketing concept is a philosophy that states that the key to business success lies in being more effective than competitors in creating, delivering, and communicating customer value to its chosen target markets. Companies whose philosophy focuses on products and selling efforts do not tend to stay around long. If a firm's management follows the philosophy known as the Marketing Concept, they develop the "right" strategies, or plans, to provide consumers with value. The significance of all this is that in order to practice marketing as we have described it, managers need information in order to determine wants and needs and to design marketing strategies that will satisfy customers in selected target markets. Furthermore, environmental changes mean that marketers must constantly collect information to monitor customers, markets, and competition.

We defined marketing research as the process of designing, gathering, analyzing, and reporting information that may be used to solve a specific problem. The AMA defines marketing research as the function that links the consumer, customer, and public to the marketer through information—information used to identify and define marketing opportunities and problems; generate, refine, and evaluate marketing actions; monitor marketing performance; and improve the understanding of marketing as a process. *Market* research is different from *marketing* research. Market research is a subset of marketing research and refers to applying marketing research to a specific geographical area, or market.

The purpose of marketing research is to link the consumer to the marketer by providing information that can be used in making marketing decisions. Not all firms use marketing research, and sometimes marketing research leads to the wrong decisions. But, marketing research has been around for many years and is growing—it has passed the "test of the marketplace."

The uses of marketing research are to (1) identify and define marketing opportunities and problems; (2) generate, refine, and evaluate marketing actions; (3) monitor marketing performance; and (4) improve our understanding of marketing. Most marketing research is considered to be applied research in that it is conducted to solve specific problems. A limited number of marketing research studies are considered basic research in that they are conducted to expand the limits of our knowledge. We classified marketing research studies using the above four types of uses of marketing research and we identified specific types of marketing research studies that would be found within each type of use of marketing research.

Marketing research is one of four subsystems making up a marketing information system (MIS). Other subsystems include internal reports, marketing intelligence, and decision support systems. Marketing research gathers information not available through the other subsystems. Marketing research provides information for the specific problem at hand. Marketing research is conducted on a project basis as opposed to an ongoing basis.

KEY TERMS

Marketing (p. 4)

Marketing concept p. 6)

Marketing strategy (p. 7)

Marketing research (p. 7)

Market research (p. 8)

Purpose of marketing research (p. 8)

Basic research (p. 12)

Applied research (p. 12)

Marketing information system (p. 12)

Internal reports system (p. 14)

Marketing intelligence system (p. 14)

Marketing decision support system (DSS) (p. 14)

Marketing research system (p. 15)

Online research (p. 15)

Web-based research (p. 16)

Online survey research (p. 16)

REVIEW QUESTIONS/APPLICATIONS

1. What are some examples of professional organizations in the marketing research field?
2. What is marketing? Explain the role of marketing research in the process of marketing management.
3. Give some examples of products that have failed.
4. Why are philosophies important to decision makers? What is the marketing concept?
5. What is strategy, and why is marketing research important to strategy makers?
6. Define marketing research. Define market research.
7. What is the purpose of marketing research?
8. Name the uses of marketing research.
9. Which use of marketing research is considered basic research?
10. Give two examples of the types of studies in each of the four classes of marketing research studies provided in this chapter.
11. Distinguish among MIS (marketing information system), marketing research, and DSS (decision support system).
12. Name three hot topics facing the research industry.
13. What is the difference between online research, Web-based research and online survey research?
14. Explain why marketers are concerned about increasing respondent resentment to invasions of privacy.
15. Go to your library, either in person or online, and look through several business periodicals such as *Advertising Age, Business Week, Fortune,* and *Forbes.* Find three examples of companies using marketing research.
16. Select a company in a field in which you have a career interest and look up information on this firm in your library or on the Internet. After gaining some knowledge of this company and its products and services, customers, and competitors, list five different types of decisions that you believe this company's management may have made within the past two years. For each decision, list the information the company's executives would have needed to make these decisions.
17. What are the differences between online research, Web-based research, and online survey research? Give some examples of how a manager in a firm may use each of these three types of research.
18. Think of the following situations. What component of the marketing information system would a manager use to find the necessary information?
    a. A manager of an electric utilities firm hears a friend at lunch talk about a new breakthrough in solar panel technology she read about in a science publication.
    b. A manager wants to know how many units of three different products in the company sold during each month for the past three years.
    c. A manager wants to estimate the contribution to company return on investment earned by 10 different products in the company product line.
    d. A manager is considering producing a totally new type of health food. But he would like to know if consumers are likely to purchase the new food, at which meal they would most likely eat the food, and how they would prefer the food to be packaged.
19. Assume you are the manager of a successful marketing research company located in Southern California. Discuss how the hot topics in marketing research, presented in this chapter, may affect your firm.

APPLE POLISHES OFF THE PIRATES[32]

Apple's iPod Can Play Thousands of Songs

Apple Computer, Inc. wants customers to believe that its Apple computers can be used as digital entertainment centers. One of their steps into the digital entertainment foray was the popular iPod, a portable MP3 player that allows up to several thousand songs to be downloaded from various Internet sources in a matter of minutes. The songs are downloaded to a computer and then transferred to the iPod. Songs can be picked, mixed, and burned on to a CD, saved on an Apple computer or a PC, or transferred to a CD.

Several problems with downloading songs have arisen for MP3 users. Some of the downloading sites do not have permission from the recording artists and recording companies to offer the songs; therefore, their legality is questionable. These sites are called "pirate music sites." Other sites have permission but charge subscription fees or limit the number of times a song can be burned onto a CD.

Apple Computer itself raised the ire of some in the recording industry with its original marketing slogan for digital users: "Rip. Mix. Burn." In other words, rip off the record companies by downloading songs for free, mix your favorite songs, and burn a CD. Steve Jobs has made amends with the industry with a new online record store called iTunes. He has won the approval of all five major record labels and believes that his new music store will revolutionize the music industry.

iTunes offers more that 200,000 tracks and charges 99¢ per song and $9.99 per album. There is no subscription fee; a song can be burned onto a CD an unlimited number of times; and songs can be transferred to an unlimited number of iPods. iTunes proffers 30-second previews of all songs to allow customers to listen to a song before purchasing it and is integrated into Apple's digital music jukebox software. Users can pick, purchase, download, organize, and listen with one application. This move may launch Apple from computer company to entertainment company.

What information did managers at Apple need to have in order to make the decision to offer this service? Consider the following questions.

1. Would this situation justify the use of marketing research? Why? Why not?
2. Are consumers concerned enough with the legality and ethicality of the "music pirates" to pay for songs rather than downloading for free?
3. If consumers would pay for the tracks, how much would they pay?
4. Are current online sites enough of a hassle to warrant a new competitor in the market?

GYM CITY[33]

Ronny McCall was a director of a state-run rehabilitation program. Running the program had given him great insights on the benefits of staying fit through exercise programs. He also saw that exercise clubs, health clubs, and gyms were not only growing but also seemed to be fully used throughout the day. Although nearing retirement, Ronny was only in his mid-50s and was interested in starting a gym in his city.

Ronny had observed the existing health clubs and gyms in his city for some time. He knew they had built new, large facilities with ample, modern equipment in the newer suburban areas of the city. In fact, the national chains had completely surrounded the city in the suburbs. He understood why they had moved out to the suburbs. He reasoned that the average age in the suburbs was much younger than in the central city. He figured the chains were trying to capture the youth market. He noticed their ads contained young models and youth-oriented copy. He noticed that the radio and TV strategies of the chains targeted the younger generation. There was no question that the gym-chain managers knew what they were doing. At all six gym/health clubs located in the suburbs, the parking lots seemed to be filled from early in the morning until late at night.

Ronny decided to use a geodemographic information system (GIS) program that would allow him to examine demographic profiles in different areas of the city. The GIS program confirmed his observations. The suburbs had lower average ages, about 30. But, while using the GIS program, he noticed that there was a fairly large, heavily populated area of the central city that had a much higher income than any of the suburbs and that there were no health clubs or gyms near this area of the city. However, the residents in the area were older than those in the suburbs. The GIS program showed that the average age in the area Ronny defined was about 50. Would the older generation work out?

Want to know more about GIS? Go to http://www.gis.com.

Ronny's wife, Lucy, showed him additional research conducted by Roper Starch Worldwide for the International Health, Racquet & Sportsclub Association (IHRSA). The IHRSA is a Boston-based, nonprofit trade association, and its objective in the research was to determine whether consumers have a different perception of fitness than they did 10 or 15 years ago when the emphasis on working out was to produce a hard-body look. The IHRSA felt that consumers today are less interested in the pursuit of being "buff" and more interested in the health and emotional benefits derived from exercise. The Roper Starch Worldwide research findings confirmed this change. More people were involved in exercise to reduce emotional stress and to prevent health problems. Also, the findings showed that, of the adults surveyed, 9 percent already were health club members and 18 percent were current members or had been members within the past five years. The research provided the following table, which shows membership in health/fitness clubs by age.

Membership in Health/Fitness Clubs by Age

Age	Current Members	Never a Member/ Not a Member for Years
18–29	10%	15%
30–39	33%	23%
40–49	22%	23%
50–59	17%	15%
60–69	9%	9%
70+	7%	15%
Median age	41	44

Percentages do not add up to 100 because not all those surveyed responded to the question.
Source: IHRSA.

1. Based on the research provided in the case, should Ronny McCall pursue his dream of developing a gym in the central city? Why or why not?

2. What other information should Ronny McCall seek?

2

The Marketing Research Process

Carroll College: An Overview of the Marketing Research Process

Shirley Ann Baker is Director of International Programs at Carroll College in Montana. The Carroll College International program is top-notch and has a successful track record. Still, Baker was interested in improving the International program and wanted to get feedback from current and former students that would enable her to make changes that would lead to the most significant improvements. She had already met with the president of the college, Dr. Thomas Trebon, about the importance of the International program to the college and the decision to use outside research. After talking with several of her peer directors around the country, Baker called the research firm of TLG. TLG CEO Robert Smith and Account Executive Jeff Williams met with Baker several times before deciding that research would be appropriate.

Every research project is different. Yet, there are enough similarities among the projects that we can identify a process that most research projects will follow. Having a knowledge of this process is most important in helping researchers identify not only the activities they must undertake to conduct the project, but the order of those activities. Before going further with the Carroll College project, Robert Smith and Jeff Williams

sat down and discussed the Carroll Project in terms of an 11-step marketing research process. As they discussed each step they made decisions that would be necessary to carry out the research project. They both knew from experience that their decisions were not final and, in fact, would likely be altered several times in carrying out the project. Nevertheless, the 11-step process gave them an ideal "road map" for planning the project.

T he above example illustrates the importance of knowing the steps necessary to carry out a marketing research project. While not making all the decisions for the research project, Robert Smith and Jeff Williams are aided in their research planning by knowing the steps they will need to use in the proposed research project for Carroll College. Marketing researchers are familiar with the steps in the marketing research process. In this chapter we will introduce you to these important steps, and these steps will serve as a framework for the rest of this book.

THE MARKETING RESEARCH PROCESS

An Eleven-Step Process

In Chapter 1 you learned what marketing research is and the role it plays in aiding managers in making marketing decisions. You are now ready to learn the steps in the marketing research process. There is value in characterizing research projects in terms of successive steps. First, the steps give researchers and nonresearchers an overview of the entire research process. Second, they provide a procedure in the sense that a researcher,

It is very important for you to learn the 11 steps in the marketing research process.

by referring to the steps, knows what tasks to consider and in what order. By introducing you to these steps we are also giving you a preview of what is in store for you as you read this book. We identify the 11 **steps in the marketing research process** in Figure 2.1.[1] The steps are (1) establish the need for marketing research, (2) define the problem, (3) establish research objectives, (4) determine research design, (5) identify information types and sources, (6) determine methods of accessing data, (7) design data-collection forms, (8) determine the sample plan and size, (9) collect data, (10) analyze data, and (11) prepare and present the final research report. We will discuss each of these steps in the following paragraphs but, first, you need to understand there are some caveats associated with using a step-by-step approach to understanding the process of marketing research.

Caveats to a Step–by–Step Process

While we think that 11 steps is a good number of steps to explain the marketing research process adequately, others may use fewer, or more, steps.

▶ **Why 11 Steps?** You should know that there are caveats to presenting all research projects in an 11-step process. First, while we conceptualize the research process as 11 steps, others may present the process in fewer steps or more steps. There is nothing sacred about 11 steps. We could present research as three steps; defining the problem, collecting and analyzing data, and presenting the results. We think this oversimplifies the research process. Or, we could present you with 20-plus steps. In our opinion, this

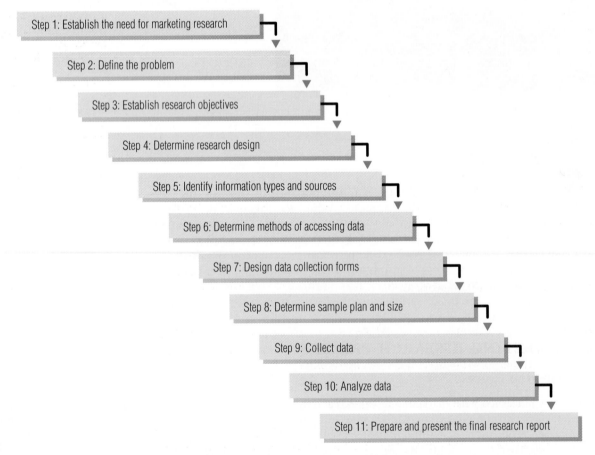

FIGURE 2.1
11 Steps in the Marketing Research Process

would provide more detail than is needed. We think that 11 steps is explicit enough without being overly detailed. But you should know that everyone does not present the research process in the same way we have presented it here.

▶ **Not All Studies Use All 11 Steps.** A second caveat is that not all studies follow all 11 steps. Sometimes, for example, a review of secondary research alone may allow the researcher to achieve the research objectives. Our 11 steps assume that the research process examines secondary data and continues on to collect primary data.

▶ **Few Studies Follow the Steps in Order.** Our third caveat is that most research projects do not follow an orderly, step-by-step process. Sometimes, after beginning to gather data, it may be determined that the research objectives should be changed. Researchers do not move, robot-like, from one step to the next. Rather, as they move through the process, they make decisions as to how to proceed in the future, which may involve going back and revisiting a previous step.

While you are forewarned about using a "list" approach, remember that our 11 steps are very useful in understanding the marketing research process. In our opening vignette, the researchers at TLG benefit greatly by knowing the steps of the research process. Knowing the steps in the process helps them design a better research project for their client. In the following paragraphs we will briefly discuss the 11 steps. Also, at the beginning of each chapter we will provide you with a list of the 11 steps and we will highlight "where you are" on the list depending on the topics covered in the chapter. See "Where We Are" in the margin.

Step 1: Establish the Need for Marketing Research

The need for marketing research arises when managers must make decisions and they have inadequate information. Not all decisions will require marketing research. Research takes time and costs money. Managers must weigh the value that may possibly be derived from conducting marketing research and having the information at hand with the cost of obtaining that information. Fortunately, most situations do not require research, because if they did, managers would be mired down in research instead of making timely decisions.

In the Carroll College situation, it was clearly established that Carroll had a fine International program. However, the college administration thought that offering its own students opportunities to study abroad and being exposed to students from diverse cultures was an essential ingredient in preparing Carroll graduates for their role in a global economy. The president placed high priority on the program and wanted to take the right steps to expand the program. Baker had years of experience in running the program but knew that she and the president needed to assess different alternatives if they were going to find the most efficient ways to effectively increase the presence of the International program on the campus. Together, Baker and Trebon, decided that the benefits of the research would far outweigh the costs. However, sometimes it is determined that it is not appropriate to use marketing research. The following section describes circumstances that indicate that research is not needed.

When Is Marketing Research Not Needed?

▶ **The Information Is Already Available.** Managers make many decisions. Many of these decisions are routine and the manager has the experience to make the decision without any additional information. When decisions do require additional information remember that there are other components of the Marketing Information System that

---

Not all marketing research projects require all 11 steps.

Many marketing research projects do not follow the 11 steps in exact order.

At the beginning of each chapter we will provide you with a list of the 11 steps and we will highlight "Where We Are" on the list depending on the topics covered in the chapter.

Where We Are
1 Establish the need for marketing research
2 Define the problem
3 Establish research objectives
4 Determine research design
5 Identify information types and sources
6 Determine methods of accessing data
7 Design data-collection forms
8 Determine sample plan and size
9 Collect data
10 Analyze data
11 Prepare and present the final research report

Ultimately, decision makers must decide whether or not they need marketing research information to make their decisions. Shirley Baker and President Thomas Trebon of Carroll College make the decision to use marketing research.

Can the needed information be obtained from the internal reports system? From the marketing intelligence system? From the decision support system? All of these information systems are ongoing sources of information. If these do not supply the information, marketing research may be needed.

the manager may use. Can the needed information be obtained from the internal reports system? From the marketing intelligence system? From the decision support system? All of these information systems are ongoing sources of information. Marketing managers can quickly and inexpensively (low variable cost) access this information. Consider the following example. Shirley Baker has a great deal of information in Carroll's internal reports system. She knows where Carroll's international students come from and she knows where Carroll students have studied abroad in the past. The college's intelligence system helps her identify trends and issues in international education. Most of this information relates to issues arising from stricter rules for visas since the terrorist attacks in the United States in 2001. Her decision support system can help her answer "what if" questions such as how much impact would it have on applicants to require a higher (or lower) grade point standard for admission? However, none of these sources could provide her with information on where potential programs are and, more importantly, what factors international students and Carroll students thought were the most important in deciding to enter an international studies program. When information is not available the researcher should consider conducting marketing research.

Sometimes the need to respond quickly to competition means there isn't time to conduct marketing research.

▶ **The Timing Is Wrong to Conduct Marketing Research.** Time often plays a critical role in decision making, and that is true with marketing research as well. It may be that there is not enough time to conduct marketing research. Consider this situation. The candy bar business is highly competitive. Mars introduces a new flavor and sales skyrocket. Market share is gained at the expense of competitors such as Hershey. Should managers at Hershey launch marketing research to determine if the new flavor is acceptable to the market? No. There isn't time. Mars's new product is all the evidence that should be needed to demonstrate that the new flavor has market acceptance. Instead of conducting research, Hershey needs to launch a competitive product, with the same flavor as the new successful Mars brand, to take back some of the losses they have already experienced.

Time may also be a factor for products that are nearing the end of their life cycle. When products have been around for many years and are reaching the decline stage of their life cycle, it may be too late for research to produce valuable results.

In our Carroll College example, there is time to conduct research. There is no need to make decisions about changing the program within a matter of days or even weeks. Secondly, since the president wishes to place a high priority on developing the program, it is time to begin the research.

▶ **Funds Are Not Available for Marketing Research.** Small firms or firms that are having cash-flow problems may not conduct marketing research simply because they cannot afford it. Research, if conducted properly, can be expensive. A study gathering primary data for a representative sample can cost hundreds of thousands of dollars. Also, many times the total cost of research is not fully appreciated. Conducting the research is one cost but, to be useful, firms must also consider what it may cost to *implement* the research recommendations. The owner of a pizza restaurant saved money for a research project but was then unable to fund any of the recommendations (should offer drive-through and delivery service). In this case, the research money was wasted.

Carroll College has funds that they may use to improve the quality of their programs. They made the decision to improve the quality of the educational experience of all their students through expanding international studies.

▶ **Costs Outweigh the Value of Marketing Research.** Managers should always consider the cost of research and the value they expect to receive from conducting it. Although costs are readily estimated, it is much more difficult to estimate the value that research is likely to add. As an example, consider a decision as to how best to package a new brand of toothpaste. The packaging required to send a few sample boxes to a new-products trade show would certainly not warrant research. The packaging needs only to ensure safe transit. If the packaging fails, little is lost and recovery is simple. However, what about the packaging of the toothpaste itself? The toothpaste must sit on a shelf among many other brands, many of which have packaging that is easily recognized by brand-loyal customers. Chances are, a consumer quickly scanning the toothpaste section will see his or her favorite brand and make the purchase without even being aware of the existence of the new brand. If research can identify a package design that will draw greater attention and promote awareness of the brand on the shelf, sales will go up. This gives the research value. How much value? Managers must try to estimate what impact there will be on sales if 2 out of 10 shoppers are aware of the brand instead of 1 out of 20. Though placing a dollar figure on value is difficult, value *can* be estimated and a more informed decision may be made justifying or not justifying marketing research. Some managers fail to compare research cost with its value, which is a mistake.[2]

When Will Research More Likely Have Greater Value? Some guidelines for answering this question are: Will the research help clarify problems or opportunities? Will research identify changes that are occurring in the marketplace among consumers and/or competitors? Will research clearly identify the best alternative to pursue among a set of proposed alternatives? Will the research help your brand establish a competitive advantage?[3] Once a decision is made that research is needed, managers (and researchers) must properly define the problem and the research objectives.

Carroll College has determined that research will add value greater than its costs. Furthermore, the research will help identify opportunities; are there colleges and universities who are looking to give their students experiences in the United States for educational programs currently being offered by Carroll? Can current Carroll

Small firms or firms that are having cash-flow problems may not conduct marketing research simply because they cannot afford it. Research, if conducted properly, can be expensive.

Though placing a dollar figure on value is difficult, value *can* be estimated and a more informed decision may be made justifying or not justifying marketing research.

students obtain coursework and program-specific training that Carroll does not currently offer in other countries? Are there countries and programs that current and future Carroll students will more likely take advantage of than the programs currently offered at Carroll? Are there employers who will consider graduates who have particular international experiences and/or language skills to be more valuable? These are all considerations that research can explore. Research can also identify and assess the likelihood of success of the many other program-alternative decisions that Carroll must make; what methods of communication will be the most effective in attracting international students to Carroll or in attracting Carroll students to international opportunities? Clearly, much may be gained through the research Carroll has decided to undertake.

Step 2: Define the Problem

Defining the problem is the most important step, because if the problem is incorrectly defined, all else is wasted effort.

If a decision is made to conduct marketing research, the second step is to define the problem. This is the most important step, because if the problem is incorrectly defined, all else is wasted effort. For this reason, clients and researchers must give high importance to properly defining the problem.

To help us better understand the problem, consider the following examples: "Which of three proposed TV advertising commercials will generate the highest level of sales of our line of cookies?" "Which media, or combination of media, should we use to promote our line of cookies?" "What message should we use in our promotions to gain sales for our line of cookies?" "What should be our overall marketing strategy for our line of cookies?" "Should we be in the cookie business?" As you can see, problems may vary considerably from being specific and narrowly focused (i.e., Which of three TV ads should we use?) to being very general and not narrowly focused (i.e., Should we even be in the cookie business?). Using our Carroll College example, should the problem be narrowly focused, such as, "Which of three proposed methods of communication to potential international program students elicit the greatest number of applications? Or, should the problem be, "Does Carroll College need to have an international program?" Now, perhaps, you are beginning to see that properly defining the problem is often difficult. This is why we devote all of Chapter 4 to the subject.

Problems stem from two primary sources: gaps between what is *supposed* to happen and what *did* happen and gaps between what *did* happen and what *could* have happened (opportunities).

Problems stem from two primary sources: gaps between what is *supposed* to happen and what *did* happen and gaps between what *did* happen and what *could* have happened. When we have a gap between what is supposed to happen and what did happen, we normally refer to this as "failure to meet our objective." For example, our objective is to have 200 students participating in our International program and we have only 145 enrolled. Or, our sales goal for last quarter was $400,000 and we sold $380,000. This is how we normally think of "problems." However, consider our second gap; a gap between what did happen and what could have happened. We did have 200 students participating in our International program this year but we could have had 500 students in the program. We had sales last quarter of $400,000 but we could have had sales of $750,000. We normally refer to this type of gap as an opportunity.

Step 3: Establish Research Objectives

Research objectives, when achieved, provide the information necessary to solve the problem.

Research objectives, although related to and determined by the problem definition, are set so that, when achieved, they provide the information necessary to solve the problem. Let's consider the following example. Independent insurance agents typically belong to a state association called, for instance, the Independent Insurance Agents of Iowa. The association is responsible for educational programs, lobbying with state insurance boards, and technical advice. If the association was concerned with responding to the needs of its members, it would be reasonable for problems to be defined as (1) are the associations' services valued by the members and (2) which services should be revised?

A good way of setting research objectives is to ask, "What information is needed in order to solve the problems?" Because the association's services are in place, the research objectives would translate as follows:

> Determine the average importance level of each service.
> Determine the average level of satisfaction for each service.

You should notice that these research objectives are different from the defined problems. Yet, when the information is gathered as a result of carrying out these research objectives, the problems are solved. Research objectives state what the researchers must do in terms of research in order to provide the information necessary to solve the problem. By collecting the information requested by the first two research objectives, the association is in a position to rank its services based on how important they are to members, and it can identify which highly important services have low satisfaction levels and need revision. Alternatively, the association can identify services that should not be revised, indicated by high satisfaction with highly important services, if they exist.

Let's take a look at how we might set our research objectives for the Carroll College example. Baker has long been aware that a significant percentage (between 20 and 40% of incoming freshmen) of Carroll students express interest in pursuing an international program agenda but fewer than 2% actually take advantage of the program. There is a gap between the number of students who are interested in an international program and the number who actually have an international program experience. At TLG, Smith and Williams now determine the research objective that will provide the information to solve this problem. Their proposed research objective is: "Conduct representative surveys among samples of Carroll freshmen, sophomores, juniors, and seniors to determine what obstacles they percieve as keeping them from taking advantage of an international program experience." As you can see, if TLG provides Baker with this information she will be in a much better position to design programs that overcome perceived obstacles preventing many students from taking part in the program.

> Research objectives state what the researchers must do in order to carry out the research.

Step 4: Determine Research Design

Almost every research project is different, but there are enough similarities among research projects to enable us to categorize them by the research methods and procedures used to collect and analyze data. There are three types of these categories, which are referred to as research designs: (1) exploratory research, (2) descriptive research, and (3) causal research.

Exploratory research is defined as collecting information in an unstructured and informal manner. It is often used when little is known about the problem. Analyzing secondary data in a library or over the Internet is one of the most common ways of conducting exploratory research. An executive reading about demographic trends forecast for the next five years in *American Demographics* would be an example of conducting exploratory research. A manager observing the lines of customers awaiting service at a bank would be an example of exploratory research.

Descriptive research designs refer to a set of methods and procedures that describes marketing variables. Descriptive studies portray these variables by answering who, what, where, when, and how questions. (They do not, however, answer Why? This is done by causal research designs). These types of research studies may describe such things as consumers' attitudes, intentions, and behaviors or the number of competitors

> There are three types of research-design categories, which are referred to as research designs:
> (1) exploratory research,
> (2) descriptive research, and
> (3) causal research.
>
> Exploratory research is defined as collecting information in an unstructured and informal manner. It is often used when little is known about the problem.
>
> Descriptive research designs refer to a set of methods and procedures that describes marketing variables. Descriptive studies portray these variables by answering who, what, where, when, and how questions. They do not, however, answer why?

TLG Account Executive Jeff Williams and CEO Robert Smith determine the appropriate research objectives for the Carroll College research project.

and their strategies. Although most descriptive studies are surveys in which respondents are asked questions, sometimes descriptive studies are observation studies that observe and record consumers' behavior in such a way as to answer the problem. When Bissell Inc. conducted marketing research on the Steam Gun, an elongated cleaning device that used steam to remove stubborn dirt, the company gave the product to families and then observed them using the product in their homes. In addition to learning that they needed to change the name, the company learned several important lessons that led them to successfully market the Steam N Clean.[4]

Causal research allows us to isolate causes and effects. Causal designs answer the question of Why? We call causal research designs "experiments."

The final research design, **causal research**, allows us to isolate causes and effects. They answer the question of Why? We call causal research designs **experiments**. Some researchers conducted an experiment on the effects of Yellow Page ads. The experiment allowed them to conclude that color is better than black and white and that photos are better than line art at causing more favorable customer attitudes and perceptions of quality and credibility. The experiments also showed that these relationships varied across product categories.[5] This is powerful information to companies that spend huge sums of money on Yellow Pages ads each year. We discuss causal designs in Chapter 5.

It is very likely TLG will use two types of research designs for Carroll College: exploratory and descriptive.

Which research design is TLG likely to propose for the Carroll College project? Very likely they will propose at least two of these designs. First, they will do exploratory research to ensure that they know what is going on around the world in terms of international studies programs. They will learn if other colleges and universities have excelled with their programs. They will find out what factors in other countries are encouraging or discouraging international studies among college students. They will determine if there are already published reports on international studies programs. Exploratory research will be very helpful but it is unlikely to help them solve all their research objectives. Second, they will likely need descriptive research. Why? Think about the research objective we discussed in step 3. TLG will need to conduct descriptive research to "describe" the obstacles Carroll students have in terms of actually taking part in international studies.

Step 5: Identify Information Types and Sources

Since research provides information to help solve problems, researchers must identify the type and sources of information they will use in step 5. There are two types of information: **primary information** (information collected specifically for the problem at hand) and **secondary information** (information already collected). Secondary information should always be sought first since it is much cheaper and faster to collect than primary information. A company franchising car washes, for example, may use secondary data to make decisions about where to locate new car washes based on the number of vehicles per square mile and the number of existing car washes in different market areas. This is information that has been collected and is available in published sources for a small fee. Sometimes research companies collect information and make it available to all those wishing to pay a subscription to get the information. Referred to as syndicated data, Nielsen Media Research's TV Ratings reports the numbers of persons who watch different TV programs, and is an example of this type of information. Both these types of secondary information are discussed in Chapters 6 and 7. However, sometimes secondary data are inadequate. What if our car-wash franchiser wanted to know how car owners in Austin, Texas, would respond to a one-price ticket good for as many car washes as needed in a year? This information is not available. What if a particular college wanted to know what its own students felt about a proposed program? Primary data must be collected specifically for these problems. Beginning with Chapter 8, the rest of this book teaches you how to gather, analyze, and report primary data.

There are two types of information: primary information (information collected specifically for the problem at hand) and secondary information (information already collected).

Almost everyone has heard of the "Nielsen TV ratings," yet few people know much about them. Where can you find ratings? How are ratings collected? Are the ratings accurate measurements of TV audiences? What is a rating and what is a share? Does Nielsen Media Research cancel TV programs? Here is your opportunity to learn about a well-known, though little understood, firm in the marketing research industry. To answer these and other questions, go to: http://www.nielsenmedia.com/index.html. As a suggestion, go to FAQ. Also take a look at the options under Quick Links.

Active Learning

Nielsen Media Research provides information on how many persons watch television programs. Printed with the permission of Nielsen Media Research, New York.

Step 6: Determine Methods of Accessing Data

Accessing data may be accomplished through a variety of methods. Methods of accessing secondary data have greatly improved over the past few years. Not only has the quantity of information available increased; but, perhaps more significantly, the Internet has vastly improved our ability to easily and quickly retrieve the information from online information services and from the Web sites of organizations providing such information. Improvements in search engines such as Google make online searching very effective and efficient. Still, much valuable information is available at your local library. Not all information is electronic. Books are still a good resource for information.

You will learn more about secondary information sources used by marketing researchers in Chapter 6.

While secondary data is relatively easy to access, accessing primary data is much more complex. When the researcher must communicate with respondents there are three main choices of accessing data: (1) have a person ask questions (i.e., conduct an in-home survey or a telephone survey), (2) use a computer-assisted method (i.e., computer assisted telephone interview [CATI] or online survey delivered to an e-mail address), and (3) allow respondents to answer questions themselves without computer assistance (i.e., mail survey). There are several methods of accessing data within the three broad choices, and each of these, along with their pros and cons are discussed in Chapter 9. Of course we could consider a fourth major type of accessing data—a hybrid, or a mix of two or more of the above methods.

What if your research objective requires you to observe a consumer rather than communicate with the consumer? Then you would be using "observation" to access your data. We discuss this in Chapter 8.

Research objectives often help spell out what method will be used to access data. As illustrated by our Carroll College example, if a research objective requires that the sample be representative, this means that everyone in the population (i.e., all Carroll students) must be able to be included in the sample. You cannot use online surveys unless all students have online access. You cannot use telephone surveys unless all students have telephones. So, if these conditions did exist, you would have to access the students by mail. On the other hand, a research objective that requires in-depth interviews with a few students could be achieved with personnel interviewing people who volunteered in response to an e-mail, telephone call, or personal request.

Step 7: Design Data-Collection Forms

The design of the data-collection form that is used to ask and record information gathered in marketing research projects is critical to the success of the project. Even when the correct problem has been defined and the most appropriate research design planned, asking the wrong questions, or asking the right questions in the wrong order, will destroy the usefulness of the research effort. Whether the research design requires that respondents be asked questions or that their behavior be observed, standardized forms, called questionnaires, record the information. A questionnaire's apparent simplicity (writing a list of questions) is very deceptive. Care must be taken to design a questionnaire that will cooperatively elicit objective information from the respondents. This means avoiding both ambiguous and leading questions. Additional considerations must be made for observation studies. In recent years, software programs have been made available to researchers to assist in creating surveys. Some of the newer software programs allow users to post the surveys on the Web, and data are automatically downloaded into a statistical package such as SPSS when respondents complete answers to the survey questions. One such software program is WebSurveyor.

TLG must be very careful in designing their data-collection forms. They know that the form they design will be influenced by the method they use to access data (step 6). Questions written for use over the telephone differ from questions written for face-to-face

---

Sidebar notes:

When the researcher must communicate with respondents there are three main choices of accessing data: (1) a person asks the questions, (2) a computer assists in asking the questions, and (3) respondents answer on their own. Of course, a fourth option is a hybrid, or mix of the above three modes.

If your research objective does not require you to communicate with the consumer, you may want to collect data by observing consumers.

Care must be taken to ask the questions that will generate information needed to solve the research objectives and to ask them clearly and without bias.

WebSurveyor is a software program and service designed to help researchers design questionnaires, administer them over the Internet, and collect and analyze data.

interviews. And, if they elect to use the Internet, they will have access to computer software programs such as WebSurveyor to help them in their task. They must choose their wording carefully so as to not have leading questions. They must design their questionnaire in a way that encourages students to respond and to provide information. They know that they will benefit from pretesting the survey on a sample of college students prior to finalizing the form. You will learn about preparing an objective questionnaire in Chapter 11.

Step 8: Determine Sample Plan and Size

Normally marketing research studies are undertaken to learn about a population by taking a sample, a subset, of that population. Heinz uses a sample of homemakers to learn about the cooking preferences of all homemakers. Yanmar Diesels studies a sample of diesel mechanics in order to learn the preferences about engine design for purposes of repair and maintenance. A population consists of the entire group about which the researcher wishes to make inferences based on information provided by the sample data. A population could be "all department stores within the Portland, Oregon, metropolitan statistical area," or it could be "College students enrolled in Carroll College during the spring 2007 term." Populations should be defined by the research objectives. The **sample plan** refers to the process used to select units from the population to be included in the sample. A sample plan, for example, would tell TLG how to select Carroll College students for its sample from among all Carroll College students. There are different sample plans, and each has advantages and disadvantages. The sample plan determines how representative the sample is of the population. You will learn how to select the appropriate sample plan depending on the research objectives in Chapter 12. **Sample size**, as the name implies, refers to determining how *many* elements of the population should be included in the sample. As a rule, the larger the sample the better, but you can have a sample that is too large, which wastes research dollars. The size of the sample determines the accuracy of the sample results. In Chapter 13 you will learn how to calculate a sample size that is just large enough to give you accurate results. There are research firms, such as Survey Sampling International and STS Samples, that help researchers with their sample plans and sample size problems. Marketing Research Insight 2.1 illustrates the services of Survey Sampling International and illustrates how a firm may sample in many countries around the globe.

Step 9: Collect Data

Data collection is very important because, regardless of the data analysis methods used, data analysis cannot "fix" bad data.[6] Data are usually gathered by trained interviewers who are employed by field-data-collection companies to collect primary data. Many possible errors, called **nonsampling errors** because they are attributable to factors other than sampling errors, may occur during data collection. Such errors include selecting the wrong sample elements to interview, selecting subjects who refuse to participate or are simply not at home when the interviewer calls, interviewing subjects who intentionally give out the wrong information, or hiring interviewers who cheat and fill out fictitious survey questionnaires. Even interviewers who honestly complete their interviews may make inadvertent nonsampling errors by copying down the wrong information on their survey form. Needless to say, good marketing researchers must be aware of the errors that may occur during data collection and should implement industry-accepted controls to reduce these errors. For example, by implementing a control called "validation," researchers may minimize the likelihood of a nonsampling error caused by a field worker cheating and making up data as reportedly coming from a

2.1 Sampling Around the World

Survey Sampling International (SSI) began operations in 1977 and is a major player in the marketing research industry. The company provides services that allow clients, both companies conducting their own research as well as other marketing research firms, solve complex sampling problems. Using the firm's SSI-SNAP® program, clients may design their own sample plans online and receive samples electronically in a matter of minutes. The company has access to huge databases and can provide client firms with RDD (random-digit-dialed) samples

Survey Sampling International

for households or business firms. They offer samples that have been screened for disconnected numbers and they also provide a service, LITe® samples, which targets selected populations such as pet owners or frequent travelers.

Responding to globalization, SSI now offers sampling services in over 20 countries around the world. This is a significant undertaking, as the various differences in infra-

Canada is the second-largest country in the world. It is in northern North America, bordering the North Atlantic Ocean and North Pacific Ocean, north of the United States. Canada is a self-governing dominion with ties to the British crown. The capital city is Ottawa.

The population is approximately 31,592,805. The bulk of the population (68%) is between the ages of 15 and 64 years; nearly 19% is 14 years and younger; and nearly 13% is 65 years and older. The languages spoken are English 59.3% (official), French 23.2% (official), and other 17.5%. The country has 16,840,000 Internet users.

Source: The World Factbook 2002 and Wikipedia: The Free Encyclopedia

structure makes sampling much more complex. Just think of the differences between countries in address formats, telephone numbering systems, and information sources containing databases of mailing addresses, telephone numbers, and Internet addresses.

Visit the SSI website at **www.surveysampling.com**. Go to "Sampling Solutions by Country" and see to which countries SSI offers sampling services.

---

respondent. Validation means that 10% (industry standard) of all respondents in a marketing research study are randomly selected, recontacted, and asked if they indeed took part in a research study. Unlike sampling error, you cannot measure the amount of non-sampling error that may exist in a study. Therefore, it is important to know the possible causes of nonsampling error so that appropriate steps, such as validation, can be taken to limit its occurrence. You will learn the causes of nonsampling errors and how to reduce those errors in Chapter 14.

Data analysis involves entering data into computer files, inspecting the data for errors, and running tabulations and various statistical tests.

Step 10: Analyze Data

Once data are collected, data analysis is used to give the raw data meaning. **Data analysis** involves entering data into computer files, inspecting the data for errors, and running tabulations and various statistical tests. The first step in data analysis is **data cleaning**, which is the process by which the raw data are checked to verify that the

Data cleaning is the process by which the raw data are checked to verify that the data have been correctly input from the data-collection form to the computer software program.

Mktg. Inc. is a marketing research firm that specializes in data collection. By permission, Mktg. Inc. Visit the company Web site at **www.mktginc.com**.

data have been correctly input from the data-collection form to the computer software program. Typically, data analysis is conducted with the assistance of a computerized data analysis program such as SPSS. You will learn how to conduct basic descriptive data analysis in Chapter 15, how to make statistical inferences from your data in Chapter 16, how to determine if there are significant differences in Chapter 17, how to determine if there are significant associations in Chapter 18, and how to make predictions in Chapter 19. You will learn all of these types of data analysis using the SPSS software that comes with this book.

Step 11: Prepare and Present the Final Research Report

The last step in the marketing research process is to prepare and present the final research report—one of the most important phases of marketing research. Its importance cannot be overstated because it is the report, or its presentation, that properly communicates the study results to the client. Sometimes researchers not only turn in a written research report but they also make an oral presentation of the research methods used to conduct the study as well as the research findings to their client. In Chapter 20 we show you how to write a marketing research report, and we provide you with suggestions on how to give an oral presentation.

When TLG prepares their research report and makes their oral presentation to Shirley Baker and President Trebon at Carroll College they will make a special effort to ensure that they have addressed every research objective identified in the early stages of the research project. If they clearly communicate the information they have gathered to satisfy these research objectives, Baker and Trebon will be well on their way to launching a major, and likely highly successful, rennovation in the International program at Carroll.

The last step in the marketing research process is to prepare and present the final research report—one of the most important phases of marketing research. Its importance cannot be overstated because it is the report, or its presentation, that properly communicates the study results to the client.

In most cases, marketing research firms prepare a written research report and they make an oral presentation to the client and staff.

SOME FINAL COMMENTS ON THE MARKETING RESEARCH PROCESS

We do not mean to imply that all marketing research processes are as straightforward as we suggest in the Carroll College case. At the same time, many marketing research projects *are* as straightforward as we have shown here. However, the point we want to make is that there is great diversity in marketing research projects. A research project designed to produce a new name for a new type of razor blade is very different from a research project designed to forecast sales in units for a brand-new product. Yet, as we told you at the beginning of this chapter, the steps in the research process still provide you with a good framework for understanding marketing research. In Chapter 3 we continue our introduction to marketing research. You are about to learn about the industry itself as well as the ethical issues facing the industry.

SUMMARY

There is great variability in marketing research projects. Some studies are limited to a review of secondary data; others require complex designs involving large-scale collection of primary data. But even with this diversity of research projects, there are enough commonalities among these projects to enable us to characterize them in terms of "steps of the research process." There is value in characterizing research projects in terms of successive steps. First, the steps give researchers and nonresearchers an overview of the entire research process. Second, they provide a procedure in the sense that a researcher, by referring to the steps, knows what tasks to consider and in what order. The steps are (1) establish the need for marketing research, (2) define the problem, (3) establish research objectives, (4) determine research design, (5) identify information types and sources, (6) determine methods of accessing data, (7) design data collection forms, (8) determine sample plan and size, (9) collect data, (10) analyze data, and (11) prepare and present the final research report.

While there are definite advantages to presenting the marketing research process in a step-by-step fashion, there are caveats. First, there is nothing magic about our "11 steps." We could use fewer steps and make the steps more general, or we could have many more steps by increasing the specificity of the steps. Second, not all studies follow all 11 steps. Many problems may not require, for example, the collection of primary data, data analysis, and so on. Our 11 steps assume that the research process examines secondary data and continues on to collect primary data. Our third caveat is that the steps are seldom followed in the same order. Rather, the steps are more interactive. That is, after collecting some data, the researcher may decide that the problem needs to be redefined, and the process may start over. The case of Carroll College is presented throughout the chapter to illustrate application of the 11-step research process in a marketing research project.

KEY TERMS

- 11 Steps in the marketing research process (p. 24)
- Exploratory research (p. 29)
- Descriptive research (p. 29)
- Causal research (p. 30)
- Experiments (p. 30)
- Primary information (p. 31)
- Secondary information (p. 31)

Sample plan (p. 33)   Data analysis (p. 34)
Sample size (p. 33)   Data cleaning (p. 34)
Nonsampling errors (p. 33)

REVIEW QUESTIONS/APPLICATIONS

 1. What are the steps in the marketing research process?
 2. Use an example to illustrate that the steps in the marketing research process are not always taken in sequence.
 3. Explain why firms may not have a need for marketing research.
 4. Why is defining the problem the most important step in the marketing research process?
 5. Explain why research objectives differ from the definition of the problem.
 6. What are the three types of research that constitute research design?
 7. Which part of the research process ensures that the sample is representative?
 8. Which part of the research process ensures the accuracy of the results?
 9. Go to the Internet and do a search for marketing research firms. Look through their Web pages. Can you identify examples of what they are presenting to you as relating to steps in the research process?
10. Go to your library or the Internet and look for examples of firms conducting a marketing research study. There are many examples reported in periodicals such as *Advertising Age, Marketing News, Business Week*, and *Forbes*. Typically, these articles will mention a few details of the research project itself. Identify as many of the steps in the marketing research process as possible that are referred to in the articles you find.
11. Observe any business in your community. Examine what it does, what products or service it provides, its prices, its promotion, or any other aspect of its business. Try to determine whether or not you, if you managed the business, would have conducted research to determine the firm's products, their design, features, prices, promotion, and so on. If you decide that you would not have conducted marketing research on a given area, explain why.

NV MY MPG[7]

If the license plates "NV MY MPG" and "DRIVE HY" (See www.hybridcars.com top 10 vanity plates) mean nothing to you, you probably are not a hybrid driver. The segment of our population that is driving one of a variety of hybrid vehicles would know that you should "envy my miles per gallon" (www.hybridcars.com); and well, the second license tag should need no explanation now.

HowStuffWorks.com says a hybrid vehicle combines two sources of power; in the case of a hybrid automobile, "the gasoline–electric hybrid car is just that—a cross between a gasoline-powered car and an electric car" (http://auto.howstuffworks.com/hybridcar1.htm). Though the first successful hybrid electric car was developed by Ferdinand Porsche in the late 1920s, a major manufacturer did not begin producing such a car until Honda and Toyota produced the Insight and the Prius in the 1990s (http://www.wordiq.com/definition/Hybrid_car).

In the 21st century, hybrids have seen exponential growth in sales. Hybridcars.com reports the following sales figures:

- 9350 in 2000
- 20,287 in 2001
- 35,000 in 2002
- 47,525 in 2003,
- 88,000 in 2004

and by 2010 one of twenty cars sold in America will be hybrids (http://www.hybridcars.com/sales-numbers.html).

Currently, there are 6 hybrid automobiles available on the market, and estimates are that the number will be in the teens soon. With celebrities ranging from Will Ferrell to Leonardo DiCaprio (http://www.hybridcars.com/celebrities.html) joining the ranks of car owners who are earning up to 68 mpg on the highway (http://www.hybridcars.com/mileage.html) while protecting the environment, hybrids might just make all of us "ATPCL-AMRCN"—atypical Americans.

Jane Akin read the article listed above on an informational Web site. Jane works in the Marketing Research department for an American car company, and she notices that Ford is the only American car company that offers a hybrid automobile—an SUV. She thinks that it is time that her company joined the hybrid race with a sedan.

Jane also finds the following survey results on www.hybridcars.com:

2004 Hybridcars.com Survey		2003 Oregon Survey	
Would you recommend your hybrid to a friend?			
96% Yes		98% Yes	
Reasons you bought a hybrid?			
80%	Reduce foreign oil dependency	89%	Pollute the air less
78%	Pollute the air less	77%	Emit less climate-changing CO_2
74%	Save money on gas	73%	Appealing technology
71%	Emit less climate-changing CO_2	71%	Save money on gas
What do you like best?			
75%	Fuel savings	68%	Technology, style, and handling
70%	Environmental benefits	53%	Fuel savings (gas mileage)
What do you like least?			
33%	Nothing disliked	7.5%	Mileage less than advertised
22%	Fear of maintenance costs	5.5%	Limited storage space
16%	Mileage less than advertised	5.4%	The car is smaller than they'd like

Source: http://www.hybridcars.com/survey.html

1. What questions with regard to marketing research should Jane ask herself?

2. Discuss Jane's idea with regard to the first 6 steps of the marketing research process

This case will appear throughout the book. It will be used to illustrate concepts covered in the chapter in which the case appears.

THE HOBBIT'S CHOICE: A RESTAURANT

Jeff Dean is a restaurant supply sales representative. He works in a large metropolitan area and calls on many of the restaurant owners in the city. His dream is to one day own his own restaurant. He had saved a substantial amount of his earnings during his 15 years in the restaurant-supply business and had recently gone over some financial figures with his banker. He and the banker both agreed that he had enough capital to get serious about investing in his dream. His banker, Walker Stripling, was very optimistic about Dean's potential for success, even though he had seen many failed attempts in the restaurant business. Stripling had confidence in Dean because he thought that because of his restaurant-supply experience, few people knew the restaurant business as well as Dean did.

Dean's idea was not try to compete with everyone else. There were too many restaurants that, except for their décor and a few menu items, offered little new to the market. He had seen many of the "me-too" restaurants falter after a short time of operation. His plan was to offer something not currently available in the market, even though the city was fairly large. Dean had traveled extensively during his career. His primary purpose in traveling had been to attend trade shows in the restaurant-supply business. There were usually several of these a year, and Dean had been diligent about attending these shows as he learned about new products and services his supplier firms were offering for him to sell to his local restaurants. While attending the trade shows, Dean and some of his friends made a habit of visiting restaurants of all types in the various cities. Dean was familiar with restaurants in New Orleans, San Francisco, Dallas, Miami, New York, and many of the other major cities in the United States. These cities all had restaurants like the restaurants he had as clients at home, and they had these same types of restaurants by the dozens. But there was one type of restaurant these cities had that was missing from his own metro area. His city did not have a fine, upscale restaurant featuring the finest entrées, drinks, and desserts in an elegant atmosphere. He had visited with the owners of these types of restaurants in several of the cities in which he traveled. Many had been very willing to talk with him about what they had learned and how they operated. Dean had planned his restaurant for several years. He took the best ideas from the restaurants he had visited and put them into his plan. His restaurant would be called "The Hobbit's Choice." Dean was a fan of the author J.R.R. Tolkien, and he thought the reference to the Hobbits would be perfect in a name for an upscale restaurant. The Hobbits, characters in Tolkien's writings, were portrayed as good, fun-loving people whose lives primarily centered around eating.

1. What reasons would you give for Jeff Dean to not conduct any marketing research?

2. What reasons would you give for Jeff Dean to conduct marketing research?

3. If you were Jeff Dean, what would you do in terms of not conducting or conducting marketing research? Why?

3

The Marketing Research Industry

Jack J. Honomichl on the Marketing Research Industry

INSIDE RESEARCH®

Jack J. Honomichl[1] knows more about the marketing research industry than anyone we know. When he was inducted into the Market Research Council's Hall of Fame he was described as having "defined the marketing research industry." He is President of The Marketing Aid Center, and he publishes "Inside Research," a monthly newsletter for marketing research industry executives. He publishes the most authoritative information on revenues of the industry in his annual reports, "The Honomichl Top 50" and the "Honomichl Global Top 25." We feature both of these reports in this chapter. For these reasons, we felt it appropriate to have Mr. Honomichl begin your first lesson in learning about the marketing research industry. We asked Mr. Honomichl to provide you with his insights on the marketing research industry, which you will find in the following paragraphs.

The research industry is maturing, becoming more transparent, and professional. While the worldwide marketing/advertising/public opinion research industry planted its seeds in the 1920s, it didn't really bloom until after WWII, in the 1950s. And then, basically, it consisted of hundreds of relatively small, privately owned firms that didn't disclose their revenues; there was no industry sense of self.

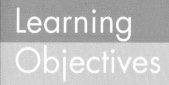

Jack J. Honomichl, President,
Marketing Aid Center and
Member of the Market
Research Council's Hall
of Fame.

Then came a surge of consolidation, and this accelerated in the 1990s. Specifically, during the 15-year period, 1990–2004, there were—worldwide—502 instances of research firms changing ownership, mostly through acquistion. This was not just the little guys; many of the world's largest firms changed ownership too, some two or more times. This trend continues—through the first four months of 2005 there were 26 more turnovers.

The end result is that, today, mostly through acquisition, there have come to be a handful of research behemoths with operations in dozens of countries around the world and annual revenues in excess of $1 billion. Many of these firms are publicly listed or operate as subsidiaries of publicly listed parent companies. So, their revenues are in the public domain, along with statements of profitability and executive remuneration. The industry, then, is more and more a glass house.

This also means that more and more people working in research now share the accouterments of corporate America—pension plans, health benefits, personnel (human resource) departments, and promotion opportunities around the world. They have become multinational and multicultural, with all that implies.

On top of all that, there now comes a movement toward accreditation of marketing research professionals. Long talked (and argued) about, there has finally come to be an industry-sponsored vehicle to obtain accreditation for individuals who wish to make marketing research a career.

Launched in early 2005, and spearheaded by the Marketing Research Association, there came to be a program leading to Professional Researcher Certification, consisting of courses and procedures that enable interested parties, mostly at their own pace, to garner the knowledge deemed desirable to move up through various stages of "professionalism" and a certificate to hang on the wall or to be touted in resumes. You will read more about this new certification program in this chapter.

Long-time practitioners now have a procedure through which they can be "grandfathered" in, and relatively young people can proceed to step up the ladder as they see fit—and are able. It will take years for this program to shake down and have a widespread impact—but it is a start, and very well thought out by professionals who wish the very best for the marketing research industry.

Now you know that the marketing research industry has evolved from small individually owned companies to large, publicly owned firms operating around the world and you know there is a new certification program to serve the industry. The purpose of this chapter is to provide you with additional information about the marketing research industry. We begin by giving a brief historical perspective of marketing research. Next, we consider the structure of the industry by examining the types of firms in the industry and we look at firm size by introducing you to **The Honomichl Global Top 25**, which contains the top 25 marketing research firms in the world in terms of revenues. We also show you "The Honomichl Top 50," which shows the top 50 marketing research firms in the United States in terms of revenue. We next look at evaluations of the industry. How has the research industry performed, and what suggestions have been made to improve the industry? We also provide you with some detailed information on the Marketing Research Association's certification program. Finally, we examine the ethical issues facing the industry. When you finish this chapter, you will have finished our three-chapter introduction to marketing research. Some of you may have become interested in marketing research as a career. If you want to know more about a career in the industry, we encourage you to read the Appendix on careers that we have provided for you at the end of this chapter.

THE MARKETING RESEARCH INDUSTRY

Evolution of the Industry

▶ **The Beginnings.** Robert Bartels, a marketing historian, wrote that the earliest questionnaire surveys began as early as 1824, and in 1879 a study was conducted by N. W. Ayers and Company to study grain production by states for a client. However, Bartels believes the first continuous and organized research was started in 1911 by **Charles Coolidge Parlin**, a schoolmaster from a small city in Wisconsin. Parlin was hired by the Curtis Publishing Company to gather information about customers and markets to help Curtis sell advertising space. Parlin was successful, and the information he gathered led to increased advertising in Curtis's *Saturday Evening Post* magazine.[2] Parlin is recognized today as the "Father of Marketing Research," and the AMA provides an award each year at the annual marketing research conference in his name.

> The first continuous and organized research was started in 1911 by Charles Coolidge Parlin, who was hired by the Curtis Publishing Company to gather information about customers and markets to help Curtis sell advertising space.

> While there are a few reported instances of the use of marketing research in the early days of the history of the United States, it was not until the 1930s that marketing research efforts became widespread.

> When the Industrial Revolution led to manufacturers producing goods for distant markets, the need for marketing research emerged.

▶ **Growth of the Need.** While there are a few reported instances of the use of marketing research in the early days of the history of the United States, it was not until the 1930s that marketing research efforts became widespread. The reason for this was that prior to the Industrial Revolution businesses were located close to the consumers. In an economy based on artisans and craftsmen involved in barter exchange with their customers, there was not much need to "study" consumers. This is because business owners saw their customers daily. They knew their needs and wants and their likes and dislikes. However, when the Industrial Revolution led to manufacturers producing goods for distant markets, the need for marketing research emerged. Manufacturers in Boston needed to know more about the consumers, and their needs, in "faraway" places like Denver and Atlanta. A. C. Nielsen started his firm in 1922. In the 1930s colleges began to teach courses in marketing research, and during the 1940s Alfred Politz introduced statistical theory for sampling in marketing research.[3] Also, during the 1940s, Robert

Charles Coolidge Parlin
(1872-1942)
Inducted 1953

Read more about Charles Coolidge Parlin by going to: **www.advertisinghalloffame. org/** and then go to Members and search under "p."

Merton introduced focus groups, which today, represent a large part of what is known as "qualitative marketing research." Computers revolutionized the industry in the 1950s.[4] By the 1960s marketing research had not only gained acceptance in the organization but it also was recognized as being a key to understanding distant and fast-changing markets. It was needed for survival.

Since the 1960s the marketing research industry has seen technological advances, in the form of many new products and services, which have increased productivity in the industry. As you learned in Chapter 1, the research industry is truly a global one. As firms spread their business throughout the markets of the world, the marketing research industry followed those firms to their distant markets.

By the 1960s marketing research had not only gained acceptance in the organization but it also was recognized as being a key to understanding distant and fast-changing markets. It was needed for survival.

The Marketing Research Industry Today

▶ **World Revenues.** The marketing research industry accounts for approximately $21.5 billion spent annually to better understand customers, markets, and competitors. In 2004 the world's top 25 marketing/advertising/public opinion firms accounted for $13.3 billion of total revenues—about 62%. The growth rate in revenues among the top 25 firms from 2003 to 2004 after adjusting sales for inflation was 2.5%. As we have seen for several years now, the top 25 are gaining more of a concentration of industry sales because of acquisition. From January 2004 to June 2005, the Top 25 acquired 48 firms. Table 3.1 is a list of the top 25 global research organizations compiled by Jack Honomichl and reported as the Honomichl Global top 25 annually in the *Marketing News*.[5]

The top 25 firms are from all over the world. Home countries include Brazil, the Netherlands, Japan, Germany, France, the United Kingdom, and the United States. Reflecting the true global nature of marketing research, 67% of the total revenues generated by the global top 25 firms in 2004 came from operations/subsidiaries outside

Mr. Honomichl's report is highly regarded as the best measure of revenue and change in the marketing research industry. You can view "The Honomichl Top 50" table at www.marketingpower. com/honomichl.

TABLE 3.1 — 2004 Honomichl Top 25 Global Research Organizations

Rank 2004	Rank 2003	Organization	Headquarters	Parent Country	Web Site (www.)	No. of Countries with Subsidiaries/Branch Offices[1]	Global Research Revenues[2] (US$ millions)	Percent Change from 2003[3]	Revenues from Outside Parent Country (US$ in millions)	Percent of Global Revenues from Outside Home Country
1	1	VNU N.V.	Haarlem	Netherlands	vnu.com	81	$3,429.2	−4.0%	3394.7*	99%*
2	2	Taylor Nelson Sofres Plc.	London	U.K.	tns-global.com	70	1,720.6	2.0	1,430.6	83.2
3	3	IMS Health Inc.	Fairfield, Conn.	USA	imshealth.com	76	1,569.0	5.9	998.0	63.6
4	4	The Kantar Group	Fairfield, CT	U.K.	kantargroup.com	61	1136.3*	2.1*	776.0*	68.3*
5	5	GfK Group	Nuremberg	Germany	gfk.com	59	835.5	6.6	541.5	64.8
6	6	Ipsos Group S.A.	Paris	France	ipsos.com	41	753.2	7.5	633.8	84.2
7	7	Information Resources Inc.	Chicago, Ill.	USA	infores.com	18	572.8	3.3	193.2	33.7
8	9	Synovate	London	U.K.	synovate.com	46	499.3	1.1	407.7	81.7
9	10	NOP World	London	U.K.	nopworld.com	8	407.1	−1.3	297.3	73.0
10	8	Westat Inc.	Rockville, Md.	USA	westat.com	1	397.8	4.3		
11	11	Arbitron Inc.	New York, N.Y.	USA	arbitron.com	3	296.6	6.1	11.9	4.0
12	***	INTAGE Inc.**	Tokyo	Japan	intage.co.jp	2	246.2	11.4	1.6	0.9
13	-	Harris Interactive Inc.	Rochester, N.Y.	USA	harrisinteractive.com	6	208.9	8.6	54.1	25.9
-	15	Wirthlin Worldwide	McLean, Va.	USA	harrisinteractive.com	-	155.4	10.7	38.7	25.2
14	12	Maritz Research	St. Louis, Mo.	USA	maritzresearch.com	4	185.3	22.6	48.7	26.3
15	13	Video Research Ltd.**	Tokyo	Japan	videor.co.jp	3	177.2	−0.9	2.3	1.3
16	14	J.D. Power and Associates	Agoura Hills, Calif.	USA	jdpa.com	8	167.6	15.8	34.1	20.3
17	16	Opinion Research Corp.	Princeton, N.J.	USA	opinionresearch.com	6	147.5	12.4	56.5	38.3
18	18	The NPD Group Inc.	Port Washington, N.Y.	USA	npd.com	11	139.2	18.4	28.7	20.6
19	20	Market & Opinion Research Int'l	London	U.K.	mori.com	2	81.0	12.2	2.4	3.0
20	21	Lieberman Research Worldwide	Los Angeles, Calif.	USA	lrwonline.com	2	77.7	22.9	10.5	13.5
21	22	Dentsu Research Inc.	Tokyo	Japan	dentsureseach.co.jp	1	69.9	14.5	0.2	0.3
22	-	IBOPE Group	Rio de Janeiro	Brazil	ibope.com.br	15	64.5	34.3	14.3	22.1
23	24	Nikkei Research Inc.	Tokyo	Japan	nikkeiresearch.com	5	53.0	−5.0		
24	25	Burke, Inc.	Cincinnati, Ohio	USA	burke.com	1	43.4	10.2	6.3	14.5
25	23	Abt Associates Inc.	Cambridge, Mass.	USA	abtassociates.com	1	41.5	−23.2		
		Total					$13,320.3	4.8%	$8,944.4	67.2%

*Estimated by Top 25

**For fiscal year ending March 2005

***INTAGE now consolidates its total company revenues. On this basis it would have ranked 12th in '03.

[1] Includes countries which have subsidiaries with an equity interest or branch offices, or both.

[2] Total revenues that include non-research activities for some companies are significantly higher. This information is given in the individual company profiles.

[3] Rate of growth from year to year has been adjusted so as not to include revenue gains or losses from acquisitions or divestitures. See company profiles for explanation. Rate of growth is based on home country currency and includes currency exchange effects.

the home country. The largest research firm in the world is VNU NV, which is based in Haarlem, the Netherlands. This firm, which owns both ACNielsen and Nielsen Media Research has revenues of over $3 billion, of which only 1% comes from the Netherlands.[6]

"The Honomichl Top 50"

▶ **Revenues of the U.S. Firms.** The top 50 U.S.-based firms are reported each year in the **Honomichl Top 50**, reported in *Marketing News*. The rankings are based on revenues earned by these firms from U.S. operations only. Honomichl reported that the top 50 earned total revenues in the United States of $6.3 billion in 2004; this was an increase of 10.0% over 2003. More importantly, the Honomichl report also shows the growth rate in the industry from 1988 to 2004 to be a healthy 5.17%. Council of American Survey Research Organizations (CASRO) has many member firms not large enough to make the top 50, and when CASRO firms are added, the total number of U.S.-based research firms climbs to 197. When U.S. revenues for these additional firms are added to the top 50 firms' revenue, the total climbs to $6.9 billion in 2004, an increase from $6.4 billion in 2003.[7] This represents an increase of 6.4% after an adjustment for inflation.[8] Table 3.2 shows the Honomichl Top 50.

The Honomichl Top 50 firms based in the United States are also highly involved in international research. These 50 firms earned $6.3 billion from U.S.-based revenues, but their total worldwide revenues totaled $13.3 billion. In other words, the Honomichl Top 50 U.S.-based firms earned 52.7% of their total revenues from operations outside the United States. As you have already learned, the marketing research industry is global in its operations.[9]

The Honomichl Top 50 U.S.-based firms earned 52.7% of their total revenues from operations outside the United States. As you have already learned, the marketing research industry is global in its operations.

Strategic alliances allow firms with strong expertise in one area to form partnerships with firms offering expertise in other areas.

▶ **Competition in the Industry Is Very Keen.** Inefficient or ineffective firms are quickly removed by market forces. In recent years there has been a growth in strategic alliances among competitor firms. **Strategic alliances** allow firms with strong expertise in one area to form partnerships with firms offering expertise in other areas. For example, a firm with a strength in client consultation may form an alliance with a firm specializing in data collection and another firm specializing in data analysis. The combination of these strengths means higher levels of competition in the industry. These alliances may be formed through acquisition, merger, or contractual agreements. Acquisition helped Synovate form strategic alliances. Synovate was formed in 2001 as Aegis Research in London. Synovate now owns, in the United States, the former Market Facts, BAI Global, Strategy Research Corp., MarkTrend Research Inc., Copernicus Inc., and IMR Research Inc.[10] These firms allow Synovate to operate in the United States with several companies offering distinct competencies in the market.

Classifying Firms in the Marketing Research Industry

In the marketing research industry we refer to providers of marketing research information as **research suppliers**. There are several ways we can classify suppliers. We use a classification developed by Naresh Malholtra,[11] slightly modified for our purposes here. This classification system is shown in Figure 3.1. As shown in this figure, suppliers may be classified as either internal or external.

Internal Suppliers

An **internal supplier** means an entity within the firm that supplies marketing research. It has been estimated that firms spend roughly 1% of sales on marketing research, whether it is supplied internally or externally.[12] Most large firms such as Kraft Foods,

TABLE 3.2   2004 Honomichl Top 50 U.S. Market Research Organizations

U.S. Rank 2004	U.S. Rank 2003	Organization	Headquarters	Web Site: WWW.
1	1	VNU Inc.	New York, NY	vnu.com
2	2	IMS Health Inc.	Fairfield, CT	imshealth.com
3	4	Westat Inc.	Rockville, MD	westat.com
4	5	TNS U.S.	New York, NY	tns-global.com
5	3	Information Resources Inc.	Chicago, IL	infores.com
6	6	The Kantar Group	Fairfield, CT	kantargroup.com
7	7	Arbitron Inc.	New York, NY	arbitron.com
8	8	NOP World US	New York, NY	nopworld.com
9	9	Ipsos	New York, NY	ipsos-na.com
10	10	Synovate	Chicago, IL	synovate.com
11	-	Harris Interactive Inc.	Rochester, NY	harrisinteractive.com
-	13	*Harris Interactive Inc.*	*Rochester, NY*	*harrisinteractive.com*
-	20	*Wirthin worldwide*	*McLean, VA*	*harrisinteractive.com*
12	11	Maritz Research	Fenton, MO	maritzresearch.com
13	12	J.D. Power and Associates	Westlake Village, CA	jdpower.com
14	14	The NPD Group Inc.	Port Washington, NY	npd.com
15	16	GfK Group USA	Nuremberg, Germany	gfk.com
16	15	Opinion Research Corp.	Princeton, NJ	opinionresearch.com
17	17	Lieberman Research Worldwide	Los Angeles, CA	lrwonline.com
18	18	Abt Associates Inc.	Cambridge, MA	abtassociates.com
19	21	Market Strategies Inc.	Livonia, MI	marketstrategies.com
20	22	Burke Inc.	Cincinnati, OH	burke.com
21	30	comScore Networks Inc.	Reston, VA	comscore.com
22	24	MORPACE International Inc.	Farmington Hills, MI	morpace.com
23	25	Knowledge Networks Inc.	Menlo Park, CA	knowledgenetworks.com
23	34	OTX Research	Los Angeles, CA	otxresearch.com
25	23	ICR/Int'l Communications Research	Media, PA	icrsurvey.com
26	36	Directions Research Inc.	Cincinnati, OH	directionsrsch.com
27	28	National Research Corp.	Lincoln, NE	nationalresearch.com
28	32	Marketing Research Services Inc.	Cincinnati, OH	mrsi.com
29	29	Lieberman Research Group	Great Neck, NY	liebermanresearch.com
30	33	Peryam & Kroll Research Corp.	Chicago, IL	pk-research.com
31	-	National Analysts Inc.	Philadelphia, PA	nationalanalysts.com
32	-	Public Opinion Strategies	Alexandra, VA	pos.org
33	27	Walker Information	Indianapolis, IN	walkerinfo.com
34	39	The PreTesting Co. Inc.	Tenafly, NJ	pretesting.com
35	19	C&R Research Services Inc.	Chicago, IL	crresearch.com
36	35	Flake-Wilkerson Market Insights LLC	Little Rock, AR	mktinsights.com
37	37	Data Development Worldwide	New York, NY	datadw.com
38	41	Schulman, Ronca & Bucuvalas Inc.	New York, NY	srbi.com
39	45	Cheskin	Redwood Shores, CA	cheskin.com
40	38	RDA Group Inc.	Bloomfield Hills, MI	rdagroup.com
41	47	Marketing Analysts Inc.	Charleston, SC	marketinganalysts.com
42	46	Market Probe Inc.	Milwaukee, WI	marketprobe.com
43	44	Savitz Research Companies	Dallas, TX	savitzresearch.com
44	42	The Marketing Workshop Inc.	Norcross, GA	mwshop.com
45	48	Ronin Corp.	Princeton, NJ	ronin.com
46	49	MarketVision Research Inc.	Cincinnati, OH	marketvisionresearch.com
47	-	Rti-DFD Inc.	Stamford, CT	rti-dfd.com
48	-	Q Research Solutions Inc.	Old Bridge, NJ	qresearchsolutions.com
49	50	Data Recognition Corp.	Maple Grove, MN	datarecognitioncorp.com
50	-	Phoenix Marketing International	Rhinebeck, NY	phoenixmi.com
		Total		
		All other (138 CASRO companies not included in the Top 50)****		
		Total (188 companies)		

(continued)

*Estimated by Top 50
**U.S. and WW revenues may include non-research activities for some companies that are significantly higher. See individual company profiles for details.
***Rate of growth from year to year has been adjusted so as not to include revenue gains or losses from acquisitions or divestitures. See company profiles for explanation.
****Total revenues of 138 survey research companies that provide financial information on a confidential basis to the Council of American Survey Research Organizations (CASRO). Also, 35 of Top 50 companies have 44 CASRO members.

TABLE 3.2 — 2004 Honomichl Top 50 U.S. Market Research Organizations (Continued)

U.S. Research Revenues ** ($ in millions)	Percent Change From 2003 ***	WW Research Revenues** ($ in millions)	Non-U.S. Research Revenues** ($ in millions)	Percent Non-U.S. Revenues
$1,794.4	11.5%	$3,429.2	$1,634.8	47.7%
571.0	6.2	1569.0	998.0	63.6
397.8	4.3	397.8		
396.0	8.1	1732.7	1336.7	77.2
379.6	−2.2	572.8	192.2	33.6
365.7*	6.4*	1136.3*	770.6*	67.8*
284.7	4.8	296.6	11.9	4.0
213.0	3.6	408.5	195.4	47.9
193.9	7.8	752.8	558.9	74.2
193.5	0.4	499.3	305.8	61.3
154.8	2.5	208.9	54.1	25.9
116.7	5.1	155.4	38.7	24.9
38.1	−5.0	53.5	15.4	28.8
136.6	25.4	185.8	48.7	26.3
133.5	12.1	167.6	34.1	20.4
110.5	14.2	139.2	28.7	20.6
93.0	3.9	834.6	741.6	88.9
91.5	8.0	147.5	56.5	38.3
67.2	16.5	77.7	10.5	13.5
41.5	−19.7	41.5		
37.9	10.5	39.5	1.6	4.1
37.1	17.8	43.4	6.3	14.5
34.9	40.9	34.9		
31.1	15.2	34.5	3.4	9.9
29.8	14.6	29.8		
29.8	56.0	29.8		
29.0	−2.4	29.4	0.4	1.4
27.3	55.1	27.3		
26.7	9.4	29.7	3.0	10.1
25.4	14.4	25.4		
25.1	4.2	25.5	0.4	1.6
22.5	6.6	22.7	0.2	0.1
22.3	1.2	22.3		
21.2	116.3	21.2		
20.4	−19.0	23.8	3.4	14.3
19.8	21.5	20.4	0.6	2.9
19.7	7.0	19.7		
18.8	5.6	18.8		
18.3	4.6	20.7	2.4	11.6
17.2	11.0	17.2		
16.5	38.7	19.0	2.5	13.2
15.4	−9.4	17.0	1.6	9.4
15.2	33.3	15.6	0.4	2.6
14.1	20.5	24.6	10.5	42.7
14.0	3.7	14.0		
13.9	−5.4	13.9		
13.5	25.0	13.9	0.4	2.8
11.8	11.3	11.8		
11.5	7.5	11.5		
11.2	27.3	11.2		
10.8	6.9	10.8		
10.6	46.5	10.6		
$6,291.0	10.0%	$13,307.7	$7,015.6	52.7%
656.6****	9.1%	737.7	81.1	11.0%
$6,947.6	9.9%	$14,012.8	$7,096.7	50.5%

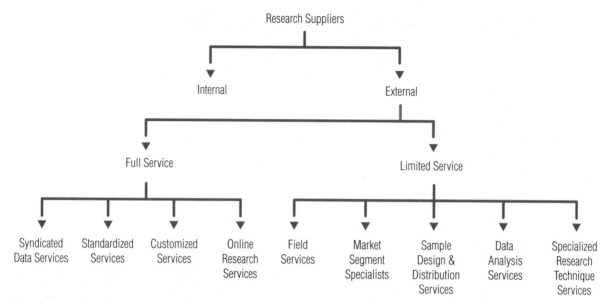

FIGURE 3.1
A Classification of Marketing Research Suppliers

IBM, Kodak, General Mills, General Motors, Ford, and DaimlerChrysler have research departments of their own.

How Do Internal Suppliers Organize the Research Function?

Internal suppliers of marketing research can elect to use several organizing methods to provide the research function. They may (1) have their own formal departments, (2) have no formal department but make at least a single individual or a committee responsible for marketing research, or (3) assign no one responsibility for conducting marketing research.

▶ **Organizing the Formal Department of Internal Suppliers.** Most large organizations have the resources to staff their own formal marketing research departments. Firms with higher sales volumes (over $500 million) tend to have their own formal marketing research departments, and many large advertising agencies have their own formal research departments.[13] Companies with their own research department must justify the large fixed costs of supporting the personnel and facilities. The advantage is that the staff is fully cognizant of the firm's operations and the changes in the industry, which may give them better insights into identifying opportunities and problems suitable for marketing research action.

Marketing research departments are usually organized according to one or a combination of the following functions: area of application, marketing function, or the research process. By "area of application," we mean these companies organize the research function around the areas to which the research is being applied. For example, some firms serve both ultimate consumers and industrial consumers. Therefore, the marketing research department may be organized into two divisions: consumer and industrial. Other areas of application may be brands or lines of products or services. Second, marketing research may be organized around functional areas (the 4 Ps) such as product research, ad research, pricing research, channel of distribution research, and so on. Finally, the research function may be organized around steps of the research process, such as data analysis or data collection.

Internal suppliers may (1) have their own formal departments, (2) have no formal department but make at least a single individual or a committee responsible for marketing research, or (3) assign no one responsibility for conducting marketing research.

Marketing research departments are usually organized according to one or a combination of the following functions: area of application, marketing function, or the research process.

▶ **Organizing When There Is No Formal Department.** If internal supplier firms elect not to have a formal marketing research department, there are many other organizational possibilities. When there is no formal department, responsibility for research may be assigned to existing organizational units such as departments or divisions. A problem with this method is that research activities are not coordinated; a division conducts its own research and other units of the firm may be unaware of useful information. One way to remedy this is to organize by having a committee or an individual assigned marketing research to ensure that all units of the firm have input into and benefit from any research activity undertaken. In some cases, committees or individuals assigned to marketing research may actually conduct some limited research, but typically their primary role is that of helping other managers recognize the need for research and coordinating the purchase of research from external research suppliers. Obviously, the advantage here is limiting fixed costs incurred by maintaining the full-time staff required for an ongoing department. In some organizations no one may be assigned to marketing research. This is rare in large companies, but it is not at all unusual in smaller firms. In very small firms, the owner/manager plays many roles, ranging from strategic planner to salesperson to security staff. He or she must also be responsible for marketing research, making certain to have the right information before making decisions.

> It is rare to find no one responsible for marketing research in large organizations; small business owners who see their customers daily conduct their own "informal" research constantly.

External Suppliers

External suppliers are outside firms hired to fulfill a firm's marketing research needs. Both large and small firms, for-profit and not-for-profit, and government and educational institutions purchase research information from external suppliers.

> External suppliers are outside firms hired to fulfill a firm's marketing research needs.

GETTING TO KNOW THE INDUSTRY STRUCTURE OF THE MARKETING RESEARCH INDUSTRY

You get an excellent picture of the structure of the marketing research industry by examining the two Honomichl tables presented in this chapter. By "industry structure" we are referring to the number of firms, the size of the firms, and the different types of firms. One conclusion we can draw from the Honomichl information is that this industry, as compared with industries such as retailing or auto manufacturing, consists of relatively small firms. Furthermore, there is one very large firm and a few other large firms and then size drops off substantially. But, there are other insights into the industry that you are not getting by examining the Honomichl reports. For example, how many *other* firms are there? And, what are the different *types* of firms in the industry? There are, of course, many other research firms in the marketing research industry beyond the top 50 in the United States and the top 25 in the world. Likewise there are many types of firms. We want you to get an appreciation of the numbers and types of firms by examining some other sources. One excellent way to learn more about the industry structure is to look at some online directories of marketing research firms. Take a look at the New York chapter of the American Marketing Association's Web site and look through the *Greenbook*, a directory of marketing research firms. Go to **www.greenbook.org** and click on the picture of the *Greenbook*. Explore this Web site and you will get a better understanding of the number and different types of supplier firms. Also, visit the different "directory" listings at **www.quirks.com**. You can also use the *Honomichl Top 50* or *Honomichl Top Global 25* reports and go to the Web sites of some of these firms. How do they organize themselves? (Read the following section.) You can often tell how companies organize themselves by the way they list their products and services.

Active Learning

Go to **www.greenbook.org** and click on the picture of the *Greenbook*. Explore this Web site and you will get a better understanding of how to classify external supplier firms. Also visit the different "directory" listings at **www.quirks.com**.

How Do External Suppliers Organize?

Like internal supplier firms, external supplier firms organize themselves in different ways. These firms may organize by function (data analysis, data collection, etc.), by type of research application (customer satisfaction, advertising effectiveness, new product development, etc.), by geography (domestic vs. international), by type of customer (health care, government, telecommunications, etc.), or by some combination of these. We also see research companies changing their organizational structure to accommodate changes in the environment. For example, as online research grew in the past several years, Burke, Inc. added a division to Burke Marketing Research called Burke Interactive. Finally, many companies use multiple bases for organizing. Opinion Research Corporation (ORC) is organized by geography, type of research application, and function. ORC's three divisions are ORC International, which conducts global marketing research; ORC Macro, which specializes in global social research such as health issues; and ORC ProTel, which is a provider of teleservices.[14]

Classifying External Supplier Firms

As you may recall from Figure 3.1, we can classify all external supplier firms into two categories: full-service or limited-service firms. In the following paragraphs we will define these two types of firms and give you some examples of each.

▶ **Full–Service Supplier Firms. Full–service supplier firms** have the ability to conduct the entire marketing research project for the buyer firms. Full-service firms will often define the problem, specify the research design, collect and analyze the data, and prepare the final written report. Typically, these are larger firms that have the expertise as well as the necessary facilities to conduct research studies in their entirety. VNU NV, for example, offers services in more than 100 countries and has more than 38,000 employees.[15] The company can provide marketing research services in many areas. TNS-Global has over 13,000 employees and offices in 70 countries. The company offers a full range of services, including market measurement, market analysis, market segmentation, advertising, communications, new product development, brand performance and a host of other services.[16] The Kantar Group (TKG) operates around the world, with several research businesses, including Millward Brown Group, Research International, The Ziment Group, IMRB International, Lightspeed Research, and Mattson Jack Group.[17] These divisions, among others, give TKG the ability to conduct many different forms of research. Most of the research firms found in the Honomichl Global Top 25 and Honomichl Top 50 would qualify as full-service firms.

▶ **Syndicated Data Service Firms. Syndicated data service firms** collect information that is made available to multiple subscribers. They supply information, or data, in standardized form (information may not be tailored to meet the needs of any one company) to a large number of companies, known as a syndicate. Therefore, these companies offer syndicated data to all subscribing members of the syndicate. Information Resources, Inc. and ACNielsen are two large syndicated data services firms. We will discuss syndicated data service firms in greater detail in Chapter 7.

▶ **Standardized Service Firms. Standardized service firms** provide syndicated marketing research services, as opposed to syndicated data, to clients. Each client gets different data, but the *process* used to collect the data is standardized so that it may be offered to many clients at a cost less than that of a custom-designed project. TNS, or Taylor Nelson Sofres PLC, offers a service, AdEval, which pretests ads. The system evaluates performance and provides diagnostics to show why the ad does or does not work.[18] Synovate's ProductQuest service assists in developing new products and improving existing products.[19] ACNielsen, and several other companies, offer the service of test marketing.

▶ **Customized Service Firms. Customized service firms** offer a variety of research services that are tailored to meet the client's specific needs. Each client's problem is treated as a unique research project. Customized service firms spend considerable time with a client firm to determine the problem and then design a research project specifically to address the particular client's problem.

Customized service firms offer a variety of research services that are tailored to meet the client's specific needs.

▶ **Online Research Services Firms. Online research services firms** specialize in providing services online. We define **online research** as the use of computer networks, including the Internet, to assist in any phase of the marketing research process, including development of the problem, research design, data gathering, analysis, and report distribution. Virtually all research firms today use online research in the sense that they make use of online technology in at least one or more phases of the research process. These firms would be better categorized in one of the other types of firms shown in Figure 3.1. However, there are many firms that *specialize* in online services. Their "reason for being" is based on the provision of services online. Affinova, for example, exists because it has proprietary software that allows consumers to design preferred product attributes into new products online. InsightExpress® was formed by NFO, Inc. in 1999 to allow clients to easily develop questionnaires and quickly conduct surveys online. The firm has grown rapidly and now offers many innovative services online. Knowledge Networks came into being because its founders wanted to provide clients with access to probability samples online. Active Group was formed to conduct focus groups online. Certainly, there are overlapping categories in Figure 3.1. We do not claim that the categories are mutually exclusive. In fact, we could argue that some of these, because they specialize in one step of the research process, could be placed in one of the limited-service supplier categories that follow.

We define online research as the use of computer networks, including the Internet, to assist in any phase of the marketing research process, including development of the problem, research design, data gathering, analysis, and report distribution.

Read about Affinova's ability to design products online at **www.affinova.com**.

Online services firms specialize in providing marketing research services online, such as surveys, concept testing of new products, and focus groups.

Keep in mind that there are overlapping categories in Figure 3.1. We do not claim that the categories are mutually exclusive.

InsightExpress® has grown rapidly and offers many innovative marketing research services online. Visit InsightExpress® at **www.insightexpress.com**. By permission, InsightExpress®.

Research for the Right Decision

▶ **Limited-Service Supplier Firms. Limited-service supplier firms** specialize in one or, at most, a few marketing research activities. Firms can specialize in types of marketing research techniques such as eye-testing and mystery shopping, or specific market segments such as senior citizens, or certain sports segments such as golf or tennis. The limited-service suppliers can be further classified on the basis of their specialization. These include field services, market segment specialists, sample design and distribution services, data analysis, and specialized research technique service suppliers. Many of these limited-service firms specialize in some form of online research.

Limited-service supplier firms typically specialize in one or, at most, a few marketing research activities.

Field service firms specialize in collecting data. These firms typically operate in a particular territory, conducting telephone surveys, focus group interviews, mall intercept surveys, or door-to-door surveys. Because it is expensive and difficult to maintain interviewers all over the country, firms will use the services of field service firms in order to quickly and efficiently gather data. There is specialization even within firms that specialize in field services. Some firms, for example, conduct only in-depth personal interviews; others conduct only mall-intercept surveys. Some firms, such as Irwin Research Associates and

Field service firms specialize in collecting data.

Visit both Irwin Research Associates (**www.irwinservices.com**) and Mktg. Inc. (**www.mktginc.com**).

Knowledge Networks, while it offers many services, may be classified as an online research services firm. Visit Knowledge Networks at **www.knowledgenetworks. com**. By permission, Knowledge Networks.

Market segment specialists collect data for special market segments, such as African Americans, Hispanics, children, seniors, gays, industrial customers, or a specific geographic area within the United States or internationally.

Sample design and distribution firms specialize in providing samples to firms that are conducting research studies.

Survey Sampling, Inc. (SSI) is one of the oldest and best-known firms specializing in providing samples to marketing research firms. SSI is also an example of a company using online research. Users can design their sample plan online (see SSI SNAP) and receive their samples online. Go to www.ssi.com.

Specialized research technique firms address very specific needs such as eye-tracking, package design, or brand name testing.

Mktg. Incorporated, are known as **phone banks** because they specialize in telephone surveying and have large numbers of telephone interviewers working in central locations.

Other limited-service firms, called **market segment specialists**, specialize in collecting data for special market segments, such as African Americans, Hispanics, children, seniors, gays, industrial customers, or a specific geographic area within the United States or internationally. Strategy Research Corporation specializes in Latin American markets. JRH Marketing Services, Inc. specializes in marketing to ethnic markets, especially to black markets. Other firms specialize in children, mature citizens, pet owners, airlines, beverages, celebrities, college students, religious groups, and many other market segments. C&R Research has a division, called "Latino Eyes," that specializes in U.S. Hispanic and Latin American markets. They have another division specializing in kids, tweens, and teens, called "KidzEyes," and another division specializing in the 50-years-and-over market, called "Sage Advice."[20] By specializing, these limited-service suppliers capitalize on their in-depth knowledge of the client's target market.

Survey Sampling Inc. and Scientific Telephone Samples (STS) are examples of limited-service firms that specialize in **sample design and distribution**. It is not uncommon, for example, for a company with an internal marketing research department to buy its sample from a firm specializing in sampling and then send the samples and a survey questionnaire to a phone bank for completion of the survey. This way, a firm may quickly and efficiently conduct telephone surveys using a probability sample plan in markets all over the country. Survey Sampling, Inc. provides Internet samples, business-to-business samples, global samples, and samples of persons with characteristics that are hard to find (low-incidence samples).

There are limited-service marketing research firms that offer **data analysis services**. Their contribution to the research process is to provide the technical assistance necessary to analyze and interpret data using the more sophisticated data analysis techniques such as conjoint analysis. SDR Consulting, SPSS MR, and Applied Decision Analysis LLC are examples of such firms.

Specialized research technique firms provide a service to their clients by expertly administering a special technique. Examples of such firms include The PreTesting Company, which specializes in eye movement research. Eye movements are used to determine the effectiveness of ads, direct-mail pieces, and other forms of visual promotion. Other firms specialize in mystery shopping, taste tests, fragrance tests, creation of brand names, generating new ideas for products and services, and so on.

We should not leave this section without saying that our categorization of research suppliers does not fit every situation. Many full-service firms fit neatly into one of our

Go to **www.pretesting.com**. Click on "Eye Movement Recording," and watch the presentation. Examine its other highly specialized services. By permission, The PreTesting Company.

categories. TNS, for example, is a large, full-service firm. It also offers very specialized data analysis services. Also, there are other entities supplying research information that do not fit neatly into one of our categories. For example, universities and institutes supply research information. Universities sponsor a great deal of research that could be classified as marketing research.

CHALLENGES TO THE MARKETING RESEARCH INDUSTRY

The marketing research industry has been the subject of constructive criticism over the years.[21] These reviews are mixed. Earlier reviews would indicate that, although the marketing research industry is doing a reasonably good job, there is room for improvement.[22] More recent reviews, however, are not as complimentary.[23] Recently, Professor Don E. Schultz has claimed that the industry is in a "death spiral" and blames marketing research for the decline in marketing. Read more about Schultz's views in Marketing Research Insight 3.1. Critics Mahajan and Wind suggest, however, that marketing research is not fundamentally flawed but that many executives misapply research.[24] They misapply research by not having research professionals involved in high-level, strategic decision making. Instead, too many executives view marketing research as a commodity to be outsourced to "research brokers," who are hired to conduct a component of the

> Some industry critics believe marketing research can add more value if marketing researchers are more involved in upper-level strategic decisions rather than be used merely as providers of research services, viewed as commodities.

MARKETING RESEARCH INSIGHT   **PRACTICAL INSIGHTS**

3.1 Marketing Research Deserves Blame for Marketing's Decline[a]

Marketing and Marketing Research Have Lost Importance in the Organization

Proctor & Gamble declared "Marketing is broken." Booz, Allen Hamilton, Inc., a consulting firm, stated "The failure of so many CMO's . . . indicates a serious disparity between companies' needs and marketing's proffered solutions." The *Harvard Business Review* suggested "Too much showmanship . . . too little expertise." Even the AMA changed the definition of marketing in 2004 (see Chapter 1). Schultz says that marketing managers bemoan their loss of power and prestige in the organization. He refers to a leading marketing academic, Philip Kotler, who says that marketers, once responsible for conceptualization and implementation of the 4Ps have been reduced to one P: promotion.

Schultz believes this marginalization of marketing has been brought about by two primary forces: overemphasis on supply-chain management and organizational structure.

Supply-chain management, by stressing economies of scale and excellence in logistics, with the assumption that

lower prices will attract consumers, means that marketing's former role of representing the consumer is lost. Marketing is now viewed as being an after-the-fact function that moves the goods, using promotional tools, at the end of the supply chain. Consumers are unimportant in the process. The assumption is that if we get the product to them at a low price, they will acquire it. Consequently, knowledge of consumers, is less important. Secondly, firms that are organized in a functional structure—i.e., finance, operations, marketing, etc. departments—view marketing as just another

Don E. Schultz is President of Agora, Inc. and Professor Emeritus-in-Service, Northwestern University. Dr. Schultz is widely recognized as a leader in the field of Integrated Marketing Communications.

(continued)

function that has constraints and responsibilities like the other functional areas. Each function has its own knowledge and skills and operates in a "silo," with little interaction across functions. Each function reports up to top management. By being just another of several functions reporting to top management, marketing has become less important, as has its components, including marketing research. Consequently, marketing research has importance only within marketing.

Marketing Research Is Too "Tool"-Oriented

Marketers and marketing researchers have contributed to the demise of their own importance in the organization because, in recent years, they have come to view themselves not as managers but as staff members who supply management with information and materials generated by their tools. External suppliers of marketing research, by focusing on their tools, have furthered this perception. Unfortunately, too often the research problem is defined in terms of being compatible with one of the existing tools ("We can use conjoint analysis to solve this problem"). Researchers too readily apply a tool instead of focusing on the more complex strategic issues facing the firm. The end result is that marketing researchers are used to supplying "ingredients" instead of being involved in making strategic decisions.

Schultz believes that marketing research today provides few real insights about customers. The overused set of tools, often selected to be implemented by the lowest bidder, provides more sophisticated analysis on irrelevant data but does not help the firm hear the "voice of the consumer."

Why the Importance of Marketing and Marketing Research Should Increase

Schultz believes that marketing and marketing research should become more important in the future for two reasons. First, top management will demand more measured,

quantitative results from organizational investments. Marketing researchers have an opportunity to demonstrate to management how management systems such as Six Sigma, Economic Value Added (EVA), and Balanced Scorecards add value for the customer. Second, the power is switching from sellers to consumers. Overproduction, oversupply, over-retail-stored, new distribution systems, and new sources of information for the consumer have switched power from manufacturers to retailers. Marketing research can help firms switch from understanding how to cut costs to understanding what values drive consumers' purchasing power.

Suggested Remedy

Shultz does offer a suggestion for improvement. First, firms must adopt a demand-chain market approach rather than a supply-chain management system. While supply-chain management will remain important, firms can compete with the likes of Wal-Mart and Dell, powerhouses of low-cost, supply-chain focus, by better understanding customers and the values they seek in the marketplace. In order for this to happen, marketing research must, instead of being a staff function, become an integrated, process-driven senior management activity that controls and directs the entire business strategy for the entire organization.

[a]This material is based upon two sources: Schultz, D. E. (2005). MR deserves blame for marketing's decline. *Marketing News*, February 15th, 7 and Schultz, D.E., Schultz, H. F., and Haigh, D. (2004). A roadmap for developing an integrated, audience-focused, market research-driven organization. *ESOMAR World Congress*, September, 2004. Readers seeking more information on Schultz's suggested remedy are encouraged to read the ESOMAR paper.

research process when they should be involved in the entire process. To remedy the situation, Mahajan and Wind, highly regarded in academics and business consulting, recommend that researchers (1) focus on diagnosing problems, (2) use information technology to increase speed and efficiency, (3) take an integrative approach, and (4) expand the strategic impact of marketing research.

Marketing Researchers Should Focus on Diagnosing Problems

Marketing researchers need to diagnose market needs first and then test proposed alternative solutions to market needs.

Mahajan and Wind suggest that marketing researchers should stop using marketing research only to test solutions, such as testing a specific product or service. Instead, researchers should diagnose the market. As an example, consider that customers did not "ask" for a Sony Walkman or a minivan. Marketing researchers would not have known about these products by asking customers what they wanted. Without having ever seen these products, it is unlikely that customers would have been able to articulate the product characteristics. But had marketing researchers focused on diagnosing the market in terms of unserved markets and unarticulated needs in those markets, they may have produced these products. The Walkman was successful because it met an unserved market's need for portable entertainment. The minivan was successful because it met an unserved market's need for additional space in family vehicles. Marketing research can improve by properly diagnosing the market first, then testing alternative solutions to meet the needs discovered in the market. Baker and Mouncey likewise suggest that marketing researchers should provide insight into the market and redirect the key focus to understanding the customer-brand relationship.[25]

Marketing Researchers Should Speed Up Marketing Research by Using Information Technology

Roger D. Blackwell, a long-time marketing consultant, has stated that the marketing research cycle must be stepped up because of fierce competition.[26] It has long been recognized that there is a trade-off between quickly producing marketing research information and doing research in a thorough manner. Marketing researchers want time to conduct projects properly. However, Mahajan and Wind point out that researchers must remember that time is money. Real dollar losses result from introducing products and services to the marketplace too late. So much so, in fact, that many companies cut many corners in the research they conduct or do not do any marketing research at all. This, of course, often leads to disaster, and it has been labeled "death-wish" marketing.[27] The suggested prescription is for marketing researchers to make use of information technology (IT) for speed and economical efficiency. This is exactly why online research has become such a significant part of the research industry.[28] Decision Analysts, Inc. allows companies to test product concepts quickly using online respondents. Using their online technology, InsightExpress® conducts very rapid concept tests for testing new product and service ideas. We already mentioned Affinova as an online research company. Affinova uses online research to allow potential consumers to be involved in designing new products online. They can do this in a fraction of the time it would take using non-online methods. Harris Interactive, Knowledge Networks, Greenfield Online, and many others allow surveys to be conducted online. All of these firms use IT to speed up and reduce the cost of research.

Online research has grown significantly because it can speed up the research process.

Marketing Researchers Should Take an Integrative Approach

Marketing researchers have created silos, which separate themselves from other information. For example, by separating research into qualitative and quantitative research, researchers tend to use one or the other when, in fact, more insights may be gained by integrating the two approaches. Other silos are created when decision support systems are not linked with marketing research. Firms should integrate experiments they conduct instead of conducting one-shot projects that investigate a single issue. Mahajan and Wind also suggest greater integration of marketing research with existing databases and other information sources such as customer complaints, other studies of product/service quality, and external databases. In other words, marketing researchers would improve their results by taking a close look at all existing information instead of embarking on isolated research projects to solve a problem. When you read Marketing Research Insight 3.1 you should have noted that Don E. Schultz also believes "silos" are a problem.

Marketing researchers would improve their results by taking a close look at all existing information instead of embarking on isolated research projects to solve a problem.

Marketing Researchers Should Expand Their Strategic Impact

Schultz, in Marketing Research Insight 3.1, would agree with Mahajan and Wind that marketing research has become too comfortable in providing standard reports using simple measures. Jack J. Honomichl has also levied this same criticism.[29] This information, although useful, does not allow marketing research to contribute to the important central issues of determining overall strategy. Research becomes relegated to a lower-level function providing information for lower-level decisions. As an example, Mahajan and Wind refer to marketing research periodically providing a report on market shares. Although this information is useful for making tactical decisions for each brand, marketing research should be providing information such as defining the market. Should the company look at a broader market than the one defined? Should global market share be considered? How can the company get more from total spending in the market? These are broader, more strategic issues that, if addressed properly by marketing research, would add value to the function of marketing research.

Other Criticisms

There have been several other investigations of the research industry over the years. Some of these reviews have been made by knowledgeable persons' critiques and others have asked buyers of marketing research studies whether the value of the research performed by the suppliers in the industry is worthwhile. Criticism has focused on the following areas of concern: There is a lack of creativity, the industry is too survey-oriented, the industry does not understand the real problems that need studying, market researchers show a lack of concern for respondents, the industry has a cavalier attitude regarding nonresponse error, the price of the research is high relative to its value, and academic marketing research should be more closely related to actual marketing management decisions.[30]

Critical reviews are good for the industry. John Stuart Mill once said that "custom is the enemy of progress."[31] One entire issue of *Marketing Research*, edited by Chuck Chakrapani, was devoted to a number of articles questioning customary practices in marketing research.[32] The debate these articles stirred is good for the industry. In summary, the basic conclusion of these evaluations is that the industry has performed well, but there is room for improvement. We discuss some of the suggestions for improvement in the following paragraphs.

Suggested Improvements: Certification, Auditing, and Education

Even though there have been criticisms of the marketing research industry, the industry has performed well by the toughest of all standards, the test of the marketplace. As we noted earlier in this chapter, annual revenues in the research industry now total over $21 billion, and these revenues, with few exceptions, have been increasing each year. Clients obviously see value in the marketing research that is being generated. However, the industry is not complacent. Many suggest that the problems are created by a very small minority of firms, most of which simply are not qualified to deliver quality marketing research services. There is obviously a concern among buyers and suppliers with the lack of uniformity in the industry as well. In a study of buyers' and suppliers' perceptions of the research industry, Dawson, Bush, and Stern found that the key issue in the industry is a lack of uniform quality; there are good suppliers and there are poor suppliers.[33]

William D. Neal, Senior Partner and Cofounder of SDR Consulting and former Chairman of the Board of Directors of the American Marketing Association, spent many tireless years nurturing the concept of certification for the marketing research industry. Mr. Neal has received many honors for his contributions to the profession including awards from the Marketing Research Association and the American Marketing Association.

Visit SDR Consulting at **www.sdr-consulting.com**. By permission, SDR Consulting.

▶ **Certification. Certification** is a designation that indicates the achievement of some minimal standard of performance. For many years, it has been argued that marketing research attracts practitioners who are not fully qualified to provide adequate service to buyer firms due in large part to the fact that there have been no formal requirements, no education level, no degrees, no certificates, no licenses, and no tests of any kind required to open a marketing research business. Certainly, the vast majority of research firms have staffs thoroughly trained in research methods and have years of excellent performance. However, many industry observers have stated that it is those few firms with unqualified personnel and management that tarnish the industry's image. Some believe many of the problems come from individuals in public relations, consulting, or advertising agency firms who conduct marketing research without the proper training and background. The certification movement was led by the efforts of William D. Neal, former Chairman of the Board of Directors of the American Marketing Association and Senior Partner and Cofounder of SDR Consulting.

Other professions, such as accounting, real estate, and financial analysis, have learned that certification programs can raise the overall level of competence within an industry.[34] Years ago it was proposed by Alvin Achenbaum[35] as well as Patrick Murphy and Gene Laczniak[36] that marketing researchers have a designation of certified public researchers (CPRs), analogous to CPAs or CFAs. Those arguing against certification pointed out that it would be difficult, if not impossible, to agree on defining certification standards, particularly for the creative aspect of the research process.[37]

To articulate the reason for certification we asked Professor Stephen W. McDaniel, a researcher with an interest in the area of certification for marketing researchers, to provide you with his views on why certification is needed in the profession. His response is in Marketing Research Insight 3.2.

The marketing research industry discussed certification programs for many years.

3.2 Should Marketing Researchers Be Certified?

- If you needed an audit done on your company's financial records, would you hire someone who had not earned a CPA?
- What if you had a large fortune and needed some financial planning advice? Would you hire someone who was not an authorized Certified Financial Planner?
- Would you want your child taught algebra by someone not certified to teach math?
- Would it matter to you that the person arriving in an ambulance at the scene of your car wreck was not certified as an Emergency Medical Technician?

Most of us would feel a lot better if the accountant, financial planner, teacher, or medical worker had been verified by a reputable certification organization to have the skills necessary for the job we were entrusting them to do. How about in the field of marketing research?

- Suppose you need a comprehensive national marketing research study to help you decide whether to launch a new product, the sales of which could potentially run into the millions. Would it matter to you that the marketing researcher who wants to do this study for you does not have a certification in the marketing research field?

Without certification, anybody can put up a sign, print up some letterhead stationery, and run a yellow page ad calling themselves "Marketing Researchers." This person may never have had a marketing course in college, or any course in college. But they can hand out professional-looking business cards with "Marketing Researcher" after their name, and they can hire themselves out to do any kind of marketing research someone will pay them to do. Without a certification program in the field of marketing research there is no formal process for determining whether this "Marketing Researcher" has the business knowledge and marketing expertise to plan the appropriate scientific marketing research study for the marketing problem at hand. There is no formal process for determining whether this "Marketing Researcher" has the statistical training to perform the appropriate quantitative analysis on the data and correctly interpret the results. There is no formal process for validating whether this "Marketing Researcher" has the necessary understanding of marketing and the marketing research process to provide sound recommendations.

In recent years this subject has been debated extensively, and national studies have been carried out on marketing research professionals, asking their opinion of marketing research certification. Overall, those in the marketing research field see several benefits from implementing a marketing research certification process. But they also have some concerns. Some of the concerns follow.

Problems with Certification

- **Disagreements on standards for certification.** What should be the basis for becoming certified? Should it be a test? If so, what areas should be covered on the test? Marketing research is a broad field with various specializations (e.g., focus-group research, statistical analysis, Internet research). Is it necessary for someone to be an expert in all these areas? Should marketing research experience be required? If so, how much experience? Is an advanced college degree required or is an undergraduate degree sufficient? Should certification be for just new researchers, and should established researchers be "grandfathered" in?
- **Difficulty in implementation.** Who should be the certifying agency—the American Marketing Association, the Marketing Research Association, or some other organization? How should possible testing be done?
- **Cost.** Is the value worth the cost for certification? Those desiring to become certified will have a cost of money and time.
- **No assurance of competency.** Will certification eliminate incompetent researchers? Probably not. Anybody can study to pass a test and then forget everything or not apply what they learned.

Even though there are obstacles to overcome, and problems will arise in the process, there are also many benefits to implementing a certification process for the marketing research field. A few of these follow.

Benefits of Certification

- **Higher level of professionalism.** Certification will raise the standards for the entire marketing research industry. The designation "Professional Researcher Certification" will communicate a professionalism that currently does not always exist among research practitioners.
- **More credibility.** The credibility of individual marketing researchers will be raised and the level of trust in research processes and findings will be increased. Overall, marketing researchers will be more knowledgeable and qualified. The number of incompetent researchers will no doubt be reduced.
- **Better image.** The marketing research industry will be viewed more positively and will be awarded more respect from consumers, the business community, and government regulators.
- **Higher ethical standards.** Not only will those going through the certification process be sensitive to the ethical issues involved in the research process, but ethical standards can be more easily set and enforced. The threat of decertification will be a strong motivator of ethical behavior.
- **Better client service.** Those paying the bill for the research will be better served. Overall, research studies will more likely be better designed and implemented, with results more valid and reliable.

On balance, it seems the benefits for developing and implementing a professional certification program for the marketing research field clearly offset the problems or concerns people may have. You have already learned that a leading proponent of certification is William D. Neal of SDR Consulting. Mr. Neal contends, "We are part of a profession that is at least 60 years old. It's time we started acting like a profession and put a certification program in place." Such action will mean that we can feel confident not only about the person doing our taxes, handling our investments, teaching our kids, or treating our injuries, but also about the person helping us decide whether to market that new product. I endorse the Marketing Research Association's Professional Researcher Certification.

Stephen W. McDaniel, Ph.D., Professor of Marketing, Mays Business School, Texas A&M University.

▶ **Marketing Research Association Begins Professional Researcher Certification**
Having read Professor McDaniel's rationale for certification you have a better appreciation for the new certification program for marketing researchers now being provided by the MRA. This is a significant event for the research industry. The MRA's Certification Workgroup, led by Chair Joan Burns of Teradyne, Inc., took great care to plan the program and coordinated many persons and industry associations. The certification program takes into consideration the diversity of research represented in the industry. Marketing Research Insight 3.3 gives you many of the details of the new certification program.

▶ **Auditing.** An alternative to certification is **auditing**. The concept is to have the work produced by marketing research firms subject to an outside, independent review for the sake of determining the quality of the work. An audit would involve procedures such as retabulation from raw data of a random sample of descriptive surveys, validation of a sample of questionnaires, and even checking questionnaires for evidence of selling under the guise of marketing research.[38] (We discuss the latter in the section on ethics below.) Though proposed several years ago for the marketing research industry, the audit concept has lain dormant and we doubt, given the MRA's PRC certification program, that an industry-wide auditing program will emerge in the industry.

3.3 Professional Researcher Certification

By Jessica Wilson

February 28, 2005, was a significant day for the marketing research industry. On this day, the Marketing Research Association (MRA) announced its new certification program, the Professional Researcher Certification. The paragraphs below contain the essentials of the program. Interested parties should consult the MRA Web Site, which is also shown below.

Certification Overview

Who Designed the Certification Program?
The MRA assumed the leadership role in developing the certification program. However, to ensure widespread industry input and participation, the Certification Task Force included both MRA and non-MRA members. Members included representatives from MRII, IMRO Division of MRA, CMOR and AMA. Also, Task Force members represented all segments of the marketing research industry from Data Collectors to End Users.

What Is the Certification Designed to Do?
The certification program is designed to accomplish the following three objectives:

- reflect all segments of the marketing research profession

- be recognized by industry-related associations and experts
- meet all requirements of NOCA (certification authorization entity) and IACET (CEU [continuing education unit] authorization entity)

Who Benefits from Certification?
The MRA certification program is beneficial for both the individual and the industry. For the individual, it will be a means of differentiating oneself from others. A "badge" of competence in the given areas gives assurance to others that the certified individual meets some minimal level of knowledge and experience. The certification program benefits the industry in that it aids in the development of a pool of well-trained, competent marketing researchers, thereby improving standards in the industry.

Certification Recognizes the Diversity with the Industry

In order to address the diversification of the work collectively known as "marketing research," job descriptions throughout the industry were analyzed and sorted into categories consisting of levels of responsibility, levels of specialized knowledge, and levels of required knowledge. The three major segments are: Data Collection, Research Suppliers/Providers, and End Users. And there are subgroups within each industry segment such as the subgroups of Mall, Telephone, Online, and Ethnographic Research within the Data Collection segment. Then, within each subgroup there are job titles. For example, for the Data Collection segment subgroup of Mall the job titles include: Facility Owner, Facility Manager, Supervisor and so on. The skills required for a title within a subgroup of a particular segment determined the criteria for certification as well as the requirements for maintaining certification.

Criteria for Levels of Certification

Certifications are awarded at three levels of experience and knowledge. Each level and their respective criteria are:

Expert
Candidates are expected to have a thorough and detailed knowledge and comprehension of topics classified for this level. Applicants must have no known ethics

complaints in the past three years, and must currently be a member of at least one marketing research professional organization. Applicants must also have five or more years' experience in a senior-level or equivalent position and have attended at least one industry conference in the past three years.

Practitioner
Candidates are expected to have a working knowledge and comprehension of the topics classified for this level. Applicants must have no known ethics complaints in the past three years. Topics at the expert level are central or mainstream and arise frequently in day-to-day professional practice. Applicants must also provide documentation of each skill area on the application, document hours for each skill area on application, list courses/conferences related to skill area on application.

Associate
Candidates are expected to have a basic understanding of the topics classified at this level. These topics may arise less frequently in day-to-day practice or are emerging, specialty, or peripheral topics. Candidates are expected to have a general familiarity with those topics and understand their broad implications. Applicants must also have at least one year in current or similar position, one letter of recommendation, and no known ethics complaints in the past three years and must document hours for each skill area upon application.

Examination
An exam developed by the Certification Development Committee is required for all applicants, excluding grandfathering applicants. Exams will be developed using resources within the profession and based on topic areas directly related to the skills and knowledge required for a specific position. A list of study guides will be provided for approved applicants. All exams will be reviewed and critiqued by the Committee, some of whom have taken the exams. This is to ensure the accuracy and appropriateness of the questions that comprise the exams. These exams will test the comprehension of topics central or mainstream to the candidate's daily professional practice.

Maintaining Certification
Knowledge and skills acquired through CEUs (Continuing Education Credits) will be the primary method for maintaining accreditation and advancing to a different level of

accreditation. In order to maintain certification, individuals must accrue a specified number of contact hours in the field in which they are certified. Contact hours can be earned by attending an approved educational program, such as an MRA national or chapter educational event or activity that offers programming in research skills, management, or support skills. With such education, individuals can develop skills in order to keep up with industry trends and techniques.

Grandfathering
Current marketing researchers may be eligible for certification without taking an exam as long as they satisfy all criteria. The ability to grandfather is allowed only during a two-year period after the certification process began.

Certification versus Accreditation?
Certification applies to individuals. Accreditation applies to an organization. A company may become accredited if it can show evidence of and maintain standards set by the accreditation agency. The MRA program addresses certification of individuals. However, the MRA also intends to sponsor an accreditation program.

Want to Learn More about Professional Researcher Certification?
Go to the MRA's Web site at **www.mra-net.org**. See the menu item "Certification."

Source: This paper was adapted from information provided by the MRA, particularly from materials posted on its Web site at **www.mra-net.org**. Also, much of the material was adapted from the writings of Joan Burns of Teradyne, Inc., who was the Chair of the Certification Workgroup. See, for example: Burns, J. (2005). Certification: the five key questions. Retrieved April 19, 2005, from the Marketing Research Association Web site at **www.mra-net.org**.

MRA Executive Director Larry Hadcock has spearheaded and supervised the development of the new Professional Researcher Certification. MRA Staff Members Linda Schoenborn and Elyse Gammer have shared major responsibility as well.

The marketing research industry has, for many years, offered many educational opportunities for its members. Certification, by requiring CEUs to maintain certification, will likely have a positive effect on educational programs in the industry.

Any review of the industry would agree that the industry is being responsive to its many challenges.

▶ **Education.** The marketing research industry has, for many years, offered many educational opportunities for its members. Certification, by requiring CEUs to maintain certification, will likely have a positive effect on educational programs in the industry. Several industry organizations offer programs designed to increase the knowledge and skills of those in the industry. The AMA, for example, sponsors several programs, including their annual Marketing Research Conference. Second, the AMA sponsors the Advanced School of Marketing Research, which is a program conducted at Notre Dame University designed to benefit the analyst, project supervisor, or manager of marketing research. Yet another AMA program is an annual conference that focuses on advanced analytical techniques. Also, the Marketing Research Association started an introductory program on marketing research several years ago. Coordinated at the University of Georgia, this program is designed to develop the research skills of those being transferred into marketing research or those who want to enter the profession. The Marketing Research Association (MRA), Council for the Association of Survey Research Organizations (CASRO's CASRO University), Qualitative Research Consultant's Associaton (QRCA), the Advertising Research Foundation (ARF), British Market Research Association, Australian Market & Social Research Society, Market Research Society of New Zealand and several other industry associations have many excellent training classes and programs frequently scheduled to meet industry needs. Several universities now offer master's-level training in marketing research. (See Appendix B at the end of this chapter). Certain firms also provide excellent training for the industry. The Burke Institute, a division of Burke, Inc., has, for many years, provided training programs that are highly regarded in the industry. The institute teaches classes throughout the year on a number of topics, including online research, multivariate techniques, questionnaire design, focus-group moderating, basic marketing research, and many others. Any review of the industry would show that the industry is being responsive to its many challenges.

ETHICS AND MARKETING RESEARCH

The marketing research industry is not immune to ethical issues.

As in most areas of business activity, there exist many opportunities for unethical (and ethical) behavior in the marketing research industry.[39] A study by the Ethics Resource Center of Washington, DC, states that the most common ethical problem in the total workplace is "lying to employees, customers, vendors or the public" (26 percent), followed by "withholding needed information" from those parties (25 percent). Only 5 percent of those in the study reported having seen people giving or taking "bribes, kickbacks, or inappropriate gifts." Ninety percent of American workers "expect their organizations to do what is right, not just what is profitable." But one in eight of those polled said they "feel pressure to compromise their organization's ethical standards." And among these respondents, nearly two thirds said pressure "comes from top management, their supervisors and/or coworkers."[40] Unfortunately, the marketing research industry is not immune to ethical problems.[41] Our purpose here is to introduce you to the areas in which unethical behavior have existed in the past and hopefully to give you some framework for thinking about how you will conduct yourself in the future when confronted with these situations. We think these ethical issues are so important that we call your attention to them throughout this book using the ethical issue icon that you see at the beginning of this section.

Ethics may be defined as a field of inquiry into determining what behaviors are deemed appropriate under certain circumstances as prescribed by codes of behavior that are set by society. Society determines what is ethical and what is not ethical. In some cases, this is formalized by our institutions. Some behavior, for example, is so wrongful that it is deemed illegal by statute. Behavior that is illegal is unethical, by definition. However, there are many other behaviors that are considered by some to be unethical but are not illegal. When these types of behaviors are not spelled out by some societal institution (such as the justice system, legislature, Congress, regulatory agencies such as the FTC, etc.), then the determination of whether the behaviors are ethical or unethical is open to debate.

Your Ethical Views Are Shaped by Your Philosophy: Deontology or Teleology

There are many philosophies that may be applied to explain one's determination of appropriate behavior given certain circumstances. In the following discussion we use the two philosophies of deontology and teleology to explain this behavior.[42] **Deontology** is concerned with the rights of the individual. Is the behavior fair and just for each individual? If an individual's rights are violated, then the behavior is not ethical.[43] For example, consider the marketing research firm that has been hired to study how consumers are attracted to and react to a new form of in-store display. Researchers, hidden from view, record the behavior of unsuspecting shoppers as they walk through the supermarket. A deontologist considers this form of research activity unethical because it violates the individual shopper's right to privacy. The deontologist would likely agree to the research provided the shoppers were informed beforehand that their behavior would be recorded, giving them the option to participate or not to participate.[44]

On the other hand, **teleology** analyzes a given behavior in terms of its benefits and costs to society. If there are individual costs but group benefits, then there are net gains, and the behavior is judged to be ethical.[45] In our example of the shopper being observed in the supermarket, the teleologist might conclude that, although there is a violation of the right to privacy among the shoppers observed (the cost), there is a benefit if the company learns how to market goods more efficiently, thus reducing long-term marketing costs. Because this benefit ultimately is shared by many more individuals than those whose privacy was invaded during the original study, the teleologist would likely declare this research practice to be ethical.

Thus, whether you view a behavior as being ethical or unethical depends on your philosophy. Are you a deontologist or a teleologist? It's difficult to answer that question until you are placed in an ethically sensitive situation. One thing that is for certain is that you will come across ethically sensitive situations during your career. Will you know it's an ethically sensitive situation? How will you respond? We hope you will at least know when you are in an ethically sensitive situation in marketing research. The rest of this section is devoted to teaching you this sensitivity.[46]

Ethical Behavior in Marketing Research

As noted previously, there are many ways a society may prescribe wanted and unwanted behaviors. In business, if there are practices that are not illegal but are nevertheless thought to be wrong, trade associations or professional organizations will often prescribe a **code of ethical behavior**. This has been the case in marketing and, more specifically, in marketing research. The American Marketing Association

We think these ethical issues are so important that we call your attention to them throughout this book using the ethical issue icon that you see here.

Ethics may be defined as a field of inquiry into determining what behaviors are deemed appropriate.

One's philosophy usually determines appropriate, ethical behavior.

One philosophy is called deontology, which focuses on the rights of the individual. If an individual's rights are violated, then the behavior is not ethical.

Teleology is a philosophy that focuses on the trade-off between individual costs and group benefits. If benefits outweigh costs, the behavior is judged to be ethical.

The British Market Research Association has a code of ethics. Visit its Web site at www.bmra.org.uk. Check out the "BRMA Code of Conduct." Visit the Market Research Society of New Zealand at www.mrsnz.org.nz. See their "Code of Practice." Visit the Australian Market and Social Research Society at www.mrsa.com. Read "Our Code."

Sugging refers to "selling under the guise of a survey." Frugging refers to "fund-raising under the guise of a survey."

Sugging is illegal.

Frugging is unethical.

(**www.marketingpower.com**), the Council of American Survey Research Organizations (**www.casro.org**), the Qualitative Research Consultants Association (**www.qrca.org**), the Marketing Research Association (**www.mra–net.org**), and the Canadian-based Professional Market Research Society (**www.pmrs–aprm.com**) all have codes of ethics. The European-based ESOMAR, the European Society for Marketing Research (**www.esoniar.nl**) also has a code of ethics.

All over the world, marketing research organizations are striving to achieve ethical behavior among practitioners of marketing research.

▶ **Codes of Ethics.** As noted previously, several associations have codes of ethics.[47] However almost all of these different organizations have codes which address the following areas:

- prohibiting selling (Sugging) or fund-raising (Frugging) under the guise of conducting research;
- maintaining research integrity by avoiding misrepresentation and omission of pertinent research data;
- treating outside clients and suppliers fairly.

▶ **Sugging and Frugging.** The first provision of the AMA code deals with prohibiting selling or fund raising under the guise of conducting research. **Sugging** refers to "selling under the guise of a survey." Typically, sugging occurs when a "researcher" gains a respondent's cooperation to participate in a research study and then uses the opportunity to attempt to sell the respondent a good or service. Most consumers are quite willing to provide their attitudes and opinions of products and services in response to a legitimate request for this information. Suggers (and Fruggers), however, take advantage of that goodwill by deceiving unsuspecting consumers. Consumers soon learn that their cooperation in answering a few questions has led to their being subjected to a sales presentation. In sugging and frugging there is no good-faith effort to conduct a survey for the purpose of collecting and analyzing data for specific purposes. Rather, the intent of the "fake" survey is to sell or raise money. Of course, these practices have led to the demise of the pool of cooperative respondents. The Telemarketing and Consumer Fraud and Abuse Prevention Act of 1994 made sugging illegal. Under this act, telemarketers are not allowed to call someone and say they are conducting a survey, and try to sell a product or service. Although telemarketers are not able to legally practice sugging, the act does not prohibit sugging via the mail.[48] **Frugging** is closely related to sugging and stands for "fund-raising under the guise of a survey." Because frugging does not involve the sale of a product or service, it is not covered in the Telemarketing and Consumer Fraud and Abuse Prevention Act of 1994, but it is widely considered to be unethical. Actually, sugging and frugging are carried out by telemarketers or other direct marketers. Researchers do not practice sugging and frugging. However, we cover this topic because both sugging and frugging are unethical treatments of potential respondents in marketing research.

The marketing research industry recognizes that it must attempt to influence legislation in a way that will be favorable for the industry. For example, the industry fought hard to protect consumers from sugging and frugging. Also, when Do Not Call bills were first introduced, the industry worked hard to educate lawmakers about the difference between telemarketers and researchers. Much of this work has been conducted by CMOR, the Council for Marketing and Opinion Research. CMOR was founded in 1992 by four industry associations: The American Marketing Association, The Council of Survey Research Organizations, The Marketing Research Association, and The Advertising Research Federation. We asked CMOR's Director of Government Affairs,

Brian Dautch, to tell you about CMOR. You will learn what he has to say in Marketing Research Insight 3.4.

▶ **Research Integrity.** Sometimes research is not totally objective. Information is withheld, falsified, or altered to protect vested interests.

Marketing research information is often used in making significant decisions. The outcome of the decision may have an impact on future company strategy, budgets, jobs, organization, and so forth. With so much at stake, the opportunity exists for a lack of total objectivity in the research process. The loss of **research integrity**, defined as performing research that adheres to accepted standards, may take the form of withholding information, falsifying data, altering research results, or misinterpreting the research findings in a way that makes them more consistent with predetermined points of view. As one

---

MARKETING RESEARCH INSIGHT

ETHICAL ISSUES

3.4 CMOR: Government Affairs, Policy Analysis, and Lobbying

CMOR
Promoting and Advocating Survey and Opinion Research

The Council for Marketing and Opinion Research, or CMOR, was founded in 1992. Its core missions were (a) government affairs and (b) respondent cooperation.

As CMOR's Director of Government Affairs, I was responsible for establishing the Council's first-ever office in the Washington, DC, area. February 23, 2004, was the official opening day of our DC office. While CMOR had always been known for *tracking* legislation at the state and federal level, a decision was made to become more active in presenting our industry's case directly to lawmakers and regulators.

In this capacity, we have continued to follow legislation from all around the country, and have influenced the language, scope, and impact of many laws around the United States. On the federal level, we have successfully worked with both parties in the House of Representatives as well as the Senate on multiple bills. This impact has ranged from laws that would have an impact on our members' ability to fax potential respondents, to obtaining clear and helpful interpretations from the Federal Trade Commission (FTC) to avoid negative interpretations of their enforcement of Do Not Call laws.

In between, we have worked on issues such as the "spyware" bill pending in front of the House and Senate through 2004 and 2005. Spyware, in primary example, is the surreptitious installation of software on one's computer, which then tracks the user's online keystrokes in hopes of stealing personal information. While the initial version of the bill would have had a negative impact on cookies, HTML, and other nonspyware aspects of online activity and commerce, we have worked to eliminate these broad inclusions and to limit the bill to spyware specifically.

Now that CMOR is well established in Washington, we have continued to expand our base of contacts. This has allowed us to take part in coalitions, working groups, and conferences all over town, and engage many like-minded companies, associations, and individuals in productive dialog.

By permission, CMOR.

Brian Dautch received his law degree from Case Western Reserve University. He has spent over 10 years of his professional career analyzing legislation and lobbying tactics. Mr. Dautch is a resident of Washington, DC.

75

researcher stated, "I refused to alter research results and as a result I was fired for failure to think strategically."[49] A recent example illustrates how research integrity is a serious issue. Forrester Research, Inc. released a report concluding that developing and deploying Web-based portal applications is substantially less expensive using Microsoft technology than it is using a Linux/J2ee combination. When it was learned that the research was funded by Microsoft it brought about skepticism on the part of several CEOs, including one who stated "I'm not a big fan of any of those marketing research firms. I don't believe them to be independent." Forrester CEO George Colony stated that the company was taking steps to "tighten" its internal processes and its integrity policy.[50]

The impetus for a breach in research integrity may come from either the supplier or buyer. If a research supplier knows that a buyer will want marketing research services in the future, the supplier may alter a study's results or withhold information, so that the study will support the buyer's wishes. Breaches of research integrity need not be isolated to those managing the research project. Interviewers have been known to make up interviews and to take shortcuts in completing surveys. In fact, there is some evidence that this is more of a problem than was once thought.[51] Maintaining research integrity is regarded as one of the most significant ethical issues in the research industry. In a study of 460 marketing researchers, Hunt, Chonko, and Wilcox found that maintenance of research integrity posed the most significant problem for one-third of those sampled.[52]

▶ **Treating Others Fairly.** Several ethical issues may arise in the practice of marketing research that center around how others are treated. Suppliers, buyers, and the public may be treated unethically.

Buyers. In the Hunt, Chonko, and Wilcox study cited previously, the second most frequently stated ethical problem facing marketing researchers was fair treatment of buyer firms. Passing hidden charges to buyers, overlooking study requirements when subcontracting work out to other supplier firms, and selling unnecessary research are examples of unfair treatment of buyer firms. By overlooking study requirements, such as qualifying respondents on specified characteristics or verifying that respondents were interviewed, the supplier firm may lower its cost of using the services of a subcontracting field service firm. A supplier firm may oversell research services to naive buyers by convincing them to use a more expensive research design.

Sharing confidential and proprietary information raises ethical questions. Virtually all work conducted by marketing research firms is confidential and proprietary. Researchers build up a storehouse of this information as they conduct research studies. Most ethical issues involving confidentiality revolve around how this storehouse of information, or "background knowledge," is treated. One researcher stated, "Where does 'background knowledge' stop and conflict exist [as a result of work with a previous client]?"[53] It is common practice among research supplier firms to check their existing list of buyer-clients to ensure that there is no conflict of interest before accepting work from a new buyer.

> Sharing of "background knowledge" among firms raises ethical questions.

> Marketing researchers try to avoid conflicts of interest by not working for two competitors.

Suppliers. *Phony RFPs.* Buyers also abuse suppliers of marketing research. A major problem exists, for example, when a firm with internal research capabilities issues a **request for proposals (RFP)** from external supplier firms. External firms then spend time and money developing research designs to solve the stated problem, estimating costs of the project, and so on. Now, having collected several detailed proposals outlining research designs and costs, the abusing firm decides to do the job internally. Issuing a call for proposals from external firms with no intention of doing the job outside is unethical behavior.

Failure to Honor Time and Money Agreements. Often buyer firms have obligations such as agreeing to meetings or the provision of materials needed for the research project. Supplier firms must have these commitments from buyers in a timely fashion in order to keep to their time schedules. Buyer firms sometimes abuse their agreements to deliver personnel or these other resources in the time to which they have agreed. Also, buyers sometimes do not honor commitments to pay for services. Although this happens in many industries, research suppliers do not have the luxury of repossession, although there are, of course, legal recourses.

The Public. Sometimes researchers are asked to do research on products thought to be dangerous to society. Ethical issues arise as researchers balance marketing requirements with social issues. This is particularly true in the areas of product development and advertising. For example, marketing researchers have expressed concern over conducting research on advertising to children. Some advertising has had the objective of increasing the total consumption of refined sugar among children via advertising scheduled during Saturday morning TV programs. Other ethical concerns arise when conducting research on products researchers thought were dangerous to the public, such as certain chemicals, cigarettes, alcohol, and sugar.

Ethical concerns arise when marketing researchers are asked to conduct research on advertising to children or on products they feel are dangerous to the public, such as certain chemicals, cigarettes, alcohol, or sugar.

Some marketing research firms take a proactive position on helping their clients implement strategy that considers ethical issues. For example, ABACO Marketing Research in São Paulo, Brazil, incorporates ethical considerations in their evaluations of clients' promotional materials. Their AD-VISOR® service provides ethical scores and compares them with norms, thus allowing clients to understand consumers' ethical evaluations of proposed communication messages.

▶ **Respondents.** Respondents are the "lifeblood" of the marketing research industry. Respondent cooperation rates have been going down, and the industry is concerned with the ethical treatment of the existing respondent pool.[54] In 1982, some of the organizations that organized CMOR began monitoring survey response cooperation. CMOR

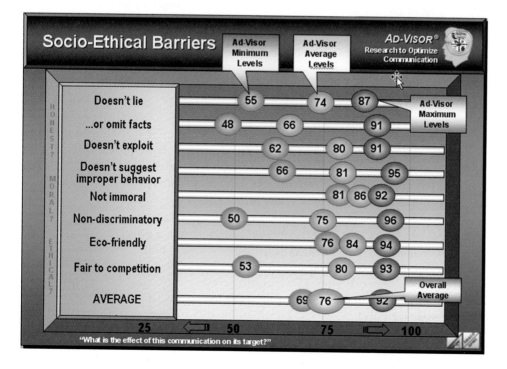

Marketing research firms, like ABACO, can take a proactive position on ethical issues. ABACO helps clients ensure that their communication messages meet certain ethical standards. Visit ABACO's Web site at **www.abacoresearch.com**. By permission, ABACO Marketing Research.

surveys a large number of consumers from time to time to determine the percentage of the population that has refused to take part in a survey in the past year. The percentages have risen sharply: 1982 (15 percent), 1992 (31 percent), 1999 (40 percent), and in 2002 the percentage was 45 percent.[55] CMOR has reported that their figures for the 2003 study show a sharp increase in nonresponse.[56] Marketing researchers must honor promises made to respondents that the respondent's identity will remain confidential or anonymous if they expect respondents to cooperate with requests for information in the future.

▶ **Respondent Fairness.** In the following paragraphs we consider some of the issues marketing researchers must face in order to treat respondents fairly.

Deception of Respondents. Respondents may be deceived during the research process. Kimmel and Smith point out that **deception** may occur during subject recruitment (they are not told the true identity/sponsor of the research, etc.), during the research procedure itself (they are viewed without their knowledge, etc.), and during postresearch situations (there is a violation of the promise of anonymity). Also, these authors suggest that there are serious consequences to this deception.[57]

An example of where deception is used in marketing research is mystery shopping. **Mystery shopping** is the practice of gathering competitive intelligence by sending people posing as customers to gather price and sales data from unsuspecting employees. Shing and Spence argue that though the information given out by the mystery shopper is not confidential, it is still given under false pretenses.[58] Mystery shopping is widely used in industry, and many would argue that it is not unethical. Few, however, would argue that it does not involve deception. Our purpose is to make certain you know when you are dealing with an issue that is ethically sensitive.

Confidentiality and Anonymity. One way of gaining a potential respondent's trust is by promising confidentiality or anonymity. **Confidentiality** means that the researcher knows who the respondent is but does not identify the respondent with any information gathered from that respondent to a client. So the respondent's identity is confidential information known only by the researcher. A stronger appeal may be made under conditions of **anonymity**. The respondent is, and remains, anonymous or unknown. The researcher is interested only in gathering information from the respondent and does not know who the respondent is. Ethical issues arise when the respondents are promised confidentiality and anonymity and the researcher fails to honor this promise.

Invasions of Privacy. Marketing research, by its nature, is invasive. Any information acquired from a respondent results in some degree of invasiveness. Ethical issues, some of them legal, abound in the area of invading others' privacy. Two areas that are most responsible for consumer concern are unsolicited telephone calls and spam. Since marketing researchers rely heavily on telephone surveys and, more recently, online survey research, both these areas are significant to the market research industry.

Unsolicited Telephone Calls. Telemarketers' abuse of consumer privacy by flooding consumers with unsolicited telephone calls has resulted in consumers' putting pressure on Congress for relief. In the summer of 2003, the FTC introduced a national "Do Not Call" registry (**www.donotcall.gov**). Research firms, calling for consumers' opinions only, have been excluded from the "Do Not Call" legislation.[59] The Do Not Call registry seems to work reasonably well. However, organizations that are excluded from the "do not call" legislation must understand that they cannot abuse the privilege they have gained. CMOR continues to work to keep research firms excluded; however, marketing researchers must work especially hard to encourage consumer goodwill and to ensure that they are viewed separately from telemarketers.

Spam. When online survey research became a possibility by accessing respondents via the Internet, some organizations viewed this as an easy, fast way to gather survey information. They were little concerned with ethical issues when they obtained e-mail lists to target survey recipients. They began sending out thousands of surveys to unwary persons. The practice of sending unwanted e-mail is called "spamming." An electronic message has been defined as **spam** if (1) the recipient's personal identity and context are irrelevant because the message is equally applicable to many other potential recipients; (2) the recipient has not verifiably granted deliberate, explicit, and still revocable permission for it to be sent; and (3) the transmission and reception of the message appear to the recipient to give a disproportionate benefit to the sender.[60] The name *spam* comes from a Monty Python skit in which a restaurant customer is deluged with many, repeated requests (sung by waiters) to order the canned, luncheon meat, Spam. Finally, the customer yells: "I don't want any Spam."[61]

Online Survey Research and Spam. The practice of sending spam threatens online survey research. Potential respondents, flooded with unwanted e-mails, will come to regard all but the most personal messages as trash. Marketing research organizations fight to reduce spam. Though the "Can Spam Act" was passed in 2003, two years later it was estimated that 60% of all e-mail that enters in-boxes everyday is spam![62] A **"Do Not Spam"** registry, allowing citizens to register their e-mail addresses to avoid spamming, similar to the "Do Not Call" registry, has been considered by the FTC. However, in June 2004 the FTC recommended not to establish such a register. The FTC cited as their primary reason lack of an effective authentication system and the inability to enforce the registry. In fact, the report stated that there was a high likelihood that such a list would be obtained by spammers and those registering would receive more spam![63] Marketing research firms have not been included in the definitions of spam abusers and have not, thus far, been included in any anti-spam legislation. In addition to marketing research organizations there are consumer organizations to fight it such as CAUCE, Coalition Against Unsolicited Commercial Email (**http://www.cauce.org/**) and MAPS, Mail Abuse Prevention System (**www.mail.abuse.org**).

Since improper online surveying could be considered spam, the marketing research industry has worked hard to establish codes of ethics dealing with proper online surveying. The Interactive Marketing Research Organization (IMRO) and CASRO have been leaders in this effort. Some of the key issues for marketing researchers to consider if they are doing online survey research are discussed in Appendix A.

In conclusion, marketing research firms are working hard to protect the privacy of their respondents. The firms in the industry realize that they must rely on consumer cooperation for information requests. In order to achieve a cooperative pool of potential respondents, marketing researchers must attempt to separate themselves from unscrupulous direct marketers. The industry has been considering developing and using an "industry identifier" such as a "Your Opinion Counts" to help consumers more easily identify legitimate marketing research firms. While this idea has been around for several years,[64] it is being discussed again among industry leaders. Those in the industry think that respondent cooperation is becoming such a problem that CMOR has created a position, Director of Respondent Cooperation.[65] However, in the meantime, the future is cloudy in terms of how legal actions will affect research. Already, research firms, realizing that respondents are their "lifeblood," are moving in the direction of recruiting their own panels of willing respondents. Recruiting and maintaining a panel requires a considerable investment. **Panel equity**, the value of

The name *spam* comes from a Monty Python skit in which a restaurant customer is deluged with many, repeated requests to order canned Spam. Finally, the customer yells: "I don't want any Spam."

The practice of sending spam threatens online survey research. Potential respondents, flooded with unwanted e-mails, will come to regard all but the most personal messages as trash.

Appendix A will teach you what is necessary to conduct online survey research that is not considered to be spam.

In an attempt to help consumers distinguish marketing research firms from unscrupulous direct marketers such as telemarketers and spammers, the industry is considering a "industry identifier" similar to the "Good Housekeeping" seal of approval.

Realizing that respondents are their "lifeblood," many research firms are recruiting their own panels of willing respondents, which requires a considerable investment. The value of panels, known as panel equity, may become very important in the future.

readily available access to willing respondents, may become more and more important in the future. Marketing research firms, recognizing the value they have in panels, will make even greater efforts to ensure fair and ethical treatment of their panel respondents.

SUMMARY

This chapter covered four introductory topics. First, it reviewed how the marketing research industry evolved. Although surveys were conducted for business purposes in the early 1800s, Charles Coolidge Parlin is given credit for conducting the first continuous and organized research for the Curtis Publishing Company beginning in 1911. Parlin is recognized as the "Father of Marketing Research." Prior to the Industrial Revolution there was little need for formal marketing research. Business proprietors, barterers, and artisans knew their customers. Once mass production made possible by the Industrial Revolution led to producing goods for distant markets, managers needed information about these distant markets. By the 1930s the marketing research industry was becoming widespread, and by the 1960s the practice of marketing research gained wide approval as a method for keeping abreast of fast-changing, distant markets.

The research industry today is a $21.5 billion industry, with firms operating all over the globe. The Honomichl Global Top 25 is a listing of the top 25 firms, in terms of revenue, operating around the world. The Honomichl Top 50 is a list of U.S.-based firms ranked by revenues generated in the United States. Strategic alliances in the industry make it a very competitive industry. VNU, which owns ACNielsen and Nielsen Media Research, is the largest marketing research firm in the world.

The research industry may be broadly classified as research buyers and suppliers. Suppliers may be internal (research is provided by an entity within the firm) or external. Internal suppliers organize by having their own formal departments, having a committee or individual responsible for research, or by not having anyone responsible. Formal departments of internal supplier firms typically organize by area of application (i.e., business to consumer, business to business, product a, product b, etc.), marketing function (product research, promotion research, etc.) or the research process (i.e., data collection, data analysis). External supplier firms may be classified as full-service or limited-service firms. Each of these types has several other classifications of firms. These firms may organize by function (data analysis, data collection, etc.), by type of research application (customer satisfaction, advertising effectiveness, new product development, etc.), by geography (domestic versus international), by type of customer (health care, government, telecommunications, etc.), or some combination of these. External supplier firms may be classified into two categories: full-service and limited-service firms. Full-service supplier firms have the ability to conduct the entire marketing research project for the buyer firms. Limited-service supplier firms specialize in one or, at most, a few marketing research activities. There are different types of both full-service and limited service firms.

The marketing research industry's performance is reviewed, or evaluated, from time to time. These reviews are mixed. Earlier reviews would indicate that, although the marketing research industry is doing a reasonably good job, there is room for improvement. More recent reviews, however, are not as complimentary. Suggestions are made for improvements, including researchers becoming more involved in diagnosing market needs, speeding up the research process, integrating research with all departments, and being less involved with their "tools" and more involved in strategy decisions, among others. Some suggested solutions have included certification for marketing research professionals to ensure a minimum standard of training and experience or an auditing system to ensure consistency of performance across the industry. In February 2005, the Marketing Research Association launched the first certification program. Individuals completing the requirements will earn their Professional Researcher Certification. The industry offers many varied educational programs from industry professional organizations such as CASRO, MRA, ARF, and the AMA. Also, there are private educational programs of excellent quality such as the Burke Institute.

Ethical issues in marketing research are more important today than ever. A number of ethical issues are present in the practice of marketing research. Ethics is defined as a field of inquiry into determining what behaviors are deemed appropriate under certain circumstances, as prescribed by codes of behavior that are set by society. How you respond to ethically sensitive situations depends on your philosophy: deontology or teleology. Several organizations in the research industry have codes of ethical behavior for both buyers and suppliers of research. Sugging is illegal. Frugging is very unethical. Ethical issues include research integrity, treating others (buyers, suppliers, the public, and respondents) fairly. Respondent fairness issues include deception, confidentiality, and invasions of privacy. Unsolicited telephone calls and e-mail spam are an invasion of privacy. Special standards, reported in Appendix A, are provided to online survey marketing researchers to protect the privacy of online respondents. In the future, we can probably expect more legislation affecting access to respondents. Research companies, faced with a declining pool of willing respondents in the general public, will rely more heavily on recruiting their own panel members. We believe that by recruiting and maintaining their own panels of respondents, research companies will come to value their "panel equity" and we will see even fairer treatment of respondents in the future. Appendix A is provided to examine how the research industry is conducting online surveying without spamming. Appendix B is provided for readers who are interested in a career in marketing research.

KEY TERMS

Charles Coolidge Parlin (p. 42)
Honomichl Global Top 25 (p. 42)
Honomichl Top 50 (p. 45)
Strategic alliances (p. 45)
Research suppliers (p. 45)
Internal supplier (p. 45)
External suppliers (p. 49)
Full-service supplier firms (p. 50)
Syndicated data service firms (p. 50)
Standardized service firms (p. 50)
Customized service firms (p. 51)
Online research services firms (p. 51)
Online research (p. 51)
Limited-service supplier firms (p. 51)

Field service firms (p. 51)
Phone banks (p. 52)
Market segment specialists (p. 52)
Sample design and distribution (p. 52)
Data analysis services (p. 52)
Specialized research technique firms (p. 52)
Certification (p. 57)
Professional Researcher Certification (PRC) (p. 59)
Auditing (p. 59)
Ethics (p. 63)
Deontology (p. 63)
Teleology (p. 63)

Code of ethical behavior (p. 63)
- Sugging (p. 64)
- Frugging (p. 64)
Research integrity (p. 65)
Requests for proposals (RFPs) (p. 66)
- Deception (p. 68)
- Mystery shopping (p. 68)
Confidentiality (p. 68)

Anonymity (p. 68)
Spam (p. 69)
Do Not Spam registry (p. 69)
Panel equity (p. 69)
Can Spam Act (p. 78)
- Opt-out (p. 78)
- Opt-in (p. 78)

REVIEW QUESTIONS/APPLICATIONS

1. Describe why Jack Honomichl thinks that more and more research firms are "glass houses."
2. Who is given credit for conducting the first continuous and organized marketing research? (He is also known as the "Father of Marketing Research.")
3. Explain why marketing research was not widespread prior to the Industrial Revolution.
4. The marketing research industry, worldwide, is about a $_____ billion industry. Marketing research in the United States is about a $_____ billion industry.
5. We categorized firms as internal and external suppliers of marketing research information. Explain what is meant by each, and give an example of each type of firm.
6. Distinguish among full-service, limited-service, syndicated data services, standardized services, customized service, and online research services firms.
7. How would you categorize the following firms?
   a. a firm specializing in marketing to kids (6–12)
   b. a firm that specializes in a computerized scent generator for testing reactions to smells
   c. a firm that offers a package for running test markets
   d. a firm that offers clients samples drawn according to the client's sample plan
   e. a firm that collects data over the Internet
8. What makes an online marketing research firm different from other marketing research firms?
9. What is the advantage in a firm having its own formal marketing research department? Explain three different ways such a department may be internally organized.
10. On evaluating the marketing research industry, what was suggested in the text as indicating there is room for improvement?
11. What were given as recommendations for improving marketing research by Professors Mahajan and Wind?
12. What have been some suggested remedies for improving the marketing research industry?
13. Do you agree or disagree with Professor Stephen W. McDaniel's answer to the question: "Should marketing researchers be certified?" Why?
14. What are the two fundamental philosophies that can be used as a basis for making ethical decisions?
15. Name four ethical issues facing the marketing research industry.
16. Go to the Web sites for any three companies listed in the Honomichl 50. Study the Web sites and compare and contrast the services the three firms offer.
17. Look up "marketing research" in your Yellow Pages directory. Given the information provided in the Yellow Pages, can you classify the research firms in your area according to the classification system of research firms we used in this chapter?

18. Comment on each practice in the following list. Is it ethical? Indicate your reasoning in each case.

   a. A research company conducts a telephone survey and gathers information that it uses later to send a salesperson to the home of potential buyers for the purpose of selling a product. It makes no attempt to sell the product over the telephone.

   b. Would your answer to (a) change if you found out that the information gathered during the telephone survey was used as part of a "legitimate" marketing research report?

   c. A door-to-door salesperson finds that by telling people that he is conducting a survey they are more likely to listen to his sales pitch.

   d. Greenpeace sends out a direct-mail piece described as a survey and asks for donations as the last question.

   e. In the appendix of the final report, the researcher lists the names of all respondents who took part in the survey and places an asterisk beside the names of those who indicated a willingness to be contacted by the client's sales personnel.

   f. A list of randomly generated telephone numbers is drawn in order to conduct a telephone survey.

   g. A list of randomly generated e-mail addresses is generated using a "Spambot" (an electronic "robot" that searches the Internet looking for and retaining e-mail addresses) in order to conduct a random online research project.

   h. Students conducting a marketing research project randomly select e-mail addresses of other students from the student directory in order to conduct their term project.

CASE **3.1**

ABR MARKETING RESEARCH

The authors wish to thank Dr. Harriet Bettis-Outland, Assistant Professor of Marketing, University of West Florida for revising this case.[66]

It was late Friday evening in December, and Barbara Jefferson, a senior research analyst for ABR Marketing Research, was working furiously to complete the media plan portion of the Precision Grooming Products report. PGP was considering introducing a men's hair gel, which required demographic characteristics and media habits of male hair gel users. In addition, attitudinal information about product attributes such as oiliness, stickiness, masculinity, and fragrance was needed.

The findings were to be presented Monday afternoon, and a long series of problems and delays had forced Barbara to stay late on Friday evening to complete the report. Complicating matters, Barbara felt that her boss, Michelle Barry, expected the statistical analysis to be consistent with ABR's initial recommendations to Precision. Barbara, Michelle, and David Miller, from Precision's advertising agency, were to meet Monday morning to finalize ABR's presentation to Precision.

Back in September, Barbara had recommended that 250 users of men's hair gel products be surveyed from each of 15 metropolitan areas. Phillip Parker from Precision's marketing department had argued that conclusions about local usage in each city would not be accurate unless each city's sample size was proportional to its population. In other words, sample sizes for larger cities should be larger than for smaller cities. Furthermore, Phillip feared that males in metropolitan areas differed from males in rural areas with regard to usage or other important characteristics. Barbara finally convinced Phillip that sample sizes proportional to population would mean only 25 to 50 interviews in some smaller cities, which would be too few to draw statistically valid conclusions. Furthermore, expanding the survey to include rural users would have required committing more money to the project—money Precision didn't want to spend.

In October, a Des Moines, Iowa, pretest revealed that the questionnaire's length was driving the cost per completed interview to about $18. Total expenses would be well over budget if that cost held for the 15 metro areas. If the survey costs exceeded $65,000 (counting the pilot study), then precious little money would be left for the focus groups, advertising, and packaging pretesting in ABR's contract with Precision (see Table A.1).

Since Precision was a new account with big potential, a long-term relationship with them would be valuable. (Business at ABR had been slow this past year.) Feeling "under the gun," Barbara met with Michelle and Phillip, who agreed to reduce the sample to 200 men in only 11 metropolitan areas.

In early November, a new problem arose. After surveying eight metro areas, Barbara discovered that her assistant had accidentally deleted all questions on media habits from the questionnaire given to ABR's vendor for the phone interviews. When told of the missing questions problem, Michelle and Phillip became visibly angry at the vendor. After much discussion, they decided there was too little time to hire a new vendor and resample the eight areas. Therefore, they agreed to re-insert the media questions for the remaining three cities and just finish the survey.

Barbara's task now was to make the most of the data she had. Because responses from each of the three cities were reasonably similar, and each city was in a different region (East, West, and Midwest), Barbara felt confident that the three-city data were representative. Therefore, she decided to base the media plan on the large differences between her results and the national averages for adult men—making sports magazines and newspapers the primary vehicles for Precision's advertising. (See Table A.2.)

Barbara's confidence in the media plan was bolstered by a phone conversation with David Miller. Until a short time ago, his agency had handled the advertising for Village Toiletries, so he had valuable information about this competitor's possible responses to Precision's new product. David liked Barbara's recommendations, thought Phillip would also approve, and agreed to support the media plan in Monday's meeting. Indeed, Barbara thought, David had been a big help.

The Precision project had put a great deal of stress on Barbara, who hated spending evenings away from her family—especially near the holidays! If the presentation went well and more business was stirred up, then Barbara suspected that she would be spending even more evenings away from her family. But if the presentation went poorly or the data-collection errors became an issue, then Precision might look elsewhere for market research, thus jeopardizing Barbara's future with ABR. Either way, she was not feeling too comfortable.

TABLE A.1 Proposed Budget	
Phone survey (including pilot study)	$ 58,000
Focus-group study	8,000
Advertising pretesting	25,000
Package pretesting	14,000
Miscellaneous expenses	5,000
Proposed total expenses	$110,000

TABLE A.2 Comparison of Media Habits: Three City Sample of Male Hair Gel Users vs U.S. Adult Males		Three-City Sample	All U.S. Men
Magazines: At least one subscription of . . .	News	28%	19%
	Entertainment	4%	3%
	Sports	39%	20%
	Other	9%	6%
Newspaper subscription (at least one daily)		35%	14%
Favorite radio format	Pop	41%	38%
	Country	21%	30%
	Jazz	15%	17%
	Easy listening	7%	6%
	News/talk	5%	4%
	Other	11%	5%
Hours watching television per week	Dramas	6.3	8.4
	Comedies	7.8	7.3
	News	1.1	3.9
	Other	2.3	3.9
	Total	17.5	23.5

1. After you have thoroughly read the case, write down what you believe are the issues in the case.

2. For each issue you write down identify how important you believe the issue to be ranging from 7 (very important) to 1 (unimportant).

CREATING THIEVES IN THE NAME OF RESEARCH!

Several years ago a company developed a device that was said to use subliminal auditory messages that would affect behavior. The company had received a great deal of publicity in the press by claiming that its "black boxes" would play subliminal messages over a company's sound system and that these messages could, for example, cause real estate agents to get more listings and cause shoppers and employees to reduce shoplifting. When retailers learned there was a way to reduce their high costs due to shoplifting, the company making the black box received numerous calls to install it. Executives viewed this wonderful new product as a way of stimulating employees to excel and, for retailers, curbing shoplifting without the use of invasive tactics. But some asked "Does this new method, based on subliminal messages, actually work?"

One of your authors was involved in a marketing research project designed to measure the effects of subliminal messages on shoplifting behavior. The research design consisted of researchers recruiting respondents passing by an office building to take part in a study of the "attitudes and opinions of the public." Respondents were then told that if they agreed to complete the short survey they would be given a choice of several nice gifts, including a watch, pen set, or expensive glassware. Respondents agreeing to the study were then escorted into a private "research office," given a bogus survey measuring attitudes and opinions, and shown a large supply of the free gifts nearby. As the respondents began to take the survey, the researcher interrupted them to tell the respondents that they had to take a break and asked if it would be OK with the respondent to "Just select one of the free gifts and lock the door when you leave." Surrounded by many nice products and without any supervision, this situation was designed to create the maximum likelihood that someone would steal. On a random basis, half of the respondents were exposed to a subliminal message consisting of the same message the black-box company claimed would reduce shoplifting. The other half of the respondents were not exposed to any message. If the subliminal message worked, there would be less stealing when the subliminal message was being played than in the condition when the message was not played.

1. Do you think this study is ethical? Why? Why not?

2. If you think the study is ethical, what is your philosophy? If unethical, what is your philosophy?

3. Do you think deception is used in the study? If so, what type of deception?

4. Should this study have been conducted? Why or why not?

5. If you felt this study should not have been conducted, under what circumstances would you agree to a study designed to measure the effects of the subliminal black-box technology?

Marketing Research and Spam Surveys

As we have noted previously, the Internet provides researchers with the ability to access millions of potential respondents. However, how they access these potential respondents is critical in determining whether unethical practices are being used. In this appendix we present information that clarifies when an e-mailed survey is or is not ethical.

CAN SPAM ACT

After Congress heard complaints that half of all e-mail traffic is spam, spam is increasing, U.S. firms alone lose $10 billion annually in lost productivity and cost for spam-filtering software, and testimony that 70% of e-mail users report that spam e-mails

The "Can Spam Act" is not likely to "can" spam.

make the online experience annoying,[67] it passed what is known as the **Can Spam Act**. The act became effective, January 2, 2004. This legislation does not make all spam illegal. Rather, it requires spam to be truthful and will give government agencies authority to fine, and, in some cases, imprison offenders. It requires spammers to use real e-mail addresses (many presently disguise their true identity) and to provide proper subject lines indicating the true nature of the e-mail message. The law also forbids "harvesting": the gathering of e-mail addresses without owner's awareness. Many agree that the Can Spam Act will be ineffective because most spammers operate in foreign countries and will not be subject to U.S. law. Also some believe the act harms other efforts to curb spam because it supersedes states' laws, some of which are strict (e.g., those in California). At least one legal expert believes that the remedy to spam will have to come from technology instead of the legal system.[68] The significance for the marketing research industry is that spam will continue, and this will further alienate potential respondents from attempts by legitimate online marketing research firms requesting them to respond to online research requests.

OPT-OUT VS. OPT-IN STANDARDS[69]

There is an ongoing debate regarding what practices actually constitute invasions of privacy. Slowly, legislation is being adopted around the world that helps to define this issue. One common theme in the legislation has been the individual's right of consent. One consent standard is the **opt-out** standard. Under this standard, individuals are given the opportunity to not be contacted again and/or to limit the manner in which information they provide may be used. On the other hand, the alternative standard, to **opt-in**, means that individuals must specifically and affirmatively consent to a specified activity, such as being given an online survey via their e-mail. Opt-in is referred to as "active consent" and has been preferred by many privacy advocates for the reason that it allows the individual full control; that is, respondents never receive the survey unless they have opted to take it. Others argue that the ability to opt-out, also known as "passive consent," provides ample control to individuals.

Legislative bodies will likely continue the debate as to which standard, opt-in versus opt-out, should be used in privacy laws. The marketing research industry has been self-regulating through codes of standards using the opt-in standard. CMOR, IMRO, and CASRO have been industry leaders in helping to shape not only ethical standards for the industry but also in trying to ensure that legislation passed to deal with telemarketers does not include legitimate marketing researchers.

WHAT DOES THE CASRO CODE OF ETHICS SAY ABOUT ONLINE SURVEY RESEARCH AND SPAMMING?

Marketing researchers cannot send unsolicited e-mails. Consumers sent e-mails should have a "reasonable expectation" of receiving the e-mail.

▶ **Who May be Surveyed?** We summarize procedures that marketing research firms should follow in order to conduct online survey research without spamming. As a general rule, marketing research organizations believe that survey research organizations should not use unsolicited e-mails (spam) to recruit respondents for surveys. And, in order to send e-mail surveys, research organizations are required to verify that individuals contacted for research by e-mail have a reasonable expectation that they will be contacted by e-mail for research. CASRO states that such a reasonable expectation can be assumed when *all* of the following conditions exist.[70]

(1) A substantive preexisting relationship exists between the individuals contacted and the research organization, the client, or the list owners contracting the research (the latter being so identified). Examples would include when there has been a business transaction or correspondence with the e-mailed person and that person has voluntarily supplied his/her e-mail address for future research, marketing, or correspondence contact. The relationship must be evident to the person being e-mailed, and the client firm, or the research firm, must be identified.

(2) Individuals have a reasonable expectation, based on the preexisting relationship, that they may be contacted for research. This means that there must be a sufficient belief, based on the preexisting relationship, then an individual may be contacted via e-mail for purposes of research.

(3) Individuals are offered the choice to be removed from *all* future e-mail contact in each invitation (opt-out standard).

(4) The invitation list excludes all individuals who have previously taken the appropriate and timely steps to request the list owner to remove them. In other words, researchers or clients must maintain a "Do Not E-mail" registry.

> **Gathering E-Mail Addresses.** Codes practiced in the research industry prohibit research organizations from using subterfuge in obtaining e-mail addresses of potential respondents, such as using technologies or techniques to collect e-mail addresses without individuals' awareness. Research organizations are prohibited from using false or misleading return e-mail addresses when recruiting respondents over the Internet. CASRO's code further states: When receiving e-mail lists from clients or list owners, research organizations are required to have the client or list provider verify that individuals listed have a reasonable expectation that they will receive e-mail contact, as defined above.

See what IMRO has to say in their Code of Ethics. Go to **www.imro.org** and go to Code of Ethics.

CASRO's code of ethics identifies conditions under which consumers may be sent e-mails from marketing research firms.

Appendix B

Careers in Marketing Research

Maybe you have been thinking about marketing research as a career choice. There are many career opportunities in the industry, and we have prepared this appendix to give you some information about those career choices. More importantly, we give you some sources to pursue additional information about a career in the marketing research industry. We highly recommend that you also go to the following Web Sites:

Marketing Research Association: www.mra-net.org. Go to Education & Events; Education; Career Guide Pt. I and Career Guide Pt. II., Universities offering Masters Degrees in Marketing Research.

Council for Survey Research Organizations: **www.casro.org**. Go to "College & Universities" for a list of schools offering programs in marketing research.

WHAT IS THE OUTLOOK FOR THE INDUSTRY?

Before you seek employment in any industry you should ask about the total outlook for the industry. Buggy-whip manufacturing is not exactly a growth industry! What are the growth rates in the industry? What do the experts have to say about the future of the industry?

A good place to find information about the outlook of an industry is the *Occupational Outlook Handbook*. You can access it online at **www.bls.gov/oco/home.htm**. Look under the category "Professional and related" and then under "market and survey researchers." Or, just type in "marketing research" in the search box.

The *Occupational Outlook Handbook* forecasts jobs in economics and marketing research to grow "faster than average" (21 to 35 percent) through 2012. Demand for qualified market research analysts should be healthy because of an increasingly competitive economy. Marketing research provides organizations valuable feedback from purchasers, allowing companies to evaluate consumer satisfaction and more effectively plan for the future. As companies seek to expand their market and consumers become better informed, the need for marketing professionals will increase.

Opportunities for market research analysts with graduate degrees should be good in a wide range of employment settings, particularly in marketing research firms, as companies find it more profitable to contract out for marketing research services rather than support their own marketing department. Other organizations, including financial services organizations, health care institutions, advertising firms, manufacturing firms producing consumer goods, and insurance companies may offer job opportunities for market research analysts.

Opportunities for survey researchers should be strong as the demand for market and opinion research increases. Employment opportunities will be especially favorable in commercial market and opinion research as an increasingly competitive economy requires businesses to more effectively and efficiently allocate advertising funds.[71]

WHAT ARE THE SALARIES?

Another question you should ask is how much the people in this profession earn. Like many professional services, salaries vary widely in the marketing research industry. Nevertheless, we can give you some general guidelines. The *Occupational Outlook Handbook* separates marketing research analysts from survey researchers. The primary difference is that analysts are involved with the total research process, and their definition of survey researchers closely matches what we discuss in this chapter as field-data-collection firms (limited-service firms). Median annual earnings of market research analysts in 2002 were $53,810. The middle 50 percent earned between $38,760 and $76,310. The lowest 10 percent earned less than $29,390, and the highest 10 percent earned more than $100,160. Median annual earnings in the industries employing the largest numbers of market research analysts in 2002 were as follows:

Management of companies and enterprises	$56,750
Insurance carriers	$46,700
Other professional, scientific, and technical services	$46,380
Management, scientific, and technical consulting services	$44,580

Median annual earnings of survey researchers in 2002 were $22,200. The middle 50 percent earned between $17,250 and $38,530. The lowest 10 percent earned less than $15,140, and the highest 10 percent earned more than $57,080. Median annual earnings of survey researchers in 2000 were $52,470 in computer and data processing services and $18,780 in research and testing services.[72]

Another source stated that entry-level job opportunities are dwindling in the marketing research industry because companies want people who can hit the ground running. The starting salaries for individuals with undergraduate degrees in business or statistics are around $40,000 per year. With more experience, researchers can earn six-figured salaries. On average, in 1999, researchers earned $87,000, a 5.3 percent increase over 1998. Also, 82 percent of marketing researchers earned more than $60,000 in 1999.[73]

WHAT KINDS OF JOBS ARE THERE?

OK, so you are still interested! What types of jobs are there in the marketing research industry? We suggest you go to the MRA Web site at **http://www.mra-net.org** and click on "Education and Events" and then on "Education" and then "Career Guide I" and "Career Guide II." Once you are familiar with these guides, go to the Honomichl 50 table in this chapter, and go to the Web sites of the companies listed. Most of them will have a "Careers with Us" or similar link. Check out the types of jobs they are describing. You should, of course, go to your career center and find out what resources your college or university has to help you find the job you want.

WHAT ARE THE REQUIREMENTS?

Do you have what it takes? The traits associated with the most successful and effective marketing researchers include the following: curiosity, high intelligence, creativity, self-discipline, good interpersonal and communication skills, the ability to work under strict time constraints, and feeling comfortable working with numbers. The field is becoming gender-neutral. Information Resources, Inc. (IRI) prefers a degree in marketing or a related area. Although an undergraduate degree is required, there has been a trend in some firms toward requiring postgraduate degrees. Most universities do not offer a degree in marketing research. There are some, reported later, that are quite good. Thus, an M.B.A. with a marketing major is one of the more common combinations for people employed in marketing research. Other possibilities are degrees in quantitative methods, sociology, or economics. Undergraduate training in mathematics or the physical sciences is a very suitable (and employable) background for anyone considering a career in marketing research.

ARE YOU INTERESTED IN A MASTER'S DEGREE IN MARKETING RESEARCH?

Graduate degrees are highly recommended in the marketing research industry. Go to the CASRO Web site at **www.casro.org** and click on "Colleges and Universities." Also, go to the MRA Web site at **www.mra-net.org** and click on "Education & Events" and then "Education." You will find "Universities Offering Masters of Market Research Programs."

Defining the Problem and Determining Research Objectives

Defining Problems Correctly Is Needed to Solve the Problems

Golfers the world over know the premier magazine in the golf industry, *Golf Digest*. Golf Digest Companies also publishes three other highly successful magazines targeting different markets of golf readers; *Golf World, Golf for Women*, and the trade magazine, *Golf World Business*. Publishers often conduct marketing research. Their managers need information to help them evaluate readership, preferences for features, interest levels in cover stories, and so on. They also conduct research to help their advertisers make better promotional decisions. While most golfers are familiar with *Golf Digest*, very few know that Golf Digest Companies is also a marketing research company. Their Corporate Marketing and Research Department, headed by V.P. Jon Last, is a full service research/marketing consulting firm. Not only does this department supply the four magazines with information, they also solve problems for clients such as manufacturers of golf equipment, travel destination resorts, financial services, pharmaceuticals, and apparel.

To help potential advertisers make decisions, Golf Digest Companies' Corporate Marketing and Research Department can provide them with important information such as how much time readers spend reading different magazines, how "involved" readers are with the magazine, preferences for different magazines, and, of course, number of sales of magazines. No matter what project Golf

■ To understand when marketing research is needed
■ To understand the importance of properly defining the problem
■ To know the two sources of problems and how to recognize them
■ To understand the difference between a symptom and a problem
■ To realize there are different types of problems
■ To know the role the researcher should play in defining the problem
■ To understand the role of ITBs and RFPs
■ To examine a process of defining the problem and research objectives in a case situation
■ To understand the role of research objectives

Learning
Objectives

GolfDigest

The Marketing Challenge

Callaway GOLF

The Process of Buying Drivers

Callaway GOLF

- Declining market share in the woods category
- Need to understand the importance of various marketing mix elements
- Need to understand consumer perceptions to re-define strategy

Digest Companies Marketing Research Department takes on, they fully understand the importance of properly defining the problem. As their motto says, Golf Digest "takes the time" to do the research properly. By accurately identifying the problems facing client Callaway Golf, research objectives were created that led to generating the information needed to solve the problems.

As you read through the chapter, you will have a better understanding of how Golf Digest Companies' Corporate Marketing and Research Department determined these problems for their client, Callaway Golf.

The previous chapters introduced you to the steps in the marketing research process. In this chapter, we are ready to begin taking those steps. We will take a closer look at the first step, establishing the need for marketing research. Second, we will look at the second step in the process, which many believe is the most important of all the steps—defining the problem and determining research objectives. In this chapter we will examine the nature of the problem itself by looking at the importance of the problem, its sources, methods for recognizing the problem, the role of symptoms, types of problems, the role of the researcher, impediments to properly defining the problem, and the role of ITBs and RFPs. We will also illustrate the process of problem definition and determining research objectives and the research proposal. Finally, we get you involved in determining the problem(s) and research objectives using your integrated case: The Hobbit's Choice.

ESTABLISHING THE NEED FOR MARKETING RESEARCH

When Is Marketing Research Not Needed?

We pointed out in Chapter 2 that marketing research is not needed for every decision. We also noted that this was a good thing. Otherwise, managers would constantly be involved in conducting marketing research instead of making decisions to run their companies. As a review, we said that marketing research should not be used when: (a) the information is already available (remember that there are those other components of the marketing information system providing information as well); (b) the timing is wrong which may mean that a competitive response is immediately needed; (c) funds are not available; (d) costs of research are greater than the value of the information generated by the research. While the value of research information is hard to quantify, managers should attempt to do this before making a decision to use marketing research.

DEFINE THE PROBLEM

The Importance of Properly Defining the Problem

Properly defining the problem is *the* most important step in the marketing research process.

Sometimes problems are easy to define, such as: "What are the media habits of the heavy users of our brand?" Sometimes problems are very difficult to define, for example: "Our sales are increasing but our market share is going down. Is there a problem, and if so, what is it?" But regardless of how difficult or easy it is to define the problem we can state that properly defining the problem is *the* most important step in the marketing research process. While this may sound like a dramatic statement, it is indeed true. Why? You have learned that there are 11 steps in the marketing research process. You also learned that, after determining whether or not research is needed, defining the problem is the next step in the process. If the wrong problem is defined, what impact does this have on the rest of the research process? Everything else is wrong! It doesn't matter if you collect data properly, analyze it properly, and report it in a meaningful fashion if it addresses the wrong problem. Great care must be exercised in properly defining the problem. Let's look at a couple of examples to illustrate improper problem definition.

▶ **How Can We Beat Burger King?** McDonald's conducted marketing research for a new burger, the McDonald's Arch DeLuxe. The burger, targeted for adults, received a less-than-hoped-for result, even though McDonald's spent large sums of money on marketing research. What happened? The analysis points to "improper problem definition." McDonald's management was eager to match the Burger King Deluxe burger. All research was focused on measuring consumer preferences for different sizes and tastes of hamburgers. McDonald's researchers would likely have been better off not defining the problem as "How can we beat Burger King" but, instead, focusing on adult fast-food customers' preferences and diet preferences. They may have produced a product that was better-tasting than the Burger King product but they did not come up with a product that appealed to adults. Improperly defining the problem leads to lost time and money.[1]

▶ **How Can We Win a Taste Test?** Another example, well known among researchers, from Coke, also illustrates the costs and wastes associated with improper problem definition. Coke was continually losing in taste tests against Pepsi, a cola with a sweeter taste than Coke. Though Coke had significant market share and an established brand name, its executives defined their problem as not having a product as tasty as that of their major competitor. This led to over four years of research, during which they developed a sweet-tasting cola. The new flavored beverage beat the competitor's cola in taste test after taste test. Thinking they had solved the "taste test problem," Coke management dropped its old product and introduced the new, sweeter-tasting cola. To their surprise, sales plummeted and consumers, missing their old drink, protested by the thousands. What happened? Many market experts believe Coke did not define the problem correctly. They defined the problem as "How can we beat the competitor in taste tests?" instead of "How can we gain market share against our competitors?" They already had a sizable share of the market with their non-sweet-flavored cola. When they stopped producing the old drink, their customers had only the sweet-flavored beverage to buy, which they didn't want; they had already shunned sweeter-tasting Pepsi in favor of Coke. Losing the taste tests led Coke's marketing managers to improperly define the problem; they wanted to beat their competitors. They did, but by dropping their existing product in favor of the new "better-tasting" cola, they lost their own customers. With 20/20 hindsight, they should have kept their existing Coke product and introduced a new brand to compete for the market preferring a sweeter cola. Eventually they did reintroduce the old cola as Coke Classic and they kept the new, sweeter version. By not focusing research on the right problem, management learned a hard lesson and wasted much time and millions of dollars.[2] These examples illustrate the importance of properly defining the problem. Not only does improper problem definition waste valuable resources such as time and money, but it also prevents proper marketing research information that may set management on the right track sooner and, as we saw in the case of Coke, another problem is lost goodwill from brand-loyal customers.

Lawrence D. Gibson is well known in marketing research for emphasizing the importance of properly defining the problem and research objectives. He conducts seminars on this topic. Read what he has to say about the importance of this step in the marketing research process in our Marketing Research Insight 4.1.

> A problem well defined is a problem half solved. A bad problem definition dooms the entire project from the start.

Two Sources of Problems

First, we must understand that problems may come from two different sources. A **problem** exists when a gap exists between what was supposed to happen and what did happen.[3] Failure to meet an objective, for example, creates a gap between what was supposed to happen and what actually did happen. This situation is what we normally think of when we use the term *problem*. The manager must now determine what course of action to take in order to close the gap between the objective and actual performance. The second type of problem, however, is not often immediately recognized as a "problem." This second type of problem, called an **opportunity**, occurs when there is a gap between what did happen and what could have happened. This is an opportunity because the situation represents a "favorable circumstance or chance for progress or advancement."[4] Put another way, a **marketing opportunity** has been defined as an area of buyer need or potential interest in which a company can perform profitably.[5] For example, our sales were $X but *could* have been $Y had we introduced a new, more competitive product. Even though we refer to this as an opportunity, managers still have a problem in that they must determine whether and how to take advantage of an opportunity.

> Managers recognize problems when gaps exists between what was *supposed* to happen and what *did* happen or when there is a gap between what *did* happen and what *could have* happened.

> An opportunity is a form of a problem in that managers must determine whether and how to take advantage of them.

4.1

The Importance of Defining the Problem Properly

Lawrence D. Gibson says that: "A problem well defined is a problem half solved says an old but still valid adage. How a problem is defined sets the direction for the entire project. A good definition is necessary if marketing research is to contribute to the solution of the problem. A bad definition dooms the entire project from the start and guarantees that subsequent marketing and marketing research efforts will prove useless. Nothing we researchers can do has so much leverage on profit as helping marketing define the right problem."[a]

This quote illustrates the importance of properly defining the problem. If inadequate attention is given to problem definition, the rest of the marketing research process is without value. Marketing researchers can add to their clients' profits, and thus become more valuable, if they focus on properly defining their clients' problems.

Lawrence D. Gibson is Independent Consultant and Senior Associate of Eric Marder Associates, Inc. Mr. Gibson worked as marketing research director at General Mills for 20 years. He has experience as an advertising agency researcher and consultant/supplier for companies such as General Motors, Amoco, and Motorola. He has worked all over the world and has been a leader in several industry associations. For the AMA, Mr. Gibson teaches a tutorial: "Problem Solving with Marketing Research."

[a]Personal communication with Lawrence D. Gibson. Also see: Gibson, L.D. (1998, Spring). Defining marketing problems: don't spin your wheels solving the wrong puzzle. *Marketing Research, 10*(4):5–12.

Recognizing the Problem

Unless managers have a control system, they will not likely identify problems arising from failure to meet objectives. Managers must also be aware of opportunities; unless they have a system for monitoring opportunities they will not likely identify these problems.

Good managers will be aware of problems, or they will soon cease to hold management positions. For managers to recognize a problem they must be knowledgeable of objectives and actual performance. They should be setting objectives and have a control system in place to monitor performance. This is just sound management practice. Many experienced managers would agree that what is worse than discovering you have a problem is to continue to operate in ignorance of the problem. Unless managers have a control system, they will not likely identify problems arising from failure to meet objectives. Regarding opportunities, managers must also be aware of opportunities; and unless they have a system for monitoring opportunities, sometimes referred to as a process of **opportunity identification**, they will not likely identify these problems.[6] Table 4.1 shows the sources, examples, and systems needed to recognize problems.

Some marketing management problems come from a failure to meet objectives, and other problems stem from determining if and how to take advantage of opportunities. In either case, managers must select the proper course of action from several alternative choices.

The Role of Symptoms in Problem Recognition

Managers and researchers must be careful to avoid confusing symptoms with problems.

The key lesson is that symptoms are not problems. Rather, symptoms should be used to alert managers to recognize problems.

The classic statement "We have a problem—we are losing money" illustrates why researchers and managers, in properly defining problems, must be careful to avoid confusing symptoms with problems. The problem is not that "we are losing money." Rather, the problem may be found among all those factors that cause us to make (or lose) money; the manager, with help from the researcher, must identify all those possible causes in order to find the right problem(s).

Symptoms are changes in the level of some key monitor that measures the achievement of an objective (e.g., our measure of customer satisfaction has fallen 10% in each

TABLE 4.1	Problem Recognition	
Sources of Problems	**Examples**	**System Required in Order to Recognize Gap**
Gap between what is *supposed* to happen and what *did* happen (Failure to meet objectives)	Sales calls below target number	Control system based on setting objectives and evaluating them against actual performance
	Sales volume below quota Return on investment (ROI) below goal	
Gap between what *did* happen and what *could* happen (Should we and how do we take advantage of opportunities?)	Increase in sales if we change product features	System for identification of opportunities
	Increase in profits if we expand into new territory	
	Increase in ROI if we diversify into growing new field	

of the past two months. In this case, the role of the symptom is to alert management to a problem; there is a gap between what should be happening and what is happening. A symptom may also be a perceived change in the behavior of some market factor that implies an emerging opportunity. A pharmaceutical company executive sees a demographic forecast that the number of teenagers will increase dramatically over the next 10 years. This may be symptomatic of an opportunity to create new drugs designed for teen problems such as acne or teenage weight problems. Note that symptoms may be *negative* but still bring about opportunities; the forecast for teens is that their numbers will shrink in the next 10 years. Should the company shift R&D from developing new drugs for teens to the growing aging Baby Boomer market? Both types of symptoms should be identified by either the control system (objectives/monitoring) or by the system in place for opportunity identification. The key lesson, however, is that symptoms are not problems; they should be used to alert managers to recognize problems.

Types of Problems

Not all problems are the same. We have already established that the sources of problems may differ: some arise through recognition of a failure to meet an objective and others from the recognition of an opportunity. We can also characterize problems in terms of their being specific versus general. Some problems are very specific: The Director of Marketing Research at Kraft Foods may want to know "What is the best package design to create awareness and interest in our Maxwell House coffee brand?" or "Which of three new cookies recipes is the most preferred?" Sometimes the problem can be very general: "Should we change our entire marketing plan?" "Should we even be in the coffee business?" Clearly, these two extremes illustrate there are wide differences in the types of problems confronting managers. Generally, the more specific the problem the easier the marketing researcher's task. When a problem is defined very narrowly and in

Problems can range from being very general to being very specific.

specific terms by management, it is much easier for the researcher to transform this type of problem into a well-defined and specific research objective. Alternatively, the researcher has a much more challenging task when confronted with the vague, general problem stated by management.

The Role of the Researcher in Problem Definition

Regardless of the type of problem, the researcher has an obligation to help managers ensure they are defining the problem correctly. This is particularly true when the researcher is called in by the manager who already has the problem defined in very specific terms. The manager who thinks the problem is coming up with a better cookie recipe may be startled to learn that total cookie sales have been falling for the past five years. Perhaps the researcher should ask the question of the manager: "Are you sure you should be in the baked cookie business?" Problem definition expert, Lawrence D. Gibson, wrote: "Researchers must resist the temptation to 'go along' with the first definition suggested. They should take the time to conduct their own investigation and to develop and consider alternative definitions."[7] This additional investigation may take the form of a situation analysis. A **situation analysis** is a form of preliminary research undertaken to gather background information and gather data pertinent to the problem area that may be helpful in properly defining the problem. (We will discuss several methods of conducting exploratory research, used in a situation analysis, when we introduce you to this type of research design in Chapter 5).

> Researchers must resist the temptation to accept the first problem defined. They should conduct their own research to determine if there are alternative problems.

The researcher should be interested in the long-term welfare of the client. Because researchers are accustomed to dealing with problem definition, they should help managers define the problem accurately. By doing so, the research they provide will add real value to the client's bottom line helping to ensure the long-term relationship.

Impediments to Problem Definition

You've read some examples illustrating how companies have not defined the problem correctly. Properly defining the problem is hampered by two factors: managers fail to recognize the importance of communicating and interacting closely with researchers and the differences between researchers and managers may hamper communications.

▶ **Failure to Change Behavior for Problem-Definition Situations.** Managers sometimes do not recognize that they need to change their normal behavior in order to properly define the problem. Managers are accustomed to dealing with outside suppliers efficiently. Suppliers are asked to present their products/services, they are evaluated against established purchasing criteria, and a decision is made. A minimum of interaction and involvement is required to make most purchasing decisions, and this is viewed as desirable; it leads to accomplishing business activities efficiently. Unfortunately, this behavior does not necessarily change when dealing with an external supplier of marketing research. Though not as probable, to some extent, you could say this is true in behavior dealing with other divisions within the same firm, as would be the case when an internal marketing research department is supplying the marketing research. Recall that we discussed marketing research acting as a "silo" in Chapter 3. Chet Kane refers to this problem by saying that managers commission marketing research projects without being involved with them. He states that managers should be involved in designing the research and actually go out into the field and listen to some of the consumer responses first-hand. Kane says that had managers been more involved in the research they would have known that the positive findings of research for "clear" products (clear beer, clear mouthwash, and clear cola) were based on the novelty or "fad" of the clear products. Had the managers been more involved with the research process they would have understood this. Instead, the "clear" products were failures.[8]

Managers must understand that to find possible causes for changing symptoms or to identify and determine the likelihood of success of pursuing opportunities requires in-depth communications over an extended period of time. Often, to be effective, this process is slow and tedious. Managers often are unaware of the required change in their behavior, and this causes difficulties in identifying the real problem. Veteran researchers are well aware of this situation and it is up to them to properly inform management of their expected role and the importance of this initial step in the research process.

▶ **Differences between Managers and Researchers.** Marketing managers and marketing researchers see the world differently because they have different jobs to perform and their backgrounds differ markedly. For example, managers possess line positions; researchers are in staff positions. Managers are responsible for generating profits; researchers are responsible for generating information. Managers are trained in general decision making, and researchers are trained in research techniques. All of these differences hinder communications between two parties at a time when in-depth, continuous communications and trust are required. However, these differences have improved over the years and are growing smaller. The reason is that college students today, tomorrow's managers, are in a better position to learn and have greater appreciation for the technical side of marketing research. Many of the analyses you will learn using the Statistical Package for the Social Sciences (SPSS), for example, were once available only to computer specialists who could write the code required to run these analyses on mainframe computers. You will be far better equipped to communicate with marketing researchers than your predecessors.

Before proceeding we wanted to give you some additional insights from a professional on properly defining the problem. We asked Ron Tatham, a man with 30 years' experience in the marketing research industry, to share his insights on this topic. Ron was CEO of Burke, Inc. and interacted with many managers in trying to determine the proper problem. Dr. Tatham wrote Marketing Research Insight 4.2 for you. Read it and you will benefit from his great insights into this important, yet difficult, step in the marketing research process.

Managers are accustomed to dealing with suppliers in an efficient manner. They must change this behavior when working with marketing research suppliers in order to properly identify the problem.

Managers historically have been generalists and researchers have been technical specialists.

The Role of ITBs and RFPs

ITBs are "invitations to bid." Alternatively, some firms use **RFPs**, which stands for "requests for proposals." Companies use these documents to alert research firms that they would like to receive bids or proposals to conduct research. In either case, the role of the researcher and manager is changed in the problem definition process. When a company uses an ITB or RFP they have already defined the problem and, in some cases, the research objectives. At the very least, management has thought through much of the issues revolving around defining the problem. This means that much of the dialogue normally necessary between researchers and managers may be avoided. For example, managers in a firm decide they need to assess customer satisfaction in a way that will allow them to prescribe remedial actions. The problem has been defined. They submit an ITB or RFP to several research firms who now bid on doing the necessary research.

Although RFPs and ITBs are all different, they contain some common elements. Commonly found sections are the following:

■ *Introduction.* Identification of the company or organization that originates the RFP, with background information about the company.
■ *Scope of proposal.* Description of the basic problem at hand.

4.2 Insights Based on 30 Years of Defining the Problem and Research Objectives

The problem definition, if properly developed, contains all the elements of the final report except the findings and recommendations. If this sounds obtuse, I will explain what I mean by "problem definition."

First of all I cringe when I hear a manager say to a researcher, "Here is what I want to know: [fill in the blank with the manager's desired information]. To be somewhat diplomatic, I ask "what decision are you trying to make using that information?" Most often the manager just stares at me and says "what do you mean?" My response is along the lines of "if you aren't making a decision, you don't need the information. If you are making a decision, are you sure this is the information that will best help you make that decision?"

Choose any management request for information and the request must be predicated on a decision. The manager's job is to maintain and increase the value of his company or his brand. Every bit of knowledge acquired must be targeted at making the decisions that will lead to strengthening value. Managers cannot just "want to know something," they must want to make decisions!

This leads me to the key elements that guide the manager and the research task. They are described below.

What is the decision? You cannot formulate the decision without specifying the alternatives that allow the decision.

1 *Example:* I want to choose the better of two proposed advertising claims. Here the alternatives are clear and a priori. (This leaves a lot unsaid, but we explain later.)

2 *Example:* I want to choose between two formulations for my product. One formulation is more expensive but provides greater benefit to the customer. Because this is a very mature category with a very small range of prices we believe we would have to substantially increase volume at the current price to warrant the more expensive formulation.

3 *Example:* I want to choose the best way to express my product's benefit to this target market. Here we implicitly express that alternatives could exist but they are not stated. (Again, more to come.)

What are the alternatives? In example 1, the alternatives were presented to the researcher. In example 2 the alternatives are clear. In example 3, deciding on alternatives to be examined becomes a research project in itself. Typically, exploratory qualitative research will aid the researcher in deciding which alternatives should be carried forward. In other words, if we cannot specify the alternatives, we must formulate another research effort to decide (here is our decision again!) on what the alternatives should be.

What information is needed and what is an appropriate unit of measurement that will allow the decision to be made? In example 1, the manager wants to choose the better of two proposed advertising claims. What is a better claim? Is it more memorable? Is it more relevant? Is it more believable? Is the best claim the least often misinterpreted? Is it more likable? Is it more persuasive in encouraging certain actions from the recipient? Is it more persuasive in encouraging certain statements of intention from the recipient? Just what is "better"? If you look around the research world, there is little agreement on what constitutes a better claim at the testing stage. The researcher is often saddled with the task of measuring the quality of the claims and with defining what a better claim should be. It would be helpful if the firm has a history of testing claims and has reached agreement on what constitutes a "better" claim. In the end the definition of "better" must be based on consensus or the decision cannot be made.

The specification of the information needed should include who has it, in what frame of reference they have it, how capable they are of giving it to us accurately, and whether they are willing to give it to us accurately. For an example of frame of reference, in a pharmaceutical company the manager may think of a particular drug in terms of dosage, form, differentiating characteristics from the nearest competitor, etc. The physician from whom they must gather information thinks first in terms of a patient's symptoms, the disease severity, possible interaction with other drugs, willingness to comply with treatment, etc. The pharmaceutical manager must think of the information needed from the physician's frame of reference, not their own.

What is the action standard? Example 2 illustrates the need for specific action standards. Assume that we have defined the unit of measurement as intention to buy after use of the product (imagine having people use a bar of soap for a week, small businesses using a new cleaning product, giving free samples of a manufacturing supply material to customers, etc.). How large a difference allows us to choose the new formulation and reduce the risk of making the wrong decision? We all know that low-cost products with short purchase cycles elicit intentions to buy that are closer to reality than high-cost, longer-purchase-cycle products. The minimum overstatement of likelihood to buy is probably in the 20 to 30% range and the maximum is close to 80 to 90%. We have to agree on not only what we will measure but on how we will use the measurement to make a decision as well. One might say, "We have past evidence in this category that a 10% difference in stated buying intention translates to a 2% difference in sales in the marketplace. Therefore, since we need a 3% difference in sales to support the new formulation, we must see a 15% minimum difference in stated buying intention between the two test products to allow us to choose the more expensive formulation."

When I think of a marketing problem I always think of these things:

- The decision
- The alternatives
- The information to be captured and the respondent's frame of reference.
- The unit of measurement
- The action standard that allows me to make the decision

If I can write a clear discussion of these five items after meeting with marketing management, to complete the final report all I need are the findings. Since I have an action standard, the findings matched against the action standard tells me the appropriate recommendation.

I have been working in marketing research for over 30 years. The number of times that a manager has come to me and said "here is the decision I need to make" and then goes on to explain how the decision is to be made is so rare as to be notable. Most of the time I hear the manager say, "This is what I would like to know." In these cases, after discussing the problem definition process from decision to action standard, the manager typically completely changes what he or she wants. You can think of "This is what I would like to know" as the manager's attempt to solve a problem that they really have not defined in a rigorous way. When the researcher accepts this "what I want to know" at face value, they often end the research with a presentation to management that elicits this comment,

"very interesting, I learned a lot about the market but I am not sure what to do next."

When the researcher uses the problem definition sequence explained earlier, the researcher gives a report that allows management to focus on how to follow through on the decision, not how to make the decision. How to make the decision was determined at the problem definition stage. This often leads to the researcher being a part of the decision-making team as opposed to the researcher being a passive provider of information.

From a purely economic point of view, following these guidelines will also reduce the time and cost of research. The questionnaire will be focused as the research problem defines the information and the units of measurement. In my experience, this results in shorter questionnaires that are easier for the respondent to handle. The analysis is very focused because the action standards are specifically stated. When the action standards are not specifically stated and analysis is done by research providers, the analyst spends half or more of the analysis effort trying to understand what the client really wants. The result is often 200 pages of charts, tables, and discussion, when fewer than 10 pages would have explained the decision and supported it. In my career I have seen this process produce better decisions at a lower cost many times.

Ron Tatham, former President and CEO of Burke, Inc., is also an author, professor, and consultant. Dr. Tatham has been prominent in the marketing research industry and is widely recognized in both the industry and in academics. Prior to joining Burke, he was a professor on the Graduate Business Faculty of Arizona State University and also taught at the University of Cincinnati and Kent State University. He is coauthor of *Multivariate Data Analysis*. He has served on the Marketing Research Advisory Board at the University of Georgia, the Masters of Science in Marketing Research Advisory Board at the University of Texas at Arlington and the A. C. Nielsen Center—University of Wisconsin External Advisory Board. Tatham also is active in several professional organizations and has presented over 200 seminars and papers before professional groups.

■ *Deliverables.* Specification of the tasks to be undertaken and products to be produced and delivered to the company soliciting the proposal or bid. For example, the deliverable may be "a survey of 1000 representative recent users of the company's services, described in a report with text, tabulations, figures, and relevant statistical analyses."

■ *Evaluation criteria.* The criteria or standards that will be used to judge the proposals, often set up as a point system in which the proposal is awarded a number of points for each area based on the quality of the work that is proposed.

■ *Deadline.* The date by which the deliverables must be delivered.

■ *Bidding specifics.* Necessary items such as the due date for the proposal or bid, specific information required about the bidding company, proposal length and necessary elements (such as sample questions that may appear on the questionnaire), intended subcontract work, payment schedule, contact individual within the origination company, and so on.

ITBs are "invitations to bid" and RFPs are "requests for proposals." Companies use these documents to alert research firms that they would like to receive bids or proposals to conduct research to solve a particular problem.

As you may remember from our discussion of ethics in Chapter 3, ITBs and RFPs are sensitive issues in terms of appropriate ethical behavior. A firm that sends out phony ITBs (or RFPs) simply to get ideas for research is practicing highly unethical behavior.

Want to see some actual RFPs and ITBs? You can find them on the Internet. The Internet is a very effective medium for companies to use to broadcast their RFPs/ITBs. Supplier firms search the Web for postings of these requests and often use the Web to reply. Go to advanced search at www.google.com. At "with at least one of the words," enter ITB RFP. At "with the exact phrases" enter marketing research. You will get many hits, and that is OK. Explore and you will find actual ITBs and RFPs. You will also find some sites designed to help you write an effective ITB or RFP.

We have discussed the importance of properly defining the problem, and we have learned several things about the nature of problems; how to recognize a problem, different sources of problems, different types of problems, and impediments to properly defining the problem, as well as the role of ITBs and RFPs. Next we look at a process a researcher may use in defining the marketing manager's problem.

A PROCESS FOR DEFINING THE PROBLEM AND ESTABLISHING THE RESEARCH OBJECTIVES

There is no universally accepted, step-by-step approach used by marketing researchers to define the problem and establish research objectives. In fact, Lawrence D. Gibson, a recognized authority on defining the problem, wrote that "Defining problems accurately is more an art than science. . . ."[9] Although there are a number of problem-solving techniques that individual managers can use,[10] we will describe a process that works for the marketing manager–researcher situation. We outline this process for you in Table 4.2. But, before you examine Table 4.2, recall that there are two sources of problems; one when there is a failure to meet an objective and the other when there is an opportunity. The process for defining these two problems is different, though they both end up determining research objectives. The major difference is that for opportunities the firm must do research to determine the attractiveness and probability of success of any opportunity. This process Kotler refers to as **market opportunity analysis (MOA)**.[11] We are not going to discuss MOA here, but we want to point out that after a company conducts an MOA to identify opportunities they now have a problem in choosing from among several alternative opportunities. Which opportunity should the firm pursue, and how should the firm pursue that opportunity? If you read Ron Tatham's Marketing Research Insight 4.2 you will also see this difference in the types of

TABLE 4.2	A Process for Determining the Problem and Establishing Research Objectives When the Source of the Problem Is a Failure to Meet an Objective

- Assess the background and the manager's situation
- Clarify the symptoms of the problem
- Pinpoint suspected causes of the symptom
- Specify solutions that may alleviate the symptom
- Speculate on anticipated consequences of the solutions
- Identify the manager's assumptions about the consequences of the solutions
- Assess the adequacy of information on hand to specify research objectives

problems discussed. It is at this point that the two types of problems are similar; therefore, we are going to discuss only the process involved when there is a failure to meet an objective. As you will see, the problem and research objectives are intertwined. The problem-definition process ends up with definitions of the research objectives.

Assess the Background and the Manager's Situation

The process may begin with the researcher learning about the industry, the competitors, key products or services, markets, market segments, and so on. The researcher should start with the industry in order to determine if any symptoms, to be identified later, are associated with the entire industry or only with the manager's firm. The researcher should then move to the company itself: the history of the company, its performance, products/services, unique competencies, marketing plans, customers, major competitors, and so on.

Also, the researcher should try to find out about the manager's unique situation. Under what constraints is this manager operating? Why does this manager believe research is needed? Do other managers agree? Does this manager have a particular objective he or she is trying to achieve? At this stage, the researcher is gathering information and will have considerable homework to do after the first meeting with the manager. The researcher must conduct some exploratory research to learn more about the industry, the company, competition, and markets. Will this information conflict with the information the manager is providing? Recall Larry Gibson's and Ron Tatham's admonition that researchers should not accept the problem without question. Researchers understand the importance of properly defining the problem, and managers, if inexperienced with research, may not be aware of this issue. Researchers add value by ensuring that the proper problem is being addressed.

The researcher is gathering information and will have considerable homework to do after the first meeting with the manager. The researcher must conduct some exploratory research to learn more about the industry, the company, competition, and markets.

Clarify the Symptoms of the Problem

You have already learned that symptoms are important in helping to identify the problem. Without symptoms, problem definition is virtually impossible. The researcher needs to understand what control system is in place. Companies vary greatly in terms of defining their objectives, monitoring their results, and taking corrective action. Does the company have an adequate control system? Is the manager alert to symptoms? What are they? Are they accurate measures of performance? Are they reported in a timely fashion? You are beginning to realize, no doubt, that the researcher acts much like a detective. It is the researcher's role to explore and to question, if the problem is to be defined properly. (You may now better understand why we told you earlier that this process requires managers to change their normal behavior! They must enter into an open and trusting relationship with the researcher, and they are not accustomed to doing this with an outside supplier.)

Without symptoms, problem definition is virtually impossible.

Pinpoint Suspected Causes of the Symptom

It is important to determine *all* **possible causes.**

At this point the manager and the researcher should be in agreement about which symptom or symptoms are in need of attention. Symptoms do not just change. There is always some **cause** or causes for the change. Profits do not go down by themselves. Sales do not drop without customers doing something differently from what they have done in the past. Satisfaction scores do not drop without some underlying cause. It is important to determine *all* **possible causes**. If only a partial list of causes is made, it is possible that the real cause will be overlooked. In this case the problem will not be defined properly and all research efforts will be wasted. We will next look at an example of University Estates apartments to help illustrate the problem-definition process.

▶ **University Estates: An Example of the Problem–Definition Process.**
University Estates is an apartment complex that targets students attending a nearby college. Last year, University Estates experienced a decline in its occupancy rate from 100 percent to 80 percent. The researcher and the manager of University Estates met and began discussing this symptom, asking themselves why the occupancy rate declined. Over the course of their discussion, they identified four general areas of possible causes: (1) competitors' actions, which had drawn prospective student residents away; (2) changes in the consumers (student target population); (3) something about the apartment complex itself; and (4) general environmental factors. The results of their brainstorming session are presented in Table 4.3. Given this long list, it was necessary to narrow down the possible causes to a small set of **probable causes**, defined as the most likely factors giving rise to the symptom.

Probable causes are those possible causes that are highly likely to be culprits.

The researcher and the University Estates manager systematically examined every possible cause listed in Table 4.3 and came to the realization that only a few could be probable causes of the decline in occupancy rate. For example, the manager was vigilant about what rents were being charged, and he knew that no competitor had lowered its rents in the past year. Similarly, no new apartment complexes had been built or opened up in the past year. Through this dialogue, the researcher and the University Estates manager narrowed the list down to two probable causes: (1) competing apartment complexes had added digital cable television in every apartment and (2) some apartment complexes had added on-site workout facilities. With a little more background investigation, it was found that only one competing apartment complex had added a workout facility, and most of the complexes, including University Estates, did not have any workout facility. Thus, the cable television deficiency of University Estates was determined to be the most probable cause for its occupancy decline.

Specify Possible Solutions That May Alleviate the Symptom

Managers have at their disposal certain resources, and these resources may provide the solutions they need to address the probable cause of the symptom. Essentially, possible **solutions** include any marketing action that the marketing manager thinks may resolve the problem, such as price changes, product modification or improvement, promotion of any kind, or even adjustments in channels of distribution. It is during this phase that the researcher's marketing education and knowledge come into play fully; often both the manager and the researcher brainstorm possible solutions.

Once again, it is for the manager to specify *all* of the solutions needed to address the probable cause of the symptom. In fact, one marketing research consultant has gone on record with this bold statement, "Unless the entire range of potential solutions is considered, chances of correctly defining the research problem are poor."[12]

TABLE 4.3	Possible Causes for University Estates' Decline in Occupancy Rate

1. **Competitors' actions**
   a. Reduced rents
   b. New or additional competitors
   c. New services
   d. New facilities
   e. Better advertising
   f. Financial deals such as no deposit

2. **Consumers (current and prospective student renters)**
   a. Loss of base numbers of students
   b. Change in financial circumstances
   c. Better living opportunities elsewhere
   d. Concern for personal safety
   e. Gravitating to condominiums
   f. Want more value for the money
   g. Negative word-of-mouth publicity

3. **University Estates itself**
   a. Traffic congestion
   b. Noisy neighbors
   c. Advertising cutback, change
   d. Aging facilities and equipment
   e. Image as "old" apartments
   f. Upkeep issues

4. **The environment**
   a. Less student financial aid
   b. Increased crime rate
   c. Housing market oversupply
   d. Change in students' preferences
   e. Cost of commuting increase
   f. Other living alternatives

▶ **Back to University Estates.** Returning to our University Estates example, the manager realized that he needed to look into *all* types of television-delivery systems. After a thorough review of the alternatives, the manager was not content to just match the competition, so he began considering a satellite television system such as DishTV's Multiple Dwelling Unit Program—with its 150 channels, four premium channels of HBO, Starz, Showtime, and Cinemax, plus pay-per-view—as one of his likely plans of action. In fact, the manager was quite pleased with his discovery that he could offer satellite television connections in every apartment because the satellite programming seemed far superior to basic cable television.

Speculate on Anticipated Consequences of the Solutions

Research on anticipated **consequences**, or most likely outcomes, of each action under consideration will help determine whether the solution is correct. For example, a solution might resolve the problem; on the other hand, it might intensify the problem if the solution is not the correct action. To avoid resolving the problem incorrectly, the manager asks "what if" questions regarding possible consequences of each marketing action being considered. These questions include the following:

■ What will be the impact not only on the problem at hand but also throughout the marketing program if a specific marketing action is implemented?
■ What additional problems will be created if a proposed solution is implemented?

Typically, the range of consequences of possible marketing actions is readily apparent. For example, if your advertising medium is changed from *People* magazine to *USA Today*, customers will either see less, see more, or see the same amount of advertising. If a nonsudsing chemical is added to your swimming pool treatment, customers will either like it more, less, or have no change in their opinions about it. Most marketing research investigates consumer consequences of marketing solutions, but it is also possible to research dealers' reactions or even suppliers' reactions, depending on the nature of the problem.

▶ **Back to University Estates.** It seemed reasonable to the University Estates manager to speculate that if University Estates added a satellite television system connection in each apartment, University Estates would be seen as more attractive than the other apartment complexes that had surged ahead in occupancy.

Identify the Manager's Assumptions About the Consequences of the Solutions

To help resolve problems, managers ask "what if" questions.

The manager's assumptions deserve researcher attention because they may be incorrect or uncertain.

As they attempt to define the problem, the manager and the researcher make certain **assumptions**, which are assertions that certain conditions exist or that certain reactions will take place if the considered solutions are implemented. For example, the manager may say, "I am positive that our lost customers will come back if we drop the price to $500," or "Our sales should go up if we gain more awareness by using advertising inserts in the Sunday paper." However, if a researcher questions a manager about his or her beliefs regarding the consequences of certain proposed actions, it may turn out that the manager is not really as certain as he or she sounds.

Conversely, the manager may be quite certain and cite several reasons why his or her assumption is valid. It is imperative, therefore, that the manager's assumptions be analyzed for accuracy.

Research will help to eliminate a manager's uncertainty, and therefore, aid in decision making.

Assumptions deserve researcher attention because they are the glue that holds the decision process together. Given a symptom, the manager *assumes* that certain causes are at fault. She or he further *assumes* that, by taking corrective actions (solutions), the problem will be resolved and the symptoms will disappear. If the manager is completely certain of all these assumptions, there is no need for research. But typically uncertainty prevails, and critical assumptions about which the manager is uncertain will ultimately factor heavily when the researcher addresses the problem. Research will help eliminate this uncertainty.

Hypotheses are statements that are taken for true for the purposes of argument or investigation.

A research project may, or may not use hypotheses. When a manager makes a statement he or she believes to be true and wants the researcher to determine if there is support for the statement, we call these statements "hypotheses."

▶ **The Role of Hypotheses in Defining the Problem. Hypotheses** are statements that are taken for true for the purposes of argument or investigation. In making assumptions about the consequences of solutions, managers are making hypotheses. For example, a successful restaurant owner uses a hypothesis that he must use X amount of food in an entrée in order to please his customers. This restaurant owner bases his decisions on the validity of this hypothesis; he makes sure that a certain quantity of food is served on every plate regardless of the menu choice. Businesspersons make decisions every day based on statements they believe to be true. Sometimes, those decisions are very important and the businessperson may not be confident that he or she is entirely correct in making the hypothesis. This is very similar to what we have been discussing in the paragraphs above about *assumptions*, isn't it? Sometimes the manager makes a specific statement (an assumption) and wants to know if there is evidence to support the statement. In the instances in which a statement is made, we may use the term *hypothesis* to describe this "statement thought to be true for purposes of a marketing research investigation." Note that not all research is conducted through hypotheses. A research question is often used to guide research. In this case, the question, not being a statement, is not considered a hypothesis. You will learn how to test hypotheses using your SPSS later on in this book. However, for now, you should understand that when a manager makes a statement he or she believes to be true and wants the researcher to determine if there is support for the statement, we call these statements "hypotheses."

▶ **Back to University Estates.** The key assumptions underlying the University Estates problem-definition meeting are that students: (1) know about and understand the advantages of satellite television over basic cable TV, and (2) want satellite television more than they want cable television in their apartments. And, most importantly, the manager was also assuming that (3) adding a satellite television connection in each apartment would render University Estates more desirable than the other apartment complexes targeting university students.

Assess the Adequacy of Information on Hand to Specify Research Objectives

As the manager and researcher go through this process, available information varies in both quantity and quality. As just noted, the manager may have information that greatly reinforces his or her beliefs, or he or she may not have anything more than an intuition. You should recall that it is the researcher's responsibility to provide information to the manager that will help resolve the manager's problem. Obviously, if the manager knows something with a high degree of certainty, it is of little value for the researcher to conduct research to reiterate that knowledge. It is vital, therefore, that the researcher assess the existing **information state**, which is the quantity and quality of evidence a manager possesses for each of his or her assumptions. During this assessment, the researcher should ask questions about the current information state and determine the desired information state. Conceptually, the researcher seeks to identify **information gaps**, which are discrepancies between the current information level and the desired level of information at which the manager feels comfortable resolving the problem at hand. Ultimately, information gaps are the basis for establishing research objectives.

Information gaps are discrepancies between the current information level and the desired information level. Information gaps are the basis for setting research objectives.

▶ **Back to University Estates.** With the University Estates situation, the manager felt quite confident about the accuracy of his information that cable television was offered by his competitors because they had advertised this new feature as well as announced this new service with signs outside the apartment complexes. Plus, he was confident that students were interested in having cable television; although, he was not sure about how much they desired the additional programming available on satellite television. Thus, the manager had an information gap because he was unsure of what the reactions of prospective University Estates residents would be if the satellite program package was included in the apartment package. Would they see it as competitive with the cable television available in the other apartment complexes? Would they want to live at University Estates more than at an apartment complex that had only basic cable?

As you may have noticed in the University Estates example, whenever an information gap that is relevant to the problem at hand is apparent to the manager, the manager and researcher come to agree that it is a research objective; that is, **research objectives** are set to gather the specific bits of knowledge that need to be gathered in order to close the information gaps. Research objectives become the basis for the marketing researcher's work. In order to formulate the research objectives, the marketing researcher considers all the current information surrounding the marketing management problem. We have created Table 4.4 to identify the information gaps and appropriate research objectives in the case of University Estates.

The manager and researcher come to agree on research objectives that are based on the information gaps.

Now, we must relate to you the most important difference between the marketing manager and the market researcher. The entire time that the dialogue is going on between the manager and the researcher, the manager is fixed on one goal: "How can I solve this problem?" However, the researcher is fixed on a different but highly related goal, "How can I gather information relevant to the problem that will help the manager

TABLE 4.4	Information Gaps and Research Objectives for University Estates	
Information Gap		**Research Objective(s)**
How will prospective residents react to the inclusion of the satellite television programming package with the base price of apartment?		*To what extent do prospective student residents want satellite television?*
Will University Estates be more competitive if it adds a satellite television package?		*Will University Estates be more attractive than competing apartment complexes if it has the satellite television programming package?*

solve his or her problem?" The researcher knows that if the right information is provided to the manager the problem will be solved. This is why we said at the beginning of this section that the problem and the research objectives are "intertwined". Next, the researcher must focus on the research proposal, which we take up next.

FORMULATE THE MARKETING RESEARCH PROPOSAL

As you have learned, the research objectives are the all-important results of the meeting(s) between the manager and researcher in their quest to resolve the problem; that is, the marketing researcher's first task is to talk to the marketing manager and to develop as complete a picture of the problem as possible. With the problem statement agreed to, the marketing researcher develops the research objectives and quickly moves to the formulation of a marketing research proposal. A **marketing research proposal** is a formal document prepared by the researcher; it serves three important functions: (1) it states the problem, (2) it specifies the research objectives, and (3) it details the research method proposed by the researcher to accomplish the research objectives. Proposals also contain (4) a time table and (5) budget.

Problem Statement

The first step in a research proposal is to describe the problem. This is normally accomplished with a single statement, rarely more than a few sentences long, called the "problem statement." The problem statement typically identifies four factors: (1) the company, division, or principals involved; (2) the symptoms; (3) the probable causes of these symptoms; and (4) the anticipated uses of the research information to be provided. The problem statement section of the formal marketing research proposal is necessary to confirm that the researcher and the manager fully agree on these important issues.

Research Objectives

After describing the problem in the marketing research proposal, the marketing researcher must reiterate the specific research objectives. As we just described, the research objectives specify what information will be collected to address information gaps that must be closed in order for the manager to go about resolving the problem. The proposal provides a mechanism to ensure that the manager and researcher both agree as to exactly what information will be gathered by the proposed research.

Research objectives must be precise, detailed, clear, and operational.

In creating research objectives, researchers must keep in mind four important qualities. Each research objective must be precise, detailed, clear, and operational. To be precise means that the terminology is understandable to the marketing manager and that it accurately captures the essence of each item to be researched. Detail is provided by elaborating, perhaps with examples, each item. The objective is clear if there is no doubt as to what will be researched and how the information will be presented to the manager. Finally, the research objective must be operational. By this we mean that the research objective should define how the construct being evaluated is actually measured. These definitions are referred to as operational definitions. An **operational definition** is a definition of a construct, such as intention to buy or satisfaction (see next section), that describes the operations to be carried out in order for the construct to be measured empirically.[13] For example, if we want to measure students' preference for apartment complex characteristics, we can do this with a 7-point rating scale for each characteristic that ranges from 1 = Strongly Not Preferred to 7 = Strongly Preferred.

▶ **The Role of Constructs.** A **construct** is an abstract idea inferred from specific instances that are thought to be related.[14] For example, marketers refer to the specific instances of someone buying the same brand 9 out of 10 times as a construct entitled "brand loyalty." A construct provides us with a mental concept that represents real world phenomena. When a consumer sees an ad for a product and states "I am going to buy that new product X," marketers would label this phenomenon with the construct called "intention to buy." Marketers use a number of constructs to refer to phenomena that occur in the marketplace. Preference, awareness, recall, satisfaction, and so on are but a few.

You can see the constructs used by Alan Grabowsky of ABACO Marketing Research in Brazil. Their program AdVisor measures "performance" of proposed communications messages such as ads by examining constructs such as impact/memorability; credibility, comprehension, and so on. Look at the questions asked for each of these contructs to see how they are operationalized.

Marketing researchers find constructs very helpful because, once it is determined that a specific construct is applicable to the problem, there are customary ways of

The researcher uses marketing constructs and envisions operational definitions of these constructs.

Alan Grabowsky is President of ABACO Research – Brazil.

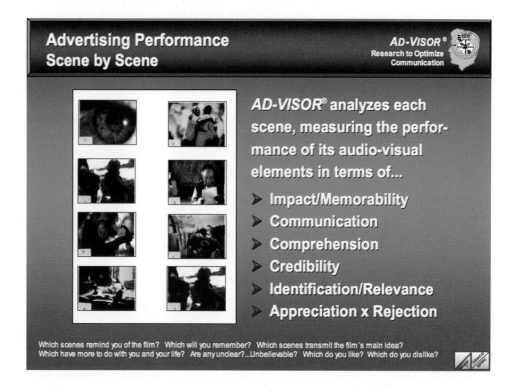

operationalizing, or measuring, these constructs. This knowledge becomes very useful in developing the research objectives. In addition, many constructs have relationships that are explained by models, and these relationships can be useful in solving problems. For example, Table 4.5 illustrates how certain constructs are related by a model referred to as the "hierarchy of effects." Note how useful this would be to you if you were the researcher in our University Estates example.

Detail the Proposed Research Method

Finally, the research proposal[15] will detail the proposed **research method**; that is, it will describe the data-collection method, questionnaire design, sampling plan, and all other aspects of the proposed marketing research in as much detail as the researcher thinks is necessary for the manager to grasp the plan. It will also include a tentative timetable and specify the cost of the research undertaking. Proposals vary greatly in format and detail, but most share the basic components we have described: problem statement; research objectives; and proposed research method, including timetable and cost. We realize that you will study in detail all of these topics in chapters that follow so we will not delve into them now.

What does a marketing research proposal look like? We have prepared Marketing Research Application 4.3, which is the proposal written for University Estates based on the way it has been described in this chapter.

PUTTING IT ALL TOGETHER USING THE INTEGRATED CASE FOR THIS TEXTBOOK

In this section, we are going to continue with our integrated case study, "The Hobbit's Choice." You were introduced to this case in Chapter 2, Case 2.2. Please go back and read this case, as the information in the case sets the scene for the description we are about to

TABLE 4.5	How the "Hierarchy of Effects" Model Can Frame Research for University Estates' Satellite Television Decision	

Hierarchy Stage	Description	Research Question
Unawareness	Not aware of your brand	What percentage of prospective student residents are unaware of satellite television?
Awareness	Aware of your brand	What percentage of prospective student residents are aware of satellite television?
Knowledge	Know something about your brand	What percentage of prospective student residents who are aware of it know that satellite television has (1) 150 channels, (2) premium channels, and (3) pay-for-view?
Liking	Have a positive feeling about your brand	What percentage of prospective student residents who know something about satellite television feel negatively, positively, or neutral about having it in their apartment?
Intention	Intend to buy your brand next	What percentage of prospective student residents who feel positively about having satellite television in their apartment intend to rent an apartment with it?
Purchase*	Have purchased your brand in the past	What percentage of the market has purchased (tried) your brand in the past?
Repurchase/Loyalty*	Purchase your brand regularly	What percentage of the market has purchased your brand more than other brands in their past five purchases?

*Not applicable to University Estates as the satellite television feature is not currently available.

MARKETING RESEARCH INSIGHT

PRACTICAL APPLICATION

4.3 Marketing Research Proposal for University Estates: Proposal to Determine the Attractiveness of Satellite Television to Prospective Student Residents of University Estates

Introduction
This proposal responds to a request on the part of the principals of University Estates, 2525 Bright Drive, New Haven, Connecticut, to provide assistance in its deliberations about adding satellite television to attract prospective university student residents.

Background
University Estates is experiencing an occupancy drop from 100% to 80%. This decline coincides with the addition of cable television now available in all of University Estates' competitors but not at University Estates. University Estates principals are contemplating the addition of a satellite tele-

vision system that will include 150 channels, four premium channels, and pay-per-view. Information is needed to assess prospective student residents' reactions to this possible additional service.

Research Objectives
Discussion with University Estates managers suggests that answers are desired to the following questions:

■ To what extent do prospective student residents want satellite television?
■ Will University Estates be more attractive than competing apartment complexes if it has the satellite television programming package?

Research Framework
Based on Research Associates' understanding of the decision facing University Estates principals, and further using the Company's experience in these types of questions, the

(continued)

Company proposes to use the "hierarchy of effects" model as a framework in which to cast the research questions to be used in the proposed survey.

This framework addresses the decision by breaking it into constructs or factors that delineate a complete picture of the factors that may facilitate or hamper the attractiveness of the satellite programming package.

Using this model, the research questions are:

- What percentage of prospective student residents are aware of satellite television?
- What percentage of prospective student residents who are aware of it know that satellite television has (1) 150 channels, (2) four premium channels, and (3) pay-per-view?
- What percentage of prospective student residents who know something about satellite television have a positive feeling (as opposed to negative or neutral feelings) about having it in their apartment?

- What percentage of prospective student residents who feel positively about having satellite television in their apartments intend to rent an apartment with it?
- Is University Estates with satellite television more attractive than competing apartment complexes with cable television?

Research Method

Research Associates proposes to undertake a telephone survey of 500 full-time university students who live off-campus. Research Associates will prepare and pretest the survey questionnaire, subcontract the telephone survey work, analyze the data, and present the findings to University Estates principals within six weeks of the execution of a contract. The cost of the proposed survey work is $10,000.

provide for you in this chapter. Again, this integrated case appears in the case section of several chapters and is the basis for most of the examples we will use in teaching you data analysis in the latter chapters of this book. Your instructor may assign these to you either as written assignments or as class discussion items throughout your course. Here is the continuation of our integrated case.

This is the second case in our integrated case series. If you have not already done so, you will need to read Case 2.2 before reading this case.

RETURN TO YOUR INTEGRATED

The Hobbit's Choice: A Restaurant to Be or Not to Be

Although Jeff Dean feels prepared for the business and is encouraged by his banker, Walker Stripling, he has several concerns. He knows that although he has learned quite a bit about restaurant operation in his area and also quite a bit about upscale restaurants from his friends in other cities, he is not sure if there is an interest in his city for such a restaurant. Even though the metro area has a population of nearly 500,000, he has no assurances that there are enough persons with the income and tastes necessary to make his business successful. He needs some additional information that would give him some inkling that a market exists. He does not want to lose the money that he has so diligently saved during the last 15 years. There are also other decisions for which he feels he needs additional information. He is not certain how to promote the restaurant in his town. Sure, the owners of the other restaurants have told him what they did, but they already had well-established reputations in their city. Where will he promote the restaurant when he first opens? Also, there are many choices to make about the design of the restaurant, the price the market is willing to pay for an upscale entrée, the best location, and so on. Now that his banker is willing to work with him and the financing is in good shape, Jeff Dean is ready to start making the other decisions needed to open The Hobbit's Choice.

Jeff Dean tells Walker Stripling that he is concerned about making the design, location, and promotion decisions. Walker tells him his experience with existing restaurant clients will not be of much help because Jeff's restaurant concept is so new to the market. Walker suggests that Jeff call the local office of CMG Research. CMG is a full-service firm that offers custom-designed research studies. The research firm has been in business for over 30 years and has offices in several cities around the country. Walker gave Jeff a business card from CMG Research, and later in the day, Jeff calls CMG and is referred to Cory Rogers, project director.

Cory Rogers asks Jeff Dean to generally explain what he is looking for from CMG. After Jeff explains that he is interested in gathering some research to help him make some decisions about opening an upscale restaurant in the area, Cory tells him that he will check to ensure there are no conflicts of interest with other clients and will get back in touch. The next day, Cory calls and asks that Jeff spend one and one-half hours with him.

Later that day, Jeff visits the offices of CMG and is greeted by Cory Rogers. Cory has arranged a comfortable, quiet meeting place and has asked his staff assistant to please not disturb him during the meeting with Jeff. Cory encourages Jeff to talk freely about his concept and assures him that the company has no other clients interested in such a business and that everything Jeff says will be kept in strict confidence. Jeff explains everything to Cory, including his desire to open the restaurant after having worked in the industry for 15 years. Cory asks probing questions that center around the steps Jeff will have to take to go into business. Even though Jeff assures Cory that the financing is set and that Walker Stripling at First Bank is enthusiastic about the plans, Cory covers all the details of the financial plans as well. Jeff is surprised when almost two hours have passed so quickly and is surprised again when Cory says, "I would like to investigate some of these issues more thoroughly and then we will need another fairly long meeting right away." Jeff enthusiastically agrees, and another appointment is made.

At the second meeting Jeff is impressed with how informed Cory is about the restaurant business. It is apparent that overnight Cory has learned many facts about the business, such as the importance of tracking food costs, table turnover rates, and financial ratios and operating expense norms for the restaurant business. He has also ordered a marketing research report that was prepared last year about upscale restaurants in general. Jeff feels assured that CMG is a good choice, and the two men continue their discussion about the decisions that would be necessary to open and operate The Hobbit's Choice.

The second meeting is structured around some issues that Cory says are key to the success or failure of The Hobbit's Choice restaurant.

Is There Demand for an Upscale Restaurant and at What Price Level?

Cory feels that one of the key issues deals with demand. Are there adequate numbers of customers in their metro area to generate profitable revenue? Cory tells Jeff that, based on his research, several successful upscale restaurants operate in metro areas as large as theirs. However, Cory is quick to point out that there are big differences in markets in terms of consumer preferences and income levels. Population alone is not a good predictor of success, but at least there is evidence that other metro areas of 500,000 support upscale restaurants. The two individuals spend the rest of the appointment discussing operating expenses for the restaurant. Cory tells Jeff he will e-mail him an Excel spreadsheet with a break-even analysis based on their assumptions about operating costs and possible entrée prices. The break-even analysis will tell Jeff how many customers he will need to have weekly in order to break even. Different revenues are included for lunch and dinner meals. The next day, Jeff receives the break-even analysis and calls Cory for another meeting. He tells Cory that he is excited because he feels the break-even figure is easily achievable.

Cory Rogers feels the best way to start off the meeting with Jeff Dean is to make certain that Jeff has not placed too much faith, at this point, in their break-even analysis. Cory points out to Jeff that the purpose of the break-even analysis, at this stage, is to see if they are dealing with a reasonable number of restaurant patrons required to break even. He explains that sometimes

CMG has to advise clients, after a rough break-even analysis, that they do not recommend going further with the project even though it means losing their business. "Our philosophy at CMG," Cory states, "is that you will come back to us when you need research in the future. We want to provide research that leads to success." He tells Jeff he views this as only a very rough start that basically has informed them to continue with the planning. Jeff agrees that this exercise is necessary, and he thanks Cory for being up-front with him. The last thing Jeff wants is to be led down the path to failure. Cory says what they want to do is to get some other inkling, some measurement from this market, that consumers in their town will support an upscale restaurant. And they want some idea of what this market would be willing to pay for a dinner meal in an upscale restaurant. "We're making a big assumption that the price per meal we've entered in our break-even analysis is valid. I would hypothesize that people in our city would expect an evening dinner entrée to be priced at $18, but I don't have any supporting data."

Cory Rogers then shows Jeff Dean a forecasting model to predict the number of customers expected to patronize a restaurant. One of the most important components in the forecasting model is a measure of the percentage of consumers in the market who stated that they would very likely patronize the restaurant and the average amount these same persons were spending, per capita, in restaurants per month. Also, another important component is the average price consumers would expect to pay for a dinner entrée. Cory explains that they would have to conduct research in their city to determine the amount of these required components to be entered into the forecasting model. Cory tells Jeff, "If we can collect valid and reliable information on likelihood to patronize your restaurant, average amount spent in restaurants per month, and the average price to be paid per entrée, we can create a much more accurate break-even analysis and compare that with the number of patrons you can expect. This is the information we need in order to determine if you will have adequate demand for The Hobbits' Choice." In fact, Cory had already made some estimates of demand using the forecasting model. He tells Jeff that if only 4 percent of heads of households in the 12 ZIP code area claimed they were "very likely" to patronize the restaurant and if these same people spent an average of $200 per month in restaurants and were willing to pay an average of $18 for an à la carte entrée, then the model predicted a very successful restaurant operation.

What About Design and Operating Characteristics?

At their next meeting, Cory refers back to questions Jeff raised in their first meeting. Jeff had told Cory there were a number of design and operating characteristics that he had seen in other restaurants but he didn't know what he should use in The Hobbit's Choice. How elegant should the décor be? Should there be live entertainment such as a jazz combo? Should the restaurant have a water view? Should the wait staff be formally dressed in tuxedos? Should the menu include a variety of choices, including exotic entrées not found in other restaurants such as elk, bison, or truffles? Would traditional desserts be desirable, or should they offer unusual desserts served with fanfare, such as flaming Bananas Foster or Baked Alaska? Would patrons view valet parking as a convenience or an extra expense? And what about driving time? Jeff thought if he located in a central section of the city, people from all over the metro area would come if they didn't mind the driving time.

Cory's background research reveals that Jeff is correct in having concerns about all these issues. Successful upscale restaurants in other cities have such a variety of design and operating characteristics that it is impossible to tell what each market values. For example, one very successful, very expensive restaurant has the barest of décor. Its plain brick walls and wooden furniture seem to add to the ambiance for customers in this city. On the other hand, a similar restaurant in terms of menu and prices in another city has very formal décor, with curtained walls and large, original antique, upholstered furniture, and expensive chandeliers. Yet another restaurant has no entertainment, and another has a jazz combo during dinner hours. It seems that each restaurant owner has discovered what his or her local market desires: this, no doubt, was at least part of the reason for their many years of success in the competitive restaurant business. "Well, we are going to have to rely a great deal on your own personal decisions in terms of how you will specifically design and operate your business," says Cory. "But, we will be able to get some good feedback from our local market when we collect the information we will need to determine demand. I'm just concerned that we don't have a clear handle on the design and operational characteristics that consumers will think important when patronizing a restaurant. We will have to think more about how to clearly determine what these are and how consumers describe them."

Where to Locate The Hobbit's Choice Restaurant

Jeff is well aware of the old axiom in retail business: The most important three factors for success in retailing are location, location, and location! Even though he knows his restaurant will be unique in the market, the location has to be considered convenient to his patrons. "You are right," says Cory Rogers, "many customers will be willing to drive far out of their way for a unique experience once or maybe even a couple of times. But everything we know about the restaurant business tells us that, if you want repeat business, you must be within a reasonable driving time of your primary target market." This makes perfect sense to Jeff. In almost every case, the owners of the successful upscale restaurants told him, "Sure, we get some business from the out-of-town tourists like yourself, but 80 percent of our revenue comes from our local, repeat customers."

Cory Rogers lays out a map of the city showing the 12 ZIP code areas of the metro area. Along with the map, Cory has acquired demographic information on each ZIP code, and he categorized them into four groups based on their commonalities. He summarized the information on the ZIP codes as follows:

Location A: ZIP Codes 1, 2. Low-income, older population located in the south-southeastern part of the city. Cory and Jeff both clearly rule out this part of the city.

Location B: ZIP Codes 3, 4, and 5. Located in the northwestern part of the city with high-income, older population of retirees and established professionals. Essentially, these are families with inherited wealth, professionals, and entrepreneurs. There is also a growing population of young professionals and managers who are upwardly mobile. Cory explains that these younger families are moving into the area and renovating older homes. Jeff thinks this could possibly be a good area in which to locate. He expresses some concern about an older population and older homes. He recalls how neighborhoods seemed to decline as homes get old. Cory suggests they keep an open mind about this area since the incomes are so high.

Location C: ZIP Codes 6, 7, 8, and 9. Almost double the population of areas 3, 4, and 5 who live in the eastern part of the city along the shoreline. These are young, upwardly mobile and older, upper-middle-class households with occupations in management, government, and young entrepreneurs. This is Jeff's part of town and he feels that this area represents an excellent opportunity. Although the incomes are not as high as in ZIP codes 3, 4, and 5, there are almost twice as many people and they have above-average incomes. Jeff comments that he has told several of his neighbors about his upscale restaurant idea and, without exception, they have each vowed to patronize the business. Also, Jeff is convinced that a waterfront view was important, and this is the only section of town where waterfront property could be acquired. Again, Cory suggests they keep an open mind.

Location D: ZIP Codes 10, 11, and 12. Middle-class neighborhoods; primarily laborers with occupations in the building and manufacturing trade who are located in the western part of the city. Jeff and Cory quickly eliminate this area as an alternative along with ZIP code 12, which is primarily an industrialized southwestern part of the city with relatively few permanent residents.

Jeff notes that the demographic information available suggests either a location somewhere within ZIP codes 3, 4, and 5 or within 6, 7, 8, and 9. Unfortunately, the two sets of ZIP codes are not close to one another. Cory tells Jeff the decision is going to be one or the other, not a central location. He also explains that they need information from the market to determine which area represents the best location. Once they make the decision about the area in which to locate, they can start dealing with choosing the specific site because there seem to be good alternatives in both the areas. Cory tells Jeff he is going to start working on a questionnaire that will address the issues they have discussed up to this point. The two set up another meeting for a week later.

How to Promote The Hobbit's Choice Restaurant

At their next meeting Jeff reminds Cory that they have not fully discussed his questions regarding how best to promote the restaurant. He is most concerned about which media and programming to select rather than ad copy. He feels comfortable about what to say in his promotional messages, but he is not confident that he knows where to say it. They discuss some ideas for preopening publicity and some direct marketing. Cory recommends a local ad agency to help with these decisions and to actually do some of the work. Jeff eagerly accepts the suggestions, knowing that he will be very involved with all the details of getting the restaurant operational. Jeff asks, "But, after the grand opening, where am I going to direct my advertising?" After some discussion, the two agree that Jeff will be using all the media from time to time: radio, television, newspaper, and perhaps the local city magazine. Jeff says he knows which medium to use and where to place the message for virtually every type of restaurant in town. He knows where the fast-food restaurants run their ads, where the cafeterias run their ads, where the restaurant/lounges run their ads, and so on. But he does not have a clue about where to place ads for The Hobbit's Choice.

Cory next shows Jeff the questionnaire he has been working on. It contains the questions needed to measure likelihood of patronizing the restaurant and the other issues the two had agreed needed addressing. Cory then identifies each medium, and the two discuss the alternatives. For radio, there are many stations from which to choose, and each provides a listenership study that gives some demographics on the audience of their station. But, even with many stations, Cory and Jeff agree they all break down into these station formats: country and western, jazz, easy listening, rock, and talk radio. Each station provides demographic information on its listeners by income. So, once Jeff Dean knows what type of programming to select, he will then need to know which specific stations to select that offer the desired type of programming. By knowing if there are differences in income between customers with different intentions to patronize the restaurant, Dean will be able to select the appropriate radio stations.

For television, few local ad opportunities exist except during daytime television, local sporting events, and the news. They both agree that news broadcasts were likely to be the most appealing, but which news broadcast will hit their target market? There was a morning, 7:00 A.M. time slot, a noon slot, early evening (6:00 P.M.), and late evening (10:00 P.M.) slot. As for the newspaper, which section did most members of the target market read? Editorial? Business? Local? Sports? Health, Living and Entertainment? Classifieds? Jeff noted that the sports section seems to be a good place to promote restaurants. As far as the local city magazine, Jeff's primary concern is whether or not the target market subscribes to it. It is an attractive, high-quality publication, but it is expensive, and he has never heard how many subscribers the magazine has. He wonders if more than a handful of subscribers will read an expensive ad in the magazine. Jeff recalls that three years ago when the magazine started, the owner gave away many copies in order to develop interest. But for the past two years the magazine has been mailed only to actual subscribers. Cory tells Jeff that he will take the notes from this meeting and add questions to the survey questionnaire he is working on to address the questions Jeff has about promoting The Hobbit's Choice. Cory tells Jeff that if he had answers to the questions they had discussed and advice from an ad agency, Jeff should be in good shape as far as promotion decisions.

Finally, Cory said, "Now I need to put together some standard demographic questions we will ask on the survey. These demographics will help us do a number of things. First, they can tell us about the sample we selected. We will prepare a demographic profile of the sample. We want to know on which group of people we are basing your decisions. Second, we will be able to profile the likely patrons of The Hobbit's Choice. This will help us more clearly understand your target market and will be helpful to you when you make future decisions, such as does the restaurant appeal more to females than males and knowing if media habits vary between males and females. Jeff thanks Cory and leaves the meeting feeling more confident than ever that he is on the road to realizing his dream.

TABLE 4.6	Marketing Problems for the Hobbit's Choice Restaurant

Problem Item	Description
Will the restaurant be successful?	Will there be adequate revenue to allow the restaurant to be profitable?
How should the restaurant be designed?	How elegant should the décor be? Should there be a waterfront view?
What operating characteristics should the restaurant have?	What type of live music should be played? How should the wait staff dress? Should unusual menu items be offered?
Where should the restaurant be located?	Are customers willing to drive more or less than 30 minutes?
What are effective and efficient promotional choices?	Where should ads for the restaurant be placed for radio, TV, and newspaper? Should ads be placed in the city magazine?
What is the profile of the target market?	What are the demographic and lifestyle profiles of those who are most likely to patronize the restaurant?

We realize that this case has a great deal of information, but we have included subheadings to show the major concerns of the case. In fact, the subheadings are clues to the primary marketing problems being faced by Jeff Dean in his quest to build and operate The Hobbit's Choice. You will find the six major marketing problems facing Jeff Dean in his Hobbit's Choice Restaurant vision identified in Table 4.6. You will be challenged to use this information to design research objectives in Case 4.2.

SUMMARY

This chapter begins with a discussion of the first step of the 11-step marketing research process; establishing the need for marketing research. Establishing the need for marketing research involves knowing when and when not to conduct marketing research. Marketing research is not needed when information to make a decision is already available, the timing is wrong, there are insufficient funds, and costs outweigh the value of doing research. Several reasons are provided to illustrate when you should conduct marketing research because the research is likely to have great value; among these are when research will help clarify problems or opportunities, identify changes in the marketplace, identify the best alternative to action, and help establish a competitive advantage.

Defining the problem, step 2, though often difficult, is the most important of all the steps in the marketing research process. A bad problem definition will doom the entire project. There are two sources of problems. One arises when there is a gap between what was supposed to happen and what did happen. This type of problem is attributed to failure to meet an objective. The second type of problem arises when there is a gap between what did happen and what could have happened. We refer to this type of problem as an opportunity. Managers recognize problems either through monitoring of control systems or through systems to recognize opportunities. Symptoms are not problems. Rather, symptoms are changes in the level of some key monitor that measures the achievement of an objective. Symptoms alert managers to problems. Problems may be general or specific and the researcher is responsible for ensuring that management has properly defined the problem. In some cases, a situation analysis is required to help define the problem. Problem definition is sometimes impeded because (a) managers fail to change their normal behavior of dealing with outside suppliers in an efficient manner during problem-solving situations, and (b) managers are usually generalists and researchers tend to be technical. ITBs are "invitations to bid." Alternatively, some firms use RFPs, which stands for "requests for proposals." Companies use these documents to alert research firms that they would like to receive bids or proposals to conduct research.

The process for defining the problem when the source of the problem is a failure to meet objectives is: (1) assess the background and the manager's situation, (2) clarify the symptoms of the problem, (3) pinpoint suspected causes of the symptom, (4) specify solutions that may alleviate the symptom, (5) speculate on anticipated consequences of the solutions, (6) identify the manager's assumptions about the consequences of the solutions, and (7) assess the adequacy of information on hand to specify research objectives. When faced with an opportunity, management should conduct a market opportunity analysis to determine which opportunities to pursue with additional marketing research. A case example of University Estates apartments was discussed in the chapter to illustrate the process in defining the problem when there has been a failure to reach an objective. Hypotheses are statements that are taken for true for the purposes of argument or investigation. In making assumptions about the consequences of solutions, managers are making hypotheses. When managers are not confident about the assumptions they are making, they may seek information through marketing research to help them to confirm, or disconfirm, the hypothesis they are using to make decisions. Both problem-definition processes lead to generating research objectives. Research objectives gather the specific bits of knowledge needed to close information gaps.

Marketing research proposals are formal documents prepared by the researcher serving the functions of stating the problem, specifying research objectives, detailing the research method and specifying a time table and budget. Research proposals typically identify marketing constructs and the operational definitions specifying how the constructs will be measured. A construct is an abstract idea inferred from specific instances that are thought to be related. Marketers use a number of constructs to refer to phenomena that occur in the marketplace. Preference, awareness, recall, and satisfaction are but a few. Marketing researchers find constructs very helpful because, once it is determined that a specific construct is applicable to the problem, there are customary ways of operationalizing, or measuring, these constructs. This knowledge becomes very useful in developing the research objectives. In addition, many constructs have relationships that are explained by models and these relationships can be useful in solving problems. The chapter ends with the integrated case, The Hobbit's Choice.

KEY TERMS

Problem (p. 87)
Opportunity (p. 87)
Marketing opportunity (p. 87)
Opportunity identification (p. 88)
Symptoms (p. 88)
Situation analysis (p. 90)

ITBs (p. 91)
RFPs (p. 91)
Market opportunity analysis (p. 94)
Cause (p. 96)
Possible causes (p. 96)
Probable causes (p. 96)

Solutions (p. 96)
Consequences (p. 97)
Assumptions (p. 98)
Hypotheses (p. 98)
Information state (p. 99)
Information gaps (p. 99)

Research objectives (p. 99)
Marketing research proposal (p. 100)
Operational definition (p. 101)
Construct (p. 101)
Research method (p. 102)

Action standard – know whats in box

REVIEW QUESTIONS/APPLICATIONS

1. Name the situations in which marketing research is not needed.
2. Name the situations in which marketing research is needed.
3. Explain why defining the problem is the most important step in the marketing research process.
4. Give an example of a research project that was conducted with the wrong problem definition.
5. What are the two sources of marketing problems?
6. Explain how managers should recognize they have a problem.
7. What is the role of symptoms in problem recognition?
8. Explain how problems may vary, and give some examples.
9. What is the role of the researcher in problem definition?
10. Explain the impediments to problem definition.
11. Discuss the differences between managers and researchers.
12. What are ITBs and RFPs used for?
13. Discuss the ethical problem with phony ITBs or RFPs.
14. What is the process for determining the problem and establishing research objectives?
15. Explain how the process for determining the problem and establishing research objectives differs when a manager is faced with an opportunity instead of a failure to reach an objective.
16. What is the difference between a possible cause and a probable cause?
17. What is the role of a hypothesis in defining the problem?
18. Why is the information state important to resolving a problem?
19. What are the components of the marketing research proposal?
20. Sony is contemplating expanding its line of 3-inch and 6-inch portable televisions. It thinks there are three situations in which this line would be purchased: (1) as a gift, (2) as a set to be used by children in their own rooms, and (3) for use at sporting events. How might the research objective be stated if Sony wished to know what consumers' preferences are with respect to these three possible uses?
21. Take the construct of channel (that is, "brand") loyalty in the case of teenagers viewing MTV. Write at least three different definitions that indicate how a researcher might form a question in a survey to assess the degree of MTV loyalty. One example is "Channel loyalty is determined by a stated preference to view a given channel for a certain type of entertainment."
22. You just started a new firm manufacturing and marketing MP3 players. Since your design offers more storage and several other features at two-thirds the cost of the lowest priced competitor your sales have been very good and it has been difficult to keep up with production. Describe the systems you need to put into place in order to detect problems your firm may have now or in the future.
23. The local Lexus dealer thinks that the four-door sedan with a list price in excess of $50,000 should appeal to Cadillac Seville owners who are thinking about buying a new automobile. He is considering a direct-mail campaign with personalized packages to be sent to owners whose Cadillac Sevilles are over two years old. Each

package would contain a professional video of all the Lexus sedan's features and end with an invitation to visit the Lexus dealership. This tactic has never been tried in this market. State the marketing problem and indicate what research objectives would help the Lexus dealer understand the possible reactions of Cadillac Seville owners to this campaign.

AJ RESEARCH

Five years ago, when Allison James started her marketing research firm, she had no idea she would be working with so many clients at one time. You are her new research assistant. She asks you to review her five new clients to determine the research objectives for each of their problems. The five new clients and their marketing research problems are as follows.

1. Wired, Inc., an electronics firm, has developed a new flat-screen television that will sell for one-third of the price of those currently on the market. *Problem:* Will there be enough demand to offset the large fixed costs of retooling to make the new television sets?

2. Wacky Znacks, a large snack foods firm, has made a name for itself with wild flavored snacks like licorice cookies and jalapeno sunflower seeds. *Problem:* They feel that customers expect even wilder flavors. Wacky Znacks wants to know what consumer reactions would be to even more unusual flavored snacks, i.e., watermelon-flavored corn chips and barbeque-flavored chewing gum.

3. Wild About Toys is a large toy firm that enjoys surprising consumers with innovative new toys. They have developed an edible clay for children. *Problem:* Will parents want to purchase a toy that their children can also eat?

4. Jimmy Roberts wants to start a small catalog business that caters to new parents. He wants to offer a variety of high-quality, higher-priced items. *Problem:* So many different baby products exist. Roberts needs to start with a limited product line. With which products should he start his business?

5. The Better Butter company has spent many years researching and developing a butter product that the company believes is truly superior to other butters on the market. *Problem:* There are a plethora of butter products. How can Better Butter package its product to call attention to it while portraying the idea of a superior product.

Using the information above, determine the research objectives for each client.

THE HOBBIT'S CHOICE RESTAURANT

The background description for this case is found on pages 38–39.

1. For each of the problems specified in Table 4.6 (page 109) identify a corresponding research objective.

2. For each of your research objectives, identify relevant constructs and possible ways to measure each construct.

3. Go back and reread Marketing Research Insight 4.2. You will see that Ron Tatham discusses a concept he calls the "action standard." What is an action standard? Identify the action standard in the Hobbit's Choice case for determining if there will be adequate demand.

Research Design

Proper Research Design Is Essential to Valid Research Recommendations

Lawrence D. Gibson, Eric Marder Associates, Inc.

Some years ago, General Mills introduced "new, improved" Trix and promptly lost more than one-third of its Trix volume. The lost sales were recaptured a few months later when original Trix was reintroduced.

The superiority of "new, improved" Trix seemed conclusively demonstrated in test after test. Consumers liked it better than old Trix at the 99 percent confidence level in each of three in-home paired-comparison product tests. They preferred the new product in a major central location taste test at the 97 percent confidence level. They rated each of three product variations superior at the 99 percent confidence in a second set of three in-home paired-comparison tests. Four taste tests of final plant-produced product confirmed the superiority of new Trix: three at 95 percent and one at 85 percent confidence levels.

How could consumer testing have been so wrong? Couldn't consumers tell which product they liked better? Was there "taste tiring"? Was it possible that consumers were deliberately misleading us? Were our interviewers cheating?

No. The problem was much simpler. Our research design was wrong. We had simply asked consumers the wrong question. We asked consumers to choose between new Trix and old Trix—a choice they were never going to have in the real world. New Trix was *replacing* old Trix and new Trix would compete with Corn Flakes and Cheerios. Preference for new Trix over old Trix was irrelevant. New Trix should have been tested against its real

Learning Objectives

- To understand what research design is, it's significance and types
- To learn how exploratory research design may be used and the methods to conduct exploratory research
- To know the fundamental questions addressed by descriptive research and the two major types of descriptive research
- To know the different types and uses of panels in marketing research
- To explain what is meant by causal research, experiments, and experimental design
- To know the different types of test marketing and how to select test market cities

competitors, Corn Flakes and Cheerios, while old Trix was also tested against Corn Flakes and Cheerios in a matched consumer group.

The lesson to be learned is straightforward. If research is to predict real-world choices, the choice in research design must be structurally the same as the choice in the real world. Proper research design is essential to valid research recommendations.

Mr. Gibson is an independent consultant and senior associate at Eric Marder Associates, Inc. He is a frequent contributor to the literature on marketing research and is widely respected in the industry for his thought-provoking ideas. By permission, Lawrence D. Gibson

Marketing research methods vary widely. Some projects are taste tests of new, improved versions of existing products like Mr. Gibson's Trix example you just read. Others are experiments of food tasting held in "kitchen-like" labs, focus groups composed of young mothers with infants or nationally representative sample surveys, among many others. Yet other research projects require only that we do library research to examine existing sources of information. How do we know which type of research project to design? Once we know the problem and we have defined our research objectives we are in a position to determine the appropriate research design. This chapter introduces you to the three basic types of research design. You will learn about why research design is important to researchers as well as exploratory, descriptive, and causal designs. When you complete this chapter you should be able to determine which of the three research designs is appropriate given your research objectives.

RESEARCH DESIGN

A research design is a set of advance decisions that makes up the master plan specifying the methods and procedures for collecting and analyzing the needed information.

Each type of study has certain advantages and disadvantages, and one method may be more appropriate for a given research problem than another. How do marketing researchers decide which method is the most appropriate? After thoroughly considering the problem and research objectives, researchers select a **research design**, which is a set of advance decisions that makes up the master plan specifying the methods and procedures for collecting and analyzing the needed information.

The Significance of Research Design

Although every problem and research objective may seem to be unique, there are usually enough similarities among problems and objectives to allow us to make some decisions in advance about the best plan to use to resolve the problem.

There are some basic marketing research designs that can be successfully matched to given problems and research objectives. In this way, they serve the researcher much like the blueprint serves the builder.

Marketing researcher David Singleton of Zyman Marketing Group, Inc. believes that good research design is the first rule of good research.[1] Every research problem is unique. In fact, one could argue that, given each problem's unique customer set, area of geographical application, and other situational variables, there are so few similarities among research projects that each study should be completely designed as a new and independent project. In a sense this is true; almost every research problem is unique in some way or another, and care must be taken to select the most appropriate set of approaches for the unique problem and research objectives at hand. However, there are reasons to justify the significance placed on research design.

First, although every problem and research objective may seem to be unique, there are usually enough similarities among problems and objectives to allow us to make some decisions in advance about the best plan to use to resolve the problem. Second, there are some basic marketing research designs that can be successfully matched to given problems and research objectives. In this way, they serve the researcher much like the blueprint serves the builder.

Once the problem and the research objective are known, the researcher selects a research design. The proper research design is necessary for the researcher to achieve the research objective. However, as you learned from the opening vignette by Lawrence D. Gibson, the wrong research design may lead to disaster.

THREE TYPES OF RESEARCH DESIGNS

The choice of the most appropriate design depends largely on the objectives of the research.

The choice of research design is dependent on how much we already know about the problem and research objective. The less we know, the more likely it is that we should use exploratory research.

Research designs are classified into three traditional categories: exploratory, descriptive, and causal. The choice of the most appropriate design depends largely on the objectives of the research. It has been said that research has three objectives: to gain background information and to develop hypotheses, to measure the state of a variable of interest (for example, level of brand loyalty), or to test hypotheses that specify the relationships between two or more variables (for example, level of advertising and brand loyalty). Note also that the choice of research design is dependent on how much we already know about the problem and research objective. The less we know, the more likely it is that we should use exploratory research. Causal research, on the other hand, should be used only when we know a fair amount about the problem and we are looking for causal relationships among variables associated with problem and/or research objectives. We shall see how these basic research objectives are best handled by the various research designs. Table 5.1 shows the three types of research designs and the basic research objective that would prescribe a given design.[2]

TABLE 5.1	The Basic Research Objective and Research Design	

Research Objective	Appropriate Design
To gain background information, to define terms, to clarify problems and hypotheses, to establish research priorities	Exploratory
To describe and measure marketing phenomena	Descriptive
To determine causality, to make "if–then" statements	Causal

Research Design: A Caution

We pause here, before discussing the three types of research design, to warn you about thinking of research design solely in a step-by-step fashion. Some may think that it is implied in this discussion that the order in which the designs are presented—that is, exploratory, descriptive, and causal—is the order in which these designs should be carried out. This is incorrect. First, in some cases, it may be perfectly legitimate to begin with any one of the three designs and to use only that one design. Second, research is an "iterative" process; by conducting one research project, we learn that we may need additional research, and so on. This may mean that we need to use multiple research designs. We could very well find, for example, that after conducting descriptive research, we need to go back and conduct exploratory research. Third, if multiple designs are used in any particular order (if there is an order), it makes sense to first conduct exploratory research, then descriptive research, and finally causal research. The only reason for this order pattern is that each subsequent design requires greater knowledge about the problem and research objectives on the part of the researcher. Therefore, exploratory research may give one the information needed to conduct a descriptive study, which, in turn, may provide the information necessary to design a causal experiment.

All three research designs are normally used by research firms. At Ask Jeeves, for example, researchers conduct *exploratory* research for client firms who want to know how their proposed sales strategies may work for online advertising conducted on Ask Jeeves. They also conduct *descriptive* studies designed to describe the type of competition and characteristics of the competitors in an industry for their clients, and finally, they conduct *experiments* to determine the effects different marketing and advertising campaigns promoting Ask Jeeves may have on Ask Jeeves' brand awareness.[3]

Exploratory Research

Exploratory research is most commonly unstructured, informal research that is undertaken to gain background information about the general nature of the research problem. By unstructured, we mean that exploratory research does not have a predetermined set of procedures. Rather, the nature of the research changes as the researcher gains information. It is informal in that there is no formal set of objectives, sample plan, or questionnaire. Other, more formal, research designs are used to test hypotheses or measure the reaction of one variable to a change in another variable. Yet, exploratory research can be accomplished by simply reading a magazine or even observing a situation. For example, an 18-year-old college student sitting in line at McDonald's drive-through awaiting a cheeseburger saw an old dilapidated truck, loaded with junk, with a sign "Mark's Hauling." This observation set in motion Brian Scudamore's ideas to launch

Exploratory research is most commonly unstructured, informal research that is undertaken to gain background information about the general nature of the research problem.

a new type of junk service called "1-800-GOT-JUNK?" Soon he was making so much money he dropped out of college. The company expects revenues of $100 million in 2006.[4] Exploratory research is very flexible in that it allows the researcher to investigate whatever sources he or she desires and to the extent he or she feels is necessary in order to gain a good feel for the problem at hand.

Exploratory research is usually conducted when the researcher does not know much about the problem and needs additional information or desires new or more recent information. Often exploratory research is conducted at the outset of research projects.

Uses of Exploratory Research

Exploratory research is used in a number of situations: to gain background information, to define terms, to clarify problems and hypotheses, and to establish research priorities.

▶ **Gain Background Information.** When very little is known about the problem or when the problem has not been clearly formulated, exploratory research may be used to gain much-needed background information. Even for very experienced researchers it is rare that some exploratory research is not undertaken to gain current, relevant background information. There is far too much to be gained to ignore exploratory information.

▶ **Define Terms.** Exploratory research helps to define terms and concepts. By conducting exploratory research to define a question such as, "What is satisfaction with service quality?" the researcher quickly learns that "satisfaction with service quality" is composed of several dimensions—tangibles, reliability, responsiveness, assurance, and empathy. Not only would exploratory research identify the dimensions of satisfaction with service quality but it could also demonstrate how these components may be measured.[5]

▶ **Clarify Problems and Hypotheses.** Exploratory research allows the researcher to define the problem more precisely and to generate hypotheses for the upcoming study. For example, exploratory research on measuring bank image reveals the issue of different groups of bank customers. Banks have three types of customers: retail customers, commercial customers, and other banks for which services are performed for fees. This information is useful in clarifying the problem of the measurement of bank image because it raises the issue of for which customer group bank image should be measured.

Exploratory research can also be beneficial in the formulation of hypotheses, which are statements describing the speculated relationships among two or more variables. Formally stating hypotheses prior to conducting a research study is very important to

Margin notes:

Exploratory research is usually conducted when the researcher does not know much about the problem and needs additional information or desires new or more recent information.

Exploratory research is used in a number of situations: to gain background information, to define terms, to clarify problems and hypotheses, and to establish research priorities.

When very little is known about the problem or when the problem has not been clearly formulated, exploratory research may he used to gain much-needed background information.

Exploratory research helps to define terms and concepts.

ensure that the proper variables are measured. Once a study has been completed, it may be too late to state which hypotheses are desirable to test.

▶ **Establish Research Priorities.** Exploratory research can help a firm prioritize research topics. A summary account of complaint letters by retail store may tell management where to devote their attention. One furniture store chain owner decided to conduct research on the feasibility of carrying office furniture after some exploratory interviews with salespeople revealed that their customers often asked for directions to stores carrying office furniture.

Methods of Conducting Exploratory Research

A variety of methods are available to conduct exploratory research. These include secondary data analysis, experience surveys, case analysis, focus groups, and projective techniques.

▶ **Secondary Data Analysis.** By **secondary data analysis**, we refer to the process of searching for and interpreting existing information relevant to the research objectives. Secondary data are those that have been collected for some other purpose. Your library and the Internet are full of secondary data, which include information found in books, journals, magazines, special reports, bulletins, newsletters, and so on. An analysis of secondary data is often the "core" of exploratory research.[6] This is because there are many benefits to examining secondary data and the costs are typically minimal. Furthermore, the costs for search time of such data are being reduced every day as more and more computerized databases become available. Knowledge of and ability to use these

> Exploratory research allows the researcher to define the problem more precisely and to generate hypotheses for the upcoming study.

> Exploratory research can help a firm prioritize research topics.

> A common method of conducting exploratory research is to examine existing information.

> For some examples of secondary data often used in marketing research, see **www.secondarydata.com**, a Web site developed by Decision Analyst, Inc.

Exploratory research can be very informal. Brian Scudamore's observation of an old pickup gave him the idea to start the very successful franchise, 1-800-GOT-JUNK? Visit the company's Web site at **www.1800gotjunk.com**.

databases are already mandatory for marketing researchers. You will learn more about how to search for secondary data and also some key examples of secondary data in Chapter 6.

▶ **Experience Surveys. Experience surveys** refer to gathering information from those thought to be knowledgeable on the issues relevant to the research problem. Volvo, believing that in the past autos had been designed by and for males, asked 100 women what they wanted in a car. They found some major differences between what women want and what is available, and they plan on introducing a "Volvo for women."[7] If the research problem deals with difficulties encountered when buying infant clothing, then surveys of mothers or fathers with infants may be in order. Experience surveys differ from surveys conducted as part of descriptive research in that there is usually no formal attempt to ensure that the survey results are representative of any defined group of subjects. Nevertheless, useful information can be gathered by this method of exploratory research.

> Experience surveys refer to gathering information from those thought to be knowledgeable on the issues relevant to the research problem.

▶ **Case Analysis.** By **case analysis**, we mean a review of available information about a former situation(s) that has some similarities to the present research problem. Usually, there are few research problems that do not have some similarities to some past situation.[8] Even when the research problem deals with a radically new product, there are often some similar past experiences that may be observed. For example, when cellular telephones were invented but not yet on the market, many companies attempted to forecast the rate of adoption by looking at adoption rates of consumer electronic products such as televisions and VCRs. A wireless communications company, 21st Century Telesis, used data from a low-power, neighborhood phone system that was very successful in Japan to help it market cellular phones to young people in Japan.[9] Researchers must be cautious in using former case examples for current problems. For example, cases dealing with technology-based products just a few years ago may be irrelevant today. The Internet and the widespread use of computers has totally changed the public's use and attitudes toward technical products and services.

> Researchers should use former similar case situations cautiously when trying to apply them to the present research objectives.

▶ **Focus Groups.** A popular method of conducting exploratory research is through **focus groups**, which are small groups of people brought together and guided by a moderator through an unstructured, spontaneous discussion for the purpose of gaining information relevant to the research problem.[10] Although focus groups should encourage openness on the part of the participants, the moderator's task is to ensure that the discussion is "focused" on some general area of interest. For example, the Piccadilly Cafeteria chain periodically conducts focus groups all around the country. The conversation may seem "freewheeling," but the purpose of the focus group may be to learn what people think about some specific aspect of the cafeteria business, such as the perceived quality of cafeteria versus traditional restaurant food. This is a useful technique for gathering some information from a limited sample of respondents. The information can be used to generate ideas, to learn the respondents' "vocabulary" when relating to a certain type of product, or to gain some insights into basic needs and attitudes.[11]

> Focus groups are small groups of people brought together and guided by a moderator through an unstructured, spontaneous discussion for the purpose of gaining information relevant to the research objectives.

▶ **Projective Techniques.** Borrowed from the field of clinical psychology, **projective techniques** seek to explore hidden consumer motives for buying goods and services by asking participants to project themselves into a situation and then to respond to specific questions regarding that situation. One example of such a technique is the sentence completion test. A respondent is given an incomplete sentence such as, "John Smith would never dye his hair because. . . . " By completing the sentence, ostensibly to represent the feelings of the fictitious Mr. Smith, the respondent projects himself or herself into the situation. Another example is the "cartoon test." A respondent is given a cartoon

> Projective techniques seek to explore hidden consumer motives for buying goods and services by asking participants to project themselves into a situation and then to respond to specific questions regarding that situation.

Marketing research firm The Opinion Suites of Richmond, Virginia, conducts a focus group in their facility. By permission of, The Opinion Suites. Visit The Opinion Suites at **www.opinionsuites.com**.

with an empty balloon (used to capture statements made by cartoon characters) above a cartoon character and is asked to state what the cartoon character is saying by filling in the balloon. Marketers know that, by using the cartoon test, respondents are more likely to make statements on behalf of Mr. Smith such as "I don't care if I am dying my hair, I'm not going to look old!" Or, "I don't care if I am getting old, I'm not going to stoop to dying my hair!" More likely, if asked directly, respondents will make statements such as "some people do (dye hair) and some people don't," "I don't care what other people do." This illustrates the value of projective techniques; by talking about "others," respondents may divulge feelings about themselves that they may not divulge in a direct question. As one marketing researcher put it: "with projective techniques, they [consumers] lay down their defenses . . . [T]he window to their psyche is opening up."[12] Projective techniques are the least used of the different types of exploratory research but, nevertheless, they can play an important role given the right problem and research objective.

A concluding word about exploratory research is that some form of it should almost always be used at least to some extent. Why? First, exploratory research, particularly secondary data analysis, is fast. You can conduct quite a bit of exploratory research online within a matter of minutes using online databases or using a search engine to surf the Net. Second, compared with collecting primary data, exploratory research is cheap. Finally, sometimes exploratory research either provides information to meet the research objective or assists in gathering current information necessary to conduct either a descriptive or causal research design. Therefore, few researchers embark on a research project without doing some exploratory research.

> Exploratory research should almost always be used because it is fast and inexpensive, and it may help in designing the proper descriptive or causal research study.

Descriptive Research

Descriptive research is undertaken to obtain answers to questions of who, what, where, when, and how. When we wish to know *who* our customers are, *what* brands they buy and in what quantities, *where* they buy the brands, *when* they shop, and *how* they found out about our products, we turn to descriptive research. Descriptive research is

> Descriptive research is undertaken to obtain answers to questions of who, what, where, when, and how.

also desirable when we wish to project a study's findings to a larger population. If a descriptive study's sample is representative, the findings may be used to predict some variable of interest, such as sales.

Classification of Descriptive Research Studies

There are two types of descriptive studies: cross-sectional studies and longitudinal studies.

Cross-sectional studies measure units from a sample of the population at one point in time.

Because cross-sectional studies are one-time measurements, they are often described as "snapshots" of the population.

There are two basic descriptive research studies available to the marketing researcher: cross-sectional and longitudinal. **Cross–sectional studies** measure units from a sample of the population at one point in time. A study measuring your attitude toward adding a required internship course in your degree program, for example, would be a cross-sectional study. Your attitude toward the topic is measured at one point in time. Cross-sectional studies are prevalent in marketing research, outnumbering longitudinal studies and causal studies. Because cross-sectional studies are one-time measurements, they are often described as "snapshots" of the population.

As an example, of a cross-sectional study many companies test their proposed advertising by using "storyboards." A storyboard consists of several drawings depicting the major scenes in a proposed ad as well as the proposed advertising copy. Companies can quickly and inexpensively test different ad appeals, copy, and creative elements through the use of storyboards by getting consumers' reactions to them. Consumers are shown the storyboard for a proposed ad and are then asked several questions, usually designed to measure their interest and understanding of the advertising message. Typically, a question is asked that measures the consumer's intentions to purchase the product after viewing the storyboard. Dirt Devil tested a proposed ad by using the AdInsights[SM] service offered by online research firm InsightExpress®. InsightExpress® allows firms to pretest promotional messages before the client firms have to spend large sums on media purchases, and they can perfect their promotional messages before they expose their messages to the competition. AdInsights[SM] may be used for all forms of promotional messages, including radio, television, and print ads. These cross-sectional studies provide client firms with useful

By showing a sample of online consumers proposed ads and getting their evaluations, client firms may use InsightExpress®' AdInsights[SM] to modify promotional materials before placing them in the media. AdInsights[SM] studies are examples of cross-sectional research. Visit InsightExpress® at **www.insightexpress.com**. By permission, InsightExpress®.

information. In at least one situation, evaluation scores for a proposed ad were increased 219% after the ad was revised as a result of using AdInsight's[SM] cross-sectional studies.

Cross-sectional studies come in many varieties; they may be based on small or very large samples. Their samples may or may not be representative of some larger population. Often when cross-sectional studies are based on fairly large sample sizes that are representative of some population they are referred to as sample surveys.[13] **Sample surveys** are cross-sectional studies whose samples are drawn in such a way as to be representative of a specific population. ABC often conducts surveys on some topic of interest to report on the evening news. The surveys' samples are drawn such that ABC may report that the results are representative of the population of the United States and that the results have a "margin of error of + or − 3%." So sample surveys may be designed so that their results are representative and accurate, within some margin of error, of the true values in the population. (You will learn how to do this by studying this book.) Sample surveys require that their samples be drawn according to a prescribed plan and to a predetermined number. Later on, you will learn about these sampling plans and sample size techniques.

Longitudinal studies repeatedly measure the same sample units of a population over a period of time. Because longitudinal studies involve multiple measurements, they are often described as "movies" of the population. While cross-sectional studies are far more prevalent, longitudinal studies are used by almost 50 percent of businesses using marketing research.[14] To ensure the success of the longitudinal study, researchers must have access to the same members of the sample, called a panel, so as to take repeated measurements. **Panels** represent sample units of the population who have agreed to answer questions at periodic intervals. Maintaining a representative panel of respondents is a major undertaking.

Several commercial marketing research firms develop and maintain consumer panels for use in longitudinal studies. Typically, these firms attempt to select a sample that is representative of some population. Firms such as Information Resources, Inc. and ACNielsen have maintained panels consisting of hundreds of thousands of households for many years. In many cases these companies will recruit panel members such that the demographic characteristics of the panel are proportionate to the demographic characteristics found in the total population according to Census Bureau statistics. Sometimes these panels will be balanced demographically not only to the United States in total but also within each of various geographical regions. In this way, a client who wishes to get information from a panel of households in the Northwest can be assured that the panel is demographically matched to the total population in the states making up the northwestern region. Many companies maintain panels to target market segments such as "dog owners," "kids" (ages 6 to 14); see **www.KidzEyes.com**). Note that panels are not limited to consumer households. Panels may consist of building contractors, supermarkets, physicians, lawyers, universities, or some other entity.

Online research created the opportunity for several new companies to emerge offering panels recruited to respond to online queries. In addition to C&R Research, another company is Lightspeed Research, which offers clients panels of consumer households. Greenfield Online is another firm that offers other marketing research firms access to its online panel of consumers.

There are two types of panels: continuous panels and discontinuous panels. **Continuous panels** ask panel members the same questions on each panel measurement. **Discontinuous panels** vary questions from one panel measurement to the next.[15] Continuous panel examples include many of the syndicated data panels that ask panel members to record their purchases, using diaries or scanners. The essential point is that panel members are asked to record the *same* information (grocery store purchases) over and over. Discontinuous panels, sometimes referred to as **omnibus** ("including or covering many things or classes") **panels** may be used for a variety of purposes, and the information collected by a discontinuous panel varies from one panel measurement to

Sample surveys are cross-sectional studies whose samples are drawn in such a way as to be representative of a specific population.

Longitudinal studies repeatedly measure the same sample units of a population over a period of time. Because longitudinal studies involve multiple measurements, they are often described as "movies" of the population.

Panels represent sample units of the population who have agreed to answer questions at periodic intervals.

Several commercial marketing research firms develop and maintain consumer panels for use in longitudinal studies.

Visit Lightspeed Research at us.lightspeedpanel.com and Greenfield Online at www.greenfield.com.

Continuous panels ask panel members the same questions on each panel measurement. Discontinuous panels vary questions from one panel measurement to the next.

Discontinuous panels are sometimes referred to as omnibus ("including or covering many things or classes") panels.

Some firms have panels designed to gather information from specific target populations. C&R Research has a panel that gathers information, with parental or guardian consent, from kids aged 6 to 17. This helps their clients see the world through KidzEyes! Visit C&R Research at **www.crresearch.com**.

The advantage of discontinuous (omnibus) panels are that they represent a group of persons who have made themselves available for research. The discontinuous panel provides clients with a source of information that may be quickly accessed for a wide variety of purposes.

the next. How longitudinal data are applied depends on the type of panel used to collect the data. Essentially, the discontinuous panel's primary usefulness is that it represents a large group—people, stores, or some other entity that is agreeable to providing marketing research information. Discontinuous panels, like continuous panels, are also demographically matched to some larger entity, implying representativeness as well. Therefore, a marketer wanting to know how a large number of consumers, matched demographically to the total U.S. population, feel about two different product concepts may elect to use the services of an omnibus panel. The advantage of discontinuous (omnibus) panels are that they represent a group of persons who have made themselves available for research. In this way, then, discontinuous panels represent existing sources of information that may be quickly accessed for a wide variety of purposes.

The UWF/Listener Group Panel is a discontinuous, or omnibus, panel that accesses panel members once a quarter. Visit the panel at **www.uwf.edu/panel**. Printed with the permission of University of West Florida and The Listener Group.

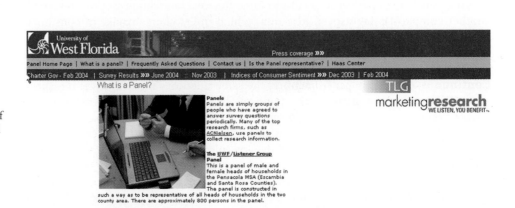

We just used the UWF/Listener Group panel as an example of a discontinuous panel. Go to the website at **www.uwf.edu/panel**. Read what the website has to say about what a panel is, how often panel members may be contacted, and how the panel protects the privacy of its panel members and take a look at the kinds of information the panel has collected by looking at some of the survey results. Finally, you need to start learning about how representative marketing research studies are. For the UWF/Listener Group panel, how representative are the results and how can the panel members determine if the results are representative?

Active **Learning**

The continuous panel is used quite differently from the discontinuous panel. Usually, firms are interested in using data from continuous panels because they can gain insights into changes in consumers' purchases, attitudes, and so on. For example, data from continuous panels can show how members of the panel switched brands from one time period to the next. Studies examining how many consumers switched brands are known as **brand-switching studies**.

To illustrate the importance of using continuous panel data to gain insights into how consumers change dog treat brands, we compare longitudinal data taken from a continuous panel with data collected from two cross-sectional sample surveys. Figure 5.1 shows data collected from two separate cross-sectional studies, each having a household sample size of 500. (Cross-sectional data are referenced as "survey 1" or "survey 2.") Look at how many families used each brand in survey 1 (gold) and then see how many families used each brand in survey 2 (purple). What would we conclude about the dog treat brands from examining these two cross-sectional studies? (1) Pooch Plus has lost market share because only 75 families indicated that they purchased Pooch Plus in the second survey as opposed to 100 Pooch Plus families in the first survey; and (2) apparently,

Firms are interested in using data from continuous panels because they can gain insights into changes in consumers' purchases, attitudes, and so on.

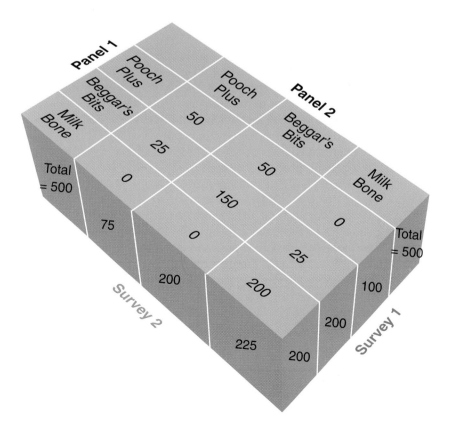

FIGURE 5.1
The Advantage of Longitudinal Studies versus Cross-Sectional Studies

Pooch Plus has lost out to Milk Bone dog treat brand, which increased from 200 to 225 families. Note that Beggar's Bits remained the same. This analysis would lead most brand managers to focus on the strategies that had been used by Milk Bone (since it is "obvious" that Milk Bone took share from Pooch Plus) to increase market share for Pooch Plus.

Now, having reached a conclusion from the two cross-sectional surveys, let's look at the data assuming we had used longitudinal research. When we examine the longitudinal data, we reach quite a different conclusion from the one we reached by looking at the two cross-sectional studies. Looking at panel 1 total (gold) and panel 2 total (purple), we see the same data that we saw in the two cross-sectional surveys. Panel 1 totals show us that Pooch Plus had 100 families, Beggar's Bits had 200 families, and Milk Bone had 200 families. (This is exactly the same data found in our first cross-sectional survey.) Now, we later return for a second measurement of the same families in panel 2 and we find the totals are Pooch Plus, 75 families; Beggar's Bits, 200 families; and Milk Bone, 225 families. (Again, we have the same totals as shown by survey 2 data.) But the real value of the continuous panel longitudinal data is found in the changes that occur between panel 1 and panel 2 measurements. With longitudinal data, we can examine how each family changed from panel 1 to panel 2 and, as we shall see, the ability to measure change is very important in understanding research data. To see how the families changed, look again at panel 1 totals (gold) and then look at the data inside the figure (blue) at the panel 2 results. In panel 1 (gold) we had 100 families using Pooch Plus. How did these families change by the time we asked for panel 2 information? Looking at the data on the inside of the figure (blue) and reading across for Pooch Plus, we see that 50 families stayed with Pooch Plus, 50 switched to Beggar's Bits, and none of the original panel 1 Pooch Plus families switched to Milk Bone. Now look at the 200 families in panel 1 (gold) who used Beggar's Bits. In panel 2 data (blue) we see that 25 of those 200 families switched to Pooch Plus, 150 stayed with Beggar's Bits, and 25 switched to Milk Bone. Finally, all of the 200 Milk Bone families in panel 1 stayed loyal to Milk Bone in panel 2. So, what does this mean? It is clear that Pooch Plus is competing with Beggar's Bits and not with Milk Bone. Milk Bone's total shares increased but at the expense of Beggar's Bits, not Pooch Plus. The brand manager should direct his or her attention to Beggar's Bits, not Milk Bone. This, then, is quite different from the conclusion reached by examining cross-sectional data. The key point we are making here is that because longitudinal data allow us to measure the change being made by each sample unit between time periods, we gain much richer information for analysis purposes. It is important to note, at this point, that this type of brand-switching data may be obtained only by using the continuous panel. Because different questions are asked, discontinuous panels do not allow for this type of analysis.

Market tracking studies are those that measure some variable(s) of interest, such as market share or unit sales, over time.

Another use of longitudinal data is that of market tracking. **Market tracking studies** are those that measure some variable(s) of interest, such as market share or unit sales, over time. By having representative data on brand market shares, for example, a marketing manager can "track" how his or her brand is doing relative to a competitor's brand's performance. Every three years the American Heart Association (AHA) conducts what it calls the "National Acute Event Tracking Study." The AHA collects data using a panel to track changes in unaided awareness of heart attack and stroke warning signs. By tracking consumers' awareness of heart attack and stroke warning signs, the AHA can determine the effectiveness of its promotional materials designed to communicate these signs to the public.[16]

Causal Research

Causality may be thought of as understanding a phenomenon in terms of conditional statements of the form "If x, then y." If Yellow Page ads are in color, then consumer attitudes toward the product will be higher than if the ad is in black and white.

Causality may be thought of as understanding a phenomenon in terms of conditional statements of the form "If x, then y." These "if–then" statements become our way of manipulating variables of interest. For example, if the thermostat is lowered, then the air will get cooler. If I drive my automobile at lower speeds, then my gasoline mileage will increase. If I spend more on advertising, then sales will rise. As humans, we are constantly trying to understand the world in which we live. Likewise, marketing managers are always trying to determine what will cause a change in consumer satisfaction, a gain in market share, or an increase in sales. In one recent experiment, marketing researchers investigated how color versus noncolor and different quality levels of graphics in Yellow Page ads caused changes in consumers' attitudes toward the ad itself, the company doing the advertising, and perceptions of quality. The results showed that color and high-quality photographic materials cause more favorable attitudes. But the findings differ depending on the class of product being advertised.[17] This illustrates how complex cause-and-effect relationships are in the real world. Consumers are bombarded on a daily and sometimes even hourly basis by a vast multitude of factors, all of which could cause them to act in one way or another. Thus, understanding what causes consumers to behave as they do is extremely difficult. Nevertheless, there is a high "reward" in the marketplace for even partially understanding causal relationships. Causal relationships are determined by the use of experiments, which are special types of studies. Many companies are now taking advantage of conducting experiments online.[18]

> **Experiments can be conducted using online research.**

EXPERIMENTS

An **experiment** is defined as manipulating an independent variable to see how it affects a dependent variable, while also controlling the effects of additional extraneous variables. **Independent variables** are those that the researcher can control *and* wishes to manipulate. Some independent variables include level of advertising expenditure, type of advertising appeal (humor, prestige), display location, method of compensating salespersons, price, and type of product. **Dependent variables**, on the other hand, are variables over which we have little or no direct control, yet we have a strong interest in them. We cannot change these variables in the same way that we can change independent variables. A marketing manager, for example, can easily change the level of advertising expenditure or the location of the display of a product in a supermarket, but he or she cannot easily change sales, market share, or level of customer satisfaction. These variables are typically dependent variables. Certainly, marketers are interested in changing these variables. But because they cannot change them directly, they attempt to change them through the manipulation of independent variables. To the extent that marketers can establish causal relationships between independent and dependent variables, they enjoy some success in influencing the dependent variables.

Extraneous variables are those that may have some effect on a dependent variable but yet are not independent variables. To illustrate, let's say you and your friend wanted to know if brand of gasoline (independent variable) affected gas mileage in automobiles (dependent variable). Your "experiment" consists of filling up your two cars, one with brand A, the other with brand B. At the end of the week, you learn that brand A achieved 18.6 miles per gallon and brand B achieved 26.8 miles per gallon. Do you have a causal relationship: Brand B gets better gas mileage than brand A? Or could the difference in the dependent variable (gas mileage) be due to factors other than gasoline brand (independent variable)? Let's take a look at what these other extraneous variables may be: (1) One car is an SUV and the other is a small compact! (2) One car was driven mainly on the highway and the other was driven in the city in heavy traffic. (3) One car has never had a tune-up and the other was just tuned up. We think you get the picture.

> **An experiment is defined as manipulating an independent variable to see how it affects a dependent variable, while also controlling the effects of additional extraneous variables.**

> **Independent variables are those that the researcher can control *and* wishes to manipulate. Independent variables could include level of advertising expenditure, type of advertising appeal, display location, method of compensating salespersons, price, and type of product.**

> **Dependent variables are variables over which we have little or no direct control, yet we have a strong interest in manipulating them. Examples include net profits, market share, or employee or customer satisfaction.**

> **Extraneous variables are those that may have some effect on a dependent variable but yet are not independent variables.**

Let's look at another example. Imagine that a supermarket chain conducts an experiment to determine the effect of type of display (independent variable) on sales of apples (dependent variable). Management records sales of the apples in its regular produce bin's position and then changes (manipulates the independent variable) the position of the apples to end-aisle displays and measures sales once again. Assume sales increased. Does this mean that if we change display position of apples from the produce bins to end-aisle displays, sales will increase? Could there be other extraneous variables that could have affected the sales of the apples? What would happen to apple sales if the weather changed from rainy to fair? If the apple industry began running ads on TV? If the season changed from summer to fall? Yes, weather, industry advertising, and apples packed in school lunch boxes are viewed in this example as extraneous variables, having an effect on the dependent variable, yet themselves not defined as independent variables. As this example illustrates, it would be difficult to isolate the effects of independent variables on dependent variables without controlling for the effects of the extraneous variables. Unfortunately, it is not easy to establish causal relationships but it can be done. In the following section we will see how different experimental designs allow us to conduct experiments.

Experimental Design

An experimental design is a procedure for devising an experimental setting such that a change in a dependent variable may be attributed solely to the change in an independent variable.

An **experimental design** is a procedure for devising an experimental setting such that a change in a dependent variable may be attributed solely to the change in an independent variable. In other words, experimental designs are procedures that allow experimenters to control for the effects on a dependent variable by an extraneous variable. In this way, the experimenter is assured that any change in the dependent variable was due only to the change in the independent variable.

Let us look at how experimental designs work. First, we list the symbols of experimental design:

You should carefully study the symbols of experimental design. Without a good grasp of the meaning of these symbols, you will have difficulty with the following sections.

O = The measurement of a dependent variable

X = The manipulation, or change, of an independent variable

R = Random assignment of subjects (consumers, stores, and so on) to experimental and control groups

E = Experimental effect, that is, the change in the dependent variable due to the independent variable

Time is assumed to be represented horizontally on a continuum.

Subscripts, such as in O_1, or O_2, refer to different measurements made of the dependent variable.

Measurements of the dependent variable taken prior to changing the dependent variable are called "pretests" and those taken after are called "posttests".

When a measurement of the dependent variable is taken prior to changing the independent variable, the measurement is sometimes called a **pretest**. When a measurement of the dependent variable is taken after changing the independent variable, the measurement is sometimes called a **posttest**.

A "true" experimental design is one that truly isolates the effects of the independent variable on the dependent variable while controlling for effects of any extraneous variables.

There are many research designs available to experimenters. In fact, entire college courses are devoted to this one topic. But our purpose here is to illustrate the logic of experimental design, and we can do this by reviewing three designs, of which only the last is a true experimental design. A **"true" experimental design** is one that truly isolates the effects of the independent variable on the dependent variable while controlling for effects of any extraneous variables. However, the first two designs we introduce you to are not true experimental designs. We introduce you to the first two designs to help you understand the real benefits of using a true experimental design. The three designs we discuss are after-only; one-group, before–after; and before–after with control group.

After–Only Design

The **after–only design** is achieved by changing the independent variable and, after some period of time, measuring the dependent variable. It is diagrammed as follows:

$$X \quad O_1$$

where X represents the change in the independent variable (putting all of the apples in end-aisle displays) and the distance between X and O represents the passage of some time period. O_1, represents the measurement, a posttest, of the dependent variable (recording the sales of the apples). Now, what have you learned about causality? Not very much! Have sales gone up or down? We do not know because we neglected to measure sales prior to changing the display location. Regardless of what our sales are, there *may* have been other extraneous variables that may have had an effect on apple sales. Managers are constantly changing things "just to see what happens" without taking any necessary precautions to properly evaluate the effects of the change. Hence, the after-only design does not really measure up to our requirement for a true experimental design.

Designs that do not properly control for the effects of extraneous variables on our dependent variable are known as **quasi-experimental designs**. Note that in the after-only design diagram there is no measure of E, the "experimental effect" on our dependent variable due solely to our independent variable. This is true in all quasi-experimental designs. Our next design, the one-group, before–after design, is also a quasi-experimental design, although it is an improvement over the after-only design.

One–Group, Before–After Design

The **one–group, before–after design** is achieved by first measuring the dependent variable, then changing the independent variable, and, finally, taking a second measurement of the dependent variable. We diagram this design as follows:

$$O_1 \quad X \quad O_2$$

The obvious difference between this design and the after-only design is that we have a measurement of the dependent variable prior to and following the change in the independent variable. Also, as the name implies, we have only one group (a group of consumers in one store) on which we are conducting our study.

As an illustration of this design, let us go back to our previous example. In this design, our supermarket manager measured the dependent variable, apple sales, prior to changing the display location. Now, what do we know about causality? We know a little more than we learned from the after-only design. We know the change in our dependent variable from time period 1 to time period 2. We at least know if sales went up, down, or stayed the same. But what if sales did go up? Can we attribute the change in our dependent variable solely to the change in our independent variable? The answer is "no"—numerous extraneous variables, such as weather, advertising, or time of year, could have caused an increase in apple sales. With the one-group, before-after design, we still cannot accurately measure E, the "experimental effect," because this design does not control for the effects of extraneous variables on the dependent variable. Hence, the one-group, before-after design is also not a true experimental design; it is a quasi-experimental design.

Control of extraneous variables is typically achieved by the use of a second group of subjects, known as a control group. By **control group**, we mean a group whose subjects have not been exposed to the change in the independent variable. The **experimental group**, on the other hand, is the group that has been exposed to a change in the independent variable. By having these two groups as part of our experimental design, we can overcome many of the problems associated with the quasi-experimental designs presented thus far. We shall use the following true experimental design to illustrate the importance of the control group.

Before–After with Control Group

The **before–after with control group** design may be achieved by randomly dividing subjects of the experiment (in this case, supermarkets) into two groups: the control group and the experimental group. A pretest measurement of the dependent variable is then taken on both groups. Next, the independent variable is changed only in the experimental group. Finally, after some time period, posttest measurements are taken of the dependent variable in both groups. This design may be diagrammed as follows:

$$\text{Experimental group (R)} \quad O_1 \quad \times \quad O_2$$
$$\text{Control group (R)} \qquad\qquad O_3 \qquad O_4$$

where:

$$E = (O_2 - O_1) - (O_4 - O_3).$$

In this true experimental design, we have two groups. Let's assume we have 20 supermarkets in our supermarket chain. Theoretically, if we randomly divide these stores into two groups—10 in the experimental group and 10 in the control group—then the groups should be equivalent; that is, both groups should be as similar as possible, each group having an equal number of large stores, and small stores, an equal number of new stores and old stores, an equal number of stores in upper-income neighborhoods and lower-income neighborhoods, and so on. Note that this design assumes that the two groups are equivalent in all aspects. An experimenter should take whatever steps are necessary to meet this condition if he or she uses this design. There are methods for gaining equivalency other than randomization. Matching on criteria thought to be important, for example, would aid in establishing equivalent groups. When randomization or matching on relevant criteria does not achieve equivalent groups, more complex experimental designs should be used.[19]

Looking back at our design, the R indicates that we have randomly divided our supermarkets into two equal groups—one a control group, the other an experimental group. We also see that pretest measurements of our dependent variable, apple sales, were recorded at the same time for both groups of stores as noted by O_1 and O_3. Next, we see by the X symbol that only in the experimental group of stores were the apples moved from the regular produce bins to end-aisle displays. Finally, posttest measurements of the dependent variable were taken at the same time in both groups of stores, as noted by O_2 and O_4.

Now, what information can we gather from this experiment? First, we know that $(O_2 - O_1)$ tells us how much change occurred in our dependent variable during the time of the experiment. But was this difference due solely to our independent variable, X? No, $(O_2 - O_1)$ tells us how many dollars in apple sales may be attributed to (1) the change in display location and (2) other extraneous variables, such as the weather, apple industry advertising, and so on. This does not help us very much, but what does $(O_4 - O_3)$ measure? Because it cannot account for changes in apple sales due to a change in display location (the display was not changed), then any differences in sales as measured by $(O_4 - O_3)$ must be due to the influence of other extraneous variables on apple sales. Therefore, the difference between the experimental group and the control group, $(O_2 - O_1) - (O_4 - O_3)$, results in a measure of E, the "experimental effect." We now know that if we change apple display locations, then apple sales will change by an amount equal to E. We have, through experimentation using a proper experimental design, made some progress at arriving at causality.

Now that you understand the rudiments of experimental design you are ready to see how experiments are conducted in the marketing research industry. ACNielsen's Market Decisions conducts experiments for clients. Read Marketing Research Insight 5.1. You will see how Market Decisions uses the concept of control versus experimental (test) groups to see how a change in the independent variable affects the dependent variable.

As we noted earlier, there are many other experimental designs and, of course, there are almost limitless applications of experimental designs to marketing problems. An experimenter, for example, could use the before–after with control group design to measure the effects of different types of music (independent variable) on total purchases made by supermarket customers (dependent variable). Although we have demonstrated how valuable experimentation can be in providing us with knowledge, we should not accept all experiments as being valid. How we assess the validity of experiments is the subject of our next section.

How Valid Are Experiments?

How can we assess the validity of an experiment? An experiment is valid if (1) the observed change in the dependent variable is, in fact, due to the independent variable, and (2) if the results of the experiment apply to the "real world" outside the experimental setting.[20] Two forms of validity are used to assess the validity of an experiment: internal and external.

MARKETING RESEARCH INSIGHT

PRACTICAL INSIGHTS

5.1

Experiments at ACNielsen

ACNielsen's Market Decisions has the expertise to conduct experiments for clients. Clients want to know what impact a change in packaging, price, in-store merchandising support, and shelf facing, among a number of other independent variables, will have on the dependent variable, sales.

Market Decisions offers a Controlled Store Test (CST), which allows clients to see, in market, how changes in their marketing mix elements cause an effect on consumer response. Market Decisions divides stores into control groups (called Control Panels) and experimental groups (Test Panels). In the Test Panels, the independent variable is manipulated (see left: shelf facings are set horizontally)

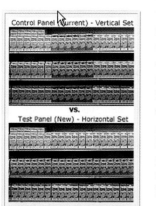

Control Panel (Current) - Vertical Set

vs.

Test Panel (New) - Horizontal Set

while remaining the same in the Control Panels.

To make sure that Control Panels of stores are equivalent, or matched, to Test Panel stores, Market Decisions uses a proprietary statistical model using prior actual activity data. For example, to ensure that the Control and Test Panels are equivalent they examine data from the panels from the previous year and then divide them into "twin" groups for control and test. By controlling for extraneous variables, the resulting data allows clients to understand how a change in their selected independent variable affects the dependent variable of interest.

To ensure that the experiments are run properly, the ACNielsen field collection staff use strict controls and processes to ensure all the test conditions are performed to exacting standards.

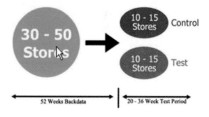

Visit ACNielsen's Market Decisions at **www.marketdec.com**. By permission, ACNielsen™.

An experiment is valid if (1) the observed change in the dependent variable is, in fact, due to the independent variable, and (2) if the results of the experiment apply to the "real world" outside the experimental setting.

Internal validity is concerned with the extent to which the change in the dependent variable was actually due to the independent variable.

Experiments lacking internal validity have little value.

Internal validity is concerned with the extent to which the change in the dependent variable was actually due to the independent variable. This is another way of asking if the proper experimental design was used and if it was implemented correctly. To illustrate an experiment that lacks internal validity, let us return to our apple example. In the experimental design, before–after with control group, we made the point that the design assumes that the experimental group and the control group are, in fact, equivalent. What would happen if the researcher did not check the equivalency of the groups? Let us suppose that, by chance, the two groups of supermarkets had customers who were distinctly different regarding a number of factors such as age and income. This difference in the groups, then, would represent an extraneous variable that had been left uncontrolled. Such an experiment would lack internal validity because it could not be said that the change in the dependent variable was due solely to the change in the independent variable. Experiments lacking internal validity have little value because they produce misleading results. Sometimes organizations will conduct studies and present them as "experiments" in order to intentionally mislead others.

External validity refers to the extent to which the relationship observed between the independent and dependent variables during the experiment is generalizable to the real world.[21] In other words, can the results of the experiment be applied to units (consumers, stores, and so on) other than those directly involved in the experiment? There are several threats to external validity. How representative is the sample of test units? Is this sample really representative of the population? In addition, there exist many examples of the incorrect selection of sample units for testing purposes. For example, executives, headquartered in large cities in cold winter climates, have been known to conduct "experiments" in warmer, tropical climes during the winter. Although the experiments they conduct may be internally valid, it is doubtful that the results will be generalizable to the total population.

Another threat to external validity is the artificiality of the experimental setting itself. In order to control as many variables as possible, some experimental settings are far removed from real-world conditions.[22] If an experiment is so contrived that it produces behavior that would not likely be found in the real world, then the experiment lacks external validity.

If an experiment is so contrived that it produces behavior that would not likely be found in the real world, then the experiment lacks external validity.

Types of Experiments

Laboratory experiments are those in which the independent variable is manipulated and measures of the dependent variable are taken in a contrived, artificial setting for the purpose of controlling the many possible extraneous variables that may affect the dependent variable.

Laboratory experiments are desirable when the intent of the experiment is to achieve high levels of internal validity.

We can classify experiments into two broad classes: laboratory and field. **Laboratory experiments** are those in which the independent variable is manipulated and measures of the dependent variable are taken in a contrived, artificial setting for the purpose of controlling the many possible extraneous variables that may affect the dependent variable.

To illustrate, let's consider a study in which subjects are invited to a theater and shown test ads, copy A or B, spliced into a TV "pilot" program. Why would a marketer want to use such an artificial, laboratory setting? Such a setting is used to control for variables that could affect the purchase of products other than those in the test ads. By bringing consumers into a contrived laboratory setting, the experimenter is able to control many extraneous variables. For example, you have learned why it is important to have equivalent groups (the same kind of people watching copy A as those watching copy B commercials) in an experiment. By inviting preselected consumers to the TV pilot showing in a theater, the experimenter can match (on selected demographics) the consumers who view copy A with those who view copy B, thus ensuring that the two groups are equal. By having the consumers walk into an adjoining "store," the experimenter easily controls other factors such as the time between exposure to the ad copy and shopping and the consumers' being exposed to other advertising by competitive brands. As you have already learned, any one of these factors, left uncontrolled, could have an impact on the dependent variable. By controlling for these and other variables, the experimenter can be assured that any changes in the dependent variable were due solely to differences in the independent variable, ad copy A and B. Laboratory experiments, then, are desirable when the intent of the experiment is to achieve high levels of internal validity.

There are advantages to laboratory experiments. First, they allow the researcher to control for the effects of extraneous variables. Second, compared to field experiments, lab experiments may be conducted quickly and with less expense. Obviously, the disadvantage is the lack of a natural setting and, therefore, there is concern for the generalizability of the findings to the real world. For instance, blind taste tests of beer have found that a majority of beer drinkers favor the older beers such as Pabst, Michelob, or Coors, yet new beer brands are introduced regularly and become quite popular,[23] so the generalizability of blind taste tests is questionable.

Field experiments are those in which the independent variables are manipulated and the measurements of the dependent variable are made on test units in their natural setting. Many marketing experiments are conducted in natural settings, such as in supermarkets, malls, retail stores, and consumers' homes. Let's assume that a marketing manager conducts a *laboratory* experiment to test the differences between ad copy A, the company's existing ad copy, and a new ad copy, copy B. The results of the laboratory experiment indicate that copy B is far superior to the company's present ad copy A. But, before spending the money to use the new copy, the manager wants to know if ad copy B will create increased sales in the real world. She elects to actually run the new ad copy in Erie, Pennsylvania, a city noted as being representative of the average characteristics of the U.S. population. By conducting this study in the field, the marketing manager will have greater confidence that the results of the study will actually hold up in other real-world settings. Note, however, that even if an experiment is conducted in a naturalistic field setting in order to enhance external validity, the experiment is invalid if it does not also have internal validity.

The primary advantage of the field experiment is that of conducting the study in a naturalistic setting, thus increasing the likelihood that the study's findings will also hold true in the real world. Field experiments, however, are expensive and time-consuming. Also, the experimenter must always be alert to the impact of extraneous variables, which are very difficult to control in the natural settings of field experimentation.

The example we just cited of using Erie, Pennsylvania, for a field experiment would be called a "test market." Much of the experimentation in marketing, conducted as field experiments, is known as test marketing. For this reason, test marketing is discussed in the following section.

TEST MARKETING

Test marketing is the phrase commonly used to indicate an experiment, study, or test that is conducted in a field setting. Companies may use one or several test market cities, which are geographical areas selected in which to conduct the test. There are two broad classes of uses of test markets: (1) to test the sales potential for a new product or service and (2) to test variations in the marketing mix for a product or service.[24] Although test marketing is very expensive and time-consuming, the costs of introducing a new product on a national or regional basis routinely amount to millions of dollars. The costs of the test market are justified if the results of the test market can improve a product's chances of success. Sometimes the test market results will be sufficient to warrant further market introductions. Sometimes the test market identifies a failure early on and

The advantages of laboratory experiments are that they allow for the control of extraneous variables and they may be conducted quickly and less expensively than field experiments.

A disadvantage of laboratory experiments is that they are conducted in artificial settings

Field experiments are those in which the independent variables are manipulated and the measurements of the dependent variable are made on test units in their natural setting.

Even if an experiment is conducted in a naturalistic field setting in order to enhance external validity, the experiment is invalid if it does not also have internal validity.

The primary advantage of the field experiment is that of conducting the study in a naturalistic setting, thus increasing the likelihood that the study's findings will also hold true in the real world. Field experiments, however, are expensive and time-consuming.

Test marketing is the phrase commonly used to indicate an experiment, study, or test that is conducted in a field setting.

There are two broad classes of uses of test markets: (1) to test the sales potential for a new product or service and (2) to test variations in the marketing mix for a product or service.

saves the company huge losses. The GlobalPC, a scaled-down computer targeted for novices, was tried in test markets. The parent company, MyTurn, concluded that the test market sales results would not lead to a profit and the product was dropped before the company experienced further losses.[25] Test markets are not only conducted to measure sales potential for a new product but also to measure consumer and dealer reactions to other marketing mix variables as well. A firm may use only department stores to distribute the product in one test market and only specialty stores in another test market city to gain some information on the best way to distribute the product. Companies can also test media usage, pricing, sales promotions, and so on through test markets. Some examples of test markets conducted around the world include Coke testing a new Barq's root beer float–flavored soft drink in Mississippi and Louisiana to test the product before a nationwide launch,[26] a Thailand-based furniture company conducting test markets in India on children's furniture designed like bugs and animals,[27] Dairy Queen testing sales of irradiated ground beef patties in the United States,[28] a health-care firm testing antisting jellyfish sunscreen in the United Kingdom,[29] and airlines, such as Southwest, British Midland and Air Canada, test marketing snacks on flights around the globe.[30]

Types of Test Markets

Test markets have been classified into four types: standard, controlled, electronic, and simulated.[31] The **standard test market** is one in which the firm tests the product and/or marketing mix variables through the company's *normal* distribution channels. While they take time and expose the new product or service to competitors, they are good indicators of how the product will actually perform because they are conducted in real settings.

A standard test market is one in which the firm tests the product and/or marketing mix variables through the company's normal distribution channels.

Controlled test markets are conducted by outside, or what we call external supplier, research firms that guarantee distribution of the product through prespecified types and numbers of distributors. Companies specializing in providing this service, such as RoperASW and ACNielsen, provide dollar incentives for distributors to provide them with guaranteed shelf space. Controlled test markets offer an alternative to the company that wishes to gain fast access to a distribution system set up for test market purposes. The disadvantage is that this distribution network may or may not properly represent the firm's actual distribution system. We will look at this service again in Chapter 7 on standardized services.

Controlled test markets are conducted by outside research firms that guarantee distribution of the product through prespecified types and numbers of distributors.

Electronic test markets are those in which a panel of consumers has agreed to carry identification cards that each consumer presents when buying goods and services. These tests are conducted only in a small number of cities in which local retailers have agreed to participate. The advantage of the card is that as consumers buy (or do not buy) the test product, demographic information on the consumers is automatically recorded. In some cases, firms offering electronic test markets may also have the ability to link media viewing habits to panel members as well. In this way, firms using the electronic test market also know how different elements of the promotional mix affect purchases of the new product. Firms offering this service include Information Resources, Inc. and ACNielsen. Obviously, the electronic test market offers speed, greater confidentiality, and less cost than standard or controlled test markets. However, the disadvantage is that the test market is not the real market. By virtue of having agreed to serve as members of the electronic panel, consumers in electronic test markets may be atypical. A user firm must evaluate the issue of representativeness. Also, electronic test markets are typically situated in small cities such as Eau Claire, Wisconsin,[32] which is another representativeness consideration.

Electronic test markets are those in which a panel of consumers has agreed to carry identification cards that each consumer presents when buying goods and services.

Simulated test markets (STMs) are those in which a limited amount of data on consumer response to a new product is fed into a model containing certain assumptions regarding planned marketing programs, which generates likely product sales volume. It is claimed that IBM has suffered business failures such as the ill-fated Aptiva line of PCs because it failed to use STM research.[33] Typical STMs share the following characteristics: (1) respondents are selected to provide a sample of consumers who satisfy predetermined demographic characteristics, (2) consumers are shown commercials or print ads for the test product as well as ads for competitive products, (3) consumers are given the opportunity to purchase, or not to purchase, the test product either in a real or simulated store environment, (4) consumers are recontacted after they have had an opportunity to use the product in an effort to determine likelihood of repurchase, as well as other information relative to use of the product, (5) information from the preceding process is fed into a computer program that is calibrated by assumptions of the marketing mix and other elements of the environment. The program then generates output such as estimated sales volume, market share, and so on.[34]

There are many advantages to STMs. They are fast relative to standard test markets. STMs typically take only 18 to 24 weeks, compared with as many as 12 to 18 months for standard test markets. STMs cost only 5 percent to 10 percent of the cost of a standard test market. STMs are confidential; competitors are less likely to know about the test. Different marketing mixes may be tested and results of STMs have shown that they can be accurate predictors of actual market response. As you will see when you read Marketing Research Insight 5.2 later in this chapter, at least one marketing researcher believes we should use more STMs. The primary disadvantage is that STMs are not as accurate as full-scale test markets. They are very dependent on the assumptions built into the models.[35]

Consumer Versus Industrial Test Markets

When we think of test marketing we normally think of tests of consumer products. Test marketing, however, has been growing in the industrial market, sometimes called the business-to-business (B2B) market. Although the techniques are somewhat different between consumer and industrial test markets, the same results are sought—the timely release of profitable products.

In consumer test markets, multiple versions of a more-or-less finished product are tested by consumers. In industrial test markets, the key technology is presented to selected industrial users, who offer feedback on desired features and product performance levels. Given this information, product prototypes are then developed and are placed with a select number of users for actual use. Users again provide feedback to iron out design problems. In this way, the new product is tried and tested under actual conditions before the final product is designed and produced for the total market. The negative side of this process is the time it takes to test the product from the beginning stages to the final, commercialized stages. During this period, information on the new product is leaked to competitors, and the longer the product is being tested, the more investment costs increase without any revenues being generated. U.S. automakers, for example, take 48 to 60 months to design, refine, and begin production of a new car model. Japanese companies are able to do it in 30 months by having a development team made up of a combination of marketing and production people. DaimlerChrysler and 3M have experimented with this concept. In many firms, future industrial test marketing will be fully integrated with the new-product development process.[36]

"Lead Country" Test Markets

A **lead country test market** is test marketing conducted in specific foreign countries that seem to be good predictors for an entire continent. As markets have become more global, firms are no longer interested in limiting marketing of new products and services to their domestic market.

A lead country test market is test marketing conducted in specific foreign countries that seem to be good predictors for an entire continent.

Colgate-Palmolive used lead country test marketing when it launched its Palmolive Optims shampoo and conditioner. The company tested the product in the Philippines, Australia, Mexico, and Hong Kong. A year later, distribution was expanded to other countries in Europe, Asia, Latin America, and Africa.[37] Colgate used two countries as test markets in 1999 to test its battery-powered Actibrush for kids. These two countries brought in $10 million in sales. Colgate moved into 50 countries in 2000 and earned $115 million in sales.[38] Korea is being used as a lead country test market for digital products and services. Seongnam is a middle-class Seoul suburb with a mix of high-rise apartment blocks, restaurants, and malls. During the next three years, municipal officials plan to transform the town of 930,000 into the world's first digital city. Multiple broad-band connections will seek to do away with analog concepts—like cash and credit cards. Seongnam will start equipping citizens with digital cell phones that, in effect, pay for purchases at every store in the city. Cash-free Seongnam is one of many on-the-ground tests being launched in South Korea, a nation preoccupied with all things digital. More than half of South Korea's 15 million households have broadband service and more than 60 percent of Koreans carry cell phones. The country is now so wired that many companies can use entire urban populations as test markets for their latest digital products and services.[39]

Selecting Test Market Cities

There are three criteria that are useful for selecting test market cities: representativeness, degree of isolation, and ability to control distribution and promotion.

There are three criteria that are useful for selecting test market cities: **representativeness**, **degree of isolation**, and **ability to control distribution and promotion**. Because one of the major reasons for conducting a test market is to achieve external validity, the test market city should be representative of the marketing territory in which the product will ultimately be distributed. Consequently, a great deal of effort is expended to locate the "ideal" city in terms of comparability with characteristics of the total U.S. (or other country) population. The "ideal" city is, of course, the city whose demographic characteristics most closely match the desired total market. For instance, R. J. Reynolds chose Chattanooga, Tennessee, to test market its Eclipse "smokeless" cigarette because Chattanooga has a higher proportion of smokers than most cities, and R. J. Reynolds needed to test Eclipse with smokers.[40]

When a firm test markets a product, distribution of the product and promotion of the product are isolated to a limited geographical area, such as Tulsa, Oklahoma. If the firm advertises in the *Tulsa World* newspaper, the newspaper not only covers Tulsa but also has very little "spillover" into other sizable markets. Therefore, the company, along with its dealers, competitors, and so on, is not likely to get many calls from a nearby city wanting to know why it cannot buy the product. Distribution has been restricted to the test market, Tulsa. Some markets are not so isolated. If you were to run promotions for a product test in the *Los Angeles Times*, you would have very large spillover of newspaper readership outside the Los Angeles geographical area. Note that this would not necessarily be a problem as long as you wanted to run the test in the geographical area covered by the *Los Angeles Times* and you also had arranged for the new product to be distributed in this area.

The ability to control distribution and promotion depends on a number of factors. Are the distributors in the city that is being considered available and willing to cooperate? If not, is a controlled test market service company available for the city? Will the media in the city have the facilities to accommodate your test market needs? At what costs? All of these factors must be considered before selecting the test city. Fortunately, because it is desirable to have test markets conducted in a city because it brings in additional revenues, city governments as well as the media typically provide a great deal of information about their city to prospective test marketers.

A good example of the application of these three criteria is McDonald's test market of its all-you-can-eat breakfast bar. The test was conducted in Atlanta and Savannah, Georgia, which are representative southeastern cities where McDonald's has control over its outlets and where the promotional media are specific to those markets. The buffet was found to increase weekend family breakfast sales.[41]

Pros and Cons of Test Marketing

The advantages of test marketing are straightforward. Testing product acceptability and marketing mix variables in a field setting provides the best information possible to the decision maker prior to actually going into full-scale marketing of the product. Because of this, Philip Kotler has referred to test markets as the "ultimate" way to test a new product.[42] Test marketing allows for the most accurate method of forecasting future sales, and it allows firms the opportunity to pretest marketing mix variables.

Test marketing allows for the most accurate method of forecasting future sales, and it allows firms the opportunity to pretest marketing mix variables.

There are, however, several negatives to test marketing. First, test markets do not yield infallible results. There have been many instances in which test market results have led to decisions that proved wrong in the marketplace. No doubt, there have probably also been many "would-be successful" products withheld from the marketplace because of poor performances in test markets. Much of this problem, however, is not due to anything inherent in test marketing; rather, it is a reflection of the complexity and changeability of consumer behavior. Accurately forecasting consumer behavior is a formidable task. Also, competitors intentionally try to sabotage test markets. Firms will often flood a test market with sales promotions if they know a competitor is test marketing a product. When PepsiCo tested Mountain Dew Sport drink in Minneapolis in 1990, Quaker Oats Company's Gatorade counterattacked with a deluge of coupons and ads. Mountain Dew Sport was yanked from the market, although Pepsi says Gatorade had nothing to do with the decision.[43] These activities make it even more difficult to forecast the normal market's response to a product.

Test markets do not yield infallible results.

Another problem with test markets is their cost. Estimates are that the costs exceed several hundred thousand dollars even for limited test markets. Test markets involving several test cities and various forms of promotion can easily reach well over six figures. Finally, test markets bring about exposure of the product to the competition. Competitors get the opportunity to examine product prototypes and to see the planned marketing strategy for the new product via the test market. If a company spends too much time testing a product, it runs the risk of allowing enough time for a competitor to bring out a similar product and to gain the advantage of being first in the market. In spite of these problems, the value of the information from test marketing makes test marketing a worthwhile endeavor.

Test markets are expensive, expose the new product or service to competitors, and take time to conduct.

Test markets may create ethical problems. Companies routinely report test marketing results to the press, which allows them access to premarket publicity. But, are negatives found in the test market always reported or only the good news? Companies, eager to get good publicity, may select test market cities they think will return favorable results. Perhaps the company already has a strong brand and market power in the market. Is this method of getting publicity ethical? *The Wall Street Journal* has addressed these issues and the Advertising Research Foundation has published "Guidelines for Public Use of Market and Opinion Research" in an attempt to make reporting of test markets more candid.[44] For a practitioner's view of the problems associated with test marketing, read our Marketing Research Insight 5.2.

MARKETING RESEARCH INSIGHT

5.2

Test Marketing in Practice: Some Hidden Difficulties

By Lawrence D. Gibson, Eric Marder Associates, Inc.

We asked Mr. Lawrence D. Gibson what insights he would like to share with you and one of the topics he chose was test marketing. Here you get some insights as to just how difficult it is to conduct and interpret test markets.

The practical difficulties of test marketing start with design. Typically these so-called experiments use only one or two "representative," markets and the attempt to find such representative markets is frustrating. It is not hard to choose markets that are nationally representative of income or ethnicity or product class consumption, but it is very difficult to pick markets that will later prove to be representative of the demand for the particular new product being tested.

This difficulty was demonstrated in an experiment conducted some years ago at General Mills. Starting with a large set of new cereal introductions, the new product national share for the introductory year was projected from the introductory year share in each of the company's 26 sales regions, each pair of regions, and each trio. In other words, each region, pair, and trio was treated as if it had been the test market for the new cereal.

The findings were startling. The average projection error for these large (4%) regions was about 25%. (Note this error band does not include any error associated with projecting forward in time.) None of the regions was accurate for more than one or two new cereals; nor was any region consistently high or low. While the error band declined significantly for pairs and trios, the most accurate single region was New York, the best pair was New York and Chicago, and the best trio was New York, Chicago, and Los Angeles. Clearly these regions were most accurate because they were the largest parts of the United States—not because they were the most representative.

Translating the national marketing plan into the test market presents several logical issues. Should the test market receive the level of advertising and promotion that it would actually receive in the national plan or should it receive the average level of the national plan? Should it receive the absolute level of the national plan, or should it receive the share of product class advertising of the plan? What local media and promotion vehicles can be substituted for the national media that may not be available locally?

Meanwhile, competitors inevitably follow the test market and consider how they will react. They may try to destroy the test with a major competitive response; they may simply read the results and plan their own future response; they may, if they have a similar new product in development, read the test and immediately introduce their new product nationally. In any event, they can learn as much from the test as the sponsor.

When the time and cost of test marketing are considered together with the difficulties just cited, the resulting inaccuracy, the inevitable security breach, and the unknown future competitive response, traditional test marketing becomes almost impossible to justify in Bayesian terms. Less expensive, even if less accurate, simulated test market procedures seem very attractive.

So you thought New York City, "The Big Apple," was different from your hometown? Think again!

SUMMARY

Research design refers to a set of advance decisions made to develop the master plan to be used in the conduct of the research project. There are three general research designs: exploratory, descriptive, and causal. Each of these designs has its own inherent approaches. The significance of studying research design is that, by matching the research objective with the appropriate research design, a host of research decisions may be predetermined. Therefore, a research design serves as a "blueprint" for researchers.

Selecting the appropriate research design depends, to a large extent, on the research objectives and how much information is already known about the problem. If very little is known, exploratory research is appropriate. Exploratory research is unstructured, informal research that is undertaken to gain background information; it is helpful for more clearly defining the research problem. Exploratory research is used in a number of situations: to gain background information, to define terms, to clarify problems and hypotheses, and to establish research priorities. Reviewing existing literature, surveying individuals knowledgeable in the area to be investigated, relying on former similar case situations, conducting focus groups, and projective techniques are methods of conducting exploratory research. Focus groups are conducted by having a small group of persons guided by a moderator through a spontaneous, unstructured conversation that focuses on a research problem. Exploratory research should almost always be used because it is fast, inexpensive, and sometimes resolves the research objective or is helpful in carrying out descriptive or causal research.

If concepts, terms, and so on are already known and the research objective is to describe and measure phenomena, then descriptive research is appropriate. Descriptive research measures marketing phenomena and answers the questions of who, what, where, when, and how. Descriptive studies may be conducted at one point in time (cross-sectional) or several measurements may be made on the same sample at different points in time (longitudinal). Longitudinal studies are often conducted using panels. Panels represent sample units of people who have agreed to answer questions at periodic intervals. Continuous panels are longitudinal studies in which sample units are asked the same questions repeatedly. Brand-switching tables may be prepared based on data from continuous panels. Market tracking studies may be conducted using data from continuous panels.

The second type of panel used in longitudinal research is the discontinuous panel. Discontinuous, sometimes called omnibus, panels are those in which the sample units are asked different questions. The main advantage of the discontinuous panel is that research firms have a large sample of persons who are willing to answer whatever questions they are asked. The demographics of panel members are often balanced with regard to the demographics of larger geographical areas they are to represent, such as a region or the entire United States. Marketing research firms such as Information Resources, Inc. and ACNielsen have maintained panels for many years.

Sometimes the research objective requires the researcher to determine causal relationships between two or more variables. Causal relationships provide relationships such as "If x, then y." Causal relationships may be discovered only through special studies called "experiments". Experiments allow us to determine the effects of a variable, known as an independent variable, on another variable, known as a dependent variable. Experimental designs are necessary to ensure that the effect we observe in our dependent variable is due, in fact, to our independent variable and not to other variables, known as extraneous variables. The validity of experiments may be assessed by internal validity and external validity.

Laboratory experiments are particularly useful for achieving internal validity, whereas field experiments are better suited for achieving external validity. Test marketing is a form of field experimentation. Test market cities are selected on the basis of their representativeness, isolation, and the degree to which market variables such as distribution and promotion may be controlled. Various types of test markets exist (standard, controlled, electronic, simulated, consumer, industrial, and lead country) and, although test markets garner much useful information, they are expensive and not infallible.

KEY TERMS

Research design (p. 116)
Exploratory research (p. 117)
Secondary data analysis (p. 119)
Experience surveys (p. 120)
Case analysis (p. 120)
Focus groups (p. 120)
Projective techniques (p. 120)
Descriptive research (p. 121)
Cross-sectional studies (p. 122)
Sample surveys (p. 123)
Longitudinal studies (p. 123)
Panels (p. 123)
Continuous panels (p. 123)
Discontinuous panels (p. 123)
Omnibus panels (p. 123)
Brand-switching studies (p. 125)
Market tracking studies (p. 126)
Causality (p. 126)
Experiment (p. 127)
Independent variables (p. 127)
Dependent variables (p. 127)
Extraneous variables (p. 127)
Experimental design (p. 128)

Pretest (p. 128)
Posttest (p. 128)
"True" experimental design (p. 128)
After-only design (p. 129)
Quasi-experimental designs (p. 129)
One-group, before–after design (p. 129)
Control group (p. 129)
Experimental group (p. 129)
Before–after with control group (p. 130)
Internal validity (p. 132)
External validity (p. 132)
Laboratory experiments (p. 132)
Field experiments (p. 133)
Test marketing (p. 133)
Standard test market (p. 134)
Controlled test markets (p. 134)
Electronic test markets (p. 134)
Simulated test markets (p. 134)
Lead country test market (p. 135)
Representativeness (p. 136)
Degree of isolation (p. 136)
Ability to control distribution and
   promotion (p. 136)

REVIEW QUESTIONS/APPLICATIONS

1. How would you match research designs with various research objectives?
2. Give some examples illustrating the uses of exploratory research.
3. What type of research design answers the questions of who, what, where, when, and how?
4. What are the differences between longitudinal studies and cross-sectional studies?
5. In what situation would a continuous panel be more suitable than a discontinuous panel? In what situation would a discontinuous panel be more suitable than a continuous panel?
6. Explain why studies of the "if–then" variety are considered to be causal studies.
7. What is the objective of good experimental design? Explain why certain designs are called "quasi-experimental designs."
8. Explain the two types of validity in experimentation and also explain why different types of experiments are better suited for addressing one type of validity versus another.
9. Distinguish among the various types of test marketing.
10. Think of a job that you have held. List three areas in which you, or some other person in the organization, could have benefited from having information generated by research. What would be the most appropriate research design for each of the three areas of research you have listed?
11. Design an experiment. Select an independent variable and a dependent variable. What are some possible extraneous variables that may cause problems? Explain

how you would control for the effects these variables may have on your dependent variable. Is your experiment a valid experiment?

12. The Maximum Company has invented an extra-strength, instant coffee brand to be called "Max-Gaff" and positioned to be stronger-tasting than any competing brands. Design a taste-test experiment that compares Max-Gaff to the two leading instant coffee brands to determine which brand consumers consider to taste the strongest. Identify and diagram your experiment. Indicate how the experiment is to be conducted, and assess the internal and external validity of your experiment.

13. Coca-Cola markets PowerAde as a sports drink that competes with Gatorade. Competition for sports drinks is fierce where they are sold in the coolers of convenience stores. Coca-Cola is thinking about using a special holder that fits in a standard cooler but moves PowerAde to eye level and makes it more conspicuous than Gatorade. Design an experiment that determines whether the special holder increases the sales of PowerAde in convenience stores. Identify and diagram your experiment. Indicate how the experiment is to be conducted and assess the internal and external validity of your experiment.

14. SplitScreen is a marketing research company that tests television advertisements. SplitScreen has an agreement with a cable television company in a medium-sized city in Iowa. The cable company can send up to four different television ads simultaneously to different households. SplitScreen also has agreements with the three largest grocery store chains, which will provide scanner data to SplitScreen. About 25 percent of the residents have SplitScreen scan cards that are scanned when items are bought at the grocery store and that allow SplitScreen to identify who bought which grocery products. For allowing SplitScreen access to their television hookups and their grocery purchases information, residents receive bonus points that can be used to buy products in a special points catalog. Identify and diagram the true experimental design possible using the SplitScreen system. Assess the internal and external validity of SplitScreen's system.

QUALITY RESEARCH ASSOCIATES

Sam Fulkerson of Quality Research Associates reviewed notes of meetings with his clients during the last week.

Monday/A.M. Discussion with Janey Dean, Director of Marketing for the Hamptons Bank. Dean is interested in knowing more about a bank image study. Informed her that we had not conducted such a study but that I would meet with her in a week and discuss how to proceed. Dean wants to hire us for advice; her own staff may actually do the image study. Next meeting set for 15th at 2:30pm.

Tuesday/P.M. Met with Cayleigh Rogers, Business Manager for Wesleyan College. College is considering a football team and the president wants some indication from alums if they favor it and if they would be willing to send a donation to help with start-up costs. The president of the college also wants to know if present students will support a football team. Call him back for follow up meeting.

Wednesday/A.M. Met with Lawrence Brown of M&M Mars. Brown is brand manager for a new candy bar, and he needs advice on promotional methods in the candy bar business. Specifically, he would like to know what promotional methods have been used over the past five years by candy bar brands and how those promotions had an impact on sales. Advised Brown I would contact some other research suppliers and get back to him.

Wednesday/P.M. Tom Greer visited office. Tom also with M&M Mars. Company interested in going into cereal line and wants information fast on how consumers will react to candy-flavored cereal company has developed. Company's own taste tests have been favorable, but Greer wants reaction from a larger sample of consumers from around the country. Would like this information within a month. Important: Company already has the samples ready for mailing.

Thursday/A.M. Meeting with Phyllis Detrick of McBride's Markets. McBride has a chain of 150 supermarkets in eight states. Company is spending several million dollars a year on advertising. Detrick wants to know what she can do with the advertising copy and layout of the ads that will generate the most attention. She conducted some exploratory research and found that potential consumers who were reading the paper don't recall seeing the McBride ads. Specifically, she wants to know if adding color is worth the expense. Will color ads generate greater attention? We set up joint meeting with the McBride Advertising Manager, who will bring in all of their newspaper ads for the past 6 months.

Thursday/P.M. Meeting with Carolyn Phillips, French Yarbrough, and Jeff Rogers. All three are part of a start-up company that has been working on a new toothbrush storage and sanitation device. The new product steam sanitizes the toothbrushes overnight to make them virtually germ-free. Two years ago we conducted exploratory research in the form of focus groups. We followed that up with a survey of a representative sample of households within the city. The survey showed the respondents a picture of the device and asked them if they would be willing to pay $x to buy it. Thus far, all had gone well and all studies indicated "go." Now, Phillips, Yarbrough, and Rogers think they are ready to introduce the product to the country. They have had several discussions with large retail chains. All of the chain buyers are interested, but they want more evidence that the market will accept the devices. One chain buyer said "I want to know if people will walk in our stores and buy these off the shelf." Also, Phillips, Yarbrough, and Rogers have narrowed their national promotion campaigns down to two choices but they aren't certain which one will gain them the most customers.

Friday/A.M. No client meetings. Work on research designs.

1. What research design do you think Sam Fulkerson should select for each of his clients?
2. For each research design you specify in question 1, describe the reason(s) you selected it.

THE HOBBIT'S CHOICE: RESEARCH DESIGN

In the case presented to you in Chapter 4 we learned that Jeff Dean had a second meeting with Cory Rogers at CMG Research. After the first meeting Cory had conducted some research on the restaurant business. He had learned about tracking food costs, table turnover rates, and financial ratios and operating expense norms for restaurants. In addition, Cory had ordered a marketing research report on upscale restaurants.

We also learned that some of the critical issues centered around the following: (a) determining demand, (b) determining the best choice of restaurant design and operating characteristics, (c) determining where to locate the restaurant, and (d) determining how to promote The Hobbit's Choice restaurant.

1. What type of research design did Cory Rogers use to be prepared for the second meeting with his client, Jeff Dean? What are some methods that he likely used?

2. Consider the second paragraph at the start of the case, which refers to the critical issues in the case. Would exploratory research be the most appropriate research design to choose, given the research objectives that would be generated, to provide the information necessary to resolve these issues? Explain why or why not.

3. If you elected not to use exploratory research design in question 2, which of the two remaining research designs would be more appropriate—descriptive or causal? Select one and provide the rationale for your choice.

4. How does selection of the research design you chose in question 3 aid Cory Rogers in planning the research project for The Hobbit's Choice restaurant?

Using Secondary Data and Online Information Databases

Secondary Data Add Value to Primary Data

As you will learn in this chapter, one of the advantages of secondary data is that they often add additional insights to reports containing primary data. Robert D. Aaron is president and cofounder of Aaron/Smith Associates, Inc., an Atlanta-based research and information services firm. Mr. Aaron says that many marketing researchers are being asked by their clients to provide more than just the results of a primary data survey or focus group. So in addition to designing questionnaires, collecting data, and analyzing the numbers, marketing researchers need to be able to add value to their own results by including information that originates from outside their organization. Secondary data is a good way to add value to marketing research reports. You can find secondary data on your own or order it from firms like MarketResearch.com.

Aaron states that with the proliferation of online databases, it is relatively easy to enhance primary research with secondary data without ever leaving your desk. Integrating secondary and primary research allows the market researcher to provide a much broader and higher-quality product that meets more of the information user's needs. Aaron suggests that researchers can find much more usable information if they do the proper research of secondary data sources. He makes some suggestions for how to go about this:

Do Your Secondary Research Homework in the Beginning of the Project. Many researchers, when they take on a new client, have to learn about an industry and

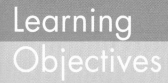

There are firms that specialize in providing clients with secondary data. Go to **www.marketresearch.com** and see how managers can find secondary information on almost any topic. By permission, MarketResearch.com.

its issues. With this information you can go to your clients with your own independent understanding of the problem, not just the one they give you.

Secondary Research Can Help You Design Your Research Objectives and Questions. The issues that come up in the published literature are often the same kinds of issues that you will be asking questions about.

Put Your Primary Data in Context. Your results may be similar to those obtained by others who have reported their findings in publications or press releases. Compare and contrast findings in the secondary research literature with your new primary data findings.

Adding information to your report will add value. External information, in the form of secondary data, provides a context for your results. Even if it is information that is already known to your client, it is often very useful to summarize information from a few well-known sources before launching into a discussion of your own findings. It provides a starting place, and it lends credibility to your report, says Aaron.

By permission, Robert D. Aaron, Aaron/Smith Associates.

Marketing researcher Robert D. Aaron demonstrates the importance of secondary data and online databases to marketing researchers. As he points out above, even when the project involves collecting primary data, marketing researchers should first consult secondary data. He also points out how online information databases have made this task much easier for the researcher. In this chapter you will learn how to distinguish secondary data from primary data. We will illustrate the usefulness of secondary data and discuss how it may be classified. We will introduce you to the advantages and disadvantages of secondary data. We will then introduce you to some strategies for effectively and efficiently searching for secondary data, including strategies for searching online information databases. Finally, we point out some of the most important secondary data sources for marketing researchers.[1]

SECONDARY DATA

Primary Versus Secondary Data

Primary data refers to information that is developed or gathered by the researcher specifically for the research project at hand.

Secondary data have previously been gathered by someone other than the researcher and/or for some purpose other than the research project at hand.

As presented in Chapter 3, data needed for marketing management decisions can be grouped into two types: primary and secondary. **Primary data** refers to information that is developed or gathered by the researcher specifically for the research project at hand. **Secondary data** have previously been gathered by someone other than the researcher and/or for some purpose other than the research project at hand. As commercial firms, government agencies, or community service organizations record transactions and business activities, they are creating a written record of these activities in the form of secondary data. When consumers fill out warranty cards, register their boats, automobiles, or software programs, this information is stored in the form of secondary data. It is available for someone else's secondary use. The evolution of the Internet has done more to bring fast and easy access of secondary data to end users than anything since the Gutenberg press. Since the mid-1980s virtually all documents have been electronically produced, edited, stored, and made accessible to users. For several years firms have concentrated on bringing this information to users through specialized services. Today many of these firms offer these services via the Internet. Although some services are available only through a subscription, the Internet provides an incredible stock of free secondary data. Yet, with all the information available to Internet users today, this will likely be viewed as very primitive when Internet2 becomes widely available. Some compare the information highway today to what Internet2 will offer as similar to how a cart path compares to an eight-lane superhighway![2] We think secondary data access through the Internet, another form of online research, will continue to grow and become more and more important in the marketing researcher's toolbox.

Secondary data access through the Internet, another form of online research, will continue to grow and become more and more important in the marketing researcher's toolbox.

Uses of Secondary Data

There are so many uses of secondary data that it is rare for a marketing research project to be conducted without including some secondary data. Some projects may be totally based on secondary data.

There are so many uses of secondary data that it is rare for a marketing research project to be conducted without including some secondary data. Some projects may be totally based on secondary data. The applications of secondary data range from predicting very broad changes in a culture's "way of life" to very specific applications such as selecting a street address location for a new car wash. Decision Analyst, Inc., a marketing research firm, has a Web site devoted entirely to secondary data. Suggested applications include economic trends forecasting, insights on industries, corporate intelligence, international data, public opinion, and historical data, among others. Marketers are very interested in knowing secondary data in terms of demographic data to help them forecast the size of the market in a newly proposed market territory. A researcher may use secondary data to determine the population and growth rate in almost any geographical area. Government agencies are interested in knowing secondary data to help them make public policy decisions. The Department of Education needs to know how many 5-year-olds will enter the public school system next year. Health-care planners need to know how many senior citizens will be eligible for Medicare during the next decade. Sometimes secondary data can be used to evaluate market performance. For example, since gasoline and fuel taxes collected per gallon are available in public records, petroleum marketers can easily

Go to www.secondarydata.com at Decision Analyst, Inc. to see the many uses of secondary data for marketing research

Decision Analyst, Inc. provides a Web site giving you access to secondary data that may be useful for marketing research projects.

Decision Analyst, Inc.

determine the volume of fuels consumed in a county. Articles are written on virtually every topic, and this storehouse of secondary data is available to marketers who want to understand a topic more thoroughly even though they themselves may not have first-hand experience. Much secondary data are available concerning the lifestyles, including purchasing habits, of demographic groups. Since these demographic groups tend to make similar purchases and have similar attitudes, they have been scrutinized by marketers. The most significant of these demographic groups for decades has been the "baby-boomer" population, defined as those born between 1946 and 1964. As the "boomers" enter mid and senior age status, other demographic groups, such as the Gen Xers, are also studied by marketers. Our Marketing Research Insight 6.1 illustrates how secondary data on demographic groups are important to marketers.

MARKETING RESEARCH INSIGHT   **PRACTICAL INSIGHTS**

6.1

Are You Watching Ozzie Osbourne with Your Parents? You May Be a Gen Yer!

Much secondary marketing research seeks demographic information. Derived from the Greek word *demos*, "demographics" refers to the study of the population. Normally included are population size, density, growth, income, ethnic background, housing, and retail sales, among other factors. Demographic analysis based on age offers many insights into the marketplace and it is highly predictable. We know today how many 16-year-olds there will be in 2021! For many decades marketers have followed baby boomers, persons born from 1946 to 1964. Boomers make up a large percentage of the population, and their demands in the marketplace have followed them through the years. In the 1950s there was a huge demand for schools to educate boomers coming of school age. Textbooks, Boy and Girl Scout uniforms, and toys experienced high growth rates. Rock and roll replaced Frank Sinatra, Perry Como, and Dean Martin when the young boomers reached their teens. The recording industry faced a large market of boomers between 12 and 18 years of age who wanted an alternative to their parents' preferences for Big Band and crooner music. Elvis Presley met the demands of this new market better than anyone else.

Indeed, one could argue that if it hadn't been for the young boomers demanding a change in music, Elvis would have had a normal life driving a truck in Memphis. As the boomers aged, they created unprecedented, but predictable demands on colleges and universities, the job market, housing, recreation, and now, retirement- and health-related goods and services.

There is a new force in demographics. Gen Y represents a group almost as large as the boomers and is expected to be as powerful as a shaper of business decisions in the future. Though there is some disagreement among demographers as to the exact size, most agree that Gen Yers represent the 72 million Americans born between 1977 and 1994. The estimated spending income of this group is $187 billion annually. But, unlike the Boomers, Gen Yers may prove to be the most unpredictable and marketing-resistant group known to U.S. marketers. With many in their early 20s, a large percentage of Gen Yers are still living at home with their parents. They shun traditional media in preference for video games, DVDs, and Web sites.

Because Gen Yers represent such a large population and still influence their younger counterparts, marketers are keenly interested in them. Honda tried to target them with its Element, which they positioned as a "dorm room

(continued)

on wheels." Chrysler did the same with its PT Cruiser. Gen Yers were not impressed. Both cars sold, but to a much older market. Gen Yers, however, are predictable when it comes to technology. They are heavy users of all forms of technology. Cell-phone manufacturers are watching Gen Yers closely to identify hot new trends for the rest of the market. Cell phones featuring video and speaker attachments are already on the market. Jupiter Research reports that 18- to 24-year-olds spend an average of 10 hours a week online, 10 hours watching TV, and 5 hours listening to the radio. They also spend considerably more time online messaging, playing games, and downloading music than their older counterparts.

Gen Yers, having been exposed to 3000 marketing messages a day (making some 23 million in their lives thus far), are immune to traditional advertising. One advertiser said that when you do a focus group with 21-year-olds, they tell you the advertiser's strategy. In other words, they see right through the ads. Instead of viewing ads for information, as the boomers do, they view them for entertainment. Advertisers, to get their attention, must make the ads entertaining, using word-of-mouth and stealth marketing.

Gen Yers are viewed as being a powerful force in the market today. They not only influence their younger siblings, but, surprisingly, they influence their boomer parents. MTV reports, for example, that parents are watching rocker Ozzie Osbourne and his family right along with their Gen Y kids! Marketers will rely heavily on secondary data to track Gen Yers in the years ahead.

Source: Portions adapted from Weiss, M. J. (2003, September 1). To be or not to be. *American Demographics*. Retrieved from LexisNexis on October 30, 2003.

CLASSIFICATION OF SECONDARY DATA

Since so much secondary information is available, every marketing researcher must learn to properly manage these data. However, the stock of information available can be overwhelming. Marketing researchers must learn to properly handle secondary data. They must know the classifications of secondary data as well as the advantages and disadvantages, and they must know how to evaluate the information available to them.

Internal Secondary Data

Internal secondary data are data that have been collected within the firm. Such data include sales records, purchase requisitions, and invoices.

Secondary data may be broadly classified as either internal or external. **Internal secondary data** are data that have been collected within the firm. Such data include sales records, purchase requisitions, and invoices. Obviously, a good marketing researcher always determines what internal information is already available. You may recall from Chapter 1 that we referred to internal data analysis as being part of the internal reports system of a firm's marketing information system (MIS). Today a major source of internal data is databases that contain information on customers, sales, suppliers, and any other facet of business a firm may wish to track. Kotler defines **database marketing** as the process of building, maintaining, and using customer (*internal*) databases and other (*internal*) databases (products, suppliers, resellers) for the purpose of contacting, transacting, and building relationships (italics added).[3] The use of internal databases has grown dramatically for several years.

Internal Databases

A database refers to a collection of data and information describing items of interest to the database owner.

Before we discuss internal and external databases, we should understand that a **database** refers to a collection of data and information describing items of interest.[4] Each unit of information in a database is called a **record**. A record could represent a customer, a supplier, a competitive firm, a product, an individual inventory item, and so on. Records are composed of subcomponents of information called **fields**. As an example, a company having a database of customers would have *records* representing each customer. Typical *fields* in a customer database would include name, address, telephone number, e-mail address, products purchased, dates of purchases, locations where purchased, warranty information, and any other information the company thought was important. Although you can have a noncomputerized database, the majority of databases are computerized because they contain large amounts of information and their use is facilitated by computer capability to edit, sort, and analyze the mass of information.

> Databases are composed of records that represent a unit of information. Subcomponents of information in records are called "fields."

 Internal databases are databases consisting of information gathered by a company during the normal course of business transactions. Marketing managers normally develop internal databases about customers, but databases may be kept on any topic of interest, such as products, members of the sales force, inventory, maintenance, and supplier firms. Companies gather information about customers when they inquire about a product or service, make a purchase, or have a product serviced. Think about the information you may have provided to marketing firms: your name, address, telephone number, fax number, e-mail address, credit card number, banking institution and account number, and so on. Coupled with a knowledge of what products you have purchased in the past and with other information provided by government and other commercial sources, many companies know quite a bit about you. Companies use their internal databases for purposes of direct marketing and to strengthen relationships with customers called **CRM, customer relationship management**.[5]

> Internal databases, built with information collected during the normal course of business, can provide invaluable insights for managers.

 Internal databases can be quite large. Dealing with the vast quantities of data has been a problem with managing information from internal databases. **Data mining** is the name for software that is now available to help managers make sense out of seemingly senseless masses of information contained in databases.[6] However, even simple databases in small businesses can be invaluable. One study showed that almost half of retail firms have some sort of database containing information about their customers.[7]

 Databases can tell managers which products are selling, report inventories, and profile customers by stock keeping unit (SKU). Coupled with geodemographic information systems (GIS), databases can provide maps indicating ZIP codes in which the most profitable and least profitable customers reside. Internal databases, built with information collected during the normal course of business, can provide invaluable insights for managers. We shall discuss GIS more completely in the next chapter.

 What companies do with information collected for their internal databases can present ethical problems. Should your credit card company share the information on what types of goods and services you bought with anyone who wants to buy that information? Should your Internet service provider be able to store information on which Internet sites you visit? As more consumers have grown aware of these privacy issues, more companies have adopted privacy policies.[8]

> What companies do with information collected in their internal databases can present ethical problems.

External Secondary Data

▶ **Published Sources. External secondary data** are data obtained from outside the firm. We classify external data into three sources: (1) published, (2) syndicated services data, and (3) databases. **Published sources** are those sources of information that are prepared for public distribution and are normally found in libraries or through a variety of other entities such as trade associations, professional organizations, or companies. Published sources are available in a number of formats, including print, CD-ROM, and online via the Internet. Many publications that were formerly available in print only are becoming available in electronic format. Magazines available electronically are called

> Published sources are those sources of information that are prepared for public distribution and are normally found in libraries or through a variety of other entities.

e-zines; journals are called e-journals. Published sources of secondary information come from the government (*Census of the Population*), nonprofit organizations (chambers of commerce, colleges and universities), trade and professional associations (CASRO, AMA, IMRO, MRA), and for-profits (*Sales & Marketing Management* magazine, Prentice Hall, McGraw-Hill, and research firms). Many research firms publish secondary information in the form of books, newsletters, white papers, or special reports.

> **Understanding the functions of the different types of publications can help you find the secondary data you need.**

The sheer volume of published sources makes searching this type of secondary data difficult. However, understanding the functions of the different types of publications can be of great help to you in successfully searching published secondary information sources. Table 6.1 depicts the different types of publications and gives you their function as well as an example.

Today many libraries enter their holdings of books and other publications in electronic records whose fields are searchable electronically. These electronic libraries allow researchers to search secondary data quickly, conveniently, inexpensively, and thoroughly. Most electronic libraries have information available in two broad categories: catalogs and indexes. A **catalog** consists of a list of a library's holdings of books. (Catalogs sometimes also list the periodicals to which the library subscribes.) Therefore, catalogs are useful for finding *books* by subject, author, title, date of publication, or publisher. **Indexes** are records compiled from periodicals and contain information on the contents of periodicals recorded in fields such as author, title, keywords, date of publication, name of periodical, and so on. Sometimes an index contains the entire contents of the periodical (called full-text indexes). Such indexes are not normally constructed by a library. Rather, they are provided by companies that make them available to libraries or other organizations. We shall talk more about these when we discuss online information databases.

> **A catalog consists of a list of a library's holdings of books.**

> **Indexes are records compiled from periodicals and contain information on the contents of periodicals recorded in fields such as author, title, keywords, date of publication, name of periodical, and so on.**

▶ **Syndicated Services Data. Syndicated services data** are provided by firms that collect data in a standard format and make them available to subscribing firms. Such data are typically highly specialized and are not available in libraries for the general public. The suppliers syndicate (sell) the information to multiple subscribers, thus making the costs more reasonable to any one subscriber. Examples include Arbitron's radio listenership data, Nielsen Media Research's Television Rating Index, and Information Resources, Inc.'s InfoScan report of products sold in retail stores. In all these cases, these firms supply subscribing firms with external secondary data. We devote more attention to syndicated data services firms in Chapter 7.

> **Syndicated services data are provided by firms that collect data in a standard format and make them available to subscribing firms. Such data are typically highly specialized and are not available in libraries for the general public.**

▶ **External Databases. External databases** are databases supplied by organizations outside the firm. They may be used as sources for secondary data. Some of these databases are available in printed format but, in recent years, many databases are now available online. **Online information databases** are sources of secondary data searchable by search engines online. Some online databases are available free of charge and are supplied as a service by a host organization. However, many online information databases are available from commercial sources that provide subscribers password (or IP address identification) access for a fee. These databases have grown dramatically since the 1980s. During the 1990s and early 2000s many of the companies supplying external databases of secondary data have merged. We have fewer companies, but each one is much larger, with the larger firms offering subscribers access to billions of records of information. Different databases are often packaged together by vendors that produce the software that retrieves the information. Sometimes called "aggregators" or "databanks," these services or vendors may offer a wide variety of indexes, directories, and statistical and full-text files all searched by the same search logic. Such services include Factiva, Gale Group, ProQuest, First Search, LexisNexis, and Dialog, among others. Business databases comprise a significant proportion of these databanks.

> **External databases are databases supplied by organizations outside the firm, and they may be used as sources for secondary data.**

> **Online information databases are sources of secondary data searchable by search engines online. Examples include Factiva, Lexis-Nexis, ProQuest, and Gale Group.**

TABLE 6.1	Understanding the Function of Different Types of Publications Can Make You a Better User of Secondary Data

1. Reference Guides

Function: Refer to *types* of other reference sources and recommended specific titles. Guides tell you where to look to find different types of information.

Example: *Encyclopedia of Business Information Sources.* Detroit: Gale Group, 1970–Present

2. Indexes and Abstracts

Function: List periodical articles by subject, author, title, keyword, etc. Abstracts also provide summaries of the articles. Indexes allow you to search for periodicals by the topic of your research.

Example: *ABI/Inform.* Ann Arbor, MI: Proquest. 1971–present

3. Bibliographies

Function: Lists varied sources such as books, journals, etc. on a particular topic. Tell you what is available, in several sources, on a topic.

Example: *Recreation and Entertainment Industries, an Information Source Book.* Jefferson, NC: Macfarland, 2000

4. Almanacs, Manuals, and Handbooks

Function: These types of sources are "deskbooks" that provide a wide variety of data in a single handy publication.

Example: *Wall Street Journal Almanac.* New York: Ballantine Books. Annual.

5. Dictionaries

Function: Define terms and are sometimes available for special subject areas.

Example: *Concise Dictionary of Business Management.* New York: Routledge, 1999

6. Encyclopedias

Function: Provide essays, usually in alphabetical order, by topic.

Example: *Encyclopedia of Busine$$ and Finance.* New York: Macmillan, 2001

7. Directories

Function: List companies, people, products, organizations, etc. usually providing brief information about each entry.

Example: *Career Guide: Dun's Employment Opportunities Directory.* Parsippany, NJ: Dun's Marketing Services. Annual.

8. Statistical Sources

Function: Provide numeric data, often in tables, pie charts, and bar charts.

Example: *Handbook of U.S. Labor Statistics.* Lanham, MD: Bernan Press. Annual

9. Biographical Sources

Function: Provide information about people. Useful for information on CEOs, etc.

Example: *D&B Reference Book of Corporate Management.* Bethlehem, PA: Dun & Bradstreet, 2001

10. Legal Sources

Function: Provide information about legislation, regulations, and case law.

Example: *United States Code.* Washington, DC: Government Printing Office

ADVANTAGES OF SECONDARY DATA

Obtained Quickly

There are five main advantages of using secondary data. First, it can be obtained quickly, in contrast to collecting primary data, which may take several months from beginning to end. You can go to the Internet and quickly find a great deal of secondary data at no expense.

The five advantages of secondary data are that secondary data can be obtained quickly and inexpensively, are usually available, enhance primary data collection, and can sometimes achieve the research objective.

As illustrated by the Web page of MarketResearch.com at the beginning of the chapter, a manager can quickly obtain reports on almost any topic by using the services of firms like MarketResearch.com. By permission, MarketResearch.com.

Inexpensive Relative to Primary Data

Second, collecting secondary data is inexpensive when compared with collecting primary data. Though there are certainly costs for collecting secondary data, these costs are but a fraction of the costs for collecting primary data. Primary data collection is seldom achieved without spending at least a few thousand dollars and, depending on the research objective, hundreds of thousands or even millions of dollars. Even purchasing secondary data from commercial vendors is inexpensive relative to primary data.

Secondary Data Are Usually Available

A third advantage of secondary data is that they are usually available. No matter what the problem area may be, someone, somewhere has probably dealt with it, and some information is available that will help the researcher in his or her task. Availability is one reason that many predict secondary data will grow in importance in marketing research applications. Not only is the amount of data growing but the ability to search billions of records to find the right data is improving with computer technology.

Secondary Data Enhance Primary Data

As our chapter-opening vignette describes, secondary data enhances existing primary data. Simply because researchers use secondary data does not mean that they will not collect primary data. In fact, in almost every case, the researcher's task of primary data collection is aided by first collecting secondary data. A secondary data search can familiarize the researcher with the industry, including its sales and profit trends, major competitors, and the significant issues facing the industry.[9] A secondary data search can identify concepts, data, and terminology that may be useful in conducting primary research. A bank's management, for example, hired a marketing research firm; together, management and the research team decided to conduct a survey measuring the bank's image among its customers. A check of the secondary information available on the measurement of bank image identified the components of bank image for the study. Also, the research team, after reviewing secondary information, determined there were three sets of bank customers: retail customers, commercial accounts, and other correspondent banks. When the researchers mentioned this to bank management, the original objectives of the primary research were changed in order to measure the bank's image among all three customer groups.

Secondary Data May Achieve the Research Objective

Finally, not only are secondary data faster to obtain, more convenient to use, and less expensive to gather than primary research, but they also may achieve the research objective! For example, a supermarket chain marketing manager wants to allocate TV ad dollars to the 12 TV markets in which the chain owns supermarkets. A quick review of secondary data will show him or her that retail sales on food is available by TV market area. Allocating the TV budget based on the percentage of food sales in a given market would be an excellent way to solve the manager's problem and satisfy the research objective.

DISADVANTAGES OF SECONDARY DATA

Although the advantages of secondary data almost always justify a search of this information, there are caveats associated with secondary data. Five of the problems associated with secondary data include incompatible reporting units, mismatch of the units of measurement, differing definitions used to classify the data, the timeliness of the secondary data, and the lack of information needed to assess the credibility of the data reported. These problems exist because secondary data have not been collected specifically to address the problem at hand but have been collected for some other purpose. Consequently, the researcher must determine the extent of these problems before using the secondary data. This is done by evaluating the secondary data. We discuss the first four disadvantages in the following paragraphs. Evaluation of secondary data is discussed in the next section.

Incompatible Reporting Units

Secondary data are provided in reporting units such as county, city, metro area or metropolitan statistical area (MSA), state, region, ZIP code, and so on. A researcher's use of secondary data often depends on whether the reporting unit matches the researcher's need. For example, a researcher wishing to evaluate market areas for the purpose of consideration for expansion may be pleased with data reported at the county level. A great deal of secondary data are available at the county level. But, what if another marketer wishes to evaluate a two-mile area around a street address that is proposed as a site location for a retail store? County data would hardly be adequate. Another marketer wishes to know the demographic makeup of each ZIP code in a major city in order to determine which ZIP codes to target for a direct mail campaign. Again, county data would be inappropriate. While inappropriate reporting units are often problems in using secondary data, more and more data are available today in multiple reporting units. Data at the ZIP +4 level are becoming more widely available. Also, as we will see in the next chapter, GIS offers marketers access to data in arbitrarily defined reporting units. The latter would be very useful for the marketer wishing to know the demographics within a two-mile ring around a street address. Nevertheless, sometimes secondary data are available, but in the wrong reporting unit.

> Secondary data are provided in reporting units such as county, MSA, state, region, ZIP code, and so on. A researcher's use of secondary data often depends on whether the reporting unit matches the researcher's need.

Measurement Units Do Not Match

Sometimes secondary data are reported in measurement units that do not match the measurement unit needed by the researcher. In analyzing markets, for example, marketing researchers are typically interested in income levels. Available studies of income may measure income in several ways: total income, income after taxes, household income, and per-capita income. Or consider a research project that needs to categorize businesses by size in terms of square footage. Secondary data sources, however, classify businesses in terms of size according to sales volume, number of employees, profit level, and so on. Much information in the United States is recorded in American units of measurement (feet, pounds, etc.), yet most of the rest of the world uses metric units (meter, kilograms, etc.). The United States is slowly becoming metric.[10]

> Sometimes measurement units reported in secondary data do not match the unit needed by the researcher. For example, income is reported as per capita instead of per household.

Class Definitions Are Not Usable

The class definitions of the reported data may not be usable to a researcher. Secondary data are often reported by breaking a variable into different classes and reporting the frequency of occurrence in each class. For example, the "Survey of Buying Power"

> Secondary data are often reported by breaking a variable into different classes and reporting the frequency of occurrence in each class. Sometimes the classes reported are not useful for the researcher's purpose.

reports the variable, effective buying income (EBI), in three classes. The first class reports the percentage of households having an EBI between $20,000 and $34,999, and the final class reports the percentage of households having an EBI of $50,000 and over. For most studies, these classifications are applicable. However, it is doubtful that Beneteau, Inc., a manufacturer of sailing yachts in South Carolina, could use these income classifications to help it target potential customer markets. Because Beneteau's average customer is thought to have an EBI in excess of $75,000, Beneteau could not use the data reported because of the way the EBI classes were defined. What does the researcher do? Typically, if you keep looking you can find what you need. For example, Beneteau can obtain secondary data that would solve its problem by purchasing *Demographics USA*, by the same publishers of the "Survey of Buying Power." It would find that *Demographics USA* provides information on EBI up through categories of $150,000 or more.[11]

Data Are Outdated

Sometimes, the "right" secondary data are found but it is dated. Researchers must always decide if they should use out-dated secondary data.

Sometimes a marketing researcher will find information reported with the desired unit of measurement and the proper classifications, however, the *data are "out-of-date."* Some secondary data are published only once. However, even for secondary data that are published at regular intervals, the time that passed since the last publication can be a problem when applying the data to a current problem. Ultimately, the researcher must make the decision as to whether or not to use the data.

EVALUATING SECONDARY DATA

Hopefully, you have learned that not everything you read is true. In order to properly use secondary data, you must evaluate that information before you use it as a basis for making decisions. A reader must be most cautious when using an Internet source because few quality standards are applied to most Internet sites. To determine the reliability of secondary information, marketing researchers must evaluate it. This is done by answering the following five questions:

- What was the purpose of the study?
- Who collected the information?
- What information was collected?
- How was the information obtained?
- How consistent is the information with other information?[12]

A discussion of each question follows.

What Was the Purpose of the Study?

Studies are conducted for a purpose. Unfortunately, studies are sometimes conducted in order to "prove" some position or to advance the special interest of those conducting the study. Many years ago, chambers of commerce were known for publishing data that exaggerated the size and growth rates of their communities. They did this to "prove" that their communities were a good choice for new business locations. However, after a few years, they learned that few people trusted chamber data, and today chambers of commerce publish reliable and valid data. But the lesson is that you must be very careful to determine whether the entity publishing the data acted in a fair and unbiased manner. Consider the example of disposable diapers. The disposable diaper industry was created in the 1960s. Environmental concerns became alarming as information became available about the forecasts of huge mountains of disposable diapers that would take 50 years to decompose. Consequently, during the late 1980s, the number of customers buying old-fashioned cloth diapers doubled. Also, more than a dozen state legislatures were considering various bans, taxes, and even warning labels on disposable diapers. Then "research studies" were produced on the environmental effects of disposable versus cloth diapers. It seemed that the "new" research proved that cloth diapers, by adding detergent by-products to the water table, were more harmful to the environment than the ever-lasting plastic disposables! Soon after several of these studies were made available to legislators, the movement against disposables was dead. Who conducted the studies? Procter & Gamble. P&G, owning the lion's share of the market for disposable diapers, commissioned the consulting firm of Arthur D. Little, Inc. to conduct a study of disposable versus cloth diapers. The study found that disposable diapers were no more harmful to the environment than reusable cotton diapers. Another favorable study for the disposables was conducted by Franklin Associates, whose research showed disposables were not any more harmful than cloth diapers. But who sponsored this study? The American Paper Institute, an organization with major interests in disposable diapers. But wait, before you become too critical of the disposable diaper folks, let's consider some other "scientific" studies. In 1988, a study was published that showed disposable diapers as being "garbage" and contributing to massive buildups of waste that was all but impervious to deterioration. Who sponsored this study? The cloth diaper industry! Another study published in 1991 found cloth diapers to be environmentally superior to disposable diapers. Guess who sponsored this study? Marketing Research Application 6.2 provides us with more examples that illustrate why it is important for you to know the true purpose behind secondary data.

Who Collected the Information?

Even when you are convinced that there is no bias in the purpose of the study, you should question the competence of the organization that collected the information. Why? Simply because organizations differ in terms of the resources they command and their quality control. But how do you determine the competency of the organization that collected the data? First, ask others who have more experience in a given industry. Typically, creditable organizations are well known in those industries for which they conduct studies. Second, examine the report itself. Competent firms will almost always provide carefully written and detailed explanations of the procedures and methods used in collecting the information contained in the report. Third, contact previous clients of the firm. Have they been satisfied with the quality of the work performed by the organization?

> Research studies are often published and become part of secondary data. However, not all research studies are conducted in a totally objective manner. You must ask who conducted the study.

What Information Was Collected?

There are many studies available on topics such as economic impact, market potential, feasibility, and the like. But what exactly was measured in these studies that constitutes impact, potential, or feasibility? There are many examples of studies that claim to provide information on a specific subject but, in fact, measure something quite different. Consider a study conducted by a transit authority on the number of riders on its bus line. On examination of the methods used in the study, the number of riders was not counted at all. Rather, the number of tokens was counted. Since a single rider may use several tokens on a single destination route requiring transfers to other buses, the study overestimated the number of "riders." Or consider a study

> It may be very important to know exactly what was measured in a report before using the results.

MARKETING RESEARCH INSIGHT

ETHICAL ISSUES

6.2

It Ain't Necessarily So!

Many times research studies are reported in secondary data and sometimes what they report "ain't necessarily so," according to authors Murray, Schwartz, and Lichter's book (*It Ain't Necessarily So: How Media Make and Unmake the Scientific Picture of Reality*).[13] These authors illustrate their point by citing a study undertaken by an "activist" group called the Food Research and Action Center whose aim, the authors report, is to highlight the problem of hunger and to increase government spending to fight hunger. The study reported that one out of eight children had gone hungry at some point in the previous year. But the researchers did not measure "hunger" in any direct manner. Instead they used a "proxy" measure of hunger. They measured what people *said* about hunger. (The Census Bureau uses income as a proxy measure of hunger.) Was their measure an accurate one? Even if it were an accurate measure of actual hunger, CBS Network incorrectly reported the results of the study by stating that the study found one in eight American children under the age of 12 is going hungry (tonight). This is a totally different picture than the number of children who reported being hungry in the past year.[14] Other studies report that coffee is associated with disease, whereas others report that coffee prevents disease.[15]

In another book, Cynthia Crossen, a reporter and editor with the *Wall Street Journal*, writes about the truthfulness of research information. Her conclusions were interesting and led her to title the book *Tainted Truth: The Manipulation of Fact in America*.[16] She warns that, even though Americans have a fascination with research information, we must understand that much of the "research" we use to help us to buy, elect, advise, acquit, and heal has been created not to expand our knowledge but to sell a product or advance a cause of the sponsor of the research. Furthermore, if the research results contradict a sponsor's agenda, the results

are routinely suppressed. Crossen gives some compelling evidence for her thesis, including a study that found that 62 percent of Americans want to keep the penny in circulation. The sponsor? The zinc industry (most pennies are made with zinc). Another study found that 70 percent of cellular telephone users reported that the cellular phones made them more successful in business. The sponsor? Motorola. Even studies to test the effectiveness of new drugs are often sponsored by the pharmaceutical company selling the drug! Crossen believes that the explosion of "tainted truth" has come from money. Money is used to "sponsor" (buy) research studies and that even once independent and objective institutions such as universities have given in to the monetary pressures. Few researchers escape the pressures of financial support and they are influenced, whether knowingly or not, by trying to please their financial sponsors. Results can be manipulated by subtle means known to researchers.

Crossen has raised an important ethical issue for the research industry. Are research results totally independent and objective? Crossen's book is one among several that deal with research not being objectively prepared or presented.[17]

Study says Coffee is Good for You! Study says Coffee is Bad for You!

of "advertising effectiveness." How was effectiveness measured? Was it the sales of the product the week after the ad was run? Was it the percentage of consumers who named the brand name the day after the ad was run? Is this distinction important? It may be or it may not be, depending on how the study's user intends to use the information. The important point here is that the user should discover exactly what information was collected!

How Was the Information Obtained?

You should be aware of the methods used to obtain information reported in secondary sources. What was the sample? How large was the sample? What was the response rate? Was the information validated? As you will learn throughout this book, there are many alternative ways of collecting primary data, and each may have an impact on the information collected. Remember that, even though you are evaluating secondary data, this information was gathered as primary data by some organization. Therefore, the alternative ways of gathering the data had an impact on the nature and quality of the data. It is not always easy to find out how the secondary data were gathered. However, as noted earlier, most reputable organizations that provide secondary data also provide information on their data-collection methods. If this information is not readily available and your use of the secondary data is very important to your research project, you should make the extra effort to find out how the information was obtained.

> Evaluate the method used to collect the primary data now available to you as secondary data. You will be much better at doing this when you finish this course.

How Consistent Is the Information with Other Information?

In some cases, the same secondary data are reported by multiple, independent organizations, which provides an excellent way to evaluate secondary data sources. Ideally, if two or more independent organizations report the same data, you can have greater confidence in the validity and reliability of the data. Demographic data, for example, for metropolitan areas (MAs), counties, and most municipalities are widely available from more than one source. If you are evaluating a survey that is supposedly representative of a given geographic area, you may want to compare the characteristics of the sample of the survey with the demographic data available on the population. If you know, based on U.S. census data, that there are 45 percent males and 55 percent females in a city and a survey, which is supposed to be representative of that city, reports a sample of 46 percent males and 54 percent females, then you can be more confident in the survey data. It is indeed rare, however, that two organizations will report exactly the same results. Here you must look at the magnitude of the differences and determine what you should do. If all independent sources report very large differences of the same variable, then you may not have much confidence in any of the data. You should look carefully at what information was collected, how it was collected, and so on for each reporting source. For example, if you were to get the number of businesses in a county from Survey Sampling, Inc. and compare that number to the number of businesses reported by the governmental publication *County Business Patterns* (CBP), you would see a marked difference. Specifically, Survey Sampling's number of businesses would be much larger than the number reported by CBP. Why?[18] The answer is found by asking the questions "What information was actually collected?" and "How was this information obtained?" As it turns out, neither organization actually counts the numbers of businesses in a given area. CBP counts the number of firms submitting payroll information on their employees. Some firms may not report this information and other small firms with "no paid employees" (whose owners are the employees) are excluded from CBP data. Therefore, the CBP surrogate indicator used to count the number of business firms is going to have a downward bias because it does not count all firms. On the other hand, Survey Sampling counts the number of business firms by adding up the number of businesses listed in the Yellow Pages.

This brings up the question, "What is a business firm?" One franchise organization may run the McDonald's in a city, yet the Yellow Pages lists nine locations. Is this one business or nine? Survey Sampling would list this as nine separate businesses. Therefore,

> If two or more sources of secondary data differ you should investigate why they differ. Did they measure the same entity? Did they use different methods to collect their data?

Survey Sampling's estimates of the number of businesses has an upward bias. Which data source should be used? It would depend on the purpose of your study and how the information would be used. Either source of information may be appropriate for use as long as the user understands exactly what the information represents. The key point is that you must adequately evaluate the various data sources so that you are in a position to select the information that will give you the most valid and reliable results.

A final word about evaluating information sources is that you may be able to get some help in terms of evaluations by others. For example, books are often reviewed and those reviews are published. Also, many journals contain articles that are reviewed by editorial board members to assess their quality before publication. Also, journals typically do not accept advertising and, consequently, may be more objective in printing information that may not be favorable to other interests. However, it is far more difficult to evaluate other sources of secondary data such as magazine articles, Web sites, or special reports.

LOCATING SECONDARY DATA SOURCES

How does one go about the actual task of locating secondary data sources? We suggest you follow the approach outlined below.[19]

Step 1. Identify what you wish to know and what you already know about your topic. This is the most important step in searching for information. Without having a clear understanding of what you are seeking, you will undoubtedly have difficulties. Clearly define your topic: relevant facts, names of researchers or organizations associated with the topic, key papers and other publications with which you are already familiar, and any other information you may have.

Step 2. Develop a list of key terms and names. These terms and names will provide access to secondary sources. Unless you already have a very specific topic of interest, keep this initial list long and quite general. Use business dictionaries and handbooks to help develop your list. Be flexible. Every time a new source is consulted, you may have to use a new selection of terms.

In printed sources as well as databases, it is important to use correct terminology to locate the most relevant resources. In many cases, the researcher must think of related terms or synonyms for a topic. For example, one database may use the term *pharmaceutical industry* to describe that industry, whereas another may use the term *drug industry*. In addition, the source may require that a broader term be used. *Pharmaceutical industry* may be listed as part of the *chemical industry*. However, there may be a need to use a narrower term. For example, if one is researching a database on the *drug industry*, it would be foolish to put in the term *drugs* because almost everything in that database would include that term. Perhaps a specific drug may be a wiser choice.

Many databases have lists of the terms or subject headings they assign to records of information, such as books or articles. These lists are called thesauri, dictionaries, or subject headings lists. In most library catalogs the Library of Congress (LC) Subject Headings are used. These are standard (sometimes called "controlled") terms that are consistently used to describe a particular subject. For example, the term *real property* is standard in the LC Subject Headings instead of the term *real estate*. Using a standard subject heading should result in a more efficient search. Marketing Research Insight 6.3 shows you how to find a standard subject heading using *ABI Inform Global*.

Active Learning

USING ONLINE INFORMATION SERVICE DATABASES TO FIND STANDARD SUBJECT HEADINGS

Go to your university's library home page and access the online databases. If your university subscribes to ABI/INFORM Global you can use the example we used in Marketing Research Insight 6.3. Regardless of the database you use, try to find their "standard subject

ONLINE APPLICATION

6.3 Finding a Standard Subject Heading: A Way to Improve Your Information Searching Skills

How many times have you used an online information service database only to end up frustrated that you could not find what you really needed? Problems of two types occur. First, you get thousands of "hits," which requires that you read through huge amounts of information still searching for what you wanted to find in the first place. Second, you get information that has your key search terms contained within the article but the articles do not have anything to do with what you really want. Sound familiar? You need to learn an important skill in searching online information databases: finding the *standard subject heading*.

Imagine that you had several persons who were well trained in evaluating and interpreting the contents of information sources such as books, manuals, special reports, magazine articles, journal articles, and so on. Next, imagine if you had these well-trained persons to look through everything that has been published and to place all the books, articles, reports, and so on that pertained to your topic in one stack. So, you now have all publications on your topic in one category and now imagine that this information is all scanned into an electronic database that you can now search using any one or a combination of search strategies. Wow! Think this would improve your information search skills? The good news is that this has already been done for you. You just need to learn how to take advantage of what we shall call *standard subject headings*.

Databases have a field called the *subject* field. When a new piece of information arrives, be it a book, journal article, or whatever, that information is evaluated to determine its subject matter. For example, let's say there is an article entitled "The Pod Squad." The title can be very misleading. In fact, if someone were doing a search about police *squads* or *iPods*, this article would appear in a results list (along with thousands of other nonrelevant information sources). But why is it misleading? Because the subject of the article is a recent upscale restaurant design phenomenon! If you were interested in finding information about restaurants, chances are you would not find this article using key terms in the title field of your database search engine. But, because those "people who are working for you" have looked over this article and correctly placed it in the category of restaurants, we are going to find it. So, **standard subject headings** are specific words or phrases that are used to properly categorize the subject matter of records as they are entered into databases. Let's see how you would do it using ABI/INFORM Global, a popular online database owned by ProQuest.

In ABI/INFORM Global, you can use the "Basic Search" if you don't really know much about your topic. However basic searches are not very productive if you know enough about your topic to enable you to conduct a more efficient search. In fact, if you enter "restaurant" for a basic search you will get over 75,000 hits! So how do you find a "standard subject heading" in ABI/INFORM Global? First, go to "Advanced Search." Then click on the drop-down menu on the right of the first row where it presently reads "Citation and abstract." (This is referring to the citation and abstract fields of the records in the database.) From the drop menu,

ProQuest

Basic Search	Advanced Search	Topic Guide	Publication Search	Marked List : 0 documents My Research Summary

Databases selected: ABI/INFORM Global

Advanced Search

Tools: Search Tips Browse Topics

		Subject ⌄ Browse subjects
AND ⌄		Citation and abstract ⌄
AND ⌄		Citation and abstract ⌄

Add a row | Remove a row   [Search] [Clear]

(continued)

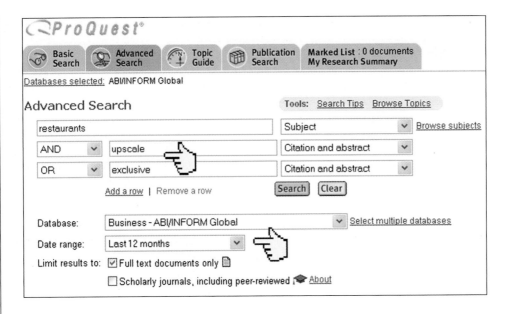

select the "Subject" field. You will then see a new choice on the right—"Browse Subjects." Click "Browse Subjects" and this opens a dialogue box that allows you to enter the words that you suspect may identify the predetermined subject category—what we call a "standard subject heading." Experiment by entering "upscale dining" or "upscale restaurants." You will find that these are NOT standard subject headings but you will find that "restaurants" is a standard subject heading!

If you conduct this search you will find that you have discovered ALL records in the database that have something to do with restaurants even though they may not have "restaurant" in the title, citation, or abstract. Your "standard subject heading" has allowed you to find this set of articles. But, you still have a problem; there are over 26,000 hits!! So, we need to narrow the search and "drill down" to find the articles we are truly interested in. What are other terms that will help you narrow your search?

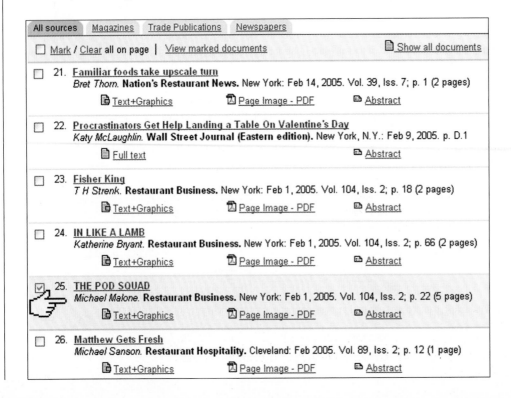

Aren't we interested in "upscale" OR "exclusive" restaurants? We can add these terms to the search by entering them in the next two rows as shown below. But, wait! Before we conduct this search, are we really interested in what was going on 5 or 10 years ago? No, we want current articles. So we can *limit* records by setting the "Date Range" to "Last 12 months." Also, we only want full articles to read so we can also limit our search to "Full text Documents Only."

Now we are really becoming better information searchers! We have "drilled down" to 93 hits, and many of these articles will be relevant; that is, they will help us learn a lot more about upscale, exclusive restaurants. Note

that one of the hits we got is "The Pod Squad," which is not recognizable as an article about restaurants, much less upscale or exclusive restaurants.

Although this is just one database from several hundred, a good researcher learns to look for lists of standard subject headings whether they are called thesaurus terms, subject headings or terms. It is also important to check all guide screens and instructions that are made available by each database. Notice that in the preceding example ABI/INFORM Global gives you "Search Tips" under "Tools." You will become a much better information searcher if you study those tips before you search. Happy searching!

heading" list. As we stated previously, standard subject headings are called different things depending on the database. In some they are called "thesauri" and in others they are listed under "dictionaries." They may have the name "subject" associated with them as we saw in ABI/INFORM Global. You may have to enter a search for the "subject" field in order to find the standard subject headings. What's the best way to discover how to find them? Read those "search tips"! Think of a term paper you must write, or perhaps you are working on the Hobbit's Choice case in this textbook, or maybe you are just interested in knowing more about a particular topic. Read Marketing Research Insight 6.3 first and make sure you understand the concept of "standard subject headings." Next, access an online database and conduct a search using the standard subject heading that best represents your search topic.

If you do the search we did in Marketing Research Insight 6.3, make sure you take a look at the article "The Pod Squad." Pretty interesting idea, isn't it? Do you think it would work in the Hobbit's Choice restaurant?

Keyword searching is usually available for searching a database, but using a keyword often retrieves too many false results. A keyword search means that the computer will retrieve a record that has that word anywhere in the record. For example, if someone is searching for the word *banks*, it could be the name of a person, a business, a type of bank, a bank of dirt (hill), or any other use of that word. Sometimes to avoid false results the searcher may simply want to search one field in the record, as described later in "Field Searching." Keywords may also be used to lead one to better terms to use. If one retrieves a long list of sources, it is wise to select an item that is relevant and examine its record to identify the standard subject heading assigned to that item. Submitting that subject heading should retrieve a much more relevant list of sources. (See Marketing Research Insight 6.3.)

Step 3. Begin your search using several of the library sources, such as those listed in Table 6.2. If you need help in selecting the appropriate sources or databases, refer to Table 6.1 and review the functions of different types of publications.

Search Strategies Used for Searching Online Information Databases

To better understand how to search online databases, the researcher should understand how databases are organized. A common vendor, also known as an aggregator or databank, may provide many databases. For example, the vendor ProQuest provides ABI/INFORM Global and the *Wall Street Journal*. An actual hierarchy exists in the organization of these databases. For example:

Top level—Databank (sometimes called "aggregator") = ProQuest
Second level—Databases = ABI/INFORM Global
Third level—Records = the units describing each item in the database
Fourth level—Fields = parts of the record, such as author, title, Standard Industrial Classification (SIC) number, and so on
Fifth level—Words or numbers = the text of the fields

Usually all databases from the same databank are searched similarly. There may be several methods (basic, advanced, and command) of searching databases. A basic search is often sufficient when searching for books in a catalog or when searching small databases; however, it is often advisable to use the advanced mode when searching for journal articles or complex ideas, so that search refinements can be used.

Most databanks use the same search features, but other databanks may use different symbols or interfaces to retrieve results. An interface is the "look and feel" of the database that actually helps the searcher know how to submit a search. Each database has a help screen that is always useful. The following examples of the search techniques are those for a typical library catalog, but each databank, such as First Search, Factiva, and others, may use different searching symbols to accomplish the same results.

Boolean Logic

Boolean logic allows the establishment of relationships between words and terms in most databases. Typical words used as operators in Boolean logic are AND, OR, and NOT. The following examples illustrate the use of Boolean logic:

Operator	Requirements	Examples	
AND	Both terms are retrieved	chemical AND Industry	Exxon AND financial
OR	Either term is retrieved	drug OR pharmaceutical	outlook OR forecast
NOT	Eliminates records containing the second term	Cherokee NOT jeeps	drugs NOT alcohol

Field Searching

Field searching refers to searching records in a database by one or more of its fields. Databases are collections of records, which consist of fields designated to describe certain parts of the record. Searching "by field" may make a search more efficient.

For example, if a title is known, a search of the title field should find the desired record. Terms entered as "subjects" may be restricted to specific subject headings (e.g., Library of Congress Subject Headings in most library catalogs), depending on the database. Most databases also allow the use of keyword searching, which searches every word in a record.

Most electronic databases use the same search strategies for searching databases, but they often vary in the keystrokes designated to perform the search. For example, on the Internet, the keyword "real estate" should be submitted with quotes surrounding the phrase so that the exact sequence of words will be searched; however, to get the same keyword phrase in some library catalogs, one would submit: "real ADJ estate." ADJ refers to *adjacent*.

Proximity Operators

The preceding *"real estate"* example demonstrates one of the proximity operators that are available to enhance keyword searching. **Proximity operators** allow the searcher to indicate how close and in which order two or more words are to be positioned within the record. Examples of proximity operators are:

Operator	Requirements	Examples
ADJ	Adjoining words in order	Electronic ADJ Commerce
NEAR	Adjoining words in any order	Bill NEAR Gates
SAME	Both terms are located in the field of the record	Microsoft SAME legal

Truncation

Another feature of database searching is **truncation**, which allows the root of the word to be submitted, retrieving all words beginning with that root. The term "forecast?" would retrieve "forecasting, forecasts, forecaster," and so on. The question mark is the truncation symbol for some databases, but other databases may use an asterisk, a plus sign, a dollar sign, or other symbol. In some cases truncation symbols may not be useful. For example, if one wanted "cat" in singular or plural, submitting "cat?" would retrieve "cat, cats, catch, catastrophe," and so on. Using the search "cat OR cats" would be preferred.

Nesting

It is essential that the computer translate the search statement correctly. **Nesting** is a technique that indicates the order in which a search is to be done. For example, if one wishes to search for microcomputers or personal computers in Florida, one would submit "Florida AND (microcomputer? OR personal ADJ computer?)," indicating that "Florida" should be combined with either term. The parentheses nest the two terms as one. Without the parentheses, "Florida" would be combined with "microcomputer," but every instance of the words "personal computer" would be added to the results. In search engines, there are text boxes that serve much like parentheses to aid in keeping similar terms together.

Limiting

Limiting allows for restricting searches to only those database records that meet specified criteria. For example, searches may be limited to a search of records containing a specific language, location, format, and/or date. These limitations are usually available on the advanced search screen of databases. When searching for current materials, the date limitation is most important to retrieve the correct results.

Step 4. *Compile the literature you have found, and evaluate your findings.* Is it relevant to your needs? Perhaps you are overwhelmed by information. Perhaps you have found little that is relevant. Rework your list of keywords and authors. If you have had little success or your topic is highly specialized, consult specialized directories, encyclopedias, and so on, such as the ones listed in this chapter. The librarian may be able to recommend the most appropriate source for your needs.

Step 5. *If you are unhappy with what you have found or are otherwise having trouble and the reference librarian has not been able to identify sources, use an authority.* Identify some individual or organization that might know something about the topic. Publications such as *Who's Who in Finance and Industry, Consultants and Consulting Organizations Directory, Encyclopedia of Associations, Industrial Research Laboratories in the United States,* and *Research Centers Directory* may help you identify people or organizations that specialize in your topic. Do not forget university faculty, government officials, and business executives. Such individuals are often delighted to be of help.

There are several keys to a successful search. First, be well informed about the search process. Reading this chapter is a good place to start. Second, you must be devoted to the search. Do not expect information to fall into your lap; be committed to finding it. Finally, there is no substitute for a good, professional librarian. Do not be afraid to ask for advice.

Step 6. Report results. You may be successful in locating data, but if the information is not properly transmitted to the reader, the research is worthless. It is important to outline the paper or report, correctly compose it, and accurately reference the sources that were used. See Chapter 20 for instructions on how to properly write a research report.

KEY SOURCES OF SECONDARY DATA FOR MARKETERS

We hope you understand by now that there are thousands of sources of secondary data that may be relevant to business decisions. In Table 6.2, we provide you with some of these major sources that are useful in marketing research. However, there are a few

TABLE 6.2	Secondary Information Sources on Marketing

I. Reference Guides

Encyclopedia of Business Information Sources

Detroit: GaleGroup, Annual. For the researcher, this lists marketing associations, advertising agencies, research centers, agencies, and sources relating to various business topics. It is particularly useful for identifying information about specific industries.

II. Indexes

ABI/INFORM Global

Ann Arbor, MI: ProQuest, 1971–. Available online, this database indexes and abstracts major journals relating to a broad range of business topics. Electronic access to some full-text articles is also available. ABI/INFORM Global may be complemented by ABI/INFORM Archive; ABI/INFORM Dateline; ABI/INFORM Trade & Industry and may be searched alone or in tandem with any or all of these databases at subscribing libraries.

Business File ASAP

Detroit: Gale Group, 1980–. Available online. This index covers primarily business and popular journals and includes some full-text articles.

Wilson Business Full Text

New York: H. W. Wilson, 1986. Available online. The print version is *Business Periodicals Index* (1958–). This basic index is useful for indexing the major business journals further back in time than other indexes.

III. Dictionaries and Encyclopedias

Dictionary of Marketing Terms

Hauppauge, NY: Barron's, 2000. Prepared by Jane Imber and Betsy Ann Toffler, this dictionary includes brief definitions of popular terms in marketing.

Encyclopedia of Consumer Brands

Detroit: St. James Press, 1994. For consumable products, personal products, and durable goods, this source provides detailed descriptions of the history and major developments of major brand names.

IV. Directories

Bradford's Directory of Marketing Research Agencies and Management Consultants in the United States and the World

Middleberg, VA: Bradford's, Biennial. Indexed by type of service, this source gives scope of activity for each agency and lists names of officers.

Broadcasting and Cable Yearbook

New Providence, NJ: R. R. Bowker, Annual. A directory of U.S. and Canadian television and radio stations, advertising agencies, and other useful information.   (continued)

sources that are so important that they deserve some extra attention. In the next few paragraphs we give you additional information about Census 2000 and other government publications, the North American Industrial Classification System (NAICS), which is replacing the Standard Industrial Classification (SIC) system, the "Survey of Buying Power," *Demographics USA*, and the Lifestyle Market Analyst.

Census 2000: Census of the Population

The U.S. Decennial Census, the **Census of the Population**, is considered the "granddaddy" of all market information. Even though the census is conducted only once every 10 years, census data serve as a baseline for much marketing information that is

TABLE 6.2	Secondary Information Sources on Marketing (Continued)

Directories in Print

Detroit: Gale Research, Annual. Provides detailed information on business and industrial directories, professional and scientific rosters, online directory of databases, and other lists. This source is particularly useful for identifying directories associated with specific industries or products.

Gale Directory of Publications and Broadcast Media

Detroit: Gale Research, Annual. A geographic listing of U.S. and Canadian newspapers, magazines, and trade publications, as well as broadcasting stations. Includes address, edition, frequency, circulation, and subscription and advertising rates.

V. Statistical Sources

Datapedia of the United States, 1790–2005

Lanham, MD: Bernan Press, 2001. Based on the *Historical Statistics of the United States from Colonial Times* and other statistical sources, this volume presents hundreds of tables reflecting historical and, in some cases, forecasting data on numerous demographic variables relating to the United States.

Demographics USA—"Survey of Buying Power"

New York: *Sales & Marketing Management* magazine, Annual. A compilation of data published in *Sales & Marketing Management* magazine, which includes statistics on population, income, retail sales, effective buying income, etc., for counties, cities, and metropolitan areas. (This source is discussed at length later in this chapter.)

Editor and Publisher Market Guide

New York: Editor and Publisher, Annual. Provides market data for more than 1,500 U.S. and Canadian newspaper cities covering facts and figures about location, transaction, population, households, banks, autos, etc.

Market Share Reporter

Detroit: Gale Research, Annual. Provides market share data on products and service industries in the United States.

Standard Rate and Data Service

Des Plaines, IL: SRDS, Monthly. In the SRDS monthly publications (those for consumer magazine and agrimedia, newspapers, spot radio, spot television) marketing statistics are included at the beginning of each state section.

provided in the "in-between" years. Firms providing secondary data commercially, such as ESRI and the "Survey of Buying Power," make adjustments each year to report current information. Besides market data, census data are used to make many governmental decisions about things such as highway construction, health-care services, educational needs, and, of course, redistricting.

The taking of a census of the U.S. population began in 1790. Prior to 1940, everyone had to answer all the questions that the census used. In 1940, the long form—a form that goes out only to a sample of respondents—was introduced as a way to collect more data, more rapidly, and without increasing respondent burden. In Census 2000, the long form went to one in six housing units. As a result, much of the census data are based on statistical sampling. A great deal of effort went into promoting Census 2000 to the citizenry of the United States due to growing concerns over privacy and declining participation rates in the census since 1970.[20] You can view Census data online at **www.census.gov**.

The census is composed of a short form, which every household received, and a long form, which is sent to one in six households. You can see both forms at www.census.gov/dmd/www/2000quest.html.

Other Government Publications

The U.S. government publishes a huge volume of secondary data. Most of these publications are produced in the U.S. Government Printing Office (GPO). You can visit its Web site at **www.gpoaccess.gov/index.html**. The **Statistical Abstract of the United States** is a convenient source of statistical secondary data, and it is now available online at **www.census.gov/statab/www/**.

North American Industry Classification System (NAICS)

The **North American Industry Classification System (NAICS)**, pronounced "nakes," and is not actually a source in and of itself. By this, we mean that NAICS is not information per se; rather, it is a coding system that can be used to access information. All marketing research students should be familiar with it because it will be used by so many secondary data sources. NAICS is replacing the **Standard Industrial Classification (SIC)** system. (We discuss both here because data based on the SIC will be around for

Visit the Bureau of the Census home page and you can find secondary data on many subjects. What is the population of the U.S. right now? What is the population of your hometown? Find out at www.census.gov!

United States Census 2000	Your Gateway to Census 2000 · Census 2000 EEO Tabulations · Summary File 4 (SF 4) · Summary File 3 (SF 3)
People	Estimates · American Community Survey · Income · Poverty · Health Insurance Coverage · Projections · Housing · International · Genealogy
Business	Economic Census · NAICS · Survey of Business Owners · Government · E-Stats · Foreign Trade | Export Codes · Local Employment Dynamics
Geography	Maps · TIGER · Gazetteer
Newsroom	Releases · Facts for Features · Minority Links · Multimedia · Cinco de Mayo · Older Americans Month
Special Topics	Census Calendar · Training · For Teachers · Statistical Abstract · Our Strategic Plan · FedStats

several years.) The SIC was created in the mid-1930s, when the government required all agencies gathering economic and industrial data to use the same system for classifying businesses. The SIC was a system that classified establishments by the type of activity in which they were engaged. Codes describing a type of business activity were used to collect, tabulate, summarize, and publish data. Each industry was assigned a code number, and all firms within that particular industry reported all activities (sales, employment, etc.) by this assigned code. The SIC divides all establishments into 11 divisions. Divisions are then subdivided into a second level of classification dividing the industry into "major groups." Major groups are numbered consecutively 01 through 99. Division A, for example, contains major groups 01 through 09. A major group within division A is agricultural production-crops; this is major group 01. Division B contains major groups 10 through 14: 10 is metal mining, 11 is coal mining, and so on. Each major group is further divided into two other categories, which provide greater specificity of classification.[21]

The SIC is being replaced by NAICS as a result of the North American Free Trade Agreement (NAFTA). The system will allow reports conducted by the Mexican, Canadian, and U.S. governments to share a common language for easier comparisons of international trade, industrial production, labor costs, and other statistics. NAICS will have improvements over the SIC and yet will allow for comparative analyses with past SIC-based data. In fact, Dun & Bradstreet is marketing software that provides a crossover from SIC codes to NAICS codes.[22] NAICS will classify businesses based on similar production processes; special attention is being given to classifying emerging industries such as services and high technology, and more classifications will be assigned to certain industry groups such as eating and drinking places. Under the SIC, all restaurants—beaneries, caterers, hamburger stands, and five-star restaurants—fall under the same category: Eating and Drinking Places. NAICS will break this down into several categories, which will be more useful to researchers.[23]

> The SIC is being replaced by NAICS as a result of the North American Free Trade Agreement (NAFTA).

NAICS groups the economy into 20 broad sectors, as opposed to the 11 SIC divisions. Many of these new sectors reflect recognizable parts of the SIC, such as the Utilities and Transportation section broken out from the SIC Transportation, Communications, and Utilities division. Because the service sector of the economy has grown so much in recent years, the SIC division for Services Industries has been broken into several new sectors, including Professional, Scientific, and Technical Services; Management, Support, Waste Management, and Remediation Services; Education Services; Health and Social Assistance; Arts, Entertainment, and Recreation; and Other Services except Public Administration. Other new NAICS sectors are composed of combinations of pieces from more than one SIC division. For example, the new information sector is composed of components from Transportation, Communications and Utilities (broadcasting and telecommunications); Manufacturing (publishing); and Services Industries (software publishing, data processing, information services, and motion pictures and sound recording).

> NAICS groups the economy into 20 broad sectors, as opposed to the 11 SIC divisions.

The NAICS uses a six-digit classification code instead of the old SIC four-digit code. The additional two digits allow for far greater specificity in identifying special types of firms. However, the six-digit code is not being used by all three NAFTA countries. The three countries agreed on a standard system using the first five digits and the sixth digit is being used by each country in a manner allowing for special user needs in each

> The NAICS uses a six-digit classification code instead of the old SIC four-digit code.

> Visit the NAICS site, which allows you to convert SIC codes to NAICS codes, at **www.census.gov/epcd/ www/naics.html**.

Knowing a NAICS number that represents a type of business will allow you to find all kinds of secondary information about the firms in that business.

country. Note that the NAICS code does not tell you anything per se. However, knowing a NAICS number that represents a type of business will allow you to find all kinds of secondary information about the firms in that business.

The "Survey of Buying Power" is an annual survey that is published every August in *Sales & Marketing Management* magazine. Visit *Sales & Marketing Management* magazine's Web site at **www.salesandmarketing.com**.

BPI is an indicator of the relative market potential of a geographic area. The BPI is an index number that represents a market's percentage of the total buying power in the United States.

"Survey of Buying Power"

The **"Survey of Buying Power"** is an annual survey that is published every August in *Sales & Marketing Management* magazine. The survey contains data for the United States on population, income, and retail sales for food, eating and drinking places, appliances, and automotives. These data are broken up into metropolitan (MSA), county, and city levels, and media market levels. Five-year projections are also provided. Because the data for the survey are extrapolated from census data, the data are current with each year's publication. In addition to the general data, the survey also reports the **effective buying income (EBI)** and the **buying power index (BPI)**.

EBI is defined as disposable personal income. It is equal to gross income less taxes and, therefore, reflects the effective amount of income available for expenditure on goods and services. This is important, because taxes differ widely depending on geographic location. BPI is an indicator of the relative market potential of a geographic area. It is based on the factors that make up a market: people, ability to buy, and willingness to buy. The BPI is an index number that represents a market's percentage of the total buying power in the United States.

▶ **How to Calculate the Buying Power Index (BPI).** The BPI is one of the main reasons that managers and researchers find the "Survey of Buying Power" so useful. With all the demographic information available to marketers, the BPI is useful because it takes the three factors making up a market (people, ability to buy, and willingness to buy) and calculates those factors into a quantitative index that represents the buying power of a market. We provide you the formula and illustrate how to calculate the BPI as follows:

$$\text{BPI} = (\text{Population of Market Area A} / \text{Total U.S. Population}) \times 2$$
$$+ (\text{EBI of Market Area A} / \text{Total U.S. EBI}) \times 5$$
$$+ (\text{Retail Sales of Market Area A} / \text{Total U.S. Retail Sales}) \times 3$$

The market areas that can be selected are regions, states, counties, MSAs, cities, or DMAs (Designated Market Areas represent television markets). Population is used to represent the market factor: *people*. EBI is used to represent the market factor: *ability to buy*. However, since *willingness to buy*, the third market factor, is a mental construct representing something consumers are going to do in the future, the "Survey of Buying Power" (SBP) uses a surrogate indicator of what consumers will buy. The surrogate is past retail sales, which is used because what people bought yesterday is a good indicator of what they will buy today. The foregoing formula gives you the BPI that, as we've said, is an index number. For example, the BPI for a large market, such as Chicago or Los Angeles, may be around 3.3333. This means that 3.3333 percent of the nation's total buying power is within that market. Casper, Wyoming, may have a BPI around 0.026. This means that Casper has 0.026 percent of the nation's buying power.

A major advantage of the SBP is that it provides demographic data updated each year, provides five-year projections and the BPI, which quantifies markets.

Advantages of the "Survey of Buying Power." First, a major advantage of the SBP is that it provides demographic data updated each year. Second, it also provides five-year projections each year. Third, by calculation of the index numbers making up the BPI, the SBP quantifies markets. Like all index numbers, the BPI is useful when used to evaluate a market over a time period. This could be achieved by plotting the BPI for a market over a five-year period. In this way, a manager or researcher would have an indication as to the trend in buying power for that market area. A second useful way to use the BPI is to compare one market with other markets. The BPI represents a quantifiable measure of markets' buying power and, therefore, is an objective measure that is useful for comparing markets. Specific uses of the BPI include selection of new markets, dividing markets into sales territories having equal buying power, and allocating media expenditure based on the potential buying power in a market. A fourth advantage of the SBP is that it is inexpensive and easy to access.

Disadvantages of the SBP. There are two weaknesses of using data reported in the "Survey of Buying Power." As we mentioned earlier, one disadvantage of using secondary data is that the data may not be classified in categories useful to the user. The example we gave was that data for EBI is reported in the SBP in only three categories, the last being $50,000 and over. Limited categories of data reported in the SBP can be overcome by using another publication, *Demographics USA*. A second disadvantage of the SBP lies in the logic of the calculation of the BPI. The BPI is a general index in that it uses the entire population, all levels of EBI, and total retail sales in a market area. However, for some products, a general BPI may not be an accurate predictor of buying power. Again, by knowing which secondary data source to consult, researchers can sometimes remedy shortcomings of one source of secondary data with another. We explain how *Demographics USA* overcomes the problem of the SBP's "general BPI" next.

> There are two weaknesses of using data reported in the "Survey of Buying Power."
>
> One disadvantage of using secondary data is that the data may not be classified in categories useful to the user.
>
> A second disadvantage of the SBP lies in the logic of the calculation of the BPI.

Demographics USA

Another useful source of secondary data is found in the publication **Demographics USA**.[24] Published by Bill Communications, the same company that publishes the "Survey of Buying Power," *Demographics USA* is much more expansive than the SBP. It not only provides much more detailed information, but it also overcomes some of the disadvantages of the SBP. First, as we noted earlier, the SBP has a limited number of categories by which it reports data. *Demographics USA* expands these categories. For example, it reports EBI in seven categories, with the highest category being "$150,000 and above." Instead of providing only the general BPI, *Demographics USA* offers other market indexes, such as **Total business BPI, high-tech BPI, manufacturing BPI, BPI for economy-priced products, BPI for moderately priced products, BPI for premium-priced products, BPI for business-to-business markets**, and **BPI for high-tech markets**.

> *Demographics USA* is much more expensive than the SBP. It not only provides much more detailed information, but it also overcomes some of the disadvantages of the SBP.
>
> Instead of providing only the general BPI, *Demographics USA* offers other market indexes.

Even with these additional choices of market indexes, some firms may want to calculate their own customized BPI. A **customized BPI** is an index that uses market factors selected for their relevancy to a particular product or service in terms of how they best represent the buying power for that particular product or service. As an example, let's suppose you were making a decision about locations for new dealerships for a new luxury automobile. Which markets represent the highest buying power for a luxury automobile? You might be predisposed to using the premium-priced products index from *Demographics USA*, but let's say you want an even better indicator of buying power for your very expensive new luxury car. A customized BPI may consist of (1) households with incomes of $75,000 or more, (2) automobile sales, and (3) households with members 35–64 years old. Of course, you would now have the problem of actually calculating your customized BPI for each market you want to consider. Another

> A customized BPI is an index that uses market factors selected for their relevancy to a particular product or service in terms of how they best represent the buying power for that particular product or service.

advantage of *Demographics USA* is the specificity of the geographic detail of the reporting units. In addition to providing the standard reporting units (Metropolitan Statistical Areas (MSAs), Designated Market Areas (DMAs), etc.), *Demographics USA* also provides data by ZIP code and information about the business market, such as the number of establishments within nine business categories (e.g., agriculture, manufacturing, retailing, and services).

Lifestyle Market Analyst

The Lifestyle Market Analyst is a printed source of information that analyzes several dozen lifestyle categories such as Avid Book Readers, Own a Cat, Take Cruise Ship Vacations, and Golf.

A unique source of secondary data is the **Lifestyle Market Analyst**. This printed source of information analyzes several dozen lifestyle categories such as Avid Book Readers, Own a Cat, Take Cruise Ship Vacations, Golf, Own a Camcorder, Have Grandchildren, Shop by Catalog/Mail, Stock/Bond Investments, Improving Health, and Donate to Charitable Causes. Information is organized into sections that have different objectives. First, you can examine markets (defined as DMAs). Not only will you get some standard demographic data for the DMA but you will also be able to determine the dominant (and least dominant) lifestyles in that market. This information helps "paint a personality portrait" of a market for users who otherwise see only a sea of numbers describing markets. Another section of the book focuses on each lifestyle. There you will find the demographic profile of the participants in that lifestyle category as well as other information. For example, to understand the lifestyle of a bicycling enthusiast, one may answer the following questions:

- What are the demographics of bicyclists?
- In what other activities are bikers involved?
- Which markets have the heaviest concentration of bikers?
- Which magazines do bikers read?

As another example, a *Lifestyle Market Analyst* profile of boating/sailing enthusiasts reveals that they also enjoy scuba diving, snow skiing, recreation vehicles, vacation property, and fishing, but they have little interest in devotional reading or needlework. Obviously, this type of consumer is an appropriate target for outdoor equipment sales.

SUMMARY

Data may be grouped into two categories: primary and secondary. Primary data are gathered specifically for the research project at hand. Secondary data are data that have been previously gathered for some other purpose. There are many uses of secondary data in marketing research and sometimes secondary data are all that is needed to achieve the research objectives. Secondary data may be internal, which means they are data already gathered within the firm for some other purpose. Data collected and stored from sales receipts such as customer names, types, quantities and prices of goods or services purchased, delivery addresses, shipping dates, salesperson making the sale, and so on would be an example of internal secondary data. Storing internal data in electronic databases has become increasingly popular, and these data may be used for database marketing. Databases are composed of records, which contain subcomponents of information called fields. Companies use information recorded in internal databases for purposes of direct marketing and to strengthen relationships with customers. The latter is a process known as CRM, customer relationship management. External secondary data are data obtained from sources outside the firm. These data may be classified as (1) published, (2) syndicated services data, and (3) databases. There are different types of published secondary data such as reference guides, indexes and abstracts, bibliographies, almanacs, manuals and handbooks, and so on. Different types of secondary data have different functions, and understanding the different functions is useful in researching secondary data. Syndicated services data are provided by firms that collect data in a standard format and make them available to subscribing firms. An example would be Nielsen Media Research's Television Rating Index. Online information databases are sources of secondary data searchable by search engines online. When several databases are offered under one search engine, the service is called either an aggregator or a databank. Examples include LexisNexis and ProQuest.

Secondary data have the advantages of being quickly gathered, being readily available, being relatively inexpensive, adding helpful insights should primary data be needed, and sometimes being all that is needed to achieve the research objective. Disadvantages are that the data are often reported in incompatible reporting units (county data are reported when ZIP code data are needed), measurement units do not match researchers' needs (household income is reported and per-capita income is needed), class definitions are incompatible with the researchers' needs (income is reported in classes up to $50k but the researchers need to know what percent of the population earns $75k or more), and secondary data may be outdated. Evaluation of secondary data is important; researchers must ask certain questions in order to ensure the integrity of the information they use: What was the true purpose of the study? Who collected the information? What information was collected? How was the information obtained? Is the information compatible with other information?

Finding secondary data involves understanding what you need to know and understanding key terms and names associated with the subject. Indexes and bibliographies may first be consulted; they list sources of secondary information by subject. Consult the sources and evaluate the information. Make use of computerized data searches from databases, if available. A good way to increase searching skills of online information databases is to learn how to find standard subject headings. Seek the services of a reference librarian to help you improve your searching skills.

Using online information databases requires understanding how these databases are organized and the fundamental search strategies used including Boolean logic, field searching, proximity operators, truncation, nesting, and limiting. Knowing how to find standard subject headings within a database is a key to successful information searching.

Examples of important secondary data for business decisions are the *Census of the Population* from the U.S. Bureau of the Census and the *Statistical Abstract of the United States*, both of which are available online. The North American Industry Classification System (NAICS) is replacing the Standard Industrial Classification (SIC) system as the government's classification system for business. Because NAICS groups businesses into 20 sectors (instead of the 11 used by the SIC) and uses codes of up to six digits to classify businesses (instead of the four-digit code used by the SIC), NAICS offers a classification system that is much better than SIC at specifying types of industries. A privately produced secondary data source that is useful to marketers is the "Survey of Buying Power" (SBP). The SBP is useful because it provides a quantitative index, called the buying power index (BPI), to measure the buying power of various geographical markets in the United States. Demographics in the SBP are updated annually. A second privately produced source of secondary information is *Demographics USA*, which provides useful demographic information that is updated annually. In addition to calculating the BPI (as is provided in the SBP), *Demographics USA* provides several other indexes to quantify the buying power of both industrial and retail markets. Firms may also calculate customized BPIs that are specifically formulated to measure the buying power for their specific product or service. The *Lifestyle Market Analyst* is a unique publication in that it provides information on lifestyles. It contains information on several dozen lifestyles, such as bicycling enthusiasts, dog owners, snow skiing enthusiasts, and so on. Demographic profiles of each lifestyle are reported along with what other lifestyle interests (and non-interests) apply.

KEY TERMS

Primary data (p. 146)
Secondary data (p. 146)
Internal secondary data (p. 148)
Database marketing (p. 148)
Database (p. 148)
Record (p. 148)
Fields (p. 149)
Internal databases (p. 149)
CRM, customer relationship management (p. 149)
Data mining (p. 149)
External secondary data (p. 149)
Published sources (p. 149)
Catalog (p. 150)
Indexes (p. 150)
Syndicated services data (p. 150)
External databases (p. 150)
Online information databases (p. 150)
Standard subject headings (p. 159)
Boolean logic (p. 162)
Field searching (p. 162)
Proximity operators (p. 162)
Truncation (p. 163)
Nesting (p. 163)

Limiting (p. 163)
Census of the Population (p. 165)
Statistical Abstract of the United States (p. 166)
North American Industry Classification System (NAICS) (p. 166)
Standard Industrial Classification (SIC) system (p. 166)
"Survey of Buying Power" (p. 168)
Effective buying income (EBI) (p. 168)
Buying power index (BPI) (p. 168)
Demographics USA (p. 169)
Total business BPI (p. 169)
Hi-tech BPI (p. 169)
Manufacturing BPI (p. 169)
BPI for economy-priced products (BPI) (p. 169)
BPI for moderately-priced products (p. 169)
BPI for premium-priced products (p. 169)
Business-to-Business (BPI) (p. 169)
High-tech markets BPI (p. 169)
Customized BPI (p. 169)
Lifestyle Market Analyst (p. 170)

REVIEW QUESTIONS/APPLICATIONS

1. Describe how secondary data may add value to primary data.
2. What are secondary data, and how do they differ from primary data?
3. Describe some uses of secondary data.
4. How would you classify secondary data?
5. What are databases, and how are they organized?
6. What is database marketing, and what is CRM?
7. What are three types of external secondary data?
8. What is the difference between a library catalog and an index?

9. What are online information databases? Name three of them.

10. What are the five advantages of secondary data? Discuss the disadvantages of secondary data.

11. How would you go about evaluating secondary data? Why is evaluation important?

12. Discuss how you would go about locating secondary data in your own library.

13. What is a standard subject heading? Explain why knowing how to find a standard subject heading would help increase your information searching skills when using online information databases.

14. Explain what is meant by Boolean logic? Proximity operators?

15. Why would searching by field help you efficiently search online information databases?

16. Describe the purposes of the *U.S. Census of the Population.*

17. Briefly identify some sources of secondary data.

18. Go to your library and find a copy of the "Survey of Buying Power." Find the BPI for your county. Explain what this number represents. Discuss why it would be a useful number to evaluate a market.

19. Go online to your favorite search engine (i.e., Ask Jeeves, Google, Yahoo, etc.) and enter "demographics." Go to some of these sites, and describe the kind of information you are receiving. Why would this information be considered secondary data?

20. Access the *Statistical Abstract of the United States* online, and find information relevant to any topic you are currently studying.

21. Select an industry and go to the NAICS website identified in this chapter. Find the NAICS number that represents your industry. Discuss how you could use this number.

22. Suppose you were the marketing director for a luxury car manufacturer. Discuss what factors you would consider in building a customized BPI that could be used to evaluate markets for future dealerships.

23. Go to **easidemographics.com**. Look for sample studies, and find an example of a ring study. What disadvantage of printed secondary data does this feature overcome?

24. Explain how a marketer of boats could use the *Lifestyle Market Analyst.*

CASE 6.1

PURE-AQUA SYSTEMS

Ronny McCall and Lucy Moody were considering a new business of supplying residential homes with bottled water. They knew the public was growing wary of tap water, and they also knew that many consumers were aware that about one-third of the bottles of water purchased in stores were filled with tap water. They had investigated a new distillation system based on heating water and collecting the condensation. Such a system has the advantage of producing the cleanest water. Even water taken from sewage water, once heated and recondensed, is perfectly clean. Traditional distillation systems operated at high costs, but McCall and Moody had developed a new system that could distill large quantities of water at costs comparable to other water-filtering systems. The two entrepreneurs scanned secondary information for clues as to how public opinions were changing in terms of their attitudes toward tap water. The problem with some of the information they found was that the secondary information was reported for markets outside their proposed area of operation, Pensacola, Florida.

Lucy, always searching secondary information sources, found an article in the local newspaper about a new study conducted by the local university in a joint venture with a marketing research firm. The two had worked together to create a panel of consumers that were reportedly representative of the two-county MSA—the market Lucy and Ronny had targeted. Excited, Lucy told Ronny about the story; together, they went to the Web site at **www.uwf.edu/panel**. There they found results of a study, conducted in November 2003, which asked a key question important to Lucy and Ronny's bottled water venture. The question asked the respondents to rate the tap-water quality in their home. The two were startled at the results. In one county almost 24% had rated the tap water as either "bad" or "poor." They knew that home-delivered-water companies were successful in other markets for which they had discovered secondary data showing that as little as 10% of the population rated the tap water as "bad" or "poor."

McCall and Moody discussed what the survey results meant to them. Was this an indication that there was a need for their service in the Pensacola market area? "Wait a minute," says Ronny. "Before we go ahead and invest our nest egg in this project, how do we know these secondary data are really representative of the population?"

1. How would you evaluate the secondary data referred to in this study (without visiting the Web site)?

2. Go to the Web site (**www.uwf.edu/panel**) and search for information that would help you evaluate the secondary data reported. What can you find to either support or refute the representativeness of the data?

3. Given your answers to questions one and two above, do you think Ronny McCall and Lucy Moody should continue to investigate their proposed bottled water venture?

YOUR INTEGRATED **CASE**

CASE **6.2**

THE HOBBIT'S CHOICE: A RESTAURANT

After the first meeting between Jeff Dean and Cory Rogers of CMG Research, Cory decided to conduct some secondary data analysis on the restaurant business. He knew he could benefit from doing this because he could conduct the research quickly and inexpensively, and he also knew he was very likely to find information in these secondary data sources that would be helpful to his client, Jeff Dean. First, Cory walked into CMG's library. The library had a reference guide, the *Encyclopedia of Business Information Sources*, almanacs, handbooks, and special business dictionaries. In addition, Cory had Internet access in his office.

1. Based on the published sources available in CMG's library, which book would you recommend as the first book Rogers should consult? The second book? Why?

2. Conduct a search of the Internet that you think Cory would have conducted. Describe the kind of information you retrieved about the restaurant industry, and provide the Web sites from which you gathered the information.

3. Based on the information you retrieved from your Internet search, did you find any examples illustrating the weaknesses of secondary data? What are the weaknesses?

4. Assuming that Cory earns $55,000 a year, estimate what CMG's costs are for Cory doing the search that you conducted over the Internet. You can exclude other fixed costs such as the costs of Internet access, building, utilities, and so on. Just estimate the amount of Cory's salary allocated to the search.

7

Standardized Information Sources

Donofrio's Coffee Uses a Standardized Service to Locate Coffee Shops

Community™ Tapestry™ is a lifestyle segmentation database offered by ESRI. This is an example of a standardized information service.

Heather Donofrio had a successful chain of coffee shops targeted to young, urban professionals. Donofrio's Coffee operates in three states located in the Northeast. By carefully planning locations Heather had never experienced a failure. Rob, Heather's husband, had started a process of franchising Donofrio's Coffee. Soon after Rob made Donofrio's Coffee available for franchising the couple received many requests from potential franchisees. Heather knew how important location was to the success of her business but knew she and Rob were limited in being able to help franchisees from all over the country make the right location decision. The Donofrios needed help in choosing the most suitable locations for the new Donofrio's Coffee shops. After considering several marketing research companies, Heather decided to use the services of ESRI (ESRI). David Huffman, Managing Director of ESRI explained their services to Heather. ESRI could use the Community Tapestry segmentation database to profile the current Donofrio's Coffee customers. Tapestry is a lifestyle segmentation database that classifies all U.S. residential ZIP codes into 65 segments based on selected demographic variables. For example, one segment is *Laptops and Lattes*, who are affluent, single, renters free of home ownership and childrearing. Another segment is *Metro Renters* who are young— one third still in their 20s—well-educated and beginning their professional careers in

■ To learn how to distinguish standardized information from other types of information
■ To know the differences between syndicated data and standardized services
■ To understand the advantages and disadvantages of standardized information
■ To see some of the various areas in which standardized information may be applied
■ To understand some specific examples of standardized information sources in each of four areas of application
■ To know the meaning of single-source data

Learning Objectives

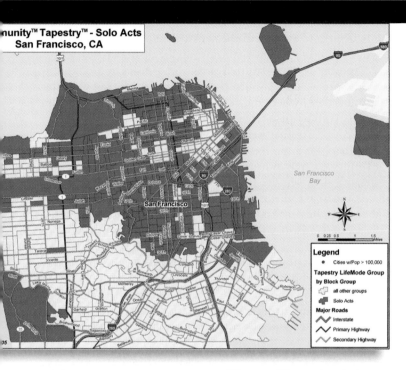

ESRI's segmentation system, Community™ Tapestry™, can identify the types of people by the neighborhoods where they live. This block group geography level map illustrates the location of metro San Francisco residents classified in Tapestry's LifeMode *Solo Acts* summary group.

urban areas. Other segments include *Salt of the Earth, Trendsetters*, and *Main Street USA*. For a broader view of markets, the 65 Community Tapestry segments can be grouped into 12 LifeMode summary groups based on similar demographic and consumption patterns. For example, the *High Society* summary group is made up of 7 of the 65 segments and includes *Top Rung, Surburban Splendor*, and *Connoisseurs*, among others. The 65 segments can also be grouped into 11 urbanization summary groups based on population density. Examples include *Metro Cities, Urban Outskirts*, and *Rural*. ESRI has worked for over thirty years in refining their segmentation system methods.

The Donofrios were sold on ESRI when Huffman explained to them that 75% of their customers were in the *Solo Acts* Life Mode summary group, which consisted of just 5 of the 65 Tapestry segments. Further, ESRI could provide the Donofrios with a map of the United States that identified the neighborhoods in which these 5 segments dominated. By using ESRI Tapestry segmentation service, the Donofrios were ready to help franchisees locate successful Donofrio's Coffee shops.

Visit ESRI's Tapestry at **www.esri.com**.

Where We Are
1 **Establish the need for marketing research**
2 **Define the problem**
3 **Establish research objectives**
4 **Determine research design**
5 Identify information types and sources
6 **Determine methods of accessing data**
7 **Design data collection forms**
8 **Determine sample plan and size**
9 **Collect data**
10 **Analyze data**

Locating new Donofrio's Coffee shops using Community Tapestry illustrates the topic of this chapter, standardized information. In this case, ESRI Business Information Solutions provides a standard process, the Community Tapestry system, to help clients better understand their customers and locate where new potential customers reside. In this chapter we are going to introduce you to the different types of standardized information: syndicated data and standardized services. We begin by defining what we mean by these types of standardized information.

WHAT IS STANDARDIZED INFORMATION?

Standardized information is a type of secondary data in which the data collected and/or the process of collecting the data are standardized for all users. There are two broad classes of standardized information: syndicated data and standardized services.

Syndicated data are data that are collected in a standard format and made available to all subscribers. The Nielsen TV ratings, for example, consist of data on TV viewing collected using a standardized method. The resulting data are made available to anyone wishing to purchase the information. **Standardized services** refers to a standardized marketing research *process* that is used to generate information for a particular user.

ESRI's Community Tapestry is a standardized *process* that is used to profile residential neighborhoods. This information is purchased by clients desiring to better understand who their customers are, where they are located, how to find them, and how to reach them. We discuss both of these types of information next.

Syndicated data are a form of external, secondary data that are supplied from a common database to subscribers for a service fee. Recall from our discussion of the types of firms in the marketing research industry in Chapter 3 that we call firms providing such data "syndicated data service firms." Such information is typically detailed information that is valuable to firms in a given industry and is not available in libraries. Firms supplying syndicated data follow standard research formats that enable them to collect the same standardized data over time. These firms provide specialized, routine information needed by a given industry in the form of ready-to-use, standardized marketing data to subscribing firms. We mentioned the Nielsen TV ratings earlier. As another example, Arbitron supplies syndicated data on the number and types of listeners to the various radio stations in each radio market. This standardized information helps advertising firms reach their target markets; it also helps radio stations define audience characteristics by providing an objective, independent measure of the size and characteristics of their audiences. With syndicated data, both the process of collecting and analyzing the data and the data themselves are standardized; that is, neither is varied for the client.[1] On the other hand, standardized services rarely provide clients with standardized data. Rather, it is the *process* they are marketing. The application of that standardized process will result in different data for each client. For example, a standardized service may be measurement of customer satisfaction. Instead of a user firm trying to "reinvent the wheel" by developing its own process for measuring customer satisfaction, it may elect to use a standardized service for measuring customer satisfaction. This is also true for several other marketing research services such as test marketing, naming new brands, pricing a new product, or using mystery shoppers.

Sidebar notes

Standardized information is a type of secondary data in which the data collected and/or the process of collecting the data are standardized for all users. Two broad classes of standardized information are syndicated data and standardized services.

Syndicated data are data that are collected in a standard format and made available to all subscribers.

Standardized services refers to a standardized marketing research *process* that is used to generate information for a particular user.

With syndicated data, the data and the process used to generate the data are standardized across all users. With standardized services, the process of collecting data is standardized across all users.

ADVANTAGES AND DISADVANTAGES OF STANDARDIZED INFORMATION

Syndicated Data

One of the key advantages of syndicated data is shared costs. Many client firms may subscribe to the information; thus, the cost of the service is greatly reduced to any one subscriber firm. When costs are spread across several subscribers, other advantages result. Because syndicated data firms specialize in the collection of standard data and because their viability, in the long run, depends on the validity of the data, the quality of the data collected is typically very high. With several companies paying for the service, the syndicating company can go to great lengths to gather a great amount of data as well.

Another advantage of syndicated data comes from the routinized systems used to collect and process the data. This means that the data are normally disseminated very quickly to subscribers because these syndicated data firms set up standard procedures and methods for collecting the data over and over again on a periodic basis. The more current the data, the greater their usefulness.

Although there are several advantages to syndicated data, there are some disadvantages. First, buyers have little control over what information is collected. Since the research is not custom research for the buyer firm, the buyer firm must be satisfied that the information received is the information needed. Are the units of measurement correct? Are the geographical reporting units appropriate? A second disadvantage is that buyer firms often must commit to long-term contracts when buying standardized data. Finally, there is no strategic information advantage in purchasing syndicated data because all competitors have access to the same information. However, in many industries, firms would suffer a serious strategic disadvantage by not purchasing the information.

> **Advantages of syndicated data are shared costs, high quality of the data, and speed with which data are collected and made available for decision making.**

> **Disadvantages of syndicated data are that there is little control over what data are collected, buyers must commit to long-term contracts, and competitors have access to the same information.**

Standardized Services

The key advantage of using a standardized service is taking advantage of the experience of the research firm offering the service. Often a buyer firm may have a research department with many experienced persons but no experience in a particular process that is now needed. Imagine a firm setting out to conduct a test market for the very first time. It would take the firm several months to gain the confidence needed to conduct the test market properly. Still, lessons would be learned by trial and error. Taking advantage of others' experiences with the process is a good way to minimize potential mistakes in carrying out the research process.

A second advantage is the reduced cost of the research. Because the supplier firm conducts the service for many clients on a regular basis, the procedure is efficient and far less costly than if the buyer firm tried to conduct the service itself. A third advantage is the speed of the research service. The efficiency gained by conducting the service over and over translates into reduced turnaround time from start to finish of a research project. The speed with which the service is conducted by standardized services firms is usually much faster than if the buyer firm were to conduct the service on its own.

> **Advantages of standardized services are using the experience of the firm offering the service, reduced cost, and increased speed of conducting the service.**

There are disadvantages of using standardized services as well. "Standardized" means "not customized." The ability to customize some projects is lost when using a standardized service. Although some services offer some customization, the ability to design a project for the project at hand is lost when using a standardized service. Second, the company providing the standardized service may not know the idiosyncrasies of a particular industry and, therefore, there is a greater burden on the client to ensure that the standardized service fits the intended situation. Client firms need to be very familiar with the service provided, including what data are collected on which population, how the data are collected, and how the data arc reported before they purchase the service.

> **Disadvantages of standardized services are the inability to customize services and the service firm not being knowledgeable about the client's industry.**

APPLICATION AREAS OF STANDARDIZED INFORMATION

Although there are many forms of standardized information that may have many applications, we will illustrate four major application areas in the remainder of this chapter. We will explore the use of standardized information applied to measuring consumer attitudes and opinion polls, defining market segments, conducting market tracking, and monitoring media usage and promotion effectiveness.

Measuring Consumer Attitudes and Opinion Polls

Several firms offer measurements of consumer attitudes and opinions on various issues. The **Yankelovich Monitor**, started in 1971, measures changing social values and how these changes affect consumers. It has specialized in generational marketing and studied matures, baby boomers, and Gen Xers.[2] The data are syndicated, meaning they are available to anyone who wishes to purchase the data, and the information can be used for a variety of marketing management decisions. Data are collected annually through 90-minute in-home interviews and a one-hour questionnaire among 2500 men and women aged 16 and over using a nationally representative sample.[3] A number of topics are included, such as activism, sex, nutrition, doctors, women, stress, work, television, shopping, simplification/escape, newspapers, and so on.[4] Yankelovich also measures attitudes and values of the youth market, Hispanic market, and African-American market.[5]

The **Harris poll** measures consumer attitudes and opinions on a wide variety of topics. Owned by Harris Interactive, the Harris poll started in 1963 and is one of the longest-running, most respected surveys of consumer opinion. Harris polls are conducted on topics such as the economy, environment, politics, world affairs, legal issues, and so on. Polls are taken weekly and, because many of the same questions are asked over and over, the Harris poll is a good source to identify trend lines. Since these data are standardized information, we use it as another example of syndicated data. However, client firms may have Harris Interactive conduct customized surveys.[6]

The **Gallup poll** surveys public opinion, asking questions on domestic issues, private issues, and world affairs, such as "Do you consider the income tax you have to pay this year to be fair?" (Although 85 percent said "yes" in 1943, only 58 percent said "yes" in 2002.) Business executives can track attitudes toward buying private brands or attitudes toward credit by following questions asked in the Gallup poll. The Gallup poll is available each year, and back issues covering each year begin with 1935.[7] Like the Harris poll, the Gallup Organization can conduct customized surveys for clients. However, we treat the Gallup poll here as syndicated data, since it collects attitude and opinion information and makes that information available to all who wish to purchase it. Visit its Web site and view some poll results. This will give you an idea of the service provided by the Gallup Organization.

Defining Market Segments

Defining market segments requires placing customers sharing certain attributes (age, income, stage in the family life cycle, etc.) into homogeneous groups or market segments. Once in these groups, marketers gather information about the members of the market, compiling profiles of the attributes describing the consumers that make up each segment. Marketers can then decide which segments are currently being served or not served by the competition. They can also determine the size, growth trends, and profit potential of each segment. Using these data, a segment, or group of segments, can be targeted for marketing.

Several standardized information sources provide marketers with information about customers in the market. Some of these sources provide information on members of the industrial market, and others provide information on members of the consumer market.

The Yankelovich Monitor measures changing social values and how these changes affect consumers. Visit Yankelovich at www.Yankelovich.com.

Companies can use HarrisInteractive to receive information on consumer attitudes and opinions. Go to www.HarrisInteractive.com.

We treat the Gallup poll here as syndicated data, since it collects attitude and opinion information and makes that information available to all who wish to purchase it. See examples of Gallup surveys at www.gallup.com.

▶ **Providing Information on Members of the Industrial Market.** A great deal about the industrial market can be learned through the use of the Standard Industrial Classification (SIC) system and the North American Industry Classification System (NAICS), the government's method of classifying business firms (discussed in Chapter 6). Although achieving the basic objectives of allowing you to identify, classify, and monitor standard statistics about certain member firms, the SIC falls short of allowing you to target customers in a highly specific industry. NAICS partially remedies this problem by going from the SIC's four-digit code to a six-digit code. NAICS allows users to select more specific types of firms instead of the broad categories available through SIC codes.

> NAICS allows marketers to define industry types more specifically than the SIC classification system.

One standardized information service firm supplies additional information that allows the user to make even better use of the government's classification systems. **Dun's Market Identifiers (DMI)**, published by Dun & Bradstreet, provides information on over 4 million firms that it updates monthly. The real benefit of DMI is its service that provides eight-digit codes to classify businesses. By having more digits, the service can provide many more categories of firms than other classification systems. This is important if a firm is trying to target specific business firms, however narrow their classification.

> By classifying firms using an eight-digit code, Dun & Bradstreet offers a standardized information service that allows firms to locate all firms in a narrowly defined industry group.

For example, one marketing researcher worked with a manufacturing firm, BasKet Kases, a manufacturer of wooden gift baskets, to secure a listing of all firms that wholesale gift baskets for the purposes of targeting these firms with a marketing campaign. Using the SIC Classification Manual, it was determined that SIC numbers with a 51 prefix were wholesalers of nondurable goods. By examining all of the 51 prefix descriptions, the SIC code of 5199 was found to represent wholesalers of "miscellaneous, nondurable goods," which included baskets. Without additional information, a list of firms with an SIC code of 5199 would have included wholesalers of all types of baskets, including wooden baskets for shipping fruit, freight, and so on. However, with the use of the additional codes supplied by DMI, it was found that the eight-digit code 51990603 represented "wholesalers of gift baskets." This was exactly what the researcher was seeking. By finding the firms sharing this eight-digit code, the researcher was able to identify 45 wholesale firms of gift baskets in the United States for BasKet Kases.

▶ **Providing Information on Members of the Consumer Market.** Many standardized information services are available to help marketers understand the consumer market. Information on segmenting consumers by personality trait[8] is available through SRI Consulting Business Intelligence's (SRIC-BI's) **VALS** program. Consumers are placed in one of eight segments based on their answers to the "VALS Questionnaire," which measures their psychological and demographic characteristics.

> VALS is a standardized service that offers a system for segmenting consumers by psychological characteristics and four demographics.

SRIC-BI works with its clients in a variety of ways. Generally, they start by working to identify the VALS consumer groups who are most naturally attracted to their client's products and services. This is done through customized surveys or by looking at national syndicated data. The VALS battery of attitude items is integrated into Mediamark's *Survey of American Consumers*, which asks questions about hundreds of products and services from toothpaste to cars to media preferences. Once manufacturers, service providers, and advertisers know the distribution of VALS types that use their products/services they can select an appropriate consumer target. Manufacturers, service providers and advertisers can design their advertising messages for the target by using VALS "power words and images" that appeal to their target. Marketers can also apply VALS to direct market solicitation using GeoVALS to identify ZIP codes or block groups that have large concentra-

> Learn more about VALS at **www.sric-bi.com/VALS/.**

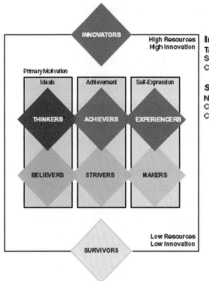

VALS is a system of segmenting consumers based on personality traits that are correlated with purchase behavior. These personality traits are used to explain consumer motivations in the marketplace.

Source: SRI Consulting Business Intelligence

By understanding consumer motivations in the different VALS segments, marketers gain insights into all phases of the marketing process from new-product development and entry-stage targeting to communications strategy and advertising. By permission, SRI Consulting Business Intelligence.

The Segments

VALS™ segments the U.S. English-speaking population age 18 or older into eight consumer groups. Their primary motivation and ability to express themselves in the marketplace distinguish the groups.

Innovators

Innovators are successful, sophisticated, take-charge people with high self-esteem. Because they have such abundant resources, they exhibit all three primary motivations in varying degrees. They are change leaders and are the most receptive to new ideas and technologies. Their purchases reflect cultivated tastes for upscale, niche products and services.

Thinkers   Motivated by ideals; high resources

Thinkers are mature, satisfied, comfortable, and reflective. They tend to be well educated and actively seek out information in the decision-making process. They favor durability, functionality, and value in products.

Believers   Motivated by ideals; low resources

Believers are strongly traditional and respect rules and authority. Because they are fundamentally conservative, they are slow to change and technology averse. They choose familiar products and established brands.

Achievers   Motivated by achievement; high resources

Achievers have goal-oriented lifestyles that center on family and career. They avoid situations that encourage a high degree of stimulation or change. They prefer premium products that demonstrate success to their peers.

Strivers   Motivated by achievement; low resources

Strivers are trendy and fun loving. They have little discretionary income and tend to have narrow interests. They favor stylish products that emulate the purchases of people with greater material wealth.

Experiencers   Motivated by self-expression; high resources

Experiencers appreciate the unconventional. They are active and impulsive, seeking stimulation from the new, offbeat, and risky. They spend a comparatively high proportion of their income on fashion, socializing, and entertainment.

Makers   Motivated by self-expression; low resources

Makers value practicality and self-sufficiency. They choose hands-on constructive activities and spend leisure time with family and close friends. Because they prefer value to luxury, they buy basic products.

Survivors

Survivors lead narrowly focused lives. Because they have the fewest resources, they do not exhibit a primary motivation and often feel powerless. They are primarily concerned about safety and security, so they tend to be brand loyal and buy discounted merchandise.

tions of their target consumers in them. In addition, VALS can be integrated into focus group screeners and can be used to hypothesize about entry-stage targets for new product development efforts.

You can determine your VALS type by completing the VALS survey online at www.sric-bi.com/VALS/. You can also learn more about the other VALS types at this Web site.[9] Since cultural differences exist, VALS is available in the United States as U.S. VALS, Japan as Japan VALS, and Great Britain as U.K. VALS.

Geodemographics is the term used to describe the classification of arbitrary, usually small, geographic areas in terms of the characteristics of their inhabitants. Aided with computer programs called **GIS** (geodemographic information systems), geodemographers can access huge databases and construct profiles of consumers residing in geographic areas determined by the geodemographer. Instead of being confined to consumer information recorded by city, county, or state, geodemographers can produce this information for geographic areas thought to be relevant for a given marketing application (such as a proposed site for a fast-food restaurant).

Firms specializing in geodemographics combine census data with their own survey data or data that they gather from other sources. Claritas Inc. is the firm that pioneered geodemography. By accessing ZIP codes and census data regarding census tracts, census block groups, or blocks, which make up a firm's trading area(s), Claritas can compile much information about the characteristics and lifestyles of the people within these trading areas. Or a firm may give Claritas a descriptive profile of its target market and Claritas can supply the firm with geographic areas that most closely match the prespecified characteristics. This service is referred to as **PRIZM$_{NE}$** (potential ratings index for ZIP markets). The PRIZM system defines every neighborhood in the United States at the household level in terms of 66 demographically and behaviorally distinct segments. By knowing which segments make up a firm's potential customers, Claritas can help target promotional messages to consumers making up those segments. Marketing Research Insight 7.1 gives you some background information on Claritas and describes some of its standardized services that can be used for market segmentation.

Active **Learning**

Geodemographics **is the term used to describe the classification of arbitrary, usually small, geographic areas in terms of the characteristics of their inhabitants.**

Firms specializing in geodemographics combine census data with their own survey data or data that they gather from other sources. PRIZM$_{NE}$ is a standardized information service that categorizes neighborhoods at the household level into one of 66 different segments.

By permission, Claritas Inc.

Through PRIZM NE, you will discover many pieces of behavioral and lifestyle information about your best customers. Knowing where they live, the products they purchase, what they like to do in their free time and their media preferences helps you communicate with them more effectively. It also gives you the ability to find more customers just like them.

PRACTICAL INSIGHTS

7.1 Claritas Standardized Services for Market Segmentation

Founded in 1971, Claritas Inc. is widely regarded as the leading provider of precision marketing solutions, developed, in part, through intricate customer segmentation systems and other data delivery and analysis software/Internet systems. The company serves clients within the automotive, financial services, media, retail, real estate, restaurant, telecommunications, and energy/utilities industries, many of which are major *Fortune* 500 companies. Claritas is a division of the VNU Marketing Information Group (VNU/MIG), an established leader in providing a wide variety of industries with innovative, precision-marketing solutions, including geodemographic information and qualitative audience research. VNU/MIG is a subsidiary of VNU Inc., which also includes ACNielsen, Nielsen Media Research, Spectra Marketing Services, Scarborough Research and VNU Business Publications.

With information generated through its segmentation systems and databases, Claritas enables businesses to address key marketing issues, such as:

- Who are my best customers and prospects?
- How many are there and where do they live?
- What is the most effective way to reach them?
- Which markets, locations, or industries offer the most potential?

- How should I allocate marketing resources to maximize my return on investment?

Some Claritas Products Used for Market Segmentation:

PRIZM$_{NE}$ (New Evolution)—Defines every neighborhood in the United States at the household level in terms of 66 demographically and behaviorally distinct segments. A precision tool for lifestyle segmentation and analysis, PRIZM$_{NE}$ offers an easy way to identify, understand, and target consumers.

P$YCLE$_{NE}$ (New Evolution)—A market segmentation system that differentiates households in terms of financial behavior. The 58-segment system predicts which households will use which types of financial/insurance products and services.

ConneXions—A household-level segmentation system for targeting video, voice, and data services.

By permission Claritas Inc.

Active Learning

Let's take a closer look at the services offered by Claritas. First, find out how Claritas would describe the types of people who live in your home area ZIP code in terms of their 66 PRIZM$_{NE}$ segments. Go to **www.mybestsegments.com.** Look at the top of the screen and click on "ZIP code Look-Up" tab. Enter your five-digit ZIP code, and don't forget to enter the code that Claritas provides for you underneath the ZIP Code entry blank. You will then get a display that shows as many as five different lifestyle PRIZM$_{NE}$ segments in your home ZIP code area. Click on each one and learn a little about the people in that segment. Don't be surprised if the descriptions match you or your neighbors!

Second, let's take a look at some case study examples using Claritas' services. Go to the Claritas home page at **www.claritas.com.** Click on "Products and Services" and then "Segmentation." Next, click on "View a listing of Claritas' segmentation case studies." Claritas has provided several examples illustrating their services across several different industries, including retail, restaurant, financial services, nonprofit, travel, and several others. Pick an industry, or company, in which you have an interest and see how Claritas used one of its standardized information services to help them solve problems.

ESRI is another geodemography firm that we introduced at the beginning of this chapter. We asked GIS Expert, Tony Burns, Retail & Commercial Industry Solution Manager, ESRI, to tell you about GIS and its application to retailing. In Marketing Research Insight 7.2 Mr. Burns discusses GIS and describes one application of GIS; defining a trading area.

Conducting Market Tracking

By **tracking studies** we mean studies that monitor, or track, a variable over time. For example, companies conduct market tracking to track sales of their brands as well as sales of competitors' brands over time. The "tracks" moving up and down or remaining stable serve as important monitors of how the market is reacting to a firm's marketing mix. Many variables may be monitored in a tracking study, including market share, customer satisfaction levels, measures of promotional spending, prices, stockouts, inventory levels, and so on.

> Tracking studies are those that monitor, or track, a variable such as sales or market share over time.

You may ask why a company needs to know what its own sales are. Wouldn't a company know, through sales receipts, how much it has sold of a particular product? Although a company may monitor its own sales, sales measured by a firm's own sales receipts provide an incomplete picture. By monitoring only its own sales, a firm does not know what is going on in the channel of distribution. Products are not distributed instantaneously. Rather, inventories are built up and depleted at various rates among the different distributors. Just because household sales of a product increase does not mean that a producer will experience a sales increase for that product. To really know what is happening in the industry, marketers need to monitor the movement of goods at the retail level. Recognizing this need, market tracking is conducted at both the retail-store level and at the household level. And tracking studies, as noted, also provide data on competitors' brands that otherwise would not be available to management. So, for these reasons, tracking studies are an important service provided by research firms.[10] Data are collected by scanners and by retail-store audits. We provide examples of each in the following paragraphs.

> Tracking studies can tell a firm how well its own products are selling in retail outlets around the world and also provide sales data for competitors' products.

▶ **Market Tracking at the Retail Level.** *ACNielsen Scantrack Services.* ACNielsen's Scantrack Services is based on syndicated retail **scanning data** and is recognized as an industry standard in terms of providing tracking data gathered from the stores' scanners. There are three components of Scantrack Services. First, **Scantrack Basic Services** collects data weekly from approximately 4800 food, drug, and mass-merchandise stores representing about 800 different retailers in 52 markets in the United States. ACNielsen Scantrack Basic Services tracks thousands of products as they move through retail stores, allowing brand managers to monitor sales and market share and to evaluate marketing strategies. Scantrack reports can be provided at many different levels of information. For example, a report may be ordered for just one category of products across the 52 U.S. markets.[11] Or a report can be generated for one brand in a single market. The other two Scantrack services provide tracking data for products sold in drugstores and mass merchandiser stores through its **PROCISION** tracking service and also for convenience stores through its **C–Store Plus Service**.[12]

> ACNielsen's Scantrack Services provide firms with tracking data based on scanner-collected data. Visit ACNielsen at www.acnielsen.com. You can learn more about Scantrack Services at www.acnielsen .com/products/reports/ scantrack/.

InfoScan Custom Store Tracking. Information Resources, Inc. (IRI) syndicated data service, **InfoScan Custom Store Tracking**, gathers data with the use of scanners in supermarkets, drugstores, and mass merchandisers. InfoScan collects data weekly in

> IRI's InfoScan Custom Store Tracking provides firms with tracking data based on scanner-collected data. Visit IRI at www.infores.com.

7.2

Why Is Geography Important in Retail Management?

GIS is a technology much like word processing or data mining. Technology has continuously played a major role in just about every business, and if it hasn't, it should. In the information age that we live in, technology's role has become increasingly important. However, for technology to be accepted into the mainstream markets, it must be beneficial, show an ROI, and be easy to use and affordable. If technology doesn't meet these requirements, it won't be adopted by business.

For many years, GIS wasn't a mainstream technology; in fact, just the term *geodemographic information systems* sounded too complex and difficult for any business to comprehend and resulted in GIS not being quickly integrated into organizations' day-to-day operations. GIS required staff specifically trained in GIS, and the cost justifications to do this weren't there. Businesses didn't want this complexity added to everything else they had to do to be successful. In businesses that did acquire the technology, its primary use was for sales and marketing. GIS was used more as a mapping system than as an analytical and modeling tool, and it typically wasn't integrated into other systems currently in use. Now, however, GIS is becoming part of the mainstream. Why? Because the software has become easier to use, the cost of data has come down in price, and systems are easier to use, they don't require GIS specialists, and they truly do benefit an organization. They help the bottom line, and business has discovered that there are certain things that only a GIS can do better than manual methods: drive-time analysis, market penetration, and trade-area delineation, to name a few. In other words, GIS is becoming mainstream because the technology criteria have been met.

The biggest advantage of GIS for retailers is that it inherently focuses the retailer's attention on where the problems are and where the solution will come from. Instead of analyzing everything in the world, GIS focuses the attention on the pieces of geography where solutions lie. Analysis such as creating the trade area and drive time cannot be done manually but adds significant value to a retailer because it defines the area of strength, market presence, and source of revenue, and gives a better understanding of customers' shopping behavior. Instead of worrying about the entire universe, a retailer can focus on the small geography and the consumers/customers in that geography who are or who should be his or her customers. With a high degree of accuracy, the system can estimate the potential for an existing retail location as well as for a prospective location. A GIS cannot ensure victory over the competition, but it can help point retailers in the right direction and give insights about where their market or trade area is the strongest.

Customer-Based Market Analysis: Using GIS to Define the Trading Area

Location, location, location have been the three most important words in retail. Typically this has addressed the location of the store, but it has come to refer also to the location of the customer. Think about it—if you know where your customers live, you not only have more information than most retailers and a significant advantage over most of your competitors, but you also have a significant set of data that can be used to define your store trade area. You now have the ability to profile your customers, the ability to identify new store locations that have demographics similar to those of your best store, and the ability to measure your market penetration.

The customer's address is the genesis of all the power of GIS in the retail industry. It gives the location of the customer. From that location, the point can be geocoded (the address can be placed on an electronic map), and from that geocode, tremendous amounts of data become available about that point.

The proximity of customers to the retail store is important, and so is drive time to the store, i.e., the normal amount of time it takes the customers to get from their homes to the store. Retailing success is all about convenience.

A GIS is used to define the store's trade area as the area where the closest customers live. The exact cutoff is arbitrary but most retailers use a cutoff of about 50% of the total customers for the Primary Trade Area and 80% for the Secondary Trade Area. Anyone who lives outside these areas by definition lives outside the trade area. We are not excluding these outside-trade-area customers from buying in the store, but they normally are not as profitable to market to. If we marketed to all the customers who had purchased in the store in the last 12 months, and broke the results into three groups, Primary Trade Area, Secondary Trade Area, and Outside the Trade Area, the highest responders will normally be

Primary, followed by Secondary, with the Outside customers responding the least. It is important to know where your customers come from, and GIS is the tool that allows us to do this.

Since there is a 50% probability of the next customer coming from the Primary Trade Area and an 80% probability that the next customer will come from the Primary/Secondary Trade Area, it is critical to learn as much as possible about those areas.

Understanding the geographies and dynamics of the retail trade area and the behavior of the consumers is critical to a retailer's success in today's extremely competitive marketplace.

Sales aggregated to the Zip code level as shown on the map.

Trade area for the store shown in the example below. Trade area based on customer revenue for one year and calculated as 40%, 60%, and 80%. This shows where the revenue comes from.

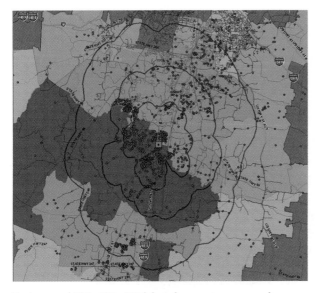

Trade areas (40%, 60%, 80%) based on customer annual spending and drive time. The underlying colors represent sales aggregated to the Zip code level, with the darkest blue having the highest concentration of sales and customers. Customers are shown as red dots.

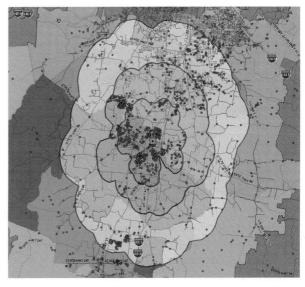

Approximately 80% of this store's revenues come from within a 20-minute-or-less drive.

Courtesy of ESRI.

over 32,000 stores and provides subscribers access to information across many InfoScan categories. Data may be analyzed across major categories as well.[13]

The primary advantage of scanning data is that the data are available very quickly to decision makers. There is a minimum delay from the time the data are collected and the time the information is available to decision makers. The disadvantage is that a company may have products distributed through smaller stores that do not have scanners. However, as the market changes some marketing research firms emerge to provide information on new trends. Such is the case with natural and organic food products being sold through natural foods supermarkets. As you will read in Marketing Research Insight 7.3, **SPINS** is a marketing research company that provides scanner tracking data for natural and organic foods.

PRACTICAL INSIGHTS

7.3

SPINS Uses Scanner Data to Track Natural and Organic Foods

As new trends emerge marketing research firms develop services to satisfy the new information needs. Natural and organic foods have been growing as a part of the total food budget and it is likely that the trend will continue. SPINS, a San Francisco, California, marketing research firm has become a specialist in providing information on natural and organic foods. They offer tracking services for products such as teas, yogurts, diet aids, vitamins and minerals, tofu, juices, pastas, milk, energy bars, baby food, and cereals. This firm offers several services, including a scanner tracking service partnered with ACNielsen to develop a Scantrack tracking service called SPINS Natural Track. This service tracks product movement through food, drug, and mass channels of distribution. ACNielsen/SPINS Natural Track Reports allows decision makers to:

■ Identify which natural brands are growing in mainstream channels.
■ Evaluate which mainstream markets are most important to natural products.
■ Assess the performance and growth of your brand and product's category in key mainstream markets.
■ Pinpoint which product categories are ripe for new natural product entry.

■ Determine market share of natural products to overall category.

Another SPINS service, SPINScan, tracks natural and organic products through natural product supermarkets. This service allows decision makers to identify and evaluate natural brands' performance and growth, including evaluating categories and determining market shares in the natural product supermarket channel.

Read more about SPINS services at their Web site: **www.spins.com**.

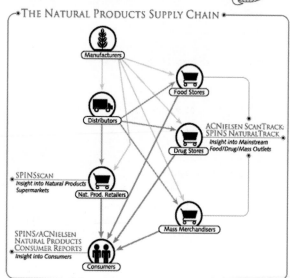

services overview

By permission, SPINS.

In retail-store audits, auditors record merchandising information needed for tracking studies.

Retail-Store Audits. Some tracking services do not rely solely on data collected in retail stores by scanners. **Retail-store audits** also are used. In retail-store audits, auditors are sent to stores to record merchandising information needed for tracking studies. Store audits are particularly useful for smaller stores that do not have scanner equipment, such as convenience stores. Sales are estimated by calculating the following:

Beginning Inventory + Purchases Received − Ending Inventory = Sales

Auditors not only record this information for many products but also note other merchandising factors, such as the level and type of in-store promotions, newspaper advertising, out-of-stock products, and shelf facings of products. Like data collected by scanning services, data collected by audit are stored in a common database and made available to all who subscribe.

▶ **Market Tracking at the Household Level.** Information is gathered in homes using scanning devices, diaries, and audits. In-home scanner devices are provided to panel members who agree to scan the UPC codes on products they have purchased. Other services ask panel members to record purchases in diaries that are subsequently mailed back to the research firm. Finally, a few research firms collect data by actually sending auditors into homes to count and record information. Almost all of these methods rely on consumer household panels whose members are recruited for the purpose of recording and reporting their household purchases to one of the standardized data services firms. We shall give you some examples of each.

Information Resources, Inc.'s ScanKey Consumer Network Household Panel. Information Resources, Inc. also maintains a panel of consumer households that record purchases at outlets by scanning UPC codes on the products purchased. Using IRI's handheld ScanKey scanning wand, panel members record their purchases, and this information is transmitted via telephone link back to IRI. In the summer of 2005, IRI had 70,000 shoppers as part of its consumer panel. Like many panels, an advantage of this panel is that it provides not only information on products purchased but also purchase data that are linked to the demographics of the purchasers.[14]

ACNielsen Homescan Panel. The **ACNielsen Homescan Panel** recruits panel members who use handheld scanners to scan all bar-coded products purchased and brought home from all outlets, including warehouse clubs and convenience stores. Panel members also record the outlet at which all the merchandise was purchased and which family member made the purchase, as well as price and causal information such as coupon usage. This panel allows ACNielsen to track data on products whether they are bought in a store with or without scanners and from any store and from any type of store whether it be a warehouse club, supermarket, mail-ordered product or a product purchased over the Internet. It also allows the company to provide data on products with and without UPC codes. The Homescan Panel consists of households that are demographically and geographically balanced and projectable to the total United States. In addition, local markets can be tracked. ACNielsen's Worldwide Panel Service also provides home tracking services for 18 countries around the world.[15]

Diary. The use of diaries to collect data appears to be decreasing. This is likely due to falling response rates. Consumers seem to be less willing to complete diaries recording their purchases or media habits.[16] However, some companies offer tracking data collected by household diaries. Each panel member is asked to complete a **diary** containing information such as the type of product, name brand, manufacturer or producer, model number, description, purchase price, store from which the item was purchased, and information about the person making the purchase. This information can then be used to estimate important factors such as market share, brand loyalty, brand switching, and demographic profile of purchasers. The panel members are typically balanced geographically to the United States and regions of the United States. Nielsen Media Research uses diaries to collect data on television viewing and Arbitron, the radio ratings company, uses diaries to collect data. We will discuss both of these services in greater depth in a later section of this chapter.

Audit. Some companies conduct an **audit**, collecting data from households by sending auditors into homes. NPD's Complete Kitchen Audit records ingredients, kitchen utensils, and appliances in homes. The information is provided to manufacturers of kitchen products and food producers.[17]

Information for tracking studies is gathered in homes using scanning devices, or through the use of diaries and even home audits.

IRI's ScanKey Consumer Network Household Panel has members who scan products they purchase and send the data back to IRI to be used in tracking studies.

Learn more about ACNielsen's Homescan Panel at www. acnielsen.com/products/ reports/homescan/.

Some services gather tracking data by having panel members record their purchases in a household diary.

Some firms collect tracking data by sending auditors into panel members' homes to actually count and record data.

▶ **Turning Market Tracking Information into Intelligence.** One of the disadvantages of today's information technology is that a user of information can easily be swamped with information, producing "information overload." You can imagine the quantity of information that could flow to a manufacturer who subscribes to tracking data. The information flows in frequently and in large quantities. Various companies have created a host of products to help decision makers use vast quantities of information for intelligent decisions. Variously labeled "decision support systems," "data mining systems," "expert systems," and the like, these systems use analytical tools to attach meaning to data, allowing managers to make decisions in response to quickly changing market conditions. Some examples include **IRI's Builder services** and **ACNielsen's Category Business Planner**. Category Business Planner is a Web-based category planning tool that aids managers in making better decisions based on sales information of products in the consumer packaged goods industry. What is unique about Category Business Planner is that it allows a manufacturer to move from retailer to retailer to view how its product is performing within each retailer's proprietary view of the category containing the product. This allows a manufacturer to evaluate product performance the same way a retail customer would evaluate the manufacturer's product, allowing them to better collaborate when developing their business plans for each product category.[18]

Monitoring Media Usage and Promotion Effectiveness

Business firms typically conduct studies to measure their effectiveness, readership, listenership, and so on. This information is useful to firms contemplating advertising expenditures. Because there is a need for some objective measure of promotional effectiveness, several syndicated data service companies have evolved over the years to supply such information to subscribing firms. Some of these services specialize in a particular medium; a few others conduct studies on several forms of media. A discussion of both types of these organizations follows.

▶ **Tracking Downloaded Music, Videos, and Recorded Books.** ACNielsen's **SoundScan** tracks music downloaded online from several online music stores such as Apple's iTunes.[19] Likewise, ACNielsen's **VideoScan** and **BookScan** track prerecorded videos and books. This is an example of a research firm innovating services in response to changing products and distribution systems.[20]

▶ **Television.** The **Nielsen Television Index (NTI)** has been the major provider of TV ratings since 1950. Nielsen Media Research provides the NTI and it is owned by VNU, a Netherlands-based publishing and research firm. VNU also owns the marketing research firm ACNielsen. Television ratings data are reported for **DMAs (Designated Market Areas)**. DMAs were designed by Nielsen to represent geographical areas that represent the various TV markets. There are 210 DMAs in the U.S.[21]

Few TV watchers have been unaffected by the Nielsen Television Index; their favorite show has been canceled or, because the index showed a large audience, the show has run for many years. Obviously, firms in the TV industry are constantly trying to achieve higher viewership than their competition. High viewership allows them to charge higher prices to advertise during the more popular programs.

For most DMAs Nielsen Media Research uses a diary in which families record their television viewing habits. However, in 56 DMAs television viewing is measured with the **people meter**, an electronic instrument that automatically measures when a TV set is on and who is watching which channel. Family members are asked to enter their names (by codes) into the people meter each time they watch TV. Data from the people meter are transmitted directly back to Nielsen, allowing the firm to develop estimates

The people meter records what TV program a household member is watching.

Nielsen Media Research is a world famous TV ratings company. The company also offers several other services that you can learn about at the Nielsen Media Research Web site at **www.nielsenmedia .com/index.html**. Courtesy of Nielsen Media Research.

of the size of the audience for each program by reporting the percentage of TV households viewing a given show.[22] NTI reports a rating and a share for each program telecast. A rating is the percentage of households that have at least one set tuned to a given program for a minimum of 6 minutes for each 15 minutes the program is telecast. A share is the percentage of households with at least one set tuned to a specific program at a specific time.

The Nielsen Television Index also provides subscribers with other audience characteristic information that allows potential advertisers to select audiences that most closely match their target markets' characteristics. Ratings are reported by the number of households, by whether the women are employed outside the home, by age group for women (18+, 12–24, 18–34, 18–49, 25–54, 35–64, 55+), by age group for men (18+, 18–34, 18–49, 25–54, 35–65, 55+), and by age group of children (children ages 2 and older, ages 6 to 11, and teenagers).

Monitoring the number of persons watching TV programs is a syndicated data service provided by the Nielsen Television Index.

▶ **Radio.** Since 1964, radio listenership has been measured by **Arbitron**. The company's national and regional panel members complete diaries reporting radio listening for one week. Panel members record information in a weekly paper-and-pencil diary. They indicate the time of day; how long the station was tuned in; which station was on; where the listening was done (at home, in a car, at work, or other place); and the panel member's age, gender, and home address. Although paper-and-pencil diaries are still being used, Arbitron has been testing a **Portable People Meter (PPM^{SM})** system, in the United States. The meter is the size of a pager, which automatically records stations listened to. (We have more to say about the PPM in the upcoming section on multimedia services). Data from the diaries are used to measure and report a number of variables indicative of radio listenership. Listenership is measured in 15-minute intervals and data are also reported by age and gender to aid in profiling audience characteristics. Subscribers to Arbitron Radio Market Reports can view the data on the computer and select the output formats in which they wish to view the data. How can radio stations and businesses use this information to formulate marketing strategy? For instance, knowing where a person is listening may affect the type of message an advertiser wishes to use. A station with a high concentration of in-car listening may appeal to car dealers, auto parts stores, transmission repair shops, and tire stores. Understanding where the listening occurs is also helpful in determining programming elements such as traffic reports, contests, newscasts, and other information and entertainment segments. Arbitron also conducts other customized marketing research studies to suit individual clients' needs.[23]

Arbitron provides syndicated data on radio station listening using panels who record the stations to which they are listening in diaries. Arbitron is testing the Portable People Meter that automatically records audio and video signals to which a person carrying the meter is exposed.

▶ **Print. NOP World's Starch Readership Service** is known as the most widely used source for measuring the extent to which magazine ads are seen and read. Starch conducts personal interviews with a minimum sample of 100 readers of a given issue of a magazine, trade publication, or newspaper. Interviews are carried out in 20 to 30 urban

NOP World's Starch Readership service provides syndicated data on magazine readership. Visit Starch Readership Service at **www.nopworld.com.** Go to Centers for Excellence/ Marketing Effectiveness/ Products and Services. While you are there, take a look at all the standardized services provided by NOP World.

Arbitron's Chinese–English Diary is just one way that Arbitron ensures that diverse populations are represented in Arbitron studies. By permission, Arbitron.

localities for each magazine issue analyzed. Interviews are conducted only with respondents who have read the issue prior to the interview. Therefore, Starch readership studies are not designed to determine the number of readers who read a particular issue of a magazine. Rather, Starch determines what readers saw and read in a study issue when they first looked through it. Starch studies over 25,000 ads in 400 individual print publications a year and interviews more than 40,000 people annually. Starch then uses the following readership levels in its reports:

> Noted—The percentage of issue readers who remember having previously seen any part of the advertisement in the study issue.
> Associated—The percentage of issue readers who not only noted the ad but also saw or read some part of it that clearly indicated the brand or advertiser.
> Read Some—The percentage of issue readers who read any part of the ad's copy.
> Read Most—The percentage of issue readers who read one-half or more of the written material in the advertisement.

In addition to these readership levels, Starch reports a number of other analytical measures, such as an ad's rank, which shows the relative standing of an ad in terms of its Noted and Associated percentages to all other ads in the magazine issue. In addition to evaluating individual ads, Starch also analyzes the impact of many other variables on readership such as ad size, number of pages, black and white, color, special position (cover, center spread, etc.), and product category, among several others.[24] To further help marketers make decisions about what comprises a good ad, Starch also provides another syndicated data service called Adnorms. **Adnorms** provides readership scores by type of ads. For example, Adnorms could calculate the average readership scores for one-page, four-color computer ads appearing in *Business Week*. This allows an advertiser to compare his or her ad scores with the norm. In this way, advertising effectiveness may be assessed. Users learn the effect of ad size, color, and even copy on readership.[25]

▶ **Multimedia.** Some standardized information sources firms provide information on a number of media. **Simmons National Consumer Study** provides information on media usage linked to product usage. About 27,000 consumers are interviewed in the study. Media habits are related to product usage among 450 product categories, such as apparel, automotive, computers, and travel. Over 8000 brands are studied. In addition, psychographic and demographic data are collected. The information allows users to determine the viewing/listening media habits of users of certain product categories and brands.

Earlier we discussed Arbitron with regard to radio. However, Arbitron's Portable People Meter (PPM) is a measure of multimedia, including TV, radio, satellite radio, and the Web. The company's development of the PPM could prove to be a significant innovation in today's world, where consumers are exposed to a variety of media types in a variety of locations other than in their own living rooms. The PPM has been under development since 1992, and Arbitron has been testing the device extensively.[26] It is currently being used internationally to measure media; the BBM in Canada is using the PPM to measure French language television. In addition it is being used in Belgium, Norway, and Kenya. The PPM system uses an encoder at a radio or television station, which embeds a code into the audio portion of the signals. The encoders can also be used for audio streaming over the Web. When a survey respondent carries the meter and is exposed to a medium's broadcast, the meter captures the code identifying the exposure. Additional encoders can be added to stations with multiple feeds (digital and analog). Since the codes are different, the meter identifies the platform. In the evening, respondents are asked to place their PPM in a base unit that recharges it and records the data collected so that it may be transmitted via modem to Arbitron. Arbitron panel members are encouraged to wear the PPM a minimum of 8 hours a day. The PPM may allow Arbitron to measure audiences for radio, television, cable, satellite, video games, CDs, VCR tapes, and even audio on the Internet. With recent technological advances making more media alternatives available (more channels on TV, satellite radio, wireless Internet, and so on), there is a growing demand for multimedia measurement services.[27]

> Simmons National Consumer Study provides information on media usage linked to product usage. You can learn more about the services provided by Simmons by going to www.smrb.com/.

> Arbitron's Portable People Meter (PPM) could prove to be a significant innovation in today's world, where consumers are exposed to a variety of media types in a variety of locations other than in their own living rooms.

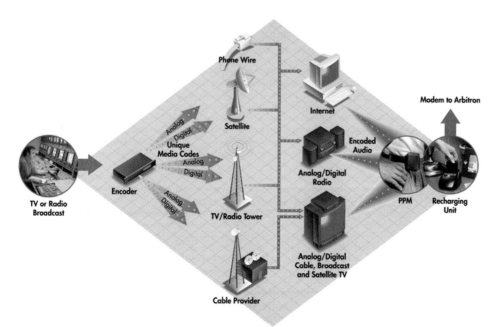

Arbitron's Portable People Meter is designed to be carried by panel members and to record encoded signals from various media sources. In this way Arbitron can measure media exposure from multiple sources whether the panelist is in or out of their home. By permission, Arbitron.

SINGLE-SOURCE DATA

Single-source data are recorded continuously from a panel of respondents to measure their exposure to promotional materials (usually TV as well as in-store promotions) and subsequent buying behavior. Armed with this information, marketers know whether consumers who saw one of their ads actually bought their product.

Several technological developments have led to the development of single-source data, including the universal product code (UPC) and scanning equipment that electronically records and stores data gathered at the point of purchase. As we shall explain in the following paragraphs, when coupled with computer and MIS technological developments, powerful "single-source" databases are built that are capable of providing a wealth of information on consumer purchases down to the UPC level.

Single-source data are data that contain information on several variables such as promotional message exposure, demographics, and buyer behavior. Single-source data can help managers determine causal relationships between types of promotions and sales.

Although scanner-based databases can provide up-to-the-minute reports on the sale of virtually any consumer product by store, date, time of day, price, and so on, these same powerful databases cannot provide any information about *who* bought the product. However, several marketing research services, such as Information Resource's BehaviorScan, can supply demographic data on the consumers' purchasing of various products. **BehaviorScan** is a standardized service that consists of panels of consumers in several cities around the United States who are provided with an electronic card that is scanned as they check out of participating retailers. BehaviorScan can control TV ads sent to its panel members. Having the ability to know which ads panelists have been exposed to and also knowing which products these same panelists have purchased gives BehaviorScan subscribers access to powerful causal data. Thus, from a single data source, a marketer may obtain information about media exposure as well as purchases. Consequently, with single-source data, marketers have not only the ability to determine who is purchasing what, when, and where, but they also know the media and in-store promotions to which the buyers were exposed. Therefore, from this one database (single source) marketers should have the ability to answer cause-and-effect questions concerning how marketing mix variables actually affect sales.

When the concept of single-source data was introduced a few years ago, some thought it would revolutionize the marketing research industry. Others believed that it would not be so revolutionary and that there would always be a place for traditional marketing research studies. Today, single-source studies are a small part of total research studies, but their use is growing. ITV's tvSPAN, for example, recently expanded its single-source service from 750 households to 3000 households.[28] As technology improves and as these systems earn confidence among users, we are likely to see single-source services grow even more.[29]

Single-source data are data that contain information on several variables such as promotional message exposure, demographics, and buyer behavior. Single-source data can help managers determine causal relationships between types of promotions and sales.

IRI's BehaviorScan is an example of a standardized service source for single-source data.

While single-source data have not replaced traditional marketing research studies during the past decade, use of the service is increasing.

SUMMARY

Standardized information is a type of secondary data in which the data collected and/or the process of collecting the data are standardized for all users. There are two classes of standardized information. Syndicated data are data being collected in a standard format and being made available to all subscribing users. An example would be the Nielsen TV ratings. Standardized services offer a standardized marketing research process that is used to generate information for a particular user.

Community Tapestry is a system of classifying residential neighborhoods by ZIP codes into 65 different segments. That process is standardized; it is the same for all users of Community Tapestry. The information from the process is then applied to generate different data for each user. With syndicated data, the data are the same for each user and with standardized services the process of generating data for each user is the same.

Syndicated data have the advantages of sharing the costs of obtaining the data among all those subscribing to the service, high data quality, and the speed with which data are collected and distributed to subscribers. Disadvantages are that buyers cannot control what data are collected, buyers must commit to long-term contracts, and there is no strategic information advantage to buying syndicated data because the information is available to all competitors.

Standardized services have the advantage of use of the supplier firm's expertise in the area, reduced costs, and speed with which supplier firms can conduct the service. The disadvantages of standardized services are that the process cannot easily be customized, and the supplier firm may not know the idiosyncrasies of the industry in which the client firm operates.

Four major areas in which standardized information sources may be applied are measuring consumers' attitudes and opinions, defining market segments in both the industrial/business-to-business markets as well as the consumer market, conducting market tracking studies, and monitoring media usage and promotion effectiveness. The Harris poll is an example of a syndicated data source providing information on consumers' attitudes and opinions. Many firms offer standardized services that define consumer market segments. Examples include ESRI's Community Tapestry, Clarita's $PRIZM_{NE}$, and VALS. Some firms offer GIS services, which allow for the analysis of markets in arbitrarily defined units. ACNielsen's Scantrack Basic Services is an example of a syndicated data source for tracking the sales of consumer product goods sold in retail stores. Other standardized services track goods by collecting data from consumer households. Arbitron radio listenership studies are an example of a syndicated data source for monitoring radio listenership.

Single-source information sources use sales data recorded by scanners that record sales at the UPC level by brand, store, date, price, and so on. Those data are then coupled with information on the buyer's demographics and media exposure. Having information on who bought what, where, and when after being exposed to promotional materials in one single database may give marketers the ability to answer important cause-and-effect questions on, for example, which marketing mix variable X caused the sale of product Y. IRI's BehaviorScan is an example of a standardized service providing single-source information. Using BehaviorScan, marketers can test the effects of different TV campaigns as well as in-store promotional materials.

KEY TERMS

Standardized information (p. 178)
Syndicated data (p. 178)
Standardized services (p. 178)
ESRI's Community Tapestry (p. 178)
Yankelovich Monitor (p. 180)
Harris poll (p. 180)
Gallup poll (p. 180)
Dun's Market Identifiers (DMI) (p. 181)
VALS (p. 181)

Geodemographics (p. 183)
GIS (p. 183)
$PRIZM_{NE}$ (p. 183)
$P\$YCLE_{NE}$ (p. 184)
ConneXions (p. 184)
Tracking studies (p. 185)
Scanning data (p. 185)
Scantrack Basic Services (p. 185)
PROCISION (p. 185)

C-Store Plus Service (p. 185)
InfoScan Custom Store Tracking (p. 185)
SPINS (p. 187)
Retail-store audits (p. 188)
ScanKey Consumer Network Household
   Panel (p. 189)
ACNielsen Homescan Panel (p. 189)
Diary (p. 189)
Audit (p. 189)
IRI's Builder services (p. 190)
ACNielsen's Category Business Planner
   (p. 190)
SoundScan (p. 190)
VideoScan (p. 190)

BookScan (p. 190)
Nielsen Television Index (NTI) (p. 190)
DMAs (Designated Market Areas)
   (p. 190)
People meter (p. 190)
Arbitron (p. 191)
Portable People Meter (PPM) (p. 191)
NOP World's Starch Readership Service
   (p. 192)
Adnorms (p. 192)
Simmons National Consumer Study
   (p. 193)
Single-source data (p. 194)
BehaviorScan (p. 194)

REVIEW QUESTIONS/APPLICATIONS

1. What is meant by "standardized information"?
2. Distinguish between syndicated data and standardized services.
3. What are the advantages and disadvantages of syndicated data?
4. What are the advantages and disadvantages of standardized services?
5. Name four broad types of applications of standardized information and give an example of each.
6. Explain how the standardized service, Dun's Market Identifiers (DMI) could be helpful in a marketing research application.
7. What is geodemography, and how can it be used in marketing decisions? Give an example.
8. Explain why VALS would be considered a standardized information service.
9. What are tracking studies? Give an example of how managers would use tracking study data.
10. Describe ACNielsen's Scantrack Basic Services.
11. What is a panel that gathers information from consumers by asking them to scan the UPC codes (bar codes) on goods they purchase and bring home?
12. Explain how "information overload" of tracking information can be alleviated through software also offered as standardized services.
13. Name the standardized information services designed to gather data on downloaded music. Prerecorded video sales. Prerecorded book sales. Natural and organic food sales.
14. What company provides syndicated data on TV ratings?
15. What is the firm that is best known for conducting studies of radio listenership? Briefly describe the service it provides.
16. What is single-source data?
17. Go to the Web sites of three marketing research companies. Review their list of products and services offered. Which of these are standardized services? Syndicated data? Custom research offerings?
18. Imagine you are a potential franchisee for a Donofrio's Coffee franchise (see beginning of chapter). Evaluate the Donofrios use of the standardized service Community Tapestry to help you make your decision about where to locate your franchise Donofrio's Coffee.

19. Review the kinds of information gathered by **www.gallup.com**. Go to the Web site and look at some of the former studies they report. How could a marketing manager use some of this information?

20. Go to a search engine such as Google, Yahoo, or AskJeeves. Look up "GIS." Describe some of the applications of GIS that some of the sites have described.

21. Describe how a marketing manager could make use of single-source data to make (a) pricing decisions and (b) in-store promotions decisions.

22. Contact a radio or TV station or perhaps a newspaper in your town. Ask managers how they measure listenership, viewership, or readership and for what purposes they use this information. In most cases, these firms will be happy to supply you with a standard package of materials answering the preceding questions.

23. Given what you know about syndicated services, which firm would you call on if you had the following information needs?

    a. You want to know which magazines have the heaviest readership among tennis players.

    b. You have decided to conduct a test market but you have no research department within your firm and no experience in test marketing.

    c. You need to know how a representative sample of U.S. households would answer seven questions about dental hygiene.

    d. You are thinking about a radically new advertising theme but you are very concerned about consumer reaction to the new theme. You want some idea as to how the new theme will have an impact on sales of your frozen dinners.

PREMIER PRODUCTS, INC.

Premier Products, Inc. (PPI) is a large multinational firm with several product divisions including foods, over-the-counter drugs, and household products. The firm has over 1000 products and distributes through grocery stores, mass merchandisers, and convenience stores in the United States, Canada, and Western Europe. Products are marketed under different brand names but all are marked with the PPI family brand name. The company is headquartered in the United States and has six regional offices. There is a marketing research department with a staff of 26 people at company headquarters. The department is primarily responsible for quarterly reports and answering the information requests of divisional managers who are responsible for creating new products and ensuring profitable product performance. Each divisional manager, working with brand managers, develop their own marketing programs and make all their decisions regarding product additions and deletions, pricing, distribution, and promotion of the different brands. PPI's V.P. of Marketing Research is Stephanie Williamson.

Dale Hair, Division Manager for the Dairy Foods line of products met with Williamson and explained that she needed better information to help them target customers for direct mail campaigns consisting primarily of new product awareness messages and cents-off coupons. Hair could describe the general demographic characteristics of her primary target market thanks to previously conducted marketing research. She needed help with this for the U.S. market.

Joy Schurr, a brand manager for a line of soups, was interested in knowing what was happening in terms of consumers' attitudes toward brand name versus privately branded soups. PPI's brand, "Bowl-A-Soup" had been on the market for almost 35 years and was a well established global brand. Schurr had been concerned about comments from many of the supermarket chain managers who were considering private brands. She wanted to know if consumer attitudes were shifting to more in favor of private, usually less-expensive, brands versus national or global brands.

Lisa Henson, Division Manager, had a new product under development—a device for replacing light bulbs in ceilings that was simple to use and very effective. However, Henson was concerned that the distribution for this product would fall outside of PPI's present distribution network of supermarkets, mass merchandisers, and convenience stores. While some of the company's mass merchandiser customers would likely carry the product, she felt distribution would be too limited to ensure a profitable return. She was interested in knowing more about hardware stores as a possible distribution strategy for the new product. However, calling on hardware stores would be too expensive if PPI had only the one product to offer. Henson wanted to know if there were wholesalers of light bulbs and light-related products who called on hardware stores and other retail stores.

1. Should Stephanie Williamson assign any, or all, of these tasks to her twenty six member staff?

2. Can you recommend a standardized information service that Williamson may consider for Dale Hair?

3. What would you recommend for Joy Schurr?

4. What would you recommend for Lisa Henson?

MAGGIE J'S DOG TREATS

Maggie J's Dog Treats are sold all over the United States. Distribution is through grocery stores and a few large mass merchandising chains such as Wal-Mart and Target Stores. Mike Hall is V.P. of marketing for the company. Hall has been concerned with the level of competition in dog treat brands in the past few months. More and more competitors are trying innovative marketing programs. Mike has commissioned an ad agency to develop a national promotional campaign. The agency has presented four different sets of TV ads, each based on a different marketing strategy. To be integrated with the TV ads are a series of in-store promotions. The four in-store promotion campaigns are each stand-alone campaigns. In other words, any one of them may be run simulaneously with any one of the four proposed TV ad campaigns.

The agency made their final presentation to Mike and the other officers of the company. Essentially they must choose between the four different TV ad/in-store promotion campaigns. Hall and the other officers are very pleased with the creative work conducted by the ad agency. All four campaigns are equally appealing. All four campaigns are consistent with the key benefits of Maggie J's treats; dogs like them and they have high nutritive value. The officers know that the selection of the right campaign is important since they are going to allocate several million dollars to the campaign. They also know it is important because they believe it will be important for them to maintain or increase market share in light of the extreme, recent competition. "This is a case in which even a very small difference in effectiveness may play a major role in the success of our brand," says Hall. After several hours of debate it was clear that no one, even with many years in the dog treat business, could clearly determine which of the four campaigns should be selected. Finally, Executive V.P. Jack Russell stated "We need to run this by Ron Stillman. He's responsible for marketing research. Maybe Ron can help us decide what to do."

The following day the officers met with Ron Stillman and reviewed the four TV ad campaigns and the four in-store promotion campaigns. Ron agreed that even a small difference in the effectiveness of the campaigns could make a significant difference in market share, profits, and ROI. Stillman also pointed out that it was possible that there could be a significant "interaction" effect between the TV campaigns and the in-store promotions. In other words, we may find that a particular TV campaign performs significantly better when it is run with a particular in-store promotion.

Maggie J's did not have their own marketing research department. However, Stillman was responsible for assisting managers in determining whether or not research was needed and in selecting the right outside supplier firm and service to use. Stillman stated that he would make some calls and gather some information from different research suppliers. A meeting was set up for the following Friday morning to consider Stillman's proposed suggestions for conducting marketing research.

1. Do you think it is appropriate to conduct marketing research?

2. Should Ron Stillman consider a standardized information service? What are the arguments for and against using a standardized information service?

3. Should Ron Stillman consider standardized data or a standardized service?

4. Which particular standardized information service, discussed in this chapter, do you think Ron Stillman should recommend? Why?

Observation, Focus Groups, and Other Qualitative Methods

Golf Digest Companies use Pluralistic Research to Solve Callaway Golf's Problems

We opened Chapter 4 on Defining the Problem and Determining Research Objectives with an example of Golf Digest Companies' Corporate Marketing and Research Department conducting research for their client, Callaway Golf. We saw that Callaway was experiencing a decline in sales of their woods, and they needed to know the importance of their marketing mix elements as well as how to use consumer perceptions to redefine their strategy. As you can see by the image on the next page, Golf Digest Companies elected to use a combination of qualitative and quantitative research. We call the use of both these approaches, pluralistic research. Focus groups, completing diaries describing purchase protocols, and in-depth interviews are considered three qualitative research methods. The quantitative study was collecting data from Golf Digest Companies' Clubhouse Panel. Pluralistic research allows researchers to gain from the advantages of both quantitative research and qualitative research. Using a pluralistic approach, Golf Digest Companies was able to provide their client with insights that helped them solve their problems.

By permission, Golf Digest Companies, New York, NY

- To understand basic differences between quantitative and qualitative research techniques
- To see how pluralistic research may be used to solve problems
- To learn the pros and cons of using observation as a means of gathering data
- To discover what focus groups are and how they are conducted and analyzed
- To become acquainted with online focus groups and their advantages
- To become familiar with other qualitative methods used by marketing researchers

Learning Objectives

The RRC Solution

4 PHASE STUDY:

- Focus Groups

- Quantitative study with Clubhouse panel

- Purchaser diaries

- Depth interviews

Qualitative research methods are sometimes referred to as the "soft side" of marketing research. In this chapter we will learn how to distinguish between qualitative and quantitative research as well as the various methods used in conducting qualitative research. You will also learn that each qualitative method has its place in the marketing research process, and that each has its unique advantages and disadvantages as well. Because focus groups are a popular qualitative marketing research technique, an in-depth discussion of them is included. We begin with a discussion of quantitative, qualitative, and pluralistic research.

QUANTITATIVE, QUALITATIVE, AND PLURALISTIC RESEARCH

The means of data collection during the research process can be classified into three broad categories: quantitative, qualitative, and pluralistic.

Quantitative research is defined as research involving the use of structured questions in which the response options have been predetermined and a large number of respondents is involved.

Qualitative research involves collecting, analyzing, and interpreting data by observing what people do and say. Observations and statements are in a qualitative or nonstandardized form.

Qualitative research techniques afford rich insight into consumer behavior.

The means of data collection during the research process can be classified into three broad categories: quantitative, qualitative, and pluralistic. There are vast differences between the first two methods, and it is necessary to understand their special characteristics in order to make the right selection. To start, we briefly define these two approaches, and then we describe pluralistic research.

Quantitative research is the traditional mainstay of the research industry, and it is sometimes referred to as "survey research." For our purposes in this chapter, **quantitative research** is defined as research involving the use of structured questions in which the response options have been predetermined and a large number of respondents is involved. When you think of quantitative research, you might envision a nationwide survey conducted with telephone interviews. That is, quantitative research often involves a sizable representative sample of the population and a formalized procedure for gathering data. The purpose of quantitative research is very specific, and this research is used when the manager and researcher have agreed that precise information is needed. Data format and sources are clear and well defined, and the compilation and formatting of the data gathered follows an orderly procedure that is largely numerical in nature.

Qualitative research, in contrast, involves collecting, analyzing, and interpreting data by observing what people do and say. Observations and statements are in a qualitative or nonstandardized form. Because of this, qualitative data can be quantified, but only after a translation process has taken place. For example, if you asked five people to express their opinions on a topic such as gun control or promoting alcoholic beverages to college students, you would probably get five different statements. But after studying each response, you could characterize each one as "positive," "negative," or "neutral." This translation step would not be necessary if you instructed them to choose predetermined responses such as "yes" or "no." Any study that is conducted using an observational technique or unstructured questioning can be classified as qualitative research, which is becoming increasingly popular in a number of research situations.[1]

Why would you want to use such a "soft" approach? Occasionally, marketing researchers find that a large-scale survey is inappropriate. For instance, Procter & Gamble may be interested in improving its Tide laundry detergent, so it invites a group of homemakers to sit down with some of Tide's marketing personnel and brainstorm how Tide could perform better or how its packaging could be improved or discuss other features of the detergent. Listening to the market in this way can generate excellent packaging, product design, or even product positioning ideas. As another example, if the Procter & Gamble marketing group were developing a special end-of-aisle display for Tide, it might want to test one version in an actual supermarket environment. It could place one in a Safeway grocery store located in a San Francisco suburb and videotape shoppers as they encountered the display. The marketing group would then review the videotape and see if the display generated the types of responses they hoped it would. For instance, did shoppers stop there? Did they read the copy on the display? Did they pick up the displayed product and look at it? Qualitative research techniques afford rich insight into consumer behavior.[2]

With the rush to online quantitative research that produces huge amounts of data, qualitative research is sometimes overlooked.[3] However, it is our goal in this chapter to show you the value of qualitative research techniques and, as you will see very soon, to convince you of the need for qualitative research and quantitative research to work hand in hand.

Although there are proponents of both types of research, many marketing researchers have adopted **pluralistic research**, which is defined as the combination of qualitative and quantitative research methods in order to gain the advantages of both. With pluralistic research, it is common to begin with exploratory qualitative techniques as, for example, in-depth interviews of selected dealers or a series of focus group discussions with customers in order to understand how they perceive your product and service as compared with those of competitors. Even an observational study could be used if it is helpful in understanding the problem and bringing to the surface issues in the research project. These activities often help crystallize the problem or otherwise open the researcher's eyes to factors and considerations that might be overlooked if he or she rushed into a full-scale survey. The qualitative phase serves as a foundation for the quantitative phase of the research project because it provides the researcher with first-hand knowledge of the research problem. Armed with this knowledge, the researcher's design and execution of the quantitative phase are invariably superior to what they might have been without the qualitative phase. With pluralistic research, the qualitative phase serves to frame the subsequent quantitative phase, and in some cases, a qualitative phase is applied after a quantitative study to help the researcher understand the findings in the quantitative phase. As an example, The Arizona Republic newspaper has used online focus groups for brainstorming, and the outcomes of these sessions are then used to devise online surveys. Through this pluralistic approach, The Arizona Republic has identified which topics are considered to be most important to its readers of the local news section of the paper. This information allowed the editors to make certain they covered the information readers thought to be most important.[4]

> Pluralistic research is defined as the combination of qualitative and quantitative research methods in order to gain the advantages of both.

> Often with pluralistic research, the qualitative phase serves to frame, or help in the design of, the subsequent quantitative phase. And in some cases, a qualitative phase is applied after a quantitative study to help the researcher understand the findings in the quantitative phase.

The pluralistic approach is becoming increasingly popular, especially with emerging and complex marketing phenomena such as online shopping behavior. We have provided Marketing Research Insight 8.1 that shows how a pluralistic program combined qualitative and quantitative research techniques to yield an understanding of the differences between men and women online as well as identifying different online segments with each gender.

Observation Techniques

Qualitative techniques include the class of **observation methods**—techniques in which the researcher relies on his or her powers of observation rather than communicating with a person in order to obtain information. Observation requires something to observe, and because our memories are faulty, researchers depend on recording devices such as videotapes, audiotapes, handwritten notes, or some other tangible record of what is observed. As we describe each observation technique, you will see that each is unique in how it obtains observations.

> One qualitative research technique is to observe others rather than communicate with them. Researchers observe behavior and record what they see.

▶ **Types of Observation** At first glance, it may seem that observation studies can occur without any structure; however, it is important to adhere to a plan so that the observations are consistent and comparisons or generalizations can be made without worrying about any conditions of the observation method that might confound the findings. There are four general ways of organizing observations: (1) direct versus indirect, (2) disguised versus undisguised, (3) structured versus unstructured, and (4) human versus mechanical.

> There are four general ways of organizing observations: (1) direct versus indirect, (2) disguised versus undisguised, (3) structured versus unstructured, and (4) human versus mechanical.

▶ **Direct Versus Indirect** Observing behavior as it occurs is called **direct observation**.[5] For example, if we are interested in finding out how much shoppers squeeze tomatoes to assess their freshness, we can observe people actually picking up the tomatoes. Direct observation has been used by Kellogg to understand breakfast rituals, by a Swiss chocolate maker to study the behavior of "chocoholics," and by the U.S. Post

> Observing behavior as it occurs is called "direct observation."

8.1 Pluralistic Research Identifies Online Buyer Segments and Distinct Purchasing Behaviors

Because online purchase behavior is an emerging phenomenon, a pluralistic approach that uses both qualitative research techniques and quantitative methods is the most appropriate way to investigate it. Accordingly, market researchers combined the following research techniques as a strategy to reveal online buyer market segments.

Focus groups, which are moderated discussions conducted with groups of 8 to 12 online buyers, were used to gain a basic understanding of online buying such as why, where, when, and how often. The focus groups uncovered basic differences between male and female online buyers.

Depth interviews, which are personal interviews lasting from 30 to 45 minutes, were then used in order to probe motivations for online purchasing, including functional as well as emotional reasons for buying online. These depth interviews also sought to tap into personal styles for online information search and processing.

An online survey was conducted via e-mail invitations to about 40,000 Internet users. The online questionnaire contained questions about demographics, lifestyle, Internet usage, preferences for Internet delivery formats, and importance of various Internet content types (such as news, entertainment, travel, family, etc.).

The online survey data were subjected to various analyses, and they resulted in the discovery of five distinct female online user segments as well as five separate male online user segments. The segments and their key differences are noted in the following table.

ONLINE SEGMENTS AND KEY DIFFERENCES REVEALED BY PLURALISTIC RESEARCH

SEGMENT	PERCENT	DEMOGRAPHICS	KEY ONLINE USAGE	ONLINE FAVORITES
Female Segments				
Social Sally	14%	30–40, college educated	Making friends	Chat and personal Web space
New Age Crusader	21%	40–50, highest income level	Fight for causes	Books and government information
Cautious Mom	24%	30–45, with children	Nurture children	Cooking and medical facts
Playful Pretender	20%	Youngest, many are students	Role play	Chat and games
Master Producer	20%	Tends to be single	Job productivity	White pages and government information
Male Segments				
Bits and Bytes	11%	Young and single	Computers and hobbies	Investments, discovery, software
Practical Pete	21%	40ish, some college, above-average income	Personal productivity	Investments, company listings
Viking Gamer	19%	Young or old, least college education	Competing and winning	Games, chat, software
Sensitive Sam	21%	Highest education and income of males	Help family and friends	Investments, government information
World Citizen	28%	50 and older, most with college education	Connecting with world	Discovery, software, investments

These are only thumbnail descriptions of these 10 different online market segments. Much more detail is provided in the original descriptions,[6] and it is important to note that such complete understanding of these emerging online types is possible only through the use of pluralistic research.

Office's advertising agency to come up with the advertising slogan "We Deliver."[7] It has also been used by General Mills to understand how children eat breakfast, leading to the launch of "Go-Gurt," a midmorning snack for schoolchildren.[8]

In order to observe types of hidden behavior, such as past behavior, we must rely on indirect observation. With **indirect observation**, the researcher observes the effects or results of the behavior rather than the behavior itself. Types of indirect observations include archives and physical traces.

Archives. **Archives** are secondary sources, such as historical records, that can be applied to the present problem. These sources contain a wealth of information and should not be overlooked or underestimated. Many types of archives exist. For example, records of sales calls may be inspected to determine how often salespersons make cold calls. Warehouse inventory movements can be used to study market shifts. Scanner data may afford insight on the effects of price changes, promotion campaigns, or package size changes.

Physical Traces. **Physical traces** are tangible evidence of some event. For example, we might turn to "garbology" (observing the trash of subjects being studied) as a way of finding out how much recycling of plastic milk bottles occurs. A soft-drink company might do a litter audit in order to assess how much impact its aluminum cans have on the countryside. A fast-food company such as Wendy's might measure the amount of graffiti on buildings located adjacent to prospective location sites as a means of estimating the crime potential for each site.[9]

▶ **Disguised Versus Undisguised** With **disguised observation**, the subject is unaware that he or she is being observed. An example of this method might be a "mystery shopper" who is used by a retail store chain to record and report on sales clerks' assistance and courtesy. One-way mirrors and hidden cameras are a few of the other ways that are used to prevent subjects from becoming aware that they are being observed. This disguise is important because if the subjects were aware of the observation, it is possible that they would change their behavior, resulting in observations of atypical behavior. If you were a store clerk, how would you act if the department manager told you that he would be watching you for the next hour? You would probably be on your best behavior for the next 60 minutes. Disguised observation has proved illuminating in studies of parents and children shopping together in supermarkets.[10] With direct questions, parents might feel compelled to say that their children are always on their best behavior while shopping.

Sometimes it is impossible for the respondent to be unaware of the observation, and this is a case of **undisguised observation**. Laboratory settings, observing a sales representative's behavior on sales calls, People Meters (Nielsen Media Research's device that is attached to a television set to record when and to what station a set is tuned), and Arbitron's Personal Portable Meter, must all be used with the subject's knowledge. Because people might be influenced by knowing they are being observed, it is wise to always minimize the presence of the observer to the maximum extent possible.

The use of observation raises ethical questions. Should people being observed be informed of the observation, and, if so, what changes might they make in their behavior in order to appear "normal" or conform to what they think is expected? The researcher wants to observe behavior as it actually occurs even if it is unusual or out of the ordinary. However, people being observed might feel uncomfortable about their habits or actions and try to act in more conventional ways. For instance, if a family agrees to have its television set wired so a researcher can track what programs the family watches, will the parents make sure that the children watch mainly wholesome

Sidebar notes:

With indirect observation, the researcher observes the effects or results of the behavior rather than the behavior itself. Types of indirect observations include archives and physical traces.

With disguised observation the subject is unaware that he or she is being observed.

When the respondent knows he or she is being observed this is known as undisguised observation.

The use of observation raises ethical questions. Should people being observed be informed of the observation, and, if so, what changes might they make in their behavior in order to appear "normal" or conform to what they think is expected?

shows, such as those on the Disney Channel? Sometimes researchers resort to deceit in order to observe people without their knowledge, but this is an unethical practice. The ethical practice is to inform people ahead of time and give them an "adjustment period" or, if such a period is not feasible, to fully debrief them of the observation afterward.

▶ **Structured Versus Unstructured** When using **structured observation** techniques, the researcher identifies beforehand which behaviors are to be observed and recorded. All other behaviors are "ignored." Often a checklist or a standardized observation form is used to isolate the observer's attention to specific factors. These highly structured observations typically require a minimum of effort on the part of the observer.

> The researcher identifies which behaviors are to be observed and recorded in structured observation.

Unstructured observation places no restriction on what the observer would note. All behavior in the episode under study is monitored. The observer just watches the situation and records what he or she deems interesting or relevant. Of course, the observer is thoroughly briefed on the area of general concern. This type of observation is often used in exploratory research. For example, Black and Decker might send someone to observe carpenters working at various job sites as a means of better understanding how the tools are used and to help generate ideas as to how to design the tools for increased safety.

> In using unstructured observation there are no predetermined restrictions on what the observer records.

▶ **Human Versus Mechanical** With **human observation**, the observer is a person hired by the researcher, or, perhaps, the observer is the researcher. However, it is often possible, desirable, and economical[11] to replace the human observer with some form of static observing device, as in **mechanical observation**. This substitution may be made because of accuracy, cost, or functional reasons. Auto traffic counts may be more accurate and less costly when recorded by machines that are activated by car tires rolling over them. Besides, during rush hour, a human observer could not count the number of cars on most major metropolitan commuter roads. Nor would it be possible to count the number of fans entering a gate at a professional football title game, so turnstile counts are used instead. Scanning devices are used to count the number and types of products sold (see Chapter 7). Mechanical devices may also be used when it is too expensive to use human observers. For example, we mentioned earlier that the People Meter is used instead of a human observer to record families' television viewing habits for Nielsen Media Research. As these examples illustrate, mechanical observation has moved into the high-technology area, and the combination of telecommunications, computer hardware, and software programs has created a very useful research tool.

Appropriate Conditions for the Use of Observation

Certain conditions must be met before a researcher can successfully use observation as a marketing research tool. These conditions are: the event must occur during a short time interval, the observed behavior must occur in a public setting, and when the possibility of faulty recall rules out collecting information by asking the person.

> *Short time interval* means that the event must begin and end within a reasonably short time span. Examples include a shopping trip in a supermarket or waiting in a teller line at a bank.

Short time interval means that the event must begin and end within a reasonably short time span. Examples include a shopping trip in a supermarket, waiting in a teller line at a bank, purchasing a clothing item, or observing children as they watch a television program. Some decision-making processes can take a long time (for example, buying a home), and it would be unrealistic in terms of the time and money required to observe the entire process. Because of this factor, observational research is usually limited to scrutinizing activities that can be completed in a relatively short time span or to observing certain phases of those activities with a long time span.

> *Public behavior* refers to behavior that occurs in a setting the researcher can readily observe such as shopping in a grocery store or shopping with children in a department store.

Public behavior refers to behavior that occurs in a setting the researcher can readily observe. Actions such as cooking, playing with one's children at home, or private worshipping are not public activities and are, therefore, not suitable for observational studies such as those described here.

Faulty recall occurs when actions or activities are so repetitive or automatic that the respondent cannot recall specifics about the behavior under question. For example, people cannot recall accurately how many times they looked at their wristwatch while waiting in a long line to buy a ticket to a best-selling movie, or which FM radio station they listened to last Thursday at 2:00 P.M. Observation is necessary under circumstances of faulty recall to fully understand the behavior at hand. Faulty recall is one of the reasons that companies have experimented for many years with mechanical devices to observe these behaviors.[12] Recall our discussion of Arbitron's new Portable People Meter in Chapter 7. This is another example of observing behavior under conditions of faulty recall.

Advantages of Observational Data

Ideally, the subjects of observational research are unaware they are being studied. Because of this they react in a natural manner, giving the researcher insight into actual, not reported, behaviors. As previously noted, observational research methods also mean that there is no chance for recall error. The subjects are not asked what they remember about a certain action. Instead, they are observed while engaged in the act. In some cases, observation may be the only way to obtain accurate information. For instance, children who cannot yet verbally express their opinion of a new toy will do so by simply playing or not playing with the toy. Retail marketers commonly gather marketing intelligence about competitors and about their own employees' behaviors by hiring the services of "mystery shoppers" who pose as customers but who are actually trained observers.[13] In some situations, data can be obtained with better accuracy and less cost by using observational methods as opposed to other means. For example, counts of in-store traffic can often be made by means of observational techniques more accurately and less expensively than by using survey techniques.

Such advantages of observational research methods should not be interpreted as meaning that this technique is always in competition with other approaches. A resourceful researcher will use observation techniques to supplement and complement other techniques.[14] When used in combination with other techniques, each approach can serve as a check on the results obtained by the other. Actually, observation of humans in their natural context is the approach that has been used by anthropologists for over 100 years and is an accepted method of conducting marketing research.[15]

Limitations of Observational Data

The limitations of observation are the limitations inherent in qualitative research in general. With direct observation, typically only small numbers of subjects are studied and usually under special circumstances, so their representativeness is a concern.[16] This factor, plus the subjective interpretation required to explain the observed behavior, usually forces the researcher to consider his or her conclusions to be tentative. Certainly, the greatest drawback of all observational methods is the researcher's inability to pry beneath the behavior observed and to interrogate the person on motives, attitudes, and all of the other unseen aspects of why what was observed took place.

To recap, a limitation of observation is that motivations, attitudes, intentions, and other internal conditions cannot be observed. Only when these feelings are relatively unimportant or are readily inferred from the behavior is it appropriate to use observational research methods. For example, facial expression might be used as an indicator of a child's attitudes or preferences for various types of fruit drink flavors because children often react with conspicuous physical expressions. But adults and even children usually

Observation should be used when consumers cannot recall their behaviors, such as knowing how many different Web pages they accessed while shopping online. Inability to recall such behaviors is known as "faulty recall."

Observation research has the advantage of seeing what consumers actually do instead of relying on their self-report of what they think they do.

Sometimes data can be obtained at less cost and more accurately by using observation methods.

Even though there are several advantages of observational research, observation methods should not be used without considering other research methods. A resourceful researcher will use observation techniques to supplement and complement other techniques.

One disadvantage of observational research is that few persons are normally observed. Researchers must be concerned about the issue of how accurately those observed represent all consumers in the target population.

Interpretation of observed behavior is subjective.

The major disadvantage of observation research is the inability to determine consumers' motives, attitudes, and intentions.

conceal their reasons and true reactions in public, and this fact necessitates a direct questioning approach because observation alone cannot give a complete picture of why and how people act the way they do.

FOCUS GROUPS

Focus groups are small groups of people brought together and guided by a moderator through an unstructured, spontaneous discussion for the purpose of gaining information relevant to the research problem.

A popular method of conducting exploratory research is through **focus groups**, which are small groups of people brought together and guided by a moderator through an unstructured, spontaneous discussion for the purpose of gaining information relevant to the research problem.[17] Although focus groups should encourage openness on the part of the participants, the moderator's task is to ensure the discussion is "focused" on some general area of interest. For example, the Piccadilly Cafeteria chain periodically conducts focus groups all around the country. The conversation may seem "freewheeling," but the purpose of the focus group may be to learn what people think about some specific aspect of the cafeteria business, such as the perceived quality of cafeteria versus traditional restaurant food. We provide you with Marketing Research Insight 8.2, which gives you an example of how this free-wheeling, brainstorming interaction takes place. Notice the improvements that are suggested for Fujifilm's digital cameras.

The focus group moderator's task is to ensure the discussion is "focused" on some general area of interest.

Focus groups represent a useful technique for gathering some information from a limited sample of respondents. The information can be used to generate ideas, to learn the respondents "vocabulary" when relating to a certain type of product, or to gain some insights into basic needs and attitudes.[18] Focus groups represent 85 to 90% of the total money spent on qualitative research.[19] Focus groups have become so popular in marketing research that every large city has a number of companies that specialize in performing focus group research. You can be assured that you will encounter focus group research if you become a practicing marketing manager. "Almost nothing gets done without them,"[20] says Bill Hillsman, a successful advertising executive whose campaigns have worked for the Minnesota Twins, the Dales shopping centers, and Arctic Cat snowmobiles. Focus groups are an invaluable means of regaining contact with customers when marketers have lost touch, and they are very helpful in learning about new customer groups.

Information from focus groups can be used to generate ideas, to learn the respondents' "vocabulary" when relating to a certain type of product, or to gain some insights into basic needs and attitudes.

How Focus Groups Work

Focus groups may be either traditional or nontraditional.

Focus group facilities have a one-way mirror or cameras, which allow clients in an adjoining room to watch the focus group without influencing what the focus group members say or do.

Focus groups can be of several types. **Traditional focus groups** select about 6 to 12 persons and meet in a dedicated room, with a one-way mirror for client viewing, for about two hours. In recent years, **nontraditional focus groups**[21] have emerged that differ in that they may be online with clients observing on computer monitors in distant locations; may have 25 or even 50 respondents; allow client interaction with participants; last four or five hours and take part outside of traditional facilities, such as in a park. We will discuss online focus groups in more detail in the following paragraphs. A marketing research firm offering traditional focus groups typically will have a **focus group facility**, which is a set of rooms especially designed for focus groups. The focus group is conducted in a room that seats about 10 people (optimal size is thought to be somewhere between 6 and 12 participants) and a moderator. A wall in the room has a one-way mirror. The one-way mirror allows clients in the adjoining room to watch the focus group without influencing what the focus group members say or do. Some facilities use video cameras in the focus group room, which allow clients to observe the focus group from another room or even a distant location. Microphones are built into the walls or ceiling or otherwise set in the center of the table, and videotape equipment often operates from an inconspicuous location.

8.2
What a Brainstorming Focus Group "Sounds" Like

Background: Fujifilm is considering redesigning its digital cameras and film to make them more user-friendly, and it is using focus group research to understand what problems consumers encounter when using digital cameras. Here is part of the transcript. Notice how the moderator directs or focuses the discussion, and notice also how the focus group participants stimulate each others' comments.

> **Moderator:** What other problems have you encountered with your digital camera?
>
> **Mary:** Well, we have a digital camera that has a lot of automatic features such as focusing and sensing when the flash should be used. Oh, and it has a red eye feature that eliminates those red demon eyes that people have when you use a regular flash.
>
> **Moderator:** What about problems with the camera? Let's talk about difficulties or frustrations with your digital camera.
>
> **Mary:** Oh, it is a bit of a problem to hook up my USB cable to it. The "plug-in" thingy only goes one way and it takes me a couple of tries to get it right.
>
> **Sally:** Yes, and sometimes you use up all of your storage capacity without warning. I have lost one or two good photo opportunities because my digital camera was full.
>
> **Gene:** Yes, I agree. It's a pain having to review your shots and decide which ones to delete so you can free up more storage space.

> **Mary:** I bet there is some way that they could make a storage cartridge that would snap into the camera when you run out of storage space.
>
> **Gail:** Yes, but first I would want them to give me some warning that I was about to run out. With conventional cameras, you can see how many shots you have taken and easily figure out how many you have left before you need to change the film.
>
> **Gene:** Yes, I agree that it would be great to have a counter that would tell me how many shots I have left. When I use my digital camera, I take two or three snaps of the same shot to make sure I will have one good one, so I often find that I am out of storage space. And the pop-in extra cartridge would be great, too.
>
> **Gail:** Yes, that's what we need—a countdown feature and maybe a warning tone or beep when I am close to using up all of the storage space in the cartridge I have in the camera.
>
> **Moderator:** Can you think of any other ways that the companies that market digital cameras might be able to change their products so they are more helpful to you?
>
> **Sally:** I have a problem seeing details in my pictures when I use the viewer in bright sunlight. I have to put my hand over the viewer screen like a visor to shade it so I can see the detail. I practically have to run inside in order to see if I took a good picture.
>
> **Moderator:** What else about the photo reviewing system? Does anyone have any ideas on a better system?

In the past, companies have tried to hide or disguise the equipment they used to record respondents' reactions. This was done in an attempt to remove any feelings of self-consciousness or awkwardness that might result in the respondents' interviews by being taped. However, such a practice is unethical, and few participants are tricked anyway. Now it is common practice to let participants know about the recording aspect when they are recruited. If they have any objections, they can decline at that time.

Focus group participants are interviewed by **moderators**, often referred to as **Qualitative Research Consultants** (QR or QRC).[22] The training and background of the moderator or QRC is extremely important for the success of the focus group.[23] QRCs have the responsibility of creating an atmosphere that is conducive to openness, yet they must make certain the participants do not stray too far from the central focus of the study. A good moderator must have excellent observation, interpersonal, and communication skills to recognize and overcome threats to a productive group discussion. He or she must be

It is unethical to conceal cameras or other methods of viewing or recording focus groups.

Focus group participants are interviewed by moderators, often referred to as Qualitative Research Consultants (QR or QRC).

The Opinion Suites in Richmond, VA, has modern focus group facilities. By permission, The Opinion Suites.

prepared, experienced, and armed with a detailed list of topics to be discussed.[24] It is also helpful if the focus group moderator can eliminate any preconceptions on the topic from his or her mind. The best moderators are experienced, enthusiastic, prepared, involved, energetic, and open-minded.[25] With an incompetent moderator, the focus group can become a disaster. Some trade secrets of successful moderators may be found in Table 8.1.

QRC's prepare the focus group report.

QRC's also must prepare a **focus group report** that summarizes the information provided by the focus group participants relative to the research questions. Two important factors must be remembered when analyzing the data. First, some sense must be made by translating the qualitative statements of participants into categories and then reporting the degree of consensus apparent in the focus groups.[27] Second, the demographic and buyer behavior characteristics of focus group participants should be judged against the target market profile to assess to what degree the groups represent the target market.

Focus group information is evaluated by an analyst who carefully observes the recorded tapes several times, transcribing any relevant statements that seem evident. These statements are then subjected to closer evaluation. This evaluation is based on the analyst's knowledge of the history and statement of the problem plus his or her own interpretation of the responses. A detailed report is prepared for the client's review.

There is a professional organization of QRCAs at www.qrca.org.

The focus group report reflects the qualitative aspect of this research method. It lists all themes that have become apparent, and it notes any diversity of opinions or thoughts expressed by the participants. It will also have numerous verbatim excerpts provided as evidence.[28] In fact, some reports include complete transcripts of the focus group discussion. This information is then used as the basis for further research studies or even for more focus groups. If the information is used for subsequent focus groups, the client uses the first group as a learning experience, making any adjustments to the discussion topics as needed to improve the research objectives. Although focus groups may be the only type of research used to tackle a marketing problem or question, they are also used as a beginning point for quantitative research efforts; that is, a focus group phase may be used to gain a feel for a specific survey that will ultimately generate standardized information from a representative sample.

TABLE 8.1	Focus Group Moderators' "Tricks of the Trade"

The following trade secrets were divulged by experienced focus group moderators at a recent panel at the annual conference of the Qualitative Research Consultants Association.[26]

Question	Tricks of the Trade
How do you make your groups great every time?	■ Be prepared. ■ Be energized. ■ Be nice but firm. ■ Make sure *everything* about the experience is comfortable.
How do you build rapport quickly?	■ Make meaningful eye contact during each person's introduction. ■ Learn and remember names. ■ Let them create their own name cards. ■ Welcome folks as they come into the room, and use small talk.
How do you bring a drifting group back into focus?	■ Tell them the topic is "for another group" and that they need to focus on the topic for this group. ■ Make a note and tell them that they will come back to this topic if there is time. ■ Tell them the topic is "interesting" but not the subject at hand and refer to the next question. ■ Suggest that they can talk about it on their own after the focus group is over.
How do you get them to talk about deeper things than top-of-the-mind answers?	■ Play naïve or dumb and ask them to help you understand by explaining. ■ Use probes such as "Tell us more about that," or "Can you go deeper on that?" ■ Ask for specifics such as "Tell me about the last time that you. . . ." ■ Pair them up and give them 10 minutes for each pair to come up with a solution or suggestion.
What about management of the "back room" where your clients are observing?	■ Orient clients with a 10-miute overview of focus groups, research objectives, and what to expect. ■ Check with the client(s) during breaks, written exercises, and so on to make sure things are going well. ■ Have an associate or colleague there to work with the client(s). ■ If you don't have an associate for the back room, ask the client to select one person to be the point person to communicate with you.

Moderators of focus groups are extremely important to the success of focus groups. Well-trained and experienced moderators at The Opinion Suites maintain an atmosphere that encourages openness while at the same time remaining focused on the subject matter. Training and experience of moderators is vitally important. By permission, The Opinion Suites.

QUALITATIVE RESEARCH CONSULTANT'S ASSOCIATION

First, make sure you read the ad for QRCA on page 213. Then go to their Web site at www.qrca.com and find the Code of Member Ethics that all members must sign. Next, read what they have to say about what qualitative research is and when to use it, and identify what QRCA shows as the methods of qualitative research. Finally, go to the menu item: *Find a QRCA Consultant/Moderator.* **Examine the** *Quick Search* **and the** *Advanced Search* **to explore ways you can find someone who specializes in qualitative research.**

Online Focus Groups

The **online focus group**, a form of nontraditional focus group, is one in which the respondents and/or the clients communicate and/or observe by use of the Internet. Typically, online focus groups allow the participants the convenience of being seated at their own computers, while the moderator operates out of his or her online focus group company. The online focus group is "virtual" in that it communicates electronically, and it does not have face-to-face contact in the traditional focus group sense. Although some experts hold that online focus groups are not equivalent to traditional focus groups, online focus groups offer many advantages and few disadvantages. The Qualitative Research Consultants Association's Online Qualitative Research Task Force published its investigations into online focus groups[29] and its major conclusions are listed in Table 8.2.

Online focus groups have the following advantages over traditional focus groups: (1) No physical set up is necessary, (2) transcripts are captured on file in real time, (3) participants can be in widely separated geographic locations, (4) participants are comfortable in their home or office environments, and (5) the moderator can exchange private messages with individual participants. Innovative approaches are possible as some researchers combine online with telephone communications for maximum effectiveness.[31]

On the flip side, there are some disadvantages to online focus groups, such as (1) observation of participants' "body language" is not possible, (2) participants cannot physically inspect products or taste food items, and (3) participants can lose interest or become distracted.[32]

Of course, as Table 8.2 indicates, both traditional and online focus groups require recruitment and compensation of participants, scheduling and notification, and a prepared and skilled moderator.

A variation of the online focus group is one that is conducted in a traditional setting, but the client watches online. With the use of streaming media and high-speed Internet connections, ActiveGroup has pioneered this research technique. For example, ActiveGroup offers clients the ability to view focus groups online using streaming video. The focus group is conducted at a traditional focus group facility with the participants seated with the moderator. This type of online focus group allows several members of the client firm to observe the focus group at their own location. This saves the client firm travel expense and time. ActiveGroup provides clients with reports and a CD-ROM of the focus group.

Since their entry into the research industry a few years ago, online focus groups have grown in popularity. While they will not replace traditional focus groups, they offer a viable research method.[33]

Advantages of Focus Groups

The four major advantages of focus groups are: (1) they generate fresh ideas; (2) they allow clients to observe their participants; (3) they may be directed at understanding a wide variety of issues, such as reactions to a new food product, brand logo, or television ad; and (4) they allow fairly easy access to special respondent groups, such as lawyers or doctors (whereas it may be very difficult to find a representative sample of these groups).

The online focus group, a form of nontraditional focus group, is one in which the respondents and/or the clients communicate and/or observe by use of the Internet. Typically, online focus groups allow the participants the convenience of being seated at their own computers, while the moderator operates out of his or her online focus group company.

Visit ActiveGroup at **www.activegroup.net**.

Focus groups generate fresh ideas, allow clients to observe them, are applicable to a wide variety of issues and allow researchers to obtain information from "hard to reach" subpopulations.

Leading the Way in Qualitative Research

QRCA is the largest body of independent qualitative research consultants in the world, with over 800 experienced qualitative research professionals from over 20 countries. All QRCA members sign the QRCA Code of Member Ethics and pledge to maintain integrity in their relationships with clients, field suppliers, and respondents. QRCA is on the forefront of trends and innovations in qualitative research worldwide. QRCA members share their resources, expertise, and knowledge to continually raise the standards of excellence in the profession.

Promoting Excellence in Qualitative Research

Go to **www.qrca.org** to "Find A Consultant" and use our other helpful resources

Qualitative Research Consultants Association, Inc.

P.O. Box 967 • Camden, TN 38320
(888) 674-7722 toll free
(731) 584-8080 • (731) 584-7882 fax

TABLE 8.2	Online Focus Groups FAQs[30]	

Question	Answer
Can online focus groups substitute for face-to-face ones?	Yes, as long as the online environment is consistent with the study's objectives.

For what situations are online focus groups best suited?	Some are:
	   Low-incidence respondents
	   Geographically dispersed respondents
	   B2B professionals

What is "lost" with oneline focus groups?	You cannot:
	   See body language
	   Show prototypes or models of products
	   Conduct taste tests

Can I recruit online focus group participants via e-mail invitation?	Yes, if they have valid e-mail accounts that they use regularly.
What incentives should I use to recruit my focus group participants?	The going rate is about $40 in cash or the equivalent, but B2B participants may require twice this amount.
How many participants should I plan for in my online focus group?	A common number is 15 to 20.
How long should it last?	Up to 90 minutes is typical.
How secure is the online focus group environment?	If you use a commercial chat program, there are password systems that can be used to maintain security.
Can my clients observe the online focus group?	Yes, there are systems in which the client(s) can observe the focus group while online at their own computers. The clients can communicate privately with the moderator online as well.
Are the moderator's skills different with an online focus group?	In addition to basic focus group moderator skills, there needs to be more care in preparation of the discussion topic guide wording to avoid misinterpretation, probes phrased to include all participants, good typing ability, and familiarity with chat room slang.
Are participants more or less candid with online focus groups?	They tend to be more candid, as they have anonymity. Also, they tend to compose answers to topic questions without reading others' responses, so the comments are unique to each participant.

Disadvantages of Focus Groups

Focus groups are not representative, and it is sometimes difficult to interpret the results of focus groups. The moderator's report is subjective and the cost per focus group participant is high.

There are three major disadvantages to focus groups: (1) focus groups do not constitute representative samples and, therefore, caution must be exercised in generalizing findings from them; (2) it is sometimes difficult to interpret the results of focus groups; the moderator's report is based on a subjective evaluation of what was said during the focus group; and (3) the cost per participant is high, though the total spent on focus group research is generally a fraction of what may be spent on quantitative research.

When Should Focus Groups Be Used?

Focus groups should be considered when the research question is one requiring something to be described.

When the research objective is to describe, rather than predict, focus groups may be an alternative. Consider the following situations: A company wants to know "how to speak" to its market; what language and terms do the customers use? What are some new ideas for an ad campaign? Will a new service we are developing have appeal to customers and how can we improve it? How can we better package our product?[34] In all these cases focus groups can describe the terms customers use, their ideas for ads, why a service appeals to them, and so on.

When Should Focus Groups Not be Used?

Because focus groups are based on a small number of persons who are not representative of some larger population, care must be exercised in using focus groups. If the research objective is to predict, focus groups should not be used. For example, if we show 12 persons in a focus group a new product prototype and find that 6 say they are going to buy it, can we predict that 50% of the population will buy our product? Hardly. Likewise, if our research is going to dictate a major, expensive decision for our company, we probably should not rely solely on the use of focus groups. If the decision is that important, research that is representative of some population and that has some known margin of error (quantitative research) should be used.

Focus groups should not be used when the research question requires a prediction or when a major decision, affecting the livelihood of the company, rests on the results of a focus group.

Some Objectives of Focus Groups

There are four main objectives of focus groups: to generate ideas; to understand consumer vocabulary; to reveal consumer needs, motives, perceptions, and attitudes about products or services; and to understand findings from quantitative studies.

Focus groups *generate ideas* for managers to consider. Krispy Kreme has conducted focus groups to help them design new product choices and stores. If managers consistently hear that their customers prefer their doughnuts but go elsewhere for gourmet coffees, this gives Krispy Kreme management ideas for changing their product mix to include gourmet coffee. Mothers talking about the difficulties in strapping children in car restraint seats give designers of these products ideas. Consumers discussing the difficulties of moving furniture gives rise to innovations in furniture designed for portability.

Focus groups generate ideas for managers to consider.

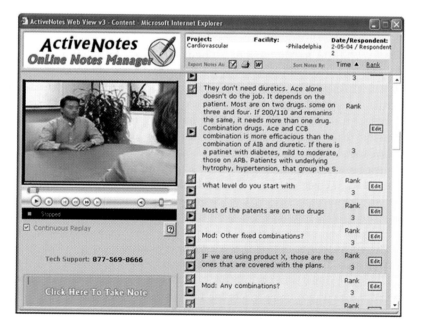

ActiveGroup gives clients the ability to observe their focus groups from remote locations by allowing clients to observe the entire focus group over the Internet. This saves clients travel expense and time. By permission of ActiveGroup.

Focus groups may be used to understand the consumers' vocabulary, needs and motives, and attitudes.

To *understand consumer vocabulary* means to use the focus group to stay abreast of the words and phrases consumers use when describing products so as to improve product or service communication with them. Such information may help in advertising copy design or in the preparation of an instruction pamphlet. This knowledge refines research problem definitions and also helps structure questions for use in later quantitative research.

To *reveal consumer needs, motives, perceptions, and attitudes* about products or services means to use the focus group to refresh the marketing team as to what customers really feel or think about a product or service. Alternatively, managers may need early customer reactions to changes being considered in products or services.[35] Focus groups are commonly used during the exploratory phase of research.[36] This application is useful in generating objectives to be addressed by subsequent research.

Focus groups may be used to better understand findings of quantitative studies.

To *understand findings from quantitative studies* means to use focus groups to better comprehend data gathered from other surveys. Sometimes a focus group can reveal why the findings came out a particular way. For example, in a bank image survey it was shown that a particular branch consistently received lower scores on "employee friendliness." Focus group research identified the problem as being several front line employees who were so concerned with efficiency that they appeared to be unfriendly to customers. The bank revised its training program to remedy the problem.

Warner-Lambert is a company that has successfully used focus groups to accomplish all four of these objectives. Its consumer health products group, which markets over-the-counter health and beauty products as well as nonprescription drugs, uses focus groups extensively.[37] In fact, Warner-Lambert uses a combination of qualitative research techniques to gain background information, to reveal needs and attitudes related to health and beauty products, to interpret the results of qualitative studies, and to stimulate brainstorming new ideas. Focus groups have been useful in understanding basic shifts in consumer lifestyles, values, and purchase patterns.

Operational Questions About Focus Groups

Before a focus group is conducted, certain operational questions should be addressed. It is important to decide how many people should take part in a focus group, who they should be, how they will be selected and recruited, and where they should meet. General guidelines exist for answering these questions. A discussion of each follows.

The optimal size of a focus group is 6 to 12 people.

▶ **What Should Be the Size of a Focus Group?** According to industry wisdom, the optimal size of a traditional focus group is 6 to 12 people. A small group (fewer than six participants) is not likely to generate the energy and group dynamics necessary for a truly beneficial focus group session. With fewer participants, it is common that one or two of the participants do most of the talking in spite of the moderator's efforts. At the same time, a small group will often result in awkward silences and force the moderator to take too active a role in the discussion just to keep the discussion alive. Similarly, a group with over a dozen participants will ordinarily prove too large to be conducive to a natural discussion. As a focus group becomes larger in size it tends to become fragmented. Those participating may become frustrated by the inherent digressions and side comments. Conversations may break out among two or three participants while another is talking. This situation places the moderator in the role of disciplinarian, in which he or she is constantly calling for quiet or order rather than focusing the discussion on the issues at hand.

Unfortunately, it is often difficult to predict the exact number of people who will attend the focus group interview. Ten may agree to participate and only 4 may show up;

14 may be invited in hopes that 8 will show up, and all 14 may arrive. Of course, if this occurs, the researcher faces a judgment call as to whether or not to send some home. In the worst case, a researcher may run into a situation in which no one attends, despite promises to the contrary. There is no guaranteed method that will ensure a successful participation ratio. Incentives (which will be discussed later) are helpful but definitely not a certain way of gaining acceptance. So although 6 to 12 is the ideal focus group size range, it is not uncommon to have some groups with fewer than 6 and some with more than 12.

▶ **Who Should Be in the Focus Group?** It is generally believed that the best focus groups are ones in which the participants share homogeneous characteristics. This requirement is sometimes automatically satisfied by the researcher's need to have particular types of people in the focus group. For instance, the focus group may be comprised of executives who use satellite phones, it may involve building contractors who specialize in building customer residences over $500,000 in value, or it might involve a group of salespeople who are experiencing some common customer service difficulty.

The need for similar demographic or other relevant characteristics in the focus group members is accentuated by the fact that the focus group participants are typically strangers. In most cases, they are not friends or even casual acquaintances, and many people feel intimidated or at least hesitant to voice their opinions and suggestions to a group of strangers. But participants typically feel more comfortable once they realize they have similarities such as their age (they may all be in their early 30s), job situations (they may all be junior executives), family composition (they may all have preschool children), purchase experiences (they may all have bought a new car in the past year), or even leisure pursuits (they may all play tennis). Furthermore, by conducting a group that is as homogeneous as possible with respect to demographics and other characteristics, the researcher is assured that differences in these variables will be less likely to confuse the issue being discussed.

Focus group members should be homogeneous.

▶ **How Should Focus Group Participants Be Recruited and Selected?** As you can guess, the selection of focus group participants is determined largely by the purpose of the focus group. For instance, if the purpose is to generate new ideas on digital camera improvements, the participants must be consumers who have used a digital camera. If the focus group is intended to elicit building contractors' reactions to a new type of central air-conditioning unit, it will be necessary to recruit building contractors. It is not unusual for companies to provide customer lists or for focus group recruiters to work from secured lists of potential participants. For instance, with building contractors, the list might come from the local Yellow Pages or a building contractor trade association membership roster. In any case, it is necessary to initially contact prospective participants by telephone to qualify them and then to solicit their cooperation in the focus group. Occasionally, a focus group company may recruit by requesting shoppers in a mall to participate, but this approach is rare.

As we noted earlier, "no shows" are a problem with focus groups, and researchers have at least two strategies to entice prospective participants. Incentives are used to encourage recruits to participate in focus groups. These range from monetary compensation for the participant's time to free products or gift certificates. Many focus group companies use callbacks during the day immediately prior to the focus group to remind prospective participants that they have agreed to take part. If one prospective participant indicates that some conflict has arisen and he or she cannot be there, it is then possible to recruit a replacement. Neither approach works perfectly, as we indicated

Selection of focus group members is determined by the purpose of the focus group.

Focus group recruiting may raise ethical issues.

earlier, and anticipating how many participants will show up is always a concern. Some focus group companies have a policy of overrecruiting, and others have lists of people they can rely on to participate, given that they fit the qualifications.

The difficulties encountered by focus group companies in recruiting focus group participants have led to some unethical practices. Some people like to participate in focus groups, and a focus group company may keep a list of willing participants. Other participants may want to take part simply for the monetary compensation, and their names may be on the focus group company's list as well. In either case, inclusion of those people who have previously participated in numerous focus groups can lead to serious validity problems. Some researchers will explicitly disallow a focus group company to use these participants because of this concern. As a matter of policy, some focus group companies will always report the last time, if ever, that each focus group member participated in a focus group. Other companies will do so only if the client firm makes an explicit request for this information.

Focus group facilities should be comfortable, allow interaction, and not have distractions.

▶ **Where Should a Focus Group Meet?** Obviously, if a group discussion is to take place for a period of 90 minutes or more, it is important that the physical arrangement of the group be comfortable and conducive to group discussion. So focus groups ideally are conducted in large rooms set up in a format suitable given the research objective. In some cases, in which it is important to have face-to-face interaction, a round table format would be ideal. Other formats are more suitable for tasting foods or beverages or for viewing video. Focus groups are held in a variety of settings. An advertising company conference room, a moderator's home, a respondent's home, the client's office, hotels, and meeting rooms at churches are all locations in which focus groups can be held. Aside from a seating arrangement in which participants can all see one another, the second critical requirement in selecting a meeting place is to find one quiet enough to permit an intelligible audiotaping of the sessions. Marketing research firms with focus group facilities like we described at the beginning of this section offer ideal settings for focus groups.

Moderators should not be hired at the last minute to run focus groups. They should thoroughly understand the research objectives.

▶ **When Should the Moderator Become Involved in the Research Project?** Moderators should not be viewed as robots needed to lead a discussion who may be hired at the last minute to run the focus groups. The focus group's success depends on the participants' involvement in the discussion and in their understanding of what is being asked of them. Productive involvement is largely a result of the moderator's effectiveness, which in turn is dependent on his or her understanding of the purpose and objectives of the interview. Unless the moderator understands what information the researcher is after and why, he or she will not be able to phrase questions effectively. It is good policy to have the moderator contribute to the development of the project's goals so as to guide the discussion topics. By aiding in the formation of the topics (questions), he or she will be familiar with them and will be better prepared to conduct the group. It is important when formulating questions that they be organized into a logical sequence and that the moderator follow this sequence to the furthest extent possible. The moderator's introductory remarks are influential; they set the tone of the entire session. All subsequent questions should be prefaced with a clear explanation of how the participants should respond, for example, how they really feel personally, not how they think they should feel. This allows the moderator to establish a rapport with participants and to lay the groundwork for the interview's structure.

▶ **Reporting and Use of Focus Group Results** As we noted earlier, focus groups report some of the subtle and obscure features of the relationships among consumers and products, advertising, and sales efforts. They furnish qualitative data on things such as consumer language; emotional and behavioral reactions to advertising; lifestyle; relationships; the product category and specific brand; and unconscious consumer motivations relative to product design, packaging, promotion, or any other facet of the marketing program under study. But focus group results are qualitative and not perfectly representative of the general population.

▶ **Final Comments on Focus Groups**　The focus group approach is firmly entrenched in the marketing research world as a mainstay technique. Because they are of reasonable total cost when compared with large-scale quantitative surveys involving a thousand or more respondents, adaptable to managers' concerns, and capable of yielding immediate results, focus groups are an appealing qualitative research method. Moreover, face-to-face focus groups are becoming common worldwide, and online focus groups are boosting the popularity of focus groups with new capabilities. They are a unique research method because they permit marketing managers to see and hear the market. Managers become so engrossed in their everyday problems and crises that they find it very refreshing to see their customers in the flesh. It is common for marketing managers to come away from a focus group session observation stimulated and energized to respond to the market's desires.

Focus group usage is growing worldwide.

We just mentioned that the use of focus groups is growing worldwide, and we have discussed the growing use of marketing research around the world in previous chapters. We asked Mr. David Kay of Toronto's Research Dimensions, Ltd. to update some of his thoughts on doing research around the globe. We think Mr. Kay's recommendations provide good, solid, no-nonsense advice. Notice what he has to say about moderators. You will find his comments in Marketing Research Insight 8.3.

MARKETING RESEARCH INSIGHT　　　　**GLOBAL APPLICATION**

8.3　Do's and Don'ts of Global Marketing Research

As we have pointed out in this book, globalization of marketing research has been a significant trend in the industry in the past decade or so. We asked David A. Kay, Principal and Founding Partner of Research Dimensions to give you some suggestions on what marketing researchers should and should not do when conducting research in global markets.

research dimensions
toronto_boston

Visit Research Dimensions at **www.researchdimensions.com**. By permission, Research Dimensions.

Language

In countries where English is not the first language, expect to conduct research in the language of the country. Use translators who specialize in marketing research translation. Also, find translators who have experience in the industry for which you are doing the research. Use "back translation"; that is, have your questionnaire translated into the local language, then have a different person translate the questionnaire back into English. You may find that "cross country skiing" becomes "skiing across many countries"!

Not being conversant in a country's language means you will likely not understand idioms or colloquialisms, especially since these can vary even by regions of a country. Local marketing researchers will understand these.

Verbal descriptors on scales do not always translate accurately. A "Poor, Good, Very Good, Excellent" scale may have different meanings in different countries. Sometimes one overcomes this problem by using numerical scale descriptors.

(continued)

Early in the "light" food revolution, we found that Canadians did not like the name LITE because they rejected it as being misspelled.

An exception may be when you are conducting market research among senior members of the business community or professional community, in which English has virtually become the international language. You may find many who have studied in the United States or in other English-speaking countries. But do not assume this is the case. Also do not assume that the English used in Australia, Jamaica, the United Kingdom, Canada, or anywhere else is the same as in the United States. Colloquialisms vary.

Style and Cultural Expectations

In most cultures there is a "positive bias" or "politeness bias" in that respondents will respond more positively in a research situation than in a real situation. But the degree of bias varies by culture. In Japan and Latin America, for example, there is a greater preference to say "yes" rather than "no" than in other areas of the world. At Research Dimensions we have learned how to "adjust" for this bias. If you base your decision on an action standard of, say, a 7.5 on an intention-to-buy scale, you may require a higher standard in another country. Or you might require different action standards for different cultural or linguistic groups within the same country.

Questions that are asked directly in the United States are taboo to ask in mixed-gender groups in other countries. Also, in some countries there are different reactions to others based on age. To avoid these problems, keep males and females separate and use younger persons to work with younger respondents and older persons to work with older respondents. In some cultures for example, younger respondents will not contradict or give a negative answer to an older moderator, regardless of how they feel about the issue being discussed. It is a matter of respect for the elder. For obvious reasons, use female moderators to interview women, even though in the United States and in many other countries it wouldn't be a concern.

Handshakes are customary in the United States. Touching is not permitted in other countries. In other countries, you will be considered unfriendly if you do not shake hands at the beginning and end of every meeting. First names are the norm in some countries and not in others. In some cultures respondents will not speak openly unless you are sharing a drink. You will be considered "distant" unless you are having a beer or glass of wine together.

Choice of a Moderator or Interviewer

In some countries moderators for focus groups are expected to be psychologists and in others they are expected to be business-oriented. Local suppliers will know what to do.

Timing of Research

Be aware of holidays. The French are unlikely to go to a focus group on July 14th, Bastille Day, as Americans are to go on Thanksgiving. The Canadian Thanksgiving is celebrated in October, not November. Local elections, sporting events, and religious holidays vary from country to country. B2B research in Europe is rarely acceptable during the month of August. Also, in some countries it is more appropriate to interview during the morning, afternoon, or evening.

Total time to conduct research outside the United States and Canada varies greatly. Double the time you normally expect to conduct research in North America and add one week. Remember, deadlines do not carry the same respect in all countries. Make sure your clients and colleagues understand this.

Contracts and Contacts

At Research Dimensions we find that, in many cases, almost everywhere, marketing research begins without a formal contract. Recruiters begin recruiting and interviewers start interviewing on the basis of a telephone call. Be careful about this. Some international contacts will agree to conduct a project without fully understanding your requirements. If you get a low bid, it may be because the company does not understand the project. Check out understanding of project requirements for both low and high bids. Also, look at alternative methods of collecting data. Door-to-door interviewing may be less expensive in some countries than telephone interviewing. Make sure you put everything in writing, and in some countries, you are expected to negotiate.

[a]We asked Mr. Kay to provide you with some fresh updates from his article on the same subject: Kay, D. A. (1996, December). Puzzles and protocols of international market research, *Communication World*, 14(1):17ff.

David A. Kay, Principal and Founding Partner, Research Dimensions

OTHER QUALITATIVE RESEARCH TECHNIQUES

Although focus group interviews and many of the observation methods we have described thus far are clearly the most frequently used qualitative research techniques, they are not the only type of nonstructured research available to marketing researchers. Other popular methods include ethnographic research, depth interviews, protocol analysis, various projective techniques, and physiological measurement.

Depth Interviews

A **depth interview** is defined as a set of probing questions posed one-on-one to a subject by a trained interviewer so as to gain an idea of what the subject thinks about something or why he or she behaves in a certain way. It is conducted in the respondent's home or possibly at a central interviewing location such as a mall-intercept facility, where several respondents can be interviewed in depth in a relatively short time. The objective is to obtain unrestricted comments or opinions and to ask questions that will help the marketing researcher better understand the various dimensions of these opinions as well as the reasons for them. Of primary importance is the compilation of the data into a summary report so as to identify common themes. New concepts, designs, advertising, and promotional messages can arise from this method.[38]

There are advantages and disadvantages to in-depth interviewing. Interviewers have the ability to probe, asking many additional questions, as a result of a respondent's response. This enables the research technique to generate rich, deep, in-depth, responses. In-depth responses may be more revealing in some research situations than say, responses to predetermined, yes–no questions typical of a structured survey. If used properly, depth interviews can offer great insight into consumer behavior.[39,40] However, this advantage also leads to the major disadvantage of in-depth interviewing which is the lack of structure in the process. Unless interviewers are well trained, the results may be too varied to give sufficient insight to the problem.

Depth interviews are especially useful when the researcher wants to understand decision making on the individual level, how products are used, or the emotional and sometimes private aspects of consumers' lives.[41,42] Obviously, the respondent in an in-depth interview is not influenced by others, as they would be in a focus group.

As noted above, in-depth interviews should be conducted by a trained fieldworker who is equipped with a list of topics or, perhaps, open-ended questions. This is necessary because the respondent is not provided a list of set responses and then instructed to select one from the list. Rather, the respondent is encouraged to respond in his or her own words, and the interviewer is trained in asking probing questions such as "Why is that so?" "Can you elaborate on your point?" or "Would you give me some specific reasons?" These questions are not intended to tap subconscious motivations; rather, they simply ask about conscious reasons to help the researcher form a better picture of what is going on in the respondent's head. The interviewer may tape-record responses or may take detailed notes. Although it is typical to do face-to-face depth interviews, they can be done over the telephone when interviewees are widely dispersed.[43] Depth interviews are versatile, but they require careful planning, training, and preparation.[44]

Laddering is a technique used in in-depth interviews in an attempt to discover how product attributes are associated with desired consumer values. Essentially, values that are important to consumers are determined, such as "good health." Next, researchers determine which routes consumers take to achieve their values, such as exercise, eating certain foods, stress reduction, and so on. Finally, researchers attempt to determine which specific product attributes are used as a means of achieving the end

A depth interview is defined as a set of probing questions posed one-on-one to a subject by a trained interviewer so as to gain an idea of what the subject thinks about something or why he or she behaves in a certain way.

that is the desired value. Through in-depth interviews researchers may learn that low-sodium foods or "white meats" are instrumental in achieving "good health.[45] The term *laddering* comes from the notion that the researcher is trying to establish the linkages, or steps, leading from product attributes to values.

The summary report for the in-depth interview will look very similar to one written for a focus group study; that is, the analyst looks for common themes across several depth interview transcripts, and these are noted in the report. Verbatim responses are included in the report to support the analyst's conclusions, and any significant differences of opinion that are found in the respondents' comments are noted as well. Again, it is vital to use an analyst who is trained and experienced in interpreting the qualitative data gathered during depth interviews.

Protocol Analysis

Protocol analysis places a person in a decision-making situation and asks them to verbalize everything they considered.

Protocol analysis involves placing a person in a decision-making situation and asking him or her to verbalize everything he or she considers when making a decision. It is a special-purpose qualitative research technique that has been developed to peek into the consumer's decision-making processes. Often a tape recorder is used to maintain a permanent record of the person's thinking. After several people have provided protocols, the researcher reviews them and looks for commonalities such as evaluative criteria used, number of brands considered, types and sources of information used, and so forth.

Protocol studies are useful in two different purchase situations. First, they are helpful for purchases involving a long time frame in which several decision factors must be considered, such as when buying a house. By having people verbalize the steps they went through, a researcher can piece together the whole process. Second, when the decision process is very short, recall may be faulty, and protocol analysis can be used to slow down the process. For example, most people do not give much thought to buying chewing gum, but if Dentyne wanted to find out why people buy spearmint gum, protocol analysis might provide some important insights regarding this purchasing behavior. A variation of the protocol technique is "customer case research," and we have provided a description and examples of its revelations in Marketing Research Insight 8.4.

Projective Techniques

Projective techniques involve situations in which participants are placed in (projected into) simulated activities in the hopes that they will divulge things about themselves that they might not reveal under direct questioning. Projective techniques are appropriate in situations in which the researcher is convinced that respondents will be hesitant to relate their true opinions.

Projective techniques involve situations in which participants are placed in (projected into) simulated activities in the hopes that they will divulge things about themselves that they might not reveal under direct questioning. Projective techniques are appropriate in situations in which the researcher is convinced that respondents will be hesitant to relate their true opinions. Such situations may include behaviors such as tipping waitresses, socially undesirable behaviors such as smoking or alcohol consumption, questionable actions such as littering, or even illegal practices such as betting on football games.

There are five common projective techniques used by marketers: the word association test, the sentence completion test, the picture test, the cartoon or balloon test, and role-playing activity. A discussion of each follows.

A word-association test involves reading words to a respondent, who then answers with the first word that comes to his or her mind.

▶ **Word–Association Test** A **word–association test** involves reading words to a respondent, who then answers with the first word that comes to his or her mind. These tests may contain over 100 words and usually combine neutral words with words being tested in ads or words involving product names or services. The researcher then looks for hidden meanings or associations between responses and the words being tested on

8.4 How Customer Care Research Leads to *Eureka!*

When a company is experiencing a customer problem that it finds very difficult to research via conventional methods, an option to try is customer case research, referred to as CCR. CCR is defined as an "exploratory, qualitative market research method that con- ducts in-depth, chronological case studies of actual purchases," and this Marketing Research Insight is based on a recent exposition of the CCR method.[46]

CCR poses seven questions to draw out consumers' stories about their experiences. More often than not, interpretation of the stories of a handful of consumers triggers a *Eureka!*-type revelation for the marketing managers involved. Here are the seven questions with the interpretations of a representative case and the *Eureka!*

CCR QUESTION	REPRESENTATIVE INTERPRETATION	EUREKA!
1. What started you on the road to making this purchase?	When asked about taking scuba lessons, many customers said they did so to prepare for a honeymoon in the Caribbean.	The scuba shop realized that brides' magazines can be an effective advertising vehicle.
2. Why did you make this purchase now?	Downtown Chicago workers said that they walk by the Chicago River tour boat docks daily but only thought about the trip when visitors were coming to stay with them.	The tour boat owners realized that they could target passersby with a "best thing to do when your relatives visit" theme.
3. What was the hardest part of this process? Was there any point where you got stuck?	It was revealed that for men, giving jewelry to a significant other was much more difficult than selecting it.	Jewelry store clerks were supplied with clever, romantic, and novel ways to use to "pop" the jewelry gift on that special person.
4. When and how did you decide the price was acceptable?	It was found that for a summer music festival those in the pavilion seats compared the price to winter indoor concerts.	The festival organizers were able to raise the pavilion seat prices with no objections.
5. Is there someone else with whom I should talk to get more of the story behind this purchase?	With B2B research, often the presumedly informed manager will say, "I am not the best one to ask. You should talk to _____."	The research should lead to the actual decision maker in the company for the product or service.
6. If you've purchased this product before, how does the story of your last purchase differ from this one?	It was determined that seeing a local television channel's news vans and news personnel around town entices curious news viewers to watch that channel's news that evening.	The local station repainted its vans with vivid colors and logo and required its visible news folks to wear easily identifiable clothing.
7. At what point did you decide you trusted this organization and this person to work in your best interests?	Prospective honeymooners are clueless about scuba equipment, but they indicated that when the salesperson asked about their specific needs, they began to trust him or her.	Sales clerks were trained to ask about and to be sensitive to the expected uses of the scuba equipment so as to build rapport with first-time customers who are potentially going to buy an expensive set of scuba equipment.

the original list. This approach is used to uncover people's real feelings about these products or services, brand names, or ad copy. The time taken to respond, called "response latency," and/or the respondents' physical reactions may be measured and used to make inferences. For example, if the response latency to the word "duo" is long, it may mean that people do not have an immediate association with the word.

Decision Analyst, Inc. uses word association tests in their battery of qualitative online research services. Anywhere from 50 to 75 words are given to online respondents as stimuli. Respondents then type the first word, association, or image that comes to mind. Sample sizes are typically 100 to 200 persons, and the entire process lasts about 30 minutes. Decision Analyst states that this projective technique is very helpful in determining awareness or exploring the imagery or other associations that are linked to brands.[47]

▶ **Sentence–Completion Test** With a **sentence–completion test**, respondents are given incomplete sentences and asked to complete them in their own words. The researcher then inspects these sentences to identify themes or concepts that exist. The notion here is that respondents will reveal something about themselves in their responses. For example, suppose that Lipton Tea was interested in expanding its market to teenagers. A researcher might recruit high school students and instruct them to complete the following sentences:

> With a sentence-completion test, respondents are given incomplete sentences and asked to complete them in their own words. The researcher then inspects these sentences to identify themes or concepts that exist.

Someone who drinks hot tea is _____.
Tea is good to drink when _____.
Making hot tea is _____.
My friends think tea is_____.

The researcher would look at the written responses and attempt to identify central themes. For instance, the theme identified for the first sentence might be "healthy," which would signify that tea is perceived as a drink for those who are health-conscious. The theme for the second sentence might be "hot," indicating that tea is perceived as a cold-weather drink, whereas the theme for the third sentence may turn out to be "messy," denoting the students' reaction to using a tea bag. Finally, the last sentence theme might be found as "okay," suggesting there are no peer pressures working to cause high-school students to avoid drinking tea. Given this information, Lipton might deduce that there is room to capitalize on the hot-tea market with teens.

Decision Analyst, Inc. also conducts sentence-completion tests online. Their service provides 50 to 75 respondents 50 to 60 incomplete sentences.[48]

> With a picture test, a picture is provided to participants, who are instructed to describe their reactions by writing a short story about the picture.

▶ **Picture Test** With a **picture test**, a picture is provided to participants, who are instructed to describe their reactions by writing a short story about the picture. The researcher analyzes the content of these stories to ascertain feelings, reactions, or concerns generated by the picture. Such tests are useful when testing pictures being considered for use in brochures, advertisements, and on product packaging. For example, a test advertisement might depict a man holding a baby, and the ad headline might say, "Ford includes driver and passenger airbags as standard equipment because you love your family." A picture test may well divulge something about the picture that is especially negative or distasteful. Perhaps unmarried male respondents cannot relate to the ad because they do not have children and have not experienced strong feelings for children. On the other hand, it may turn out that the picture has a much more neutral tone than Ford's advertising agency intended. It may be that the picture does not generate feelings of concern and safety for the family in married respondents with young children. In any case, without the use of a picture test, it would be very difficult to determine the audience's reactions.

> With a cartoon or balloon test, a line drawing with an empty "balloon" above the head of one of the actors is provided to subjects, who are instructed to write in the balloon what the actor is saying or thinking. The researcher then inspects these thoughts to find out how subjects feel about the situation described in the cartoon.

▶ **Cartoon or Balloon Test** With a **balloon test**, a line drawing with an empty "balloon" above the head of one of the actors is provided to subjects who are instructed to write in the balloon what the actor is saying or thinking. The researcher then inspects these thoughts to find out how subjects feel about the situation described in the cartoon. For example, when shown a line drawing of a situation in which one of the characters is making the statement, "Ford Explorers are on sale with a discount of $4,000 and 0% interest for 48 months," the participant is asked how the other character in the drawing would respond. Feelings and reactions of the subject are judged based on their answers.

▶ **Role–Playing Activity** With **role playing**, participants are asked to pretend they are a "third person," such as a friend or neighbor, and to describe how they would act in a certain situation or to a specific statement. By reviewing their comments, the researcher can spot latent reactions, positive or negative, conjured up by the situation. It is believed that some of the respondents' true feelings and beliefs will be revealed by this method because they can pretend to be another individual. For example, if Ray-Ban is thinking about introducing a new "Astronaut" sunglasses model with superior ultraviolet light filtration, space-age styling, and a cost of about $200, role playing might be used to fathom consumers' initial reactions. In this use of role playing, subjects could be asked to assume the role of a friend or close workmate and to indicate what they would say to a third person when they learned that their friend had purchased a pair of Astronaut sunglasses. If consumers felt the Astronaut model was over-priced, this feeling would quickly surface. On the other hand, if the space-age construction and styling were consistent with these consumers' lifestyles and product desires, this fact would be divulged in the role-playing comments.

As with depth interviews, all of these projective techniques require highly qualified professionals to interpret the results. This increases the cost per respondent compared with other survey methods. Because of this aspect, projective techniques are not used extensively in commercial marketing research, but each one has value in its special realm of application.[49]

> With role playing, participants are asked to pretend they are a "third person," such as a friend or neighbor, and to describe how they would act in a certain situation or to a specific statement. By reviewing their comments, the researcher can spot latent reactions, positive or negative, conjured up by the situation.

Ethnographic Research

Ethnographic research is a term borrowed from anthropology; it is defined as a detailed, descriptive study of a group and its behavior, characteristics, culture, etc.[50] *Ethno* means people and *graphy* means describe. Anthropologists have gained insights into human behavior by living with or among their subjects, called *immersion*, for prolonged periods to study their emotions, behaviors and reactions to the demands of everyday events. Ethnography uses several different types of research, including immersion, participant observation, and informal and ongoing in-depth interviewing. Ethnographers pay close attention to words, metaphors, symbols, and stories people use to explain their lives and communicate with one another.[51] Marketers have increasingly used ethnographic research to study consumer behavior. However, unlike anthropologists, marketing researchers do not immerse themselves for months on end. Rather, ethnographic research involves direct observation, interviews, and audio and video recordings of consumers. Ethnographic research is not done at a point in time, as most other research is conducted. One researcher, Ann-Marie McDermott of Quaestor Research, stated that she worked on a new chicken burger project. Instead of doing the normal research she decided to spend time with consumers. She went to their homes and watched them shop, cook in their homes, and eat.[52]

Ethnographic research is an area of ethical sensitivity. Researchers immersing themselves in others' homes, schools, places of work and play for purposes of recording behaviors, comments, reactions, and emotions of persons naïve to the research is unethical. As the technique grows in marketing research, researchers must be adept in skills necessary to be "present and known" without interfering with normal behavior.

> Ethnographic research is a term borrowed from anthropology; it is defined as a detailed, descriptive study of a group and its behavior, characteristics, culture, etc. *Ethno* means people and *graphy* means describe.

> Ethnographers pay close attention to words, metaphors, symbols, and stories people use to explain their lives and communicate with one another. Marketers have increasingly used ethnographic research to study consumer behavior.

Fortunately, most behaviors marketers are interested in are public behaviors—shopping, cooking, and eating, for example. Such public behaviors are easily observed.

Physiological Measurement

Physiological measurement involves monitoring a respondent's involuntary responses to marketing stim-uli via the use of electrodes and other equipment.

Physiological measurement involves monitoring a respondent's involuntary responses to marketing stimuli via the use of electrodes and other equipment. Most people who are monitored find the situation strange, and they may experience uneasiness during the monitoring. Because of this factor and the necessary hardware, this technique is rarely used in marketing research.

We briefly describe two physiological measures to round out this chapter on qualitative research: the pupilometer and the galvanometer. The **pupilometer** is a device that attaches to a person's head and determines interest and attention by measuring the amount of dilation in the pupil of the eye. It actually photographs the movement of a person's pupil when he or she views different pictures. Theoretically, a person's pupil enlarges more with an interesting image than when an uninteresting one is viewed. Eye-tracking has a new application in the Internet marketing arena. For example, AT&T has begun to use eye-tracking coupled with depth interviewing to understand how AT&T customers interact with its customer service Web site.[53]

The pupilometer is a device that attaches to a person's head and determines interest and attention by measuring the amount of dilation in the pupil of the eye.

The galvanometer is a device that determines excitement levels by measuring the elec-trical activity in the respon-dent's skin.

The **galvanometer** is a device that determines excitement levels by measuring the electrical activity in the respondent's skin. It requires electrodes or sensing pads to be taped to a person's body in order to monitor this activity. When a person encounters an interesting stimulus, the electrical impulses in the body become excited. Physiological measures are useful under special circumstances, such as testing sexually oriented stimuli about which many people are embarrassed or may not tell the truth, and they require special skills to be administered correctly. There are two disadvantages to using physiological measurement techniques. First, the techniques are unnatural, and subjects may become nervous and emit false readings. Second, even though we know that the respondent reacted to the stimulus, we do not know if the response was positive or negative.[54]

Other Qualitative Research Techniques

There are many other qualita-tive research techniques other than those we have identified in this chapter.

The various techniques described thus far are in no way a complete list, for a number of other techniques are used to study human behavior. Plus, there are promising analytical techniques for interpreting the marketing strategy implications of qualitative data.[55] However, each new-to-marketing-research qualitative research technique brings with it a need to understand the theoretical and practical aspects of that technique in order to apply it properly, so it is best to hire a specialist with expertise in the particular qualitative research technique. Indeed, companies that specialize in these new techniques report that clients are cautious about them at first.[56] At the same time, qualitative techniques are fast and relatively inexpensive, and companies such as Bissell, which changed the name of its cleaner unit from the Steam Gun to Steam N' Clean after qualitative research found that children would want to use a Steam Gun to threaten their siblings, have found qualitative research to be very satisfactory when funds are low and time is short.[57]

SUMMARY

This chapter described the various qualitative research techniques used by marketing researchers. Quantitative research uses predetermined structured questions with predetermined structured response options. It is also normally characterized by the use of large samples. Qualitative research is much less structured than quantitative approaches. Qualitative research involves collecting, analyzing, and interpreting data by observing what people do or say. The observations and statements are in a qualitative or unstructured, nonstandardized form. The advantage of qualitative research is that it allows researchers to gather deeper, richer information from respondents. Pluralistic research involves using both qualitative and quantitative research methods.

Observation is a qualitative research technique in which researchers observe what consumers do rather than communicate with them. We described four general types of observation alternatives as direct versus indirect, disguised versus undisguised, structured versus unstructured, and human versus mechanical. We noted that the circumstances most suitable to observational studies are instances of (1) short time interval, (2) public behavior, and (3) lack of recall. Ethical issues arise in observation studies when respondents are not aware they are being observed. The primary advantage of observation is that researchers record what respondents actually do instead of relying on their recall of what they think they do. The limitations of observation studies is that they often rely on small samples, so representativeness is a concern. Another disadvantage is the subjective interpretation required to explain the behavior observed. Researchers do not know consumers' movtives, attitudes, or intentions.

We next described the use of focus groups, or moderated small-group discussions. Focus groups represent a very popular form of research. The major task of the moderator is to ensure free-wheeling and open communication yet focusing on the research topic. We provided excerpts from a focus group in Marketing Research Insight 8.2. Traditional focus groups use about 6 to 12 persons in a dedicated room, with a one-way mirror for client viewing. In recent years, there have been many innovations comprising what we call nontraditional focus groups. An example would be online focus groups in which clients may observe a focus group from a distant location via video streaming over the Internet. Another form of online focus group allows the participants to participate from their homes or any remote location where they observe and respond to others in the focus groups via chat rooms. Focus groups have the following advantages: (1) they generate fresh ideas; (2) they allow clients to observe their participants; and (3) they may be directed at understanding a wide variety of issues. Disadvantages include lack of representativeness, subjective evaluation of the meaning of the discussions and high costs per participant. Focus groups should be used when there is a need to describe marketing phenomena. They should not be used when there is a need to predict a phenomenon such as how many persons will actually buy a new product evaluated by focus groups. Four main objectives of focus groups are to generate ideas; to understand consumer vocabulary; to reveal consumer needs, motives, perceptions, and attitudes on products or services; and to better understand findings from quantitative studies.

The chapter presents several operational issues in running focus groups. We noted that a focus group should include from 6 to 12 participants sharing similar characteristics. Recruiting and selection may be problems because of "no shows." Focus group facilities exist in most major cities, but any large room with a central table can be used. The moderator's role is key to a successful focus group and he or she should become involved early on in the research project.

We wrapped up the chapter with descriptions of some of the other qualitative techniques used in marketing research. Depth interviews, for instance, have been adapted to probe into consumer motivations and hidden concerns. Protocol analysis induces participants to "think aloud" so the researcher can map the decision-making process being used while a consumer goes about making a purchase decision. Projective techniques, such as word association, sentence completion, or role playing, are also useful in unearthing motivations, beliefs, and attitudes that subjects may not be able to express well verbally. Ethnographic research involves observing consumers in near-natural settings to observe their behaviors, relations with others, and emotions. Finally, there are some physiological measurements such as pupil movement or electrical activity in the skin that can be used in special circumstances to better understand consumer reactions.

KEY TERMS

Quantitative research (p. 202)
Qualitative research (p. 202)
Pluralistic research (p. 203)
Observation methods (p. 203)
Direct observation (p. 203)
Indirect observation (p. 205)
Archives (p. 205)
Physical traces (p. 205)
Disguised observation (p. 205)
Undisguised observation (p. 205)
Structured observation (p. 206)
Unstructured observation (p. 206)
Human observation (p. 206)
Mechanical observation (p. 206)
Focus group (p. 208)
Traditional focus group (p. 208)
Nontraditional focus group (p. 208)
Focus group facility (p. 208)

Moderators (p. 209)
Qualitative Research Consultants (p. 209)
Focus group report (p. 210)
Online focus group (p. 212)
Depth interview (p. 221)
Laddering (p. 221)
Protocol analysis (p. 222)
Projective techniques (p. 222)
Word-association test (p. 222)
Sentence-completion test (p. 224)
Picture test (p. 224)
Balloon test (p. 224)
Role playing (p. 225)
Ethnographic research (p. 225)
Physiological measurement (p. 226)
Pupilometer (p. 226)
Galvanometer (p. 226)

REVIEW QUESTIONS/APPLICATIONS

1. Define quantitative research. Define qualitative research. List the differences between these two research methods. What is pluralistic research?
2. What is meant by an "observation technique"? What is observed, and why is it recorded?
3. Indicate why disguised observation would be appropriate for a study on how parents discipline their children when dining out.
4. Describe a traditional focus group.
5. Describe two formats of online focus groups.
6. Describe at least three different uses of focus groups.
7. How are focus group participants recruited, and what is a common problem associated with this recruitment?
8. Should the members of a focus group be similar or dissimilar? Why?
9. Describe what a focus group company facility looks like and how a focus group would take place in one.
10. Should the marketing manager client be a focus group moderator? Why or why not?
11. Indicate how a focus group moderator should handle each of the following cases: (a) A participant is loud and dominates the conversation; (b) a participant is obviously suffering from a cold and goes into coughing fits every few minutes; (c) two participants who, it turns out, are acquaintances, persist in a private conversation about their children; and (d) the only minority representative participant in the focus group looks very uncomfortable with the group and fails to make any comments.

12. What should be included in a report that summarizes the findings of a focus group?

13. Indicate the advantages and disadvantages of client interaction in the design and execution of a focus group study.

14. What is laddering? Discuss how it may be used in marketing research.

15. What is ethnographic research? Discuss how a marketing researcher could get into an ethically sensitive situation using the technique.

16. What is meant by the term *projective* as in *projective techniques*?

17. Describe (a) sentence completion, (b) word association, and (c) balloon test. Create one of each of these that might be used to test the reactions of mothers whose children are bed-wetters to absorbent underpants that their children would wear under their nightclothes.

18. Johnny Walker Red Label Scotch is concerned about the shifting attitudes of the public regarding the consumption of alcohol. However, managers think that scotch whiskey may be seen differently because it is normally consumed in small quantities as opposed to beer, wine, or even other hard liquors, such as vodka. Select two projective techniques. First, defend your use of a projective technique. Second, describe in detail how your two chosen techniques would be applied to this research problem.

19. Your university is considering letting an apartment management company build an apartment complex on campus. To save money, the company proposes to build a common cooking area for every four apartments. This area would be equipped with an oven, burners, microwave oven, sink, food preparation area, garbage disposal, and individual mini-refrigerators with locks on them for each apartment. Two students would live in each apartment, so eight students would use the common cooking area. You volunteer to conduct focus groups with students to determine their reactions to this concept and to brainstorm suggestions for improvements. Prepare the topics list you would have as a guide in your role as moderator.

BACKROADS ADVENTURE EXPERIENCE

Backroads is a unique travel service that specializes in guided biking, walking, and multisport trips in the most beautiful and exotic places on the globe. Backroads is unique in that it combines very-high-quality lodging and gourmet cuisine with athletic activities. Most Backroads tours are six days, five nights such as the following European tours: Provence Walking, Loire Valley Biking, and Ireland Multisport. There are Asia-Pacific tours such as Bali Multisport, Latin American tours such as Costa Rica Walking, African tours like Morocco Multisport, and North American tours such as Vermont Walking or Yellowstone/Tetons Multisport. Each Backroads trip is set up with 5 to 10 start-and-end dates that are scheduled for peak season when the weather is most favorable and the sights are most spectacular.

Backroads is dedicated to excellence, and even though its trips are popular and many are sold out, it believes in constantly monitoring its customers. Backroads has commissioned a company to conduct focus groups with its "first-timers," or individuals who have gone on a Backroads tour for the first time in the past six months. Here is an excerpt from the transcript of the first focus group. This group was comprised of single males and females between the ages of 25 and 40 and took place in San Francisco, California.

Moderator: Does anyone else have a reaction to his or her Backroads trip?

John: Yes, I really enjoyed my trip because everything was planned out from dawn to bedtime, and all of the equipment—bikes, kayaks, and snorkeling gear—was provided.

Curtis: I absolutely agree. It was so nice not to worry about lining up the equipment rentals at the local places or worrying that the equipment will be really bad. Backroads equipment is first class, and its guides are outstanding. They know everything there is to know about the area.

Jill: I did have difficulty lining up my transportation to and from the departure point. I did the Dordogne Biking trip, and I had to get to Brive, France, on my own. Getting flights to Paris at high tourist season is not fun at all, and I almost lost it at DeGaulle Airport because everything was so confusing.

Peter: Same with me. I did the New Zealand Multisport in January, so the season was not a problem, but the cost was a lot more than I expected. Those Backroads tour prices are not cheap to begin with, and they do not include the transportation to and from the departure point. So, I spent probably $2,500 more than I expected to.

John: Wow, that's a lot. I did multisport on the Monterey Peninsula, so I just jumped into my Lexus and I was there in less than two hours.

Amber: My strongest reaction is that I think the singles group trips are perfect. I have done sport trips with mixed groups, and you are always being held back by the slow ones. The complainers are the worst. Two years ago in Thailand with a different sport tour company, all we heard was constant whining from a spoiled 12-year-old all the way from Bangkok to Chang Mai.

Jill: The Backroads singles group tours are the best. I met someone special, and we have plans to do the San Juan Biking tour together this coming October.

Peter: Oh, I did that one last year, but I gained 5 pounds. The gourmet food on the Backroads trips was so good, and I enjoyed it so much.

Using these excerpts as representative of the entire focus group transcript, answer the following questions.

1. How is Backroads perceived? That is, what are its apparent strengths?

2. What are some areas of possible service improvement for Backroads?

3. Are the findings of this focus group generalizable to all of Backroads' "first-timers?" Why or why not?

THE HOBBIT'S CHOICE RESTAURANT

This is your integrated case described on pages 104–108.

Cory Rogers, project director at CMG Research, was excited because he had just talked to Jeff Dean on the phone, and Jeff had given him the go-ahead to conduct some focus groups on The Hobbit's Choice Restaurant project. To refresh his memory on the project, Cory checked his notes, searching for a summary table that he and Jeff had devised in the problem definition phase. Here is the table of problems based upon what you read in Chapter 4.

Marketing Problems for The Hobbit's Choice Restaurant

Problem Item	Description
Will the restaurant be successful?	Will a sufficient number of people patronize the restaurant?
How should the restaurant be designed?	What about decor, atmosphere, specialty entrées and desserts, wait staff uniforms, reservations, special seating, and so on?
What should be the average price of entrées?	How much are patrons willing to pay for the standard entrées as well as for the house specials?
What is the optimal location?	How far from their homes are patrons willing to drive, and are there any special location features (such as waterfront, ample parking, etc.) to take into consideration?
What is the profile of the target market?	What are the demographic and lifestyle profiles of those who are going to patronize The Hobbit's Choice?
What are the best promotional media?	What advertising media should be used to best reach the target market?

1. Which one of these marketing problem areas should be addressed with focus group research, and why?

2. What types of informants should be recruited for these focus groups?

3. Draft a focus group topic list that a moderator could use as a guide when conducting these focus groups.

9

Survey Data-Collection Methods

Conducting a Survey on the "Roof of the World"

The Himalayas are the highest mountains in the world, and they include Mount Everest, the highest point on the globe. Situated in the midst of this inconvenient location is Nepal's Sagarmatha National Park, which is renowned for its high-altitude vistas, trekking, ecotourism, and adventure trips. However, while tourism is a boon to the local economy, it perhaps has devastating long-term consequences. For example, tourism in Nepal has been associated with the decline in traditional customs and lifestyles of the local Sherpa culture, and the need for heating and cooking fuel has been identified as the cause of the widespread deforestation of this once pristine area. Other issues include waste and trash disposal, which has overwhelmed the low-capacity infrastructure in this area as well as severe crowding of highways, markets, and accommodation facilities in peak season. A huge worry are health-related concerns, as tourists are prone to the normal traveler's illnesses, plus they are prey to high-altitude sicknesses caused by decreased oxygen content and pressure at most of the locations in Nepal's Sagarmatha National Park. As would be expected, this part of the world is very remote, with very limited access points, but it does attract tourists from all corners of the globe.

A research program[1] was initiated to investigate several research objectives pertaining to tourism in the Himalayas, namely, (1) origins of tourists, (2) motivations to visit, (3) travel expectations, (4) health consequences, and (5) satisfaction with the

Learning Objectives

Research investigates the effects of ecotourism on the culture of Nepal.

experience. Because of the unique nature of the research, the researchers pondered the problem of how to collect responses from tourists who visit Nepal's Sagarmatha National Park (SNP). Dr. Ghazali Musa, a business faculty member at the University of Malaysia, led the research project, and he has graciously provided the following description of the data-collection method used, and, more important, the reasons for its use.

"Data were collected for three separate seasons: rainy season, peak season, and winter season. The Jorsalle entrance to the SNP was chosen for data collection. The venue is appropriate, as all tourists who visit the Park have to leave through the Jorsalle entrance. So tourists could be selected randomly because all of them had to register their names with Park officials before leaving the Park. After leaving the park the majority headed for Lukla to take planes to Kathmandu. However, some bypassed Lukla by walking straight to Jiri and taking the bus to Kathmandu. Hence, collecting data in Lukla would not be random."

"The process of selecting the tourists to participate in the study depended on the season. During the rainy season, as the number of visitors to the park was very low, all the tourists leaving the park were requested to participate in the study. A total of 250 questionnaires were delivered during the season. The tourists were given options to return the questionnaires at Himalaya Lodge in Lukla or at tourist offices in Kathmandu or to post them to the sponsoring university.

"During the October peak season data were collected for 10 days. During data collection the average number of tourists leaving the park each day ranged from 100 to 200. We distributed 25 questionnaires a day for the purpose of capturing people with different experiences and circumstances. Since the number of visitors leaving the park far exceeded the number of questionnaires that could be delivered, we selected tourists randomly. By using the guideline of the number of tourists leaving the park on the previous day, we quantified what should be the ratio of questionnaire distribution during the next day. If 100 tourists left the park the previous day on the next day we chose one of every four trekkers leaving the Park to take part in the study. Those selected would be approached and asked to participate in the study. Sometimes complimentary local apples were given to those who were willing to take part. Again the avenue of return was similar to that during the data collection during the rainy season.

"During the winter season, data collection at the Jorsalle entrance was impossible because of weather circumstances. So, questionnaires were distributed randomly at Lukla airport. Another set of questionnaires were administered by the owner of the Himalaya Lodge. The lodge was chosen as the venue of the final data collection because it is the biggest lodge in Lukla. Many tourists on camping holidays stay in the lodge as a treat on their last day in the harsh environment of the mountains. This feature allowed all types of tourist to be captured in the study: individuals, groups, budget trekkers and trekkers who seek for comfort. Since the winter season is also a low season, the owner was requested to distribute the questionnaires to all the guests. Tourists returned the completed questionnaires to the lodge reception desk. The lodge owner then posted all the completed questionnaires to the researchers."

As you are learning in this course, there are many different ways of conducting marketing research studies. In previous chapters, we discussed different forms of research such as focus groups, experiments, and descriptive research. There are many ways of gathering information among these various types of studies. Respondent behavior is observed and recorded by the researcher in observation studies. Some studies use physiological measurements, such as eye-movement tracking devices. Other studies may use passive electronic means to gather data such as Arbitron's Portable People Meter (PPM) or The Pretesting Company's "WhisperCode" which is a device placed in homes and automobiles that automatically records TV, radio, or Internet commercials to which respondents are exposed. However, in many studies, marketers must communicate with large numbers of respondents. Communication is necessary to learn what respondents are thinking; their opinions, preferences, or planned intentions. Large numbers of respondents may be required in order to collect a large enough sample of important subgroups or to ensure that the study accurately represents some larger population. Sometimes, as our opening vignette describing data-collection methods used to survey visitors to Nepal's Sagarmatha National Park illustrates, the researcher must design the data-collection method(s) around the special circumstances of the group to be surveyed in order to obtain a reasonably sample of respondents.

Surveys involve interviews with a large number of respondents using a pre-designed questionnaire. This chapter focuses on data collection methods used for surveys.

Surveys involve interviews with a large number of respondents using a predesigned questionnaire.[2] In this chapter we focus on the various methods used to collect data for surveys.

This chapter begins with a short discussion on why surveys are popular and advantageous. Next, it describes the four basic survey modes: (1) person-administered surveys, (2) computer-assisted surveys, (3) self-administered surveys, and (4) mixed-mode, sometimes called "hybrid," surveys. We discuss the advantages and disadvantages of each of these methods, and we present you with the various alternative methods of collecting data within each of these basic data-collection methods. For example, person-administered surveys may be conducted through mall intercepts or by telephone. Finally, we discuss factors a market researcher should consider when deciding which data-collection method to use.

ADVANTAGES OF SURVEYS

Compared with observation or other qualitative methods, survey methods allow the collection of significant amounts of data in an economical and efficient manner; and they typically involve large sample sizes. There are five advantages of using survey methods: (1) standardization, (2) ease of administration, (3) ability to tap the "unseen," (4) suitability to tabulation and statistical analysis, and (5) sensitivity to subgroup differences (see Table 9.1).

> Key advantages of surveys include standardization, ease of administration, ability to tap the "unseen," suitability to tabulation and statistical analysis, and sensitivity to subgroup differences.

Surveys Provide for Standardization

Because questions are preset and put in a particular arrangement on a questionnaire, survey methods ensure that all respondents are asked the same questions and are exposed to the same response options for each question. Moreover, the researcher is assured that every respondent will be confronted with questions that address the complete range of information objectives driving the research project.

Surveys Are Easy to Administer

Sometimes an interviewer is used, and survey modes are easily geared to such administration. On the other hand, the respondent may fill out the questionnaire unattended. In either case, the administration aspects are much simpler than, for instance, conducting a focus group or using depth interviews. Perhaps the simplest case is a respondent answering questions in an online survey. All the researcher needs to do is design the questionnaire, publish it on the Internet, and invite prospective respondents to fill it out.

> Online surveys are self-administered, the simplest form of administration for researchers.

Surveys Get "Beneath the Surface"

The four questions of what, why, how, and who help uncover "unseen" data. For instance, we can ask a working parent to tell us how important the location of a preschool was in his or her selection of the child's preschool. We can inquire as to how many different preschools he or she seriously considered before deciding on one, and we can easily gain an understanding of the person's financial or work circumstances

TABLE 9.1	Five Advantages of Surveys
Advantage	**Description**
Provides standardization	All respondents react to questions worded identically and presented in the same order. Response options (scales) are the same, too.
Easy to administer	Interviewers read questions to respondents and record their answers quickly and easily. In some cases, the respondents fill out the questionnaires themselves.
Gets "beneath the surface"	It is possible to ask questions about motives, circumstances, sequences of events, or mental deliberations.
Easy to analyze	Large sample sizes and computer processing allows quick tallies, cross-tabulations, and other statistical analyses.
Reveals subgroup differences	Respondents can be divided into segments or subgroups for comparisons in the search for meaningful differences.

Surveys allow researchers to compare market segments.

with a few questions on income, occupation, and family size. Much information that marketing researchers desire is unobservable and requires direct questions.

Surveys Are Easy to Analyze

Questionnaire design programs include statistical analysis packages as a natural extension of survey research.

The marketing researcher ultimately must interpret the patterns or common themes sometimes hidden in the raw data he or she collects. Statistical analysis, both simple and complex, is the preferred means of achieving this goal, and large cross-sectional surveys perfectly complement these procedures. Qualitative methods, in contrast, prove much more frustrating in this respect because of their necessarily small samples, need for interpretation, and general approach to answering marketing managers' questions. Increasingly, questionnaire design software includes the ability to perform simple statistical analyses, such as tabulations of the answers to each question, as well as the ability to create color graphs summarizing these tabulations.

Surveys Reveal Subgroup Differences

Because surveys involve large numbers of respondents, it is relatively easy to "slice" up the sample into demographic groups or other subgroups and then to compare them for market-segmentation implications. In fact, the survey sample design may be drawn up to specifically include important subgroups as a means of looking at differences in market segments.

FOUR ALTERNATIVE TYPES OF DATA COLLECTION

We must alert you to the fact that the data-collection step in the marketing research process is in the midst of great change. There are two reasons for this change. First, for the past two decades, there has been a dramatic decline in the willingness of the general public to take part in surveys, and second, computer and telecommunications technology have advanced significantly and opened new, efficient ways for marketing researchers to collect data. With respect to declining survey response rates, in a recent article, Roger Tourangeau[3] has identified the major reasons for this trend. The factors underlying a growing unwillingness in the U.S. public to take part in surveys are: use of "gatekeepers" such as answering machines, caller ID, and call blocking (for example, it is estimated that 11 million Americans have moved exclusively to mobile phones and 64 million households are on the Federal "do-not-call list[4]"), reduced amounts of free time, decline in the public's engagement with important issues, rising percentages of foreign-born Americans who are not fluent in English, and increases in the numbers of elderly who have comprehension and expression difficulties. There is also a growing desire for privacy among Americans. Indeed, the declining cooperation rates are being experienced worldwide, not just in the United States. These rising nonresponse rates have caused marketing researchers to rethink the use of "traditional" data-collection methods.

Plus, technology has opened doors to new methods, although, technology has not solved the problem of the decline in cooperation rates Figure 9.1 depicts how the traditional data-collection methods that were standard as recently as 10 years ago have been transformed by computer and telecommunications technology into new and better data-collection methods. As you look at Figure 9.1, you may not recognize some of the terminology it uses; however, after reading the rest of this chapter, you will become acquainted with these terms.

To repeat, there are four major modes of collecting survey information from respondents: (1) Have a person ask the questions, either face-to-face or voice-to-voice without any assistance from a computer. (2) Have a computer assist or direct the questioning in a face-to-face or voice-to-voice survey. (3) Allow respondents to fill out the questionnaire themselves, without computer assistance. (4) Some combination of two or more of the above three modes. We will refer to these four alternatives as person-administered, computer-administered, self-administered, and mixed-mode surveys, respectively. Each one has special advantages and disadvantages that we describe in general before discussing the various types of surveys found within each category. Specific advantages and disadvantages of these various types are discussed later.

The four basic survey modes are: (1) person-administered surveys, (2) computer-assisted surveys, (3) self-administered surveys, and (4) mixed-mode or "hybrid."

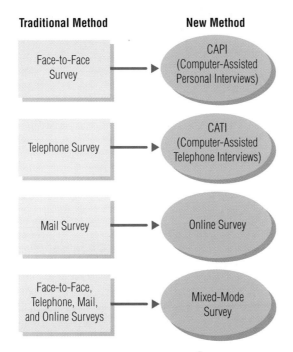

FIGURE 9.1
The Impact of Technology on Data-Collection Methods

Person-Administered Surveys (without Computer Assistance)

A **person-administered survey** is one in which an interviewer reads questions, either face-to-face or over the telephone, to the respondent and records his or her answers. It was the primary administration method for many years. However, its popularity has fallen off as communications systems have developed and computer technology has advanced. Nevertheless, person-administered surveys are still used, and we describe the advantages and disadvantages associated with these surveys next.

▶ **Advantages of Person-Administered Surveys.** Person-administered surveys have four unique advantages: They offer feedback, rapport, quality control, and adaptability.[5] They also have higher response rates than telephone or mail surveys, they permit a variety of techniques (such as card sorting) that are cumbersome with other data-collection methods, and they overcome illiteracy or poor ability to read the language.[6]

Feedback. Interviewers often must respond to direct questions from respondents during an interview. Sometimes respondents do not understand the instructions, they may not hear the question clearly, or they might become distracted during the interview. A human interviewer may be allowed to adjust his or her questions according to verbal or nonverbal cues. When a respondent begins to fidget or look bored, the interviewer can say, "I have only a few more questions." Or if a respondent makes a comment, the interviewer may jot it down as a side note to the researcher.

Rapport. Some people distrust surveys in general, or they may have some suspicions about the survey at hand. It is often helpful to have another person present to develop some rapport with the respondent early on in the questioning process. Another person can create trust and understanding that nonpersonal forms of data collection cannot achieve.

A person-administered survey is one in which an interviewer reads questions, either face-to-face or over the telephone, to the respondent and records his or her answers.

Without a personal interviewer present, respondents may fail to understand survey questions.

Quality Control. An interviewer sometimes must select certain types of respondents based on gender, age, or some other distinguishing characteristic. Personal interviewers may be used to ensure respondents are selected correctly. Alternatively, some researchers think that respondents are more likely to be truthful when they respond face-to-face.

Personal interviewers can build rapport with respondents who are initially distrustful or suspicious.

Adaptability. Personal interviewers can adapt to respondent differences. It is not unusual, for instance, to find an elderly person or a very young person who must initially be helped step by step through the answering process in order to understand how to respond to questions. Interviewers are trained, however, to ensure that they do not alter the meaning of a question by interpreting the question for a respondent. In fact, interviewers should follow precise rules on how to adapt to different situations presented by respondents.

Personal interviewers can adapt to differences in respondents, but they must be careful not to alter the meaning of a question.

▶ **Disadvantages of Person-Administered Surveys.** The drawbacks to using human interviewers are human error, slowness, cost and interview evaluation.

Humans Make Errors. Human interviewers may ask questions out of sequence; they may change the wording of a question, which may change its meaning altogether. Humans can make mistakes recording the information provided by the respondent. Human interviewers may make any number of errors when they become fatigued or bored from repetition.

Slow Speed. Collecting data using human interviewers, particularly door-to-door interviewing, is slower than other modes. Although pictures, videos, and graphics can be handled by personal interviewers, they cannot accommodate them as quickly as computers. Often personal interviewers simply record respondents' answers using pencil and paper, which necessitates a separate data-input step to build a computer data file. But increasing numbers of data-collection companies have shifted to the use of laptop computers that immediately add the responses to a data file.

High Cost. Naturally, the use of a face-to-face interviewer is more expensive than mailing the questionnaire to respondents or having them respond to an online questionnaire. Ideally, personal interviewers are highly trained and skilled and their use overcomes the expense factor. A less expensive person-administered survey is a telephone interview.

Fear of Interview Evaluation. Another disadvantage of person-administered surveys is that the presence of another person may create apprehension,[7] called **interview evaluation**, among certain respondents. We discuss this concept more fully in the following section.

The disadvantages of person-administered surveys are: human errors, slow data collection, high cost, and "interview evaluation" apprehension among respondents.

Computer-Administered Surveys

Computer technology represents an attractive and viable option with respect to survey mode, and new developments occur almost every day. Although person-administered surveys are still the industry mainstay, computer-administered survey methods are growing very rapidly and will surpass person-administered surveys in the very near future, if they have not already (exact figures are unavailable). Because of their significant advantages, computer-assisted surveys are spreading to other survey types. For instance, a computer may house questions asked by a telephone interviewer, or a questionnaire may be posted on the Internet for administration. Basically, a **computer-administered survey** is one in which computer technology plays an essential role in

A computer-administered survey is one in which computer technology plays an essential role in the interview work.

the interview work. Here, either the computer assists an interview or it interacts directly with the respondent. In the case of Internet-based questionnaires, the computer acts as the medium by which potential respondents are approached, and it is the means by which respondents submit their completed questionnaires. As with person-administered surveys, computer-administered surveys have their advantages and disadvantages.

▶ **Advantages of Computer–Administered Surveys.**   There are variations of computer-administered surveys. At one extreme, the respondent answers the questions on his or her personal computer, often online, and the questions are tailored to his or her responses to previous questions, so there are no human interviewers. At the other end, there are computer programs in which a telephone or personal interviewer is prompted by the computer about which questions to ask and in what sequence. Regardless of which variation is considered, at least five advantages of computer-administered surveys are evident: speed; error-free interviews; use of pictures, videos, and graphics; real-time capture of data; and reduction of anxieties caused by "interview evaluation" concern (respondents' concern that they are not answering "correctly").

Computer-administered surveys are fast, error-free, capable of using pictures or graphics, able to capture data in real time, and less threatening for some respondents.

Speed.   Perhaps the greatest single advantage of computer-assisted data collection is its ability to gather survey data very quickly. The computer-administered approach is much faster than the human interview approach. Computers can quickly jump to questions based on specific responses, they can rapidly dial random telephone numbers, and they can easily check on answers to previous questions to modify or otherwise custom-tailor the interview to each respondent's circumstances. The speed factor translates into cost savings, and there is a claim that Internet surveys are about one-half the cost of mail or phone surveys.[8]

Error-Free Interviews.   Properly programmed, the computer-administered approach guarantees zero interviewer errors, such as inadvertently skipping questions, asking inappropriate questions based on previous responses, misunderstanding how to pose questions, recording the wrong answer, and so forth. Also, the computer becomes neither fatigued nor bored, and it never cheats.

Use of Pictures, Videos, and Graphics.   Computer graphics can be integrated into questions as they are viewed on a computer screen. So rather than having an interviewer pull out a picture of a new type of window unit air conditioner, for instance, computer graphics can show it from various perspectives. High-quality video windows may be programmed to appear so the respondent can see the product in use or can be shown a wide range of visual displays.

The real-time capture of data by computer-administered surveys is an important advantage of this data-collection method.

Real-Time Capture of Data.   Because respondents are interacting with the computer, the information is entered directly into a computer's data storage system and can be accessed for tabulation or other analyses at any time. Once the interviews are finished, final tabulations can be completed in a matter of minutes. This feature is so beneficial that some interview companies have telephone interviewers directly linked to computer input when they conduct their interviews.

Interview evaluation occurs when the interviewer's presence creates anxieties in respondents, which may cause them to alter their normal responses.

Reduction of "Interview Evaluation" Concern in Respondents.   Interview evaluation may occur when another person is involved in the interviewing process and some respondents are apprehensive about whether they are answering "correctly." Even when responding to questions from a perfect stranger, some people become anxious about the possible reaction of the interviewer to their answers. They may be concerned about how the interviewer evaluates their responses. This may be especially present when the questions deal with personal topics such as personal hygiene, political opinions, financial matters, and even age. The presence of a human interviewer may cause a respondent to answer differently than they would in a nonpersonal data collection mode. Some respondents, for example, try to please the interviewer by saying what they think the interviewer wants to hear. In any case, some researchers believe that respondents will provide more truthful answers to potentially sensitive topics when interacting with a machine.

Finally, an emerging advantage of online surveys is that when online surveys are coupled with opt-in or "permission marketing," they are becoming known for their high response rates; that is, when there is a panel or a database of a firm's customers who have agreed to respond to online survey requests from a research firm or the company, studies have shown that respondents are more cooperative and more actively involved in the survey and that response-inducements such as prenotifications and personalization are unnecessary.[9]

▶ **Disadvantages of Computer–Administered Surveys.** The primary disadvantages of computer-assisted surveys are that they require some level of technical skill and setup costs may be significant.

Technical Skills May Be Required. There is a wide range of computer-assisted methods available to marketing researchers. While the simplest options require minimal technical skills and students taking marketing research courses can master them in a matter of an hour or less, there are more sophisticated versions that require considerable skill to ensure that the systems are operational and free of errors.

> The disadvantages to computer-assisted data collection are the requirement of technical skills and high setup costs.

Setup Costs Can Be High. Though computer technology can result in increases in productivity, there can be high setup costs associated with getting some systems in place and operational. With the most sophisticated computer-administered survey types, such as a computer-assisted telephone interview (CATI) system, programming and debugging must occur with each survey. One software evaluator has estimated that two days of setup time by an experienced programmer was fairly efficient.[10]

Depending on what type of computer-administered survey is under consideration, these costs, including the time associated with them, can render computer-administered delivery systems for surveys less attractive than other data-collection options. On the other hand, there are a number of moderate- to low-cost computer-administered options, such as Web-based questionnaires with user-friendly development interfaces that are fueling the rush toward more and more online research around the world. Without much effort and using a Web-based questionnaire that respondents fill out simply by going online and accessing the appropriate Web site, a researcher can realize considerable cost savings.

> Some types of computer-administered surveys incur relatively high setup costs, but others are very reasonable and easy to use.

Self-Administered Surveys (without Computer Assistance)

A **self-administered survey** is one in which the respondent completes the survey on his or her own. It is different from other survey methods in that there is no agent—human or computer—administering the interview.[11] So, we are referring to the prototypical "pencil-and-paper" survey here. Instead, the respondent reads the questions and responds directly on the questionnaire. Normally, the respondent goes at his or her own pace, and in most instances he or she selects the place and time to complete the interview. He or she also may decide when the questionnaire will be returned. As with other survey methods, those that are self-administered have their advantages and disadvantages.

> A self-administered survey is one in which the respondent completes the survey on his or her own: there is no agent—human or computer—administering the interview.

Self-administered surveys have three important advantages: reduced cost, respondent control, and no interviewer-evaluation apprehension.

▶ **Advantages of Self-Administered Surveys.** Self-administered surveys have three important advantages: reduced cost, respondent control, and no interviewer-evaluation apprehension.

Reduced Cost. By eliminating the need for an interviewer or an interviewing device such as a computer program, there can be significant savings in cost.

Respondent Control. Respondents can control the pace at which they respond, so they may not feel rushed. Ideally, a respondent should be relaxed while responding, and a self-administered survey may effect this relaxed state.

No Interview-Evaluation Apprehension. As we just noted, some respondents feel apprehensive when answering questions, or the topic may be sensitive, such as gambling,[12] smoking, or dental work. The self-administered approach takes the administrator, whether human or computer, out of the picture, and respondents may feel more at ease. Self-administered questionnaires have been found to elicit more insightful information than face-to-face interviews.[13]

The disadvantages of self-administered surveys are respondent control, lack of monitoring, and high questionnaire requirements.

If respondents misunderstand or do not follow directions, they may become frustrated and quit.

▶ **Disadvantages of Self-Administered Surveys.** The disadvantages of self-administered surveys are lack of respondent control, lack of monitoring, and high questionnaire requirements.

Respondent Control. As you can see, self-administration places control of the survey in the hands of the prospective respondent. As a result, this type of survey is subject to the possibilities that respondents will not complete the survey, will answer questions erroneously, will not respond in a timely manner, or will refuse to return the survey at all.

Lack of Monitoring. With self-administered surveys there is no opportunity for the researcher to monitor or interact with the respondent during the course of the interview. A monitor can offer explanations and encourage the respondent to continue. But with a self-administered survey, respondents who do not understand the meaning of a word or who are confused about how to answer a question may answer improperly or become frustrated and refuse to answer at all.

With self-administered surveys, the questionnaire must be especially thorough and accurate in order to minimize respondent errors.

High Questionnaire Requirements. Because of the absence of the interviewer or an internal computer check system, the burden of respondent understanding falls on the questionnaire itself. Not only must it have perfectly clear instructions, examples, and reminders throughout, the questionnaire must also entice the respondents to participate and encourage them to continue answering until all questions are complete. Questionnaire design is important regardless of the data-collection mode. However, with self-administered surveys, clearly the questionnaire must be thorough and accurate before data collection begins. You will learn more about designing questionnaires in Chapter 11.

Mixed-Mode Surveys

Mixed-mode surveys, sometimes referred to as "hybrid" surveys, use multiple data-collection methods.

Mixed-mode surveys, sometimes referred to as "hybrid" surveys, use multiple data-collection methods. It has become increasingly popular to use mixed-mode surveys in recent years. Part of this popularity is due to the increasing use of online survey research. As more and more respondents have access to the Internet, online surveys, a form of computer-assisted surveys, are often combined with some other method, such as telephone surveying, a form of person-administered surveying. With a mixed-mode approach, a researcher may use two or more survey data-collection methods to access a representative sample,[14] or methods may be used in tandem, such as use of the Internet to solicit respondents who agree to a face-to-face interview.[15]

▶ **Advantages of Mixed−Mode Surveys**

Multiple "Pluses" to Achieve Data-Collection Goal. The main benefit of mixed-mode surveys is that researchers are able to take the advantages of each of the various modes to achieve their data-collection goals. For example, one survey of a panel of households administered quarterly uses a randomly selected sample of about 800 households. Since 50% of these households have Internet service, they may be surveyed each quarter via an online survey. This gives the panel administrators the advantages associated with online surveys; they may access all the panel households with the touch of a computer key. Also, as respondents open their e-mailed questionnaires and answer, their responses are automatically downloaded to the panel's statistical package for analysis. In order to achieve a representative sample, households without Internet service must be included. Households without Internet service typically have telephones. So these panel members are surveyed each quarter via telephone. With this mixed-mode approach, the panel administrators are able to take advantage of the speed and low cost of online surveying and the advantage of reaching the total household population using telephone surveys.[16]

> The advantage of mixed-mode surveys is that researchers are able to take the advantages of each of the various modes to achieve their data-collection goals.

▶ **Disadvantages of Mixed−Mode Surveys.** There are two primary disadvantages of using mixed-mode, or "hybrid" data-collection methods.

The Survey Mode May Affect Response. One of the reasons that in the past researchers were reluctant to use mixed modes for gathering data is concern that the mode used may affect responses given by consumers. Will consumers, responding to an in-home interview with a personal interviewer respond differently from a consumer responding to an impersonal, online survey? In a study conducted by Professors Green, Medlin, and Whitten, two methods of data collection were compared: online surveys versus a traditional mail survey. While the study showed no difference in the data quality, interestingly, response rates did not vary either. This is surprising, since one of the major disadvantages with mail surveys is a low response rate.[17] Several other studies have been conducted to assess differences between data-collection methods in mixed-mode applications.[18] The results of studies addressing the question of survey mode effects on respondents are not entirely consistent, so our warning is that the researcher must assess differences in data collected to determine if the data-collection mode explains any differences that are found.

> A disadvantage of the mixed-mode survey is that the researcher must assess the effects the mode may have on response data.

Additional Complexity. Multiple modes of data collection add to the complexities of data collection.[19] For example, if you are conducting a survey online and by telephone, the wording of the instructions must be different to accommodate respondents reading instructions they themselves are to follow (for online respondents) versus a telephone interviewer reading the instructions to the respondent. Further, data from the two sources will need to be integrated into a single data set, so much care must be taken to ensure that data are compatible.

> Multi-modes of data collection add to the complexities of data collection such as differences in instructions and integration of data from different sources.

DESCRIPTIONS OF DATA−COLLECTION MODES

Now that you have an understanding of the pros and cons of person-, computer-, self-administered, and mixed-mode surveys, we can describe the various interviewing techniques used in each method. Not counting mixed-mode surveys, there are at least 11 different data-collection methods used by marketing researchers (Table 9.2):

Person-administered surveys:
1. In-home interview
2. Mall-intercept interview
3. In-office interview
4. "Traditional" telephone interview
5. Central location telephone interview

TABLE 9.2	Various Ways to Gather Data
Data-Collection Method	**Description**
In-home interview	The interviewer conducts the interview in the respondent's home. Appointments may be made ahead by telephone.
Mall-intercept interview	Shoppers in a mall are approached and asked to take part in the survey. Questions may be asked in the public area of the mall or in the mall-intercept company's facilities located in the mall.
In-office interview	The interviewer makes an appointment with business executives or managers to conduct the interview at the respondent's place of work.
"Traditional" telephone interview	Interviewers work out of their homes to conduct telephone interviews with households or business representatives.
Central location telephone interview	Interviewers work in a data-collection company's office using cubicles or work areas for each interviewer. Often the supervisor has the ability to "listen in" to interviews and to check that they are being conducted correctly.
Computer-assisted telephone interview	With a central location telephone interview, the questions are programmed for a computer screen that an interviewer reads to the respondent. Responses are entered directly into the computer program by the interviewer.
Fully computerized interview	A computer is programmed to administer the questions. Respondents interact with the computer and enter their own answers by using a keyboard, by touching the screen, or by using some other means.
Online or other Internet-based survey	Respondents fill out a questionnaire that resides on the Internet, or otherwise accesses it via the Internet, such as receiving an e-mail attachment, or downloads the file online.
Group self-administered survey	Respondents take the survey in a group context. Each respondent works individually, but they meet as a group; this allows the researcher to economize.
Drop-off survey	Questionnaires are left with the respondent to fill out. The administrator may return at a later time to pick up the completed questionnaire, or it may be mailed in.
Mail survey	Questionnaires are mailed to prospective respondents, who are asked to fill them out and return them by mail.

Computer-administered surveys:
  6. Computer-assisted telephone interview (CATI)
  7. Fully computerized interview
  8. Online and other Internet-based surveys
Self-administered surveys:
  9. Group self-administered survey
 10. Drop-off survey
 11. Mail survey

Person–Administered Interviews

There are at least five variations of person-administered interviews, and their differences are based largely on the location of the interview. These variations include the in-home interview, the mall-intercept interview, the in-office interview, and the telephone interview (which includes "traditional" and central location telephone interviews).

▶ **In-Home Interviews.** Just as the name implies, an **in-home interview** is conducted by an interviewer who enters the home of the respondent. In-home interviews take longer to recruit participants, and researchers must travel to and from respondents' homes. Therefore, the cost per interview is relatively high. Two important factors justify the high cost of in-home interviews. First, the marketing researcher must believe that personal contact is essential to the success of the interview. Second, the researcher must be convinced that the in-home environment is conducive to the questioning process. In-home interviews are useful when the research objective requires respondents' physical presence to either see, read, touch, use or interact with the research object, such as a product prototype *and* the researcher believes that the security and comfort of respondents' homes is an important element affecting the quality of the data collected. For example, the Yankelovich Youth Monitor conducts in-home interviews of children who are 6 years and older so both parents and children are comfortable with the interviewing process.[20]

> In-home interviews are used when the survey requires respondents to see, read, touch, use, or interact with a product prototype *and* the researcher believes that the security and comfort of respondents' homes is important to the quality of the data collected.

For instance, some research objectives require the respondents' physical presence in order to interact with the research object. A company develops a new type of countertop toaster oven that is designed so that it remains perfectly clean. However, in order to get the benefit of clean cooking, the oven must be configured differently for different cooking applications and the throw-away "grease-catch foil" must be placed in just the right position to work properly. Will consumers be able to follow the instructions? This is an example of a study that would require researchers to conduct surveys in the home kitchens of the respondents. Researchers would observe respondents opening the box, unwrapping and assembling the device, reading the directions, and cooking a meal. All of this may take an hour or more. Again, respondents may not be willing to travel somewhere and spend an hour on a research project. But, they would be more likely to do this in their own home. This process results in high quality interviews and facilitates rapport.

> In-home interviews facilitate interviewer–interviewee rapport.

▶ **Mall-Intercept Interviews.** Although the in-home interview has important advantages, it has the significant disadvantage of cost. The expense of in-home interviewer travel is high, even for local surveys. Patterned after "man-on-the-street" interviews pioneered by opinion-polling companies and other "high-traffic" surveys conducted in settings where crowds of pedestrians pass by, the **mall-intercept interview** is one in which the respondent is encountered and questioned while he or she is visiting a shopping mall. A mall-intercept company generally has its offices located within a large shopping mall, usually one that draws from a regional rather than a local market area. Typically, the interview company negotiates exclusive rights to do interviews in the mall and, thus, forces all marketing research companies that wish to do mall intercepts in that area to use that interview company's services. In any case, the travel costs are eliminated because the respondents incur the costs themselves by traveling to the mall. Mall-intercept interviewing has acquired a major role as a survey method because of its ease of implementation.[21] Shoppers are intercepted in the pedestrian traffic areas of shopping malls and either interviewed on the spot or asked to move to a permanent interviewing facility located in the mall office. Although some malls do not allow marketing research interviewing because they view it as a nuisance to shoppers, many do

> Mall-intercept interviews are conducted in large shopping malls, and they are less expensive per interview than are in-home interviews.

Mall intercept interviews take place while respondents are shopping.

permit mall-intercept interviews and may rely on these data themselves to fine-tune their own marketing programs.

The representativeness of mall interview samples is always an issue.

In addition to low cost, mall interviews have many of the benefits associated with in-home interviewing. Perhaps the most important advantage is the presence of an interviewer who can interact with the respondent.[22] However, a few drawbacks are associated specifically with mall interviewing, and it is necessary to point them out here. First, sample representativeness is an issue, for most malls draw from a relatively small area in close proximity to their location. If researchers are looking for a representative sample of some larger area, such as the county or metropolitan statistical area (MSA), they should be wary of using the mall intercept. Some people shop at malls more frequently than others and, therefore, have a greater chance of being interviewed.[23] Recent growth of non-mall retailing concepts such as catalogs and stand-alone discounters such as Wal-Mart mean that more mall visitors are recreational shoppers rather than convenience-oriented shoppers, resulting in the need to scrutinize mall-intercept samples as to what consumer groups they actually represent.[24] Also, many shoppers refuse to take part in mall interviews for various reasons. Nevertheless, special selection procedures called "quotas," which are described in Chapter 12 may be used to counter the problem of nonrepresentativeness.

Mall interview companies use rooms in their small headquarters areas to conduct private interviews in a relaxed setting.

A second shortcoming of mall-intercept interviewing is that a shopping mall does not have a comfortable home environment that is conducive to rapport and close attention to details. The respondents may feel uncomfortable because passersby stare at them; they may be pressed for time or otherwise preoccupied by various distractions outside the researcher's control. These factors may adversely affect the quality of the interview. Some interview companies attempt to counter this problem by taking respondents to special interview rooms located in the interview company's mall offices. This procedure minimizes distractions and encourages respondents to be more relaxed. Some mall interviewing facilities have rooms with one-way mirrors.

▶ **In-Office Interviews.** Although the in-home and mall-intercept interview methods are appropriate for a wide variety of consumer goods, marketing research conducted in the business-to-business or organizational market typically requires interviews with business executives, purchasing agents, engineers, or other managers. Normally, **in-office interviews** take place in person while the respondent is in his or her office, or perhaps in a company lounge area. Interviewing businesspersons face-to-face has essentially the same advantages and drawbacks as in-home consumer interviewing. For example, if Hewlett-Packard wanted information regarding user preferences for different features that might be offered in a new ultra-high-speed laser printer designed for business accounting firms, it would make sense to interview prospective users or purchasers of these printers. It would also be logical that these people be interviewed at their places of business.

As you might imagine, in-office personal interviews incur relatively high costs. Executives qualified to give opinions on a specific topic or individuals who would be involved in product purchase decisions must first be located. Sometimes names can be obtained from sources such as industry directories or trade association membership lists. More frequently, screening must be conducted over the telephone by calling a particular company that is believed to have executives of the type needed. However, locating those people within a large organization may be time-consuming. Once a qualified person is located, the next step is to persuade that person to agree to an interview and then set up a time for the interview. This may require a sizable incentive. Finally, an interviewer must go to the particular place at the appointed time. Even with appointments, long waits are sometimes encountered and cancellations are not uncommon because businesspeople's schedules sometimes shift unexpectedly. Added to these cost factors is the fact that interviewers who specialize in businessperson interviews are more costly in general because of their specialized knowledge and abilities. They have to navigate around gatekeepers such as secretaries, learn technical jargon, and be conversant on product features when the respondent asks pointed questions or even criticizes questions as they are posed to him or her.

▶ **Telephone Interviews.** As we have mentioned previously, the need for a face-to-face interview is often predicated on the necessity of the respondent's actually seeing a product, advertisement, or packaging sample. On the other hand, it may be vital that the interviewer watch the respondent to ensure correct procedures are followed or otherwise to verify something about the respondent or his or her reactions. If, however, physical contact is not necessary, telephone interviewing is an attractive option. There are a number of advantages as well as disadvantages associated with telephone interviewing.[25]

The advantages of telephone interviewing are many, and they explain why phone surveys are very common in marketing surveys. First, the telephone is a relatively inexpensive way to collect survey data. Long-distance telephone charges are much lower than the cost of a face-to-face interview. A second advantage of the telephone interview is that it has the potential to yield a very-high-quality sample. If the researcher uses random dialing procedures and proper callback measures, the telephone approach may produce a better sample than any other survey procedure. A third and very important advantage is that telephone surveys have very quick turnaround times. Most telephone interviews are of short duration anyway, but a good interviewer may complete several interviews per hour. Conceivably, a study could have the data-collection phase executed in a few days with telephone interviews. In fact, in the political polling industry, in which real-time information on voter opinions is essential, it is not unusual to have national telephone polls completed in a single night.

Unfortunately, the telephone survey approach has several inherent shortcomings. First, the respondent cannot be shown anything or physically interact with the research object. This shortcoming ordinarily eliminates the telephone survey as an alternative in situations requiring that the respondent view product prototypes, advertisements, packages, or anything else.

In-office interviews are conducted at executives' or managers' places of work because they are the most suitable locations.

In-office personal interviews incur costs due to difficulties in accessing qualified respondents.

Advantages of telephone interviews are cost, quality, and speed.

A second disadvantage is that the telephone interview does not permit the interviewer to make the various judgments and evaluations that can be made by the face-to-face interviewer. For example, judgments regarding respondent income based on the home they live in and other outward signs of economic status cannot be made. Similarly, the telephone does not allow for the observation of body language and facial expressions, nor does it permit eye contact. On the other hand, some may argue that the lack of face-to-face contact is helpful. Self-disclosure studies have indicated that respondents provide more information in personal interviews, except when the topics are threatening or potentially embarrassing. Questions on alcohol consumption, contraceptive methods, racial issues, or income tax reporting will probably generate more valid responses when asked in the relative anonymity of the telephone than when administered face-to-face.[26] A recent review article concluded that, compared with face-to-face interviews, telephone interviews elicit more suspicion and less cooperation, generate more "no opinions" and socially desirable answers, and foster more dissatisfaction with long interviews.[27]

The telephone is a poor choice for conducting a survey with many open-ended questions.

A third disadvantage of the telephone interview is that the marketing researcher is more limited in the quantity and types of information that he or she can obtain. Very long interviews are inappropriate for the telephone, as are questions with lengthy lists of response options that respondents will have difficulty remembering when they are read over the telephone. Respondents short on patience may hang up during interviews, or they may utter short and convenient responses just to speed up the interview. Obviously, the telephone is a poor choice for conducting an interview with many open-ended questions for which respondents make comments or give statements because the interviewer will have great difficulty recording these remarks.

Telephone interviewers must contend with the negative impression people have of telemarketers.

A last problem with telephone interviews is the growing threat to its existence by the increased use of answering machines, caller recognition, and call-blocking devices being adopted by consumers.[28] The research industry is concerned about these gate-keeping methods, and it is just beginning to study ways around them.[29] Another difficulty is that legitimate telephone interviewers must contend with the negative impression people have of telemarketers.[30]

SETTING UP CONTROLS FOR A TELEPHONE INTERVIEW

Suppose your marketing research course requires team projects, and your team decides to research when and why students at your university chose to attend it. Your five-member team will conduct telephone interviews of 200 students selected at random from your university's student directory, with each team member responsible for completing 40 interviews by calling from his or her apartment or dorm room. You have volunteered to direct the telephone interviewing. How do you propose to accomplish each of the following tasks?

Task	Write your proposed solution here
How will you train your fellow student team member interviewers?	_____
How will you ensure that they are conducting the interviews correctly?	_____
How will you make sure they conduct the interviews on time?	_____
How will you instruct them how to handle "no answers" and answering machines?	_____
How will you ensure that their completed interviews are not bogus?	_____

As you read the following descriptions of how surveys are conducted by telephone, see if your answers to these questions about your team research project are consistent with standard practices in marketing research.

Despite their shortcomings and declining response rates, telephone surveys remain popular. In fact, when monetary incentives, assurance that it is not a sales call, and a short survey is involved, response rates are quite good according to one study conducted in New Zealand.[31]

There are two types of telephone interviews: traditional and central location. As you can guess, telephone interviewing has been and continues to be greatly affected by advances in telephone systems and communications technology. As you will see, the traditional telephone approach has largely faded away, whereas the central location approach has embraced technological advances in telephone systems.

Traditional Telephone Interviewing. Technology has radically changed telephone surveys; however, it is worthwhile to describe this form of telephone interviewing as a starting point. Prior to central location and computer-assisted telephone interviewing (both of which we will describe shortly), **traditional telephone interviews** were those that were conducted either from the homes of the telephone interviewing staff or, perhaps, from telephones located in the data-collection company's offices. Everything was done mechanically; that is, interviewers entered the telephone number manually, they read questions off a printed questionnaire, they were responsible for following special instructions on how to administer the questions, and they checked off the respondent's answers on each questionnaire. Quality control was limited to training sessions, sometimes in the form of a dress rehearsal by administering the questionnaire to the supervisor or another interviewer, and to callback checks by the supervisor to verify that the respondent had taken part in the interview. Obviously, the traditional telephone interview method has great potential for errors.

Traditional telephone interviewing has great potential for errors.

In addition to the possibilities of misdialing and making mistakes in administering the questions, there are potential problems of insufficient callbacks for respondents who are not at home, and a host of other problems. Also, because the actual hours worked while performing telephone interviews are difficult to track, most interview companies opt for a "per completion" compensation system; that is, the interviewer is compensated for each questionnaire delivered to the office completely filled out. As you can imagine, there have been instances of dishonest interviewers turning in falsified results. We have prepared Marketing Research Insight 9.1 so you will learn about the ethical issues involved with interviewer cheating and some methods used in marketing research to minimize it.

Central Location Telephone Interviewing. This form of telephone interviewing is in many ways the research industry's current standard. With **central location telephone interviewing**, a field data-collection company installs several telephone lines at one location, and the interviewers make calls from the central location. Usually, interviewers have separate enclosed work spaces and lightweight headsets that free both hands so they can record responses. Everything is done from this central location. Obviously, there are many advantages to operating from a central location. For example, resources are pooled, and interviewers can handle multiple surveys, such as calling plant managers in the afternoon and households during the evening hours.

Central location interviewing is the current telephone survey standard because it affords good control of interviewers.

The reasons accounting for the prominence of the central location phone interview are efficiency and control. Efficiency is gained when everything is performed at a single location and further acquired by the benefit that multiple telephone surveys can be conducted simultaneously.

9.1 Interviewer Cheating with Traditional Telephone Interviews

A concern with traditional telephone interviewing is interviewer cheating. Although most traditional telephone interviewers are honest, only minimal control and supervision can be used with this method. Consequently, there are temptations for cheating, such as turning in bogus completed questionnaires or conducting interviews with respondents who do not qualify for the survey at hand. When traditional telephone interviewing is used, checks should be more extensive and may include the following[32]:

1 Have an independent party call back a sample of each interviewer's respondents to verify that they took part in the survey.

2 Have interviewers submit copies of their telephone logs to validate that the work was performed on the dates and in the time periods required.

3 If long-distance calls were made, have interviewers submit copies of their telephone bill with long-distance charges itemized to check that the calls were made properly.

4 If there is a concern about a particular interviewer's diligence, request that the interviewer be taken off the project.

A researcher should always check the accuracy and validity of interviews, regardless of the data collection method used, but because interview cheating is a well-known problem with traditional telephone interviews, the researcher who uses this data-collection method and fails to build checks and verification procedures into the survey is not measuring up to the ethical standards of the marketing research industry.

Apart from cost savings, perhaps the most important reason is quality control. To begin, recruitment and training are performed uniformly at this location. Interviewers can be oriented to the equipment, they can study the questionnaire and its instructions, and they can practice the interview among themselves over their phone lines. Also, the actual interviewing process can be monitored. Most telephone interviewing facilities have monitoring equipment that permits a supervisor to listen in on interviewing as it is being conducted. Interviewers who are not doing the interview properly can be spotted and the necessary corrective action taken. Ordinarily, each interviewer will be monitored at least once per shift, but the supervisor may focus attention on newly hired interviewers to ensure they are doing their work correctly. The fact that each interviewer never knows when the supervisor will listen in guarantees more overall diligence than would be seen otherwise. Also, completed questionnaires are checked on the spot as an additional quality-control check. Interviewers can be immediately informed of any deficiencies in filling out the questionnaire. Finally, there is control over interviewers' schedules. That is, interviewers report in and out and work regular hours, even if they are evening hours, and make calls during the time periods stipulated by the researcher as appropriate interviewing times.

Computer-Administered Interviews

Computer technology has had a significant impact on the telephone data-collection industry. There are two variations of computer-administered telephone interview systems. In one, a human interviewer is used, but in the other, a computer, sometimes with a synthesized or recorded voice, is used. At the same time, there are important computer-assisted interview methods that have recently emerged, which we describe in this section as well.

▶ **Computer-Assisted Telephone Interview (CATI).** The most advanced telephone interview companies have computerized the central location telephone interviewing process, and such systems are called **computer-assisted telephone interviews (CATIs)**. Although each system is unique, and new developments occur almost daily, we can describe a typical situation. Here each interviewer is equipped with a hands-free headset and is seated in front of a computer screen that is driven by the company's computer system. Often the computer dials the prospective respondent's telephone automatically, and the computer screen provides the interviewer with the introductory comments. As the interview progresses, the interviewer moves through the questions by pressing a key or a series of keys on the keyboard. Some systems use light pens or pressure-sensitive screens.

> With CATI, the interviewer reads the questions off a computer screen and enters respondents' answers directly into the computer program.

The questions and possible responses appear on the screen one at a time. The interviewer reads the question to the respondent, enters the response code, and the computer moves on to the next appropriate question. For example, an interviewer might ask if the respondent owns a dog. If the answer is "yes," there could appear a series of questions regarding what type of dog food the dog owner buys. If the answer is "no," these questions would be inappropriate. Instead, the computer program skips to the next appropriate question, which might be "Do you own a cat?" In other words, the computer eliminates the human error potential that would exist if this survey were done in the traditional or central location telephone interview modes. The human interviewer is just the "voice" of the computer.

> With CATI, the interviewer is the "voice" of the computer.

The computer can even be used to customize questions. For example, in the early part of a long interview you might ask a respondent the years, makes, and models of all cars he or she owns. Later in the interview you might ask questions about each specific car owned. The question might come up on the interviewer's screen as follows: "You said you own a Lexus. Who in your family drives this car most often?" Other questions about this car and others owned would appear in similar fashion. Questions like this can, of course, be dealt with in a traditional or central location manual interview, but they are handled much more efficiently in the computerized version because the interviewer does not need to physically flip questionnaire pages back and forth or remember previous responses.

The CATI approach also eliminates the need for editing completed questionnaires and creating computer data files by later manually entering every response with a keyboard. There is no checking for errors in completed questionnaires because there is no physical questionnaire. More to the point, in most computerized interview systems it is not permitted to enter an "impossible" answer. For example, if a question has three possible answers with codes "A," "B," and "C," and the interviewer enters a "D" by mistake, the computer will ask for the answer to be reentered until an acceptable code is entered. If a combination or pattern of answers is impossible, the computer will not accept an answer, or it may alert the interviewer to the inconsistency and move to a series of questions that will resolve the discrepancy. Data entry for completed questionnaires is eliminated because data are entered directly into a computer file as the interview is completed.

> Most CATI systems are programmed to make wrong answers impossible.

This second operation brings to light another advantage of computer-assisted interviewing. Tabulations may be run at any point in the study. Such real-time reporting is impossible with pencil-and-paper questionnaires, for which there can be a wait of several days following interviewing completion before detailed tabulations of the results are available. Instantaneous results available with computerized telephone interviewing provide some real advantages. Based on preliminary tabulations, certain questions may be dropped, saving time and money in subsequent interviewing. If, for example, over 90 percent of those interviewed answered a particular question in the same manner, there may be no need to continue asking the question.

> CATI systems permit tabulation in midsurvey.

Tabulations may also suggest the addition of questions to the survey. If an unexpected pattern of product use is uncovered in the early interviewing stages, questions can be added to further delve into this behavior. So the computer-administered telephone survey affords an element of flexibility unavailable in the traditional paper-and-pencil survey methods. Finally, managers may find the early reporting of survey results useful in preliminary planning and strategy development. Sometimes survey project deadlines run very close to managers' presentation deadlines, and advance indications of the survey's findings permit managers to organize their presentations in advance rather than all in a rush the night before. The many advantages and quick turnaround of CATI and CAPI (computer-assisted personal interviewing) make them mainstay data collection methods for many syndicated omnibus survey services.[33]

In sum, computer-administered telephone interviewing options are very attractive to marketing researchers because of the advantages of cost savings, quality control, and time savings over the paper-and-pencil method.[34]

▶ **Fully Computerized Interview (Not Online).** Some companies have developed **fully computerized interviews**, in which the survey is administered completely by a computer, but not online. With one such system, a computer dials a phone number and a recording is used to introduce the survey. The respondent then uses the push buttons on his or her telephone to make responses, thereby interacting directly with the computer. In the research industry, this approach is known as the **completely automated telephone survey (CATS)**. CATS has been successfully used for customer satisfaction studies, service quality monitoring, election day polls, product/warranty registration, and even in-home product tests with consumers who have been given a prototype of a new product.[35]

CATS are completely automated telephone surveys on a stand-alone computer, but not online.

In another system, the respondent sits or stands in front of the computer unit and reads the instructions off the screen. Each question and its various response options appear on the screen, and the respondent answers by pressing a key or touching the screen. For example, the question may ask the respondent to rate how satisfied, on a

Fully computerized interviews allow the respondent to work at his or her own pace.

scale of 1 to 10 (where 1 is very unsatisfied and 10 is very satisfied), he or she was the last time he or she used a travel agency to plan a family vacation. The instructions would instruct the respondent to press the key with the number appropriate to his or her degree of satisfaction. So, the respondent might press a "2" or a "7," depending on his or her experience and expectations. If, however, a "0" or some other ineligible key were pressed, the computer could be programmed to beep, indicating that the response was inappropriate, and instruct the respondent to make another entry.

All of the advantages of computer-driven interviewing are found in this approach, plus the interviewer expense or extra cost of human voice communication capability for the computer is eliminated. Because respondents' answers are saved in a file during the interview itself, tabulation can take place on a daily basis, and it is a simple matter for the researcher to access the survey's data at practically any time. Some researchers believe that the research industry should move to replace pen-and-paper questionnaires with computer-based ones.[36]

Fully computerized interviews have all the advantages of computer-driven interviews, and the need for an interviewer is eliminated.

▶ **Online and Other Internet–Based Interviews.** Online research may take on any of a number of faces, but the **Internet–based questionnaire**, in which the respondent answers questions online is becoming the industry standard for online surveys. For example, Procter & Gamble, which spends $150 million to conduct thousands of surveys each year, conducted 15 percent of its surveys online in 1999, and increased that to 50 percent in 2001. Plans are to continue this trend.[37] Internet-based online surveys are fast, easy, and inexpensive.[38] These questionnaires accommodate all of the standard question formats, and they are very flexible, including the ability to present pictures, diagrams, or displays to respondents. As an example, we have included a picture of the computer screen for Greenfield Online's Shelf Testing service that places respondents in a virtual shopping trip situation and lets them select and inspect various products that are on the shelf in order to make a selection. In fact, the graphics capability is a major reason why researchers tracking advertising effects prefer online surveys to telephone surveys, which have been a standard data-collection method for advertising tracking for a great many years.[39] The researcher can check the Web site for current tabulations whenever he or she desires, and respondents can access the online survey at any time of the day or night.

Online data collection is and will continue to profoundly change the marketing research landscape,[40] particularly in the case of online panels.[41] For instance, in the case of customer satisfaction, instead of "episodic" research in which a company does a large study one time per year, it allows for "continuous market intelligence" in which the survey is posted permanently on the Web and modified as the company's strategies are

Online surveys have significant advantages over traditional surveys, and their use will increase in the future.

implemented. Company managers can call up tabulated customer reactions on a daily basis.[42] Some researchers refer to this advantage of online surveys as "real-time research."[43] At least one author[44] has claimed that online research is replacing focus groups because of its ease of application to new product testing. Online surveys are generally believed to effect response quality equal to telephone or mail surveys; although, research of this belief is only now becoming evident.[45] One serendipitous aspect of online surveys is that because the researcher can monitor the progress of the online survey on a continual basis, it is possible to spot problems with the survey and to make adjustments to correct these problems. Read Marketing Research Insight 9.2 to appreciate this feature of online surveys.

Active Learning

TAKE AN ONLINE SURVEY

As you know, SRI Consulting Business Intelligence has developed a system called VALS that uses personality traits and consumer behavior constructs to categorize people into one of eight different types of individuals. To find out what type you belong to and to learn about the VALS system, go to this company's Web site at (**www.sric–bi.com/VALS/ presurvey.shtml**) and complete the online questionnaire.

MARKETING
RESEARCH
INSIGHT

ONLINE APPLICATION

9.2 Use Available Tracking Metrics to Diagnose and Correct Your Online Survey

A metric is a numerical measure that provides insight into how an online survey is performing. Recently, Jacob Brown, a principal of In-Depth, a marketing research company located in California, offered the following metrics and corrective actions for online surveys.[46]

Metric 1: What percent of people who are invited to take the survey actually go to the online survey? If this percent is lower than you expect, then reworking the invitation to take part in the survey is recommended. Improvements include:

- Make it shorter
- Take out any marketing hype
- Specify the survey topic and attempt to make it interesting to the prospective respondents
- If appropriate, include the sponsor company to add to the credibility of the invitation
- If you have an incentive, make it unambiguous

Metric 2: What percent of people who go to the survey drop out after each question? This metric will identify the questions that are most challenging or discouraging to respondents. Examine these questions to see what factors underlie the drop outs. For example, is the respondent supposed to download applets, pictures, videos, or other slow-loading content? If so, search for faster-loading alternatives. On the other hand, if a question is too complicated or involved, break it down into a simpler form.

Metric 3: Is the overall completion rate low even though you do not find individual questions with high drop-out rates? With this metric, Mr. Brown advises that you look at the total length of time and effort required to complete the survey, as it is probably too long. To cut down the length, take out superfluous or otherwise nonessential questions. You can also look at your various lists that might be in the questionnaire to see if they can be appreciably shortened.

As a final recommendation, Mr. Brown advises that every marketing researcher use a pretest before launching the full study. By applying these three metrics with a pretest using a small sample of representative prospective respondents, the researcher will be able to spot online survey problems and correct them before the full survey is launched.

Based on your reading thus far and your online survey experience with the VALS survey, you may wonder why the marketing research world is not rushing to using online surveys exclusively. While there is a definite strong trend in this direction, it is not universal. We have provided Marketing Research Insight 9.3 so you can learn why the use of Internet-based surveys in Europe is lagging behind their use in the United States.

Online surveys have the important advantages of speed and low cost, plus real-time access of data; however, there are drawbacks of sample representativeness, respondent validation, and difficulty in asking probing types of questions.

Self-Administered Surveys

Recall that a self-administered survey is one in which the respondent is in control, often deciding when to take the survey, where to take it, and how much time and attention to devote to it. Plus, with a self-administered survey, the respondent always decides what questions he or she will or will not answer; that is, the respondent fills in answers to a static copy of the questionnaire, which is what we have referred to as a "paper-and-pencil" questionnaire in previous descriptions. Probably the most popular type of self-administered survey is the mail survey; however, there are other variations that

---

MARKETING RESEARCH INSIGHT

GLOBAL APPLICATION

9.3

Why European Marketing Research Is Slower to Adopt Online Data Collection Techniques

In a recent interview, Reinier Heutink, director of research and consulting, at Interview-NSS, headquartered in Amsterdam, the Netherlands, and one of the largest marketing research companies in that country, offered his views on what has been observed as a seeming reluctance of European marketing research companies to shift to the new and emerging data-collection techniques that American research companies appear to be adopting at a very rapid pace.[47] Mr. Heutink offered the following reasons for the slow adoption of Internet-based surveys by European research companies:

- Internet penetration in Europe has trailed that in the United States.
- Europeans are more conservative when adopting new methods.
- Americans have fewer cultural barriers to overcome.
- Americans have a common language, while Europeans do not.
- The true quality of Internet-based surveys in Europe is unknown and possibly suspect.

However, it has been observed that Internet-based surveys are higher in the Netherlands and Scandinavia than in other European countries, and Mr. Heutink cited the following reasons for this phenomenon.

- Internet penetration is highest in the Netherlands and Scandinavia.
- People living in these regions are more open-minded as compared to other Europeans.
- Because population is sparsely distributed here, there is an acknowledged need to use technology to decrease distance.

Nonetheless, Mr. Heutink believes that European marketing research companies have important grounding regarding the many diversities that characterize European consumers and they have expertise in creating surveys that acknowledge and work around these many differences.

Based on his experience and opinions, Mr. Heutink makes two predictions:

- Telephone research will be a healthy data-collection method in Europe for at least the next 10 years.
- American research firms who do not accommodate the many variations in Europeans will have a difficult time conducting research in Europe.

researchers consider from time to time. These are the group self-administered survey and the drop-off survey.

Before continuing, however, we need to address a question that you may have, namely, "Why aren't Internet-based interviews categorized as 'self-administered'?" This is an excellent question, and our answer is that the sophistication of Internet-based questionnaire design software is at the state at which it does not allow respondents to avoid answering key questions. For example, the program may be set up to remind a respondent that a certain question was not answered. This prompt continues until the question is answered by the respondent. Because we consider the inability of self-administered surveys to stop respondents from "opting out" of questions to be their greatest drawback, we have not included Internet-based interviews in this group.

Group self-administered surveys economize on time and money because a group of respondents participates at the same time.

▶ **Group Self-Administered Survey.** Basically, a **group self-administered survey** entails administering a questionnaire to respondents in groups, rather than individually, for convenience or to gain certain economies. One way to be more economical is to have respondents self-administer the questions. For example, 20 or 30 people might be recruited to view a TV program sprinkled with test commercials. All respondents would be seated in a viewing room, and a videotape would run on a large television projection screen. Then they would be given a questionnaire to fill out regarding their recall of test ads, their reactions to the ads, and so on. As you would suspect, it is handled in a group context primarily to reduce costs and to provide the ability to interview a large number of people in a short time.

Variations for group self-administered surveys are limitless. Students can be administered surveys in their classes; church groups can be administered surveys during meetings; and social clubs and organizations, company employees, movie theater patrons, and any other group can be administered surveys during meetings, work, or leisure time. Often the researcher will compensate the group with a monetary payment as a means of recruiting the support of the group's leaders. In all of these cases, each respondent works through the questionnaire at his or her own pace. Granted, a survey administrator may be present, so there is some opportunity for interaction concerning instructions or how to respond, but the group context often discourages the respondents from asking all but the most pressing questions.

Drop-off surveys must be self-explanatory because they are left with the respondents, who fill them out without assistance.

▶ **Drop-Off Survey.** Another variation of the self-administered survey is the **drop-off survey**, sometimes called "drop and collect," in which the survey representative approaches a prospective respondent, introduces the general purpose of the survey to him or her, and leaves the survey with the respondent to fill out on his or her own. Essentially, the objective is to gain the prospective respondent's cooperation. The respondent is told that the questionnaire is self-explanatory, and it will be left with him or her to fill out at leisure. Perhaps the representative will return to pick up the questionnaire at a certain time, or the respondent may be instructed to complete and return it by prepaid mail. Normally, the representative will return on the same day or the next day to pick up the completed questionnaire. In this way, a representative can cover a number of residential areas or business locations in a single day with an initial drop-off pass and a later pick-up pass. Drop-off surveys are especially appropriate for local market research undertakings in which travel is necessary but limited. They have been reported to have quick turnaround, high response rates, minimal interviewer influence on answers, and good control over how respondents are selected; plus, they are inexpensive.[48] Studies have shown that the drop-off survey improves response rates with business or organizational respondents.[49]

Variations of the drop-off method include handing out the surveys to people at their places of work, asking them to fill them out at home, and then to return them the next day. Some hotel chains have questionnaires in their rooms with an invitation to fill them out and turn them in at the desk on checkout. Stores sometimes have short surveys on customer demographics, media habits, purchase intentions, or other information that customers are asked to fill out at home and return on their next shopping trip. A gift certificate drawing may even be used as an incentive to participate. As you can see, the term *drop-off* can be stretched to cover any situation in which the prospective respondent encounters the survey as though it were "dropped off" by a research representative.

▶ **Mail Survey.** A **mail survey** is one in which the questions are mailed to prospective respondents, who are asked to fill them out and return them to the researcher by mail.[50] Part of its attractiveness stems from its self-administered aspect: There are no interviewers to recruit, train, monitor, and compensate. Similarly, mailing lists are readily available from companies that specialize in this business, and it is possible to access very specific groups of target respondents. For example, it is possible to obtain a list of physicians specializing in family practice who operate clinics in cities with populations larger than 500,000 people. Also, one may opt to purchase computer files, printed labels, or even labeled envelopes from these companies. In fact, some list companies will even provide insertion and mailing services. There are a number of companies that sell mailing lists, and most, if not all, have online purchase options. On a per-mailed respondent basis, mail surveys are very inexpensive. In fact, they are almost always the least expensive survey method in this regard. But mail surveys incur all of the problems associated with not having an interviewer present, which we discussed earlier in this chapter.

Despite the fact that the mail survey is described as "powerful, effective, and efficient"[51] by the American Statistical Association, the mail survey is plagued by two major problems. The first is **nonresponse**, which refers to questionnaires that are not returned.[52] The second is **self-selection bias**, which means that those who do respond are probably different from those who do not fill out the questionnaire and return it and, therefore, the sample gained through this method is nonrepresentative of the general population. Research shows that self-selected respondents can be more interested and involved in the study topic.[53] To be sure, the mail survey is not the only survey method that suffers from nonresponse and self-selection bias.[54] Failures to respond are found in all types of surveys, and marketing researchers must be constantly alert to the possibilities that their final samples are somehow different from the original list of potential respondents because of some systematic tendency or latent pattern of response. Whatever the survey mode used, those who respond may be more involved with the product, they may have more education, they might be more or less dissatisfied, or they may even be more opinionated in general than the target population of concern.[55]

When informing clients of data-collection alternatives, market researchers should inform them of the nonresponse problems and biases inherent in each one being considered. For example, mail surveys are notorious for low response, and those respondents who do fill out and return a mail questionnaire are likely to be different from those who do not. At the same time, there are people who refuse to answer questions over the telephone, and consumers who like to shop are more likely to be encountered in mall-intercept interviews than are those who do not like to shop. Each data-collection method has its own nonresponse and bias considerations, and a conscientious researcher will help his or her client understand the dangers represented in the methods under consideration. Thus, nonresponse and the subsequent danger of self-selection bias is greatest with mail surveys, for typically mail surveys of households achieve response rates of less than 20 percent. Researchers have tried various tactics to increase the response rate, such as using registered mail, color, money, personalization, reminder postcards, and so on.[56, 57]

However, even when researchers experiment with prenotifications, incentives, or other aspects, response rates are low for mail surveys.[58] Despite this situation, special

Mail surveys suffer from nonresponse and self-selection bias.

"Self-selection bias" means that respondents who return surveys by mail may differ from the original sample.

When informing clients of data-collection alternatives, market researchers should inform them of the nonresponse problems and biases inherent in each one being considered.

types of mail surveys are viable in countries with high literacy rates and dependable postal systems.[59] There is some evidence that mail surveys with business respondents using prenotifications, incentives, and various other strategies alleviate the nonresponse problem to some extent.[60] We have prepared Marketing Research Insight 9.4, which offers recommendations for mail surveys based on the experience of a company that has achieved a good deal of success with this data-collection method.

To cope with low response to mail surveys, some companies have turned to mail panels.

One way research companies have sought to cope with the low response for mail surveys is to create a mail panel, in which respondents agree to respond to several questionnaires mailed to them over time; some see this approach as a preferred option.[61] Others are shifting to Internet communication systems that are faster and cheaper; that is, they are using electronic mail systems of various sorts. Of course, the panel members are carefully prescreened to ensure that the mail panel represents the company's target market or consumers of interest.

CHOICE OF THE SURVEY METHOD

At the outset of the discussion of the various types of interviewing used in marketing research, we made the comment that the marketing researcher is faced with the problem of selecting the one survey mode that is most suitable in a given situation. Since you have read our descriptions, you now know that each data-collection method has unique advantages, disadvantages, and special features. As a quick reference tool, and we have summarized these for you in Table 9.3.

MARKETING RESEARCH INSIGHT

PRACTICAL APPLICATION

9.4

Mail Surveys Can Work!

While you may have the impression that mail surveys do not work well because of their large nonresponse factor, there are success stories for mail surveys. The following set of recommendations is provided by Jack Semler, President and CEO of Readex Research, located in Stillwater Minnesota.

"Generally speaking, the mail survey method works best in situations in which highly representative results are required, complex or lengthy questionnaires are to be deployed, or sensitive issues need to be explored. When an appropriate mailing series is used, supported by response-enhancing tactics, response rates of 30%–50% and better are not unusual. This can be true even when very long questionnaires are sent as part of the survey process. It's also easier to gather information on such things as salary, personal data, and opinions on charged social issues using the mail survey.

"Mail can prove advantageous when used in circumstances in which potential respondents are hard to reach. For example, since a mail survey can be answered at the respondent's convenience, a busy retail store manager can participate after hours or a doctor when doing paperwork. Also, there is no worry of interviewer bias or interviewer quality.

"Most mail surveys are optimized by using three elements of the mailing series. The first is an alert letter, followed very shortly by the survey kit, which includes the actual questionnaire, introduction letter, reply envelope, and incentive. After some period of time (usually two to three weeks) a follow-up survey is sent to nonresponders. However, the actual mailing series can be varied depending on the nature of the target audience—i.e., how responsive they may be or based on the length and complexity of the questionnaire."

Printed with the permission of Jack Semler, President and CEO, Readex Research, Stillwater, MN.

	TABLE 9.3	Major Advantages and Disadvantages of Alternative Data-Collection Methods	
Method	**Major Advantages**	**Major Disadvantages**	**Comment**
In-home interview	Conducted in privacy of the home, which facilitates interviewer–respondent rapport	Cost per interview can be high; interviewers must travel to respondent's home	Often much information per interview is gathered
Mall-intercept interview	Fast and convenient	Only mall patrons are interviewed; respondents may feel uncomfortable answering questions in the mall	Mall-intercept company often has exclusive interview rights for that mall
In-office interview	Useful for interviewing busy executives	Relatively high cost per interview; gaining access is sometimes difficult	Useful when respondents must examine prototypes or samples of products
Central location telephone interview	Fast turnaround; good quality control; reasonable cost	Restricted to telephone communication	Long-distance calling is not a problem
CATI	Computer eliminates human interviewer error; simultaneous data input to computer file; good quality control	Setup costs can be high	Losing ground to online surveys and panels
Fully computerized interview	Respondent responds at his or her own pace; computer data file results	Respondent must have access to a computer and be computer literate	Many variations and an emerging method with exciting prospects
Online questionnaire	Ease of creating and posting; fast turnaround; computer data file results	Respondent must have access to the Internet	Fastest-growing method; very flexible; online analysis available
Group self-administered survey	Cost of interviewer eliminated; economical for assembled groups of respondents	Must find groups and secure permission to conduct the survey	Prone to errors of self-administered surveys; good for pretests or pilot tests
Drop-off survey	Cost of interviewer eliminated; appropriate for local market surveys	Generally not appropriate for large-scale national surveys	Many variations exist with respect to logistics and applications
Mail survey	Economical; good listing companies exist	Low response rates; self-selection bias; slow	Many strategies to increase response rate exist

But how do you decide which is the best survey mode for a particular research project? When answering this question, the researcher should always have the overall quality of the data collected as a foremost concern. Even the most sophisticated techniques of analysis cannot make up for poor data. So, the researcher must strive to choose a survey mode that achieves the highest quality of data allowable with the time, cost, and other special considerations[62] involved with the research project at hand. We wish we could provide you with a set of questions about these considerations that, when answered, would point to the single most appropriate data collection method. However, this is not possible, as researchers have to apply good judgment to narrow down the many candidates to one that best fits the circumstances. In some cases, these judgments are quite obvious, but in others, they require some careful thinking. Also, as we have indicated in our descriptions, new data-collection methods have emerged[63] and

In selecting a data-collection method, the researcher balances quality against cost, time, and other special considerations.

improvements in old ones have come about, so the researcher must constantly update his or her knowledge of these data-collection methods.

How Much Time Is There for Data Collection?

A short deadline may dictate which data-collection method to use.

Sometimes data must be collected by some very close deadline. There are many reasons for tight deadlines; a national campaign is set to kick off in four weeks and one component needs testing; an upcoming trademark infringement trial needs a survey of the awareness of the company's trademark and the trial starts in four weeks; an application for a radio license with the FCC deadline is in six weeks and a listenership study of other stations in the area must be conducted, and so on. Traditionally, if there was a very short time constraint, telephone surveys were often selected because of their speed. Today, online surveys are exceptionally fast and can accommodate all but physical handling of test products. Magazine ads, logos, and other marketing stimuli may be evaluated in online surveys. Poor choices under the condition of the short time constraint would be in-home interviews or mail surveys because their logistics require long time periods.

How Much Money Is There for Data Collection?

With a generous budget, any appropriate data-collection method can be considered, but with a tight budget, the more costly data-collection methods must be eliminated from consideration. With technology costs dropping and Internet access becoming more and more common, online survey research options have become attractive when the data-collection budget is austere. For example, there are some online survey companies that allow the client to design the questionnaire and select the target sample type and number from their panels. Here, surveys can be completed for a few hundred or a few thousand dollars, which, most researchers would agree, is a small data-collection budget. Of course, the researcher must be convinced that the panel members are those he or she desires to survey. Furthermore, the researcher must consider the incident rate and any other "cultural" factors that have a bearing on the selection of the data-collection method.

What Is the Incidence Rate?

The incidence rate, the percentage of the population that possesses some characteristic necessary to be included in the survey, affects the decision about which data-collection method to use.

By **incidence rate** we are referring to the percentage of the population that possesses some characteristic necessary to be included in the survey. Rarely are research projects targeted to "everyone." In most cases, there are qualifiers for being included in a study. Examples are registered voters, persons owning and driving their own automobile, persons 18 years of age and older, and so on. Sometimes the incidence rate is very low. A drug company may want to interview only men over 50 with cholesterol levels above 250 while on medication. A cosmetics firm may want to interview only women who were planning facial cosmetic surgery within the next six months. In low-incidence situations such as these, certain precautions must be taken in selecting the data-collection method. For example, in either of the above examples, it would be foolishly time-consuming and expensive to send out interviewers door-to-door looking for members who have the qualifications to participate in the study. A data-collection method that can easily and inexpensively screen respondents is desirable with a low-incidence-rate situation because a great many potential respondents must be contacted, but a large percentage of these would not qualify to take the survey. Of course, the marketing research industry has worked with low-incidence populations for a long time, and online panels that are maintained by research providers are often touted as affordable ways for researchers to access the low-incidence panel members who are preidentified.[64]

Are There Cultural and/or Infrastructure Considerations?

On occasion, data-collection method choice is largely affected by cultural norms and/or communication systems that are in place. These considerations have become more of an issue as more and more marketing research companies operate around the globe. For example, in Scandinavia, residents are uncomfortable allowing strangers in their homes. Therefore, telephone and online surveying is more popular than door-to-door interviewing. On the other hand, in India less than 10 percent of the residents have a telephone and online access is very low. Door-to-door interviewing is used often.[65] In Canada, where incentives are typically not offered to prospective respondents, there is heavy use of telephone surveys. Online research is slowing growing.[66] It would be very important for a firm, conducting a study in a culture about which they are unfamiliar, to consult the services of local research firms before making the data-collection method decision. Another example is a global marketing research study conducted across 100 counties with online and mail surveys to compensate for differences in Internet access and to obtain a representative sample.[67] It is interesting to note that even marketing researcher perceptions of infrastructure or cultural considerations will affect the choice of the data-collection method, as for example, take the case of marketing researchers in Spain who have historically refrained from using mail surveys in favor of face-to-face interviews. However, a recent study has revealed that the quality of mail surveys is equal to face-to-face ones with Spanish respondents.[68]

Cultural norms and/or limitations of communications systems may limit the choice of data-collection method.

What Type of Respondent Interaction Is Required?

Finally, the data-collection method selection may be influenced by any special requirements that are a vital part of the survey; that is, there might be a requirement that the respondent inspect an advertisement, package design, or logo. Or the researcher may want respondents to handle a prototype product, taste formulations, or watch a video. Typically, when there are requirements such as these built into the survey, the researcher has discussed data-collection issues early on with the client, and an agreement that time and money will not be paramount or an understanding that the data-collection method will accommodate these requirements.

For example, if the respondent needs to view photos of a logo or magazine ad, mail surveys or online surveys may be considered. If the respondent needs to observe a short video or moving graphic, online surveys may be considered. If the respondent needs to watch a 20-minute infomercial, mailed videos (with a considerable incentive!); mall intercepts or special online systems can be considered. If the respondent is required to handle, touch, feel, or taste a product, mall-intercept company services are reasonable. If a respondent is required to actually use a product in a realistic setting, in-home interviews may be the only data-collection method that will work.

If respondents need to see, handle, or experience something, the data-collection mode must accommodate these requirements.

SPSS Student Assistant:
Milk Bone Biscuits: Modifying Variables and Values

SUMMARY

In this chapter, you learned about the data-collection step in the marketing research process. The four basic survey modes used are: (1) person-administered surveys, (2) computer-assisted surveys, (3) self-administered surveys, and (4) mixed-mode, sometimes called "hybrid," surveys. Person-administered survey modes are advantageous because they allow feedback, permit rapport building, facilitate certain quality controls, and capitalize on the adaptability of a human interviewer. However, they are prone to human error, slow, and costly and sometimes produce respondent apprehension known as "interview evaluation." Computer-administered interviews, on the other hand, are faster, error-free, may have pictures or graphics capabilities, allow for real-time capture of data, and may make respondents feel more at ease because another person is not listening to their answers. Disadvantages are that technical skills are required and there may be high setup costs. Self-administered survey modes have the advantages of reduced cost, respondent control, and no interview-evaluation apprehension. The disadvantages of self-administered surveys are lack of respondent control, in that respondents may not complete the task or may complete the task in error, lack of a monitor to help guide respondents, and high demands on having a perfect questionnaire. Finally, mixed-mode surveys, sometimes referred to as "hybrid" surveys, use multiple data-collection methods. The advantage of mixed-mode surveys is that researchers are able to take the advantages of each of the various modes to achieve their data-collection goals. Disadvantages are that different modes may produce different responses to the same research question and researchers must evaluate this. Second, mixed-mode methods result in greater complexities because researchers must design different questionnaires and be certain that data from different sources all come together in a common database for analysis.

We described 11 different survey data-collection methods: (1) in-home interviews, which are conducted in respondents' homes; (2) mall-intercept interviews, conducted by approaching shoppers in a mall; (3) in-office interviews, conducted with executives or managers in their places of work; telephone interviews, either conducted (4) by an interviewer working in his or her home, or (5) from a central location by workers in a telephone interview company's facilities; (6) computer-assisted telephone interviews, in which the interviewer reads questions off a computer screen and enters responses directly into the program; (7) fully computerized interviews, in which the respondent interacts directly with a computer; (8) online and other Internet-based surveys; (9) group self-administered surveys, in which the questionnaire is handed out to a group for individual responses; (10) drop-off surveys, in which the questionnaire is left with the respondent to be completed and picked up or returned at a later time; and (11) mail surveys, in which questionnaires are mailed to prospective respondents, who are requested to fill them out and mail them back. The specific advantages and disadvantages of each data-collection mode were discussed.

The chapter noted that researchers must take into account several considerations when deciding on a survey data-collection method. The major concerns are (1) the survey time horizon, (2) the survey data-collection budget, (3) incidence rate, (4) cultural and infrastructure considerations, and (5) the type of respondent interaction required. The research project deadline, money available for data collection, and desired quality of data are taken into consideration. Ultimately, the researcher will select a data-collection method with which he or she feels comfortable and one that will result in the desired quality and quantity of information without exceeding time or budget constraints.

KEY TERMS

Survey (p. 234)
Person-administered survey (p. 238)
Computer-administered survey
  (p. 239)
Interview evaluation (p. 240)

Self-administered survey (p. 241)
Mixed-mode survey (p. 242)
In-home interview (p. 245)
Mall-intercept interview (p. 245)
In-office interviews (p. 247)

Traditional telephone interviews (p. 249)

Central location telephone interviewing (p. 249)

Computer-assisted telephone interviews (CATIs) (p. 251)

Fully computerized interviews (p. 252)

Completely automated telephone survey (CATS) (p. 252)

Internet-based questionnaire (p. 253)

Group self-administered survey (p. 256)

Drop-off survey (p. 256)

Mail survey (p. 257)

Nonresponse (p. 257)

Self-selection bias (p. 257)

Incidence rate (p. 260)

REVIEW QUESTIONS/APPLICATIONS

1. List the major advantages of survey research methods over qualitative methods. Can you think of any drawbacks? If so, what are they?

2. What aspects of computer-administered surveys make them attractive to marketing researchers?

3. What are the advantages of person-administered surveys over computer-administered ones?

4. What would be the motivation for a researcher to consider a mixed-mode survey?

5. Indicate the differences between (a) in-home interviews, (b) mall-intercept interviews, and (c) in-office interviews. What do they share in common?

6. Why are telephone surveys popular?

7. Indicate the pros and cons of self-administered surveys.

8. What advantages do online surveys have over other types of self-administered surveys?

9. What are the major disadvantages of a mail survey?

10. How does a drop-off survey differ from a regular mail survey?

11. How does the incidence rate affect the choice of a data-collection method?

12. Is a telephone interview inappropriate for a survey that has as one of its objectives a complete listing of all possible advertising media a person was exposed to in the past week? Why or why not?

13. NAPA Car Parts is a retail chain specializing in stocking and selling both domestic and foreign automobile parts. It is interested in learning about its customers, so the marketing director sends instructions to all 2000 store managers telling them that whenever a customer makes a purchase of $150 or more, they are to write down a description of the customer who made that purchase. They are to do this just for the second week in October, writing each description on a separate sheet of paper. At the end of the week, they are to send all sheets to the marketing director. Comment on this data collection method.

14. Discuss the feasibility of each of the types of survey modes for each of the following cases:

    a. Fabergé, Inc. wants to test a new fragrance called "Lime Brut."

    b. Kelly Services needs to determine how many businesses expect to hire temporary secretaries for those who go on vacation during the summer months.

    c. The Encyclopaedia Britannica requires information on the degree to which mothers of elementary school–aged children see encyclopedias as worthwhile purchases for their children.

  d. AT&T is considering a television screen phone system and wants to know people's reaction to it.

15. With a telephone survey, when a potential respondent refuses to take part or is found to have changed his or her telephone number or moved away, it is customary to simply try another prospect until a completion is secured. It is not standard practice to report the number of refusals or noncontacts. What are the implications of this policy for the reporting of nonresponse?

16. Compu-Ask Corporation has developed a stand-alone computerized interview system that can be adapted to almost any type of survey. It can fit on a personal digital assistant (PDA)–sized computer, and the respondent answers questions directly using a stylus once the interviewer has turned on the computer and started up the program. Indicate the appropriateness of this interviewing system in each of the following cases:

  a. A survey of plant managers concerning a new type of hazardous waste disposal system.

  b. A survey of high-school teachers to see if they are interested in a company's videotapes of educational public broadcast television programs.

  c. A survey of consumers to determine their reactions to a nonrefrigerated variety of yogurt.

17. A researcher is pondering what survey mode to use for a client who markets a home security system for apartment dwellers. The system comprises sensors that are pressed onto all of the windows and magnetic strips that are glued to each door. Once plugged into an electric socket and activated with a switch box, the system emits a loud alarm and simulates a barking guard dog when an intruder trips one of the sensors. The client wants to know how many apartment dwellers in the United States are aware of the system, what they think of it, and how likely they are to buy it in the coming year. Which consideration factors are positive and which ones are negative for each of the following survey modes: (a) in-home interviews, (b) mall intercepts, (c) online survey, (d) drop-off survey, and (e) CATI survey?

CASE 9.1

STEWARD RESEARCH, INC.

Joe Steward is President of Steward Research, Inc. The firm specializes in customized research for clients in a variety of industries. The firm has a centralized location telephoning facility and they have a division, "Steward Online," that specializes in online surveys. However, Joe often calls on the services of other research firms in order to provide his client with the most appropriate data-collection method. In a meeting with four project directors, Joe discusses each client's special situation.

  Client 1: A small tools manufacturer has created a new device for sharpening high-precision drill bits. High-precision drill bits are used to drill nearly perfect holes in devices such as engine blocks. Such applications have demanding specifications, and drill bits may be used only a few times before being discarded. However, the new sharpening device takes the bits back to original specifications and the bits can be resharpened and used in as many as a dozen applications. After testing the device and conducting several focus groups in order to get modifications suggestions, the client is now ready for more information on presentation methods. The project director and the client have developed several different presentation formats. The client wishes to have some market evaluation of these presentations before launching a nationwide training program of the company's 125 salesperson sales force.

Client 2: A regional bakery markets several brands of cookies and crackers to supermarkets throughout California, Nevada, Arizona, and New Mexico. The product category is very competitive, and competitors use a great deal of newspaper and TV advertising. The bakery's VP of marketing desires more analytics in making the promotional decisions for the firm. She has lamented that although she spends several million dollars a year on promotions in the four states, she has no analytics on which to evaluate the effectiveness of the expenditures. Steward's Project Director has recommended a study that will establish some baseline measures of top of mind brand awareness (called TOMA, this measure of awareness is achieved by asking respondents to name the first three brands that come to mind when thinking of a product or service category such as "cookies"), attitudes, and preferences.

Client 3: An inventor has developed a new device that sanitizes a toothbrush each time the brush is used and replaced in the device. The device uses steam to sanitize the brush and lab tests have shown the mechanism to be very effective at killing virtually all germs and viruses. The inventor has approached a large manufacturer who is interested in buying the rights to the device but would like some information first. The manufacturer wants to know if people have any concerns with toothbrush sanitization and whether or not they would be willing to purchase a countertop, plug-in device to keep their toothbrush sterile. The project director states that the manufacturer is not interested in a sample that represents the United States. They just want to know what a few hundred people think about these issues. The inventor is anxious to supply this information very quickly before the manufacturer loses interest in the idea.

1. For each of the three clients, suggest one or more data-collection methods that would be appropriate.

2. For each data-collection method you select in question 1, discuss the rationale for your choice.

3. What disadvantages are inherent in the data-collection methods you have recommended?

MACHU PICCHU NATIONAL PARK SURVEY

In Peru, there are many ruins of the temples and palaces of the Inca Indians who attained what some historians consider to be the highest accomplishments in the Americas for agriculture, engineering, monument building, and craftsmanship. Unfortunately, the Incas were no match for the Spanish who, with firearms and horses, defeated the entire Inca Empire in a matter of a few years in the 1560s.

In 1913, Hirram Bingham discovered the Inca complex called Machu Picchu, which had not been plundered by the Spanish Conquistadors; it is the best-preserved Inca ruin of its type. Located at 8000 feet above sea level on a moutain at the border of the Andes mountains and the Peruvian jungle, Machu Picchu is still very difficult to access, as it requires a three-hour mountain train ride to reach from Cusco, Peru, the closest city. Normally, tourists board the train very early in the morning in Cusco and arrive at the Machu Picchu village train station around 10 A.M. They then board busses that take 30 minutes to climb up the six-mile switchback dirt road to the entrance of Machu Picchu. With guides or on their own, tourists wander the expansive Machu Picchu ruins, have lunch at the Machu Picchu lodge located at the top of the mountain, and hurry to catch the bus down the mountain so they will not miss the one train that leaves around 3 P.M. to return to Cusco. Some tourists stay overnight at the Machu Picchu Lodge or in one of the six hotels located at the base in Machu Picchu village. At peak season, approximately 1000 tourists visit Machu Picchu daily.

Machu Picchu is a Peru national park, and since it is one of the top tourist attractions in the world, the national park department wishes to conduct a survey to research the satisfaction of tourists with the park's many features as well as their total experience on their visit to Peru. With the help of a marketing researcher who specializes in tourism research, the park department officials have created a self-administered questionnaire for its survey. Now, there is the question of how to gather the data, and some alternatives have been suggested. Using concepts in this chapter and your knowledge of data-collection methods and issues, answer each of the following questions.

1. If the questionnaire is an online survey, would it be successful? Why or why not?

2. If the park department uses a mail survey, what issues must be resolved? Would it be successful? Why or why not?

3. If the seven hotels in the Machu Picchu area each desired to know how its customers felt about the hotel's services, prices, and accommodations, how might the park department and the hotels work together on data collection to effect a mutually beneficial survey?

4. Using the knowledge that the Peru national park department has very meager resources for marketing research, suggest a different method (not online, not mail, and not partnering with the local hotels) with the potential of effecting a high response rate and high-quality responses.

This is your integrated case described on pages 104–108.

THE HOBBIT'S CHOICE RESTAURANT

Cory Rogers presented his interpretations of the focus groups he had subcontracted for Jeff Dean's The Hobbit's Choice Restaurant to get a feel for what patrons wanted in the décor, atmosphere, entrees, specialty items, and other aspects of the restaurant's operation. Jeff was impressed with the amount of information that had been collected from just three focus groups. "Of course," noted Cory, "we have to take all of this information as tentative because we talked with so few folks, and there is a good chance that they are just a part of your target market. But we do have some good exploratory research that will guide us in the survey."

Jeff agrees with Cory's assessment, and asks, "What's next?" Cory says, "I need to think about how we will gather the survey data. There are several options that I must consider in order to make the best choice to survey the entire metropolitan area."

1. Is a mail survey a good choice? Why or why not?

2. Should Cory recommend a telephone survey? What are the pros and cons of telephone data collection for The Hobbit's Choice Restaurant survey?

3. What about an online survey? Compare the use of an online survey to a telephone survey, and recommend one for Cory to use.

10

Measurement in Marketing Research

How Do You Measure Customer Satisfaction?

The consumer behavior construct of customer satisfaction is central to the marketing concept, and it is a strategic goal of practically every marketing organization imaginable. For a very long time, marketing researchers have wrestled with the question, "How do you measure customer satisfaction?" Two marketing principals of Maritz Research have recently reviewed this area and offered their opinions.[1] This opening vignette summarizes their position on this important question. To begin, they offer the criteria for a customer-satisfaction scale, and specifically, they state that it must:

- Be reliable, meaning that respondents' answers should be consistent
- Be valid, meaning that it should actually measure how satisfied respondents are
- Be metric (a concept explained later in this chapter)
- Apply to a wide variety of products and services
- Be easy for respondents to relate to and remember during interviews

The authors continue in their article by specifying the general policies of Maritz Research with respect to customer-satisfaction measurement scales. Specifically, the response scale should:

- Be symmetrically unbalanced, meaning having a number of positive degrees of satisfaction with dissatisfaction measured as a single scale position at the "bottom" of the scale

Learning Objectives

- To appreciate the considerations used by the researcher to determine which question format will be used for a particular question
- To understand the basics of measurement regarding people, places, and things
- To recognize the four types of scales used by marketing researchers
- To examine question formats commonly used in marketing research
- To comprehend why reliability and validity are concerns when designing and administering questions intended to measure concepts

Maritz Research has devised ways to measure customer satisfaction.

- Not have a midpoint at which the respondent can indicate that he/she is "neither dissatisfied nor satisfied" (because the scale is unbalanced on the postive side and a neutral position does not fit this arrangement)
- Have 5 scale points at a minimum (although up to 10 scale points are permissible if consistent with respondents' abilities and appropriate for the data-collection method)
- Be fully word-anchored, meaning that each scale position should have a verbal description

The recommended satisfaction response scale is as follows:

Overall, how satisfied are you with _____? Please check only one box

Not at All Satisfied	Slightly Satisfied	Somewhat Satisfied	Very Satisfied	Completely Satisfied
☐	☐	☐	☐	☐

However, the authors point out that the circumstances of the survey must be taken into account when deciding on the customer-satisfaction response scale. For instance, if there is reason to believe that respondents are familiar with the brand or company being measured, it is acceptable to use a bipolar balanced scale such as the following

Completely Dissatisfied	Somewhat Dissatisfied	Neither Satisfied nor Dissatisfied	Somewhat Satisfied	Completely Satisfied
☐	☐	☐	☐	☐

This chapter is the first of two devoted to the questionnaire-design phase of the marketing research process. Its primary goal is to develop the foundation for understanding measurement in marketing research. This is done by first describing the six question–response formats available, defining basic concepts in measurement, and then, explaining the various scale formats commonly used in marketing research. Next, we describe some "workhorse" scale formats that are often used by marketing researchers. Finally, we offer some recommendations—similar to the customer-satisfaction scale formats recommended by the Maritz Research executives in the example above—as to what scale format to use when you are measuring various constructs typically included in marketing research projects.

BASIC QUESTION–RESPONSE FORMATS

Designing a questionnaire from the ground up is akin to a composer creating a song, an author writing a novel, or an artist painting a landscape—it requires creativity. Still, there are some basic aspects of questionnaire design that can be described. This chapter is concerned with the response side of questions on a questionnaire, and it will introduce you to measurement issues. To begin, you should be aware of the three basic question–response formats from which a researcher has to choose: open-ended, closed-ended, and scaled-response questions. Figure 10.1 illustrates the three types and indicates two variations for each one. Pros and cons of each format are provided in Table 10.1. A description of each format follows.

Open–Ended Response Format Questions

Question response formats can be open-ended, close-ended, or scaled.

An **open-ended question** presents no response options to the respondent. Rather, the respondent is instructed to respond in his or her own words. The response depends, of course, on the topic. An **unprobed format** seeks no additional information from the respondent. With an unprobed response format, the researcher wants a simple comment or statement from the respondent, or perhaps the researcher simply wants the respondent to indicate the name of a brand or a store.[2] On the other hand, the researcher may use a **probed format,** which includes a **response probe** instructing the interviewer to ask for additional information, saying, for instance, "Can you think of anything more?"

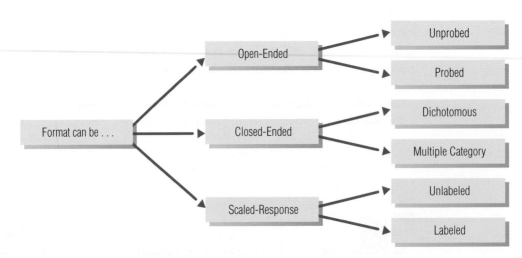

FIGURE 10.1
A Diagram of Six Alternative Question–Response Formats

TABLE 10.1	Pros and Cons of Alternative Response Formats			
Response Format	**Example Question**	**Pros**	**Cons**
Unprobed open-ended question	*"What was your reaction to the Sony DVD player advertisement you last saw on television?"*	Allows respondent to use his or her own words.	Difficult to code and interpret. Respondents may not give complete answers.
Probed open-ended question	*"Did you have any other thoughts or reactions to the advertisement?"*	Elicits complete answers.	Difficult to code and interpret.
Dichotomous closed-ended question	*"Do you agree or disagree with the statement 'Sony DVD players are better than Panasonic DVD players'?"*	Simple to administer and code.	May oversimplify response options.
Multiple category closed-ended question	*"If you were to buy a DVD player tomorrow, which brand would you be most likely to purchase? Would it be: a. Panasonic b. General Electric c. Sony d. JVC, or e. Some other brand?"*	Allows for broad range of possible responses. Simple to administer and code.	May alert respondents to response options of which they were unaware. Must distinguish "pick one" from "pick all that apply."
Unlabeled scaled-response question	*"On a scale of 1 to 7, how would you rate the Sony DVD player on ease of operation?"*	Allows for degree of intensity/ feelings to be expressed. Simple to administer and code.	Respondents may not relate well to the scale.
Labeled scaled-response question	*"Do you disagree, strongly disagree, agree, or strongly agree with the statement 'Sony DVD players are a better value than General Electric DVD players'?"*	Allows for degree of intensity/ feelings to be expressed. Simple to administer and code. Respondents can relate to the scale.	Scale may be unfamiliar or have more levels than respondents can relate to easily.

The intent here is to encourage the respondent to provide information beyond the initial and possibly superficial first comments.

Closed-Ended Response Format Questions

The **closed-ended question** lists response options on the questionnaire that can be answered quickly and easily.[3] A **dichotomous closed-ended question** has only two response options, such as "yes" or "no." If there are more than two options for the response, then the researcher is using a **multiple-category closed-ended question**. Both the dichotomous and multiple-category closed-ended question formats are very common on questionnaires because they facilitate the answering process as well as data entry. They also standardize these questions' response options on the questionnaire.

Scaled-Response Questions

The **scaled-response question** uses a scale chosen by the researcher to measure the attributes of some construct under study. The response options are identified on the questionnaire. With an **unlabeled scaled-response format**, the scale may be purely numerical or only the endpoints of the scale are identified. The **labeled scaled-response format** uses a

Six basic response format options are available to the researcher.

scale in which all of the scale positions are identified with some descriptor. We describe both of these formats in detail later in this chapter.

CONSIDERATIONS IN CHOOSING A QUESTION–RESPONSE FORMAT

All of the six question formats we have just described are possible response formats for questions on a questionnaire. So how does the researcher decide which to use? At least four considerations serve to narrow the choice down: (1) the nature of the property being measured, (2) previous research studies, (3) the ability of the respondent, and (4) the scale level desired.

Nature of the Property Being Measured

The properties of the construct being measured often determine the appropriate response format.

As will become clear later in the chapter when we describe basic concepts in measurement, the inherent nature of the property of a construct often determines the question–response format. For example, if Alka Seltzer wants to know if respondents have bought its brand of flu relief medicine in the past month, the only answers are "yes," "no," and, perhaps, "do not recall." If we ask marital status, a woman is married, separated, divorced, widowed, single, or cohabiting. But when we ask how much a person likes Hershey's chocolate, we can use a scaled-response approach, because "liking" is a subjective property with varying degrees. So, some properties are preset as to appropriate responses, while others are amenable to scales that indicate gradations or levels.

Previous Research Studies

Researchers strive to use question formats that are tried and true.

On some occasions, a survey follows an earlier one, and there may be a desire to explicitly compare the new findings with the previous survey. In this case, it is customary to simply adopt the question format used in the initial study. On the other hand, a particular scale or question response format may have been developed by others who have measured the construct. Some scales are published or available for use by marketing researchers at no cost, whereas others may reside within the researcher's own company as a result of its work with several clients over time. For instance, some research companies specialize in customer-satisfaction studies, and they have refined their own scales tapping this construct.[4] In any case, if a researcher believes a question format to be suitable for the purpose of the study at hand, it is good practice to adopt or adapt it rather than inventing a new one.

Ability of the Respondent

Some respondents may relate better to one type of response format than another.

It is advantageous to match the question format with the abilities of the respondents. For instance, if a researcher thinks that the respondents in a particular study are not articulate or that they will be reluctant to verbalize their opinions, the open-ended option is not a good choice. Similarly, if the respondent is unable to rate objects on numerical scales, it is appropriate to use a label format, or perhaps to move back to a dichotomous closed-ended question format in which the respondent simply indicates "agree" or "disagree."[5]

Scale Level Desired

You will learn in subsequent chapters that certain statistical analyses incorporate assumptions about the nature of the measures being analyzed, so the researcher must bear these requirements in mind when selecting a question format. For example, if the response options are simply "yes" or "no," the researcher can report the percentage of respondents who answered in each way, but if the question asks how many times respondents used an ATM machine in the past month, the researcher could calculate an average number of times. An average is different from a percent; one reason being that a dichotomous yes–no response option is less informative than a scaled-response option such as "0," "1," "2," and so on. If a researcher desires to use higher-level statistical analyses, the question must have a scaled-response format. This point brings us to the concepts involved with measurement.

BASIC CONCEPTS IN MEASUREMENT

Questionnaires are designed to collect information gathered via **measurement**, which is defined as determining if and how much of a property is possessed by an object. For instance, a marketing manager may wish to know how a person feels about a certain product, or how much of the product he or she uses in a certain time period. This information, once compiled, can help answer specific research objectives such as determining brand usage.

> **Measurement is determining if and how much of a property is possessed by an object.**

But what are we really measuring? We are measuring properties—sometimes called "attributes" or "qualities"—of objects. Objects include consumers, brands, stores, advertisements, or whatever construct is of interest to the researcher working with a particular manager. **Properties** are the specific features or characteristics of an object that can be used to distinguish it from another object. For example, assume the object we want to research is a consumer. As depicted in Table 10.2, the properties of interest to a manager who is trying to define who buys a specific product are a combination of demographics such as age, income level, gender, and buyer behavior, which includes such things as the buyer's impressions or perceptions of various brands. Note that each property has the potential to further differentiate consumers.

TABLE 10.2	Measuring the Properties of an Object and Differentiating among Three Consumers' Properties	

The Object	Properties	Measurement Designations
A consumer	Age	35 years
(Mr. Able)	Income level	$75,000
	Gender	Male
	Brand last bought	Gillette
	Evaluation of "our" brand	"Fair"

Properties	Measurement Designations		
	Mr. Able	Ms. Black	Mr. Colby
Age	35	42	21
Income	$75,000	$65,000	$45,000
Gender	Male	Female	Male
Brand last bought	Gillette	Schick	Gillette
Evaluation of "our" brand	"Fair"	"Good"	"Excellent"

Restaurants have several properties that can be measured.

For example, Table 10.2 also compares three consumers' ages, income levels, perceptions, and sexes. Once the object's designation on a property has been determined, we say that the object has been measured on that property. Measurement underlies marketing reseach to a very great extent because researchers are keenly interested in describing marketing phenomena. Furthermore, researchers are often given the task of finding relevant differences in the profiles of various customer types.

On the surface, measurement may appear to be a very simple process. It is simple as long as we are measuring **objective properties**, which are physically verifiable characteristics such as age, income, number of bottles purchased, store last visited, and so on. They are observable and tangible. Typically, objective properties are the ones that are preset as to appropriate response options. However, marketing researchers often desire to measure **subjective properties**, which cannot be directly observed because they are mental constructs such as a person's attitude or intentions. Subjective properties are unobservable and intangible. In this case, the marketing researcher must ask a respondent to translate his or her mental constructs onto a continuum of intensity—no easy task. To do this, the marketing researcher must adapt or develop question formats that are very clear and that are used identically by the respondents. This process is known as "scale development."

Objective properties are observable and tangible. Subjective properties are unobservable and intangible, and they must be translated onto a rating scale through the process of scale development.

SCALE CHARACTERISTICS

Scale development is designing questions and response formats to measure the subjective properties of an object. There are various types of scales, each of which possesses different characteristics. The characteristics of a scale determine the scale's level of measurement. The level of measurement, as you shall see, is very important. First, however, you must learn about the four characteristics of scales: description, order, distance, and origin.

Scale characteristics are description, order, distance, and origin.

Description

Description refers to the use of a unique descriptor, or label, to stand for each designation in the scale. For instance, "yes" and "no," "agree" and "disagree," and the number of years of a respondent's age are descriptors of three different simple scales. All scales include description in the form of unique labels that are used to define the response options in the scale.

Order

Order refers to the relative sizes of the descriptors. Here, the key word is "relative" and includes such descriptors as "greater than," "less than," and "equal to." A respondent's least-preferred brand is "less than" his or her most-preferred brand, and respondents who check the same income category are the same ("equal to"). Not all scales possess order characteristics. For instance, is a "buyer" greater than or less than a "nonbuyer"? We have no way of making a relative size distinction.

> An ordered scale has descriptors that are "greater than," "less than," and "equal to" one another.

Distance

A scale has the characteristic of **distance** when absolute differences between the descriptors are known and may be expressed in units. The respondent who purchases three bottles of diet cola buys two more than the one who purchases only one bottle; a three-car family owns one more automobile than a two-car family. Note that when the characteristic of distance exists, we are also given order. We know not only that the three-car family has "more than" the number of cars of the two-car family, but we also know the distance between the two (one car).

Origin

A scale is said to have the characteristic of **origin** if there is a unique beginning or true zero point for the scale. Thus, 0 is the origin for an age scale just as it is for the number of miles traveled to the store or for the number of bottles of soda consumed. Not all scales have a true zero point for the property they are measuring. In fact, many scales used by marketing researchers have arbitrary neutral points, so they do not possess origins. For instance, when a respondent says, "No opinion," to the question "Do you agree or disagree with the statement, 'The Lexus is the best car on the road today'?" we cannot say that the person has a true zero level of agreement.

> A neutral category is not a true zero value for a scale.

Perhaps you noticed that each scale characteristic builds on the previous one; that is, description is the most basic and is present in every scale. If a scale has order, it also possesses description. If a scale has distance, it also possesses order and description, and if a scale has origin, it also has distance, order, and description. In other words, if a scale has a higher-level characteristic, it also has all lower-level characteristics. But the opposite is not true, as is explained in the next section.

LEVELS OF MEASUREMENT SCALES

You may ask, "Why is it important to know the characteristics of scales?" The answer is that the characteristics possessed by a scale determine that scale's level of measurement. Throughout this chapter, we try to convince you that it is very important for a marketing researcher to understand the level of measurement of the scale he or she selects. Let us now examine the four levels of measurement. They are nominal, ordinal, interval, and ratio. Table 10.3 shows how each scale type differs with respect to the scaling characteristics we have just discussed.

TABLE 10.3	Measurement Scales Differ by What Scale Characteristics They Possess				
		Scale Characteristic			
Level of Measurement		Description	Order	Distance	Origin
Categorical scales	Nominal	Yes	No	No	No
	Ordinal	Yes	Yes	No	No
Metric scales	Interval	Yes	Yes	Yes	No
	Ratio	Yes	Yes	Yes	Yes

There is a hierarchy of scales; ratio scales are the "highest" and nominal scales are the "lowest."

Table 10.3 also introduces two new concepts: categorical versus metric scales. A **categorical scale** is one that is typically composed of a small number of distinct values or categories such as "male" versus "female," or "married," versus "single," versus "widowed." As you can see in the table, there are two categorical scale types: nominal and ordinal. These will be described in detail in this section. The other concept is a **metric scale**, which is composed of numbers or labels that have an underlying measurement continuum. There are two metric scales that are also described in this section—interval and ratio scales.

Nominal Scales

Nominal scales simply label objects.

Nominal scales are defined as those that use only labels; that is, they possess only the characteristic of description. Examples include designations as to race, religion, type of dwelling, gender, brand last purchased, buyer/nonbuyer; answers that involve yes–no or agree–disagree; or any other instance in which the descriptors cannot be differentiated except qualitatively. If you describe respondents in a survey according to their occupation—banker, doctor, computer programmer—you have used a nominal scale. Note that these examples of a nominal scale only label the consumers. They do not provide other information such as "greater than," "twice as large," and so forth. Examples of nominal-scaled questions are found in Table 10.4A.

Ordinal Scales

Ordinal scales indicate only relative size differences between objects.

Ordinal scales permit the researcher to rank-order the respondents or their responses. For instance, if the respondent was asked to indicate his or her first, second, third, and fourth choices of brands, the results would be ordinally scaled. Similarly, if one respondent checked the category "Buy every week or more often" on a purchase-frequency scale and another checked the category "Buy once per month or less," the result would be an ordinal measurement. Ordinal scales indicate only relative size differences among objects. They possess description and order, but we do not know how far apart the descriptors are on the scale because ordinal scales do not possess distance or origin. Examples of ordinal-scaled questions are found in Table 10.4B.

Interval Scales

Interval scales use descriptors that are equal distances apart.

Interval scales are those in which the distance between each descriptor is known. For adjacent descriptors, the distance is normally defined as one scale unit. For example, a coffee brand rated "3" in taste is one unit away from one rated "4." Sometimes the researcher must impose a belief that equal intervals exist between the descriptors; that is, if you were asked to evaluate a store's salespeople by selecting a single designation from a list of "extremely friendly," "very friendly," "somewhat friendly," "somewhat unfriendly," "very

TABLE 10.4	Examples of the Use of Different Scaling Assumptions in Questions

A. Nominal-Scaled Questions

1. Please indicate your gender.   ___ Male ___ Female

2. Check all the brands you would consider purchasing.
   ___ Sony
   ___ Zenith
   ___ RCA
   ___ Curtis Mathes

3. Do you recall seeing a Delta Airlines advertisement for "carefree vacations" in the past week?
   ___ Yes   ___ No

B. Ordinal-Scaled Questions

1. Please rank each brand in terms of your preference. Place a "1" by your first choice, a "2" by your second choice, and so on.
   ___ Arrid
   ___ Right Guard
   ___ Mennen

2. For each pair of grocery stores, circle the one you would be more likely to patronize.
   Kroger versus First National
   First National versus A&P
   A&P versus Kroger

3. In your opinion, would you say the prices at Wal-Mart are
   ___ Higher than Sears,
   ___ About the same as Sears, or
   ___ Lower than Sears?

C. Interval-Scaled Questions

1. Please rate each brand in terms of its overall performance.

Brand	Rating (Circle One)									
	Very Poor								Very Good	
Mont Blanc	1	2	3	4	5	6	7	8	9	10
Parker	1	2	3	4	5	6	7	8	9	10
Cross	1	2	3	4	5	6	7	8	9	10

2. Indicate your degree of agreement with the following statements by circling the appropriate number.

Statement	Strongly Disagree				Strongly Agree
a. I always look for bargains.	1	2	3	4	5
b. I enjoy being outdoors.	1	2	3	4	5
c. I love to cook.	1	2	3	4	5

3. Please rate the *Pontiac Firebird* by checking the line that best corresponds to your evaluation of each item listed.
   Slow pickup ___ ___ ___ ___ Fast pickup
   Good design ___ ___ ___ ___ Bad design
   Low price ___ ___ ___ ___ High price

D. Ratio-Scaled Questions

1. Please indicate your age.
   ___ Years

2. Approximately how many times in the past month have you purchased anything over $5 in value at a 7-11 store?
   0   1   2   3   4   5   More (specify: ___)

3. How much do you think a typical purchaser of a $100,000 term life insurance policy pays per year for that policy?
   $_____

4. What is the probability that you will use a lawyer's services when you are ready to make a will?
   ___ percent

unfriendly," or "extremely unfriendly," the researcher would probably assume that each designation was one unit away from the preceding one. In these cases, we say that the scale is "assumed interval." As shown in Table 10.4C, these descriptors are evenly spaced on a questionnaire; as such, the labels connote a continuum and the check lines are equal distances apart. By wording or spacing the response options on a scale so they appear to have equal intervals between them, the researcher achieves a higher level of measurement than ordinal or nominal. With higher-order scales, the researcher is permitted to apply more powerful statistical techniques such as correlation analysis.

Ratio Scales

Ratio scales have a true zero point.

Ratio scales are ones in which a true zero origin exists—such as an actual number of purchases in a certain time period, dollars spent, miles traveled, number of children in the household, or years of college education. This characteristic allows us to construct ratios when comparing results of the measurement. One person may spend twice as much as another, or travel one-third as far. Such ratios are inappropriate for interval scales, so we are not allowed to say that one store was half as friendly as another. Examples of ratio-scaled questions are presented in Table 10.4D.

See if you can use the following template to figure out the scaling characteristics and scale level of a question. For each question in the first column, circle your answer to each of the questions along its row. Use these answers and the information in Table 10.3 to identify and write in the scale level.

	Answer each question by circling "Yes" or "No"							
Question	**Is There an Origin?**		**Is There Equal Distance between Adjacent Labels?**		**Is Each Label Greater than or Less than Its Adjacent Label(s)?**		**There are Labels (*Note*: All Scales Have Labels).**	**Write in the Name of the Level of Scale in the Question**
Do you own or lease your family vechicle? ____ Own ____ Lease	Yes?	No?	Yes?	No?	Yes?	No?	Yes	_____
How many times per month do you use a car wash to clean your family vehicle? ____ Times	Yes?	No?	Yes?	No?	Yes?	No?	Yes	_____
"My family vehicle is adequate for all my needs." ____ Strongly agree ____ Agree ____ No Opinion ____ Disagree ____ Strongly disagree	Yes?	No?	Yes?	No?	Yes?	No?	Yes	_____
For a family round trip of at least 500 miles where most of the driving will be on Interstate roads, would you prefer: ____ Your family vehicle ____ A rental vehicle	Yes?	No?	Yes?	No?	Yes?	No?	Yes	_____

WHY THE LEVEL OF A MEASUREMENT SCALE IS IMPORTANT

Why all the fuss over scale characteristics and the level of measurement? There are two important reasons. First, the level of measurement determines what information you will have about the object of study; it determines what you can say and what you cannot say about the object. For example, nominal scales measure the lowest information level, and therefore they are sometimes considered the crudest scales. Nominal scales allow us to do nothing more than identify our object of study on some property. Ratio scales, however, contain the greatest amount of information; they allow us to say many things about our object such as quantitatively how different it is from another object. A second important reason for understanding the level of measurement your scale possesses is that the level of measurement dictates what type of statistical analyses you may or may not perform. Low-level scales necessitate low-level analyses whereas high-level scales permit much more sophisticated analyses. In other words, the amount of information contained in the scale dictates the limits of statistical analysis. You will read more about this topic in Chapters 15 through 19.

As a general recommendation it is desirable to construct a scale at the highest appropriate level of measurement possible. Of course, appropriateness is determined by the properties of the object being measured and to some extent by the mental abilities of your respondents. As we have pointed out, some characteristics are inherently qualitative and can be measured only with a nominal scale, while other characteristics can be quantified and measured with a metric scale.

> Level of measurement is important because it determines (1) what you can or cannot say about your object and (2) which statistical analysis you may use.

WORKHORSE SCALES USED IN MARKETING RESEARCH

We noted in our opening comments that marketing researchers often wish to measure subjective properties of consumers. There are many variations of these properties, but usually they are concerned with the psychological aspects of consumers. There are various terms and labels given to these constructs, including attitudes, opinions, evaluations, beliefs, impressions, perceptions, feelings, and intentions. Because these constructs are unobservable, the marketing researcher must develop some means of allowing respondents to express the direction and the intensity of their impressions in a convenient and understandable manner. To do this, the marketing researcher uses scaled-response questions, which are designed to measure unobservable constructs. In this section, we will describe the basic scale formats that are most common in marketing research practice; that is, you will find these scale formats time and again on questionnaires; hence, we call them **workhorse scales** because they do the bulk of the measurement work in marketing research.

> Scaled-response questions are used to measure unobservable constructs.

The Intensity Continuum Underlying Workhorse Scales

Because most of these psychological properties exist on a continuum ranging from one extreme to another in the mind of the respondent, it is common practice to use scaled-response questions with an interval scale format. Sometimes numbers are used to indicate a single unit of distance between each position on the scale. Usually, but not always, the scale ranges from an extreme negative, through a neutral, and to an extreme positive designation. The neutral point is not considered zero, or an origin; instead, it is consid-

Workhorse scales are standard ones that marketing researchers rely on time and again.

ered a point along a continuum. Take a look at the examples in Table 10.5, and you will see that all of them span a continuum ranging from extremely negative to extremely positive with a "no opinion" position in the middle of the scale.

As we noted earlier, it is not good practice to invent a novel scale format with every questionnaire. Instead, marketing researchers often fall back on standard types used by the industry. These workhorse scales include the Likert scale, the lifestyle inventory, and the semantic differential, all three of which we describe next. Of course, sometimes no previous scale exists; or if one exists, it may have been developed in a context different from the one the researcher has in mind.

Marketing researchers use standard scales rather than inventing new ones for each research project.

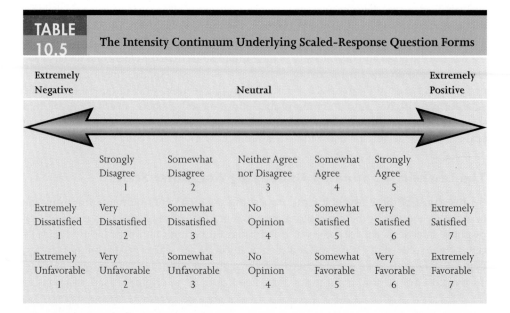

TABLE 10.5	The Intensity Continuum Underlying Scaled-Response Question Forms					
Extremely Negative			**Neutral**			**Extremely Positive**
	Strongly Disagree 1	Somewhat Disagree 2	Neither Agree nor Disagree 3	Somewhat Agree 4	Strongly Agree 5	
Extremely Dissatisfied 1	Very Dissatisfied 2	Somewhat Dissatisfied 3	No Opinion 4	Somewhat Satisfied 5	Very Satisfied 6	Extremely Satisfied 7
Extremely Unfavorable 1	Very Unfavorable 2	Somewhat Unfavorable 3	No Opinion 4	Somewhat Favorable 5	Very Favorable 6	Extremely Favorable 7

The Likert Scale

A scaled-response form commonly used by marketing researchers[6] is the **Likert scale**, in which respondents are asked to indicate their degree of agreement or disagreement on a symmetric agree–disagree scale for each of a series of statements. The value of the Likert scale should be apparent because respondents are asked how much they agree or disagree with the statement; that is, the scale captures the intensity of their feelings. With this scale, it is best to use "flat" or plain statements and let the respondent indicate the intensity of his or her feelings by using the agree–disagree response continuum position. Table 10.6 presents an example of its use in a telephone interview. You should notice the directions given by the interviewer to properly administer this scale.

The Likert-type of response format, borrowed from a formal scale development approach developed by Rensis Likert, has been extensively modified and adapted by marketing researchers, so much, in fact, that its definition varies from researcher to researcher. Some assume that any intensity scale using descriptors such as "strongly," "somewhat," "slightly," or the like is a Likert variation. Others use the term only for questions with agree–disagree response options. We tend to agree with the second opinion and prefer to refer to any scaled measurement other than an agree–disagree dimension as a "sensitivity" or "intensity" scale. But this convention is only our preference, and you should be aware that different researchers embrace other designations.

The Likert scale format measures intensity of agreement or disagreement.

The Lifestyle Inventory

There is a special application of the Likert question form called the **lifestyle inventory** (or psychographics inventory), which takes into account the values and personality traits of people as reflected in their unique activities, interests, and opinions (AIOs) toward their work, leisure time, and purchases. The technique was originated by advertising strategists who wanted to obtain descriptions of groups of consumers as a means of establishing more effective advertising. The underlying belief is that knowledge of

The lifestyle inventory measures a person's activities, interests, and opinions with a Likert scale.

TABLE 10.6	The Likert Question Format Can Be Used in Telephone Surveys, but Respondents Must Be Briefed on Its Format or Otherwise Prompted

(INTERVIEWER: READ) I have a list of statements that I will read to you. As I read each one, please indicate whether you agree or disagree with it.
Are the instructions clear? (IF NOT, REPEAT)
(INTERVIEWER: READ EACH STATEMENT. WITH EACH RESPONSE, ASK) Would you say that you (dis)agree STRONGLY or (dis)agree SOMEWHAT?

Statement	Strongly Disagree	Disagree	Neutral	Agree	Strongly Agree
Levi's Engineered jeans are good looking.	1	2	3	4	5
Levi's Engineered jeans are reasonably priced.	1	2	3	4	5
Your next pair of jeans will be Levi's Engineered jeans.	1	2	3	4	5
Levi's Engineered jeans are easy to identify on someone.	1	2	3	4	5
Levi's Engineered jeans make you feel good.	1	2	3	4	5

consumers' lifestyles, as opposed to just demographics, offers direction for marketing decisions. Many companies use psychographics as a market targeting tool.[7]

A consumer's lifestyle may be measured in terms of his or her activities, interests, and opinions.

Lifestyle questions measure consumers' unique ways of living. These questions can be used to distinguish among types of purchasers, such as heavy versus light users of a product, store patrons versus nonpatrons, or media vehicle users versus nonusers. They can assess the degree to which a person is, for example, price-conscious, fashion-conscious, an opinion giver, a sports enthusiast, child-oriented, home-centered, or financially optimistic. These attributes are measured by a series of AIO statements, usually in the form presented in Table 10.7.[8] Each respondent indicates his or her degree of agreement or disagreement by responding to the agree–disagree scale positions. In some applications, the questionnaire may contain a large number of different lifestyle statements ranging from very general descriptions of the person's AIOs to very specific statements concerning particular products, brands, services, or other items of interest to the marketing researcher.

TABLE 10.7   Examples of Lifestyle Statements on a Questionnaire

Please respond by circling the number that best corresponds to how much you agree or disagree with each statement.

Statement	Strongly Disagree		Neither Agree nor Disagree		Strongly Agree
I shop a lot for "specials."	1	2	3	4	5
I usually have one or more outfits that are of the very latest style	1	2	3	4	5
My children are the most important thing in my life.	1	2	3	4	5
I usually keep my house very neat and clean.	1	2	3	4	5
I would rather spend a quiet evening at home than go out to a party.	1	2	3	4	5
It is good to have a charge account.	1	2	3	4	5
I like to watch or listen to baseball or football games.	1	2	3	4	5
I think I have more self-confidence than most people.	1	2	3	4	5
I sometimes influence what my friends buy.	1	2	3	4	5
I will probably have more money to spend next year than I have now.	1	2	3	4	5

CONSTRUCT A COLLEGE STUDENT LIFESTYLE INVENTORY

Since you are a college student, you can easily relate to the dimensions of college student lifestyle. In this active learning exercise, take each of the following college student activities and write the Likert scale statement that could appear on a college student lifestyle inventory on a questionnaire. Be sure to word your statements as recommended in our descriptions of the Likert scale workhorse scale format.

College Lifestyle Dimension	Your Statement	Strongly Disagree	Disagree	Neither Disagree nor Agree	Agree	Strongly Agree
Studying	_____	1	2	3	4	5
Going out	_____	1	2	3	4	5
Working	_____	1	2	3	4	5
Exercising	_____	1	2	3	4	5
Shopping	_____	1	2	3	4	5
Dating	_____	1	2	3	4	5
Spending money	_____	1	2	3	4	5

The Semantic Differential Scale

A specialized scaled-response question format that has sprung directly from the problem of translating a person's qualitative judgments into quantitative estimates is the **semantic differential scale**. Like the Likert scale, this one has been borrowed from another area of research, namely semantics. The semantic differential scale contains a series of bipolar adjectives for the various properties of the object under study, and respondents indicate their impressions of each property by indicating locations along its continuum. The focus of the semantic differential is on the measurement of the meaning of an object, concept, or person. Because many marketing stimuli have meanings, mental associations, or connotations, this type of scale works very well when the marketing researcher is attempting to determine brand, store, or other images.

The construction of a semantic differential scale begins with the determination of a concept or object to be rated. The researcher then selects bipolar pairs of words or phrases that could be used to describe the object's salient properties. Depending on the object, some examples might be "friendly–unfriendly," "hot–cold," "convenient–inconvenient," "high quality–low quality," or "dependable–undependable." The opposites are positioned at the endpoints of a continuum of intensity, and it is customary, although not mandatory, to use five or seven separators between each point. The respondent then indicates his or her evaluation of the performance of the object, say a brand, by checking the appropriate line. The closer the respondent checks to an endpoint on a line, the more intense is his or her evaluation of the object being measured.

Table 10.8 shows how this was done for a survey for Red Lobster. The respondents also rated Jake's Seafood Restaurant on the same survey. You can see that each respondent has been instructed to indicate his or her impression of various restaurants such as Red Lobster by checking the appropriate line between the several bipolar adjective phrases. As you look at the phrases, you should note that they have been randomly flipped to avoid having all of the "good" ones on one side. This flipping procedure is used to avoid the **halo effect**,[9] which is a general feeling about a store or brand that can bias a

The semantic differential scale is a good way to measure a brand, company, or store image.

When using the semantic differential scale, you should control for the "halo effect."

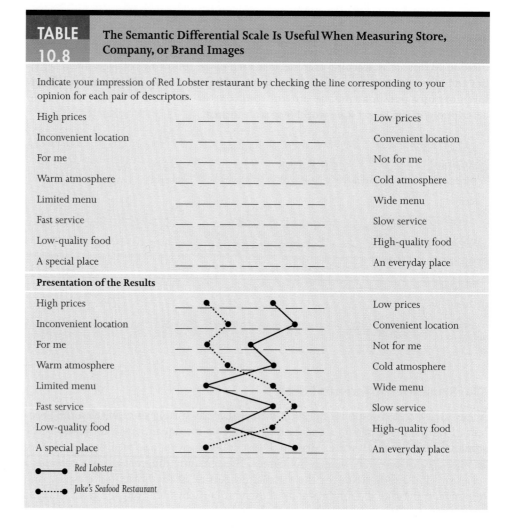

TABLE 10.8	The Semantic Differential Scale Is Useful When Measuring Store, Company, or Brand Images

Indicate your impression of Red Lobster restaurant by checking the line corresponding to your opinion for each pair of descriptors.

High prices	— — — — — — —	Low prices
Inconvenient location	— — — — — — —	Convenient location
For me	— — — — — — —	Not for me
Warm atmosphere	— — — — — — —	Cold atmosphere
Limited menu	— — — — — — —	Wide menu
Fast service	— — — — — — —	Slow service
Low-quality food	— — — — — — —	High-quality food
A special place	— — — — — — —	An everyday place

Presentation of the Results

High prices		Low prices
Inconvenient location		Convenient location
For me		Not for me
Warm atmosphere		Cold atmosphere
Limited menu		Wide menu
Fast service		Slow service
Low-quality food		High-quality food
A special place		An everyday place

●——● Red Lobster

●·····● Jake's Seafood Restaurant

respondent's impressions about its specific properties.[10] For instance, suppose you have a very positive image of Red Lobster. If all of the positive items were on the right-hand side and all the negative ones were on the left-hand side, you might be tempted to just check all of the answers on the right-hand side without reading each characteristic carefully. But it is entirely possible that some specific aspect of the Red Lobster might not be as good as the others. Perhaps the restaurant is not located in a very convenient place, or the menu is not as broad as you would like. Randomly flipping favorable and negative ends of the descriptors in a semantic differential scale minimizes the halo effect. Also, there is some evidence that when respondents are ambivalent toward the survey topic, it is best to use a balanced set of negatively and positively worded questions.[11]

One of the most appealing aspects of the semantic differential scale is the ability of the researcher to compute averages and then to plot a "profile" of the brand or company image. Each check line is assigned a number for coding. The numbers 1, 2, 3, and so on, beginning from the left side, are customary. Then, an average is computed for each bipolar pair. The averages are plotted as in Table 10.8, and the marketing researcher has a very nice graphical communication vehicle with which to report the findings to his or her client. The semantic differential scale format can be applied in various ways.

There is some evidence that the semantic differential scale (and perhaps all scales) are culturally bound; that is, scales that have been developed in a particular culture may

With a semantic differential scale, a researcher can plot the average evaluation on each set of bipolar descriptors.

not elicit the sames types of answers when used for respondents in a different culture. Read Marketing Research Insight 10.1, which describes what researchers found when they compared the use of a semantic differential scale with respondents in the United States versus respondents in Hong Kong.[12]

Other Scaled–Response Question Formats

There are a great many variations of scaled-response question formats used in marketing research. If you choose a career in the marketing research business, you will realize that each marketing research company or marketing research department tends to rely on "tried-and-true" formats that they apply from study to study. Several examples are provided in Table 10.9.

There are some very good reasons for this practice of adopting a preferred question format. First, it expedites the questionnaire design process; that is, by selecting a standardized scaled-response form that has been used in several studies, there is no need to be creative and to invent a new form. This saves both time and costs.[13] Second, by testing a scaled-response format across several studies, there is the opportunity to assess its reliability as well as its validity. Both of these topics are discussed in detail in a later section of this chapter, which introduces the basic concepts involved with reliability and validity of measurements and illustrates the methods used to assess reliability and validity.

Researchers tend to rely on "tried-and-true" scale formats.

MARKETING RESEARCH INSIGHT

GLOBAL APPLICATION

10.1

Do Different Cultures Respond Differently to Semantic Differential Scales?

Theoretically, a semantic differential scale should entice respondents to indicate their extreme opinions about the image of a company or brand; that is, the semantic differential scale, with its bipolar adjective pair for each company or brand image dimension being measured clearly affords respondents the opportunity to use either endpoint and express, for example, that a store has extremely friendly or extremely unfriendly sales personnel. So, if one group of respondents refrains from using the extreme rating positions, while another group exhibits less restraint, there is cause to believe that the lesser use of the extremes by the first group may be due to a response tendency specific to the group.

To investigate this question, researchers compared the response of respondents in Hong Kong to respondents in the United States on an identical semantic differential scale used to measure the image of a local supermarket.

Interestingly, when examining the responses to a traditional semantic differential scale such as the one described earlier in this chapter, the researchers found a general tendency in both the United States and Hong Kong respondents to not use the extreme positions on the scale. On deeper analysis, it was found that Hong Kong respondents have a somewhat more generalized tendency to not use the extreme scale positions than do U.S. respondents. To be more specific, for each of 18 supermarket image dimensions, an average of 1 percent of the Hong Kong respondents selected the extreme negative position while over 3 percent of U.S. respondents selected the extreme negative scale position. With the extreme positive scale position, an average of 4.6 percent of Hong Kong respondents chose it, while the average for U.S. respondents was over 8 percent. Albeit small, the evidence was sufficient for the researchers to conclude that there is a reasonable doubt that scales developed in Western culture will automatically transfer to other cultures, and researchers are warned to apply pretests and other means to ensure that respondents are using the full range of the response scale.

TABLE 10.9	Scaled-Response Question Formats Can Have Various Forms

Scale Name	Description and Examples
Graphic rating scale	Use of a line or pictorial representation to indicate intensity of response: Unimportant ◄- - - - - - - - - - - - - - - - - - - ► Extremely Important ☺ ☺ ☺ ☺ ☺
Itemized rating scale	Use of a numbered or labeled continuous scale to indicate intensity of response: ___ 1 ___ 2 ___ 3 ___ 4 ___ 5 Poor Fair Good Very Good Excellent ___ ___ ___ ___ ___
Stapel scale	Use of numbers, usually −5 to +5, to indicate the intensity of response: Fast checkout service −5 −4 −3 −2 −1 +1 +2 +3 +4 +5
Percentage scale	Use of percentages to indicate the intensity of response: Unlikely to purchase Likely to purchase 0% 10% 20% 30% 40% 50% 60% 70% 80% 90% 100% Very dissatisfied Very satisfied 0% 25% 50% 75% 100%

Issues in the Use of Scaled-Response Formats

Using scaled-response formats requires the researcher to answer two questions. First is the question of whether or not to include the middle, neutral response option. Our Likert scale, lifestyle, and semantic differential examples all have a neutral point, but some researchers prefer to leave out the neutral option on their scales. Valid arguments exist for both options.[14] Those arguing for the inclusion of a neutral option believe that some respondents do not have opinions formed on that item, and they must be given the opportunity to indicate their ambivalence. Proponents of not including a neutral position, however, believe that respondents may use the neutral option as a dodge or a method of hiding their opinions.[15] Eliminating the neutral position forces these respondents to indicate their opinions or feelings.

The second question concerns whether or not to use a completely symmetric scale. Sometimes, common sense causes the researcher to conclude that only the positive side is appropriate. For example, when you think of how important something is to you, you do not usually think in terms of degrees of "unimportance." In fact, for many constructs symmetric scales are awkward or nonintuitive, and should not be used.[16]

Consequently, some scales contain only the positive side, because very few respondents would make use of the negative side. When in doubt, a researcher can pretest both the complete and the one-sided versions to see whether the negative side will be used by respondents. As a general rule, it is best to pretest a sensitivity scale to make sure it is being used in its entirety. Some individuals, such as Hispanics, have tendencies to use only one end of a scale,[17] and pretests should be used to find a scale that will be used appropriately.

Figuring out what scale to use when is challenging for a neophyte marketing researcher.

WHAT SCALE TO USE WHEN

It has been our experience that when you study each workhorse scale and the other scaled-response question formats described in this chapter, each one makes sense. However, when faced with the actual decision about which scale to recommend in a given situation, it is difficult for neophyte marketing researchers to sort these scales out.

As we indicated in Chapter 4, the market researcher's mindset is geared toward the actual survey steps, and questionnaire design is a vital step that he or she must think about when formulating the marketing research proposal. We indicated in Chapter 4 that market researchers use "constructs" or standard marketing concepts, and, more important, we indicated that the researcher typically has a mental vision of how each construct will be measured. This mental vision, we indicated, is called an **operational definition**.

Since you now understand the basic concepts of measurement and have become acquainted with the workhorse scales and other scales used by market researchers, we have provided Table 10.10 as a quick reference to appropriate scales pertaining to the constructs most often measured by market researchers. You will notice that most of the scales in Table 10.10 are interval scaled because most of the constructs are attitudinal or intensity scales, and the general recommendations is to use the highest level scale possible.[18]

Of course, this is not a complete list of marketing constructs, but the constructs in Table 10.10 are often involved in marketing research undertakings.

We have included some nominally scaled constructs in Table 10.10, namely the awareness, possession, recall, and recognition constructs are measured with yes–no scales. If there is a list, and the respondent checks all that apply, the researcher can use a **summated scale**, meaning that the number of checks will be counted for each respondent, and that number will stand as the measure of the construct. For example, if there is a list of 10 kitchen appliances that a person could have in his/her kitchen, respondents with many appliances will have high summated scale numbers, while those with few will have low summated scale numbers.

TABLE 10.10 Commonly Used Scales for Selected Constructs

Construct	Response Scale
Awareness (or possession)	Yes–no OR check mark from a list of items Example: *Which of the following kitchen appliances do you own? (check all that apply.)*
Brand/store image	Semantic differential scale (with 5 or 7 scale points) using a set of bipolar adjectives Example: *Refer to example on page 284.*
Demographics	Standard demographic questions (gender, age range, income range, etc.) Examples: *Indicate your gender.* _____ *Male* _____ *Female* *What is your age range?* _____ *20 or younger* _____ *21–30* _____ *31–40* _____ *41–50* _____ *51 or older*
Frequency of use	Labeled (never, rarely, occasionally, often, quite often, very often) OR number of times per relevant time period (e.g., month) Example: *How often do you buy takeout Chinese dinners?*
Importance	Labeled (unimportant, slightly important, important, quite important, very important) OR numbered rating using 5 scale points Example: *How important is it to you that your dry cleaning service has same-day service?*
Intention to purchase	Labeled (unlikely, somewhat likely, likely, quite likely, very likely) OR 100% probability Example: *The next time you buy cookies, how likely are you to buy a fat-free brand?*
Lifestyle/opinion	Likert (strongly disagree–strongly agree with 5 scale points) using a series of lifestyle statements Example: *Indicate how much you agree or disagree with each of the following statements.* 1. *I have a busy schedule.* 2. *I work a great deal.*
Performance or attitude	Labeled (poor, fair, good, very good, excellent) OR numbered rating scale using 5 scale points OR Stapel scale using −5 to +5, or number of scale points in ability of respondents Example: *Indicate how well you think Arby's performs on each of the following features.* 1. *Variety of items on the menu* 2. *Reasonable price* 3. *Location convenient to your home*
Recall or recognition	Yes–no OR check mark from a list of items Example: *Where have you seen or heard an ad for Pets-R-Us in the past month? (check all that apply).*
Satisfaction	Labeled (not at all satisfied, slightly satisfied, somewhat satisfied, very satisfied, completely satisfied) OR 10-point satisfaction scale, where 1 = "not at all satisfied" and 10 = "completely satisfied" Note: If there is reason to believe that an appreciable number of respondents are not satisfied, the recommendation is for a symmetric balanced scale to measure the degree of dissatisfaction (completely dissatisfied; slightly dissatisfied; neither dissatisfied nor satisfied; slightly satisfied; completely satisfied) Example: *Based on your experience with Federal Express, how satisfied have you been with its overnight delivery service?*

Not at all satisfied	Slightly satisfied	Somewhat satisfied	Very Satisfied	Completely satisfied
☐	☐	☐	☐	☐

If you are still confused about which scale to use when, do not feel bad, because scales are not an easy concept to understand at first reading. While we did not include it as one of our "workhorse" scales, a very commonly used scale is the simple 5-point anchored scale. An **anchored scale** is one in which labels are identified at the opposite ends of the measurement continuum and associated only with the beginning and ending numbers of the scale. For example, a telephone interviewer might say, "Please tell me how satisfied you were with your CD-burner software, where a 1 means 'unsatisfied,' and a 5 means 'very satisfied.' " Another example is this: "Please rate the music quality of your PC's audio system, where 1 means 'poor,' and 5 means 'excellent.' " An **unanchored scale** is one in which the endpoints are not identified, for example, "Please indicate on a scale of 1 to 5 how satisfied you were with your CD-burner software." It is implicit with an unanchored scale that as the scale numbers rise, the evaluation is more positive. So, a 1 would be the least postive response, while a 5 would be the most positive response. Nevertheless, it is important to indicate how the numbers relate to the respondent's evaluation in the instructions for that rating scale.

Is 5 points the best number of scale positions? The answer is "maybe," and we have prepared Marketing Research Insight 10.2, which explains why we say "maybe."

10.2 How Many Scale Positions, or How Do You Measure a Fever?

When measuring subjective constructs such as evaluations, expectations, attitudes, opinions, and the like, marketing researchers are always confronted with the question of how many scale positions to use; that is, should the researcher use a 2-point scale, a 5-point scale, a 10-point scale, or some other number of scale positions?

The answer to question about the number of scale positions is not straightforward, and researchers do not agree.[19] For example, the opening case vignette for this chapter noted that the Maritz Research company typically uses a 5-point, fully labeled scale to measure satisfaction. At the same time, *Reader's Digest* uses a 5-point scale measuring "brand trust" in its annual consumer trust survey conducted in 18 different European countries to identify the most trusted consumer brands in at least 30 different product categories and printed in 20 languages.[20] A recent article[21] compared 2-point, 4-point, and 5-point scales and concluded that the 5-point scale performs best when used to measure a brand's performance, consumers' expectations, and, to some extent, satisfaction. At the same

time, other researchers[22] have concluded that a 10-point satisfaction scale is superior to a 5-point scale.

Why can't researchers agree? The underlying disagreement may be due to differences in the researchers' objectives; that is, no scale is perfect in every situation.[23] When a researcher needs a gross indication, the 5-point scale is useful; however, when the researcher requires a "fine resolution" measure, the 7-, 9- or 10-point scale is more appropriate. To use an analogy, when someone feels a bit ill, the first measure is usually to feel that person's forehead to quickly assess whether or not the person has a fever. This is a gross measure because it indicates only whether or not the person's forehead feels cold, cool, normal, warm or hot to the touch. So the forehead measure is analogous to a negative, neutral, or positive response to a symmetric 5-point scale. Later, when the gross touch measure determines that the person's skin temperature is not right, a thermometer is used to determine the exact body temperature of that person. Similarly, a 5-point attitude scale can detect a general tendency in respondents to be negative, neutral, or favorable, but a scale with more points will measure the degree of attitude more precisely. The researcher's objective—either a general indication or a precise degree—requires fewer or more scale positions, respectively.

RELIABILITY AND VALIDITY OF MEASUREMENTS

Reliable measures obtain identical or very similar responses from the same respondent.

Ideally, any measurement used by a market researcher should be reliable and valid. A **reliable measure** is one for which a respondent responds in the same or in a very similar manner to an identical or near-identical question. Obviously if a question elicits wildly different answers from the same person and you know that the person is unchanged from administration to administration of the question, there is something very wrong with the question.

Validity is the truthfulness of responses to a measure.

Validity, on the other hand, operates on a completely different plane than reliability; it is possible to have perfectly reliable measurements that are invalid. Validity is defined as the accuracy of the measurement: It is an assessment of the exactness of the measurement relative to what actually exists. So, a **valid measure** is one that is truthful. To illustrate this concept and its difference from reliability, think of a respondent who is embarrassed by a question about his income. This person makes under $40,000 per year, but he does not want to tell the interviewer. Consequently, he responds with the highest category, "Over $100,000." In a retest of the questions, the respondent persists in his lie by stipulating the highest income level again. Here, the respondent has been perfectly consistent (that is, reliable), but he has also been completely untruthful (that is, invalid). Of course, lying is not the only reason for invalidity. The respondent may have a faulty memory, may have a misconception, or may even be a bad guesser, which causes his responses to be inexact from reality.[24]

Face validity: Does the question "look like" it measures what it is supposed to measure?

When a researcher develops questions for his or her questionnaire, he or she uses an intuitive form of judgement called **face validity** to evaluate the validity of each question. Face validity is concerned with the degree to which a measurement "looks like" it measures that which it is designed to measure.[25] Thus, as each question is developed, there is an implicit assessment of its face validity. Often a researcher will ask a colleague to look at the questions to see if he or she agrees with the researcher's face validity judgments. Revisions strengthen the face validity of the question until it passes the researcher's subjective evaluation. Unfortunately, face validity is considered by academic marketing researchers to be a very weak test, so marketing research practitioners are faced with an ethical dilemma when they work with scales. We describe this ethical dilemma in Marketing Research Insight 10.3.

MARKETING RESEARCH INSIGHT

ETHICAL ISSUES

10.3 Why Marketing Researchers Face Ethical Issues in Scale Development

Researchers face an ethical dilemma in scale development. The proper way to develop a scale is very lengthy and expensive because there are several different criteria that should be used to assess the quality of a scale. To meet these criteria, it is expected that a scale will be developed over a series of administrations. Statistical tests are used after each one to refine the scale, and

each subsequent administration tests the new version, which leads to further refinement. It is not unusual for scales that are published in academic journals to go through three or four administrations involving hundreds of respondents. To say this more pointedly, when a marketing researcher must develop a scale to measure a marketing construct, doing it properly may take several months or even years of work.

The few marketing research firms who have pursued scale development have developed proprietary instruments that are protected by copyright; that is, they have invested the time and money in the scale development so it will be one of their marketing research services, and they will enjoy a competitive advantage over other marketing research firms because of the legal protection afforded their work by a copyright.

As you would expect, the vast majority of marketing research practitioners do not have the time and their clients are unwilling to supply the money necessary to thoroughly develop scales. So, there is an ethical dilemma when a marketing researcher must measure some marketing phenomenon, but he or she does not have the luxury of time or the resources necessary to do so properly. Proper scale development simply cannot take place because clients do not appreciate the time and cost factors. In fact, they may not even believe these procedures are warranted and will refuse to pay for them, meaning that if such tests are performed, they will reduce the marketing researcher's profits. Consequently, the vast majority of marketing researchers are forced to design their measures by relying on face validity alone, meaning that the researcher, and perhaps the client if he or she is inclined to take part, simply judges that the question developed to measure the marketing construct at hand "looks like" it is an adequate measure.

The unfortunate truth is that most marketing researcher practitioners cannot concern themselves at all with rigorous scale development that relies on time-consuming reliability or validity measurements. The standard procedure is to use measures that are well known to the researcher through his or her company's experience (refer to the Maritz Research example at the beginning of this chapter) through his or her own experience, or that are available in the marketing research literature. On the other hand, it is unethical for a researcher to find reliability and/or validity problems and not strive to resolve them. A conscientious market researcher will devote as much time and energy as possible to ensure the reliability and validity of the research throughout the entire process.

The formal development of reliable and valid measures is a long and complicated process that is largely entrusted to academic marketing researchers.[26] In other words, marketing professors who work on the cutting edge of research often labor for months and sometimes years to develop reliable and valid measures of the marketing constructs with which they are working. Fortunately, these labors are ultimately published in academic journals, which places these measures in the public domain, meaning that marketing research practitioners can use them freely.

In fact, a series of *Marketing Scales Handbooks* edited by Gordon C. Bruner II, Karen E. James, and Paul J. Hensel contains hundreds of these scales; it is published by the American Marketing Association. These handbooks save the time and effort that would need to be expended in searching for scales in journal articles or other similar academic sources. (See **www.marketingpower.com**.)

SPSS Student Assistant: Coca-Cola: Sorting, Searching, and Inserting Variables and Cases

SUMMARY

This chapter discussed the concepts involved in measurement of the subjective properties of marketing phenomena. We began by reviewing the three basic question–response option formats of open-ended, closed-ended, and scaled-response questions and then we introduced you to the four levels of scales used in marketing research: (1) nominal or simple classifications; (2) ordinal or rank order; (3) interval scales, which include number scales and other equal-appearing spaced scales; and (4) ratio scales, which have a true zero point. As you move from the lowest (nominal) to the highest (ratio) type of scale, you gain more information in measurement.

Marketing researchers have a set of commonly used scale types, and the chapter included descriptions of three of these. First, there is the Likert scale, which appears as an agree–disagree continuum with five to seven positions. Next, we described lifestyle questions, which use a Likert approach to measure people's attitudes, interests, and opinions. Third, we illustrated how the semantic differential scale uses bipolar adjectives to measure the image of a brand or a store. We also listed a number of other scaled-response question formats that are popular with marketing researchers, and we provided our recommendations about how a neophyte marketing researcher should measure each of 10 commonly researched marketing constructs such as awareness or satisfaction.

Finally, reliability and validity of measurement were discussed. Reliability is the degree to which a respondent is consistent in his or her answers. Validity, on the other hand, is the accuracy of responses. It is possible to have reliable measures that are inaccurate. Researchers use face validity, or intuitive judgment, when developing questions that "look like" they are eliciting valid answers. The American Marketing Association publishes handbooks on marketing scales that have been developed and published in journals by academic market researchers.

KEY TERMS

Know all

Open-ended question (p. 270)
Unprobed format (p. 270)
Probed format (p. 270)
Response probe (p. 270)
Closed-ended question (p. 271)
Dichotomous closed-ended question
    (p. 271)
Multiple-category closed-ended question
    (p. 271)
Scaled-response question (p. 271)
Unlabeled scaled-response format
    (p. 271)
Labeled scaled-response format (p. 271)
Measurement (p. 273)
Properties (p. 273)
Objective properties (p. 274)
Subjective properties (p. 274)
Scale development (p. 274)
Description (p. 275)
Order (p. 275)

Distance (p. 275)
Origin (p. 275)
Categorical scale (p. 276)
Metric scale (p. 276)
Nominal scales (p. 276)
Ordinal scales (p. 276)
Interval scales (p. 276)
Ratio scales (p. 278)
Workhorse scales (p. 280)
Likert scale (p. 281)
Lifestyle inventory (p. 281)
Semantic differential scale (p. 283)
Halo effect (p. 283)
Operational definition (p. 287)
Summated scale (p. 287)
Anchored scale (p. 289)
Unanchored scale (p. 289)
Reliable measure (p. 290)
Valid measure (p. 290)
Face validity (p. 290)

REVIEW QUESTIONS/APPLICATIONS

1. List each of the three basic question–response formats. Indicate the two variations for each one, and provide an example for each.
2. Identify at least three considerations that determine a question's format and indicate how each one would determine the format.
3. What is measurement? In your answer, differentiate an object from its properties, both objective and subjective.
4. Distinguish the four scale characteristics that determine the level of measurement with a scale.

5. Define the four levels of scales and indicate the types of information contained in each.

6. Explain what is meant by a continuum along which a subjective property of an object can be measured.

7. What are the arguments for and against the inclusion of a neutral response position in a symmetric scale?

8. Distinguish among a Likert scale, a lifestyle scale, and a semantic differential scale.

9. What is the halo effect, and how does a researcher control for it?

10. What is an operational definition? Provide operational defintions for the following constructs:
   a. Brand loyalty
   b. Intention to purchase
   c. Importance of "value for the price"
   d. Attitude toward a brand
   e. Recall of an advertisement
   f. Past purchases

11. How does reliability differ from validity? In your answer, define each term.

12. Mike, the owner of the convenience store Mike's Market, is concerned about low sales. He reads in a marketing textbook that the image of a store often has an impact on its ability to attract its target market. He contacts the All-Right Research Company and commissions it to conduct a study that will shape his store's image. You are charged with the responsibility of developing the store image part of the questionnaire.

   Design a semantic differential scale that will measure the relevant aspects of Mike's Market's image. In your work on this scale, you must do the following: (a) brainstorm the properties to be measured, (b) determine the appropriate bipolar adjectives, (c) decide on the number of scale points, and (d) indicate how the scale controls for the halo effect.

13. Each of the examples listed below involves a market researcher's need to measure some construct. Devise an appropriate scale for each. Defend the scale in terms of its scaling assumptions, number of response categories, use or nonuse of a "no opinion" or neutral response category, and face validity.
   a. Mattel wants to know how preschool children react to a sing-along video game in which the child must sing along with an animated character and guess the next word in the song at various points in the video.
   b. TCBY is testing five new flavors of yogurt and wants to know how its customers rate each one on sweetness, flavor strength, and richness of taste.
   c. A pharmaceutical company wants to find out how much a new federal law eliminating dispensing of free sample prescription drugs by doctors will affect their intentions to prescribe generic versus brand-name drugs for their patients.

14. Harley-Davidson is the largest American motorcycle manufacturer, and it has been in business for several decades. Harley-Davidson has expanded into "signature" products such as shirts that prominently display the Harley-Davidson logo. Some people have a negative image of Harley-Davidson because it was the motorcycle favored by the Hell's Angels and other motorcycle gangs. There are two research questions here. First, do consumers have a negative feeling toward Harley-Davidson, and, second, are they disinclined toward the purchase of Harley-Davidson signature products such as shirts, belts, boots, jackets, sweatshirts, lighters, and key chains? Design a Likert measurement scale that can be used in a nationwide telephone study to address these two issues.

15. In conducting a survey for the Equitable Insurance Company, Burke Marketing Research assesses reliability by selecting a small group of respondents, calling

them back, and readministering five questions to them. One question asks, "If you were going to buy life insurance sometime this year, how likely would you be to consider the Equitable Company?" Respondents indicate the likelihood on a probability scale (0% to 100% likely). Typically, this test–retest approach finds that respondents are within 10 percent of their initial response; that is, if a respondent indicated that he or she were 50 percent likely in the initial survey, he or she responded in the 45 percent to 55 percent range on the retest.

The survey has been going on for four weeks, and it has two more weeks before the data collection will be completed. Respondents who are retested are called back exactly one week after the initial survey. In the last week, reliability results have been very different. Now Burke is finding that the retest averages are 20 percent higher than the initial test. Has the scale become unreliable? If so, why has its previous good reliability changed? If not, what has happened, and how can Burke still claim that it has a reliable measure?

16. General Foods Corporation includes Post, which is the maker of Fruit and Fibre Cereal. The brand manager is interested in determining how much Fruit and Fibre consumers think it is helping them toward a healthier diet. But the manager is very concerned that respondents in a survey may not be entirely truthful about health matters. They may exaggerate what they really believe so they "sound" more health-conscious than they really are, and they may say they have healthy diets when they really do not.

The General Foods Corporation marketing research director suggests a unique way to overcome the problem. He suggests that they conduct a survey of Fruit and Fibre customers in Pittsburgh, Atlanta, Dallas, and Denver. Fifty respondents who say that Fruit and Fibre is helping them toward a healthier diet and who also say they are more health-conscious than the average American will be selected, and General Foods will offer to "buy" their groceries for the next month. To participate, the chosen respondents must submit their itemized weekly grocery trip receipts. By reviewing the items bought each week, General Foods can determine what they are eating and make judgments on how healthy their diets really are. What is your reaction to this approach? Will General Foods be able to assess the validity of its survey this way? Why or why not?

CASE 10.1

METRO TOYOTA OF KALAMAZOO

The Metro Toyota dealership, located in Kalamazoo, Michigan, wanted to know how people who intend to buy a new automobile in the next 12 months view their purchase. The General Sales Manager called the marketing department at the University of Western Michigan and arranged for a class project to be taken on by Professor Ann Veeck's undergraduate marketing research students. Professor Veeck had a large class that semester, so she decided to divide the project into two groups and to have each group compete against the other to see which one designed and executed the better survey.

Both groups worked diligently on the survey over the semester. They met with the Metro Toyota General Sales Manager, discussed the dealership with his managers, conducted focus groups, and consulted the literature on brand, store, and company image research. Both teams conducted telephone surveys, whose findings are presented in their final reports.

Professor Veeck offered to grant extra credit to each team if it gave a formal presentation of its research design, findings, and recommendations.

Findings of Professor Veeck's Marketing Research Teams

Team One's Findings for Metro Toyota of Kalamazoo: Importance of Features of Dealership in Deciding to Buy There

Feature	Percent Indicating "Yes"[a]
Competitive prices	86%
No high pressure	75%
Good service facilities	73%
Low-cost financing	68%
Many models in stock	43%
Convenient location	35%
Friendly salespersons	32%

[a]Based on responses to the question "Is _____(insert feature)_____ important to you when you decide on a dealership from which to purchase your new automobile?"

Image of Metro Toyota of Kalamazoo Dealership

Feature	Percent Indicating "Yes"[a]
Competitive prices	45%
No high pressure	32%
Good service facilities	80%
Low-cost financing	78%
Many models in stock	50%
Convenient location	81%
Friendly salespersons	20%

[a]Based on responses to the question "Were you satisfied with Toyota of Kalamazoo's _____(insert feature)_____ when you purchased your new automobile there?"

Team Two's Findings for Metro Toyota of Kalamazoo: Importance and Image of Metro Toyota of Kalamazoo Dealership

Feature	Importance[a]	Satisfaction[b]
Competitive prices	6.5	1.3
No high pressure	6.2	3.6
Good service facilities	5.0	4.3
Low-cost financing	4.7	3.9
Many models in stock	3.1	3.0
Convenient location	2.2	4.1
Friendly salespersons	2.0	1.2

[a]Based on a 7-point scale, where 1 = "unimportant" and 7 = "extremely important."
[b]Based on a 5-point scale, where 1 = "completely unsatisfied" and 5 = "completely satisfied."

1. Contrast the different ways these findings can be presented in graphical form to the Metro Toyota management group. Which student team has the ability to present its findings more effectively? How and why?

2. What are the managerial implications apparent in each team's findings? Identify the implications and recommendations for Metro Toyota as they are evident in each team's findings.

EXTREME EXPOSURE ROCK CLIMBING CENTER FACES THE KRAG

For the past 5 years, Extreme Exposure Rock Climbing Center has enjoyed a monopoly. Located in Sacramento, California, Extreme Exposure was the dream of Kyle Anderson, who has been into freestyle extreme sports of various types, including outdoor rock climbing, hang gliding, skydiving, mountain biking, snowboarding, and a number of other adrenalin-pumping sports. Now in his mid-30s, Kyle came to realize in the year of his 30th birthday that after three leg fractures, two broken arms, and numerous dislocations, he could not participate on the extreme edge like he used to. So, he found an abandoned warehouse, recruited two investors and a friendly banker, and opened Extreme Exposure.

Kyle's rock-climbing center has over 6500 sq. ft. of simulated rock walls to climb, with about 100 different routes up to a maximum of 50 vertical feet. Extreme Exposure's design permits the four major climbing types: top-roping, in which the climber climbs up with a rope anchored at the top; lead-climbing, in which the climber tows the rope that he or she fixes to clips in the wall while ascending; bouldering, in which the climber has no rope but stays near the ground; and rappelling, in which the person descends quickly by sliding down a rope. Climbers can buy day passes, month-long, or annual memberships. Shoes and harnesses can be rented cheaply, and helmets are available free of charge, as all climbers must wear protective helmets. In addition to individual and group climbing classes, Extreme Exposure has several group programs, including birthday parties, a kids summer camp, and corporate team-building classes.

There is a newspaper article about another rock climbing center, to be called "The Krag," that will be built in Sacramento in the next six months. Kyle notes the following items about The Krag that are different from Extreme Exposure: (1) The Krag will have climbs up to a maximum of 60 vertical feet, (2) it will have a climber certification program, (3) there will be day trips to outdoor rock climbing areas, (4) there will be group overnight and extended-stay rock climbing trips to the Canadian Rockies, and (5) The Krag's annual membership fee will be about 20% lower than the one for Extreme Exposure.

Kyle chats with Dianne, one of his Extreme Exposure members who is in marketing, during a break in one of her climbing visits, and Dianne summarizes what she believes Kyle needs to find out about his current members. Dianne's list follows.

1. What are the demographic and rock-climbing profiles of Extreme Exposure's members?

2. How satisfied are the members with Extreme Exposure's climbing facilities?

3. How interested are its members in: (a) day trips to outdoor rock climbing areas, (b) group overnight and/or extended-stay rock climbing trips to the Canadian Rockies, and (c) a rock-climber certification program?

4. What are members' opinions of the annual membership fee charged by Extreme Exposure?

5. Will members consider leaving Extreme Exposure to join a new rock-climbing center with climbs that are 10 feet higher than the maximum climb at Extreme Exposure?

6. Will members consider leaving Extreme Exposure to join a new rock-climbing center with climbs that are 10 feet higher than the maximum climb at Extreme Exposure and whose annual membership fee is 20% lower than Extreme Exposure's?

For each of Dianne's questions, identify the relevant construct and indicate how it should be measured.

11 Designing the Questionnaire

Guideposts Uses WebSurveyor to Boost Readership[1]

Guideposts, a leading publisher of inspirational books and magazines, with a total circulation of over 8 million, is a dynamic media company, constantly studying its readers' opinions to enhance existing products and develop new offerings. Guideposts has relied on traditional research methods, such as paper surveys, focus groups, and newsstand tests to measure feedback from its readers. However, these methods, while accurate, can often be costly and time-consuming.

Guideposts decided to continue conducting focus groups and paper surveys, while moving some of its paper surveys online to accelerate the information-gathering process. Guideposts initiated an online survey pilot project to compare reader opinions of various product concepts under consideration for development. "We started doing paper and online surveys at the same time, and compared the results," says Jennifer Chenail, senior research coordinator for Guideposts. "The online surveys were incredibly fast in obtaining results and much less expensive compared to mail surveys."

The adoption of the WebSurveyor solution allowed Guideposts to move additional survey projects online as well, including online surveys to test products for a catalog, online voting, and demos. For example, Guideposts formed an online

To learn more about Guideposts, visit **www.guideposts.com.**

■ To appreciate the basic functions of a questionnaire
■ To learn the "Do's" and "Do Not's" of question wording
■ To learn the basics of questionnaire organization
■ To comprehend coding of questionnaires
■ To understand the advantages of computer-assisted questionnaire design software
■ To learn how to use WebSurveyor

Learning Objectives

Guideposts is one of a great many companies that have adopted WebSurveyor as the vehicle for its online surveys.

panel of readers to probe deeper into its customer base. "We are getting a pretty high return rate," says Chenail. Now the company is building more panels using online research. From reader panels, the company has moved to online contests that have become highly popular. For example, in a joint project with a major automotive advertiser, readers were asked to judge short stories submitted by other readers. "We picked the top 10 stories, posted them on our Web site and asked readers to vote for their favorite story," says Chenail. "We got around 315,000 votes in two 10-day periods. Advertisers were blown away by that."

The company is now using WebSurveyor for a variety of business tasks, ranging from traditional research to Web site traffic analysis. "The solution is extremely flexible and we will be moving more things online in the future," says Chenail.

We are now ready to discuss questionnarie design. In this chapter you will learn the functions of a questionnaire and the process of developing one. We give you guidelines on how to word questions so they are focused and clear, and we show you how to avoid biased questions. You will also learn how to organize a questionnaire and how to apply codes, plus you will hear about the importance of pretesting your questionnaire. We introduce you to computer-assisted questionnaire design programs, and we will show you how to use WebSurveyor, a popular computer program that is used to develop a questionnaire that can be published online for use by respondents and that generates a downloadable computer file of all respondents' answers.

THE FUNCTIONS OF A QUESTIONNAIRE

A questionnaire poses the survey questions to respondents.

A **questionnaire** is the vehicle used to pose the questions that the researcher wants respondents to answer. Surely, you appreciate that questionnaires are important elements in surveys, but it might surprise you to learn that a questionnaire serves six key functions. (1) It translates the research objectives into specific questions that are asked of the respondents. (2) It standardizes those questions and the response categories so every participant responds to identical stimuli. (3) By its wording, question flow, and appearance, it fosters cooperation and keeps respondents motivated throughout the interview. (4) Questionnaires serve as permanent records of the research. (5) Depending on the type of questionnaire used, a questionnaire can speed up the process of data analysis. Online questionnaires, for example, can be transmitted to thousands of potential respondents in seconds. In the case of WebSurveyor, questionnaires can be delivered and returned online. Some printed questionnaires may be designed to allow respondents' responses to be scanned into a statistical package. (6) Finally, questionnaires contain the information on which reliability assessments may be made, and they are used in follow-up validation of respondents' participation in the survey. In other words, questionnaires are used by researchers for quality control.

Given that it serves all of these functions, the questionnaire is indeed a very important ingredient in the research process. In fact, studies have shown that questionnaire design directly affects the quality of the data collected. Even experienced interviewers cannot compensate for questionnaire defects.[2] The time and effort invested in developing a good questionnaire are well spent.[3] As you will soon learn, questionnaire development is a systematic process in which the researcher contemplates various question formats, considers a number of factors characterizing the survey at hand, and ultimately words the various questions very carefully. Questionnaire design is a process that requires the researcher to go through a series of interrelated steps.

THE QUESTIONNAIRE DEVELOPMENT PROCESS

Questionnaire design is a systematic process that requires the researcher to go through a series of considerations.

As you will soon learn, **questionnaire design** is a systematic process in which the researcher contemplates various question formats, considers a number of factors characterizing the survey at hand, ultimately words the various questions very carefully, and organizes the questionnaire's layout.

Figure 11.1 offers a flowchart of the various phases in a typical marketing research survey. The first two steps in the flowchart have been covered in this book. We have expanded and highlighted the questionnaire design steps, so you can see that there are some specific activities the researcher must execute before the questionnaire is finalized. As you can see in Figure 11.1, a questionnaire will ordinarily go through a series of drafts before it is in an acceptable final form. In fact, even before the first question is constructed, the researcher mentally reviews alternative question formats to decide which ones are best suited to the survey's respondents and circumstances. As the questionnaire begins to take shape, the researcher continually evaluates each question and its response options. Changes are made, and the question's wording is reevaluated to make sure that it is asking what the researcher intends. Also, the researcher strives to minimize **question bias**, defined as the ability of a question's wording or format to influence respondents' answers.[4] We will elaborate on question development and the minimization of question bias very soon.

Question bias occurs when the question's wording or format influences the respondent's answer.

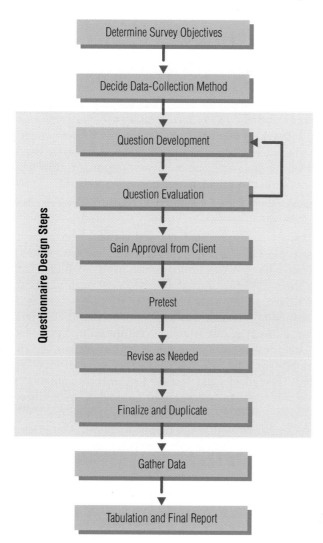

FIGURE 11.1
Steps in the Questionnaire
Development Process

For now, it is important only that you realize that with a custom-designed research study, the questions on the questionnaire, along with the questionnaire's instructions, introduction, and general layout, are systematically evaluated for potential error and revised accordingly. Generally, this evaluation takes place at the researcher's end, and the client will not be involved until after the questionnaire has undergone considerable development and evaluation by the researcher. The client is given the opportunity to comment on the questionnaire during the client approval step, in which the client reviews the questionnaire and agrees that it covers all of the appropriate issues. This step is essential, and some research companies require the client to sign or initial a copy of the questionnaire as verification of approval. Granted, the client may not appreciate all of the technical aspects of questionnaire design, but he or she is vitally concerned with the survey's objectives and can comment on the degree to which the questions on the questionnaire appear to address these objectives. Following client approval, the questionnaire normally undergoes a pretest, which is an actual field test using a very limited sample to reveal any difficulties that might still lurk in wording, instructions, administration, and so on. We describe pretesting more fully later in this chapter.[5] Revisions are made based on the pretest results, and the questionnaire is finalized.

DEVELOPING QUESTIONS

Question development is the practice of selecting appropriate response formats and wording questions that are understandable, unambiguous, and unbiased.

Question development is the practice of selecting appropriate response formats and wording questions that are understandable, unambiguous, and unbiased. Marketing researchers are very concerned with developing research questions because they measure (1) attitudes, (2) beliefs, (3) behaviors, and (4) demographics,[6] and they desire reliable and valid answers to their questions. So, question development is a tall order, so to speak, but it is absolutely vital to the success of the survey. Here is a corny example to make our point that question development is very important. How would you respond to the following question that might appear on a questonnaire?

Have you stopped trying to beat red traffic lights when you think you have the chance?
Yes ____ No ____

If you say, "Yes," it means you used to speed up when the traffic light showed yellow, and if you say, "No," it means you are still taking chances. Either way, the conclusion is that everyone who took part in the survey drove or still drives dangerously. But, we all know that everyone is not a reckless driver now or in the past, so the question wording must be flawed, and it surely is.

Developing a question's precise wording is not easy. A single word can make a difference in how study participants respond to a question, and there is considerable research to illustrate this. For example in one study, researchers let subjects view a picture of an automobile for a few seconds. Then, they asked a single question, but they changed one word. They asked, "Did you see <u>the</u> broken headlight?" to one group of participants and asked, "Did you see <u>a</u> broken headlight?" to another group. Only the "a" and the "the" were different, yet the question containing the "the" produced more "don't know" and "Yes" answers than did the "a" question.[7] Our point is that as little as a one word in a question can result in question bias that will distort the findings of the survey. Unfortunately, words that we use commonly in speaking to one another sometimes encourage biased answers when they appear on a questionnaire. Table 11.1 lists our "Ten Words to Avoid in Question Development." Again, the point to remember is that while we use these words in everyday language, they can introduce an element of bias into a questionnaire when they are used and respondents are using a literal interpretation in their efforts to answer the questions.

Some words, when taken literally, introduce question bias.

As you can see by reading Table 11.1, it is important that questions do not contain subtle cues, signals, or interpretations that lead respondents to give answers that are inaccurate. Granted, not all respondents will be influenced by question wording, but if a significant minority is affected, this bias can cause the findings to be distorted or mixed, as you saw in our broken headlight study example. You should notice with the "better-wording" questions in Table 11.1 that these do not place respondents in the awkward position of answering to extreme absolutes. The better-wording questions give respondents latitude to respond in degrees (such as how often, how important, etc.) that are more consistent with their actual deliberations or actions than are the extreme-absolute-wording versions.

Four "Do's" of Question Wording

The researcher uses question evaluation to scrutinize a possible question for its question bias.

Question evaluation amounts to scrutinizing the wording of a question to ensure that question bias is minimized and that the question is worded such that respondents understand it and can respond to it with relative ease. As we noted earlier, question bias occurs when the phrasing of a question influences a respondent to answer wrongly or with other than perfect accuracy. Ideally, every question should be examined and tested according to a number of crucial factors known to be related to question bias. To be

TABLE 11.1	Ten Words to Avoid in Question Development: Example in a Survey Performed with Purchasers of Flat Screen TVs	

Word[a]	Poor Wording	Better Wording
✓ All	Did you consider <u>all</u> the options before you decided to purchase your flat screen plasma TV?	What options did you consider when you decided to purchase your flat screen plasma TV?
Always	Do you <u>always</u> buy electronics products from Gateway?	How often do you buy electronics products from Gateway?
✓ Any	Did you have <u>any</u> concerns about the price?	To what extent was the price a concern for you?
✓ Anybody	Did you talk to <u>anybody</u> about flat screen televisions before you made your decision?	Did you talk with someone about flat screen televisions before you made your decision?
✓ Best	What is the <u>best</u> feature on your new flat screen plasma TV?	Please rate the following features of our new flat screen plasma TV on their performance for you using "poor," "fair," "good," or "excellent."
✓ Ever	Have you <u>ever</u> seen a flat screen television?	Have you seen a flat screen television in the past 30 days?
✓ Every	Do you consult *Consumer Reports* <u>every</u> time you purchase a major item?	How often do you consult *Consumer Reports* when you purchase a major item?
Most	What was the <u>most</u> important factor that convinced you it was time to make this purchase?	Please rate the following factors on their importance in convincing you it was time to make this purchase using "unimportant," "slightly important," or "very important."
✓ Never	Would you say that you <u>never</u> think about an extended warranty when making a major electronics purchase?	How often do you consider an extended warranty when making a major electronics purchase?
Worst	Is the high price the <u>worst</u> aspect of purchasing a flat screen plasma TV?	To what extent did the high price concern you when you were considering your purchase of your flat screen plasma TV?

[a]Why avoid these words? The words are *extreme absolutes,* meaning that they place respondents in a situation in which they must either agree or disagree completely with the extreme position in the question.
Source: Adapted and modified from Payne, S. L. (1980). *The Art of Asking Questions,* 2nd ed. Princeton, NJ: Princeton University Press. (First printing, 1951).

sure, question evaluation is a judgement process, but we can offer four simple guidelines, or "Do's," for question wording. We strongly advise that you do ensure that the question is: (1) focused, (2) brief, (3) simple, and (4) crystal clear. A discussion of these four guidelines follows.

▶ **The Question Should Be Focused on a Single Issue or Topic.** The researcher must stay focused on the specific issue or topic.[8] For example, take the question "What type of hotel do you usually stay in when on a trip?" The focus of this question is hazy because it does not narrow down the type of trip or when the hotel is being used. For example, is it a business or a pleasure trip? Is the hotel at a place en route or at the final destination? A more

A question should be focused.

Long and unfocused questions confuse respondents.

focused version is "When you are on a family vacation and stay in a hotel at your destination, what type of hotel do you typically use?" As a second example, consider how "unfocused" the following question is: "When do you typically go to work?" Does this mean when do you leave home for work or when do you actually begin work once at your workplace? A better question would be "At what time do you ordinarily leave home for work?"

A question should be brief.

▶ **The Question Should Be Brief.** Unnecessary and redundant words should always be eliminated. This requirement is especially important when designing questions that will be administered verbally, such as over the telephone. Brevity will help the respondent to comprehend the central question and reduce the distraction of wordiness. Here is a question that suffers from a lack of brevity: "What are the considerations that would come to your mind while you are confronted with the decision to have some type of repair done on the automatic icemaker in your refrigerator assuming that you noticed it was not making ice cubes as well as it did when you first bought it?" A better, brief form would be "If your icemaker was not working right, how would you correct the problem?" One source recommends that in order to be brief, a question be no more than 20 words in length.[9]

A question should be grammatically simple.

▶ **The Question Should Be a Grammatically Simple Sentence If Possible.** A simple sentence is preferred because it has only a single subject and predicate, whereas compound and complex sentences are busy with multiple subjects, predicates, objects, and complements. The more complex the sentence, the greater the potential for respondent error. There are more conditions to remember, and more information to consider simultaneously, so the respondent's attention may wane or he or she may concentrate on only one part of the question. To avoid these problems, the researcher should strive to use only simple sentence structure[10]—even if two separate sentences are necessary to communicate the essence of the question. Take the question, "If you were looking for an automobile that would be used by the head of your household who is primarily responsible for driving your children to and from school, music lessons, and friends' houses, how much would you and your spouse discuss the safety features of one of the cars you took for a test drive?" A simple approach is, "Would you and your spouse discuss the safety features of a new family car?" followed by (if yes), "Would you discuss safety 'very little,' 'some,' 'a good deal,' or 'to a great extent'?"

▶ **The Question Should Be Crystal Clear.**[11,12] Forgive us for stealing a line uttered by actor Tom Cruise in his movie *A Few Good Men*, but it is essential that all respondents "see" the question identically. For example, the question "How many children do you have?" is unclear because it can be interpreted in various ways. One respondent might think of only those children living at home, whereas another might include children from a previous marriage. A better question is "How many children under the age of 18 live with you in your home?" One tactic for clarity is to develop questions that use words that are in respondents' core vocabularies; that is, the general public does not use marketing jargon such as "price point" or "brand equity," so it is best to avoid words that are vague or open to misinterpretation. To develop a crystal clear question, the reseacher may be forced to slightly abuse the previous guideline of simplicity, but with a bit of effort, question clarity can be obtained with an economical number of words.[13] One author has nicely summarized this guideline: "The question should be simple, intelligible, and clear."[14]

A question should be crystal clear.

Question wording is difficult when the reseacher is conducting a survey in a foreign country. Many countries have unique cultures with completely different languages, and creating a questionnaire in the country's language is an exceptionally challenging undertaking.[15] There are, however, some general guidelines for researchers who find themselves engaged in global research projects. You will find these guidelines in Marketing Research Insight 11.1.

MARKETING RESEARCH INSIGHT

GLOBAL APPLICATION

11.1 Guidelines for Developing a Questionnaire in a Foreign Language

What about question wording in global marketing research situations, in which the researcher must create questionnaires that are in diverse languages? How can a manager avoid question bias when he/she does not speak the language of the respondents? For example, a researcher working with Delta Airlines might need to design a survey that has respondents who speak only one of the following languages: English, French, Spanish, Italian, Dutch, German, or Russian. One solution might be to design the questionnaire in some "universal" language, such as English, that many non-native English speakers can read; however, this approach is generally unsatisfactory because there are many opportunities for miscomprehension. Instead, global marketing researchers use the following steps[16] when attempting to do across-the-globe research.

- Create the questionnaire in the researcher's native language (e.g., English).
- Translate the questionnaire into the other language (e.g., German).
- Have independent translators translate it back into the native language (e.g., from German to English) to check that the first translation was accurate.
- Revise the questionnaire based on the "back translation" (into a better German version).
- If an online survey is involved, make sure that the letters and characters (such as Chinese, Japanese, or Arabic) are faithful to the language being used.
- Carefully pretest the revised questionnaire using individuals whose native tongue is the other language (e.g., natives of Germany).

Even with these precautions, there may be translation errors in which idioms or concepts do not translate well from one culture to the other.

Four "Do Not's" of Question Wording

There are four situations in which question bias is practically assured, and it is important that you learn these so you can avoid them or spot them when you are reviewing a questionnaire draft. Specifically, the question should not be (1) leading, (2) loaded, (3) double-barreled, or (4) overstated.

Do not use leading questions that have strong cues on how to answer.

▶ **The Question Should Not Lead the Respondent to a Particular Answer.** A **leading question** is worded or structured in such a way as to give the respondent a strong cue or expectation as how to answer.[17] Therefore, it biases responses. Consider this question: "Don't you see any problems with using your credit card for an online purchase?" The respondent is being led here because the question wording stresses one side (in this case, the negative side) of the issue. Therefore, the question "leads" respondents to the conclusion that there must be some problems, and, therefore, they will likely agree with the question, particularly respondents who have no opinion. Rephrasing the question as "Do you see any problems with using your credit card for an online purchase?" is a much more objective request for the respondent. Here the respondent is free—that is, not led—to respond "yes" or "no." Examine the following questions for other forms of leading questions:

As a Cadillac owner, you are satisfied with your car, aren't you?	This is a leading question because the wording presupposes that all Cadillac owners are satisfied. It places the respondent in a situation in which disagreement is uncomfortable and singles him/her out as an outlier.
Have you heard about the satellite radio system that everyone is talking about?	This is a leading question because it can condition the respondent to answer in a socially desirable manner. In other words, few people would want to admit they are clueless about something "everybody is talking about.[18]"

Do not use loaded questions that have emotional overtones.

▶ **The Question Should Not Have Loaded Wording or Phrasing.** Leading questions are biased in that they direct the respondent to answer in a predetermined way. By contrast, loaded questions are more subtle, yet, they are also biased questions. Identifying this type of bias in a question requires more judgment, because a **loaded question** has buried in its wording elements that make reference to universal beliefs or rules of behavior. It may even apply emotionalism or touch on a person's inner fears. Some researchers refer to a loaded question simply as a "biased question."[19] For example, a company marketing mace for personal use may use the question, "Should people be allowed to protect themselves from harm by using mace as self-defense?" Obviously, most respondents will agree with the need to protect oneself from harm, and self-defense is an acceptable and well-known legal defense. Eliminating the loaded aspect of this question would result in the question "Do you think carrying a mace product is acceptable for someone who believes it is needed?" As you can see, the phrasing of each question should be examined thoroughly to guard against the various sources of question bias error; with the new wording we do not load the question by mentioning protection or self-defense.

Do not use double-barreled questions, which ask two questions at the same time.

▶ **The Question Should Not Be Double-Barreled.** A **double-barreled question** is really two different questions posed as one.[20] With two questions posed together, it is difficult for a respondent to answer either one directly.[21] Consider a question asked of patrons at a restaurant "Were you satisfied with the restaurant's food and service?" How do respondents answer? If they say "yes" does that mean they were satisfied with the food? The service? A combination? The question would be much improved by asking about a single item: one question for food and another question for service. Sometimes double-barreled questions are not as obvious. Look at the following question designed to ask for occupational status:

    ____ Full-time employment
    ____ Full-time student
    ____ Part-time student
    ____ Unemployed
    ____ Retired

How does one who is retired and a full-time student answer the question? An improvement could be made by asking one question about occupational status and another about student status.[22]

▶ **The Question Should Not Use Words That Overstate the Condition.** An **overstated question** is one that places undue emphasis on some aspect of the topic. It uses what might be considered "dramatics" to describe the topic. Avoid using words that overstate conditions. It is better to present the question in a neutral tone rather than in a strong positive or negative tone. Here is an example that might be found in a survey conducted for Ray-Ban sunglasses. An overstated question might ask, "How much do you think you would pay for a pair of sunglasses that will protect your eyes from the sun's harmful ultraviolet rays, which are known to cause blindness?" As you can see, the overstatement concerns the effects of ultraviolet rays, and because of this overstatement, respondents will be compelled to think about how much they would pay for something that can prevent blindness and not about how much they would really pay for the sunglasses. A more toned-down and acceptable question wording would be, "How much would you pay for sunglasses that will protect your eyes from the sun's glare?"

> Do not use overstated questions that use words that overemphasize the case.

To be sure, there are other question wording pitfalls, but if you use common sense in developing questions for your questionnaire, you will probably avoid them. For example, it is nonsensical to ask respondents: about details they don't recall (How many and what brands of aspirin did you see the last time you bought some?); questions that invite guesses (What is the price per gallon of premium gasoline at the Exxon station on the corner?); or to predict their actions in circumstances they cannot fathom (How often would you go out to eat at this new, upscale restaurant that will be built 10 miles from your home?).

Can you identify what is "bad" about a question and correct it? Here are some questions that might appear on a questionnaire. Each one violates one of the "do's" or "do not's" of question wording about which you just read. For each "Bad" question, write in what is bad about it; that is, decide on which "do" or "do not" is violated, and write a bettter version of the question that does not have the error in it.

Active Learning

Bad Version of the Question	What's the Error?	Good Version of the Question
How do you feel about car seats for infants?	_____	_____
When your toddler wants to ride in the car with you when you run errands or pick up your older children at school, practice, or some friend's home, do you use an infant car seat?	_____	_____
If using an infant car seat is not convenient for you, or when you are in a hurry and your toddler is crying, do you still go ahead and use the infant car seat?	_____	_____

(continued)

How much do you think you should
have to pay for an infant car seat
that restrains and protects your
toddler in case someone runs into your
car or you lose control of your car and
run into a light post or some other
object?   _____   _____

Shouldn't concerned parents of toddlers
use infant car seats?   _____   _____

Since infant car seats are proven to be
exceptionally valuable, do you agree that
infant car seats should be used for your
loved ones?   _____   _____

Do you believe that good parents and
responsible citizens use infant car seats?   _____   _____

If you had an accident with your
toddler on board, do you believe an
infant car seat could protect your child
from being maimed?   _____   _____

Seasoned researchers develop a sixth sense about the "Do's" and "Do not's" we have just described; however, because the researcher can become caught up in the research process, slips do occur. This danger explains why many researchers use "experts" to review drafts of their questionnaires. For example, it is common for the questionnaire to be designed by one employee of the research company. Then it is given to another employee who understands questionnaire design for a thorough inspection for question bias. **Face validity**, that is, if the questions "look right," is assessed as well.

QUESTIONNAIRE ORGANIZATION

Now that you have learned about question development, and specifically the guidelines and things to avoid when wording questions, we can turn to the organization of the questionnaire. Normally, the researcher creates questions by taking the research objectives in turn and developing the questions that relate to each objective. In other words, the questions are developed but not arranged on the questionnaire. **Questionnaire organization** is the sequence of statements and questions that make up a questionnaire. Questionnaire organization is an important concern because the questionnaire's appearance and the ease with which respondents complete the questions have the potential to affect the quality of the information that is gathered. Well-organized questionnaires motivate respondents to be conscientious and complete, while poorly organized ones discourage and frustrate respondents and may even cause them to stop answering questions in the middle of the survey. We will describe two critical aspects of questionnaire organization: the introduction and the actual flow of questions in the questionnaire body.

> "Questionnaire organization" refers to the introduction and the actual flow of questions on the questionnaire.

The Introduction

The introduction is very important in questionnaire design. If the introduction is written to accompany a mail survey or online survey, it is normally referred to as a **cover letter**. If the introduction is to be verbally presented to a potential respondent, as in the case of a personal interview, it may be referred to as the "opening comments." Of course, each sur-

A bank may wish to disguise the fact that it is conducting a survey so as to not alert competitors.

vey and its target respondent group are unique, so a researcher cannot use a standardized introduction. In this section, we discuss the five functions to be provided by the introduction. Table 11.2 lists these five functions, and it provides examples of the sentences that you might find in a survey on personal money management software. As you read our descriptions of each function, refer back to the example in Table 11.2 and the brief explanation.

First, it is common courtesy for the interviewer to introduce himself or herself at the beginning of a survey. Note in Table 11.2 that the interviewer has identified himself or herself and the prospective respondent has been made aware that this is a bona fide survey and not a sales pitch. In addition, the sponsor of the survey should be identified.

There are two options with respect to sponsor identity. With an **undisguised survey**, the sponsoring company is identified, but with a **disguised survey**, the sponsor's name is not divulged to respondents. The choice of which approach to take rests with the survey's objectives or with the researcher and client, who agree about whether disclosure of the sponsor's name or true intent can in some way influence respondents' answers. Another reason for disguise is to prevent alerting competitors to the survey.

Second, the general purpose of the survey should be described clearly and simply. In a cover letter, the purpose may be expressed in one or two sentences. Typically, respondents are not informed of the several specific purposes of the survey, as it would be boring and perhaps intimidating to list all the research objectives. Consider a bank having a survey conducted by a marketing research firm. The actual purpose of the survey is to determine the bank's image relative to that of its competitors. However, the research firm need only say, "We are conducting a survey on customers' perceptions of financial institutions in this area." This satisfies the respondent's curiosity and does not divulge the name of the bank.

Third, prospective respondents must be made aware of how and why they were selected. Just a short sentence to answer the respondent's mental question of "Why me?" will suffice. Telling respondents that they were "selected at random" usually is sufficient.

Whether or not to use a disguised survey depends on the survey's objectives, possible undue influence with knowledge of the client, or desire to not alert competitors of the survey.

The introduction should indicate to the respondent how he or she was selected.

TABLE 11.2	The Functions of the Questionnaire Introduction		
Function	**Example**		**Explanation**
Identifies the surveyor/sponsor.	"Hello, my name is ____, and I am a telephone interviewer working with Nationwide Opinion Research Company here in Milwaukee. I am not selling anything."		The sponsor of the survey is divulged, plus the prospective respondent is made aware that this is a bona fide survey and not a sales pitch.
Indicates the purpose of the survey.	"We are conducting a survey on money management software used by individuals."		Informs prospective respondent of the topic and the reason for the call.
Explains how the respondent was selected.	"Your telephone number was generated randomly by a computer."		Notifies prospective respondent how he or she was chosen to be in the survey.
Requests for/provides incentive for participation.	This is an anonymous survey, and I would now like to ask you a few questions about your experiences with money management computer programs. It will only take a few minutes. Is now a good time?"		Asks for prospective respondent's agreement to take part in the survey at this time. (Also, here, notes anonymity to gain cooperation and gives the respondent information on how much time the survey will take.)
Determines if respondent is suitable.	"Do you use Quicken or Microsoft Money?"		Determines whether prospective respondent is qualified to take part in the survey; those who do not use either program will be screened out.

Of course, you should be ethical and tell them the actual method that was used. If their selection was not random, you should inform them as to which method was used.

Fourth, you must ask prospective respondents for their participation in the survey. With a mail survey, the cover letter might end with, "Will you please take 10 minutes to complete the attached questionnaire and mail it back to us in the postage-paid, preaddressed envelope provided?" If you are conducting a personal interview or a telephone interview, you might say something like "I would now like to ask you a few quick questions about your experiences with automotive repair shops. OK?" You should be as brief as possible yet let the respondent know that you are getting ready for him or her to participate by answering questions. This is also the appropriate time to offer an incentive to participate. **Incentives** are offers to do something for the respondent in order to increase the probability that the respondent will participate in the survey. There are various incentives that may be used by the researcher to encourage participation. As consumers have become more resistant to telemarketers and marketing researchers' pleas for information, researchers are reporting they must offer increased incentives. Offering a monetary incentive, a sample of a product, or a copy of study results are examples. Other incentives encourage respondent participation by letting them know the importance of their participation: "You are one of a select few, randomly chosen, to express your views on a new type of automobile tire." Or the topic itself can be highlighted for importance: "It is important that consumers let companies know whether or not they are satisfied."

Other forms of incentives address respondent anxieties concerning privacy. Here again, there are methods that tend to reduce these anxieties and, therefore, increase participation. As you can see in Table 11.2, one method is **anonymity**, in which the respondent is assured that neither the respondent's name nor any identifying designation will be associated with his or her responses. The second method is **confidentiality**,[23] which means that the respondent's name is known by the

Anonymity means the respondent is never identified with the data collected, while **confidentiality** means that the respondent's identity is not to be divulged to a client or any other third party.

researcher, but it is not divulged to a third party, namely, the client. Anonymous surveys are most appropriate in data-collection methods in which the respondent responds directly on the questionnaire. Any self-administered survey qualifies for anonymity as long as the respondent does not indicate his or her identity and provided the questionnaire does not have any covert identification-tracing mechanism. However, when an interviewer is used, appointments and/or callbacks are usually necessary, so there typically is an explicit designation of the respondent's name, address, telephone number, and so forth on the questionnaire. In this case, confidentiality may be required. Often questionnaires have a callback notation area for the interviewer to make notes indicating, for instance, whether the phone is busy, the respondent is not at home, or a time at which to call back when the respondent will be available. In these cases, the respondent will ordinarily be assured of confidentiality, and it is vital that the researcher guard against the loss of that confidentiality.

A fifth function of the introduction is to qualify prospective respondents. Respondents are screened for their appropriateness to take part in the survey. **Screening questions** are used to ferret out respondents who do not meet the qualifications necessary to take part in the research study.[24] Whether you screen respondents depends on the research objectives. If the survey's objective is to determine the factors used by consumers to select an automobile dealer for the purpose of purchasing a new car, you may want to screen out those who have never purchased a new car or those who have not purchased a new car within the past, say, two years by asking, "Have you purchased a new car within the past two years?" For all those who answer "no," the survey is terminated with a polite "Thank you for your time." Some would argue that you should put the screening question early on so as to not waste the time of the researcher or the respondent. This should be considered with each survey. We place screening questions as last in the introduction because we have found it awkward to begin a conversation with a prospective respondent without first taking care of the first four items we just discussed. There is some research indicating that direct screening questions for income and for the respondent the interviewer wants to speak to can result in self-selection in which qualified respondents "dodge" the survey, so it is recommended that the researcher endeavor to use a sample frame that reduces the need for screening questions.[25]

The creation of the introduction should entail just as much care and effort as the development of the questions on the questionnaire. The first words heard or read by the prospective respondent will largely determine whether he or she will take part in the survey. It makes sense, therefore, for the researcher to labor over a cover letter or opening until it has a maximum chance of eliciting the respondent's cooperation to take part in the survey.[26] If the researcher is unsuccessful in persuading prospective respondents to take part in the survey, all of his or her work on the questionnaire itself will have been in vain.[27]

> Screening questions are used to screen out respondents who do not meet the qualifications necessary to take part in the research study.

> If this topic seems familiar to you, it is because it is directly related to our discussion of the "incidence rate" in Chapter 9.

Question Flow

Question flow pertains to the sequencing of questions or blocks of questions, including any instructions, on the questionnaire. Each research objective gives rise to a question or a set of questions. As a result, questions are usually developed on an objective-by-objective basis. However, to facilitate respondents' ease in answering questions, the organization of these sets of questions should follow some understandable logic. A commonly seen sequence of questions found in questionnaires is presented in Table 11.3, and as the table title notes, there should be a logical or common-sense order to questions on a questionnaire. Of course, it should be obvious that an objective is to keep the

> Attention should be given to placing the questions developed into a logical sequence to ease respondent participation.

TABLE 11.3	The Location of Questions on a Questionnaire Is Logical		
Question Type	**Location**	**Examples**	**Rationale**
Screens	First questions asked	"Have you shopped at the Gap in the past month?" "Is this your first visit to this store?"	Used to select the respondent types desired by the researcher to be in the survey
Warm-ups	Immediately after any screens	"How often do you go shopping?" "On what days of the week do you usually shop?"	Easy to answer; shows respondent that survey is easy to complete; generates interest
Transitions (statements and questions)	Prior to major sections of questions or changes in question format	"Now, for the next few questions, I want to ask about your family's TV viewing habits." "Next, I am going to read several statements and, after each, I want you to tell me if you agree or disagree with the statement."	Notifies respondent that the subject or format of the following questions will change
Complicated and difficult-to-answer questions	Middle of the questionnaire; close to the end	"Rate each of the following 10 stores on the friendliness of their salespeople on a scale of 1 to 7." "How likely are you to purchase each of the following items in the next three months?"	Respondent has committed himself or herself to completing the questionnaire; can see (or is told) that there are not many questions left
Classification and demographic questions	Last section	"What is the highest level of education you have attained?"	Questions that are "personal" and possibly offensive are placed at the end of the questionnaire

questionnaire as short as possible, because long questionnaires have a negative effect on the response rate.[28] To begin, as we discussed with regard to the introduction's functions, the first few questions are normally screening questions, which will determine whether the potential respondent qualifies to participate in the survey based on certain selection criteria that the researcher has deemed essential. Of course, not all surveys have screening questions. A survey of the charge account customers for a department store, for example, may not require screening questions. This is true because, in a sense, all potential respondents have already been qualified by virtue of having a charge account with the store.

Once the individual is qualified by the screening questions, the next questions may serve as a "warm-up" function. **Warm-up questions** are simple and easy-to-answer questions that are used to get the respondents' interest[29] and to demonstrate the ease of responding to the research request. Ideally, warm-up questions pertain to the research objectives, but the researcher may opt for a superfluous question that is used to heighten the respondent's interest so that he or she will be more inclined to deal with the harder questions that follow.

Transitions are statements or questions used to let the respondent know that changes in question topic or format are about to happen. A statement such as "Now, I would like to ask you a few questions about your family's TV viewing habits" is an example of a transition statement. Such statements aid in making certain that the respondent understands the line of questioning. Transitions include "skip" questions. A **skip question** is one whose answer affects which question will be answered next. For example, a skip question may be "When you listen to music at home, do you usu-

Warm-up questions are used near the beginning of the survey to get the respondent's interest and demonstrate the ease of responding to the research request.

Transitions are statements made to let the respondent know that changes in question topic or format are forthcoming.

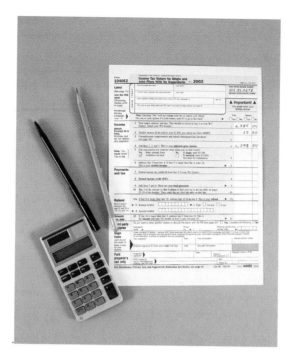

Income is a demographic question customarily placed in the last section of a questionnaire.

ally listen to the radio, use a CD player, or use some other device?" If the person responds that he or she listens to the radio, questions asking the details of CD player listening or, for example, iPod tunes are not appropriate, and the questionnaire will instruct the respondent (or the interviewer, if one is being used) to skip over or to bypass those questions. If the researcher has a great number of transition and skip questions, he can consider making a flow chart of the questions to ensure that there are no errors in the instructions.[30]

As Table 11.3 reveals, it is good practice to "bury" complicated and difficult-to-answer questions deep in the questionnaire. Scaled-response questions such as semantic differential scales, Likert-type response scales, or other questions that require some degree of mental activity such as evaluation, voicing opinions, recalling past experiences, indicating intentions, or responding to "what if" questions are found here. There are at least two reasons for this placement. First, by the time the respondent has arrived at these questions, he or she has answered several relatively easy questions and is now caught up in a responding mode in which he or she feels some sort of commitment. Thus, even though the questions in this section require more mental effort, the respondent will feel more compelled to complete the questionnaire than to break it off. Second, if the questionnaire is self-administered or online, the respondent will see that only a few sections of questions remain to be answered: the end is in sight, so to speak. If the survey is being administered by an interviewer, the questionnaire will typically have prompts included for the interviewer to notify the respondent that the interview is in its last stages. Also, experienced interviewers can sense when respondents' interest levels sag, and they may voice their own prompts, if permitted, to keep the respondent on task.

The last section of a questionnaire is traditionally reserved for classification questions. **Classification questions**, which almost always include demographic questions, are used to classify respondents into various groups for purposes of analysis. For instance, the researcher may want to classify respondents into categories based on age,

The more complicated and difficult-to-answer questions are placed deep in the questionnaire.

Demographics questions, sometimes called classification questions, are used to classify respondents into various groups for purposes of analysis.

gender, income level, and so on. The placement of classification questions such as these at the end of the questionnaire is useful because some respondents will consider certain demographic questions "personal," and they may refuse to give answers to questions about the highest level of education they attained, their age, their income level, or marital status.[31] In these cases, if the respondent refuses to answer, the refusal comes at the very end of the questioning process. If it occurred at the very beginning, the interview would begin with a negative tone, perhaps causing the person to think that the survey will be asking any number of personal questions, and the respondent may very well object to taking part in the survey at that point.[32]

While most researchers agree in principal to these question-flow recommendations, some prefer to think about questionnaire organization somewhat differently; that is, they tend to envision the questionnaire as comprised of areas of elements that can be arranged efficiently and logically while still preserving the basic question-flow suggestions you have just read. Read Marketing Research Insight 11.2 to learn about the three different questionnaire organization alternatives.

Active **Learning**

Below is a table that identifies each of the Hobbit's Choice Restaurant survey research objectives as well as a possible measurement scale to be used with each research objective. Using your newly acquired knowledge of question flow and questionnaire organization (Marketing Research Insight 11.2), for each objective, indicate in the following table where on the questionnaire you recommend to place the question(s) pertaining to that research objective. Jot down your reasoning for your location recommendation as well.

Research Objective and Description	How to Measure?	Location on the Questionnaire and Reason(s) for this Location
Will the restaurant be successful? Will a sufficient number of people patronize the restaurant?	Describe the restaurant concept and intentions to purchase there on a scale.	_____
How should the restaurant be designed? What about décor, atmosphere, specialty entrées and desserts, wait staff uniforms, reservations, special seating, and so on?	Determine respondents' preferences for each of the several possible design features on a preference scale.	_____
What should be the average price of entrées? How much are potential patrons willing to pay for the entrées as well as for the house specials?	Describe standard entrées and example house specials and obtain how much respondents are willing to purchase using price ranges.	_____
What is the optimal location? How far from patrons' homes are patrons willing to drive, and are there any special location features (such as waterfront, ample parking, etc.) to take into consideration?	Determine furthest driving distance respondents are willing to drive to the new restaurant for each location feature.	_____
What is the profile of the target market?	Ask for demographics of the respondents.	_____
What are the best promotional media? What advertising media should be used to best reach the target market?	Determine normal use of various local media such as newspaper, radio, television and obtain specifics such as what newspaper sections are read, what radio programming is listened to, and what local television news times are watched.	_____

11.2 Approaches to Question Organization on a Questionnaire

The flow of questions we have described in this chapter is generally used by questionnaire designers, but there are at least three approaches to questionnaire organization that we can describe: the funnel approach, the work approach, and the sections approach.

The **funnel approach** uses a wide-to-narrow or general-to-specific flow of questions that places inquiries at the beginning of a topic on the questionnaire that are general in nature and those requiring more specific and detailed responses later on[33]; that is, the questionnaire begins (after the screens) with general and easy-to-answer questions and proceeds to more detailed questions deeper into the questionnaire.[34] The most specific questions are personal demographic questions located at the end of the questionnaire.

The **work approach** is used when the researcher realizes that respondents will need to apply different mental effort to groups of questions. When questions tap responses that are deeper than simple recall, respondents must apply a higher degree of concentration in answering them. As we have specified in our recommendations as to question flow on a questionnaire, difficult questions are placed deep in the questionnaire. As a rule, nominal-scale questions are easier to answer than either scaled-response or open-ended questions. Open-ended questions are thought to be the most taxing questions for respondents. In fact, some researchers recommend rarely using open-ended questions or using a minimum of open-ended questions.[35] As we just noted, when the respondent encounters the work questions, he or she should be caught up in the responding mode or otherwise committed to completing the questionnaire. If this is the case, the respondent will be more inclined to expend the extra effort necessary to answer them.

Another organization scheme is to arrange the questions in logical sets on the questionnaire, referred as to the sections approach. A **sections approach** organizes questions into sets based on a common objective of the questions in the set. The sections approach is particularly useful when the researcher has several topics with a set of questions for each topic. By using sections, the researcher has a structure to cover all the topics, and the respondent's focus is concentrated on that topic in the section. For example, several questions may be measuring media habits, others may be measuring frequency of purchasing different products, and other questions may all be measuring preferences for restaurant services and features. Sometimes the research objectives define the sections. Sections could also be based on question format. All Likert questions are placed in one section, for example.

Which approach is best? There is no single questionnaire format that fits all cases. In fact, the three approaches we have just described are not mutually exclusive, and a researcher may use a combination of approaches in a single questionnaire. Also, a researcher may find that the survey topics influence the placement or approach used in question flow.[36] However, while any one or a combination of these approaches may be used, the guiding issue should be which approach best facilitates the answering of questions. Researchers can analyze questions in any sequence they wish; it's the respondents who are important here.

As we indicated earlier, designing a questionnaire is a blend of creativity and adherence to simple, common-sense guidelines. The most important principle to keep in mind, though, is to design the questionnaire's flow of questions so as to make it respondent-friendly[37] by minimizing the amount of effort necessary to respond to it while maximizing the probability that each respondent will fill it out reliably, accurately, and completely.[38] To achieve these results, the researcher selects logical response formats, provides clear directions, makes the questionnaire appearance visually appealing, and numbers all sections plus all items in each section.[39]

COMPUTER-ASSISTED QUESTIONNAIRE DESIGN

(Standardized)

Computer-assisted questionnaire design refers to software programs that allow users to use computer technology to develop and disseminate questionnaires and, in some cases, to retrieve and analyze data gathered by the questionnaire. Several companies have developed computer software that bridges the gap between composing questions on a word processor and generating the final, polished version complete with check boxes, radio buttons, and coded questions. Also, most of these software programs allow users to publish their questionnaires on the Internet and enable respondents to enter data on the Internet. The data are then downloaded and made available for analysis, and practically all of these special-purpose personal computer programs generate data files that can be exported in Excel-readable format, which is a format that the Statistical Package for the Social Sciences (SPSS) can import.

The following paragraphs illustrate how these computer-assisted questionnaire design programs work. First, however, let us point out that there are at least four distinct advantages of computer-assisted questionnaire design software packages: They are easier, faster, friendlier, and provide significant flexibility beyond that available with a traditional word processor. Given this, here are descriptions of the basic functions of a computer-assisted questionnaire design program.

Questionnaire Creation

The typical questionnaire design program will query the user on, for example, the type of question, the number of response categories, whether multiple responses are permitted, if skips are to be used, and how response options will appear on the questionnaire. The survey-creation feature sometimes takes the form of a menu of choices, or it might appear as a sequence of format inquiries for each section of the questionnaire. Usually, the program offers a list of question types such as closed-ended, open-ended, numeric, or scaled-response questions. The program may even have a question library[40] feature that provides "standard" questions on constructs that researchers often measure, such as demographics, importance, satisfaction, performance, or usage. An advanced feature is an ability for the researcher to upload graphics files of various types if these are part of the research objectives. Most computer-assisted questionnaire design programs are quite flexible and allow the user to modify question formats, build blocks or matrices of questions with the identical response format, include an introduction and instructions to specific questions, and to move the location of questions with great ease. Often, the appearance can be modified to the designer's preferences for font, background, color, and more.

Some screen captures from WebSurveyor, with our annotations will show you how this software works. First, in Figure 11.2, you can see that WebSurveyor allows the user to build the questionnaire question-by-question and holds the questions in an easy-to-navigate scrolling menu window. In Figure 11.3 you will see a question editor window feature of WebSurveyor. The user selects a question type (such as select only one, select all that apply, etc.) and the appropriate WebSurveyor question editor window appears. In Figure 11.3, the matrix question format window is visible, and it creates a rating scale repeated for several categories. Here, the researcher has identified a number of features of a pizza delivery company, and each will be rated on its importance to the respondent. When the researcher has the questionnaire at a point at which the final, published version is to be previewed, WebSurveyor lets the user see what the online survey will look like. In Figure 11.4, you can see a "check all that apply" question, a specific numeric value response question, and part of the importance ratings scale question for the pizza delivery survey.

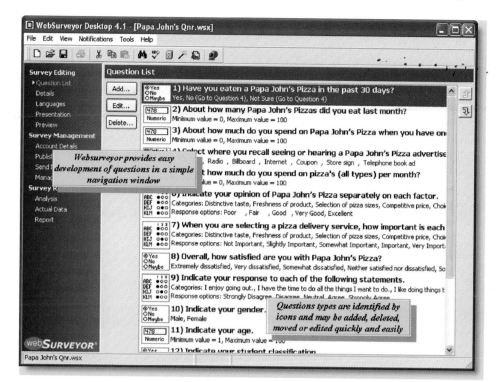

FIGURE 11.2
WebSurveyor Question
Menu Window

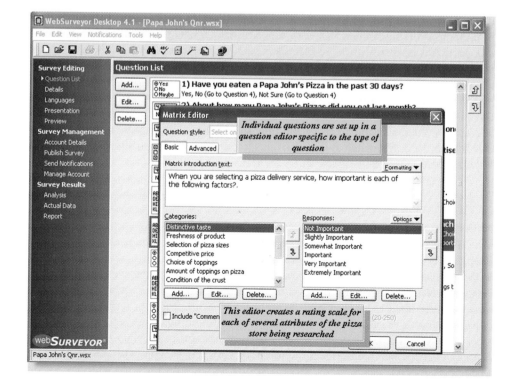

FIGURE 11.3
WebSurveyor Question
Editor Feature

FIGURE 11.4
WebSurveyor Preview
Feature

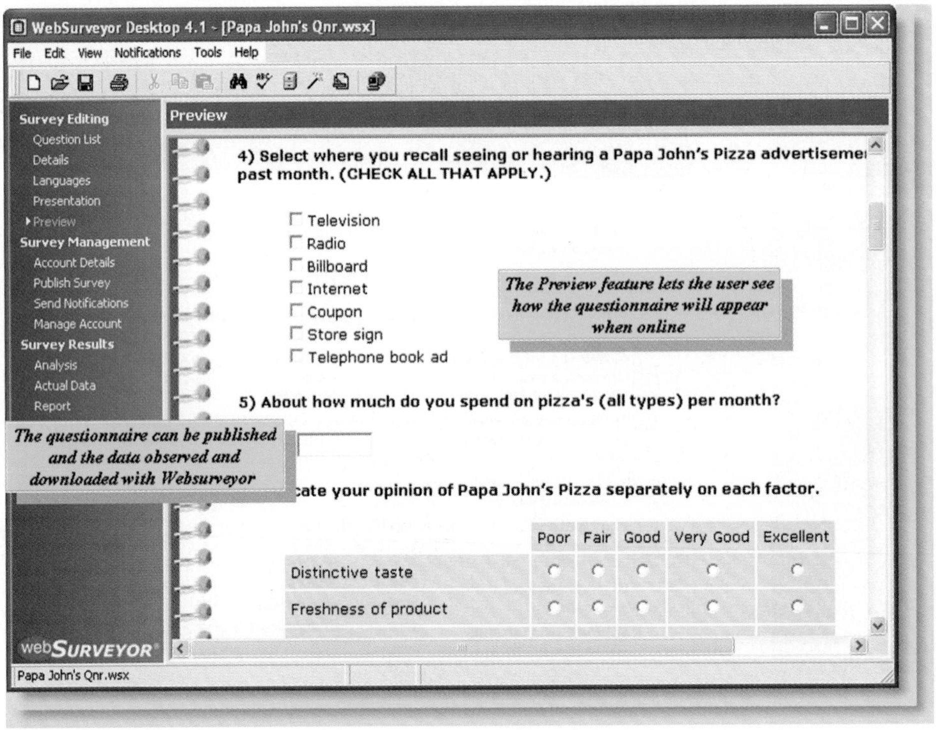

The Preview feature lets the user see how the questionnaire will appear when online

The questionnaire can be published and the data observed and downloaded with Websurveyor

Data Collection and Creation of Data Files

Computer-assisted questionnaire design programs have
question types, question
libraries, real-time data
capture, and downloadable
data sets.

Computer-assisted questionnaire design programs create online survey questionnaires that are published on the Internet via a feature of the program. Once there, the survey is ready for respondents who are alerted to the online survey with whatever communication methods the researcher wishes to use. Normally, a data file is built as respondents take part, that is, in real time. To elaborate, each respondent accesses the online questionnaire, registers responses to the questions, and, typically, clicks on a "Submit" button at the end of the questionnaire. The submit signal prompts the program to write the respondent's answers into a data file, so the data file grows in direct proportion to and at the same rate as respondents submit their surveys. Features, such as requesting an e-mail address, are often available to block multiple submissions by the same respondent. The data file can be downloaded at the researcher's discretion, and, usually, several different formats, including Excel-readable ones, are available.

Data Analysis and Graphs

Many of the software programs for questionnaire design also have provisions for data analysis, graphic presentation, and report formats of results. Some packages offer only simplified graphing capabilities, whereas others offer different statistical analysis options. In fact, it is very useful to researchers to monitor the survey's progress with these features. The graph features vary, and some of these programs enable users to create professional-quality graphs that can be saved and/or embedded in word processor report files.

The advantages of online questionnaires are astounding; however, they should be treated with the precise concerns that researchers have in mind when designing questionnaires for other data-collection methods. In fact, as you will see by reading Marketing Research Insight 11.3, one marketing research professional who has a great

ONLINE APPLICATION

11.3

How to Design a Winning Online Questionnaire by Using Best Practices

Online questionnaires afford immense advantages over questions used with other data-collection methods. The advantages of a tiny percent of the cost of telephone or mail surveys, savings of days and perhaps weeks in questionnaire design and implementation, returns in a matter of days instead of weeks, and the attractiveness of working with computer technology all combine to seduce a marketing researcher into making hasty and costly mistakes. Mr. Lee Smith, president of InsightExpress, an online research firm that has experienced great success in its field, recently listed a number of "best practices" for survey research.[41] As you will see as you read the following list of best practices, a number of them pertain to questionnaire design.

Here are Lee Smith's best practices for surveys that should be adhered to when designing and implementing online surveys:

- Carefully define the research objectives
- Make sure that the online population you will use is consistent with the respondents you wish to survey

- With respect to questionnaire length,
  - ☐ Keep it as short as possible
  - ☐ Start with a question that grabs the respondent's interest
  - ☐ The first questions should be easy to understand and easy to answer
  - ☐ Ask one thing at a time (that is, use focused questions)
  - ☐ Avoid questions that are biased (that is, not leading)
  - ☐ Avoid loaded questions
- Use invitations that gain cooperation
  - ☐ Use personalization, if possible
  - ☐ Remind the potential respondent of any relationship he or she may have with the sponsoring company
  - ☐ Tell the potential respondent why taking the time to answer the survey is worth his or her time
  - ☐ If incentives are to be used, experiment to find the one that gains the highest response rate as a reasonable cost
- Monitor the responses as they come in to ensure that the survey is working as expected, and, if not, make appropriate adjustments quickly

deal of experience with online surveys has written an article to remind marketing researchers that they should still adhere to the "best practices" of survey and questionnaire design when working with online surveys.

CODING THE QUESTIONNAIRE

A final task in questionnaire design is **coding** questions, which is the use of numbers associated with the question responses to facilitate data entry during data collection and data analysis after the survey has been conducted. The logic of coding is simple once you know the ground rules, and we have incorporated the basic rules of questionnaire coding in Table 11.4. The primary objective of coding is to represent each possible response with a unique number because numbers are easier and faster to enter into a computer file. Also, computer tabulation programs are more efficient when they process numbers.

SPSS Student Assistant:
Codes are numbers placed with question responses to facilitate data entry and analysis.

TABLE 11.4	Examples of Codes on the Final Questionnaire

1. Have you purchased a Papa John's pizza in the past month?

_____ Yes (1) _____ No (2) _____ Unsure (3)

2. The last time you bought a Papa John's pizza, did you (check only one):

_____ Have it delivered to your house?   (1)
_____ Have it delivered to your place of work?   (2)
_____ Pick it up yourself?   (3)
_____ Eat it at the pizza parlor?   (4)
_____ Purchase it some other way?   (5)

3. In your opinion, the taste of a Papa John's pizza is (check only one):

_____ Poor (1)
_____ Fair (2)
_____ Good (3)
_____ Very Good (4)
_____ Excellent (5)

4. Which of the following toppings do you typically have on your pizza? (Check all that apply.)

_____ Green pepper (0;1)   (Note: the 0;1 indicates the
_____ Onion (0;1)   coding system that will be used.
_____ Mushroom (0;1)   Typically, no precode such as this
_____ Sausage (0;1)   is placed on the questionnaire. Each
_____ Pepperoni (0;1)   response category must be defined
_____ Hot peppers (0;1)   as a separate question.)
_____ Black olives (0;1)
_____ Anchovies (0;1)

5. How do you rate the speediness of Papa John's delivery service once you have ordered? (Circle the appropriate number.)

Very   Very
Slow   1   2   3   4   5   6   7   Fast

6. Please indicate your age: _____ Years (Note: No precode is used as the respondent will write in a number.)

7. Please indicate your gender.

_____ Male (1) _____ Female (2)

Here are the basic rules for questionnaire coding:

■ Every closed-ended question should have a code number associated with every possible response.
■ Use single-digit code numbers, beginning with "1," incrementing them by 1 and using the logical direction of the response scale.
■ Use the same coding system for questions with identical response options regardless of where these questions are positioned in the questionnaire.
■ Remember that a "check all that apply" question is just a special case of a "yes" or "no" question, so use a "1" ("yes") and "0" ("no") coding system.
■ Whenever possible, set up the coding system before the questionnaire is finalized.

Table 11.4 illustrates code designations for selected questions that exemplify our code system guidelines. As you can see, when words such as "yes" and "no" are used as literal response categories, codes are normally placed alongside each response and in parentheses. For labeled scales, we recommend that the numbers match the direction of the scale. For example, notice in question 3 in Table 11.4, that the codes are 1–5, and they match the Poor–Excellent direction of the scale. If we happened to have a 5-point Likert scale with Strongly Disagree to Strongly Agree response options in our questionnaire the codes would be 1–5. With scaled-response questions in which numbers are used as the response categories, the numbers are already on the questionnaire, so there is no need to use codes for these questions.

As you examine Table 11.4, notice that there is one instance in which coding becomes slightly complicated; but, again, once you learn the basic rules, the coding is fairly easy to understand. Occasionally, a researcher uses an **"all that apply" question** that asks the respondent to select more than one item from a list of possible responses. This is the case in question 4 in Table 11.4. With "all that apply" questions, the standard approach is to have each response category option coded with a 0 or a 1. The designation "0" will be used if the category is not checked, whereas a "1" is used if it is checked by a respondent. It is as though the researcher asked each item in the list with a yes/no response [e.g., Do you usually order green peppers as topping? ____ No (0) ____ Yes (1)], but by listing them and asking "all that apply," the questionnaire is less cluttered and more efficient.

The codes for an "all that apply" question are set up as though each possible response was a "yes" or "no."

As a final comment, we will point out that it is becoming less common for codes to actually appear on the final questionnaire as the marketing research industry moves further into the high-technology side of questionnaire design and administration. There is no need for codes to appear on the questionnaire using computer-assisted questionnaire design programs because the codes are embedded in the software instructions. Still, the researcher must know how to code the responses.

PERFORMING THE PRETEST OF THE QUESTIONNAIRE

Refer back to Figure 11.1, and you will find that before finalizing the questionnaire, one last evaluation should be conducted on the entire questionnaire.[42] Such an evaluation uses a pretest to ensure that the questions will accomplish what is expected of them. A **pretest** involves conducting a dry run of the survey on a small, representative set of respondents in order to reveal questionnaire errors before the survey is launched.[43] It is very important that pretest participants are in fact representative, that is, selected from the target population under study. Before the questions are administered, participants are informed about the pretest, and their cooperation is requested in spotting words, phrases, instructions, question flow, or other aspects of the questionnaire that appear confusing, difficult to understand, or otherwise a problem. Normally, from 5 to 10 respondents are involved in a pretest, and the researcher looks for common problem themes across this group.[44] For example, if only one pretest respondent indicates some concern about a question, the researcher probably would not attempt to modify its wording, but if three mention the same concern, the researcher would be alerted to the need to undertake a revision. Ideally, when making revisions, researchers should place themselves in the respondent's shoes and ask the following questions: "Is the meaning of the question clear?" "Are the instructions understandable?" "Are the terms precise?" and "Are there any loaded

A pretest is a dry run of a questionnaire to find and repair difficulties that respondents encounter while taking the survey.

SPSS Student Assistant:
Your SPSS Data Sets Supplied
by Burns and Bush

or charged words?"[45] However, because researchers can never completely replicate the respondent's perspective, a pretest is extremely valuable.[46]

SUMMARY

This chapter described questionnaire design and some of the activities that are involved in the questionnaire design process. We noted that questionnaires serve several functions. We also advocated that the designer follow a step-by-step development process that begins with question development and includes question evaluation, client approval, and a pretest to ensure that the questions and instructions are understandable to respondents. Certain words should be avoided in question wording, and we provided our "top 10" words that you should definitely avoid because these words are absolute extremes that force respondents to totally agree or totally disagree with the question. The objective of question development is to create questions that minimize question bias, and the four "do's" in question development stress that the ideal question is focused, simple, brief, and crystal clear. Question bias is most likely to occur when question wording is leading, loaded, double-barreled, or overstated.

The organization of questions on the questionnaire is critical, including the first statements, or introduction to the survey. The introduction should: identify the sponsor of the survey, relate its purpose, explain how the respondent was selected, solicit the individual's cooperation to take part, and, if appropriate, qualify him or her for taking part in the survey. We next provided general guidelines on the flow of questions on the questionnaire and pointed out the location and roles of screens, warm-ups, transitions, "difficult" questions, and classification questions. The chapter also introduced you to the notion of coding or placing the codes to be put in the computer data file on the questionnaire itself. In addition, we described WebSurveyor, a software system that performs questionnaire design, and the chapter briefly described the features of these programs. Finally, you learned the function of and details for pretesting a questionnaire.

KEY TERMS

Questionnarie (p. 300)
Questionnaire design (p. 300)
Question bias (p. 300)
Question development (p. 302)
Question evaluation (p. 302)
Leading question (p. 306)
Loaded question (p. 306)
Double-barreled question (p. 306)
Overstated question (p. 307)
Face validity (p. 308)
Questionnaire organization (p. 308)
Cover letter (p. 308)
Undisguised survey (p. 309)

Disguised survey (p. 309)
Incentives (p. 310)
Anonymity (p. 310)
Confidentiality (p. 310)
Screening questions (p. 311)
Question flow (p. 311)
Warm-up questions (p. 312)
Transitions (p. 312)
Skip question (p. 312)
Classification questions (p. 313)
Funnel approach (p. 315)
Work approach (p. 315)
Sections approach (p. 315)

REVIEW QUESTIONS/APPLICATIONS

1. What is a questionnaire, and what are the functions of a questionnaire?
2. What is meant by saying that questionnaire design is a systematic process?
3. What is meant by "question bias"? Write two biased questions using some of the words to avoid described in Table 11.1. Rewrite each question without using the problem word.
4. What are the four guidelines, or "Do's," for question wording?
5. What are the four "Do Not's" for question wording? Describe each Do Not.
6. What is the purpose of a questionnaire introduction, and what things should it accomplish?
7. Distinguish anonymity from confidentiality.
8. Indicate the functions of (a) screening questions, (b) warm-ups, (c) transitions, (d) "skip" questions, and (e) classification questions.
9. List at least three features of computer-assisted questionnaire design programs that make them more advantageous to a questionnaire designer than the use of a word processor program.
10. What is coding, and why is it used? Relate the special coding need with "all that apply" questions.
11. What is the purpose of a pretest of the questionnaire, and how does a reseacher go about conducting a pretest?
12. Listed here are five different aspects of a questionnaire to be designed for the crafts guild of Maui, Hawaii. It is to be administered by personal interviewers who will intercept tourists as they are waiting at the Maui Airport in the seating areas of their departing flight gates. Indicate a logical question flow on the questionnaire using the guidelines in Table 11.3.
    a. Determine how they selected Maui as a destination.
    b. Discover what places they visited in Maui and how much they liked each one.
    c. Describe what crafts they purchased, where they purchased them, when they bought them, how much they paid, who made the selection, and why they bought those particular items.
    d. Specify how long they stayed and where they stayed while on Maui.
    e. Provide a demographic profile of each tourist interviewed.
13. The Marketing Club at your university is thinking about undertaking a money-making project. Coeds will be invited to compete and 12 will be selected to be in the "Girls of [insert your school] University" calendar. All photographs will be taken by a professional photographer and tastefully done. Some club members are concerned about the reactions of other students who might think that the calendar will degrade women. Taking each of the "Do Not's" of question wording, write a question that would tend to bias answers such that that the responses would tend to support the view that such a calendar would be degrading. Indicate how the question is in error, and provide a better version.
14. Using the Internet, find a downloadable trial version of a computer-assisted questionnaire design program such as WebSurveyor and become familiar with it. With

each of the following possible features of computer-assisted questionnaire design programs, briefly relate the specifics of how the program you have chosen provides the feature.

a. Question type options
b. Question library
c. Font and appearance
d. Web uploading (sometimes called "publishing")
e. Analysis, including graphics
f. Download file format options

15. Panther Martin invents and markets various types of fishing lures. In an effort to survey the reactions of potential buyers, it hires a research company to intercept fishermen at boat launches, secure their cooperation to use a Panther Martin lure under development sometime during their fishing trip that day, meet them when they return, and verbally administer questions to them. As an incentive, each respondent will receive three lures to try that day, and five more will be given to each fisherman who answers the questions at the end of the fishing trip.

   What opening comments should be verbalized when approaching fishermen who are launching their boats? Draft a script to be used when asking these fishermen to take part in the survey.

MOE'S WRAPS & SUBS

Moe's is a submarine sandwich shop that also offers wraps, which are sandwiches made with a tortilla rather than bread. There are seven Moe's units located in the greater metropolitan area, and Moe is thinking about setting up a franchise system to go "big time" with nationwide coverage. A business associate recommends that Moe first conduct a baseline survey of his seven units to better understand his customers and to spot any weaknesses that he might not be aware of. Moe meets with Bob Watts of Superior Research, Inc., and together they agree on the following research objectives. Also, Bob has convinced Moe that a telephone survey of the greater metropolitan area is the best choice.

Research Objectives for Moe's Wraps & Sub's Survey

1. How often do people purchase a meal at Moe's?
2. About how much do they spend there per visit (per individual).
3. Overall, how satisfied are they with Moe's?
 4. How do they rate Moe's Wraps & Subs' performance on the following various aspects?
   a. Competitive price
   b. Convenience of locations
   c. Variety of sandwiches
   d. Freshness of sandwich fillings
   e. Speed of service
   f. Taste of subs

   g. Taste of wraps

   h. Uniqueness of sandwiches

5. What recent advertising do they recall, and/or where do they recall noticing advertising? (Moe's uses the following advertising: Yellow Pages, billboards, newspaper ads, and coupons.)

6. Obtain a demographic profile of the sample.

Design a questionnaire for the Moe's Wraps & Subs survey that will be performed by Superior Research under Bob Watt's direction.

PARK PLACE PSYCHIATRIC HOSPITAL

Park Place Psychiatric Hospital opened last year in Tucson, Arizona. It specializes in psychiatric care and mental health services. Both inpatient and outpatient services are provided, although the hospital is quite small and can accommodate only up to 40 inpatients at any one time. The location of the hospital is in the desert, approximately 20 miles from downtown Tucson and from 10 to 30 miles away from the upscale subdivisions that are its target market. It has invested in an extensive advertising campaign using billboards, newspaper, Yellow Pages, radio spots, and a Web site. By the end of its first year of operation, Park Place has experienced only 45 percent occupancy, but it is optimistic about the future.

The management of Park Place has decided that in order to grow, it must reach out to its patient population in Tucson by being more aggressive in its program offerings. Among the services being considered is a series of seminars on selected mental health care problems and a set of companion programs that will cover the various topics more extensively. The marketing manager contacts a local research company and works with some of its personnel to formulate a list of research objectives. These objectives address his concerns about the effectiveness of the marketing program, the hospital's location situation, the decision-making process for a family member who detects another family member having a problem, and an interest in various programs and seminars. The hospital management also desires to know where Tucson residents will turn to for help when a family member exhibits symptoms of minor or major mental health problems. These research objectives are specified as follows:

■ To determine the level of interest in participating in each of the following one-time, two-hour evening group seminars to take place at the Park Place Hospital location that cost $50 each: stop smoking, weight control, stress management, substance abuse, Alzheimer's disease, understanding anxiety, and coping with teenagers.

■ To assess the degree of interest in enrolling in any two-month-long group programs previously listed (stop smoking, weight control, etc.) that cost $750 each. The programs involve two 2-hour sessions per week for 8 weeks that take place at the Park Place Hospital.

■ To evaluate where a person or family would be likely to seek help if a minor mental health problem possibly requiring professional counseling were evident with some family member (a minor mental health problem would be depression, stress, lethargy, sleeping problems, anger, or some other problem that renders the person undependable, erratic, or disoriented). The possible places to seek assistance include a religious counselor such as a minister or pastor, knowledgeable friends and acquaintances, a family lawyer, a family doctor, a psychiatric care facility, a psychologist, a social worker, local police, or some other form of assistance.

- To evaluate where a person or family would be likely to seek help if a major mental health problem possibly requiring professional counseling were evident with some family member (a major mental health problem would be severe depression, violence, bizarre behavior, self-abuse, or some other problem such that the person's well-being is in danger and/or he or she may harm others). The possible places to seek assistance include: a religious counselor such as a minister or pastor, knowledgeable friends and acquaintances, a family lawyer, a family doctor, a psychiatric care facility, a psychologist, a social worker, local police, or some other form of assistance.
- To determine if prospective clients recall recent advertising for Park Place Psychiatric Hospital, and if so, in which advertising medium.
- To evaluate the importance of location in the selection of a mental health care facility for a family member, either as an inpatient or an outpatient.
- To determine how Park Place Psychiatric Hospital's location is perceived.
- To obtain target market information.

Random telephone calls will be used to select prospective respondent households from the upscale neighborhoods that Park Place Psychiatric Hospital has identified as its target market.

1. Design a questionnaire suited for a telephone survey of 500 Tucson households to be conducted with the "adult head of the household who is responsible for the family's health care."

2. Justify your choice of the type of question response format for each question. If you have used the same format for a group of related questions, you should indicate your rationale for the group rather than for each question in the group.

3. Identify the organization aspects of your questionnaire. Identify the question flow approach you have used and indicate why; that is, identify all screening questions, warm-ups, transition questions, and skip questions that you have used.

THE HOBBIT'S CHOICE RESTAURANT

(Note: This case requires that you have read Case 4.2, The Hobbit's Choice Restaurant.)
Cory Rogers now feels he has a good grasp of the research objectives needed in order to conduct the research study for Jeff Dean. He sits down and starts working on the questionnaire that he will need. He knows he will need to write a cover letter and he knows he needs a screening question. Would everyone's opinion be useful? "Certainly not," he thinks. Why would we want the opinion of persons who rarely eat out in restaurants? Cory then turns to the other issues he knows he needs to address. He knows he needs input for the forecasting model, so several questions will

need to be designed to deal with demand assessment. Also, he needs several questions dealing with the design and operating characteristics questions as well as the advertising placement decisions. Finally, Cory knows he will have to address the location issue.

1. Carefully go over Case 4.2 and design a questionnaire for The Hobbit's Choice Restaurant.

12

Determining How to Select the Sample

I'm Sorry, I Have Hiccups, but I Do Speak English

Hotels in Switzerland are a very strange mix because of the makeup of the country. First, there is the fact that there are at least three distinct language districts in Switzerland, and depending on which district the hotel is located in, its customer service personnel will speak French, German, or Italian, and they may or may not understand English. Next, Swiss hotels differ markedly depending on their geographic location. There are hotels in the Alps mountains, hotels in the lakes region, hotels in major cities, and hotels sprinkled around the Swiss countryside. Last, and as everywhere else in the world, Swiss hotels vary by service category: from 1 to 5 stars, with 5-star hotels occupying the deluxe level and 1-star hotels of the budget variety. There is good reason to believe that while all Swiss hotels provide accommodations for travelers, there are differences in their service quality levels as a function of the English abilities of hotel personnel, location, and star rating.

In a study to determine the responsiveness of Swiss hotels, researchers from the Swiss Lausanne Institute for Hospitality Research decided to send a mock e-mail enquiry to a sample of Swiss hotels to test for differences in the responsiveness of the hotels.[1] Early on in the survey, the researchers wrestled with the problem of drawing a sample. They determined that 5700 hotels are located in Switzerland, but they could not find a database or listing for these hotels. They did, however, find that the Swiss Hotel Administration (SHA) had a listing of 2058 Swiss hotels; although, it did not have a faithful listing of the

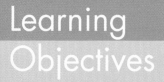

Research was used to assess the responsiveness of Swiss hotels to foreign tourists' inquiries.

budget-level hotels. Using the SWA database and taking into consideration both the language region and the star category rating of the hotels, the researchers selected what is called a "stratified" sample of 200 hotels for their study. In a nutshell, a stratified sample recognizes that there are different groups (e.g., linguistic identification) and draws subsamples from each identified group. Of course, in this study the groupings were both linguistic and star service level (1–2 stars, 3 stars, and 4–5 stars), meaning that there were nine distinct groups, called strata.

The researchers sent a mock request to each of the sampled hotels. The mock request, sent in English, inquired about the availability of special room rates for a family of four on a coming holiday weekend, and it asked about hotel services. About 25 percent of the hotels did not respond, and the researchers determined that "hiccups" were at fault, meaning Internet crashes or other response system failures were largely at fault in these cases. For those hotels who responded, the researchers found no significant differences by star category, language, hotel size, or location; however, hotels with more Web site relationship management response tools did have a better response rate. The quality of the response—measured as the use of formality—was greatly affected by hotel factors; that is, small hotels tended to answer with informal language and failed to identify the hotel sender or even the hotel's name more than larger hotels. High service rated hotels were more formal, and German-speaking hotels were more formal and more complete in their replies, as were hotels with more Web site relationship management response tools.

I nternational markets are measured in hundreds of millions of people, national markets comprise millions of individuals, and even local markets may constitute hundreds of thousands of households. To obtain information from every single person in a market is usually impossible and obviously impractical. For these reasons, marketing researchers make use of a sample. This chapter describes how researchers go about taking samples. As can be seen in our Swiss hotels example above, the sampling procedure sometimes must explicitly take into account and make provisions for the peculiarities of the whole group, or population, under study. We begin with definitions of basic concepts such as population, sample, and census. Then we discuss the reasons for taking samples. From here, we distinguish the four types of probability sampling methods from the four types of nonprobability sampling methods. Because online surveys are becoming popular, we discuss sampling aspects of these surveys. Last, we present a step-by-step procedure for taking a sample, regardless of the sampling method used.

BASIC CONCEPTS IN SAMPLES AND SAMPLING

To begin, we acquaint you with some basic terminology used in sampling. The terms we discuss here are *population, sample, sample unit, census, sampling error, sample frame,* and *sample frame error.*

Population

A **population** is defined as the entire group under study as specified by the objectives of the research project. Managers tend to have a less specific definition of the population than do researchers. This is because the researcher must use the description of the population very precisely, whereas the manager uses it in a more general way.

For instance, let us examine this difference for a research project performed for Terminix Pest Control. If Terminix were interested in determining how prospective customers were combating roaches, ants, spiders, and other insects in their homes, the Terminix manager would probably define the population as "everybody who might use our services." However, the researcher in charge of sample design would use a definition such as "heads of households in the metropolitan areas served by Terminix who are responsible for insect pest control." Notice that the researcher has converted "everybody" to "households" and has indicated more precisely who the respondents will be, in the form of "heads of households." The definition is also made more specific by the requirement that the household be in a metropolitan Terminix service area. Just as problem definition error can be devastating to a survey so can population definition error, because a survey's findings are applicable only to the population from which the survey sample is drawn. For example, if the Terminix population is "everybody who might use our services," it would include industrial, institutional, and business users as well as households. If a large national chain such as Hilton Hotels or Olive Garden Restaurants were included in the survey, then the findings could not be representative of households alone.

Sample and Sample Unit

A **sample** is a subset of the population that suitably represents that entire group.[2] Once again, there is a difference in how the manager uses this term versus how it is used by the researcher. The manager will often overlook the "suitably" aspect of this definition and assume that any sample is a representative sample. However, the researcher is trained in detecting sample errors and is very careful in assessing the degree of representativeness of the subgroup selected to be the sample.

As you would expect, a **sample unit** is the basic level of investigation; that is, in the Terminix example, the unit is a household. For a Weight Watchers survey, the unit would be one person, but for a survey of hospital purchases of laser surgery equipment, the sample unit would be the hospital purchasing agents because hospital purchases are being researched.

Census

Although a sample is a subset of a group, a **census** is defined as an accounting of the complete population. Perhaps the best example of a census is the U.S. census taken every 10 years by the U.S. Census Bureau (**www.census.gov**). The target population in the case of

---

The population is the entire group under study as defined by research objectives.

The sample is a subset of the population, and the sample unit pertains to the basic level of investigation.

A census requires information from everyone in the population.

the U.S. census is all households in the United States. In truth, this definition of the population constitutes an "ideal" census, for it is virtually impossible to obtain information from every single household in the United States. At best, the Census Bureau can reach only a certain percentage of households, obtaining a census that provides information within the time period of the census-taking activity. Even with a public-awareness promotional campaign budget of several hundred thousand dollars that covered all of the major advertising media forms such as television, newspaper, and radio, and an elaborate follow-up procedure method, the Census Bureau admits that its numbers are inaccurate.[3] The difficulties encountered by U.S. census takers are identical to those encountered in marketing research. For example, there are instances of individuals who are in transition between residences, without places of residence, illiterate, incapacitated, illegally residing in the United States, or unwilling to participate. Marketing researchers undertaking survey research face all of these problems and a host of others. In fact, researchers long ago realized the impracticality and outright impossibility of taking a census of a population. Consequently, they turned to the use of subsets, or samples, which were chosen to represent the target population.

Sampling Error

Sampling error is any error in a survey that occurs because a sample is used. Sampling error is caused by two factors: (1) the method of sample selection and (2) the size of the sample. You will learn in this chapter that some sampling methods minimize this error, whereas others do not control it well at all. Also, in the next chapter, we show you the relationship between sample size and sampling error.

Whenever a sample is taken, the survey will reflect sampling error.

Sample Frame and Sample Frame Error

To select a sample, you will need a **sample frame**, which is some master list of all the sample units in the population. For instance, if a researcher had defined a population to be all shoe repair stores in the state of Texas, he or she would need a master listing of these stores as a frame from which to sample. Similarly, if the population being researched were certified public accountants (CPAs), a sample frame for this group would be needed. In the case of shoe repair stores, a list service such as American Business Lists of Omaha, Nebraska, which has compiled its list of shoe repair stores from Yellow Pages listings, might be used. For CPAs, the researcher could use the list of members of the American Institute of Certified Public Accountants, located in New York City, which contains a listing of all accountants who have passed the CPA exam. Sometimes the researcher cannot find a list, and the sample frame becomes a matter of whatever access to the population the researcher can conceive of, such as "all shoppers who purchase at least $50 worth of merchandise at a Radio Shack store during the second week of March." Here, because some shoppers pay by credit card, some by check, and some with cash, there is no physical master list of qualified shoppers, but there is a stream of shoppers that can be sampled.

A sample frame is a master list of the entire population.

A sample frame invariably contains **sample frame error**, which is the degree to which the sample frame fails to account for all of the population. A way to envision sample frame error is by matching the list with the population and seeing to what degree the list adequately matches the targeted population. What do you think is the sample frame in our shoe repair store sample? The primary error involved lies in using only Yellow Pages listings. Not all shops are listed in the Yellow Pages, as some have gone out of business, some have come into being since the publication of the Yellow Pages, and some may not be listed at all. The same type of error exists for CPAs, and the researcher would have to determine how current the list is that he or she is using.[4]

A listing of the population may be inaccurate and thus contain sample frame error.

Whenever a sample is drawn, the amount of potential sample frame error should be judged by the researcher.[5] Sometimes the only available sample frame contains much potential sample frame error, but it is used due to the lack of any other sample frame. It is a researcher's responsibility to seek out a sample frame with the least amount of error at a reasonable cost. The researcher should also apprise the client of the degree of sample frame error involved.

REASONS FOR TAKING A SAMPLE

Taking a sample is less expensive than taking a census.

There are two general reasons a sample is almost always more desirable than a census. First, there are practical considerations such as cost and population size that make a sample more desirable than a census. Taking a census is expensive, as consumer populations may number in the millions. Even if the population is restricted to a medium-sized metropolitan area, hundreds of thousands of individuals can be involved. Even when using a mail survey, accessing the members of a large population is cost prohibitive.

Second, typical research firms or the typical researcher cannot analyze the huge amounts of data generated by a census. Although computer statistical programs can handle thousands of observations with ease, they slow down appreciably with tens of thousands, and most are unable to accommodate hundreds of thousands of observations. In fact, even before a researcher considers the size of the computer or tabulation equipment to be used, he or she must consider the various data preparation procedures involved in just handling the questionnaires or responses and transferring these responses into computer files. The sheer physical volume places limitations on the researcher's staff and equipment.

Defending the use of samples from a different tack, we can turn to an informal cost–benefit analysis to defend the use of samples. If the project director of our Terminix household survey had chosen a sample of 500 households at a cost of $10,000 and had determined that 20 percent of those surveyed "would consider" switching to Terminix from their current pest control provider, what would be the result if a completely different sample of the same size were selected in identical fashion to determine the same characteristic? For example, suppose the second sample resulted in an estimate of 22 percent. The project would cost $10,000 more, but what has been gained with the second sample? Common sense suggests that very little in the form of additional information has been gained, for if the project director combined the two samples he or she would come up with an estimate of 21 percent. In effect, $10,000 more has been spent to gain 1 percent more of information. It is extremely doubtful that this additional precision offsets the additional cost.

PROBABILITY VERSUS NONPROBABILITY SAMPLING METHODS

With probability sampling, the chances of selection are "known," but with nonprobability sampling, they are not.

In the final analysis, all sample designs fall into one of two categories: probability or nonprobability. **Probability samples** are samples in which members of the population have a known chance (probability) of being selected into the sample. **Nonprobability samples**, on the other hand, are samples in which the chances (probability) of selecting members from the population into the sample are unknown. Unfortunately, the terms "known" and "unknown" are misleading for, in order to calculate a precise probability, one would need to know the exact size of the population, and it is impossible to know the exact size of the population in most marketing research studies. If we were targeting, for example, readers of the magazine *People*, the exact size of the population changes from week to week as a result of new subscriptions, old ones running out, and fluctuations in counter sales as a function of whose picture is on the cover. You would be hard-pressed, in fact, to think of cases in which the population size is known and stable enough to be associated with an exact number.

The essence of a "known" probability rests in the sampling method rather than in knowing the exact size of the population. Probability sampling methods are those that ensure that, if the exact size of the population were known for the moment in time that sampling took place, the probability of any member of the population being selected into the sample could be calculated. In other words, this probability value is never calculated in actuality, but we are assured by the sample method that the chances of any one population member being selected into the sample could be computed.

With nonprobability methods there is no way to determine the probability even if the population size is known because the selection technique is subjective. As one author has described the difference, nonprobability sampling uses human intervention whereas probability sampling does not.[6] The following descriptions will teach you that it is the sampling method that determines probability or nonprobability sampling.

> **With probability sampling, the method determines the chances of a sample unit being selected into the sample.**

Probability Sampling Methods

There are four probability sampling methods: simple random sampling, systematic sampling, cluster sampling, and stratified sampling (Table 12.1). A discussion of each method follows.

▶ **Simple Random Sampling** With **simple random sampling**, the probability of being selected into the sample is equal for all members of the population. This sampling technique is expressed by the following formula:

Formula for Sample-Selection Probability   Probability of selection = sample size/population size

> **With simple random sampling, the probability of selection into the sample is "known" for all members of the population.**

So, with simple random sampling, if the researcher was surveying a population of 100,000 recent buyers of high-definition TVs (HDTVs) buyers with a sample size of 1000 respondents, the probability of selection for any single population member into this sample would be 1000 divided by 100,000, or 1 out of 100, calculated to be 1 percent.

There are a number of examples of simple random sampling, including the "blind draw" method and the random numbers method.

The Blind Draw Method. The **blind draw method** involves blindly choosing participants by their names or some other unique designation. For example, suppose that you wanted to determine the attitudes of students in your marketing research class toward a career in marketing research. Assume that the particular class that you have chosen as your population has 30 students enrolled. To do a blind draw, you first write the name of every student on a 3-by-5 index card, then take all of these cards and put them inside a container of some sort. Next, you place a top on the container and shake it very vigorously. This procedure ensures that the names are thoroughly mixed. You then ask some person to draw the sample. This individual is blindfolded so that he or she cannot see inside the container. You would instruct him or her to take out 10 cards as the sample. (For now, let us just concentrate on sample-selection methods. We cover sample size determination in the next chapter.) In this sample, every student in the class has an equal chance of being selected, with a probability of 10/30 or 33 percent, or 1-out-of-3 chance of being selected into that

> **The "blind draw" is a form of simple random sampling.**

TABLE 12.1	Four Different Probability Sampling Methods

Simple Random Sampling

The researcher uses a table of random numbers, random digit dialing, or some other random selection procedure that guarantees that each member of the population in the sample frame has an identical chance of being selected into the sample.

Systematic Sampling

Using a sample frame that lists members of the population, the researcher selects a random starting point for the first sample member. A constant "skip interval," calculated by dividing the number of population members in the sample frame by the sample size, is then used to select every other sample member from the sample frame. A skip interval must be used such that the entire list is covered, regardless of the starting point. This procedure accomplishes the same end as simple random sampling, and it is more efficient.

Cluster Sampling

The sample frame is divided into groups called "clusters," each of which must be considered to be very similar to the others. The researcher can then randomly select a few clusters and perform a census of each one. Alternatively, the researcher can randomly select more clusters and take samples from each one. This method is desirable when highly similar clusters can be easily identified.

Stratified Sampling

If the population is believed to have a skewed distribution for one or more of its distinguishing factors (e.g., income or product ownership), the researcher identifies subpopulations in the sample frame called "strata." A simple random sample is then taken of each stratum. Weighting procedures may be applied to estimate population values such as the mean. This approach is better suited than other probability sampling methods for populations that are not distributed in a bell-shaped pattern.

Games of chance such as this wheel are based on random numbers which underlie random sampling as well.

sample. Of course, you could use ID numbers or some other designation for each population member as long as there were no duplicates. Examples of the blind draw method with which you are familiar are: lottery numbers selected by numbered ping pong balls, a roulette wheel in a casino, and being dealt a hand in a poker game. In every case, every member of the population has the same probability of being selected.

Random Numbers Method. A more sophisticated application of simple random sampling is to use a computer-generated number based on the concept of **random numbers**, which are numbers whose random nature is assured; that is, computer programs have the ability to generate numbers without any systematic sequence to the numbers whatsoever: that is, they are random.

A random number embodies simple random sampling assumptions.

To use the random number method to draw the sample in your careers in marketing research study, assign each student in the class a number, say 1 through 30. Granted, we will select only 10 students, but every member of our population must be uniquely identified before we begin the selection process. Or you might use social security numbers because these are unique to each person. If each student is given a number from 1 to 30, it is a simple matter to use a computer program such as Microsoft Excel or SPSS to generate random numbers to draw the sample.

Marketing Research Insight 12.1 shows the steps involved in using random numbers generated by a spreadsheet program to select students from this 30-member

---

MARKETING RESEARCH INSIGHT

PRACTICAL APPLICATION

12.1

How to Use Random Numbers to Select a Simple Random Sample

STEP 1: Assign all members of the population a unique number.

NAME	NUMBER
Adams, Bob	1
Baker, Carol	2
Brown, Fred	3
Chester, Harold	4
Downs, Jane	5
. . .	↓
Zimwitz, Roland	30

STEP 2: Generate random numbers in the range of 1 to N (30 in this case) by using the random number function in a spreadsheet program such as Microsoft Excel.[7] Typically, such random number

functions generate numbers from 0.0 to 1.0, so if you multiply the random number by N and format the result as an integer, you will have random numbers in the range of 1 to N. The following set of random numbers was generated this way.

23 12 8 4 22 17 6 23 14 2 13

Select the first random number and find the corresponding population member.

In the following example, number 23 is the first random number.

STEP 3: Select the person corresponding to that number into the sample: #23—Stepford, Ann

STEP 4: Continue to the next random number and select that person into the sample: #12—Fitzwilliam, Roland

STEP 5: Continue in the same manner until the full sample is selected. If you encounter a number selected earlier, such as the 23 that occurs at the eighth random number, simply skip over it because you have already selected that population member into the sample. (This explains why eleven numbers were drawn.)

population. Beginning with the first generated random number, you would progress through the set of random numbers to select members of the population into the sample. If you encounter the same number twice within the same sample draw, the number is skipped over, because it is improper to collect information twice from the same person.

Active Learning

ARE RANDOM NUMBERS REALLY RANDOM?

Some people do not believe that random numbers are actually random. These individuals sometimes point out that certain numbers seem to repeat more frequently than other numbers in lotteries, or they claim that they have a "favorite" or "lucky" number that wins for them when gambling or taking a chance of some sort. You can test the randomness of random numbers by creating an Excel spread sheet and using its random number function. Use the following steps to perform this test.

1. Open Excel and place numbers 1–100 in cells A2–A101 with 1 in A2, 2 in A3, etc.

2. Place numbers 1–100 in cells C1–CX1, respectively.

3. Next, In cells C3–CX101, enter the Excel function =INT(RAND()*100)+1 (*Note:* you can enter this formula into cell C3, then copy it and paste the copy into cells C3–CX101. You should see numbers that are whole integers ranging from 1 to 100 in cells C2–CX101.

4. Next in cell B2, enter in =COUNTIF(C2:CX2,A2). Copy this formula and paste it into cells B2–B101. You will now see integers such as 0, 1, 2, 3, etc in column B2–B101.

5. Finally, in cell B102, enter in the formula =AVERAGE(B2:B101). Format Cell B102 to be a number with 1 decimal place.

6. Cell B102 is the average number of times that the number in Column A2–A101 appears in the corresponding row, meaning row C2–CX2 for A2 or 1, C3–CX3, for A3 or 2, and so on.

What is in cell B102? It is the average number of times out of 100 that each number from 1 to 100 appeared in its respective row. In other words, if the average in cell B102 is 1, then every number from 1 to 100 had an equal chance of being in its respective row. Stated differently, B102 is the number of chances out of 100 for any number from 1 to 100 to be selected by Excel's random number function.

You can "redraw" all 1000 random numbers in Excel by simply entering in a blank-return anywhere in the spreadsheet. Try this with cell B103 several times, and will see that the average changes slightly, but it will tend to "hover" around 1.0.

You can test the "lucky number" theory by copying row 101 into rows 105–114, and placing the lucky number into cells A105–A114. Create an average of cells B105:B114 in cell B115. Then, do several repetitions by entering in a blank-return and keep track of the numbers that appear in cell B115. You will find that it is typically 1, meaning that the lucky number has no more chance of being drawn than any of the 99 other random numbers.

Advantages and Disadvantages of Simple Random Sampling. Simple random sampling is an appealing sampling method because it embodies the requirements necessary to obtain a probability sample and, therefore, to derive unbiased estimates of the population's characteristics. This sampling method guarantees that every member of the population has an equal chance of being selected into the sample; therefore, the resulting sample, no matter what the size, will be a valid representation of the population.

Using random numbers to draw a simple random sample requires a complete accounting of the population.

However, there are some slight disadvantages associated with simple random sampling. To use either the blind draw or the random numbers approach, it is necessary to predesignate each population member. In the blind draw example, each student's name was written on an index card, whereas in the random numbers example, each student was assigned a specific number. In essence, simple random sampling necessarily begins with a complete listing of the population, and current and complete listings are sometimes difficult to obtain. If the population does not exist as an electronic list, it is also cumbersome and tedious to manually provide unique designations for each population member.

Simple Random Sampling Used in Practice. There are three practical applications in which simple random sample designs are used quite successfully: random digit dialing, computerized databases, and small populations. In fact, these three cases constitute the bulk of the use of simple random sampling in marketing research.

One instance in which simple random sampling is commonly used is through the use of random digit dialing. **Random digit dialing (RDD)** is used in telephone surveys to overcome the problems of unlisted and new telephone numbers. Unlisted numbers are a growing concern not only for researchers in the United States but in all industrialized countries such as those in Europe as well.[8,9]

In random digit dialing, telephone numbers are generated randomly with the aid of a computer. Telephone interviewers call these numbers and administer the survey to the respondent once the person has been qualified.[10] However, random digit dialing may result in a large number of calls to nonexisting telephone numbers. A popular variation of random digit dialing that reduces this problem is the **plus-one dialing procedure**, in which numbers are selected from a telephone directory and a digit, such as a "1," is added to each number to determine which telephone number is then dialed. Alternatively, the last digit can be substituted with a random number.[11]

Next, there is the possibility of selecting respondents from computer lists, company files, or commercial listing services, which have been converted into databases. Practically every database software program has a random number selection feature, so simple random sampling is very easy to achieve if the researcher has a computerized database of the population. The database programs can work with random numbers of as many digits as are necessary, so even social security numbers with nine digits are no problem. Companies with credit files, subscription lists, or marketing information systems have the greatest opportunity to use this approach, or a research company may turn to a specialized sampling company such as Survey Sampling to have it draw a random sample of households or businesses in a certain geographic area using its extensive databases.

Finally, one of the most troublesome aspects of simple random sampling is a listing of the population. Consequently, in those marketing research studies in which "small" and stable populations are involved, it is wise to use simple random sampling. For instance, the regional distributor for Anheuser-Busch desired that a customer satisfaction survey be administered to its many accounts. The distributor wanted to know how its delivery system compared to that of its key competitors: Coors Beer and Miller Beer. The Anheuser-Busch accounts were divided into "on-premises" locations, where the beer products were consumed at the location. These locations included restaurants, bars, taverns, and sports arenas. The "off-premises" locations were where buyers purchase beer and carry it away. These locations included supermarkets, convenience stores, and package stores. The beer distributor had detailed computer lists of approximately 200 on-premises clients and about 600 off-premises clients. It was a simple matter to generate two separate lists, number each account, and to use the random selection feature of Microsoft Excel to draw a sample of each type of buyer.

▶ **Systematic Sampling** In the special situation of a large population list that is not in the form of a computer database, such as a telephone book or a directory, the time and expense required to use simple random sampling are daunting. Fortunately, there is an economical alternative probability sampling method that can be used. At one time, **systematic sampling**, which is a way to select a random sample from a directory or list that is much more efficient (uses less effort) than with simple random sampling, was the most prevalent type of sampling technique used. However, its popularity has fallen

Random digit dialing overcomes problems of unlisted and new telephone numbers.

Plus-one dialing is a convenient variation of random digit dialing.

Systematic sampling is more efficient than simple random sampling.

as computerized databases and generated random number features have become widely available. Nonetheless, in the special case of a physical listing of the population, such as a membership directory or a telephone book, systematic sampling is often chosen over simple random sampling based primarily on the economic efficiency that it represents. In this instance, systematic sampling can be applied with less difficulty and accomplished in a shorter time than can simple random sampling. Furthermore, in these instances, systematic sampling has the potential to create a sample that is almost identical in quality to samples created from simple random sampling.

To use systematic sampling, it is necessary to obtain a hard-copy listing of the population. As noted earlier, the most common listing is a directory of some sort. The researcher decides on a **skip interval**, which is calculated by dividing the number of names on the list by the sample size as can be seen in the following formula:

One must calculate a "skip interval" to use systematic sampling.

Formula for Skip Interval

Skip interval = population list size/sample size

Names are selected based on this skip interval. For example, if one calculated a skip interval of 250, every 250th name would be selected into the sample. The use of this skip interval formula ensures that the entire list will be covered. Marketing Research Insight 12.2 shows how to take a systematic sample.

Why Systematic Sampling Is Efficient. Systematic sampling is probability sampling because it uses a random starting point, which ensures there is sufficient randomness in the systematic sample to approximate an equal probability of any member of the population being selected into the sample. In essence, systematic sampling envisions the list as made up of the skip interval number of mutually exclusive samples, each one of which is representative of the listed population. The random starting point guarantees that the selected sample is selected randomly.

How does the random starting point take place? One option would be to count or estimate the number of population members on the list, and to generate a random number between 1 and N (the population size). Then you would have to count the list until you

---

MARKETING RESEARCH INSIGHT

PRACTICAL APPLICATION

12.2 How to Take a Systematic Sample

STEP 1: Identify a listing of the population that contains an acceptable level of sample frame error. **Example:** The telephone book for your city

STEP 2: Compute the skip interval by dividing the number of names on the list by the sample size. **Example:** 25,000 estimated names in the phone book, sample size of 500, so skip interval = every 50th name

STEP 3: Using random number(s), determine a starting position for sampling the list. **Example:** Select:

random number for page number *Select:* random number for the column on that page *Select:* random number for name position in that column (say, Jones, William P.)

STEP 4: Apply the skip interval to determine which names on the list will be in the sample. **Example:** Jones, William P. (skip 50 names) Lathum, Ferdinand B.

STEP 5: Treat the list as "circular"; that is, the first name on the list is now the initial name you selected, and the last name is now the name just prior to the initially selected one. **Example:** When you come to the end of the phone book names (Zs), just continue by going back to the beginning (As).

came to that member's location. But a more efficient approach would be to first generate a random number between 1 and the number of pages to determine the page on which you will start. Suppose page 53 is drawn. Another random number would be drawn between 1 and the number of columns on a page to decide the column on that page. Assume the 3rd column is drawn. A final random number between 1 and the number of names in a column would be used to determine the actual starting position in that column. Let us say the 17th name is selected. From that beginning point, the skip interval would be used. The skip interval would ensure that the entire list would be covered, and the final name selected would be approximately one skip interval before the starting point. It is convenient to think of the listing as a circular file, like an old-fashioned Rolodex file, such that A actually follows Z if the list were alphabetized, and the random starting point determines where the list "begins."

The essential difference between systematic sampling and simple random sampling is apparent in the use of the words "systematic" and "random." The system used in systematic sampling is the skip interval, whereas the randomness in simple random sampling is determined through the use of successive random draws. Systematic sampling works its way through the entire population from beginning to end, whereas random sampling guarantees that the complete population will be covered but without a systematic pattern. The efficiency in systematic sampling is gained by two features: (1) the skip interval aspect and (2) the need to use random number(s) only at the beginning.

Active **Learning**

Systematic sampling is more efficient than simple random sampling because only one or a very few random numbers need to be drawn at the beginning.

TAKE A SYSTEMATIC SAMPLE USING YOUR TELEPHONE BOOK

This Active Learning exercise will give you some practice in taking a systematic sample from a "hard copy" list, such as a telephone book. For this exercise, you will use the telephone book for your area, and you will apply systematic sampling steps as though you were selecting a sample of 1000 households. Use the following steps:

1. Estimate the total number of households listed in the telephone book. You can do this estimate by:

   a. Determine the total number of pages of household listings:
   _____ pages

   b. Determine the number of columns of numbers per page:
   _____ columns

   c. Determine the average number of households listings per column (*Note*: If there are business telephone numbers mixed with the household ones, you will need to make an adjustment for this factor):
   _____ household listings

   d. Determine the estimated total number of households in your sample frame (the telephone book) by multiplying the number of pages times the number of columns times the number of household listings per column.
   _____ household numbers

   e. Determine the skip interval by dividing the number of household numbers by the sample size, 1000.
   _____ skip interval

   f. Now, use some sort of random number generator such as an Excel function or a table of random numbers (typically found in a statistics textbook) to select a random starting point in either of two ways:

      1) Select a random number between 1 and the total number of households in your sample frame, or

2) Select a random page from 1 to the number of pages in the telephone book and turn to that page. Then, select a random column from 1 to the number of columns per page, and go to that column. Finally, select a random household in that column with a random number from 1 to the number of households per column.

g. Using your skip interval, you can now select the 1000 household telephone listings.

h. The procedure you have used here assumes that every one of your 1000 randomly selected households will participate in the survey (100% response rate); however, this assumption is unrealistic. Assume that you expect a 50% response rate. What adjustment to the skip interval calculation can you make to accommodate the fact that every other prospective respondent will refuse to take part in the survey when asked?

With systematic sampling the small loss in sampling precision is counterbalanced by its economic savings.

Disadvantage of Systematic Sampling. The greatest danger in the use of systematic sampling lies in the listing of the population (sample frame). Sample frame error is a major concern for telephone directories because of unlisted numbers. It is also a concern for lists that are not current. In both instances, the sample frame will not include certain population members, and these members have no chance of being selected into the sample because of this fact.

A cluster sampling method divides the population into groups, any one of which can be considered a representative sample.

▶ **Cluster Sampling** Another form of probability sampling is known as **cluster sampling**, in which the population is divided into subgroups, called "clusters," each of which represents the entire population. Note that the basic concept behind cluster sampling is very similar to the one described for systematic sampling, but the implementation differs. The procedure identifies identical clusters. Any one cluster, therefore, will be a satisfactory representation of the population. Cluster sampling can be applied to an electonic database or when there is no electronic database of the population. It is easy to administer, and cluster sampling goes a step further in striving to gain economic efficiency over systematic sampling by simplifying the sampling procedure used. We illustrate cluster sampling by describing a type of cluster sample known as area sampling.

Area sampling uses either a one-step or a two-step approach.

Area Sampling as a Form of Cluster Sampling. In **area sampling**, the researcher subdivides the population to be surveyed into geographic areas, such as census tracts, cities, neighborhoods, or any other convenient and identifiable geographic designation. The researcher has two options at this point: a one-step approach or a two-step approach. In the **one-step area sample** approach, the researcher may believe the various geographic areas (clusters) to be sufficiently identical to permit concentrating attention on just one area and then generalizing the results to the full population. But the researcher would need to select that one area randomly and perform a census of its members. Alternatively, the researcher may use a **two-step area sample** approach to the sampling process; that is, for the first step, the researcher could select a random sample of areas, and then for the second step, he or she could decide on a probability method to sample individuals within the chosen areas. The two-step area sample approach is preferable to the one-step approach because there is always the possibility that a single cluster may be less representative than the researcher believes. But the two-step method is more costly because more areas and time are involved. Marketing Research Insight 12.3 illustrates how to take an area sample using subdivisions as the clusters.[12]

Area grid sampling is a variation of the area sampling method. To use it, the researcher imposes a grid over a map of the area to be surveyed. Each cell within the

12.3

How to Take an Area Sampling Using Subdivisions

STEP 1: Determine the geographic area to be surveyed and identify its subdivisions. Each subdivision cluster should be highly similar to all others. **Example:** There are 20 subdivisions within 5 miles of the proposed site for our new restaurant; assign each a number.

STEP 2: Decide on the use of one-step or two-step cluster sampling. **Example:** Use two-step cluster sampling.

STEP 3: (assuming two-step): Using random numbers, select the subdivisions to be sampled. **Example:** Select four subdivisions randomly, say numbers 3, 15, 2, and 19.

STEP 4: Using some probability method of sample selection, select the members of each chosen subdivision to be included in the sample. **Example:** Identify a random starting point; instruct fieldworkers to drop off the survey at every fifth house (systematic sampling).

grid then becomes a cluster. The difference between area grid sampling and area sampling lies primarily in the use of a grid framework, which cuts across natural or artificial boundaries such as streets, rivers, city limits, or other separations normally used in area sampling. Geodemography has been used to describe the demographic profiles of the various clusters.[13] Regardless of how the population is sliced up, the researcher has the option of a one-step or a two-step approach.[14]

Area sampling uses subdivisions as its clusters.

Disadvantage of Cluster (Area) Sampling. The greatest danger in cluster sampling is cluster specification error that occurs when the clusters are not homogeneous. For example, if a subdivision association used area sampling to survey its members using its streets as cluster identifiers, and one street circumnavigated a small lake in the back of the subdivision, the "Lake Street" homes might be more expensive and luxurious than most of the other homes in the subdivision. If by chance, Lake Street was selected as a cluster in the survey, it would most likely bias the results toward the opinions of the relatively few wealthy subdivision residents. In the case of one-step area sampling, this bias could be severe.

▶ **Stratified Sampling** All of the sampling methods we have described thus far implicitly assume that the population has a normal or bell-shaped distribution for its key properties; that is, there is the assumption that every potential sample unit is a fairly good representation of the population, and any who are extreme in one way are perfectly counterbalanced by opposite extreme potential sample units. Unfortunately, it is common to work with populations in marketing research that contain unique subgroupings; you might encounter a population that is not distributed symmetrically across a normal curve. With this situation, unless you make adjustments in your sample design, you will end up with a sample described as "statistically inefficient" or, in other words, inaccurate. One solution is **stratified sampling**, which separates the population into different subgroups or strata and then samples all of these subgroups.

With stratified sampling, the population is separated into different strata and a sample is taken from each stratum.

Working with Skewed Populations. A **skewed population** has a long tail on one side and a short tail on the opposite end. As such, it deviates greatly from the bell-shaped distribution that is assumed to be the case in the use of simple random, systematic, or cluster sampling. So, if any of these methods is used to draw the sample from a skewed distribution, it most certainly would be inaccurate. For example, let's take the case of a college that is attempting to assess how its students perceive the quality of its educational programs.

Stratified sampling is appropriate when we expect that responses will vary across strata, or groups in the population.

A researcher has formulated the question, "To what extent do you value your college degree?" The response options are along a 5-point scale, where 1 equals "not valued at all" and 5 equals "very highly valued." The population of students is stratified or divided by year: freshman, sophomore, junior, and senior. You would expect the response to differ by the respondent's year status because seniors probably value a degree more than do juniors, who value a degree more than do sophomores, and so on. At the same time, you would expect that seniors would be more in agreement (have less variability) than would underclassmen. This belief is due to the fact that freshmen are students who are trying out college, some of whom are not serious about completing it and do not value it highly, but some of whom are intending to become doctors, lawyers, or professionals whose training will include graduate degree work as well as their present college work. The serious freshman students would value a college degree highly, whereas the less serious ones would not. So, we would expect much variability in the freshman students, less in sophomores, still less in juniors, and the least with college seniors. The situation might be something similar to the distributions illustrated in Figure 12.1. Notice in Figure 12.1, we have portrayed the four class strata distributions as a normal curve, whereas the entire college population of all four classes as a skewed curve.

Stratified sampling is used when the researcher is working with a "skewed" population divided into strata.

With stratified random sampling, one takes a skewed population and identifies the subgroups or **strata** contained within it. Simple random sampling, systematic sampling, or some other type of probability sampling procedure is then applied to draw a sample from each stratum because we typically believe that the individual strata have bell-shaped distributions. So, it is a "divide and conquer" approach to sampling.

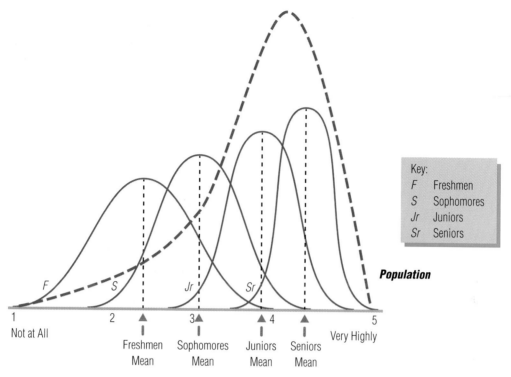

"To what extent do you value a college degree?"

FIGURE 12.1
Stratified Simple Random Sampling: Using College-Year Status as a Stratification Basis

Accuracy of Stratified Sampling. How does stratified sampling result in a more accurate overall sample? Actually, there are two ways this accuracy is achieved. First, stratified sampling allows for explicit analysis of each stratum. The college degree example illustrates why a researcher would want to know about the distinguishing differences between the strata in order to assess the true picture. Each stratum represents a different response profile, and by recognizing this, stratified sampling is a more accurate sample design.

Second, there is a procedure that allows the estimation of the overall sample mean by use of a **weighted mean**, whose formula takes into consideration the sizes of the strata relative to the total population size and applies those proportions to the strata's means. The population mean is calculated by multiplying each stratum by its proportion and summing the weighted stratum means. This formula results in an estimate that is consistent with the true distribution of the population. Here is the formula that is used for two strata:

Formula for Weighted Mean

$$\text{Mean}_{\text{population}} = (\text{mean}_A)(\text{proportion}_A) + (\text{mean}_B)(\text{proportion}_B)$$

where *A* signifies stratum *A*, and *B* signifies stratum *B*.

Here is an example. A researcher separated a population of households that rent DVDs on a regular basis into two strata. Stratum *A* was families without young children, and stratum *B* was families with young children. When asked to use a scale of 1 = poor, 2 = fair, 3 = good, 4 = very good, and 5 = excellent to rate their video/DVD rental store on its DVD selection, the means were computed to be 2.0 (fair) and 4.0 (very good), respectively, for the samples. The researcher knew from census information that families

A stratified sample may require the calculation of a weighted mean to achieve accuracy.

without young children accounted for 70 percent of the population and families with young children accounted for the remaining 30 percent. The weighted mean rating for video selection was then computed as $(.7)(2.0) + (.3)(4.0) = 2.6$ (between fair and good).

Researchers should select a basis for stratification that reveals different responses across the strata.

How to Apply Stratified Sampling. There are a number of instances in which stratified sampling is used in marketing research because skewed populations are often encountered. Prior knowledge of populations under study, augmented by research objectives sensitive to subgroupings, sometimes reveals that the population is not normally distributed. Under these circumstances, it is advantageous to apply stratified sampling to preserve the diversity of the various subgroups. Usually, a **surrogate measure**, which is some observable or easily determined characteristic of each population member, is used to help partition or separate the population members into their various subgroupings. For example, in the instance of the college, the year classification of each student is a handy surrogate. Of course, there is the opportunity for the researcher to divide the population into as many relevant strata as necessary to capture different subpopulations. For instance, the college might want to further stratify on college of study or grade point average (GPA) ranges. Perhaps professional-school students value their degrees more than do liberal arts students or high-GPA students more than average-GPA or failing students. The key issue is that the researcher should use some basis for dividing the population into strata that results in different responses across strata.

If the strata sample sizes are faithful to their relative sizes in the population, you have what is called a **proportionate stratified sample** design. Here you do not use the weighted formula because each stratum's weight is automatically accounted for by its sample size. But with **disproportionate stratified sampling**, the weighted formula needs to be used because the strata sizes do not reflect their relative proportions in the population. We have provided a step-by-step description of stratified sampling in Marketing Research Insight 12.4.

MARKETING RESEARCH INSIGHT

PRACTICAL APPLICATION

12.4

How to Take a Stratified Sample

STEP 1: Be certain that the population's distribution for some key factor is not bell-shaped and that separate subpopulations exist. **Example:** HDTV owners differ from nonowners in their use of pay-per-view movies and events, so stratify by ownership/nonownership of HDTVs.

STEP 2: Use this factor or some surrogate variable to divide the population into strata consistent with the separate subpopulations identified. **Example:** Use a screening question on ownership/nonownership of an HDTV. This may require a screening survey using random digit dialing to identify respondent pools for each stratum.

STEP 3: Select a probability sample from each stratum. **Example:** Use a computer to select simple random samples for each stratum.

STEP 4: Examine each stratum for managerially relevant differences. **Example:** Do HDTV owners differ from nonowners in their use of pay-per-view TV? *Answer:* HDTV owners average 10 times per month; nonowners average 5 times per month.

STEP 5: If stratum sample sizes are not proportionate to the stratum sizes in the population, use the weighted mean formula to estimate the population value(s). **Example:** If owners are 30 percent and nonowners are 70 percent of the population, the estimate is $(10)(.30) + (5)(.70) = 6.5$ pay-per-views per month.

Nonprobability Sampling Methods

All of the sampling methods we have described thus far embody probability sampling assumptions. In each case, the probability of any unit being selected from the population into the sample is known, even though it cannot be calculated precisely. The critical difference between probability and nonprobability sampling methods is the mechanics used in the sample design. With a nonprobability sampling method, selection is not based on probability. Instead, a nonprobability sample is based on an inherently biased selection process, typically in order to reduce the cost of sampling. So, with a nonprobability sample, the researcher has some savings but at the expense of using a sample that is not truly representative of the population.[15] There are four nonprobability sampling methods: convenience samples, judgment samples, referral samples, and quota samples (Table 12.2). A discussion of each method follows.

> With nonprobability sampling methods, some members of the population do not have any chance of being included in the sample.

▶ **Convenience Samples Convenience samples** are samples drawn at the convenience of the interviewer. Accordingly, the most convenient areas to a researcher in terms of reduced time and effort turn out to be high-traffic areas such as shopping malls or busy pedestrian intersections. The selection of the place and, consequently, prospective respondents is subjective rather than objective. Certain members of the population are automatically eliminated from the sampling process.[16] For instance, there are those people who may be infrequent visitors or even nonvisitors of the particular high-traffic area being used. On the other hand, in the absence of strict selection procedures, there are members of the population who may be omitted because of their physical appearance, general demeanor, or by the fact that they are in a group rather than alone. One author states, "Convenience samples . . . can be seriously misleading."[17]

> Convenience samples may misrepresent the population.

TABLE 12.2	Four Different Types of Nonprobability Sampling Methods

Convenience Sampling

The researcher or interviewer uses a high-traffic location such as a busy pedestrian area or a shopping mall as the sample frame from which to intercept potential respondents. Sample frame error occurs in the form of members of the population who are infrequent users or nonusers of that location. Other errors may result from any arbitrary way that the interviewer selects respondents from the sample frame.

Judgment Sampling

The researcher uses his or her judgment or that of some other knowledgeable person to identify who will be in the sample. Subjectivity enters in here, and certain members of the population will have a smaller chance of selection than will others.

Referral Sampling

Respondents are asked for the names or identities of others like themselves who might qualify to take part in the survey. Members of the population who are less well known, disliked, or whose opinions conflict with the selected respondents have a low probability of being selected.

Quota Sampling

The researcher identifies quota characteristics such as demographic or product use factors and uses these to set up quotas for each class of respondent. The sizes of the quotas are determined by the researcher's belief about the relative size of each class of respondent in the population. Often quota sampling is used as a means of ensuring that convenience samples will have the desired proportion of different respondent classes.

Mall intercepts are convenience samples.

It should be obvious that mall-intercept companies use convenience sampling to recruit respondents. For example, shoppers are encountered at large shopping malls and quickly qualified with screening questions. For those satisfying the desired population characteristics, a questionnaire may be administered or a taste test performed. Alternatively, the respondent may be given a test product and asked if he or she would use it at home. A follow-up telephone call some days later solicits his or her reaction to the product's performance. In this case, the convenience extends beyond easy access of respondents into considerations of setup for taste tests, storage of products to be distributed, and control of the interviewer workforce. In addition, large numbers of respondents can be recruited in a matter of days. The screening questions and geographic dispersion of malls may appear to reduce the subjectivity inherent in the sample design, but in fact the vast majority of the population was not there and could not be approached to take part. There are ways of reducing convenience sample selection error using a quota system, which we discuss shortly.

With a judgment sample, one "judges" the sample to be representative.

▶ **Judgment Samples Judgment samples** are somewhat different from convenience samples in concept because they require a judgment or an "educated guess" as to who should represent the population. Often the researcher or some individual helping the researcher who has considerable knowledge about the population will choose the individuals that he or she thinks constitute the sample. It should be apparent that judgment samples are highly subjective and, therefore, prone to much error.

Focus group studies often use judgment sampling rather than probability sampling. In a recent focus group concerning the need for low-fat, nutritious snacks, 12 mothers of preschool children were selected as representative of the present and prospective market. Six of the woman also had school-age children, while the other six had only preschoolers. In the judgment of the researcher, these 12 women represented the population adequately for the purposes of the focus group. It must be quickly pointed out, however, that the intent of this focus group was far different from the intent of a sample survey. Consequently, the use of a judgment sample was considered satisfactory for this particular phase in the research process for the snacks. The focus group findings served as the foundation for a large-scale regional survey conducted two months later that relied on a probability sampling method.

A referral sample asks respondents to provide the names of additional respondents.

▶ **Referral Samples Referral samples**, sometimes called "snowball samples," require respondents to provide the names of prospective respondents. Such lists begin when the researcher compiles a short list of possible respondents that is smaller than the total sample he or she desires for the study. After each respondent is interviewed, he or she is queried about the names of other possible respondents.[18] In this manner, additional respondents are referred by previous respondents. Or, as the other name implies, the sample grows just as a snowball grows when it is rolled downhill.

Referral samples are most appropriate when there is a limited and disappointingly short sample frame and when respondents can provide the names of others who would qualify for the survey. The nonprobability aspects of referral sampling come from the selectivity used throughout. The initial list may also be special in some way, and the primary means of adding people to the sample is by tapping the memories of those on the original list. Referral samples are often useful in industrial marketing research situations.[19]

Quota samples rely on key characteristics to define the composition of the sample.

▶ **Quota Samples** The **quota sample** establishes a specific quota—or percentage of the total sample for various types of individuals to be interviewed. For example, a researcher may desire the sample to be 50% males and 50% females. A quota sample is a form of nonprobability sampling used prevalently by marketing researchers who rely on mall intercepts, a convenience sample method. The quotas are determined

A referral sample is like a snowball because it grows large with each respondent's list of prospective survey participants.

through application of the research objectives and are defined by key characteristics used to identify the population. In the application of quota sampling, a fieldworker is provided with screening criteria that will classify the potential respondent into a particular quota group. For example, if the interviewer is assigned to obtain a sample quota of 50 each for black females, black males, white females, and white males, the qualifying characteristics would be race and gender. Assuming our fieldworkers were working mall intercepts, each would determine through visual inspection where the prospective respondent falls and work toward filling the quota in each of the four groups. So a quota system reduces some of the nonrepresentativeness inherent in convenience samples.

Quota samples are often used by companies that have a firm grasp on the features characterizing the individuals they wish to study in a particular marketing research project. A large bank, for instance, might stipulate that the final sample be one-half adult males and one-half adult females because in the bank's understanding of its market, the customer base is equally divided between males and females. Quota sampling need not be based solely on demographic characteristics. For example, in a survey of the usage of a public park, the quotas were set for nine different park user types using location (north, middle, and south areas of the park) and time of day (morning, midday, and afternoon).[20] In Marketing Research Insight 12.5 we have provided an example of how quota sampling was used with a convenience sample of Hong Kong schoolchildren to research their understanding of televisions.

When done conscientiously and with a firm understanding of the population's quota characteristics, quota sampling can rival probability sampling in the minds of researchers. One researcher has commented, "Probability sampling is the recommended method, but in the 'real world,' statistical inferences are often based on quota samples and other nonrandom sampling methods. Strangely, these heretical uses of statistical theory, in my experience, seem to work just as well as they do for 'purist' random samples."[22]

Quota samples are appropriate when you have a detailed demographic profile of the population on which to base the sample.

12.5

A Quota Sample Answers the Question, "Do Chinese Children Understand Television Advertising?"

Interviewing grade-school children is difficult because of their developing reading and communication skills, plus accessing these children is problematic when the researcher does not have the resources to conduct a random sample.

Consequently, a researcher directed interviewers to recruit grammar-school children in public libraries, churches, restaurants, and parks near grammar schools; that is, she used a convenience sample.[21] However, she applied a quota sample for these Hong Kong grammar school students such that the sample was balanced with 50% males and 50% females and each of seven grades (kindergarten through grade 6) were represented equally. The researcher found the following patterns of television understanding.

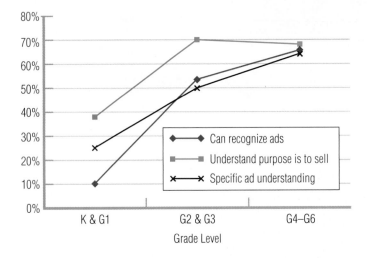

The graph reveals that by the time they have reached grade 2 or 3, almost three-quarters of Chinese children can recognize television advertising apart from television programming, and over one-half understand that its intent is to promote products, and, on average, these children can identify the key message of specific advertisements. By the 6th grade, 7 out of 10 Hong Kong children can recognize, understand the intent of, and can identify key messages for specific advertisements they encounter while watching television. The study also found that, regardless of grade level, slightly over one-half of Hong Kong children like television advertisements because of their entertainment aspects. These findings offer strong encouragement for marketers who spend large sums of money developing and positioning their television advertising on children's television programs to promote their food and drink products, toys, and other children's products.

PICTURES SAY A THOUSAND WORDS: A GRAPHICAL PRESENTATION OF SAMPLE METHODS

Figure 12.2 contains representations of each of the eight types of sample methods used in a fictitious satisfaction survey. The population in every instance is comprised of 25 consumers. One-fifth (20%) of the consumers are unsatisfied, two-fifths (40%) are satisfied, and two-fifths (40%) are indifferent or neutral about our brand. With each prob-

FIGURE 12.2
Graphical Presentations for the Various Sampling Methods

FIGURE 12.2
Continued

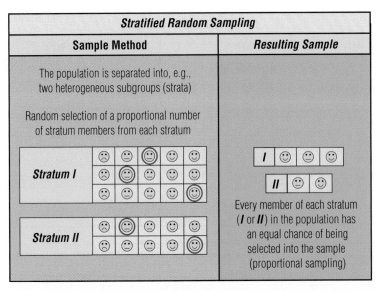

FIGURE 12.2
Continued

Referral Sampling	
Sample Method	**Resulting Sample**
Selection based on the referrals of respondents who are selected arbitrarily	Only those who are in the friendship network have a chance of being selected into the sample, resulting in error

Quota Sampling	
Sample Method	**Resulting Sample**
The population distribution is classified by demographics and/or some consumer behavior variable(s). Selection based on a quota system that ensures the population distribution, but from a convenient location like a shopping mall	Only those who pass by the convenient location have a chance of being selected into the sample, resulting in error

ability sample method (simple random sample, systematic sample, cluster sample, and stratified random sample), the resulting sample's satisfaction profile is consistent with the population; that is, each probability sample has five consumers, with one unsatisfied (20%), two satisfied (40%), and two indifferent (40%).

However, with each of the nonprobability sample methods (convenience sample, judgment sample, referral sample, and quota sample), the resulting sample's satisfaction profile is a poor representation of the population. If you look at any nonprobability sample's selection specifics, the selections are concentrated in specific areas of the population. The concentration aspect of nonprobability sampling means that some members of the population have a disproportionate chance of being selected into the sample, resulting in sample selection error.

Nonprobability samples result in a poor representation of the population.

ONLINE SAMPLING TECHNIQUES

To be sure, sampling for Internet surveys poses special challenges, but most of these issues can be addressed in the context of our probability and nonprobability sampling concepts.[23] The trick is to understand how the online sampling method in question works and to interpret the sampling procedure correctly with respect to basic sampling concepts.[24] Of course, the advantages of Internet surveys are well known and should be weighted against any sample bias expected from using the Internet context.[25]

For purposes of illustration, we will describe four types of online sampling: (1) random online intercept sampling, (2) invitation online sampling, (3) online panel sampling, and (4) other online sampling types.

Online samples apply sampling methods to online populations.

Random Online Intercept Sampling

Random online intercept sampling relies on a random selection of Web-site visitors. There are a number of Java-based or other HTML-embedded routines that will select Web-site visitors on a random basis such as time of day or random selection from the stream of Web-site visitors. If the population is defined as Web-site visitors, then this is a simple random sample of these visitors within the time frame of the survey. If the sample selection program starts randomly and incorporates a skip interval system, it is a systematic sample,[26] and if the sample program treats the population of Web-site visitors like strata, it uses stratified simple random sampling as long as random selection procedures are used faithfully. However, if the population is other than Web-site visitors, and the Web site is used because there are many visitors, the sample is akin to a mall-intercept sample (convenience sample).

Random sampling techniques can be easily applied to online populations.

Invitation Online Sampling

Invitation online sampling is when potential respondents are alerted that they may fill out a questionnaire that is hosted at a specific Web site.[27] For example, a retail store chain may have a notice that is handed to customers with their receipts notifying them that they may go online to fill out the questionnaire. However, to avoid spam, online researchers must have an established relationship with potential respondents who expect to receive an e-mail survey. If the retail store uses a random sampling approach such as systematic sampling, a probability sample will result. Similarly, if the e-mail list is a truly representative group of the population, and the procedures embody random selection, it will constitute a probability sample. However, if in either case there is some aspect of the selection procedure that eliminates population members or otherwise overrepresents elements of the population, the sample will be a nonprobability one.[28] A good example of a sampling system that overcomes this problem is Opinion Place. It uses a proprietary sampling method in which visitors learn about Opinion Place through promotions placed throughout America Online (AOL) properties, the Internet, and various rewards programs. In addition, AOL members can access the area quickly through a permanent placement in AOL Member Perks or through AOL Keyword: Opinion Place. Visitors to Opinion Place proceed through a complex, sophisticated screening process to ensure random representation across all surveys.[29]

It is advisable to have a prior relationship with potential respondents who are requested by e-mail to take part in an online survey.

Online Panel Sampling

Online panel sampling refers to consumer or other respondent panels that are set up by marketing research companies for the explicit purpose of conducting online surveys with representative samples.[30] There is a growing number of these companies, and online panels afford fast, convenient, and flexible access to preprofiled samples.[31] Typically, the panel company has several thousand individuals who are representative of a large geographic area, and the market researcher can specify sample parameters such as specific geographic representation, income, education, family characteristics, and so forth. The panel company then uses its database on its panel members to broadcast an e-mail notification to those panelists who qualify according to the sample parameters specified by the market researcher. Although online panel samples are not probability samples (an exception to this rule is found in Marketing Research Insight 12.6), they are used extensively by the marketing research industry.[32] One of the greatest pluses of online panels is the high response rate, which ensures that the final sample closely represents the population targeted by the researcher.

> **A popular approach to online sampling is for a research company to have a large number of panel members who have agreed to take part in online surveys.**

ONLINE APPLICATION

12.6 Knowledge Networks Has a Unique Online Panel that is Representative of the United States

The typical approach to recruiting an online panel involves using pop-ups and other online-only devices to contact potential respondents and request that they join the online panel. Various incentives and compensation packages are offered in order to increase the willingness of reluctant individuals to take part in the panel. Nonetheless, this approach invariably suffers from "coverage bias," meaning that not everyone has access to the Internet. In fact, it is reported that while 96% of the U.S. population owns a telephone, only about 61% of the population has ready access to the Internet.[33]

Knowledge Networks has come up with an innovative solution to the representativeness drawback that plagues online panels in general and online samples in particular.[34] First, Knowledge Networks is unique in that it uses telephone contacts to recruit its online panel members. Thus, it eliminates the coverage bias that accompanies Internet-based recruitment methods. Knowledge Networks starts with a statistically valid sample of the full U.S. population using random digit dialing (a technique described earlier in this chapter), which means that everyone in the United States has an equal chance of being on the panel. This is different from nearly all other Internet research, for which panelists are "self-selected" (i.e., volunteers).

When a person agrees to join the Knowledge Networks panel, but does not have access to the Internet, Knowledge Networks solves this problem by providing them with the hardware and connection to MSN TV, formerly known as WebTV. MSN TV is a system that uses the person's television set as the computer monitor. MSN TV uses a dial-up connection, and the keyboard and remote control device connect wirelessly to the MSN TV player. As can be seen in the photo, the result is an Internet connection that has all of the functions necessary for an online survey, including graphics capabilities. For more information about Knowledge Networks nationally representative online panels and its other products, go to their Web site: **www.knowledgenetworks.com**.

Other Online Sampling Approaches

Other online sampling approaches are feasible and limited only by the creativity of the sample designers. To identify the underlying sample method, you simply need to analyze the specifics of how potential respondents are selected. For instance, a respondent may be asked to forward the survey site to his or her friends (referral sampling), or there may be a survey page that pops up after every customer makes an online purchase (census). Regardless of the approach, if you analyze it carefully in the context of basic sampling techniques that are described in this chapter, you should be able to determine if it is a probability or a nonprobability sample.

DEVELOPING A SAMPLE PLAN

Up to this point, we have discussed various aspects of sampling as though they were discrete and seemingly unrelated decisions. However, they are logically joined together, and there is a definite sequence of steps, called the **sample plan**, that the researcher goes through in order to draw and ultimately arrive at the final sample.[35] These steps are illustrated in Figure 12.3. Now that you are acquainted with basic terms, definitions, and concepts involved with sampling, we can describe these steps in detail.

Step 1: Define the Population

A sample plan begins with the population definition.

As you know, the first step to be considered in the sampling process requires a definition of the target population under study. We indicated earlier in the chapter that the target population is identified by the marketing research study objectives; however, typically at the beginning of the sampling phase of a research project, the focus on the relevant population is necessarily sharpened. This sharpening involves the translation of vague descriptions of the target population into fairly specific demographic or other characteristics that separate the target population from other populations. The task here is for the researcher to specify the sample unit in the form of a precise description of the type of person to be surveyed.

For example, with a brand-awareness restaurant survey done for Nordic Track treadmills, it might be assumed that important descriptors helping to define the relevant population is that its members: (1) own their own homes and (2) do not belong to fitness centers. A population description can result from previous studies, or it may be the

FIGURE 12.3
Steps in the Sampling Process

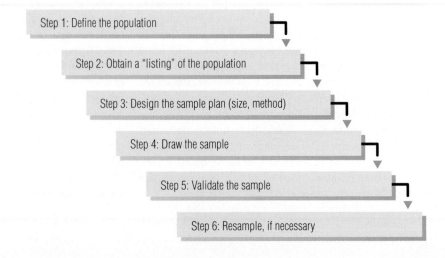

Step 1: Define the population

Step 2: Obtain a "listing" of the population

Step 3: Design the sample plan (size, method)

Step 4: Draw the sample

Step 5: Validate the sample

Step 6: Resample, if necessary

collective wisdom of marketing decision makers who have catered to this particular population for a number of years and have had the opportunity to observe members' behaviors and to listen to their comments.

Step 2: Obtain a Listing of the Population

Once the population has been defined, the researcher begins searching for a suitable list to serve as the sample frame. In some studies, candidate lists are readily available in the form of databases of various sorts—company files or records, either public or private, that are made available to the researcher. In other instances, the listing is available, at a price, from a third party. Unfortunately, it is rare that a listing is perfectly faithful to the target population. Most lists suffer from sample frame error; or, as we noted earlier, the database does not contain a complete enumeration of members of the population. Alternatively, the listing may be a distorted accounting of the population in that some of those listed may not belong to the population. As a example, consider the use of a voter registration as a sample frame for a survey about automobile driving.

The key to assessing sample frame error lies in two factors: (1) judging how different the people listed in the sample frame are from the population and (2) estimating what kinds of people in the population are not listed in the sample frame. With the first factor, screening questions at the beginning of an interview will usually suffice as a means of disqualifying those contacted who are not consistent with the population definition. As we noted in an earlier chapter, the percentage of people on a list who qualify as members of the population is referred to as the **incidence rate**. In our voter registration list example, it is a simple matter to have a qualifier question inquiring whether or not the individual has a driver's license. Since most people in the United States drive, there should be a high incidence rate. However, not every driver is registered to vote, so some drivers would not be in the sample frame, but the sample frame error would be small. So voter registration records would serve as an acceptable sample frame for this survey. If the population is global and has a low-incidence rate, researchers typically turn to compiled lists, and sampling companies such as Survey Sampling, Inc. have developed services to accommodate this especially problematic aspect of global marketing research.

Lists to be considered as sample frames should be assessed in terms of sample frame error.

Step 3: Design the Sample Plan (Size and Method)

Armed with a precise definition of the population and an understanding of the availability and condition of lists of the target population, the researcher progresses directly into the design of the sample itself. At this point, the costs of various data-collection method factors come into play; that is, the researcher begins to simultaneously balance sample design, data-collection costs, and sample size. We discuss sample size determination in the next chapter, and you will learn that it is a trade-off between the desire for statistical precision and the requirements of efficiency and economy.

Regardless of the size of the sample, the specific sampling method or combination of sampling methods to be used must be stipulated in detail by the researcher. There is no one "best" sampling method. The sample plan varies according to the objectives of the survey and its constraints.[36]

Sample size and sample method are separate steps in the sample plan.

The sampling method description includes all of the necessary steps to draw the sample. For instance, if we decided to use systematic sampling, the sampling method would detail the sample frame, the sample size, the skip interval, how the random starting point would be determined, qualifying questions, recontacts, and replacement procedures; that is, all eventualities and contingencies should be foreseen and provisions should be made for each of them. These contingency plans are most apparent in the directions given to interviewers or provided to the data-collection company. Obviously, it is vital to the success of the survey that the sampling method be adhered to throughout the entire sampling process.

Step 4: Draw the Sample

Drawing the sample is a two-phase process. First, the sample unit must be selected. Second, information must be gained from that unit. Simply put, you need to choose a person and ask him or her some questions. However, there comes the question of substitutions.[37] Substitutions occur whenever an individual who was qualified to be in the sample proves to be unavailable, unwilling to respond, or unsuitable. The question here is, "How is the substitution respondent determined?" If the marketing research project director wishes to ensure that a particular sampling method is used faithfully, the question of substitutions must be addressed. There are three substitution methods in practice: drop-downs, oversampling, and resampling.

Substitutions in the sample may be effected with "drop-downs," oversampling, or resampling.

The **drop-down substitution** is used when the researcher has a convenient listing of the entire population. Let us say that we are using a telephone directory as our sample frame, and you are the interviewer who is instructed to call every 100th name. On your first call, the person qualifies but refuses to take part in the survey. If the drop-down method of substitution is in effect, you are trained to call the name immediately following the one you just called. You will not skip 100 names but just drop down to the next one below the refusal. If that person refuses to take part, you will drop down another name and so on until you find a cooperative respondent. Then you will resume the 100 skip interval, using the original name as your beginning point. Obviously, interviewers must be provided the complete sample frame to use drop-down substitution.

Oversampling is an alternative substitution method, and it takes place as a result of the researcher's knowledge of incidence rates, nonresponse rates, and unusable responses. For example, if the typical response rate for a mail survey questionnaire hovers around 20 percent, in order to obtain a final sample of 200 respondents, 1000 potential respondents must be drawn into the mailout sample. Each data-collection method constitutes separate oversampling implications, and it is up to the marketing research project director to apply his or her wisdom to determine the appropriate degree of oversampling. Otherwise, resampling will be necessary at a later point in the marketing research study in order to obtain the desired sample size.

Incidence rates and response rates determine the need for sample substitutions.

Resampling constitutes a third means of respondent substitution. Resampling is a procedure in which the sample frame is tapped for additional names after the initial sample is drawn. Here the response rate may turn out to be much lower than anticipated, and more prospective respondents must be drawn. Of course, provision must be made not to include prospective respondents appearing in the original sample in the resample.

Step 5: Validate the Sample

Sample validation assures the client that the sample is representative, but sample validation is not always possible.

Typically, the final activity in the sampling process is the validation stage. **Sample validation** is a process in which the researcher inspects some characteristic(s) of the sample to judge how well it represents the population. Sample validation can take a number of forms, one of which is to compare the sample's demographic profile with a known profile, such as the census. With quota sample validation, of course, the researcher must use a demographic characteristic other than those used to set up the quota system. The essence of sample validation is to assure the client that the sample is, in fact, a representative sample of the population about which the decision maker wishes to make decisions. Although not all researchers perform sample validation, it is recommended when prior knowledge exists about the population's demographic profile. When no such prior information exits, validation is not possible, and the sample selection method bears the full burden of convincing clients that the sample is representative of the population.

Step 6: Resample If Necessary

When a sample fails validation, it means that it does not adequately represent the population. This problem may arise even when sample substitutions are incorporated.[38] Sometimes when this condition is found, the researcher can use a weighting scheme in the tabulations and analyses to compensate for the misrepresentation. On the other hand, it is sometimes possible to perform resampling by selecting more respondents and adding them to the sample until a satisfactory level of validation is reached.

SPSS

SPSS Student Assistant: Red Lobster: Recoding and Computing Variables

SUMMARY

This chapter described various sampling methods. It began by acquainting you with various terms such as *population, census,* and *sample frame.* A sample is taken because it is too costly to perform a census, and there is sufficient information in a sample to allow it to represent the population. We described four probability sampling methods in which there is a known chance of a member of the population being selected into the sample: (1) simple random sampling, (2) systematic sampling, (3) cluster sampling using area sampling as an example, and (4) stratified sampling. We also described four nonprobability sampling methods: (1) convenience sampling, (2) judgment sampling, (3) referral sampling, and (4) quota sampling. The growing trend to draw online samples was noted, and we related (1) random online intercept sampling, (2) invitation online sampling, and (3) other online sampling types. Finally, we described six steps needed to develop a sample plan: (1) define the relevant population; (2) obtain a listing of the population; (3) design the sample plan (size and methods); (4) draw the sample; (5) validate the sample; and (6) resample if necessary.

KEY TERMS

- Population (p. 330)
- Sample (p. 330)
- Sample unit (p. 330)
- Census (p. 330)
- Sampling error (p. 331)
- Sample frame (p. 331)
- Sample frame error (p. 331)
- Probability samples (p. 332)
- Nonprobability samples (p. 332)
- Simple random sampling (p. 333)
- Blind draw method (p. 333)
- Random numbers (p. 335)
- Random digit dialing (p. 337)
- Plus-one dialing procedure (p. 337)
- Systematic sampling (p. 337)
- Skip interval (p. 338)
- Cluster sampling (p. 340)
- Area sampling (p. 340)
- One-step area sample (p. 340)
- Two-step area sample (p. 340)
- Stratified sampling (p. 342)

- Skewed population (p. 342)
- Strata (p. 342)
- Weighted mean (p. 343)
- Surrogate measure (p. 344)
- Proportionate stratified sample (p. 344)
- Disproportionate stratified sampling (p. 344)
- Convenience samples (p. 345)
- Judgment samples (p. 346)
- Referral samples (p. 346)
- Quota sample (p. 346)
- Random online intercept sampling (p. 352)
- Invitation online sampling (p. 352)
- Online panel sampling (p. 352)
- Sample plan (p. 354)
- Incidence rate (p. 355)
- Drop-down substitution (p. 356)
- Oversampling (p. 356)
- Resampling (p. 356)
- Sample validation (p. 356)

REVIEW QUESTIONS/APPLICATIONS

1. Distinguish a nonprobability from a probability sampling method. Which one is the preferable method and why? Indicate the pros and cons associated with probability and nonprobability sampling methods.

2. List and describe briefly each of the probability sampling methods described in the chapter.

3. What is meant by the term *random*? Explain how each of the following embodies randomness: (a) blind draw, (b) use of random digit dialing, and (c) use of a computer to generate random numbers.

4. In what ways is a systematic sample more efficient than a simple random sample? In what way is systematic sampling less representative of the population than simple random sampling?

5. Distinguish cluster sampling from simple random sampling. How are systematic sampling and cluster sampling related?

6. Differentiate one-step from two-step area sampling, and indicate when each is preferred.

7. What is meant by a "skewed" population? Illustrate what you think is a skewed population distribution variable and what it looks like.

8. What are some alternative online sampling methods? Describe each.

9. Briefly describe each of the four nonprobability sampling methods.

10. Why is quota sampling often used with a convenience sampling method such as mall intercepts?

11. Describe each of the three methods of substitution for individuals who are selected into the sample but who refuse to participate in the survey or who did not qualify.

12. Provide the marketing researcher's definitions for each of the following populations:

    a. Columbia House, a mail-order house specializing in tapes and CDs, wants to determine interest in a 10-for-1 offer on jazz CDs.

    b. The manager of your student union is interested in determining if students desire a "universal" debit ID card that will be accepted anywhere on campus and in many stores off campus.

    c. Joy Manufacturing Company decides to conduct a survey to determine the sales potential of a new type of air compressor used by construction companies.

13. Here are four populations and a potential sample frame for each one. With each pair, identify (1) members of the population who are not in the sample frame and (2) sample frame items that are not part of the population. Also, for each one, would you judge the amount of sample frame error to be acceptable or unacceptable?

Population	Sample Frame
Buyers of Scope mouthwash	Mailing list of *Consumer Reports* subscribers
Listeners of a particular FM radio classical music station	Telephone directory in your city
Prospective buyers of a new day planner and prospective clients tracking kit	Members of Sales and Marketing Executives International (a national organization of sales managers)
Users of weatherproof decking materials (to build outdoor decks)	Individuals' names registered at a recent home and garden show

14. Taco Bell approaches an official at your university and proposes to locate one of its restaurants on the campus. Because it would be the first commercial interest of this sort on your campus, the administration requires Taco Bell to conduct a survey of

full-time students to assess the desirability of this operation. Analyze the practical difficulties encountered with doing a census in this situation, and provide specific examples of each one. For instance, how long might such a census take, how much might it cost, what types of students are more accessible than others, and what capacity constraints might be operating here?

15. A state lottery (weekly lottery in which players pick numbers from 1 to 20) player is curious about the randomness of winning lottery numbers. He has kept track of the winning numbers in the past five weeks and finds that most numbers were selected 25 percent of the time, but the number 6 was one of the winning numbers 50 percent of the time. Will he be more or less likely to win if he picks a 6 in this week's lottery, or will it not make any difference in his chances? Relate your answer to simple random sampling.

16. Pet Insurers Company markets health and death benefits insurance to pet owners. It specializes in coverage for pedigreed dogs, cats, or expensive and exotic pets such as miniature Vietnamese pot-bellied pigs. The veterinary care costs of these pets can be high, and their deaths represent substantial financial loss to their owners. A researcher working for Pet Insurers finds that a listing company can provide a list of 15,000 names, which includes all current subscribers to *Cat Lovers*, *Pedigreed Dog*, and *Exotic Pets Monthly*. If the final sample size is to be 1000, what should be the skip interval in a systematic sample for each of the following: (a) a telephone survey using drop-down substitution, (b) a mail survey with an anticipated 30 percent response rate, and (c) resampling to select 250 more prospective respondents? Also, assess the incidence rate for this sample frame.

17. A market researcher is proposing a survey for the Big Tree Country Club, a private country club that is contemplating several changes in its layout to make the golf course more championship caliber. The researcher is considering three different sample designs as a way to draw a representative sample of the club's golfers. The three alternative designs are:

a. Station an interviewer at the first-hole tee on one day chosen at random, with instructions to ask every 10th golfer to fill out a self-administered questionnaire.

b. Put a stack of questionnaires on the counter where golfers check in and pay for their golf carts. There would be a sign above the questionnaires, and there would be an incentive for a "free dinner in the clubhouse" for three players who fill out the questionnaires and whose names are selected by a lottery.

c. Using the city telephone directory, a plus-one dialing procedure would be used. With this procedure a random page in the directory would be selected, and a name on that page would be selected, both using a table of random numbers. The plus-one system would be applied to that name and every name listed after it until 1000 golfers are identified and interviewed by telephone.

   Assess the representativeness and other issues associated with this sample problem. Be sure to identify the sample method being contemplated in each case. Which sample method do you recommend using and why?

18. A financial services company wants to take a survey of Internet users to see if they are interested in using the company's financial-planning and asset-tracking Internet services. Previous studies have shown that Internet usage differs greatly by age, education, and gender. The total sample size will be 1000. Using actual information about Internet usage or supplying reasonable assumptions, indicate how stratified simple random sampling should be applied for each of the following stratification situations: (1) 18–25, 26–50, and 51–65 age ranges; (2) education levels of high-school diploma, some college, college degree, and graduate degree; and (3) gender: males versus females.

PEACEFUL VALLEY: TROUBLE IN SUBURBIA

Located on the outskirts of a large city, the suburb of Peaceful Valley comprises approximately 6000 upscale homes. The subdivision came about 10 years ago when a developer built an earthen dam on Peaceful River and created Peaceful Lake, a 20-acre body of water. The lake became the centerpiece of the development, and the first 2000 one-half acre lots were sold as lakefront property. Now Peaceful Valley is fully developed, with 50 streets, all approximately the same length with approximately 120 houses on each street. Peaceful Valley's residents are primarily young, professional, dual-income families with one or two school-age children.

But controversy has come to Peaceful Valley. The Suburb Steering Committee has recommended that the community build a swimming pool, tennis court, and meeting room facility on four adjoining vacant lots in the back of the subdivision. Construction cost estimates range from $1.5 million to $2 million, depending on how large the facility will be. Currently, every Peaceful Valley homeowner is billed $100 annually for maintenance, security, and upkeep of Peaceful Valley. About 75% of the residents pay this fee. To construct the proposed recreational facility, every Peaceful Valley household would be expected to pay a one-time fee of $500, and annual fees would increase to $200 based on facility maintenance cost estimates.

Objections to the recreational facility come from various quarters. For some, the one-time fee is unacceptable; for others, the notion of a recreational facility is not appealing. Some residents have their own swimming pools, belong to local tennis clubs, or otherwise have little use for a meeting room facility. Other Peaceful Valley homeowners see the recreational facility as a wonderful addition, where they could have their children learn to swim, play tennis, or just hang out under supervision.

The president of the Peaceful Valley Suburb Association has decided to conduct a survey to poll the opinions and preferences of Peaceful Valley homeowners regarding the swimming pool, tennis court, and meeting room facility concept. It is decided that a sample of 3000 heads of households in Peaceful Valley should be used in this survey.

Given this background information on the Peaceful Valley, indicate the steps necessary to implement each of the following sample methods.

1. How would you select a simple random sample of those Peaceful Valley homeowners who paid their $100 subdivision association dues last year? What, if any, sample bias, might result from this approach?

2. How would you select a one-stage cluster sample of Peaceful Valley households?

3. How would you select a systematic sample assuming that a membership directory is not available?

THE COBALT GROUP: ONLINE SURVEY FOR MYCARTOOLS

The Cobalt Group (www.cobaltgroup.com) touts itself as a leading provider of e-business products and services for the automotive industry. It claims almost 9000 Web-site clients and about the same number of parts locator clients. There are several Cobalt Group products, and a number are geared toward the automobile dealer–automobile buyer/owner relationship. One of Cobalt Group's products is MyCarTools, which provides auto dealers with the ability to give personal Web space to its auto buyers. This Web space is set up to let the car owner input his or her auto usage, to track service records, or to schedule a service appointment online. The auto dealership can use this Web space service as a direct-marketing tool of its own, for as its customers enter their information on their Web spaces, the dealership's database of owners grows. This database can be used to identify customer types and trends, to target specific customer segments with advertisements and special promotions, or even to alert customers to product recalls.

There is great potential value in MyCarTools, because it is a means of maintaining close contact with buyers of autos from the dealership over the life of their automobiles. If satisfying to the customer, this contact may well translate into a strong propensity in that customer to return to the dealership when he or she is thinking about replacing the auto. Of course, the degree of participation in MyCarTools is entirely voluntary, and it depends on a number of factors. First, the auto buyer must agree to be entered into the dealer's Web space, and, second, the buyer must have computer availability and Internet connectivity. Finally, the buyer must use the service on a regular basis.

In an online chat problem-solving forum, automobile dealers who use Cobalt Group dealership software brainstormed questions about the value of MyCarTools. The top question was, "Does the use of MyCarTools increase the propensity of a car buyer to return to the dealership where he or she bought the auto as compared to those who do not use MyCarTools?"

The Cobalt Group Special Projects Team was assigned the task of researching this question. The team immediately created an online questionnaire using WebSurveyor, but it is having difficulty deciding on the sample plan.

1. What should be the population definition for this marketing research situation?

2. Given this population definition, what should be the sample frame?

3. Should the Special Projects Team use an e-mail invitation or a Web site pop-up invitation sampling method? Why did you recommend this method over the other option?

 This is your integrated case described on pages 38–39.

THE HOBBIT'S CHOICE RESTAURANT

After some deliberation, Cory Rogers has narrowed the data-collection method for The Hobbit's Choice Restaurant down to two choices: a telephone sample or an online panel. In order for his forecasting model to work properly, Cory needs to use a sample design that will result in a sample that represents the entire greater metropolitan area.

1. Should Cory use a systematic sample using the metropolitan area telephone book as the sample frame? What are the advantages and disadvantages of this sample plan?

2. Should Cory use random digit dialing for the sample plan? What are the advantages and disadvantages of this sample plan?

3. Should Cory use a probability online panel such as the one maintained by Knowledge Networks, Inc.? With respect to sample design, what are the advantages and disadvantages involved with using this approach? (You may want to review Knowledge Networks, Inc. services by reading Marketing Research Insight 12.6 or by visiting its Web site at www.knowledgenetworks.com.)

13

Determining the Size of a Sample

How the Clients and Marketing Researchers Agree on Sample Size

In this fictitious example, we describe how sample size is determined for a survey for a water park that is thinking about adding an exciting new ride, to be called the "Frantic Flume," to its attractions.

Larry, our marketing researcher, has worked with Dana, the water park owner, to develop the research objectives and basic research design for a survey to see if there is sufficient interest in the Frantic Flume ride. Yesterday, Dana indicated that she wanted to have an accuracy level of ±3.5% because this was "just a little less accurate than your typical national opinion poll."

Larry has done some calculations and created a table that he faxed to Dana. The table looks like this.

"The Frantic Flume" Survey: Sample Size, Sample Error, and Sample Data-Collection Cost		
Sample Size	**Sample Error**	**Sample Cost[a]**
784	±3.5%	$15,680
600	±4.0%	$12,000
474	±4.5%	$9,480

Learning Objectives

- To understand the 8 axioms underlying sample size determination with a probability sample
- To know how to compute sample size using the confidence interval approach
- To become aware of practical considerations in sample size determination
- To be able to describe different methods used to decide sample size, including knowing whether or not a particular method is flawed

The marketing researcher and the owner of this water park must agree on the sample size for a survey to see if customers want a new wild water ride.

384	±5.0%	$7,680
317	±5.5%	$6,340
267	±6.0%	$5,340

[a]Estimated at $20 per completed interview

The following conversation now takes place.

Larry: "Did the fax come through okay?"

Dana: "Yes, but maybe I wish it didn't."

Larry: "What do you mean?"

Dana: "There is no way I am going to pay over $15,000 just for the data collection."

Larry: "Yes, I figured this when we talked yesterday, but we were thinking about the accuracy of a national opinion poll then, but we are talking about your water park survey now. So, I prepared a schedule with some alternative sample sizes, their accuracy levels, and their costs."

Dana: "Gee, can you really get an accuracy level of ±6% with just 267 respondents? That seems like a very small sample."

Larry: "Small in numbers, but it is still somewhat hefty in price, as the data-collection company will charge $20 per completed telephone interview. You can see that it will still amount to over $5000."

Dana: "Well, that's nowhere near $15,000! What about the 384 size? It will come to $7680 according to your table, and the accuracy is ±5%. How does the accuracy thing work again?"

Larry: "If I find that, say 70% of the respondents in the random sample of your customers want the Frantic Flume at your water park, then you can be assured that between 65% to 75% of all of your customers want it."

Dana: "And with $7680 for data collection, the whole survey comes in under $15,000?"

Larry: "I am sure it will. If you want me to, I can calculate a firm total cost using the 384 sample size."

Dana: "Sounds like a winner to me. When can you get it to me?

Larry: "I'll have the proposal completed by Friday. You can study it over the weekend."

Dana: "Great. I'll set up a tentative meeting with the investors for the middle of next week."

As you can see in the preceding conversation, there is something surprising about sample size, which refers to the number of respondents in a survey. The surprise for Dana is that the sample size does not need to be huge in order to be reasonably accurate. In fact, the Frantic Flume water park survey will have fewer than 400 respondents in the sample, yet its accuracy level is acceptable to Dana, and the cost of the survey is also reasonable to her. In the previous chapter, you learned that the method of sample selection determines its representativeness. Unfortunately, many managers falsely believe that sample size and sample representativeness are related, but they are not. By studying this chapter, you will learn that the size of a sample directly affects its accuracy or error just as Larry, the researcher, related to Dana, the client, in the preceding conversation. If discovering that a sample of 384 respondents has a ±5.0% accuracy level shocks you, do not be concerned, as this only means that you are like most marketing managers. After you read this chapter, you will understand why this sample size is appropriate for the Frantic Flume survey.

Here is a way to convince yourself that there is no relationship between the size of a sample and its representativeness of the population from which it is drawn. Suppose we want to find out what percentage of the U.S. workforce dresses "business casual" most of the workweek. We take a convenience sample by standing on a corner of Wall Street in New York City. We ask everyone who will talk to us about whether or not they come to work in business casual dress. At the end of one week, we have questioned over 5000 respondents in our survey. Are these people representative of the U.S. workforce population? No, of course they are not. In fact, conceivably they are not even representative of New York City workers because a nonprobability sampling method was used. What if we had asked 10,000 New Yorkers? No matter what its size, the sample would still be unrepresentative for the same reason.

To repeat an important point, instead of determining representativeness, the size of the sample affects the sample accuracy of results. **Sample accuracy** refers to how close a random sample's statistic (for example, mean of the responses to a particular question) is to the population's value (that is, the true mean of the population) it represents. Sample size will have a direct bearing on how accurate the sample's findings are relative to the true values in the population. If a random sample has 5 respondents, it is more accurate than if it had only 1; 10 respondents are more accurate than 5, and so forth. Common sense tells us that larger random samples are more accurate than smaller random samples. But, as you will learn in this Chapter, 5 is not 5 times more accurate than 1, and 10 is not twice as accurate as 5. The important points to remember at this time are that (1) sample size is not related to representativeness, but (2) sample size is related to accuracy. Precisely how accuracy is affected constitutes a major section of this chapter.

This chapter is concerned with methods to determine sample size. To be sure, sample-size determination can be a complicated process[1] but we have tried to make it uncomplicated and intuitive. To begin, we share with you some axioms about sample size. These statements serve as the basis for the confidence interval approach, which is the best sample size determination method to, so we describe its underlying notions of variability, allowable sample error, and level of confidence. These are combined into a simple formula to calculate sample size, and we give some examples of how the formula works. Next, we describe four other popular, but mostly incorrect, methods used to decide on a sample's size. Last, there are practical considerations and special situations that affect the final sample size, and we briefly mention some of these.

SAMPLE SIZE AXIOMS

How to determine the number of respondents in a particular sample is actually one of the simplest decisions within the marketing research process[2]; however, because formulas are used, it often appears bewildering. In reality, a sample size decision is usually a compromise between what is theoretically perfect and what is practically feasible. Although it is not the intent of this chapter to make you a sampling expert, it is important that you understand the fundamental concepts that underlie sample size decisions.[3]

There are two good reasons a marketing researcher should have a basic understanding of sample size determination. First, many practitioners have a **large sample size bias**—a false belief that sample size determines a sample's representativeness. Such practitioners ask questions such as "How large a sample should we have to be representative?" However, as you just learned, there is no relationship between sample size and representativeness. So, you already know one of the basics of sample size determination. Second, a marketing manager should have a basic understanding of sample size determination because the size of the sample is often a major cost factor, particularly for personal interviews but even with telephone surveys. Consequently, understanding how sample size is determined will help the manager better manage his or her resources.

We wish to contradict the "large sample size bias" found in many marketing research clients with Table 13.1, which lists eight axioms about sample size and how this size relates to the accuracy of that sample. An axiom is a universal truth, meaning that the statement will always be correct. However, we must point out that these axioms pertain only to probability samples, so they are true only as long as the sample in question is a random one. As we describe the confidence interval method of sample size determination, we will refer to each axiom in turn and help you understand it.

> The size of a sample has nothing to do with its representativeness. Sample size affects the sample accuracy.

TABLE 13.1	The Axioms of Sample Size and Sample Accuracy

1. The only perfectly accurate sample is a census.

2. A probability sample will always have some inaccuracy (sample error).

3. The larger a probability sample is, the more accurate it is (less sample error).

4. Probability sample accuracy (error) can be calculated with a simple formula, and expressed as a ± % number.

5. You can take any finding in the survey, replicate the survey with the same probability sample size, and you will be "very likely" to find the same finding within the ± % range of the original finding.

6. In almost all cases, the accuracy (sample error) of a probability sample is independent of the size of the population.

7. A probability sample size can be a very tiny percent of the population size and still be very accurate (have little sample error).

8. The size of a probability sample depends on the client's desired accuracy (acceptable sample error) balanced against the cost of data collection for that sample size.

THE CONFIDENCE INTERVAL METHOD OF DETERMINING SAMPLE SIZE

The confidence interval approach is the correct method by which to determine sample size.

The most correct method of determining sample size is the **confidence interval approach**, which applies the concepts of accuracy (sample error), variability, and confidence interval to create a "correct" sample size. Because it is theoretically the most correct method, it is the one used by national opinion polling companies and most marketing researchers. To describe the confidence interval approach to sample size determination, we first describe the four underlying concepts.

Sample Size and Accuracy

The only perfectly accurate sample is a census.

The first axiom, "*The only perfectly accurate sample is a census,*" is easy to understand. Accuracy is referred to as "sample error." You should be aware that a survey has two types of error: nonsampling error and sampling error. **Nonsampling error** pertains to all sources of error other than the sample selection method and sample size, so nonsampling error includes things such as problem specification mistakes, question bias, or incorrect analysis. **Sampling error** involves sample selection and sample size.[4] With a census, every member of the population is selected, so there is no error in selection. Because a census accounts for every single individual, it is perfectly accurate, meaning that it has no sample error whatsoever.

However, a census is almost always infeasible because of cost and for practical reasons. This fact brings us to the second axiom, "*A probability sample will always have some inaccuracy (sample error).*" This axiom notifies you that no random sample is a perfect representation of the population. However, it is important to remember that a random sample is nonetheless a *very good* representation of the population, even if it is not perfectly accurate.

The larger the size of the (probability) sample, the less is its sample error.

The third axiom, "*The larger a probability sample is, the more accurate it is (less sample error),*" serves notice that there is a relationship between sample size and the accuracy of that sample. This relationship is presented graphically in Figure 13.1. In this figure, sample error (accuracy) is listed on the vertical axis and sample size is noted on the horizontal one. The graph shows the accuracy levels of samples ranging in size from 50 to 2000. The shape of the graph is consistent with the third axiom, as the sample error decreases as sample size increases. However, you should immediately notice that the graph is not a straight line. In other words, doubling sample size does not result in halving the sample error. The relationship is a curved one. It looks a bit like a backward ski jump.

There is another important property of the sample error graph. As you look at the graph, note that at a sample size of around 1,000, the accuracy level drops to about ±3

FIGURE 13.1
The Relationship between Sample Size and Sample Error

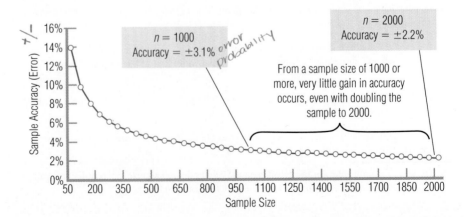

percent (actually ±3.1%), and it decreases at a very slow rate with larger sample sizes. In other words, once a sample is greater than, say 1000, large gains in accuracy are not realized with large increases in the size of the sample. In fact, if its accuracy is already ±3.1 percent, there is not much more accuracy possible.

With the lower end of the sample size axis, however, large gains in accuracy can be made with a relatively small sample size increase. For example, with a sample size of 50, the accuracy level is ±13.9 percent, whereas with a sample size of 250 it is ±6.2 percent, meaning the accuracy of the 250 sample is roughly double that of the 50 sample. But as was just described, such huge gains in accuracy are not the case at the other end of the sample size scale because of the nature of the curved relationship.

> With a sample size of 1000 or more, very little gain in accuracy occurs even with doubling or tripling the sample to 2000 or 3000.

The sample error graph was produced using the fourth axiom[5]: "*Probability sample accuracy (error) can be calculated with a simple formula and expressed as a ± % number,*" and the formula follows:

Sample-Error Formula

$$\pm \text{ Sample error \%} = 1.96 \times \sqrt{\frac{p * q}{n}}$$

This formula is simple, as n is the sample size, and there is a constant, 1.96. But what are p and q?

p and q: The Concept of Variability

When we find a wide dispersion of responses—that is, when we do not find one response option accounting for a large number of respondents relative to the other items—we say that the results have much variability. **Variability** is defined as the amount of dissimilarity (or similarity) in respondents' answers to a particular question. If most respondents indicate the same answer on the response scale, the distribution has little variability because respondents are highly similar. On the other hand, if respondents are

> Variability refers to how similar or dissimilar responses are to a given question.

> Sample size should be large with more differences evident among population members.

evenly spread across the question's response options, there is much variability because respondents a quite dissimilar.

Our sample error formula pertains only to nominal data, or data in which the response items are categorical. We recommend that you think of a yes/no question for which the responses are highly similar. The greater this similarity, the less the variability in the responses. For example, we may find that the question "The next time you order a pizza, will you use Domino's?" yields a 90–10 percent distribution split between "yes" versus "no." In other words, most of the respondents gave the same answer, meaning that there is much similarity in the responses, and the variability would be low. In contrast, if the question had resulted in a 50–50 percent split, the overall response pattern would be (maximally) dissimilar, and there would be much variability. You can see the variability of responses in Figure 13.2. With the 90–10 percent split, the graph has one high side (90%) and one low side (10%), meaning almost everyone agreed on Domino's, or with disagreement or much variability in people's answers, it has both sides at even levels (50%–50%).

The Domino's Pizza example relates to p and q in the following way:

$$p = \text{percent saying "yes"}$$
$$q = 100\% - p, \text{ or percent saying "no"}$$

In other words, p and q will always sum to 100% as in the cases of 90% + 10% and 50% + 50%.

In our sample error formula, p and q are multiplied together. The largest possible product of p times q is 2500 or 50% times 50%. You can verify this fact by multiplying other combinations of p and q, such as 90–10 (900), 80–20 (1600), or 60–40 (2400). Every one will have a result smaller than 2500, and, in fact, the most lopsided combination of 99–1 (99) yields the smallest product. So, if we assume the worst possible case of maximum variability or 50–50 disagreement, the sample-error formula becomes even simpler and can be given with two constants, 1.96 and 2500 as follows:

Sample-Error Formula with p = 50% and q = 50%

$$\pm \text{ Sample error } \% = 1.96 \times \sqrt{\frac{2500}{n}}$$

FIGURE 13.2
The Amount of Variability Is Reflected in the Spread of the Distribution

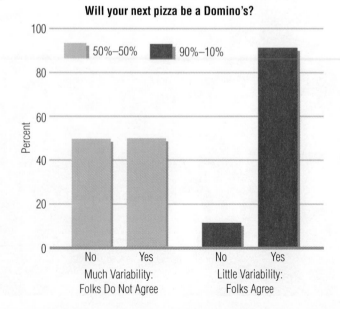

This is the formula we used to create the sample-error graph in Figure 13.1. To determine how much sample error is associated with a random sample of a given size, all you need to do is to "plug in" the sample size in this formula.

The Concept of a Confidence Interval

The fifth sample size axiom states, "*You can take any finding in the survey, replicate the survey with the same probability sample size, and you will be "very likely" to find the same finding within the ± % range of the original finding.*" This axiom is based on the concept of a "confidence interval."

A **confidence interval** is a range whose endpoints define a certain percentage of the responses to a question. A confidence interval is based on the normal or bell-shaped curve commonly found in statistics. Figure 13.3 reveals that the properties of the normal curve are such that 1.96 times the standard deviation theoretically defines the endpoints for 95 percent of the distribution.

There is a theory called the **central limit theorem** that underlies many statistical concepts, and this theory is the basis of the seventh axiom. A replication is a repeat of the original, so if we repeated our Domino's survey a great many times—perhaps 1000—with a fresh random sample of the same size, and we made a bar chart of all 1000 percents of "yes" results, the central limit theorem holds that our bar chart would look like a normal curve. Figure 13.4 illustrates how the bar chart would look if 50% of our population members intended to use Domino's the next time they ordered a pizza.

Figure 13.4 reveals that 95% of the replications fall within ±1.96 times the sample error. In our example, 1000 random samples, each with sample size (n) equal to 100 were taken and the percent of "yes" answers was calculated for each sample and all of these were plotted in line chart. The sample error for a sample size of 100 is calculated as follows:

> A confidence interval defines endpoints based on knowledge of the area under a bell-shaped curve.

Sample-Error Formula with p = 50%, q = 50%, and n = 100

$$\pm \text{ Sample error \%} = 1.96 \times \sqrt{\frac{2500}{n}}$$

$$= 1.96 \times \sqrt{\frac{2500}{100}}$$

$$= 1.96 \times \sqrt{25}$$

$$= 1.96 \times 5$$

$$= \pm 9.8\%$$

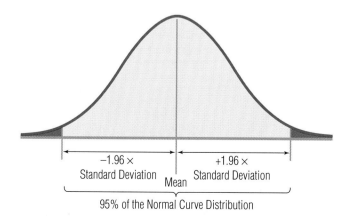

−1.96 ×
Standard Deviation   Mean   +1.96 ×
Standard Deviation

95% of the Normal Curve Distribution

FIGURE 13.3
A Normal Curve with Its 95% Properties Identified

FIGURE 13.4
Plotting the Findings of
1000 Replications of the
Domino's Pizza Survey:
Illustration of the Central
Limit Theorem

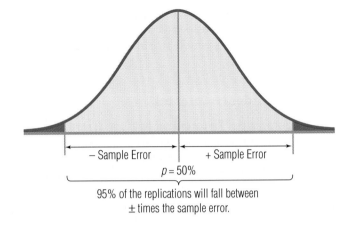

95% of the replications will fall between
± times the sample error.

The confidence interval is calculated as follows:

Confidence Interval Formula   *Confidence interval = p ± sample error*

which means that the limits of the 95% confidence interval in our example are 50% ±
9.8%, or 40.2% to 59.8%.

> The confidence interval gives the range of findings if the survey were replicated many, many times with the identical sample size.

How can a researcher use the confidence interval? This is a good time to leave the
theoretical and move to the practical aspects of sample size. The confidence interval
approach allows the researcher to predict what would be found if a survey were replicated many, many times. Of course, no client would agree to the cost of 1000 replications, but the researcher can say, "I found that 50% of the sample intends to order
Domino's the next time. I am very confident that the true population percent is between
40.2% and 59.8%; in fact, I am confident that if I did this survey over 1000 times, 95%
of the findings would fall in this range."

What if the confidence interval was too wide? In other words, what if the client
thought that a range from about 40% to 60% was not precise enough? Figure 13.5
shows how the sample size affects the shape of the theoretical sampling distribution,
and, more important, the confidence interval range.

Active **Learning**

HOW DOES THE LEVEL OF CONFIDENCE AFFECT THE SAMPLE ACCURACY CURVE?

Thus far, the sample error formula has used a z value of 1.96, which corresponds to the
95% level of confidence. However, there is another level of confidence sometimes used by
marketing researchers, and this is the 99% level of confidence, with the corresponding z
value of 2.58. For this active learning exercise, use the sample error formula with p = 50%
and q = 50%, but use a z value of 2.58, and calculate the sample error associated with sample sizes of:

100
500
1000
2000

Plot your computed sample error ± numbers that correspond to sample sizes of 100,
500, 1000, and 2000 in Figure 13.1. Connect your four plotted points with a curved line
similar to the one already in the graph. Write down two things you can conclude about the

Sample Size   Sampling Distribution (Reflective of Sample Error)

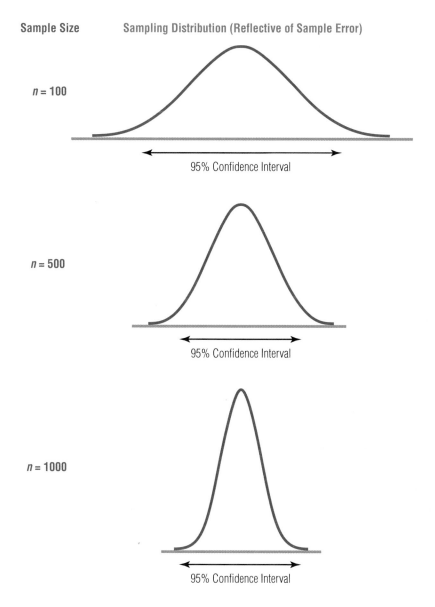

n = 100

95% Confidence Interval

n = 500

95% Confidence Interval

n = 1000

95% Confidence Interval

FIGURE 13.5
Three Sampling Distributions Showing How the Sample Error Is Less with Larger Sample Sizes

effect of a level of confidence different from 95% on the amount of sample error with samples in the range of the horizontal axis in Figure 13.3.

1. _____

2. _____

How Population Size (N) Affects Sample Size

Perhaps you noticed something that is absent in all of these discussions and calculations, and that element is mentioned in the sixth sample size axiom, "*In almost all cases, the accuracy (sample error) of a probability sample is independent of the size of the population.*" Our formulas do not include N, the size of the population! We have been calculating sample error and confidence intervals without taking the size of the population into account. Does this mean that a sample of 100 will have a sample error of ±5% (confidence interval of ±9.8%)

With few exceptions, the sample size and the size of the population are not related to each other.

for a population of 20 million people who watched the last Super Bowl, 2 million Kleenex tissue buyers, and 200,000 Scottish Terrier owners? Yes, it does. The only time that the population size is a consideration in sample size determination is in the case of a "small population," and this possibility is discussed in the last section in this chapter.

Because the size of the sample is independent of the population size, the seventh sample size axiom, "*A probability sample size can be a very tiny percent of the population size and still be very accurate (have little sample error),*" can now be understood. National opinion polls tend to use sample sizes ranging from 1000 to 1200 people, meaning that the sample error is around ±3%, or highly accurate. A sample size of 5000 yields an error of ±1.4%, which is a very small error level, yet 5000 is less than 1% of 1 million, and a great many consumer markets—cola drinkers, condominium owners, debit-card users, allergy sufferers, home gardeners, Internet surfers, and so on—are each comprised of many millions of customers. Here is one more example to drive our point home: a sample of 500 is just as accurate for the entire population of China (1.3 billion people) as it is for Montgomery, Alabama (200,000 people), as long as a random sample is taken in both cases.

THE SAMPLE-SIZE FORMULA

To compute sample size, only three items are required: variability, acceptable sample error, and confidence level.

You are now acquainted with the basic concepts essential to understanding sample-size determination using the confidence interval approach. To calculate the proper sample size for a survey, only three items are required: (1) the variability believed to be in the population, (2) the acceptable sample error, and (3) the level of confidence required in your estimates of the population values. This section will describe the formula used to compute sample size via the **confidence interval method**. As we describe the formula, we will present some of the concepts you learned earlier a bit more formally.

Determining Sample Size via the Confidence Interval Formula

As you would expect, there is a formula that includes our three required items.[6] When considering a percentage, the formula is as follows[7]:

Standard Sample-Size Formula $$n = \frac{z^2(pq)}{e^2}$$

where

> n = the sample size
> z = standard error associated with the chosen level of confidence (typically, 1.96)
> p = estimated percent in the population
> q = $100 - p$
> e = acceptable sample error

The standard sample size formula is applicable if you are concerned with the nominally scaled questions in the survey such as "yes or no" questions.

▶ **Variability: p times q** This sample-size formula is used if we are focusing on some nominally scaled question in the survey. For instance, when conducting the Domino's Pizza survey, our major concern might be the percentage of pizza buyers who intend to buy Domino's. If no one is uncertain, there are two possible answers: those who do and those who do not. Earlier, we illustrated that if our pizza buyer population has very little variability, that is, if almost everyone, say 90%, is a raving Domino's Pizza fan, this belief will be reflected in the sample size. With little variation in the population, we know that we can take smaller samples because this is accommodated by the formula by

Managers often find it hard to believe that a sample can be a very tiny proportion of a population and be very accurate at the same time.

p times q. The estimated percent in the population, p, is the mechanism that performs this translation along with q, which is always determined by p, as q = 100% − p.

▶ **Acceptable Sample Error: e**　The formula includes another factor—acceptable sample error. We hope you are not surprised at this factor, as we developed it in the previous section that explained many of the sample size axioms. **Acceptable error** is, in fact, the very same concept that was introduced to you earlier; that is, the term e is the amount of sample error that will be associated with the survey. It is used to indicate how closely to the population percentage you want the many, many replications, if you were to take them.

In other words, if we performed any survey with a p value that was to be estimated—who intends to buy from Wal-Mart, IBM, Shell, Allstate, or any such vendor versus any other vendor, the acceptable sample error notion would hold. Small acceptable sample error translates into a low percent, such as ±4% or less, whereas high acceptable sample error translates into a large percent such as ±10% or higher.

▶ **Level of Confidence: z**　Last, we need to decide on a level of confidence, or, to relate to our previous section, the percent of area under the normal curve described by our calculated confidence intervals. Thus far, we have used the constant, 1.96, because 1.96 is the z value that pertains to 95% confidence intervals. Researchers typically only worry about the 95 percent or 99 percent level of confidence. The 95 percent level of confidence is by far the most commonly used, so we used 1.96 in the examples earlier and referred to it as a constant because it is the chosen z in most cases. Also, 1.96 rounds up to 2, which is convenient in case you do not have a calculator handy, and you want to do a quick approximation of the sample size.

Actually, any level of confidence ranging from 1% to 100% is possible, but you would need to consult a z table in order to find the corresponding value. Market researchers almost never deviate from 95%, but if they do, 99% is the level likely to be

In marketing research, a 95 percent or 99 percent level of confidence is standard practice.

TABLE 13.2	Values of z for 95% and 99% Level of Confidence	
Level of Confidence		**z**
95%		1.96
99%		2.58

used. We have itemized the z values for the 99% and 95% levels of confidence in Table 13.2, so you can turn to it quickly if you need to.

We are now ready to calculate sample size. Let us assume there is great expected variability (50%) and we want ±10% acceptable sample error at the 95% level of confidence. To determine the sample size needed, we calculate as follows:

Sample Size Computed with p = 50%, q = 50%, and e = 10%

$$n = \frac{1.96^2(50 \times 50)}{10^2}$$
$$= \frac{3.84(2500)}{100}$$
$$= \frac{9600}{100}$$
$$= 96$$

Just to convince you of the use of the confidence interval approach, recall our previous comment that most national opinion polls use sample sizes of about 1100 and they claim ±3% accuracy (allowable sample error). Using the 95% level of confidence, the computations would be:

Sample Size Computed with p = 50%, q = 50%, and e = 3%

$$n = \frac{1.96^2(50 \times 50)}{3^2}$$
$$= \frac{3.84(2500)}{9}$$
$$= \frac{9600}{9}$$
$$= 1067$$

In other words, if these national polls were to be ±3% accurate at the 95% confidence level, they would need to have sample sizes of 1067 (or about 1100 respondents). The next time you read in the newspaper or see on television something about a national opinion poll, check the sample size and look to see if there is a footnote or reference on the "margin of error." It is a good bet that you will find the error to be somewhere close to ±3% and the sample size to be in the 1100 range.

What if the researcher wanted a 99% level of confidence in his or her estimates? The computations would be as follows:

99% Confidence Interval Sample Size Computed with p = 50%, q = 50%, and e = 3%

$$n = \frac{2.58^2(50 \times 50)}{3^2}$$
$$= \frac{6.66(2500)}{9}$$
$$= \frac{16650}{9}$$
$$= 1850$$

Thus, if a survey were to have ±3% allowable sample error at the 99% level of confidence, it would need to have a sample size of 1850, assuming the maximum variability (50%).

SAMPLE-SIZE-CALCULATIONS PRACTICE

While you can follow the step-by-step sample-size calculations examples we have just described, it is useful for someone just learning about sample size to perform the calculations themselves. In this Active Learning exercise, refer back to the standard sample-size formula and use it to calculate the appropriate sample size for each of the following five situations.

Situation	Confidence Level	Value of p	Allowable Error	Sample Size (Enter your Answer Below)
1	95%	65%	±3.5%	_____
2	99%	65%	±3.5%	_____
3	95%	60%	±5%	_____
4	99%	60%	±5%	_____
5	95%	50%	±4%	_____

Why all the fuss about variability, acceptable error, and confidence level? To be certain, it probably seems like we are making a mountain out of a mole hill, but consider, for a few minutes, a practical consequence of the desired sample size. Take the case of random digit dialing, and ponder how many numbers you would have to generate in order to end up with 1100 completed telephone interviews. We have provided Marketing Research Insight 13.1 to make you aware that it may take many thousands of telephone calls to obtain the desired sample size of completed telephone interviews. So, it is vital that the researcher understand the factors that affect sample size and apply them faithfully in the sample size determination formula because every additional desired completion has significant ramifications for the effort that will be necessary to accomplish that competed interview.

MARKETING RESEARCH INSIGHT

PRACTICAL APPLICATION

13.1

How Many Random Digit Dialing Telephone Numbers Do You Need?

In Chapter 12, we described random digit dialing as a practical embodiment of random sampling. You should recall that random digit dialing uses a random number generator to produce telephone numbers to be used in a telephone survey. The single most important advantage of random digit dialing is that *all* telephone numbers are eligible to be in the sample; whereas, if the telephone book was used as the sample frame, there would be no chance for unlisted numbers to be selected. Similarly, telephone numbers activated after the publication date of the telephone book would not be eligible because they would not be in the sample frame.

Random digit dialing overcomes the "missing numbers" problem; however, dialing random telephone numbers has

(continued)

its own drawbacks. For one, nonworking telephone numbers will be dialed, and business, organization, association, and other noneligible telephone numbers will be called, even if the survey is intended for households. Furthermore, even telephone numbers of households that are called may not qualify to take part in the survey, and of those who are qualified, some will refuse to participate in the survey.

So, how many random digit telephone numbers are needed to arrive at the desired sample size number of completed interviews? You can answer this question by calculating a ratio that we will call the "completion ratio." The calculation is as follows.

1 Estimate the percent of random digit dialing numbers that will be eligible households; call it "active."
2 Estimate the incidence rate for eligible households to qualify for the survey; call it "incidence."

3 Estimate what percent of households who qualify will agree to take part in the survey; call it "participate."
4 Multiply the percents: active times incidence times participate to determine the "completion ratio."

As an example, let's use an active percent of .8, an incidence of .6, and a participate percent of .4. The completion ratio is $.8 \times .6 \times .4 = .192$. The interpretation of a .192 completion ratio is to realize that 19.2% of the total random digit dialing numbers will be completed surveys. Or, to say this differently, 80.8% of the random digit dialing numbers will not result in a single completed survey.

Applying a little algebra, one finds that in order to determine how many random digit dialing numbers will be needed to achieve the desired sample size of completions may be calculated with the following formula:

Number of random digit dialing numbers = desired sample size/completion ratio

To illustrate, use our completion ratio of .192, if the desired sample size is 1100, then the calculation looks like:

Number of random digit dialing numbers =   desired sample size/completion ratio
Number of random digit dialing numbers =   1100/.192
Number of random digit dialing numbers =   5230 (rounded up)

PRACTICAL CONSIDERATIONS IN SAMPLE-SIZE DETERMINATION

Although we have discussed how variability, acceptable sample error, and confidence level are used to calculate sample size, we have not discussed the criteria used by the marketing manager and researcher to determine these factors. General guidelines follow.

How to Estimate Variability in the Population

When using standard sample-size formula with percentages, there are two alternatives: (1) expect the worst case or (2) estimate what is the actual variability. We have shown you that with percentages, the **worst case**, or most, **variability** is 50%/50%. This assumption is the most conservative one, and it will result in the calculation of the largest possible sample size.

On the other hand, a researcher may want to estimate p, or the percentage in order to lower the sample size. Remember that any p/q combination other than 50%/50% will result in a lower calculated sample size. A lower sample size means less effort, time, and cost, so there are good reasons for a researcher to try to estimate p rather than to take the worst case.

Surprisingly, information about the target population often exists in many forms. There are census descriptions available in the form of secondary data, and there are compilations and bits of information that may be gained from groups such as Chambers of Commerce, local newspapers, state agencies, groups promoting commercial development, and a host of other similar organizations. Moreover, many populations under study by firms are known to them either formally through prior research studies or

By estimating p to be other than 50%, the researcher can reduce the sample size and save money.

To estimate variability, you can use prior research, experience, and/or intuition.

informally through prior business experiences. All of this information combines to help the research project director grasp the variability in the population. If the project director has conflicting information, or is worried about the timeliness or some other aspect of the information about the population's variability, he or she may conduct a pilot study in order to estimate p more confidently.[8]

How to Determine the Amount of Acceptable Sample Error

The marketing manager knows that small samples are less accurate, on the average, than are large samples. But it is rare for a marketing manager to think in terms of sample error. So, it is almost always up to the researcher to educate the manager on what might be acceptable, or "standard," sample error.

Marketing researchers often must help decision makers understand the sample-size implications of their requests for high precision, expressed as acceptable sample error.

Translated in terms of precision, the more precise the marketing decision maker desires the estimate to be, the larger must be the sample size. So, it is the task of the marketing research director to extract from the marketing decision maker the acceptable range of allowable error sufficient for him or her to make a decision. As you have learned, the acceptable sample error is specified as a plus or minus percent. That is, the researcher might say to the marketing decision maker, "I can deliver an estimate that is within ± 10 percent of the actual figure." If the marketing manager is confused at this, the researcher can next say, "This means that if I find that 45% of the sample is thinking seriously about leaving your competitors and buying your brand, I will be telling you that between 35% and 55% of your competitors' buyers are thinking about jumping over to be your customers." The conversation would continue until the marketing manager felt comfortable with the confidence interval range.

How to Decide on the Level of Confidence

All marketing decisions are made under a certain amount of risk, and it is mandatory to incorporate the estimate of risk, or at least some sort of a notion of uncertainty, into sample-size determination. Because sample statistics are estimates of population values, the proper approach is to use the sample information to generate a range in which the population value is anticipated to fall. Because the sampling process is imperfect, it is appropriate to use an estimate of sampling error in the calculation of this range. Using proper statistical terminology, the range is what we have called the "confidence interval." The researcher reports the range and the confidence he or she has that the range includes the population figure.

Use of the 95% or 99% level of confidence is standard in sample-size determination.

As we have indicated, the typical approach in marketing research is to use the standard confidence interval of 95%. As we have also indicated, this level translates into a z of 1.96. As you may recall from your statistics course, any level of confidence between 1% and 99.9% is possible, but another level of confidence that market researchers may consider is the 99% level. With the 99% level of confidence, the corresponding z value is 2.58. The 99% level of confidence means that if the survey were replicated many, many times with the sample size determined by using 2.58 in the sample size formula, 99% of the sample ps would fall in the sample error range.

However, since the z value is in the numerator of the sample size formula, an increase from 1.96 to 2.58 will increase the sample size. In fact, for any given sample error, the use of 99% level of confidence will increase the sample size by about 73%. So, using the 99% confidence level has profound effects on the calculated sample size. Are you surprised that most marketing researchers opt for a z of 1.96?

A researcher can calculate sample size using either a percentage or a mean. We describe the percentage approach here, and we show you how to determine sample size using a mean in Marketing Research Insight 13.2. Although the formulas are different, the basic concepts involved are identical.

13.2

Determining Sample Size Using the Mean: An Example of Variability of a Scale

We have presented the standard sample size formula in this chapter, and it assumes that the researcher is working with a case of percentages (p and q). However, there are instances when the researcher is more concerned with the mean of a variable in which case the percentage sample size formula does not fit. Instead, the researcher must use a different formula for sample size that includes the variability expressed as a standard deviation; that is, this situation calls for the use of the standard deviation to indicate the amount of variation. In this case, the sample size formula changes slightly to be the following:

Sample-Size Formula for a Mean $n = \dfrac{s^2 z^2}{e^2}$

where:

  n = the sample size
  z = standard error associated with the chosen level of confidence (typically, 1.96)
  s = variability indicated by an estimated standard deviation
  e = the amount of precision or allowable error in the sample estimate of the population

Although this formula looks different from the one for a percentage, it applies the same logic and key concepts in an identical manner.[9] As you can see, the formula determines sample size by multiplying the squares of the variability (s) and level of confidence values (z) and dividing that product by the square of the desired precision value (e). First, let us look at how variability of the population is a part of the formula. It appears in the form of s, or the estimated standard deviation of the population. This means that, because we are going to estimate the population mean, we need to have some knowledge of or at least a good guess at how much variability there is in the population. We must use the standard deviation because it expresses this variation. Unfortunately, unlike our percentage sample size case, there is no "50% equals the most variation" counterpart, so we have to rely on some prior knowledge about the population for our estimate of the standard deviation.

Next, we must express e, which is the acceptable error around the sample mean when we ultimately estimate the population mean from our survey. If information on the population variability is truly unknown and a pilot study is out of the question, a researcher can use a range estimate and knowledge that the range is approximated by the mean ±3 standard deviations. On occasion, a market researcher finds he or she is working with metric scale data, not nominal data. For instance, the researcher might have a 10-point importance scale or a 7-point satisfaction scale that is the critical variable with respect to determining sample size.

Suppose, for example, that a critical question on the survey involved a scale in which respondents rated their satisfaction with the client company's products on a scale of 1 to 10. If respondents use this scale, the theoretical range would be 10, and 10 divided by 6 equals a standard deviation of 1.7, which would be the variability estimate. Note that this would be a conservative estimate, as respondents might not use the entire 1–10 scale, or the mean might not equal 5, the midpoint, meaning that 1.7 is the largest variability estimate possible in this case.[10]

How to Balance Sample Size with the Cost of Data Collection

Perhaps you thought we had forgotten to comment on the last sample size axiom, "*The size of a probability sample depends on the client's desired accuracy (acceptable sample error) balanced against the cost of data collection for that sample size.*" This is a very important axiom, as it describes the reality of almost all decisions about sample-size determination. Hopefully, you will remember that in one of the very early chapters of this textbook, we commented on the cost of the research versus the value of the research, and that there was always a need to make sure that the cost of the research did not exceed the value of the information expected from that research.

Nowhere, it seems, do the cost and value issues come into play more vividly than with sample size determination and data-collection cost considerations.[11] You just learned that using the 99% level confidence has a considerable impact on the sample size, and you also learned that for this reason market researchers almost always use the 95% level of confidence.

The researcher must take cost into consideration when determining sample size.

In order to help you understand how to balance sample size and cost, let's consider the typical sample size determination case. First, 95% level of confidence is used, so $z = 1.96$. Next, the $p = q = 50\%$ situation is customarily assumed, as it is the worst possible case of variabilty. Then, the researcher and marketing manager decide on a *preliminary* acceptable sample error level. As example, we have provided a typical case in our Frantic Flume water park conversation with Larry, the researcher, and Dana, the water park owner, at the very beginning of this chapter. In our example, the researcher and water park owner initially agreed to a ±3.5% sample error.

Using the sample-size formula, the sample size, n, is calculated as follows.

Sample Size Computed with p = 50%, q = 50%, and e = 3.5%

$$
\begin{aligned}
n &= \frac{1.96^2(50 \times 50)}{3.5^2} \\
&= \frac{3.84(2500)}{12.25} \\
&= \frac{9600}{12.25} \\
&= 784 \ (\textit{rounded up})
\end{aligned}
$$

In our example, the $15,000+ cost of data collection for 784 completed telephone interviews was not acceptable to the client, so the researcher created a table with alternative sample sizes and associated accuracy levels based on his knowledge of the standard sample size formula. While not every researcher uses a table, the acceptable sample errors and the costs of various sample sizes are most certainly discussed in order to come to an agreement on the survey's sample size.

A table that relates data-collection cost and sample error is a useful tool when deciding on the survey sample size.

When a researcher is involved with an online survey that he or she has created, the cost of the sample can be minimized by purchasing the services of a panel such as samples from the SurveySpot panel maintained by Survey Sampling, Inc. As you will learn by reading Marketing Research Insight 13.3, Survey Sampling can draw a sample of its panel members with specific demographic, lifestyle, or topic interest characteristics but that is still representative of the types of respondents the researcher wishes to have in his or her online survey.

MARKETING RESEARCH INSIGHT

ONLINE APPLICATION

13.3 Need an Internet Sample for an Online Survey? Have "Spot" Fetch One!

For a great many years, Survey Sampling, Inc. has been the leader in supplying samples to marketing researchers. In its earlier existence, Survey Sampling developed comprehensive telephone number databases for households and for businesses to which it applied random sampling procedures and it sold to marketing researchers requiring representative samples of geographic areas, or special affinities (such as golfers or gardeners), or business samples.

In an Internet research environment, Survey Sampling has moved aggressively into the recruitment of household members who join its various panels. The service is called "SurveySpot," and it operates much like a computer database of telephone numbers except the database is comprised *(continued)* of the e-mail addresses of SurveySpot panel members. Individuals who join the panel agree to take part in online surveys that they are interested in, and they receive rewards based on periodic sweepstakes drawings and by way of a frequent particpant program that accumulates points that can be redeemed for products. Individuals who join provide demographic, lifestyle, and interest area information that goes into the SurveySpot database. Survey Sampling claims that its panel is comprised of 12 million panelists, and it can identify its panelist by their demographic and other characteristics with 3500 different topics across four countries: the United States, Canada, United Kingdom, and Australia.[12] Here is a sample listing of the hobbies/interests topics by which Survey Sampling can identify groups of its SurveySpot panelists.

- Automotive work
- Crafts
- Gardening
- Gourmet cooking
- Home decorating
- Carpet preferences
- Home improvement/DIY
- Photography
- Boating/sailing
- Camping/hiking
- Cat owners
- Cultural arts/events

- Dog owners
- Fine Living network viewers
- Fishing
- Football
- Gambling
- Health and fitness
- Movie enthusiasts
- Music
- Vacation cruises
- Watches sports more than three times a week
- Wine drinking by type
- Champagne/sparkling wine drinker
- Fine Living magazine readership
- Cable food channel viewers
- Woodworking
- Yoga

To use SurveySpot, a marketing researcher creates an online survey, and then contracts with Survey Sampling to purchase some number of randomly selected SurveySpot respondents. Survey Sampling then draws the random sample and notifies those panelists who are qualified and selected at random from its panel to visit the survey site and to complete the online questionnaire. Because its panelists are motivated by topic interest and its incentive programs, Survey Sampling ensures a high percentage of participation by its panels in response to these targeted invitations to take online surveys.

OTHER METHODS OF SAMPLE-SIZE DETERMINATION

In practice, a number of different methods are used to determine sample size, including some that are beyond the scope of this textbook.[13] The more common methods are described briefly in this section. As you will soon learn, most have critical flaws that make them undesirable, even though you may find instances in which they are used and proponents who argue for their use. Since you are acquainted with the eight sample-size axioms, and you know how to calculate sample size using the confidence interval method formula, you should comprehend the flaws as we point each one out.

Arbitrary "Percent-Rule-of-Thumb" Sample Size

The **arbitrary approach** may take on the guise of a "percent-rule-of-thumb" statement regarding sample size: "A sample should be at least 5 percent of the population in order to be accurate." In fact, it is not unusual for a marketing manager to respond to a marketing researcher's sample-size recommendation by saying, "But that is less than 1 percent of the entire population!"

Arbitrary sample size approaches rely on erroneous rules of thumb.

You must agree that the arbitrary percent-rule-of-thumb approach certainly has some intuitive appeal in that it is very easy to remember, and it is simple to apply.

Surely, you will not fall into the seductive trap of the percent-rule-of-thumb, for you understand that sample size is not related to population size at all. Just to convince yourself, consider these sample sizes. If you take 5% samples of populations with sizes 10,000, 1,000,000, and 10,000,000, the ns will be 500, 50,000, and 500,000, respectively. Now, think back to the sample accuracy graph (Figure 13.1). The highest sample size on that graph was 2000, so obviously the percent rule of thumb method can yield sample sizes that are absurd with respect to accuracy. Further, you have also learned from the sample size axioms that a sample can be a very, very small percent of the total population and have very great accuracy.

In sum, arbitrary sample sizes are simple and easy to apply, but they are neither efficient nor economical. With sampling, we wish to draw a subset of the population in an economical manner and to estimate the population values with some predetermined degree of accuracy. "Percent-rule-of-thumb" methods lose sight of the accuracy aspect of sampling; they certainly violate some of the axioms about sample size, and, as you just saw, they certainly are not economical when the population under study is large.

Arbitrary sample sizes are simple and easy to apply, but they are neither efficient nor economical.

Conventional Sample-Size Specification

The **conventional approach** follows some "convention" or number believed somehow to be the right sample size. A manager may be knowledgeable of national opinion polls and notice that they are often taken with sample sizes of between 1000 and 1200 respondents. This may appear to the manager as a "conventional" number, and he or she may question a market researcher whose sample-size recommendation varies from this convention. On the other hand, the survey may be one in a series of studies a company has undertaken on a particular market, and the same sample size may be applied each succeeding year simply because it was used last year. The convention might be an average of the sample sizes of similar studies, it might be the largest sample size of previous surveys, or it might be equal to the sample size of a competitor's survey that the company somehow discovered.

A "cookie cutter" or conventional approach that uses the same sample size for every survey should not be used because each survey is unique.

Using conventional sample size can result in a sample that may be too small or too large.

The basic difference between a "percent-rule-of-thumb" and a "conventional" sample-size determination is that the first approach has no defensible logic, whereas the conventional approach appears logical. However, the logic is faulty. We just illustrated how a percent-rule-of-thumb approach such as a 5% rule of thumb explodes into huge sample sizes very quickly; however, the national opinion poll convention of 1200 respondents would be constant regardless of the population size. Still, this characteristic is one of the conventional sample-size determination method's weaknesses, for it assumes that the manager wants an accuracy of around ±3%, and it assumes that there is maximum variability in the population.

Conventional sample sizes ignore the special circumstances of the survey at hand.

Adopting past sample sizes or taking those used by other companies can be criticized as well, for both approaches assume that whoever determined sample size in the previous studies did so correctly (that is, not with a flawed method). If a flawed method was used, you simply perpetuate the error by copying it, and if the sample-size method used was not flawed, the circumstances and assumptions surrounding the predecessor's survey may be very different from those encompassing the present one. So, the conventional sample size approach ignores the circumstances surrounding the study at hand and may well prove to be much more costly than would be the case if the sample size were determined correctly.

Statistical Analysis Requirements Sample-Size Specification

Sometimes the researcher's desire to use particular statistical techniques influences sample size.

On occasion, a sample's size will be determined using a **statistical analysis approach**, meaning that the researcher wishes to perform a particular type of data analysis that has sample-size requirements.[14] In truth, the sample-size formulas in this chapter are appropriate for the simplest data analyses.[15] We have not discussed statistical procedures as yet in this textbook, but we can assure you that some advanced techniques require certain minimum sample sizes in order to be reliable, or to safeguard the validity of their statistical results.[16] Sample sizes based on statistical analysis criteria can be quite large.[17]

Even the least powerful personal computer allows for extensive "subgroup analysis,"[18] which is nothing more than a reasonably thorough investigation of subsegments within the population. As you would expect, the desire to gain knowledge about subgroups has direct implications for sample size. It should be possible to look at each subgroup as a separate population and to determine sample size for each subgroup, along with the appropriate method and other specifics to gain knowledge about that subgroup; that is, if you were to use the standard sample-size formula described in this chapter to determine the sample size, and more than one subgroup was to be analyzed fully, this objective would require a total sample size equal to the number of subgroups times the standard sample-size formula's computed sample size.[19] Once this is accomplished, all of the subgroups can be combined into a large group in order to obtain a complete population picture.

Cost Basis of Sample-Size Specification

Sometimes termed, the **all-you-can-afford approach**, this method uses cost as a basis for sample size. As you learned with our presentation on the eighth sample-size axiom, managers and marketing research professionals are vitally concerned with the costs of data collection, because they can mount quickly, particularly for personal interviews, telephone surveys, and even for mail surveys in which incentives are included in the envelopes mailed out. So it is not surprising that cost sometimes becomes the basis for sample size.

Using cost as the sole determinant of sample size may seem wise, but it is not.

Exactly how the all-you-can-afford approach is applied varies a great deal. In some instances, the marketing research project budget is determined in advance, and set amounts are specified for each phase. Here, the budget may have, for instance, $10,000 for interviewing, or it might specify $5000 for data collection. A variation is for the entire year's marketing research budget amount to be set and to have each project carve out a slice of that total. With this approach, the marketing research project director is forced to stay within the total project budget, but he or she can allocate the money across the various cost elements, and the sample size ends up being whatever is affordable within the budget.

But using the all-you-can-afford sample-size specification is a case of the tail wagging the dog; that is, instead of the value of the information to be gained from the survey being a primary consideration in the sample size, the sample size is determined by budget factors that usually ignore the value of the survey's results to management, and this approach certainly does not consider sample accuracy at all. In fact, because many managers harbor a bias in favor of large sample sizes, it is possible that their marketing research project costs are overstated for data collection when smaller sample sizes could have sufficed quite well. As can be seen in our Marketing Research Insight 13.4, unscrupulous market researchers can use this bias selfishly.

Still, you know from the last sample-size axiom, that you cannot decide on sample size without taking cost into consideration. The key is to remember *when* we consider cost. In the all-you-can-afford examples we just described, cost drives the sample size completely. When we have $5000 for interviewing and a data-collection company tells us that it charges $25 per completed interview, our sample is set at 200 respondents. Another, the correct, approach is to consider cost relative to the value of the research to the manager. If the manager requires extremely precise information, the researcher will surely suggest a large sample, and then estimate the cost of obtaining the sample. The manager, in turn, should then consider this cost in relation to how much the information is actually worth. Using the cost schedule concept, the researcher and manager can then discuss alternative sample sizes, different data-collection methods, costs, and other considerations. This is a healthier situation, for now the manager is assuming some ownership of the survey and a partnership arrangement is being forged between the manager and the researcher. The net result will be a better understanding on the part of the manager about how and why the final sample size was determined. This way cost will not be the only means of determining sample size, but it will be given the consideration it deserves.

The appropriateness of using cost as a basis for sample size depends on when cost factors are considered.

13.4   The Ethics of Sample Size

Marketing managers and other clients of marketing researchers do not have a thorough understanding of sample size. In fact, they tend to have a belief in a false "law of large sample size"; that is, they often confuse the size of the sample with the representativeness of the sample. As you know from learning about sample selection procedures, the way the sample is selected determines its representativeness, not its size. Also, as you have just learned, the benefits of excessively large samples are typically not justified by their increased costs.

It is an ethical marketing researcher's responsibility to try to educate a client on the wastefulness of excessively large samples. Occasionally, there are good reasons for having a very large sample, but whenever the sample size exceeds that of a typical national opinion poll (1200 respondents), justification is required. Otherwise, the manager's cost will be unnecessarily inflated. Unethical researchers may recommend very large samples as a way to increase their profits, which may be set at a percentage of the total cost of the survey. They may even have ownership in the data-collection company slated to gather the data at a set cost per respondent. It is important, therefore, that marketing managers know the motivations underlying the sample-size recommendations of the researchers they hire.

TWO SPECIAL SAMPLE–SIZE DETERMINATION SITUATIONS

The final section of this chapter takes up two special cases: sample size when sampling from small populations and sample size when using a nonprobability sampling method.

Sampling from Small Populations

Implicit to all sample-size discussions thus far in this chapter is the assumption that the population is very large. This assumption is reasonable because there are multitudes of households in the United States, millions of registered drivers, hundreds of thousands of persons over the age of 65, and so forth. So it is common, especially with consumer goods and services marketers, to draw samples from very large populations. Occasionally, however, the population is much smaller, and this is not unusual in the case of business-to-business marketers. This case is addressed by the condition stipulated in our fourth sample-size axiom, **"In almost all cases, the accuracy (sample error) of a probability sample is independent of the size of the population."**

With small populations, you should use the finite multiplier to determine sample size.

As a general rule, a **small population** situation is one in which the sample exceeds 5% of the total population size. Notice that a small population is defined by the size of the sample under consideration. If the sample is less than 5% of the total population, you can consider the population to be of large size, and you can use the procedures described earlier in this chapter. On the other hand, if it is a small population, the sample-size formula needs some adjustment with what is called a **finite multiplier**, which is an adjustment factor that is approximately equal to the square root of that proportion of the population not included in the sample. For instance, suppose our population size was considered to be 1000 companies, and we decided to take a sample of 500. That would result in a finite multiplier of about 0.71, or the square root of 0.5, which is [(1000 − 500)/1000]. That is, we could use a sample of only 355 (or .71 times 500) companies, and it would be just as accurate as one of size 500 if we had a large population.

The formula for computation of a sample size using the finite multiplier is as follows:

Small Population Sample-Size Formula
$$\text{Sample population sample size} = \text{sample size formula} \times \sqrt{\frac{N - n}{N - 1}}$$

Here is an example using the 1000-company population. Let us suppose we want to know the percentage of companies that are interested in a substance abuse counseling program for their employees offered by a local hospital. We are uncertain about the variability, so we use our 50–50, worst-case approach. We decide to use a 95% level of confidence, and the director of Counseling Services at Claremont Hospital would like the results to be accurate ±5%. The computations are as follows:

Sample Size Computed with p = 50%, q = 50%, and e = 5%

$$n = \frac{1.96^2(pq)}{e^2}$$
$$= \frac{1.96^2(50 \times 50)}{5^2}$$
$$= \frac{3.84(2500)}{25}$$
$$= \frac{9600}{25}$$
$$= 384$$

Now, applying the finite multiplier to adjust the sample size for a small population:

$$\text{Small population sample} = n\sqrt{\frac{N - n}{N - 1}}$$

**Example:
Sample-Size Formula
to Adjust for a Small
Population Size**

$$= 384\sqrt{\frac{1000 - 384}{1000 - 1}}$$

$$= 384\sqrt{\frac{616}{999}}$$

$$= 384\sqrt{.62}$$

$$= 384 \times .79$$

$$= 303$$

In other words, we need a sample size of 303, not 384, because we are working with a small population. By applying the finite multiplier, we can reduce the sample size by 81 respondents and achieve the same accuracy level. If this survey required personal interviews, we would gain a considerable cost savings.

Appropriate use of the finite multiplier formula will reduce a calculated sample size and save money when performing research on small populations.

Sample Size Using Nonprobability Sampling

All sample-size formulas and other statistical considerations treated in this chapter assume that some form of probability sampling method has been used. In other words, the sample must be unbiased with regard to selection, and the only sampling error present is due to sample size. Remember, sample size determines the accuracy, not the representativeness, of the sample. The sampling method determines the representativeness. All sample size formulas assume that representativeness is guaranteed with use of a probability sampling procedure.

The only reasonable way of determining sample size with nonprobability sampling is to weigh the benefit or value of the information obtained with that sample against the cost of gathering that information. Ultimately, this is a very subjective exercise, as the manager may place significant value on the information for a number or reasons. For instance, the information may crystallize the problem, it may open the manager's eyes to vital additional considerations, or it might even make him or her aware of previously unknown market segments. But because of the unknown bias introduced by a haphazard sample-selection[20] process, it is inappropriate to apply sample-size formulas. For nonprobability sampling, sample size is a judgment based almost exclusively on the value of the biased information to the manager, rather than desired precision, relative to cost.

When using nonprobability sampling, sample size is unrelated to accuracy, so cost–benefit considerations must be used.

**SPSS Student Assistant:
Noxzema Skin Cream:
Selecting Cases**

SUMMARY

We began this chapter by notifying you of the large-sample-size bias that many managers hold. To counter this myth, we listed eight sample-size axioms that relate the size of a random sample to its accuracy, or closeness of its findings to the true population value. These axioms were used to describe the confidence interval sample-size determination method, which is the most correct method because it relies on statistical concepts of variability, confidence intervals, and sample error. From the descriptions of these concepts, we moved to the standard sample-size formula used by market researchers. This formula uses variability (p and q), level of confidence (z), and acceptable sample error (e) to compute the sample size, n. We indicated that for confidence level, typically 95% or 99% levels are applied. These equate to z values of 1.96 and 2.58, respectively. For variability with percentage estimates, the researcher can fall back on a 50%/50% split, which is the greatest case of variability possible. The standard sample-size formula is best considered a starting point for deciding the final sample size, for data-collection costs must be taken into consideration. Normally, the researcher and manager will discuss the alternative sample error levels and their associated data-collection costs to come to agreement on a final acceptable sample size.

Although most are flawed, there are other methods of determining sample size: (1) designating size arbitrarily, (2) using a "conventional" size, (3) basing size on the requirements of statistical procedures to be used, and (4) letting cost determine the size. Finally, the chapter discussed two special sampling situations. With a small population, the finite multiplier should be used to adjust the sample-size determination formula. Last, with nonprobability sampling, a cost–benefit analysis should take place.

KEY TERMS

Sample accuracy (p. 364)
- Large sample size bias (p. 365)
Confidence interval approach (p. 366)
- Nonsampling error (p. 366)
- Sampling error (p. 366)
- Variability (p. 367)
- Confidence interval (p. 369)
Central limit theorem (p. 369)
Confidence interval method (p. 372)

Acceptable error (p. 373)
- Worst-case variability (p. 376)
Arbitrary approach (p. 380)
- Conventional approach (p. 381)
Statistical analysis approach (p. 382)
All-you-can-afford approach (p. 382)
Small population (p. 384)
Finite multiplier (p. 384)

REVIEW QUESTIONS/APPLICATIONS

1. Describe each of the following methods of sample-size determination and indicate a critical flaw in the use of each.
   a. Using a rule-of-thumb percentage of the population size.
   b. Using a conventional sample size, such as the typical size pollsters use.
   c. Using the amount in the budget allocated for data collection to determine sample size.
2. Describe and provide illustrations of each of the following notions: (a) variability, (b) confidence interval, and (c) acceptable sample error.
3. What are the three fundamental considerations involved with the confidence-interval approach to sample-size determination?
4. When calculating sample size, how can a researcher decide on the level of accuracy to use? What about level of confidence? What about variability with a percentage?
5. Using the formula provided in the text, determine the approximate sample sizes for each of the following cases, all with precision (allowable error) of ±5%:
   a. Variability of 30 percent, confidence level of 95%.
   b. Variability of 60 percent, confidence level of 99%.
   c. Unknown variability, confidence level of 95%.
6. Indicate how a pilot study can help a researcher understand variability in the population.

7. Why is it important for the researcher and the marketing manager to discuss the accuracy level associated with the research project at hand?

8. What are the benefits to be gained by knowing that a proposed sample is more than 5% of the total population's size? In what marketing situation might this be a common occurrence?

9. A researcher knows from experience that the average costs of various data-collection alternatives are:

Data Collection Method	Cost/Respondent
Personal interview	$50
Telephone interview	$25
Mail survey	$0.50 (per mail-out)

If $2500 is allocated in the research budget for data collection, what are the levels of accuracy for the sample sizes allowable for each data-collection method? Based on your findings, comment on the inappropriateness of using cost as the only means of determining sample size.

10. Last year, Lipton Tea Company conducted a mall-intercept study at six regional malls around the country and found that 20% of the public preferred tea over coffee as a midafternoon hot drink. This year, Lipton wants to have a nationwide telephone survey performed with random digit dialing. What sample size should be used in this year's study in order to achieve an accuracy level of ±2.5% at the 99% level of confidence? What about at the 95% level of confidence?

11. Allbookstores.com has a used textbook division. It buys its books in bulk from used book buyers who set up kiosks on college campuses during final exams, and it sells the used textbooks to students who log on to the allbookstores.com Web site via a secured credit card transaction. The used textbooks are then sent by United Parcel Service to the student.

   The company has conducted a survey of used book buying by college students each year for the past four years. In each survey, 1000 randomly selected college students have been asked to indicate whether or not they had bought a used textbook in the previous year. The results are as follows:

	Years Ago			
	1	2	3	4
Percent buying used text(s)	45	50	60	70

What are the sample-size implications of these data?

12. American Ceramics, Inc. (ACI) has been developing a new form of ceramic that can withstand high temperatures and sustained use. Because of its improved properties, the project development engineer in charge of this project thinks that the new ceramic will compete as a substitute for the ceramics currently used in spark plugs. She talks to ACI's market research director about conducting a survey of prospective buyers of the new ceramic material. During their phone conversation, the research director suggests a study using about 100 companies as a means of determining market demand. Later that day, the research director does some background using the Thomas Register as a source of names of companies manufacturing spark plugs. A total of 312 companies located in the continental United States are found in the register. How should this finding impact the final sample size of the survey?

13. Here are some numbers that you can use to sharpen your computational skills for sample size determination. Crest toothpaste is reviewing plans for its annual survey of toothpaste purchasers. With each case below, calculate the sample size pertaining to the key variable under consideration. Where information is missing, provide reasonable assumptions.

Case	Key Variable	Variability	Acceptable Error	Confidence Level
1	Market share of Crest toothpaste last year	23% share	4%	95%
2	Percent of people who brush their teeth per week	Unknown	5%	99%
3	How likely Crest buyers are to switch brands	30% switched last year	5%	95%
4	Percent of people who want tartar-control features in their toothpaste	20% two years ago; 40% one year ago	3.5%	95%
5	Willingness of people to adopt the toothpaste brand recommended by their family dentist	Unknown	6%	99%

14. Do managers really have a large-sample-size bias? Because you cannot survey managers easily, this exercise will use surrogates. Ask any five seniors majoring in business administration who have not taken a marketing research class the following questions. Indicate whether each of the following statements is true or false.

   a. A random sample of 500 is large enough to represent all of the full-time college students in the United States.

   b. A random sample of 1000 is large enough to represent all of the full-time college students in the United States.

   c. A random sample of 2000 is large enough to represent all of the full-time college students in the United States.

   d. A random sample of 5000 is large enough to represent all of the full-time college students in the United States.

   What have you found out about sample-size bias?

15. The Andrew Jergens Company markets a "spa tablet" called ActiBath, which is a carbonated moisturizing treatment for use in a bath. From previous research, Jergens management knows that 60% of all women use some form of skin moisturizer and 30% believe their skin is their most beautiful asset. There is some concern among management that women will associate the drying aspects of taking a bath with ActiBath and not believe that it can provide a skin moisturizing benefit. Can these facts about use of moisturizers and concern for skin beauty be used in determining the size of the sample in the ActiBath survey? If so, indicate how. If not, indicate why and how sample size can be determined.

16. Donald Heel is the Microwave Oven Division Manager of Sharp Products. Don proposes a $40 cash rebate program as a means of promoting Sharp's new crisp-broil-and-grill microwave oven. However, Sharp's president wants evidence that the program would increase sales by at least 25%, so Don applies some of his research budget to a survey. He uses the National Phone Systems Company to conduct a nationwide survey using random digit dialing. National Phone Systems is a fully integrated telephone polling company, and it has the capability of providing daily tabulations. Don decides to use this option, and instead of specifying a final sample size, he chooses to have National Phone Systems perform 50 completions each day. At the end of five days of fieldwork, the daily results are as follows:

	Day				
	1	2	3	4	5
Total sample size	50	100	150	200	250
Percentage of respondents who would consider buying a Sharp microwave with a $40 rebate	50	40	35	30	33

For how much longer should Don continue the survey? Indicate your rationale.

PEACEFUL LAKE SUBDIVISION SAMPLE SIZE REVISITED

The details about the Peaceful Lake Subdivision survey are found in Case 12.1 on pages 360.

Recall that the president of this subdivision has decided to conduct a survey to determine how Peaceful Lake's 6000 homeowners feel about the recreation complex that some of the residents want built. The complex will require up to $2 million in construction costs, and it will take a year to complete. To construct the proposed recreational facility, every Peaceful Valley household would be expected to pay a one-time fee of $500, and annual fees would increase to $200 based on estimates of facility maintenance cost. The president has decided on a probability sampling method, but he is reconsidering the sample size based on his recent Internet search of sample sizes.

1. What is the expected level of sample error (accuracy level) for the original sample size of 3000? Is this a large or a small error level, and why do you judge it to be small or large?

2. If the president desires the survey to be accurate to ±5% and at a 95% level of confidence, what sample size should be used? How would you adjust this sample size if the president believes that there will be a 75% response rate to the survey?

3. Should the survey be a sample or a census of Peaceful Lake Subdivision homeowners? Defend your choice. Be certain to discuss any practical considerations that enter into your choice.

THE COBALT GROUP: ONLINE SURVEY FOR MYCARTOOLS, PART II

The background for this case is found as Case 12.2 on page 360–361.

A decision is made to use a pop-up invitation that will appear randomly on every automobile dealership Web site over the course of a complete week, beginning at midnight on Sunday and ending at 11:59:59 P.M. on Saturday of that week. There are approximately 9000 automobile dealerships with Cobalt Group Web sites, but only about 2000 use the MyCarTools feature. A quick check of the Web site's database suggests that automobile dealerships experience about 100 "serious" hits per week. A "serious" hit is when the Web-site visitor stays on the site for two minutes or longer. In other words, there are about 100 × 2000, or 20,000, serious hits on these dealer Web sites in a typical week.

There is a decision to be made regarding on what percent of these serious hits the pop-up invitation should appear. The decision is complicated by the unknown factor of the response rate: what percent of the dealer Web-site visitors who are invited to move to the WebSurveyor online survey will actually fill out and submit it? Some online marketing research sources say that a 10% response rate is standard.

1. Determine the sample error (at a 95% level of confidence) that will accompany the expected sample size for each of the following alternatives.
   a. Invite every 20th visitor
   b. Invite every 10th visitor
   c. Invite every 5th visitor

2. Using what you found in your answers to the above question, and taking into consideration other factors that are related to sample size, what sample-size approach do you recommend in this case and why?

14

Data Collection in the Field, Nonresponse Error, and Questionnaire Screening

To Say "I Am Not Selling Anything" or Not to Say It: How Do Potential Respondents React?[1]

Far more than any time before, today's public is downright hostile toward telephone surveys. It is a well-documented fact that fewer and fewer people cooperate with survey requests. Furthermore, a significant portion of them feel that there are just too many such requests, while a similar significant percentage just plain believes that all survey research is just a disguised sales call, that is, sugging. This situation poses a thorny dilemma for marketing researchers in general and telephone interview companies in particular. Should the interviewer say, "I am not selling anything"?

Here are the horns of this dilemma. If the interviewer is silent about selling something, many potential respondents will be thinking that it is just a matter of time before the interviewer pops the question about buying a time-sharing unit, adding another credit card, or switching to another long-distance telephone company, so they will be on guard and obviously distracted during the interview. If the interviewer says, "I am not selling anything," then the respondent may be alerted to the fact that sometimes survey introductions are twisted into sales calls, so the respondent may be skeptical or otherwise waiting for the sales pitch. It seems that marketing researchers have no way of solving the "I am not selling anything" issue.

- To learn about total error and how nonsampling error is related to it
- To understand the sources of data-collection errors and how to minimize them
- To learn about the various types of nonresponse error and how to calculate response rate in order to measure nonresponse error
- To read about questionnaire-inspection procedures used during and after data collection

Learning Objectives

Should the interviewer say, "I am not selling anything?"

Two Dutch researchers set out to design an experiment to determine the effect of including "I am not selling anything" to the introduction to a telephone survey. Their experiment was quite ambitious, as it included 10 different market research companies belonging to the Netherlands Association for Market Research Companies who agreed to use what is called a "split-ballot" approach. With the split-ballot approach, half of the telephone interviews used the standard introduction, in which the interviewer introduced the survey, but made no mention about selling anything. With the other half of the telephone surveys, the interviewer was instructed to say specifically, "We are not selling anything." Twenty-nine different Dutch telephone surveys were included in the experiment, with slightly more than 100,000 persons contacted in total.

Using various measures of response and refusal, the Dutch researchers found the good news that the "I am not selling anything" introduction did increase the response rate and, conversely, decrease the refusal rate. The "I am not selling anything" statement did not affect the percent of respondents who terminated the survey in mid-interview. Comparing the response rates, the researchers found that the "I am not selling anything" introduction increased the response rate by 2% over the standard introduction. Further analysis revealed that the "I am not selling anything" disclosure works best when it is placed at the start of the interviewer's introduction rather than further into it. Balanced against the modest 2% increase in response rate is the fact that the "I am not selling anything" statement can be included very easily in the introduction and its cost is minimal. Thus, the researchers strongly advocate placing this statement very early in the interviewer's introductory comments.

This chapter deals with data-collection issues, including, as you have just read, factors that stimulate individuals to participate in surveys. While you learned about sample error in the previous chapter, you will learn about another source of research error in this chapter. There are two kinds of errors in survey research. The first is sampling error, which arises from the fact that we have taken a sample. You learned in Chapter 13 that you can actually control sampling error through the standard sample-size formula. But, what about the error that arises from a respondent who does not listen carefully to the question or an interviewer who is almost burned out from listening to answering machines or having a prospective respondent hang up? This is the second type of error, called nonsampling error. In this chapter we learn the sources of nonsampling error and what controls we can use to minimize it in our research.

We previously learned that we can expect to have sampling errors and that we can control for the level of sampling error. But nonsampling error cannot be measured; it can only be controlled with safeguards. So, you must understand the sources of these nonsampling errors and learn how they may be minimized. This chapter teaches you the sources of nonsampling errors. Along with a discussion of each source of error, we make suggestions on how you can minimize the negative effect of each type of error. We also teach you how to calculate the response rate in order to measure the amount of nonresponse error. We relate what a researcher looks for in preliminary questionnaire screening after the survey has been completed in order to spot respondents whose answers may exhibit bias, such as always responding positively or negatively to questions.

NONSAMPLING ERROR IN MARKETING RESEARCH

Nonsampling error is defined as all errors in a survey except those due to the sample plan and the sample size.

Data collection has the potential to greatly increase the amount of nonsampling error in a survey.

In the previous two chapters, we discussed sampling. We learned that the sample plan and sample size are important in predetermining the amount of sampling error that you will experience. The significance of understanding sampling is that we can control sampling error.[2] However, as we indicated to you, sampling error is only one of the two components of total error in a survey. The counterpart to sampling error is **nonsampling error**, which is defined as all errors in a survey *except* those attributable to the sample plan and the sample size. Nonsampling error includes the following: (1) all types of nonresponse error, (2) data-gathering errors, (3) data-handling errors, (4) data-analysis errors, and (5) interpretation errors. It also includes errors in problem definition, question wording, and, in fact, anything other than sampling error. Generally, the greatest potential for large nonsampling error occurs during the data-collection stage, so we discuss at some length errors that can occur during this stage. Also, because nonsampling error cannot be measured by a formula, as sampling error can, we describe the various controls that can be imposed on the data-collection process to minimize the effects of nonsampling error.[3]

POSSIBLE ERRORS IN FIELD DATA COLLECTION

A variety of nonsampling errors can occur during data collection. To help you learn about them, we divide these errors into two general types and further specify errors within each general type. The first general type is **fieldworker error**, defined as errors committed by the individuals who administer the questionnaires, typically interviewers.[4] The quality of fieldworkers can vary dramatically depending on the researcher's resources and the circumstances of the survey, but it is important to keep in mind that fieldworker error can occur with professional data-collection workers as well as with do-it-yourselfers. Of course, the potential for fieldworker error is less with professionals than with first-timers or part-timers.

The other general type of nonsampling error is **respondent error**, which refers to errors on the part of the respondent. These, of course, can occur regardless of the method of data collection, but some data collection methods have greater potential for respondent error than others. Within each general type, we identify two classes of error: intentional errors, or errors that are committed deliberately, and unintentional errors, or errors that occur without willful intent.[5] Figure 14.1 lists the various errors/types of errors described in this section under each of the four headings. In the early sections of this chapter, we will describe these data-collection errors, and, later, we will discuss the standard controls that marketing researchers use in order to minimize these errors.

Nonsampling errors are committed by fieldworkers and respondents.

Intentional Fieldworker Errors

Intentional fieldworker errors occur whenever a data collector willfully violates the data collection requirements set forth by the researcher. There are two variations of intentional fieldworker errors that we describe: interviewer cheating and leading the respondent. Both are constant concerns of all researchers.

Interviewer cheating occurs when the interviewer intentionally misrepresents respondents. You might think to yourself, "What would induce an interviewer to intentionally falsify responses?" The cause is often found in the compensation system.[6] Interviewers may work by the hour, but a common compensation system is to reward them by completed interviews; that is, a telephone interviewer or a mall-intercept interviewer may be paid at a rate of $5.50 per completed interview, so at the end of an interview day, he or she simply turns in the completed questionnaires, and the number is credited to the interviewer. Or the interviewers may cheat by interviewing someone who is convenient instead of a person designated by the sampling plan. Again, the by-completed-interview compensation may provide the incentive for this type of cheating.[7] At the same time, most interviewers are not full-time employees,[8] and their conscientiousness may be diminished as a result.

Interviewer cheating is a concern, especially when compensation is on a per-completion basis.

There is some defensible logic for a paid-by-completion compensation system. Interviewers do not always work like production-line workers. With mall intercepts, for instance, there are periods of inactivity, depending on mall shopper flow and respondent qualification requirements. Telephone interviewers working out of their homes may take breaks, or they may be waiting for periods of time in order to satisfy the number-of-callbacks policy for a particular survey. Also, as you may already know, the

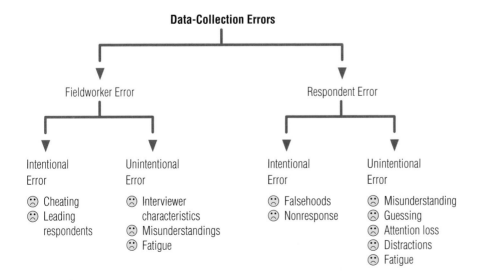

FIGURE 14.1
Data-Collection Errors Can Occur with Fieldworkers or Respondents

compensation levels for fieldworkers are low, the hours are long, and the work is frustrating at times.[9] So the temptation to turn in bogus completed questionnaires is present, and some interviewers give in to this temptation.

ARE YOU A CHEATER?

Students who read about the cheating error we have just described are sometimes skeptical that such cheating goes on. However, take the following test and see if you are just as skeptical about the cheating behavior of your fellow students. For each statement, circle "Yes" or "No" as to whether or not you think some of your fellow students have engaged in the following cheating behaviors in the past two years.

In the Past Two Years, Have Some of Your Fellow College Students Engaged in the Following Behaviors?	Do Your Fellow Students Engage in this Behavior?	
Studied a copy of an exam that was "stolen" from an earlier administration of the exam in that course.	Yes	No
Worked with other student(s) on a take-home exam or homework that was supposed to be completed individually.	Yes	No
Used crib notes or other materials that should not have been used in a closed-book, closed-notes exam.	Yes	No
Altered answers on an exam that is passed back to him/her that they then presented to the instructor to correct the "error."	Yes	No
Copied another student's homework or assignment.	Yes	No
Received information about an exam administered in an earlier section when the instructor has required those exam-takers to take a "vow of silence."	Yes	No

If you circled "Yes" a majority of times, you are consistent with most business students who have answered a variation of this test.[10] Now, if you and the majority of university students in general believe that their fellow students are cheating on examinations and assignments, don't you think that interviewers who may be in financially tight situations are tempted to cheat on their interviews?

Interviewers should not influence respondents' answers.

The second error that we are categorizing as intentional on the part of the interviewer is **leading the respondent**, and it is defined as occurring when the interviewer influences the respondent's answers through wording, voice inflection, or body language. In the worst case, the interviewer may actually reword a question so it is leading. For instance, consider the question, "Is conserving electricity a concern for you?" An interviewer can influence the respondent by changing the question to "Isn't conserving electricity a concern for you?"

There are other, less obvious instances of leading the respondent. One way is to subtly signal the type of response that is expected. If, for example, a respondent says "yes" in response to our question, the interviewer might say, "I thought you would say 'yes' because over 90% of my respondents have agreed on this issue." A comment such as this plants a seed in the respondent's head that he or she should continue to agree with the majority.

Another area of subtle leading occurs in the interviewer's cues. In a personal interview, for instance, the interviewer might ever so slightly shake his or her head "no" to questions he or she disagrees with and "yes" to those he or she agrees with while posing the question. The respondent may perceive these cues and begin responding in the expected manner signaled by the interviewer's head movements while he or she reads the questions. Over the telephone, an interviewer might give verbal cues such as "unhuh" to responses he or she disagrees with or "okay" to responses he or she agrees with, and this continued reaction pattern may subtly influence the respondent's answers. Again, we have categorized this example as an intentional error because professional interviewers are trained to avoid them, and if they commit them, they should be aware of their violations.

Unintentional Fieldworker Errors

An **unintentional interviewer error** occurs whenever an interviewer commits an error while believing that he or she is performing correctly.[11] There are three general sources of unintentional interviewer errors. These sources are interviewer personal characteristics, interviewer misunderstandings, and interviewer fatigue. Unintentional interviewer error is found in the interviewer's **personal characteristics** such as accent, sex, and demeanor. Under some circumstances, even the interviewer's voice[12] or gender[13] can be a source of bias. On the flip side, there are characteristics that distinguish outstanding interviewers. Read Marketing Research Insight 14.1 to find out what the research industry believes to be winning attributes of telephone interviewers.[14]

Interviewer misunderstanding occurs when an interviewer believes he or she knows how to administer a survey, but instead does it incorrectly. As we have described, a questionnaire may include various types of instructions for the interviewer, varying response scale types, directions on how to record responses, and other complicated guidelines that must be adhered to by the interviewer. As you can guess, there is a considerable education gap between marketing researchers who design questionnaires and interviewers who administer them. This gap can easily become a communication problem in which the

Interviewer errors can occur without the interviewer being aware of them.

Unintentional interviewer errors include misunderstandings and fatigue.

Personal characteristics such as appearance, accent, or dress, although unintentional, may cause field worker errors.

14.1 The Characteristics of Outstanding Telephone Interviewers

Telephone interviewers who experience exceptionally low refusal rates, high levels of productivity, and longevity have the following characteristics.

Work Orientation—a hard worker who considers interviewing a personal skill

Team player—works well with others

Affinity—enjoys collecting opinions on the telephone

Pride—values quality and likes to be recognized for good work

Discipline—completion-oriented and focused

Empathy—listens to respondent's answers and tailors the interview to the respondent

Command—can take charge of the interview and overcome refusals by stressing the value and purpose of the survey

Congeniality—has a likable presence

Ethics—is an honest human being

Of course, not every outstanding interviewer has all of these characteristics to the maximum degree. However, successful interviewers exhibit ample amounts of these qualities.

---

instructions on the questionnaire are confusing to the interviewer. It has been shown that interviewer experience cannot overcome poor questionnaire instructions.[15] In this circumstance, the interviewer will usually struggle to comply with the researcher's wishes, but may fail to do so to some degree or another.[16]

The third type of unintentional interviewer error pertains to **fatigue–related mistakes,** which can occur when an interviewer becomes tired. You may be surprised that fatigue can enter into something as simple as asking questions and recording answers, but interviewing is labor-intensive,[17] and it can become tedious and monotonous. It is repetitive at best, and it is especially demanding when respondents are uncooperative. Toward the end of a long interviewing day, the interviewer may be less mentally alert than earlier in the day, and this condition can cause slip-ups and mistakes to occur. The interviewer may fail to obey a skip pattern, might forget to check the respondent's reply to a question, might hurry through a section of the questionnaire, or might appear or sound weary to a potential respondent, who refuses to take part in the survey as a result.

Currently, there is a strong trend toward Web-based surveys, which eliminate the interviewer from the picture. But what happens when there is no interviewer? Read Marketing Research Insight 14.2 to see the findings of a study that compared telephone interviewing to an online questionnnaire approach.

Intentional Respondent Errors

Sometimes respondents do not tell the truth.

Intentional respondent errors occur when respondents willfully misrepresent themselves in surveys. There are at least two major intentional respondent errors that require discussion: falsehoods and refusals. **Falsehoods** occur when respondents fail to tell the truth in surveys. They may feel embarrassed, they might want to protect their privacy, or they may even suspect that the interviewer has a hidden agenda, such as suddenly turning the interview into a sales pitch. Certain topics denote greater potential for misrepresentation. For instance, the income level of the respondent is a sensitive topic for many people, marital status disclosure is a concern for women living alone, age is a delicate topic for some, and personal hygiene questions may offend some respondents. Respondents may become bored; the interview process may become burdensome; they may find the inter-

MARKETING RESEARCH INSIGHT

14.2

Can We Eliminate the Interviewer from the Survey?[18]

This chapter describes a number of unintentional and intentional interviewer errors that must be guarded against whenever an interviewer administers a survey. The obvious question to ask is, "Can we execute the survey without any interviewers?" If so, we can stop worrying about all the potential interviewer errors that can occur in a survey.

Researchers sought to compare a Web-based questionnaire with a telephone-administered one. Identical questionnaires were used. Both the telephone and the online samples were selected with probability sampling methods, so they were equivalent. The telephone survey was administered by a professional telephone interviewing company, while the Web-based survey was self-administered by individuals contacted by e-mail to take part in the survey.

The findings:

CHARACTERISTIC	WEB-SURVEY RESPONDENT	TELEPHONE-SURVEY RESPONDENT
Age	Younger	Older
Ethnicity	Anglos predominant	Hispanics predominant
Education	Fewer college graduates	More college graduates
Time in community	Less time	More time
Gender	More females	Fewer females
Response rate	32.6%	11.5%
Attitude toward the sponsor	Less positive	More positive
General attitudes	Somewhat more positive	Somewhat more negative
Cost per interview	$14	$30

The answer to our initial question is, "It may depend." There is a distinct cost benefit to Web-based surveys as, in this study, telephone interviews are twice as costly as are Web-based ones, so if cost is paramount, a Web survey is the clear correct choice. The researchers conclude, "Web surveys may be equally, if not more, accurate than telephone surveys. . . . " However, the presence of a telephone interviewer may result in subtle differences that may reflect the population and which the researcher wishes to be present in the final sample.

---

viewer irritating; or for some reason, they may want to end the interview in a hurry. So falsehoods may be motivated by a desire on the part of the respondent to deceive, or they may be mindless responses uttered just to complete the interview as quickly as possible.

The second type of intentional respondent error is nonresponse, which we have referred to at various times in your textbook. Recall that **nonresponse** is either a failure on the part of a prospective respondent to take part in the survey, premature termination of the interview, or refusals to answer specific questions on the questionnaire. In fact, nonresponse of various types is probably the most common intentional respondent error that researchers encounter. Some observers believe that survey research is facing tough times ahead because of a growing distaste for survey participation, increasingly busy schedules, and a desire for privacy.[19] By one estimate, the

> Nonresponse is defined as failure on the part of a prospective respondent to take part in a survey or to answer a question.

refusal rate of U.S. consumers is almost 50%.[20] Telephone surveyors are most concerned.[21] While most agree that declining cooperation rates present a major threat to the industry[22] some believe the problem is not as severe as many think.[23] Nonresponse in general, and refusals in particular, are encountered in virtually every survey conducted, but as you will see by reading Marketing Research Insight 14.3, sometimes extra efforts on the part of the interviewer can reduce the number of refusals. We devote an entire section to this important source of error in a later section of this chapter.

MARKETING RESEARCH INSIGHT

GLOBAL APPLICATION

14.3 Who Is "Easy" and Who Is "Hard" to Get in U.K. Surveys?[24]

Two researchers from the United Kingdom have diagrammed various types of sample members based on how difficult it is to make contact and convince them to take part in a survey. In their depiction, there are three basic types of respondent: "easy to get," "reluctant," and "difficult to contact." The latter two types combine to make up "hard to get" respondents. The diagram is as follows.

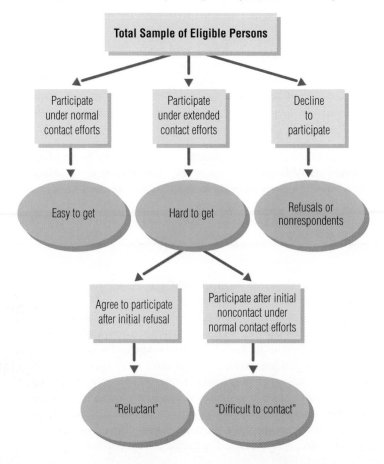

An easy-to-get respondent is one who is contacted within the standard number of contact attempts (normally three attempts are standard, but some companies use more). In other words, an easy-to-get respondent readily agrees to take part in the survey, and the interviewer makes contact with this person on the first attempt or within a few attempts. The hard-to-get respondents are those who are contacted only after repeated contact attempts beyond the interview company's normal contact attempts policy. Some hard-to-get respondents agree to take part in the survey upon contact; hence, they are simply "difficult to contact." However, there are hard-to-get individuals who, when finally asked to take part in the survey, refuse, but on listening to the interviewer's comments and persuasion (considered to be a standard part of contacting potential respondents), these individuals reverse their refusals and become willing participants. Thus, they are designated as "reluctant."

Across three major surveys taken in the United Kingdom and conducted with personal interviews, the following characteristics of the various respondent types emerged as follows:

- Hard-to-gets are considerably younger than easy-to-gets
- Hard-to-gets are more likely to be employed than easy-to-gets
- Hard-to-gets work more hours per week than easy-to-gets
- Hard-to-gets are less likely to own and occupy homes than easy-to-gets
- Difficult-to-contacts are younger than easy-to-gets
- Reluctants are no different in age from easy-to-gets
- Reluctants are no different in employment status from easy-to-gets
- Reluctants are, in general, more likely to be female

Unintentional Respondent Errors

An **unintentional respondent error** occurs whenever a respondent gives a response that is not valid, but he or she believes is the truth. There are five instances of unintentional respondent errors: respondent misunderstanding, guessing, attention loss, distractions, and respondent fatigue. First, **respondent misunderstanding** is defined as situations in which a respondent gives an answer without comprehending the question and/or the accompanying instructions. Potential respondent misunderstandings exist in all surveys. Such misunderstandings range from simple errors, such as checking two responses to a question when only one is called for, to complex errors, such as misunderstanding terminology.[25] For example, a respondent may think in terms of net income for the past year rather than income before taxes as desired by the researcher. Any number of misunderstandings such as these can plague a survey.

A second form of unintentional respondent error is **guessing**, in which a respondent gives an answer when he or she is uncertain of its accuracy. Occasionally, respondents are asked about topics they have little knowledge of or low recall about, but they feel compelled to provide an answer to the questions being posed. Here, the respondent might guess the answer. All guesses are likely to contain errors. Here is an example of guessing. If you were a respondent and were asked to estimate the amount of electricity in kilowatt hours you used last month, how many would you say you used?

A third unintentional respondent error occurs when a respondent's interest in the survey wanes, known as **attention loss**. The typical respondent is not as excited about the survey as is the researcher, and some respondents will find themselves less and less motivated to take part in the survey as they work their way through the questionnaire.

Fourth, **distractions**, such as interruptions, may occur while the questionnaire administration takes place. For example, during a mall-intercept interview, a respondent may be distracted when an acquaintance walks by and says hello. A parent answering questions on the telephone might have to attend to a toddler, or a mail survey respondent might be diverted from the questionnaire by a telephone call. A distraction may cause the respondent to get "off track" or otherwise not take the survey as seriously as is desired by the researcher.

Unintentional respondent errors include misunderstanding, guessing, attention loss, distractions, and fatigue.

Sometimes a respondent will answer without understanding the question.

Whenever a respondent guesses, error is likely.

Fifth, unintentional respondent error can take the form of **respondent fatigue**, in which the respondent becomes tired of participating in the survey. Whenever a respondent tires of a survey, deliberation and reflection will diminish. The respondent might even opt for the "no opinion" response category just as a means of quickly finishing the survey because he or she has grown tired of answering questions.

FIELD–DATA–COLLECTION QUALITY CONTROLS

Fortunately, there are precautions that can be implemented to minimize the effects of the various types of errors just described. Please note that we said "minimize" and not "eliminate," as the potential for error always exists. However, by instituting the following controls a researcher can be assured that the nonsampling error factor involved with data collection will be diminished. The field data collection quality controls we describe are listed in Table 14.1.

Control of Intentional Fieldworker Error

Intentional fieldworker error can be controlled with supervision and validation procedures.

There are two general strategies to guard against cases in which the interviewer might intentionally commit an error. These strategies are supervision and validation.[26] **Supervision** uses administrators to oversee the work of field data collection work-

TABLE 14.1 How to Control Data-Collection Errors

Error Types	Control Mechanisms
Intentional fieldworker errors	
Cheating	Supervision
Leading respondent	Validation
Unintentional fieldworker errors	
Interviewer characteristics	Selection and training of interviewers
Misunderstandings	Orientation sessions and role playing
Fatigue	Require breaks and alternative surveys
Intentional respondent errors	
Falsehoods	Ensuring anonymity and confidentiality
	Incentives
	Validation checks
	Third-person technique
Nonresponse	Ensuring anonymity and confidentiality
	Incentives
	Third-person technique
Unintentional respondent errors	
Misunderstandings	Well-drafted questionnaire
	Direct questions
Guessing	Well-drafted questionnaire
	Response options, e.g., "unsure"
Attention loss	Reversal of scale endpoints
Distractions	Prompters
Fatigue	

Close supervision can reduce field worker errors.

ers.[27] Most centralized telephone interviewing companies have a "listening in" capability that the supervisor can use to tap into and monitor any interviewer's line during an interview. The respondent and the interviewer may be unaware of the monitoring, so the "listening in" samples a representative interview performed by that interviewer. If the interviewer is leading or unduly influencing respondents, this procedure will spot the violation, and the supervisor can take corrective action, such as a reprimand of that interviewer. With personal interviews, the supervisor might accompany an interviewer to observe that interviewer while administering a questionnaire in the field. Because "listening in" without the consent of the respondent could be considered a breach of privacy, many companies now inform respondents that all or part of the call may be monitored and/or recorded.

Validation verifies that the interviewer did the work. This strategy is aimed at the falsification/cheating problem. There are various ways to validate the work. One type of validation is for the supervisor to recontact the respondent to find out whether he or she took part in the survey. An industry standard is to randomly select 10% of the completed surveys for purposes of making a callback to validate that the interview was actually conducted. A few sample questions might even be readministered for comparison purposes. In the absence of callback validation, some supervisors will inspect completed questionnaires, and, with a trained eye, they may spot patterns in an interviewer's completions that raise suspicions of falsification. Interviewers who turn in bogus completed questionnaires are not always careful about simulating actual respondents. The supervisor might find inconsistencies, such as very young respondents with large numbers of children, that raise doubts about a questionnaire's authenticity.

An industry standard is verification of 10% of the completed surveys.

Control of Unintentional Fieldworker Error

The supervisor is instrumental in minimizing unintentional interviewer error. We describe three mechanisms commonly used by professional field data-collection companies in this regard: selection and training, orientation sessions, and role playing.[28] Interviewer personal characteristics that can cause unintentional errors are best taken care of by careful selection of interviewers. Following selection, it is important to train them well so as to avoid any biases resulting from manner, appearance, and so forth. **Orientation sessions** are meetings in which the supervisor introduces the survey and questionnaire administration requirements to the fieldworkers.[29] The supervisor might highlight qualification or quota requirements, note skip patterns, or go over instructions to the interviewer that are embedded throughout the questionnaire. Finally, often as a means of becoming familiar with a questionnaire's administration requirements, interviewers will conduct **role-playing sessions**, which are dry runs or dress rehearsals of the questionnaire with the supervisor or some other interviewer playing the respondent's role. Successive role-playing sessions serve to familiarize interviewers with the questionnaire's special administration aspects. To control for interviewer fatigue, some researchers require interviewers to take frequent breaks and/or alternate surveys, if possible. In short, the more competent the field interview through training, supervision, and personal skills, the lower the potential for interviewer error.[30]

Unintentional fieldworker errors can be reduced with supervised orientation sessions and role playing.

Control of Intentional Respondent Error

To control intentional respondent error, it is important to minimize falsehoods and non-response tendencies on the parts of respondents. Tactics useful in minimizing intentional respondent error include anonymity, confidentiality, incentives, validation checks, and third-person technique.[31] **Anonymity** occurs when the respondent is assured that his or her name will not be associated with his or her answers. **Confidentiality** occurs when the respondent is given assurances that his or her answers will remain private. Both assurances are believed to be helpful in forestalling falsehoods. The belief here is that when respondents are guaranteed they will remain nameless, they will be more comfortable in self-disclosure and will refrain from lying or misrepresenting themselves.[32]

Tactics useful in minimizing intentional respondent error include anonymity, confidentiality, validation checks, and third-person technique.

Another tactic for reducing falsehoods and nonresponse error is the use of **incentives**, which are cash payments, gifts, or something of value promised to respondents in return for their participation.[33] For participating in a survey, the respondent may be paid cash or provided with a redemption coupon. He or she might be given a gift such as a ballpoint pen or a T-shirt. Here, in a sense, the respondent is being induced to tell the truth by direct payment. The respondent may now feel morally obligated to tell the truth because he or she will receive compensation. Or, he or she may feel guilty at receiving an incentive and then not answering truthfully. Unfortunately, practitioners and academic researchers are only beginning to understand how to entice prospective respondents to take part in a survey.[34]

Incentives sometimes compel respondents to be more truthful; they also discourage nonresponse.

A different approach for reducing falsehoods is the use of **validation checks**, in which information provided by a respondent is confirmed. For instance, in an in-home survey on Leap Frog educational products for preschool children, the interviewer might ask to see the respondent's Leap Frog unit and modules as a verification or validation check. A more unobtrusive validation is to have the interviewer, who is trained to be alert to untrue answers, check for old-appearing respondents who say they are young, shabbily dressed respondents who say they are wealthy, and so on. A well-trained interviewer will note suspicious answers in the margin of the questionnaire.[35]

Finally, there is a questionnaire design feature that a researcher can use to reduce intentional respondent errors. Sometimes the opportunity arises in which a **third-person**

technique can be used in a question, in which instead of directly quizzing the respondent, the question is couched in terms of a third person who is similar to the respondent. For instance, a question posed to a middle-aged man might be, "Do you think a person such as yourself uses Viagra?" Here, the respondent will most probably think in terms of his own circumstances, but because the subject of the question is some unnamed third party, the question is not seen as personal. In other words, he will not be divulging some personal and private information by talking about this fictitious other person. The third-person technique may be used to reduce both falsehoods and nonresponse.

With an embarrassing question, the third-person technique may make the situation less personal.

Control of Unintentional Respondent Error

The control of unintentional respondent error takes various forms as well, including well-drafted questionnaire instructions and examples, reversals of scale endpoints, and use of prompters. With regard to misunderstanding, well-drafted **questionnaire instructions and examples** are commonly used as a way of avoiding respondent confusion. We described these in Chapter 11 on questionnaire design. Also, researchers sometimes resort to direct questions to assess respondent understanding. For example, after describing a 5-point agree–disagree response scale in which 1 = strongly agree, 2 = agree, 3 = neither agree nor disagree, 4 = disagree, and 5 = strongly disagree, the interviewer might be instructed to ask, "Are these instructions clear?" If the respondent answers in the negative, the instructions are repeated until the respondent understands them. Guessing may be reduced by alerting respondents to response options such as "no opinion," "do not recall," or "unsure."

Ways to combat unintentional respondent error include well-drafted questionnaire instructions and examples, reversals of scale endpoints (and use of scale endpoints), and use of prompters.

A tactic we described when we discussed the semantic differential is **reversals of scale endpoints**, in which instead of putting all of the negative adjectives on one side and all the positive ones on the other side, a researcher will switch the positions of a few items. Such reversals are intended to warn respondents that they must respond to each bipolar pair individually. With agree–disagree statements, this tactic is accomplished by negatively wording a statement every now and then to induce respondents to attend to each statement individually. Both of these tactics are intended to heighten the respondent's attention.

Finally, long questionnaires often use **prompters**, such as "We are almost finished," or "That section of questions was the most difficult to answer," or other statements strategically located to encourage the respondent to remain on track. Sometimes interviewers will sense an attention lag or fatigue on the part of the respondent and provide their own prompters or comments intended to maintain the respondent's full participation in the survey.

Prompters are used to keep respondents on task and alert.

Final Comment on the Control of Data–Collection Errors with Traditional Surveys

As you can see, a wide variety of nonsampling errors can occur on the parts of both interviewers and respondents during the data-collection stage of the marketing research process. Similarly, a variety of precautions and controls are used to minimize nonsampling error. Each survey is unique, of course, so we cannot provide universally applicable guidelines. We will, however, stress the importance of good questionnaire design in reducing these errors. Also, professional field-data-collection companies, whose existence depends on how well they can control interviewer and respondent error, are commonly relied on by researchers who understand the true value of their services. Finally, technology is dramatically changing data collection and helping in the control of its errors.[36] For example, in certain research situations, there is good opportunity to use multiple data-collection methods that, in combination, derive an accurate picture of the topic being researched.

DATA COLLECTION ERRORS WITH ONLINE SURVEYS

In many ways, an online survey is similar to a self-administered questionnaire because there is no interviewer. At the same time, unless controls are in place, there can be misrepresentations in online surveys. There are three data-collection errors unique to online surveys: (1) multiple submissions by the same respondent, (2) bogus respondents and/or responses, and (3) misrepresentation of the population.

Multiple submissions. The typical online questionnaire is fast and easy to take. Unless there is a control in place, it is possible for a respondent to submit his or her completed questionniare multiple times in a matter of minutes. If the person is free to submit multiple responses, this error will result in a overrepresentation of that individual's views and opinions. The customary control for multiple submissions is to ask the respondent for his or her e-mail address, and an electronic block is activated if the e-mail address is repeated. Of course, this control does not eliminate the problem of multiple e-mail addresses from the same respondent.

Bogus respondents and responses. The anonymity of the Internet can inspire individuals to log on to a questionnaire site as a fictitious person or to disguise him/herself as another person. Under this disguise, the individual may feel inspired to give nonsense, polarized, or otherwise false responses. Coupled with the multiple submissions error, a bogus response error has the potential to create havoc with an online survey. If this concern is great, researchers turn to online panels or other options in which the respondents are prequalified or preidentified in some manner to control for bogus respondents.

Population misrepresentation. We alluded to this problem in our chapter on sample design but it must be reiterated that all consumers are not equally Internet-connected or Web-literate.[37] In fact, some segments of the population—such as elderly citizens, low-income families, folks in remote areas where Internet connections are sparse and/or expensive, and technophobic people—are not good prospects for an online survey. By the same token, some individuals are more connected than others in their respective market segments, so there is the very real possibility that, for instance, a Web-based survey of insurance agents would result in a responding sample overrepresenting those agents who are very comfortable with the Web, and underrepresenting those agents who use the Web only occasionally.

NONRESPONSE ERROR

Although nonresponse was briefly described earlier in our discussion of mail surveys, we will now describe the nonresponse issue more fully, including various types of nonresponse, how to assess the degree of **nonresponse error**, and some ways of adjusting or compensating for nonresponse in surveys. The identification, control, and adjustments necessary for nonresponse are critical to the success of a survey. Figure 14.2 shows the declining response rate experienced by the University of Michigan's Survey of Consumer Attitudes telephone surveys in the past two decades.[38] The decrease prior to 1996 was about 1% per year, but since 1996, the decline has been 1.5% per year, and the decline rate is accelerating. This pattern has prompted the authors of this study to state that "the long-term future of telephone interviewing does not appear promising."

Nonresponse has been labeled the marketing research industry's biggest problem,[39] and it is multinational in scope.[40] Compounding the problem has been the increase in the numbers of surveys, which means the likelihood of being asked to participate in a survey has increased. With several researchers chasing the same population, there is always a constant battle to keep response rates from dropping. Some industry observers

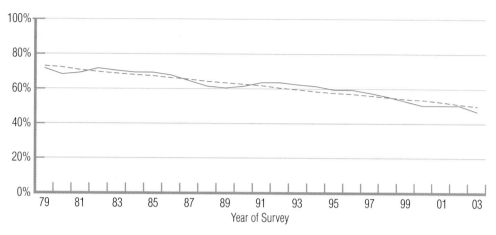

FIGURE 14.2

Nonresponse to Telephone Surveys Are on a Downward Trend (dotted line)
Source: Curtin, R., Presser, S., and Singer, E. (2005, Spring). Changes in telephone survey nonresponse over the past quarter century. *Public Opinion Quarterly*, 69(1):91.

believe that the major problems leading to nonresponse are caused by fears of invasion of privacy, skepticism of consumers regarding the benefits of participating in research, and the use of research as a guise for telemarketing. (At this point, you may want to recall our discussion of sugging and frugging in Chapter 2.)

Nonresponse is defined as a failure on the part of a prospective respondent to take part in the survey or to answer specific questions on the questionnaire. There are at least three different types of potential nonresponse errors lurking in any survey: refusals to participate in the survey, break-offs during the interview, and refusals to answer specific questions, or item omission. Table 14.2 briefly describes each type of nonresponse.

> There are three types of nonresponse errors: refusals to participate in the survey, break-offs during the interview, and refusals to answer specific questions (item omissions).

Refusals to Participate in the Survey

Refusal rates differ by area of the country as well as by demographic differences. The reasons for **refusals** are many and varied. The person may be busy, he or she may have no interest in the survey, something about the interviewer's voice or approach may have turned the person off, or the refusal may simply reflect how that person always responds to surveys. We have prepared Marketing Research Insight 14.4 so you can learn about the effect of topic interest in gaining a potential respondent's cooperation. One of the reasons for a refusal to participate is because the respondents do not want to take the time or because they regard it as an intrusion of their privacy. Refusals are a concern even with panels.[41]

> Refusals to participate in surveys are increasing worldwide.

As we mentioned previously, one way to overcome refusals is to use incentives as a token of appreciation. In a review of 15 different mail surveys, researchers found that

TABLE 14.2	The Three Types of Nonresponses with Surveys

Refusal—A prospective respondent declines to participate in the survey.

Break-off—A respondent stops answering in the middle of the survey.

Item omission—A respondent does not answer a particular question but does answer questions after that question.

MARKETING RESEARCH INSIGHT

ONLINE APPLICATION

14.4

Do Respondents Participate in Surveys Due to Topic Interest?

There is a commonly held belief that survey respondents are more inclined to take part in a survey if the topic has a high level of interest to them. Three researchers[42] set out to test this belief. They used four different surveys, each on a different topic and each with a different household population. The populations were teachers, new parents, senior citizens, and political contributors. The topics were education and schools, child care and parenting, Medicare and health issues, voting and elections, and issues facing the nation. Respondents were selected with random sampling methods, and all those selected were approached with a telephone survey. A total of 2330 respondents participated in the surveys, with an overall response rate of 63%.

The results: people do cooperate more with surveys that have topics of great interest to them. In fact, the researchers found that with a survey topic of great interest to the person, the chances of that person taking part are 40% higher than with a low-interest topic. Clearly, if a marketing researcher believes the survey topic will be interesting to potential respondents, it is vital to divulge the topic very early in the introduction. Alternatively, if the survey topic is not highly interesting to those who will be asked to participate in the survey, the researcher should give strong consideration to incentives and inducements for individuals who participate.

inclusion of a small gift, such as a $1.50 rollerball pen, increased response rates by nearly 14 percent. A second feature that contributes to refusals is the length of the questionnaire.[43] The study previously cited found that for every additional minute it takes to fill out the questionnaire, the response rate drops by 0.85%. Response rates to mail surveys are also influenced by the type of appeal that is made in the cover letter. Results from one study indicated that a social utility appeal was more effective in increasing response rates when an educational institution was the sponsor. On the other hand, an egoistic appeal was more effective when the sponsor was a commercial organization. An egoistic appeal is a suggestion that the respondent's individual responses are highly important in completing the research task.[44]

Break-Offs During the Interview

If tired, confused, or uninterested, respondents may "break off" in the middle of an interview.

A **break-off** occurs when a respondent reaches a certain point and then decides not to answer any more questions for the survey. Reasons for break-offs, as you would expect, are varied. The interview may take longer than the respondent initially believed, the topic and specific questions may prove to be distasteful or too personal, the instructions may be too confusing, a sudden interruption may occur, or the respondent may choose to take an incoming call on call-waiting and stop the interview. Sometimes with self-administered surveys, a researcher will find a questionnaire in which the respondent has simply stopped filling it out.

It is critical that well-trained interviewers be employed to carry out the surveys. In a discussion on how to improve respondent cooperation, Howard Gershowitz, senior vice president of MKTG, said, "I think the interviewers have to be taken out of the vacuum and be included in the process. Companies that are succeeding right now realize that the interviewers are the key to their success."[45] Increasingly, research providers are focusing on improved training techniques and field audits.

For any number of reasons and at any time, a respondent may break off the interview.

Refusals to Answer Specific Questions (Item Omission)

Even if a failure to participate or a break-off situation does not occur, a researcher will sometimes find that specific questions have lower response rates than others. In fact, if a marketing researcher suspects ahead of time that a particular question, such as the respondent's annual income for last year, will have some degree of refusals, it is appropriate to include the designation "refusal" on the questionnaire. Of course, it is not wise to put these designations on self-administered questionnaires, because respondents may use this option simply as a cop-out, when they might have provided accurate answers if the designation were not there. **Item omission** is the phrase sometimes used to identify the percentage of the sample that refuses to answer a particular question.[46] Research has shown that sensitive questions elicit more refusals and questions that require more mental effort garner more "don't know" responses.[47] So it is useful for a researcher to offer the "don't know" option with the latter type of questions to reduce item omissions.

Occasionally, a respondent will refuse to answer a particular question that he or she considers too personal or a private matter.

What Is a Completed Interview?

As we learned earlier, you will experience both break-offs and item omissions. At what point does a break-off still constitute a completed interview? At what level of item omission do we deem a survey to be incomplete? In other words, a researcher must have a definition or otherwise specify the criteria for a "completed interview." Almost all surveys will have some item omissions and break-offs. However, simply because a few questions remain unanswered does not mean you do not have a completed interview. But, how many questions must be answered before you have a completed interview? The answer to this question is a judgment call, and it will vary with each marketing research project. Only in rare cases will it be necessary for the respondent to answer all of the questions. In most others, the researcher will adopt some decision rule that defines completed versus not completed interviews. For example, in most research studies there are questions directed at the primary purpose of the study. Also, there are usually questions asked for purposes of adding additional insights into how respondents answered the primary questions. Such secondary questions often include a list of demographic questions. Demographics, because they are more personal in nature, are typically placed at the end of the questionnaire. Because they are not the primary focus of the study, a **completed interview** may be defined as one in which all the primary questions have been answered. In this way, you will have data for your primary questions and most of the data for your secondary questions. Interviewers can then be given a specific statement as to what constitutes a completed survey such as, "If the respondent answers through question 18, you may count it as a completion." (The demographics begin with question 19.) Likewise, the researcher must adopt a decision rule for determining the extent of item omissions necessary to invalidate a survey or a particular question.

> You must define a "completed" interview.

REDUCING NONRESPONSE ERROR

We have now learned the sources of nonresponse error and how to control for interviewer and respondent errors that may occur in surveys. Now, what can we do to ensure that we minimize nonresponse (maximize the response rate)? Each survey data-collection method represents a unique potential for nonresponse. Mail surveys historically represent the worst case, but even with these, there are many strategies used by marketing researchers to increase response rates.[48] Such strategies include **advance notification** via postcard or telephone, **monetary incentives**,[49] and **follow-up contacts**. Identification of respondents prior to mailing the survey can increase response rates for a 10-minute survey from 27.5% to 33.7%. In addition to respondent identification, if respondent cooperation can be secured in advance, the response rate can be improved to 40%. Researchers are now experimenting with other data-collection methods such as faxes, e-mail, etc., as means of increasing response rates. However, one has to contend with other problems such as a restricted population, loss of anonymity, and inability to have longer questionnaires.[50]

> Tactics such as advance notification, monetary incentives, and follow-up mailings are used to increase response rates.

To reduce the not-at-homes, busy signals, and no answers, several **callback attempts** should be made. Interviewers should be trained to write the time and date when the respondent is not at home, the phone is busy, or there is no answer. Callback attempts, usually three or four, should be made at another time and/or date. Marketing research firms have designed special forms that can keep track of the several callback attempts that may be made to obtain a completed survey from a particular respondent. This sheet allows for a total of (e.g.) four callback attempts. There are provisions to mark the time and date of the call as well as the result. The results are coded so that the data analyst can find out whether the nonresponse was due to a disconnected number, language problems, refusal to answer, and so on.

> Callback forms are essential tools tracking attempts to reduce nonresponses.

We discussed using replacement samples in Chapter 12. There are many methods that may be followed to replace samples. Essentially, they all strive to replace a nonrespondent (noncontact or refusal) with an equivalent respondent during the survey. For instance, if a telephone interviewer is given a telephone book and instructed to interview every 25th name, he or she may find that one of these people refuses to participate in the survey. To replace the nonrespondent, the interviewer can be directed to use a "drop-down" replacement procedure; that is, the interviewer will call the next name below that one rather than skipping to the next 25th name. He or she can continue calling names in this manner until a replacement is secured for the refusal. On finding a replacement, the original 25-name skip interval would be resumed. The basic strategy for treating nonresponse error during the conduct of the survey involves a combination of judicious use of incentives and persuasion to cooperate and repeated attempts to reach the original prospective respondent. Systematic replacement of respondents who, for whatever reason, do not take part in the survey, help achieve desired levels of allowable error.

Measuring Nonresponse Error in Surveys

Most marketing research studies report their response rate. The response rate essentially enumerates the percentage of the total sample for which interviews were completed. It is, therefore, the opposite of the nonresponse rate (a measure of nonresponse error). If you have a 75% response rate, then you have a nonresponse error of 25%.

For many years there was much confusion about the calculation of response rates. There was no one universally accepted definition, and different firms used different methods to calculate response rates. In fact, there were many terms in common usage, including completion rate, cooperation rate, interview rate, at-home rate, and refusal rate, among others. In 1982, however, CASRO (Council of American Survey Research Organizations) published a special report in an attempt to provide a uniform definition and method for calculating the response rate.[51]

According to the CASRO report, response rate is defined as the ratio of the number of completed interviews to the number of eligible units in the sample. Or,

CASRO Response Rate Formula (Simple Form)

$$\text{Response rate} = \frac{\text{Number of completed interviews}}{\text{Number of eligible units in sample}}$$

In many studies, eligible respondents are determined by screening or qualifying questions. For example, if we were working with a department store that was specifically concerned with its kitchenwares department, we would determine potential respondents' eligibility for the survey by asking them screening questions: "Do you shop at Acme Department Store regularly?" If the person answers, "Yes," then we would ask "Have you shopped in the kitchenwares department at any time during the past three months?" If the person answers, "Yes," to this question, then he or she is eligible to take part in the survey.

Suppose we have a sample of 1000 shoppers, and the results of the survey are:

Completions = 400
Ineligible = 300
Refusals = 100
No answer, busy, not at home = 200

This information allows you to calculate the number of sample units that are (a) eligible, (b) noneligible, and (c) not ascertained. When calculating the response rate we have the number of completions in the numerator (as usual). However, in the denominator we have the number of completions plus the percentage of those who refused and who were busy, and not-at-homes who were eligible. Because we do not talk to those who refuse (before the screening question), do not answer, have busy signals, or who are not at home, how do we determine the percentage of these people that would have been eligible? We multiply their number by the percentage of those that we did talk with who are eligible. By doing this, we are assuming that the same percentage of eligibles exist in the population of those that we did talk with (of the 700 we talked with, 0.57 were eligible) as exist in the population of those that we did not talk with (due to refusals, no answers, busy, or not-at-homes). The formula for calculating the response rate for this situation is:

CASRO Response Rate Formula (Expanded Form)

$$\text{Response rate} = \frac{completions}{completions + \left(\dfrac{completions}{completions + ineligible}\right) \times (refusals + not\ reached)}$$

Here are the calculations.

Calculation of CASRO Response Rate (Expanded Form)

$$\text{Response rate} = \frac{400}{400 + \left\{\dfrac{400}{400 + 300}\right\}\{100 + 200\}}$$

$$= \frac{400}{400 + (0.57)(300)}$$

$$= 70.0\%$$

Active **Learning**

HOW TO CALCULATE A RESPONSE RATE USING THE CASRO FORMULA

Although the CASRO formulas seems simple and straightforward, questions arise about exactly how to interpret them when dealing with individual research projects. We have created this Active Learning exercise so you can appreciate what goes into the proper calculation of a response rate.

We are providing you with this example because it seems that all research projects are unique when we are trying to calculate a response rate. For example, although the situation we present here is fairly common, we incorporate two of the response rate formulas discussed in this chapter. Our attempt here is to provide you with a generic telephone survey and to give you as much detail as possible so that you will understand how to calculate a response rate.

> **Population:** Survey of car-buying attitudes and behavior in households with telephones in Anytown, USA
> **Sampling frame:** Telephone directory
> **Eligibility of respondents:** The survey seeks information about car dealers and recent car-purchasing behavior. Your client wants information collected *only from individuals who have purchased an automobile within the past year.* Consequently, a screening question was asked at the beginning of the survey to determine if the respondent, or anyone in the household, had purchased a car within the past year.

Assume you are doing this survey as a class project and you have been assigned the task of conducting telephone interviews. You are given a list of randomly selected telephone numbers and told to fill a quota of five completions. You are instructed to make at least three contact attempts before giving up on a telephone number. Also, you are given a call record sheet where you are to write in the result of every call you attempt. So, as you call each number, you record one of the following outcomes by the telephone number and in the column corresponding to which contact attempt pertained to that particular call. The results that you can record are as follows:

> **Disconnected (D)**—Message from phone company stating number no longer in service.
> **Wrong target (WT)**—(ineligible) Number is a business phone and you are interested only in residences.
> **Ineligible respondent (IR)**—No one in household has purchased an automobile within past year.
> **Refusal (R)**—Subject refuses to participate.

Terminate (T)—Subject begins survey but stops before completing all questions.

Completed (C)—questionnaire is completed.

Busy (BSY)—phone line is busy; attempt callback at later time, unless this is your 3rd attempt.

No answer (NA)—No one answers or you encounter a telephone answering device. You may leave a message and state that you will call back later, unless this is your 3rd attempt.

Callback (CB)—Subject has instructed you to callback at more convenient time; record callback time and date and return call, unless this is your 3rd attempt.

Let us assume that your list of numbers and codes looks like the following:

Telephone Number	1st Attempt	2nd Attempt	3rd Attempt
474-2892	No answer	No answer	Completed
474-2668	Busy	Ineligible respondent	
488-3211	Disconnected		
488-2289	Completed		
672-8912	Wrong target		
263-6855	Busy	Busy	Busy
265-9799	Terminate		
234-7160	Refusal		
619-6019	Callback	Busy	Busy
619-8200	Ineligible respondent		
474-2716	Ineligible respondent		
774-7764	No answer	No answer	
474-2654	Disconnected		
488-4799	Wrong target		
619-0015	Busy	Completed	
265-4356	No answer	No answer	Completed
265-4480	Wrong target		
263-8898	No answer	No answer	No answer
774-2213	Completed		

You should note that you met your quota of 5 completed interviews with 19 telephone numbers. So, the response rate computation should not include anything about any telephone numbers that you did not have to call in your part of the survey even if these numbers were provided to you.

Look at the last code you recorded for each number and count the number of each code. (We have used color coding on your record sheet to help you find the last code for each telephone number.) Insert these numbers into the following response rate formula to determine your correctly computed response rate.

$$\text{Response rate} = \frac{C}{C + \left(\frac{C}{C + IR + WT}\right)(BSY + D + T + R + NA)}$$

$$= \underline{\hspace{2cm}}\%$$

Note how ineligibles were handled in the formula. Both *IR* and *WT* were counted as ineligibles. The logic is that the percentage of eligibles among those who were talked with is the same as among those not talked with (*BSY, D, T, R,* and *NA*).

ADJUSTING RESULTS TO REDUCE THE EFFECTS OF NONRESPONSE ERROR

Nonresponse error should always be measured, and if we assess that the degree of nonresponse is a problem, we are obliged to make adjustments. Of course, if we do not find significant nonresponse error, there is no reason to make adjustments. But, if some exists, there are at least two methods of compensating for its presence:[52] weighted averages and oversampling.[53]

Weighted Averages

Weighted averages involve applying weights, believed to accurately reflect the proportions that subgroups represent in the population, to the subgroup means to compute an overall score that adjusts for the nonresponse differences in the subgroups. This way, a weighted average is applied to adjust a sample's results to be consistent with the believed true demographic profile.

For example, if we believed the target market for a suntan lotion was really 50% married and 50% single, but a mail survey sample contained 25% married and 75% single, we could adjust the results using a 50–50 weighted average. One question on the survey may have asked, "On the average, how much would you expect to pay for a 5-oz bottle of NoSun Natural Tanning Lotion?" We find that the married respondents' average answer is $2.00, whereas the singles' average is $3.00. If we were to take the overall average of the mail survey (25–75) sample, it would be computed as $2.75 (.25 × $2.00 + .75 × $3.00), but if we applied the 50–50 true ratio, the average price would turn out to be $2.50 (.5 × $2.00 + .5 × $3.00). Nonresponse error distorted the average price, but we have adjusted using the believed true demographic profile to eliminate that source of error.

Oversampling

The second general strategy for dealing with nonresponse error in a survey is typically more expensive, but it is applied under certain circumstances. With the second strategy, the marketing researcher uses **oversampling**, which involves drawing a sample that is larger than the group to be analyzed. Please note that we are referring to an instance in which the final sample will be a good deal larger than the target sample size and not a case of drawing a large number of potential respondents in order to achieve the target sample size. The researcher then draws a subsample of respondents to match the believed profile of the target group. Alternatively, with high refusal rates for specific questions, oversampling may generate sufficient numbers of respondents who do answer these questions.

For example, using the suntan lotion example, we might send out 10,000 questionnaires and receive 2000 back, still with the incorrect 75% singles and 25% married distribution. Now, we would use our computer capabilities to select a 50–50 sample of marrieds to singles (that is, 500 of each type) out of our respondent group data set. We would not

Weighting responses by subgroup sizes is a way to compensate for nonresponse error.

Caution should be used in weighting responses, and it should be done only in unusual situations.

If a researcher believes that nonresponse will be a problem, he or she may opt to oversample in order to compensate.

need to perform the weighted averaging because the sample being analyzed is in the proper proportions. In essence, however, we would be throwing away 1000 questionnaires returned by marrieds to bring our sample into conformity with the married:single population ratio. In fact, if we greatly oversampled, we would have the opportunity to draw a subsample from the respondents that matched our believed population for several demographic factors, such as sex, age, education, income, and so forth. But with more factors, the final sample size could decrease, and more returned questionnaires would be left out of our analyses. Obviously, the best policy is to strive to reduce nonresponse error of all types to as low a level as possible by appropriate choice of survey method, use of incentives, and whatever other inducements are available to the researcher so that adjustments are not necessary. As a rule of thumb, such adjustments, though sometimes appropriate, should be avoided.

PRELIMINARY QUESTIONNAIRE SCREENING

As we have indicated, nonresponses appear in practically every survey. At the same time, there are respondents whose answers have a suspicious pattern to them. Both of these necessitate a separate phase of the data-collection stage in the marketing research process that involves the inspection of questionnaires as they are being prepared for entry into a computer file for tabulation and analysis. Researchers develop a sixth sense about the quality of responses, and they can often spot errors just by inspecting raw questionnaires. Granted, some data-collection companies provide for direct entry of responses into a computer file, and this option is becoming commonplace. It is also likely that a stack of completed questionnaires is the result, and this stack is sent to the researcher whose office might be in Omaha, Little Rock, or Boston. In either case, it is good practice to perform a screen step to catch respondent errors before tabulation of the data takes place. So, when inspecting individual respondents' answers, the researcher may be looking at a hard-copy questionnaire, or he/she may be scrutinizing the code numbers in row of a computer file.

Completed questionnaires should be screened for errors.

What to Look for in Questionnaire Inspection

What is the purpose of questionnaire checks? Despite all of the precautions described thus far, the danger still exists that problem questionnaires are included in the completed stack. So the purpose of inspection of completed questionnaires is to determine the degree of "bad" questionnaires and, if deemed advisable, to pull the ones with severe problems. Problem questionnaires are ones that fall into the following categories: They have questionable validity; they have unacceptable patterns of incompleteness; they have unacceptable amounts of apparent respondent misunderstanding; or they have other complications, such as illegible writing, damage in transit, or some other obvious problem. Five different problems that can be identified with screened completed questionnaires can be described: incomplete questionnaires, nonresponses to specific questions, yea- or nay-saying patterns, middle-of-the-road patterns, and unreliable responses. We describe each problem, and Table 14.3 summarizes each one. In industry jargon, these are "exceptions," and they signal possible field-data-collection errors to a researcher.

Problems found when screening completed questionnaires include incomplete questionnaires, nonresponses to specific questions, yea- or nay-saying patterns, middle-of-the-road patterns, and unreliable responses.

▶ **Incomplete Questionnaires** Incomplete questionnaires are those in which the later questions or pages of a questionnaire are left blank. We just described this type of nonresponse error as a "break-off," which is its common label with personal or

Some questionnaires may be only partially completed.

Questionnaires should be checked for various types of response problems.

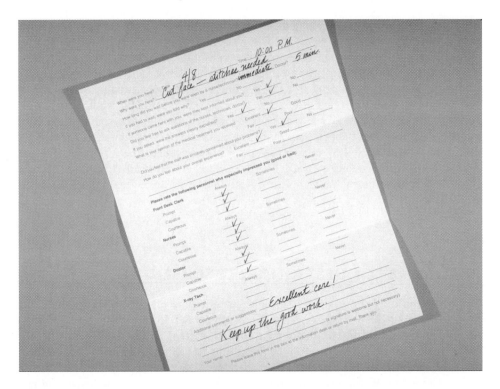

telephone interviews; that is, the researcher might find that a respondent answered the first three pages of questions, and then, for some reason, stopped. Perhaps the respondent became bored, or the questions might have been too complicated, or perhaps he or she thought the topic was too personal. The reason that the questionnaire was not completed may never be known.

When a respondent does not answer a particular question, it is referred to as an "item omission."

▶ **Nonresponses to Specific Questions (Item Omissions)**   Also, as we just noted in our descriptions of the various types of nonresponse, for whatever reasons, respondents will sometimes leave a question blank. In a telephone interview, they may decline answering a question, and the interviewer might note this occurrence with the designation "ref" (refused) or some other code.

TABLE 14.3	Types of Response Problems Found during Questionnaire Inspection
Problem Type	**Description**
Incomplete questionnaire	Questionnaire is incompletely filled out. The respondent stopped answering questions at some point (break-off).
Nonresponse to specific question	The respondent refused to answer particular question(s), but answered others before and after it (item omission).
Yea- or nay-saying pattern	Respondent exhibits a persistent tendency to respond favorably or unfavorably, respectively, regardless of the questions.
Middle-of-the-road pattern	Respondent indicates "no opinion" to most questions.
Unreliable responses	Respondent is not consistent on a reliability check.

▶ **Yea- or Nay-Saying Patterns** Even when questions are answered, there can be signs of problems. A **yea-saying** pattern may be evident on one questionnaire in the form of all "yes" or "strongly agree" answers.[54] The yea-sayer has a persistent tendency to respond in the affirmative regardless of the question, and yea-saying implies that the responses are not valid. The negative counterpart to the yea-saying is **nay-saying**, identifiable as persistent responses in the negative.

Yea-saying and nay-saying are seen as persistent tendencies on the parts of some respondents to agree or disagree, respectively, with most of the questions asked.

▶ **Middle-of-the-Road Patterns** The **middle-of-the-road pattern** is seen as a preponderance of "no opinion" responses. No opinion is in essence no response, and prevalent no opinions on a questionnaire may signal low interest, lack of attention, or even objections to being involved in the survey. True, a respondent may not have an opinion on a topic, but if one gives a great many no-opinion answers, questions arise as to how useful that respondent is to the survey.

Some respondents will hide their opinions by indicating "no opinion" throughout the survey.

▶ **Unreliable Responses** We defined *reliability* in a previous chapter as the consistency in a respondent's answers. Sometimes a researcher will deliberately include a consistency check. For instance, if a respondent encountered the question "Is the amount of electricity used by your kitchen appliances a concern to you?" the person might respond with a "yes." Later in the survey, this question appears: "When you use your electric coffee maker, toaster, or electric can opener, do you think about how much electricity is being used?" Now, suppose that respondent answers with a "no" to this question. This signals an inconsistent or **unreliable respondent**, who should be eliminated from the sample.

There are other bothersome problems that can pop up during questionnaire screening. For example, you might find that a respondent has checked more than one response option when only one was supposed to be checked. Another respondent may have failed to look at the back of a questionnaire page and thus missed all of the questions there. A third respondent may have ignored the agree–disagree scale and written in comments about energy conservation. Usually, detecting these errors requires physically examining the questionnaires.

SPSS Student Assistant: Getting SPSS Help

SUMMARY

Total error in survey research is a combination of sampling error and nonsampling error. Sampling error may be controlled by the sample plan and the sample size. Researchers must know both the sources of nonsampling error and how to minimize its effect on total errors. The data-collection phase of marketing research holds great potential for nonsampling errors. There are intentional as well as unintentional errors on the parts of both interviewers and respondents that must be regulated. Dishonesty, misunderstanding, and fatigue affect fieldworkers; falsehoods, refusals, misunderstanding, and fatigue affect respondents. We described the several controls and procedures used to overcome these sources of error.

At the same time, nonresponse errors of various types are encountered during data collection. Nonresponse error is measured by the calculation of the response rate. There are several methods for improving the response rate and thereby lowering nonresponse error. A weighted average method or oversampling may be applied to bring the sample back into alignment with the population. Once the interviews are completed, the researcher must screen them for errors. Invariably, incomplete questionnaires and refusals are present, and tendencies such as yea-saying may be seen as well.

KEY TERMS

Nonsampling error (p. 392)
Fieldworker error (p. 392)
Respondent error (p. 393)
Intentional fieldworker errors (p. 393)
Interviewer cheating (p. 393)
Leading the respondent (p. 394)
Unintentional interviewer errors
  (p. 395)
Personal characteristics (p. 395)
Interviewer misunderstanding (p. 395)
Fatigue-related mistakes (p. 396)
Intentional respondent errors (p. 396)
Falsehoods (p. 396)
Nonresponse (p. 397)
Unintentional respondent error
  (p. 399)
Respondent misunderstanding (p. 399)
Guessing (p. 399)
Attention loss (p. 399)
Distractions (p. 399)
Respondent fatigue (p. 400)
Supervision (p. 400)
Validation (p. 401)
Orientation sessions (p. 402)
Role-playing sessions (p. 402)
Anonymity (p. 402)
Confidentiality (p. 402)

Incentives (p. 402)
Validation checks (p. 402)
Third-person technique (p. 402)
Questionnaire instructions and examples
  (p. 403)
Reversals of scale endpoints (p. 403)
Prompters (p. 403)
Multiple submissions (p. 404)
Bogus respondents and responses
  (p. 404)
Population misrepresentation
  (p. 404)
Nonresponse error (p. 404)
Refusals (p. 405)
Break-offs (p. 406)
Item omission (p. 407)
Completed interview (p. 408)
Advance notification (p. 408)
Monetary incentives (p. 408)
Follow-up contacts (p. 408)
Callback attempts (p. 408)
Weighted averages (p. 412)
Oversampling (p. 412)
Yea-saying (p. 415)
Nay-saying (p. 415)
Middle-of-the-road pattern (p. 415)
Unreliable respondent (p. 415)

REVIEW QUESTIONS/APPLICATIONS

1. Distinguish sampling error from nonsampling error.
2. Because we cannot easily calculate nonsampling errors, how must the prudent researcher handle nonsampling error?
3. Identify different types of intentional fieldworker error and the controls used to minimize them. Identify different types of unintentional fieldworker error and the controls used to minimize them.
4. Identify different types of intentional respondent error and the controls used to minimize them. Identify different types of unintentional respondent error and the controls used to minimize them.
5. Define "nonresponse." List three types of nonresponse found in surveys.
6. If a survey is found to have resulted in significant nonresponse error, what should the researcher do?
7. Why is it necessary to perform preliminary screening of completed questionnaires?
8. Identify five different problems that a researcher might find while screening completed questionnaires.

9. What is an "exception," and what is typically done with each type of exception encountered?

10. Your church is experiencing low attendance for its Wednesday evening Bible classes. You volunteer to design a telephone questionnaire aimed at finding out why church members are not attending these classes. Because the church has limited funds, members will be used as telephone interviewers. List the steps necessary to ensure good data quality in using this "do-it-yourself" option of field data collection.

11. A new mall-intercept company opens its offices in a nearby discount mall, and its president calls on the insurance company where you work to solicit business. It happens that your company is about to do a study on the market reaction to a new whole life insurance policy it is considering adding to its line. Make an outline of the information you would want from the mall-intercept company president in order to assess the quality of its services.

12. Acme Refrigerant Reclamation Company performs large-scale reclamation of contaminated refrigerants as mandated by the U.S. Environmental Protection Agency. It wishes to determine what types of companies will use this service, so the marketing director designs a questionnaire intended for telephone administration. Respondents will be plant engineers, safety engineers, and directors of major companies throughout the United States. Should Acme use a professional field-data-collection company to gather the data? Why or why not?

13. You work part-time at a telemarketing company. Your compensation is based on the number of credit card applicants you sign up with the telemarketing approach. The company owner has noticed that the credit card solicitation business is slowing down, so she decides to take on some marketing research telephone interview business. When you start work on Monday, she says that you are to do telephone interviews and gives you a large stack of questionnaires to have completed. What intentional fieldworker errors are possible under the circumstances described here?

14. Indicate what specific intentional and unintentional respondent errors are likely with each of the following surveys:
    a. The Centers for Disease Control and Prevention sends out a mail questionnaire on attitudes and practices concerning the prevention of AIDS.
    b. Eyemasters has a mall-intercept survey performed to determine opinions and uses of contact lenses.
    c. Boy Scouts of America sponsors a telephone survey on American's views on humanitarian service agencies.

15. How do you define a "completion," and how does this definition help a researcher deal with "incomplete questionnaires?"

16. What is nay-saying, and how does it differ from yea-saying? What should a researcher do if he or she suspects a respondent of being a nay-sayer?

17. On your first day as a student marketing intern at the O-Tay Research Company, the supervisor hands you a list of yesterday's telephone interviewer records. She tells you to analyze them and to give her a report by 5 P.M. Well, get to it!

	Ronnie	Mary	Pam	Isabelle
Completed	20	30	15	19
Refused	10	2	8	9
Ineligible	15	4	14	15
Busy	20	10	21	23
Disconnected	0	1	3	2
Break-off	5	2	7	9
No answer	3	2	4	3

AFFILIATED GROCERS, INC.

Affiliated Grocers, Inc. (AG) is a food store wholesaler cooperative located in Cleveland, Ohio. AG operates a large warehouse distribution center and serves approximately 100 independent grocery stores in the state of Ohio. Most of these grocery stores are family-owned, medium-sized supermarkets such as Jacob's, Cravitt's, or Wimberly's, but about one-quarter have banded together in local chainlike associations such as Hi Neighbor, Blue Bonnet, or Associated Food Stores. All compete against the national food store chains such as Winn-Dixie, SuperFresh, and Kroger.

A recent statewide survey done by the Cleveland State University has revealed that the major chains dominate, accounting for over 90% of the market. Awareness of AG stores is very low; these stores represent less than 5% of grocery purchases. This finding prompted AG executives to begin a corporate identity program. They talked to a professor of marketing from Cleveland State University, who suggested that the first step is to ascertain the positions of the major grocery chains and the desires of grocery shoppers as a way of identifying positioning alternatives for AG. The professor advised AG to do a statewide survey on the grocery market as a first step. He also informed AG that he advises an American Marketing Association (AMA) student chapter that does various types of marketing projects. He suggested that AG use the AMA student members for data collection in a telephone survey as a means of holding costs down.

AG officials were skeptical of the ability of students to execute this survey, but they had very little money to devote to this project. The professor proposed a meeting with AG officials, the marketing research projects director of the student AMA chapter, and himself to discuss the matter. When he returned to campus, he informed the AMA student chapter president of the opportunity, and told her to have the marketing research projects director draft a list of the quality-control safeguards that would be used in a statewide telephone survey in which 20 student interviewers would be calling from their apartments or dorm rooms.

1. Take the role of the marketing research projects director, and draft all of the interviewer controls you believe are necessary to effect data collection comparable in quality to that gathered by a professional telephone interviewing company.

2. The AMA student chapter president calls the marketing research projects director and says, "I'm concerned about the questionnaire's length. It will take over 20 minutes for the typical respondent to complete over the phone. Isn't the length going to cause problems?" Again, take the role of the marketing research projects director. Indicate what nonresponse problems might result from the questionnaire's length, and recommend ways to counter each of these problems.

PACIFIC STATES RESEARCH: CATI OR ONLINE PANEL?

Pacific States Research, Inc. is a full-service interview company located in 10 regional malls throughout western United States, extending as far south as San Diego. Each location is equipped with a complete focus group facility that accounts for approximately 25% of Pacific States' revenues. Another 25% is derived from Pacific States' mall-intercept interviewing, and the remaining 50% of the business is obtained from centralized telephone interview services. Work has been reasonably steady in all three areas over the past five years. But the company has continually wrestled with quality problems in its telephone interview area. The major difficulty is retention of interviewers. An internal study has revealed that the average location needs six telephone interviewers to work full-time and another six part-timers who are hired as the volume of work requires. When work is slack, the full-time interviewers are laid off, and when the workload increases beyond the ability of the full-time interviewers, the part-timers are used for the time when they are needed. The average length of time full-time telephone interviewers work for Pacific States is just under six months.

Quality-control problems have affected business. One major account recently informed Pacific States that it would no longer use its services when a major error was found in how Pacific States' interviewers administered a critical question on its survey. Other accounts have complained that Pacific States is slow in turning telephone interview work around, and they have also noted errors in the work that has been done. To make matters more complicated, the marketing research trade publications are reporting a general decline in telephone research due to nonresponse problems, issues of privacy, and various "call blocking" systems that consumers can use to screen their incoming calls.

Ned Allen, the manager responsible for telephone interviewing, has met with various computer services companies about the problem. Ned is thinking of recommending that Pacific move away from centralized telephone interviewing to computer-assisted telephone interviewing (CATI). Ned has done some preliminary analysis, and he figures that CATI would greatly reduce interviewer errors. He thinks that the ease of a CATI system will probably entice interviewers to stay with Pacific longer. Also, because CATI can be integrated across all 10 locations, it would serve to spread the work evenly across the full-time interviewers. Right now, each location operates like a stand-alone data-collection company, but work is allocated to each through Pacific States' main office located in San Francisco.

Ned finds that a fully integrated CATI system would require somewhere around $250,000 in installation costs, and annual maintenance/upgrading is going to cost about $150,000. Also, Pacific States would need to levy clients a setup charge of $250 per page to convert the questionnaire to a CATI format.

Ned is also contemplating an online panel that would be representative of the "Upscale West USA." It would consist of 20,000 online panelists, with 1000 in each of the 20 largest cities in the "Upscale West" (California, Oregon, Washington, Arizona, and Nevada). The panel respondents would be upscale consumers who would be compensated in catalog buying points for responding to at least three online surveys per month. Ned estimates the annual panelist compensation cost alone would be $2 million. The programming of the online service will cost about $250,000, and the Internet fees to maintain the online panel are estimated to be about the same amount.

1. Using your knowledge of the data-collection concepts and issues described in this chapter, make a pro and con list for Ned concerning the CATI system.

2. What is your advice concerning the online panel system that is a great deal more expensive than the CATI system? Should Ned just focus his attention on the CATI system, or should he pursue the online panel idea? Why?

15

Basic Data Analysis:
Descriptive Statistics

How Long Do You Expect to Live, and What Worries You?[1]

A recent survey concerned the topic of how long Americans expect to live. According to the National Center for Health Statistics, average life expectancy is 77.3 years. However, as you can see in the pie chart here, the largest slice of the pie represents well over one-third of those surveyed who expect to live into their 80s, and close to 1 out of 5 expects to live into his or her 90s!

Only 1 person out of 4 (24%) thinks that he or she will die in his or her 70s, which is the decade corresponding to the actual life expectancy that the National Center for Health Statistics (NCHS) stipulates on its Web site.

What worries do people have about threats to their lives? The survey asked respondents to specify what ailments they think might threaten their health in the next five years. The following graph summarizes the findings, and it reveals that almost 4 out of 10 people believe that their overweight condition will adversely affect their life expectancy in the next five years. About 1 out of 3 people have real worries about high cholesterol, while 1 out of 4 worries about a heart attack, and 1 out of 5 is worried about some life-threatening form of cancer in the next five years of their lives. Did these people miss anything to worry about? Yes, they did as the NCHS lists "accidents" as the fifth largest cause of death for Americans.

Learning Objectives

Research shows that people expect to live long and active lives, but they do have concerns about health and worries about life-threatening illnesses.

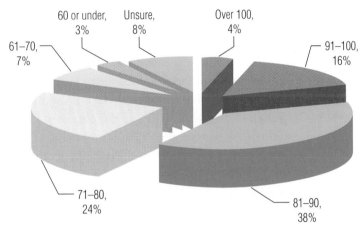

How old do you expect to live?

60 or under, 3%

Unsure, 8%

Over 100, 4%

91–100, 16%

61–70, 7%

71–80, 24%

81–90, 38%

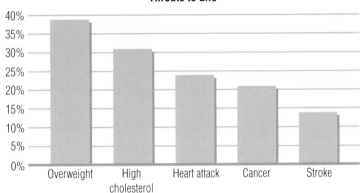

Threats to Life

Overweight — High cholesterol — Heart attack — Cancer — Stroke

Finally, the survey asked respondents about what physical conditions and afflictions are worrying them. In the following chart, it is evident that aching joints, perhaps complicated by arthritis is the number one debilitating physical condition fear for Americans, as 4 out of 10 have this on their minds. About 1 in 3 has concerns about declining vision, while about 1 in 5 has concerns about depression, hearing loss, and/or anxiety. Interestingly, the fear of AIDS is almost nonexistent for most Americans. Again we can ask if these people are worrying about the "right" physical conditions, and the question can be answered by consulting the NCHS Web site.

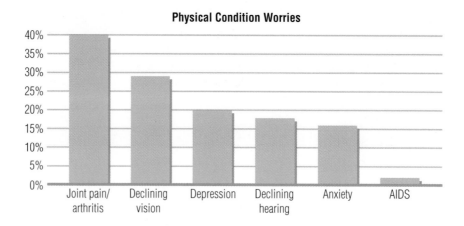

Physical Condition Worries

Our purpose in presenting these findings to you is not to increase your anxiety about these conditions and ailments, but rather to show you how survey findings can be presented and interpreted. We first used a pie chart because the age range percentages summed to 100%, and a pie chart is an effective visual aid depicting the pattern of the percentages. With our bar charts, you can easily see the relative sizes of worries about the threats to life and physical conditions, and with both the pie and bar chart findings, we interpreted the findings by using fractions or "1 out of *n*" references that are easy for you to relate to.

This chapter begins our discussion of the various statistical techniques available to the marketing researcher. As you will soon learn, these really are devices to convert formless data into meaningful information just as was done in the "How Long Do You Expect to Live, and What Worries You?" example. These techniques summarize and communicate patterns found in the data sets marketing researchers analyze. We begin the chapter by describing data coding and the code book. Then we introduce data summarization and the four functions it accomplishes. Here we preview five different types of statistical analyses commonly used by marketing researchers. Next, we define descriptive analysis and discuss measures of central tendency such as the mode, median, and mean. We also discuss measures of variability, including the frequency distribution, range, and standard deviation. It is important to understand when each measure is appropriate, so this topic is addressed. Last, we show you how to obtain the various descriptive statistics available in the Statistical Package for the Social Sciences (SPSS).

CODING DATA AND THE DATA CODE BOOK

After questionnaires are screened and exceptions are dealt with, the researcher moves to the data entry stage of the data analysis process. **Data entry** refers to the creation of a computer file that holds the raw data taken from all of the questionnaires deemed suitable for analysis. A number of data entry options exist, ranging from manual keyboard entry of each and every piece of data to computer scanning systems that scan entire sets of questionnaires and convert them to a data file in a matter of minutes. There are, in fact, integrated questionnaire design and analysis software programs, such as WebSurveyor, that include computer scanning operations in their systems.

Data entry requires an operation called **data coding**, defined as the identification of codes that pertain to the possible responses for each question on the questionnaire. Typically, these codes are numeric because numbers are quick and easy to input, and computers work with numbers more efficiently than they do with alphanumeric codes. Recall that we discussed precoding the questionnaire in Chapter 11. In large-scale projects, and especially in cases in which the data entry is performed by a subcontractor, researchers use a **data code book**, which identifies all of the variable names and code numbers associated with each possible response to each question that makes up the data set. With a code book that describes the data file, any researcher can work on the data set, regardless of whether or not that researcher was involved in the research project during its earlier stages.

With online surveys, such as the use of WebSurveyor, the data file is built as respondents submit their completed online questionnaires; that is, with a Web-based survey, the codes are programmed into the html questionnaire document, but they do not appear as code numbers such as those customarily placed on a paper-and-pencil questionnaire. In the case of Web-based surveys, the code book is vital, as it is the researcher's only map to decipher the numbers found in the data file and to correlate them to the answers to the questions on the questionnaire.

With SPSS, it is easy to obtain the coding. With the data file opened, and all of the variables and their variable labels defined, use the Utilities—File Info or Utilities—Variables commands. The first one gives a list of all variables in the SPSS output window, whereas the second one uses a window that isolates the variable information one by one (see Figure 15.1).

> Researchers use data coding when preparing and working with a computer data file.

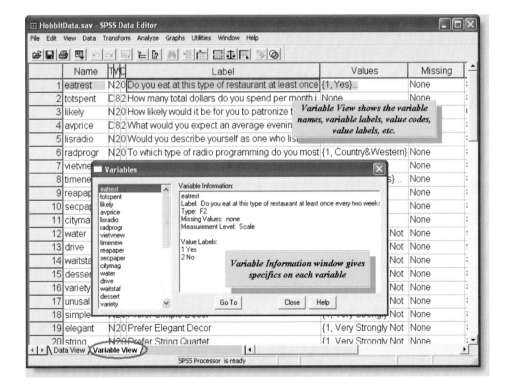

FIGURE 15.1
SPSS Variable View and Variables Window Reveal the Underlying Code Book for the Hobbit's Choice Restaurant Survey Data

TYPES OF STATISTICAL ANALYSES USED IN MARKETING RESEARCH

As you have learned through using SPSS, experimenting with the data sets we have provided, and becoming familiar with how SPSS works, marketing researchers work with data matrices. A **data matrix** is the coded raw data from a survey. These data are arranged in columns, which represent answers to the various questions on the survey questionnaire, and rows, which represent each respondent or case. The problem confronting the marketing researcher when faced with a data matrix is **data summarization**, which is defined as the process of describing a data matrix by computing a small number of measures that characterize the data set. Data summarization condenses the data matrix while retaining enough information so the client can mentally envision its salient characteristics.[2] Data summarization is actually any statistical analysis that accomplishes one or more of the following functions: (1) It summarizes the data; (2) it applies understandable conceptualizations; (3) it communicates underlying patterns; and (4) it generalizes sample findings to the population.[3] Refer to Table 15.1.

There are five basic types of statistical analyses that can be used by marketing researchers to reduce a data matrix: descriptive analysis, inferential analysis, differences analysis, associative analysis, and predictive analysis (Table 15.2). Each one has a unique role in the data analysis process; moreover, they are usually combined into a complete analysis of the information in order to satisfy the research objectives. As you can see in Figure 15.2, these techniques are progressively more complex, but at the same time, they convert raw data into increasingly more useful information as they increase in complexity.

These introductory comments will provide a preview of the subject matter that will be covered in this and other chapters. Because this is an introduction, we use the names of statistical procedures, but we do not define or describe them here. The specific techniques are all developed later in this textbook. It is important, however, that you understand each of the various categories of analysis available to the marketing researcher and comprehend generally what each is about.

Descriptive Analysis

Descriptive analysis is used to describe the variables (question responses) in a data matrix (all respondents' answers).

Certain measures, such as the mean, mode, standard deviation, and range are forms of **descriptive analysis** used by marketing researchers to describe the sample data matrix in such a way as to portray the "typical" respondent and to reveal the general pattern of responses. Descriptive measures are typically used early in the analysis process and become foundations for subsequent analysis.[4]

TABLE 15.1	The Four Functions of Data Analysis
Function	**Example**
Summarizes the data	The *average* respondent's age is . . .
Applies understandable conceptualizations	*Few respondents are younger than 30* . . .
Communicates underlying patterns	Most *satisfied customers recommend our brand* to their friends . . .
Generalizes sample findings to the population	This means that *from 70% to 80% of the target market is* . . .

TABLE 15.2	Five Types of Statistical Analysis Used by Marketing Researchers		
Type	**Description**	**Example**	**Statistical Concepts**
Descriptive (Chapter 15)	Data reduction	Describe the typical respondent, describe how similar respondents are to the typical respondent	Mean, median, mode, frequency distribution, range, standard deviation
Inferential (Chapter 16)	Determine population parameters, test hypotheses	Estimate population values	Standard error Null hypothesis
Differences (Chapter 17)	Determine if differences exist	Evaluate statistical significance of difference in the means of two groups in a sample	t test of differences, analysis of variance
Associative (Chapter 18)	Determine associations	Determine if two variables are related in a systematic way	Correlation, cross-tabulation
Predictive (Chapter 19)	Forecast, based on a statistical model	Estimate the level of y, given the amount of x	Regression

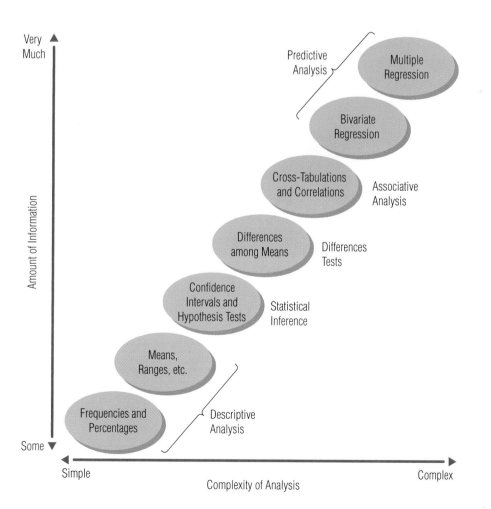

FIGURE 15.2
Levels of Analysis Used in Marketing Research

Inferential Analysis

Inferential analysis is used to generate conclusions about the population's characteristics based on the sample data.

When statistical procedures are used by marketing researchers to generalize the results of the sample to the target population that it represents, the process is referred to as **inferential analysis**. In other words, such statistical procedures allow a researcher to draw conclusions about the population based on information contained in the data matrix provided by the sample. Inferential statistics include hypothesis testing and estimating true population values based on sample information. We describe basic statistical inference in Chapter 16.

Differences Analysis

Occasionally, a marketing researcher needs to determine whether two groups are different. For example, the researcher may be investigating credit-card use and want to see if high-income earners differ from low-income earners in how often they use American Express. The researcher may statistically compare the average annual dollar expenditures charged on American Express by high- versus low-income buyers. Important market segmentation information may come from this analysis. Or he or she may run an experiment to see which of several alternative advertising themes garners the most favorable impression from a sample of target audience members. The researcher uses **differences analysis** to determine the degree to which real and generalizable differences exist in the population in order to help the manager make an enlightened decision on which advertising theme to use. Statistical differences analyses include the t test for significant differences between groups and analysis of variance. We define and describe them in Chapter 17.

Differences analysis is used to compare the mean of the responses of one group to that of another group, such as satisfaction ratings for "heavy" users versus "light" users

Differences analysis will tell you if high income owners use their American Express card account differently from lower income owers and/or for other credit card holders.

Associative Analysis

Other statistical techniques are used by researchers to determine systematic relationships among variables. **Associative analysis** investigates if and how two variables are related. For instance, are advertising recall scores positively associated with intentions to buy the advertised brand? Are expenditures on sales force training positively associated with sales force performance? Depending on the statistic used, the analysis may indicate the strength of the association and/or the direction of the association between two questions on a questionnaire in a given study. Techniques are also available if the researcher is interested in determining complex patterns of associations; these procedures are beyond the scope of this textbook. We devote Chapter 18 to descriptions of cross-tabulations and correlations that are basic associative analysis methods used in marketing research.

> Associative analysis determines the strength and direction of relationships between two or more variables (questions in the survey).

Predictive Analysis

Statistical procedures and models are available to the marketing researcher to help him or her make forecasts about future events; these fall under the category of **predictive analysis**. Regression analysis or time series analysis are commonly used by the marketing researcher to enhance prediction capabilities. Because marketing managers are typically worried about what will happen in the future given certain conditions such as a price increase, prediction is very desirable. Regression analysis is described in depth in Chapter 19.

> Predictive analysis allows one to make forecasts of future events.

It is not our intention to make you an expert in statistical analysis. Rather, the primary objective of our chapters on statistical analysis is to acquaint you with the basic concepts involved in each of the selected measures. You will certainly do basic statistical analysis throughout your marketing career, and it is very likely that you will encounter information summarized in statistical terms. So it is important for you to have a conceptual understanding of the commonly used statistical procedures. Our descriptions are intended to show you when and where each measure is appropriately used and to help you interpret the meaning of the statistical result once it is reported. We also rely heavily on computer statistical program output because you will surely encounter statistical program output in your company's marketing information system and/or summarized in a marketing research study report.

UNDERSTANDING DATA VIA DESCRIPTIVE ANALYSIS

YOUR INTEGRATED   **CASE**

The Hobbit's Choice Restaurant SPSS Data Set

We now turn to the several tools in descriptive analysis available to the researcher to describe the data obtained from a sample of respondents. In this chapter and in all other data analysis chapters, we are going to use The Hobbit's Choice Restaurant survey data set. That way, you can reconstruct the data analysis on your own with your Student Version of SPSS using the data set. To download this data set, go to the following Web site (www.prenhall.com/burnsbush) and find the data set download area.

For your information and as a quick review, the questionnaire was posted on WebSurveyor, and qualified respondents answered the questions and submitted their questionnaires in the

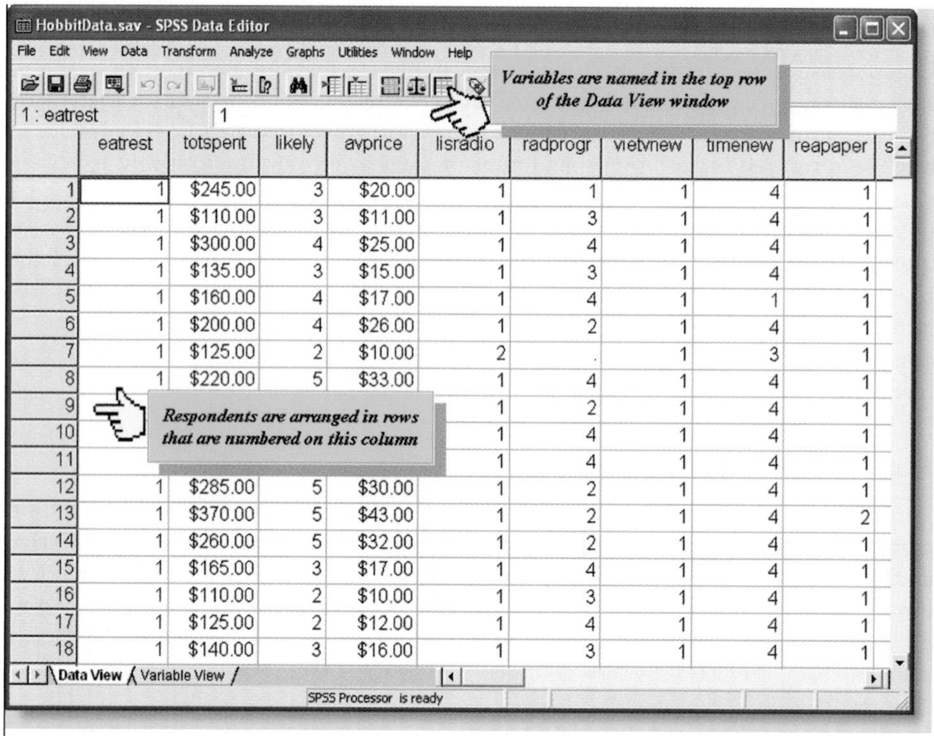

	eatrest	totspent	likely	avprice	lisradio	radprogr	vietvnew	timenew	reapaper
1	1	$245.00	3	$20.00	1	1	1	4	1
2	1	$110.00	3	$11.00	1	3	1	4	1
3	1	$300.00	4	$25.00	1	4	1	4	1
4	1	$135.00	3	$15.00	1	3	1	4	1
5	1	$160.00	4	$17.00	1	4	1	1	1
6	1	$200.00	4	$26.00	1	2	1	4	1
7	1	$125.00	2	$10.00	2	.	1	3	1
8	1	$220.00	5	$33.00	1	4	1	4	1
9					1	2	1	4	1
10					1	4	1	4	1
11					1	4	1	4	1
12	1	$285.00	5	$30.00	1	2	1	4	1
13	1	$370.00	5	$43.00	1	2	1	4	2
14	1	$260.00	5	$32.00	1	2	1	4	1
15	1	$165.00	3	$17.00	1	4	1	4	1
16	1	$110.00	2	$10.00	1	3	1	4	1
17	1	$125.00	2	$12.00	1	4	1	4	1
18	1	$140.00	3	$16.00	1	3	1	4	1

FIGURE 15.3
The SPSS Data View Window Shows the Hobbit's Choice Restaurant Survey Data Matrix

time period allotted for the online survey. The data were downloaded, imported into SPSS, set up with variable names and value labels, and cleaned. The final data set has a total of 400 respondents who answered all of the questions on the questionnaire. It exists as an SPSS data file called "hobbitdata.standard.sav." At your earliest convenience, you should download the "hobbitdata.standard.sav" file and use SPSS to examine the questions and response formats that were used in The Hobbit's Choice Restaurant survey. We will refer to some of these as we instruct you on the use of SPSS for various types of analyses described in this chapter and other chapters that follow it.

From now on, you are going to "watch over the shoulder" of the marketing researcher confronted with analyzing this data set. As you know, an SPSS data set is made up of rows and columns (in the data view window). The columns are the variables that correspond to the questions and parts of questions on the questionnaire, and the individual rows represent each respondent. Refer to Figure 15.3 to see The Hobbit's Choice Restaurant survey data in their row and column arrangement in SPSS. Of course, it is not possible to show all of the variables (columns) and respondents (rows), and Figure 15.3 shows only the first several respondents in the data set with the questions (variables) visible.

Commonly used descriptive analysis reveal central tendency (typical response) and variability (similarity of responses).

Two sets of measures are used extensively to describe the information obtained in a sample. The first set involves measures of central tendency or measures that describe the "typical" respondent or response. The second set involves measures of variability or measures that describe how similar (dissimilar) respondents or responses are to (from) "typical" respondents or responses. Other types of descriptive measures are available, but they do not enjoy the popularity of central tendency and variability. In fact, they are rarely reported to clients.

Measures of Central Tendency: Summarizing the "Typical" Respondent

The basic data summarization goal involved in all **measures of central tendency** is to report a single piece of information that describes the most typical response to a question. The term *central tendency* applies to any statistical measure used that somehow reflects a typical or frequent response.[5] Three such measures of central tendency are commonly used as data summarization devices. They are the mode, the median, and the mean. We describe each one in turn.

Three measures of central tendency are mode, median, and mean.

▶ **Mode**   The **mode** is a descriptive analysis measure defined as that value in a string of numbers that occurs most often. In other words, if you scanned a list of numbers constituting a field in a data matrix, the mode would be that number that appeared more than any other. For example, in Figure 15.3, the first variable, "eatrest," pertains to the qualifying question, "Do you eat at this type of restaurant at least once every two weeks?" Respondents who said "no" were not qualified, and they do not appear in the data set. Thus, the mode for this question is "1," the code for "yes." The mode is most appropriate for categorical data such as nominal (e.g., yes/no) or ordinal (e.g., rankings) scales.

With a string of numbers, the mode is that number appearing most often.

Let's look at a more interesting categorical question, "To which type of radio programming do you most often listen?" The response options and their codes are (1) country and western, (2) easy listening, (3) rock, (4) talk/news, and (5) no preference. A simple method is available to find the mode. First, the frequency or percentage distribution for each number in the string is tabulated, and then the researcher scans for the largest incidence, or he or she may use a bar chart or histogram as a visual aid. If you do a quick count using just the codes that can be seen for this variable in Figure 15.3, you will find that there is one 1, two 2s, two 3s, and four 4s. Since 4 is the most prevalent, then talk/news shows is the mode. (There is also a period (.) which you will learn about later in this chapter.)

You should note that the mode is a relative measure of central tendency, for it does not require that a majority of responses occurred for this value. Instead, it simply specifies the value that occurs most frequently, and there is no requirement that this occurrence is 50 percent or more. It can take on any value as long as it is the most frequently occurring number. If a tie for the mode occurs, the distribution is considered to be "bimodal." Or it might even be "trimodal" if there is a three-way tie.

▶ **Median**   An alternative measure of central tendency is the **median**, which expresses that value whose occurrence lies in the middle of an ordered set of values; that is, it is the value such that one-half of all of the other values is greater than the median and one-half of the remaining values is less than the median. Thus, the median tells us the approximate halfway point in a set or string of numbers that are arranged in ascending or descending order while taking into account the frequency of each value. With an odd number of values, the median will always fall on one of the values, but with an even number of values, the median may fall between two adjacent values.

The median expresses the value whose occurrence lies in the middle of a set of ordered values.

To determine the median, the researcher creates a frequency or percentage distribution with the numbers in the string in either ascending or descending order. In addition to the raw percentages, he or she computes cumulative percentages and, by inspecting these, finds where the 50–50 break occurs.

Let us take just the first 10 respondents that can be seen in Figure 15.3. In order to determine a median, the codes must be ordered, meaning that they cannot be categorical. We can use the likelihood of patronizing Hobbit's Choice (the variable called "likely"), which is an interval scale. There is one 2, four 3s, four 4s, and one 5. This means that the median is exactly between 4 (somewhat likely) and 3 (neither likely nor unlikely) because the 2 and 3 codes account for exactly 53 percent, and the 4 and 5 codes account for the remaining 47 percent. In our 15-respondent example, the median is 3, as it "contains" the 50 percent value.

You should notice that the median supplies more information than does the mode, for a mode may occur anywhere in the string, but the median must be at the halfway point. It should be pointed out that most frequency distributions are not symmetric, and the 50–50 point often falls on a particular value rather than between two adjacent ones.

▶ **Mean** A third measure of central tendency is the mean, sometimes referred to as the "arithmetic mean." The **mean** is the average value characterizing a set of numbers. It differs from the mode and the median in that a computation is made to determine the average. The mean is computed through the use of the following formula:

The mean is the arithmetic average of a set of numbers.

$$\text{Formula for a mean} \qquad \text{Mean } (\bar{x}) = \frac{\sum\limits_{i=1}^{n} x_i}{n}$$

where:

n = the number of cases
x_i = each individual value
Σ signifies that all the x_i values are summed

As you can see, all of the members in the set of n numbers, each designated by x_i, are summed and that total is divided by the number of members in that set. The resulting number is the mean, a measure that indicates the central tendency of those values. It approximates the typical value in the set. To compute the mean average price of a restaurant evening meal entrée, we must first sum the 15 prices visible in Figure 15.3. If you want to, you can verify that this sum is $372. Then the sum is divided by 15 respondents to yield a mean of $12.13. Because the mean is determined by taking every member of the set of numbers into account through this formula, it is more informative than the median. Means communicate a great deal of information, and they can be plotted for quick interpretations. Read Marketing Research Insight 15.1 for an illustration.

Measures of Variability: Visualizing the Diversity of Respondents

Although they are extremely useful, measures of central tendency are incomplete descriptors of the variety of values in a particular set of numbers. That is, they do not indicate the variability of responses to a particular question or, alternatively, the diversity of respondents on some characteristic measured in our survey. To gain sensitivity for the diversity or variability of values, the marketing researcher must turn to measures of variability. All **measures of variability** are concerned with depicting the "typical" difference between the values in a set of values.

Measures of variability reveal the typical difference between the values in a set of values.

It is one matter to know the mean or some other measure of central tendency, but it is quite another to be aware of how close to that mean or measure of central tendency the rest of the values fall. For example, we ascertained that the average expected cost for an entrée in an upscale restaurant such as The Hobbit's Choice is $12.13, but until we have a notion of the variability of the price estimates provided by our respondents, we are clueless about the existence of individuals who might be expecting to pay twice or three times that much. This information is vital to Jeff Dean's understanding of the price sensitivity of various market segments that might patronize The Hobbit's Choice.

GLOBAL APPLICATION

15.1 Plot Means to Illustrate Global Differences

Are U.S. teenagers different from teenagers in different countries? The answer to this question depends, of course, on the topic. Researchers who were interested in the influence of children in various purchases chose to compare the purchase influence of teenagers in Israel to that of teenagers in the U.S.[6] They selected a number of family purchase situations such as the family automobile, the family TV, and the family vacation and identified four or five subdecisions such as when to buy, where to buy, and how much to spend. They interviewed families with a 13- to 18-year-old child, and measured the child's influence on a scale in which 1 = no influence at all and 6 = complete influence. The following graph compares the average amount of influence for Israeli teenagers to that of American teenagers in the various subdecisions for a family auto purchase.

Teenagers' Influence in Family Automobile Decisions

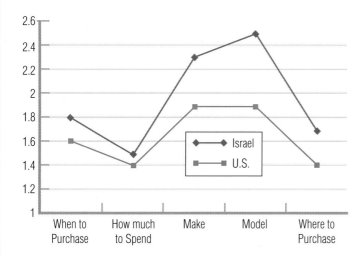

The plot line for the average influence of Israeli teens is higher than the plot line for American teens in all five subdecisions. But, is this just an isolated case? The answer is seen in the following two graphs.

Teenagers' Influence in Family TV Decisions

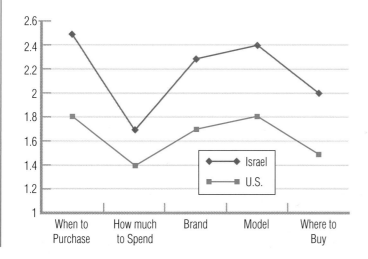

Teenagers' Influence in Family Vacation Decisions

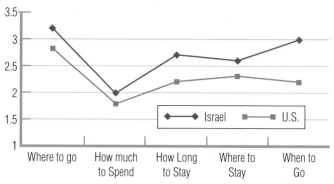

The plots of the averages show quite convincingly that teenagers in the United States have less influence than do teenagers in Israeli families in many family purchase decisions.

Thus, knowing the variability of the data could have a great impact on a marketing decision based on the data because it expresses how similar the respondents are to one another on the topic under examination. There are three measures of variability: frequency distribution, range, and standard deviation. Each measure provides its own unique version of information that helps to describe the diversity of responses.

Measures of variability include frequency distribution, range, and standard deviation.

▶ **Frequency Distribution** A **frequency distribution** is a tabulation of the number of times that each different value appears in a particular set of values. Frequencies themselves are raw counts, and normally these frequencies are converted into percentages for ease of comparison. The conversion is arrived at very simply through a quick division of the frequency for each value by the total number of observations for all of the values, resulting in a percent, called a **percentage distribution**. For instance, we stated in the example of a mode for listening to the radio that in the "lisradio" column, you will find nine 1s and one 2 (Figure 15.3). This is the frequency distribution, and to determine the percentage distribution, each frequency must be divided by the number of respondents—10 in this case. So the percentage distribution is this: yes (90%) and no (10%). Apparently, just about everyone in our 10-person example listens to the radio regularly.

A frequency (percentage) distribution reveals the number (percent) of occurrences of each number in a set of numbers.

Variability indicates how different respondents are on a common topic such as what type of fresh seafood they prefer.

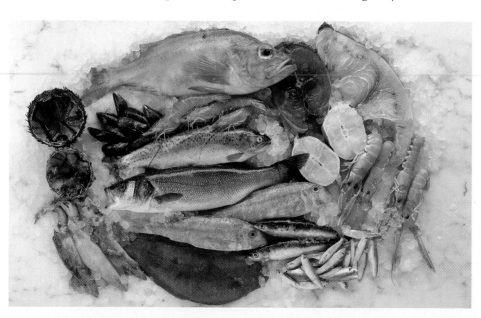

In sum, a frequency distribution affords an accounting of the responses to values in a set. It quickly communicates all of the different values in the set, and it expresses how similar the values are. The percentage distribution is often used here. Figure 13.2 on page 368 illustrates how quickly percentage distributions communicate variability when they are converted to bar charts.[7] For instance, if our percentage distribution happened to have only a few very similar values in it, it would appear as a very steep, spike-shaped histogram such as the one for our "little variability" bar graph; however, if the set of values happened to be made up of many dissimilar numbers, the histogram would be much more spread out, with small peaks and valleys. This is the case with the "much variability" bar graph. This pattern indicates a great deal of dispersion in the numbers, whereas the spiked distribution indicates little variability in the set of numbers.

▶ **Range** The **range** identifies the distance between the lowest value (minimum) and the highest value (maximum) in an ordered set of values. Stated somewhat differently, the range specifies the difference between the endpoints in a distribution of values arranged in order. The range does not provide the same amount of information supplied by a frequency distribution; however, it identifies the interval in which the distribution occurs. The range also does not tell you how often the maximum and minimum occurred, but it does provide some information on the dispersion by indicating how far apart the extremes are found. For example, if you scan the "totspent" column, representing the estimated total dollars spent in restaurants in a typical month by each of our 10 respondents in Figure 15.3, you will find the lowest number to be $110, and the highest one to be $370, so the range is 370 − 110, or $260.

The range identifies the maximum and minimum values in a set of numbers.

▶ **Standard Deviation** The **standard deviation** indicates the degree of variation or diversity in the values in such a way as to be translatable into a normal or bell-shaped curve distribution. Although marketing researchers do not always rely on the normal curve interpretation of the standard deviation, they often encounter the standard deviation on computer printouts, and they usually report it in their tables. So it is worthwhile to digress for a moment to discuss this statistical concept.

A standard deviation indicates the degree of variation in a way that can be translated into a bell-shaped curve distribution.

Table 15.3 shows the properties of a bell-shaped or normal distribution of values. As we have indicated in Chapter 13, on sample size determination, the usefulness of this model is apparent when you realize that it is a symmetric distribution: Exactly 50 percent of the distribution lies on either side of the midpoint (the apex of the curve). With

TABLE 15.3	Normal Curve Interpretation of Standard Deviation	
Number of Standard Deviations from the Mean	Percent of Area under Curve[a]	Percent of Area to Right (or Left)[b]
±1.00	68%	16.0%
±1.64	90%	5.0%
±1.96	95%	2.5%
±2.58	99%	0.5%
±3.00	99.7%	0.1%

[a]This is the area under the curve with the number of standard deviations as the lower (left-hand) and upper (right-hand) limits and the mean equidistant from the limits.
[b]This is the area left outside of the limits described by plus or minus the number of standard deviations. Because of the normal curve's symmetric properties, the area remaining below the lower limit (left-hand tail) is exactly equal to the area remaining above the upper limit (right-hand tail).

a normal curve, the midpoint is also the mean. Standard deviations are standardized units of measurement that are located on the horizontal axis. They relate directly to assumptions about the normal curve. For example, the range of one standard deviation above and one standard deviation below the midpoint includes 68 percent of the total area underneath that curve. Because the bell-shaped distribution is a theoretical or ideal concept, this property never changes. Moreover, the proportion of area under the curve and within plus or minus any number of standard deviations from the mean is perfectly known. For the purposes of this presentation, normally only two or three of these values are of interest to marketing researchers. Specifically, ± 2.58 standard deviations describes the range in which 99 percent of the area underneath the curve is found, ± 1.96 standard deviations is associated with 95 percent of the area underneath the curve, and ± 1.64 standard deviations corresponds to 90 percent of the bell-shaped curve's area. Remember, we must assume that the shape of the frequency distribution of the numbers approximates a normal curve, so keep this in mind during our following examples.

It is now time to review the calculation of the standard deviation. The equation typically used for the standard deviation is as follows:

The standard deviation embodies the properties of a bell-shaped distribution of values.

Formula for a standard deviation

$$\text{Standard deviation (s)} = \sqrt{\frac{\sum_{i-1}^{n}(x_i - \bar{x})^2}{n - 1}}$$

The squaring operation in the standard deviation formula is used to avoid the cancellation effect.

In this equation, x_i stands for each individual observation and $\bar{x}$ stands for the mean, as indicated earlier. We use the average price spent for an entrée in our 15-respondent Hobbit's Choice Restaurant survey example to illustrate the calculations for a standard deviation. We already know that the mean amount spent is $12.13. Applying the standard deviation formula, the computations are as follows:

Example of how to compute a standard deviation

$$s = \sqrt{\frac{\sum_{i-1}^{n}(x_i - \bar{x})^2}{n = 1}}$$

$$= \sqrt{\frac{(20 - 12.13)^2 + (11 - 12.13)^2 + \cdots + (11 - 12.13)^2}{10 - 1}}$$

$$= \$9.96$$

It may seem strange to square differences, add them up, divide them by $(n - 1)$, and then take the square root. If we did not square the differences, we would have positive and negative values; and if we summed them, there would be a cancellation effect; that is, large negative differences would cancel out large positive differences, and the numerator would end up being close to zero. But this result is contrary to what we know is the case with large differences: There is variation, which is expressed by the standard deviation. The formula remedies this problem by squaring the subtracted differences before they are summed. Squaring converts all negative numbers to positives and, of course, leaves the positives positive. Next, all of the squared differences are summed and divided by 1 less than the number of total observations in the string of values; 1 is subtracted from the number of observations to achieve what is typically called an "unbiased" estimate of the standard deviation. But we now have an inflation factor to worry about because every comparison has been squared. To adjust for this, the equation specifies that the square root be taken after all other operations are performed. This final step adjusts the value back down to the original measure (e.g., dollars rather than squared dollars). By the way, if you did not take the square root at the end, the value would be referred to as the **variance**. In other words, the variance is the standard deviation squared.

Now, whenever a standard deviation is reported along with a mean, a specific picture should appear in your mind. Assuming that the distribution is bell shaped, the size of the standard deviation number helps you envision how similar or dissimilar the typical responses are to the mean. If the standard deviation is small, the distribution is greatly compressed. On the other hand, with a large standard deviation value, the distribution is consequently stretched out at both ends. With our 15-respondent Hobbit's Choice sample the standard deviation was found to be $9.96. Assuming that the responses approximate a bell-shaped distribution, the range for 95 percent of the responses would be calculated to be 12.13 ± (1.96 × 9.96), which turns out to be 12.13 ± 19.52, or $0 to $31.65. That is, 95 percent of the respondents spend between $0 and $31.65.

We have prepared Marketing Research Insight 15.2 as a means of helping you remember the various descriptive statistics concepts that are commonly used by marketing researchers.

> With a bell-shaped distribution, 95 percent of the values lie within ±1.96 times the standard deviation away from the mean.

MARKETING RESEARCH INSIGHT

PRACTICAL INSIGHTS

15.2 Descriptive Statistics: What They Mean and How to Compute Them

Invariably, a researcher has to make "sense" out of a set of numbers that represents the ways respondents answered the questions in the survey. The answers are normally coded; that is, they are converted to numbers such as 1 for "yes," 2 for "no," and 3 for "maybe." Sometimes the numbers correspond to responses on a scale, such as when a respondent indicates that his or her wireless phone company rates a "4" on a 5-point scale where 1 means "poor," 2 means "fair," 3 means "good," 4 means "very good," and 5 means "excellent" service. We are using the responses to this scale in our example here.

Descriptive statistics are basic to marketing research and essential to the researcher's understanding of how the

respondents answered each question. Here is a data set comprising the answers 10 different respondents gave when asked to rate the quality of their PCS wireless phone service.

RESPONDENT	RATING	RESPONDENT	RATING
1	4	6	4
2	5	7	3
3	4	8	4
4	2	9	5
5	3	10	4

To illustrate the nine descriptive statistics concepts, the ratings of our 10 respondents are analyzed in the following table. For each finding, the poor–excellent scale is used to aid in the interpretation.

STATISTICAL CONCEPT	WHAT IS IT?	HOW DO YOU COMPUTE IT?	USING THE RATINGS EXAMPLE AND INTERPRETATION	
Frequency	The number of times a number appears in the data set	Count the number of times the number appears in the set of numbers.	As an example, the number 4's frequency is 5, so 5 respondents gave a "very good" rating.	
Frequency distribution	The number of times each different number in the set appears	Count the number of times each different number appears in the set, and make a table that shows each number, its count, and the total count (all counts totaled).	RATING 2/fair 3/good 4/very good 5/excellent Total	COUNT 1 2 5 2 10

STATISTICAL CONCEPT	WHAT IS IT?	HOW DO YOU COMPUTE IT?	USING THE RATINGS EXAMPLE AND INTERPRETATION		
Percentage distribution	The presence of each different number expressed as a percent	Divide each frequency count for each rating number by the total count, and report the result as a percent.	**RATING** 2/fair 3/good 4/very good 5/excellent Total	**PERCENT** 10% 20% 50% 20% 100%	
Cumulative distribution (frequency or percentage)	A running total of the counts or percentages	Arrange all the different numbers in descending order and indicate the sum of the counts (percentages) of all preceding numbers plus the present one.	**RATING** 2/fair 3/good 4/very good 5/excellent Total	**PERCENT** 10% 20% 50% 20% 100%	**CUM. PERCENT** 10% 30% 80% 100%
Median	The number in the set of numbers such that 50% of the other numbers are larger, and 50% of the other numbers are smaller	Use the cumulative percentage distribution to locate where the cumulative percent equals 50% or where it includes 50%.	**RATING** 2/fair 3/good 4/very good 5/excellent	**CUM. PERCENT** 10% 30% 80% ← Median 100%	
Mode	In a frequency or a percentage distribution, the number that has the largest count or percentage (ties are acceptable)	By inspection, determine which number has the largest frequency or percentage in the distribution.	The number 4 (very good) accounts for 50%, the largest of any other rating		
Mean	The arithmetic average of the set of numbers	Add up all the numbers and divide this sum by the total number of numbers in the set.	$(4 + 5 + 4 + 2 + 3 + 4 + 3 + 4 + 5 + 4)/10 = 3.8$, so the mean is just a bit below "very good"		
Range	An indication of the "spread" or span covered by the numbers	Find the lowest and highest numbers in the set and identify them as the minimum and maximum, respectively.	The minimum is 2, and the maximum is 5; so the range is 5 − 2, or 3. Respondents rate it from "fair" to "excellent."		
Standard deviation	An indication of how similar or dissimilar the numbers are in the set, interpretable under the assumptions of a normal curve of that result	Sum the square of each number subtracted from the mean, divide that sum by the total number of numbers less one, and then take the square root.	$\{((4 − 3.8)^2 (5 − 3.8)^2 ... (4 − 3.8)^2)/10 − 1\}^{1/2} = .92$ 95% of the respondents are within ± 1.6 (1.96 times .84) ratings away from average of 3.8 or between "fair" and "excellent."		

WHEN TO USE A PARTICULAR DESCRIPTIVE MEASURE

The scaling assumptions underlying a question determine which statistic is appropriate.

In Chapter 10, you learned that the level of measurement for a scale affects how it may be analyzed statistically. Remember, for instance, that nominal question forms contain much less information than do questions with interval scaling assumptions. Similarly, the amount of information provided by each of the various measures of central tendency and dispersion differs. As a general rule, statistical measures that communicate the most information should be used with scales that contain the most amount of information, and measures that communicate the least information should be used with scales that contain the least information. The level of measurement determines the appropriate measure; otherwise, the measure will be uninterpretable.

At first reading, this rule may seem confusing, but on reflection it should become clear that the level of measurement of each question dictates the measure that should be used. It is precisely at this point that you must remember the arbitrary nature of coding schemes. For instance, if on a demographic question concerning religious preference, "Catholic" is assigned a "1," "Protestant" is assigned a "2," "Jewish" is assigned a "3," and so forth, a mean could be computed. But what would be the interpretation of an average religion of 2.36? It would have no practical interpretation because the mean assumes interval or ratio scaling, whereas the religion categories are nominal. The mode would be the appropriate central tendency measure for these responses.

Table 15.4 indicates how the level of measurement relates to each of the three measures of central tendency and measures of variation. The table should remind you that a clear understanding of the level of measurement for each question on the questionnaire is essential because the researcher must select the statistical procedure and direct the computer to perform the procedure. The computer cannot distinguish level of measurement because we typically convert all of our data to numbers for ease of entry.

As you might suspect, there is much potential for misunderstanding when a researcher communicates the results of his or her descriptive analyses to the marketing manager. We have noted some of the common misconceptions held by managers in Marketing Research Insight 15.3. If a researcher knowingly allows these misunderstandings, he or she is acting unethically.

TABLE 15.4	What Descriptive Statistic to Use When		
Example Question	Measurement Level	Central Tendency (the most typical response)	Variability (how similar the responses are)
What is your gender?	Nominal scale	Mode	Frequency and/or percentage distribution
Rank these 5 brands from your 1st choice to your 5th choice	Ordinal scale	Median	Cumulative percentage distribution
On a scale of 1 to 5, how does "Starbucks" rate on variety of its coffee drinks?	Interval scale	Mean	Standard deviation and/or range
About how many times did you charge your cell phone last week?	Ratio scale	Mean	Standard deviation and/or range

15.3 Ethical Issues in Descriptive Data Analysis

The adage that "perception is reality" raises some ethical issues when marketing researchers use the terminology of descriptive statistics to communicate their findings to marketing managers. Actually, in this case we should change the adage to "misperception is reality," for the typical marketing manager, who is largely familiar with the precise meanings of statistical concepts, may well have misperceptions about them that can greatly distort how the marketing manager understands what the marketing researcher is reporting. Here are some statements that might be made by a researcher, what each statement means in terms of descriptive analysis, and possible misperceptions that might occur in a manager who is not accustomed to working with statistical terminology.

WHAT THE MARKETING RESEARCHER SAYS	WHAT THE MARKETING RESEARCHER MEANS	LIKELY MISPERCEPTION BY THE MARKETING MANAGER
"The modal answer was . . . "	The answer given by more respondents than any other answer.	Most or all of the respondents gave this answer.
"A majority responded . . . "	Over 50% of the respondents answered this way.	Most or all of the respondents gave the answer.
"A plurality responded . . . "	The answer was given by more respondents than any other answer, but less than 50% gave that answer.	A majority of respondents gave the answer.
"The median response was . . . "	The answer such that 50% answered above it and 50% answered below it.	Most respondents gave this answer or responded very close to this answer.
"The mean response was . . . "	The arithmetic average of all respondents' answers.	Most respondents gave this answer.
"There was some variability responses . . . "	Respondents gave a variety of responses with some agreement.	There was no agreement among the in the respondents.
"The standard deviation was . . . "	The value was computed by applying the standard deviation formula.	No comprehension

Remember, these are basic statistical concepts, and there are a great many more sophisticated statistics that a researcher may use to completely analyze a data set. So, there is ample opportunity for a marketing manager to miscomprehend what a marketing researcher is communicating about the statistical findings. Here are some approaches that can be used to make certain that the audience will not misunderstand the researcher's words.

1 Some companies have prepared handbooks or glossaries that define marketing research terms, including statistical concepts. They are given to clients at the onset of work.

2 Some researchers include an appendix in the final report that defines and illustrates the statistical concepts mentioned in the report.

3 Definitions of statistical concepts are included in the text of the final report where the concept is first mentioned.

4 Footnotes and annotations are included in the tables and figures that explain the statistical concepts used.

No ethical researcher would intentionally mislead a client in reporting findings, and because statistical concepts have high potential for misperceptions such as those illustrated here, ethical researchers go to considerable lengths to prevent such misunderstandings.

COMPUTE MEASURES OF CENTRAL TENDENCY AND VARIABILITY

Active Learning

This chapter has described measures of central tendency: mean, median, mode, as well as measures of variability: percentage distribution, range, and standard deviation. At the same time, you should realize that certain measures are appropriate for some scales, but inappropriate for others. Below is a data set of respondents who answered questions on a survey of portable hard drive ownership and usage. For this survey, only owners of portable hard drives were interviewed.

Respondent	For How Many Months Have You Owned Your Portable Hard Drive?	Where Did You Purchase Your Portable Hard Drive?	What Capacity is Your Portable Hard Drive (in Gigabytes)?
1	5	Internet	20
2	11	Office supply store	100
3	19	Internet	100
4	14	Computer store	40
5	5	Computer store	60
6	13	Internet	80
7	6	Internet	100
8	24	Internet	100
9	23	Computer store	20
10	5	Internet	40
11	15	Internet	60
12	24	Internet	80
13	5	Office supply store	80
14	10	Computer store	80
15	13	Internet	20
16	8	Office supply store	100
17	5	Computer store	100
18	10	Computer store	20
19	19	Office supply store	80
20	6	Computer store	20
Mean	_____	_____	_____
Standard Deviation	_____	_____	_____
Range: Maximum & Minimum	_____	_____	_____
Median	_____	_____	_____
Mode	_____	_____	_____

For your Active Learning exercise here, you must determine what measure(s) of central tendency and what measures of variability are appropriate and compute them. We have identified the relevant measures under the "Respondent" column of the data set, and your task is to write in the proper answer under each of the three questions in the survey.

RETURN TO YOUR INTEGRATED

Descriptive statistics are needed to see The Hobbit's Choice survey's basic findings.

A frequency distribution and mode are appropriate for nominal scales.

Use the Analyze—Descriptive Statistics—Frequencies procedure to produce descriptive statistics for variables with nominal or ordinal scaling.

The Hobbit's Choice Survey: Obtaining Descriptive Statistics with SPSS

Beginning with this chapter and all subsequent chapters dealing with statistical analyses, we provide illustrations with the use of SPSS in two ways. First, in your textbook descriptions, we indicate step-by-step the procedures used with SPSS to obtain the statistical analyses being described. Plus, we have included examples of SPSS output in these sections. The second way is with the use of your SPSS Student Assistant. By now, you are well acquainted with the Student Assistant. We prompt you to look at these statistical analysis sections that illustrate how to operate SPSS, as well as how to find specific statistical results in SPSS output.

Obtaining a Frequency Distribution and the Mode with SPSS

There were many questions on The Hobbit's Choice survey that had categorical response options and, thus, embodied nominal scaling assumptions. With a nominal scale, the mode is the appropriate measure of central tendency, and variation must be assessed by looking at the distribution of responses across the various response categories.

Earlier, to illustrate how to determine the mode of our 15-person Hobbit's Choice data set, we used the radio programming listening preferences variable as it is a nominal scale. We will now use this variable with the entire 400-completions data set to illustrate how to instruct SPSS to create a frequency distribution and find the mode.

Figure 15.4 shows the clickstream sequence to find a mode for the radio station listening preferences using the entire Hobbit's Choice survey data set. As you can see, the primary menu sequence is Analyze—Descriptive Statistics—Frequencies. This sequence opens up the variable selection window where you specify the variable(s) to be analyzed, and the Statistics . . . button opens up the Statistics window, which has several statistical concepts as options. Since we are working only with the mode, you would click in the check box beside the Mode. Continue will

FIGURE 15.4
The SPSS Clickstream to Obtain a Frequency Distribution and the Mode

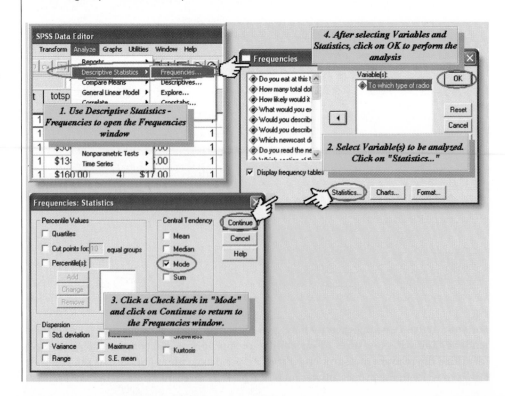

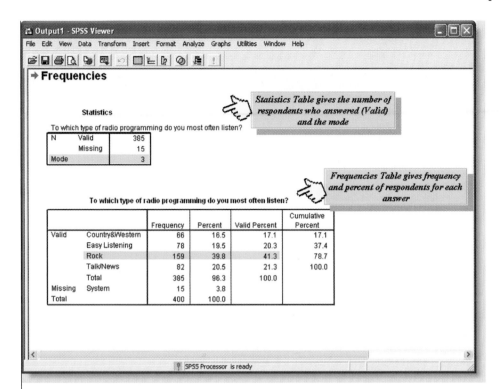

FIGURE 15.5
The SPSS Output for a
Frequency Distribution
and the Mode

close this window, and OK will close the variable selection and cause SPSS to create a frequency distribution and to identify the mode. You can see this output in Figure 15.5, where the code number of "3" is specified as the mode response, and the frequency distribution shows that rock is the most popular station format, with 159 respondents selecting it, or 39.8 percent of the total 100 percent.

As you look at the output, you should notice that the variable labels and value labels were defined, and they appear on the output. The Descriptive Statistics—Frequencies procedure creates a frequency distribution and associated percentage distribution of the responses for each question. Its output includes a statistics table and a table for each variable that includes the variable label, value labels, frequencies, percent, valid percent, and cumulative percent.

Our Hobbit's Choice Restaurant survey data set is typical because there are missing answers. As you learned in Chapter 14, it is not uncommon for respondents to refuse to answer a question in a survey or for them to be unable to answer a question. Alternatively, a respondent may be directed to skip a question if his or her previous answer does not qualify him or her for the subsequent question. If any of these occurs, and the respondent is still included in the data set, we have an instance of "missing data." This is absolutely no problem for SPSS and most other data analysis programs, but the output will be adjusted to compensate for the missing data. Read Marketing Research Insight 15.4 to learn about what SPSS specifies as "valid percent."

SPSS Student Assistant:
Descriptive Statistics for
Nominal Data: Frequencies,
Percents, Mode

Active

Use your SPSS Hobbit's Choice data set to compute the frequency distribution and percentage distribution and to identify the mode as we have just described. Use Figure 15.6 to direct your mouse clicks and selections using the radio programming listening preferences variable in the data set. Compare the SPSS output that you obtain with Figure 15.7 and make sure that you can identify the mode of 3 (Rock Music). Also, to ensure that you understand the "valid percent" output provided by SPSS for its Frequencies analysis, calculate one of the valid percents (such as for Country & Western music) and compare your result to the SPSS output valid percent (17.1% in this case). If your calculation of the valid percent does not agree with the SPSS output, reread Marketing Research Insight 15.4 to gain the proper understanding of valid percents.

FIGURE 15.6
The SPSS Clickstream to Obtain a Mean, Standard Deviation, and the Range

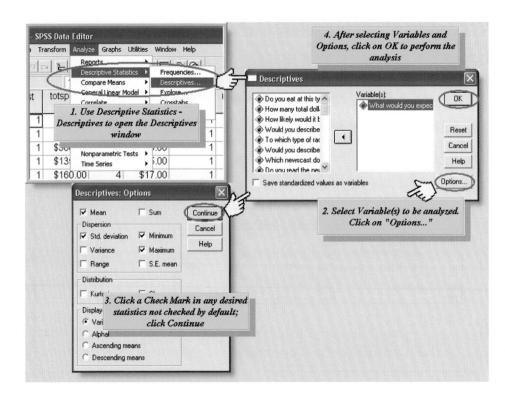

FIGURE 15.7
SPSS Output for a Mean, Standard Deviation, and the Range

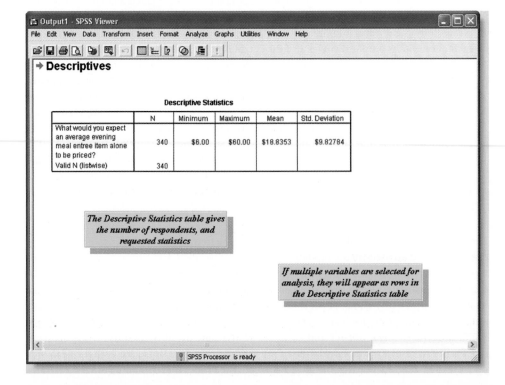

PRACTICAL APPLICATION

15.4 How SPSS Handles Missing Data

When a researcher conducts a survey, and the data set is inspected, it is not uncommon to discover some questions that respondents have failed to answer. The reasons for these omissions are varied. The respondent may have refused to answer the question, perhaps the respondent was interrupted and did not return to the last question he or she answered, or there might even have been a data entry error of some sort. Regardless of the reason, the researcher is now confronted with the problem of "missing data," or cases in which fewer respondents than the entire sample answered a question.

SPSS has a built-in procedure for missing data. First, by its convention, SPSS will denote any missing data cell in its data matrix with a "." In other words, a researcher can locate any missing data in the Data Editor by looking for period or dots in the place of numbers. Second, SPSS is programmed to omit any missing data from its analysis.

The SPSS output in Figure 15.5 first reports in its Statistics table the "N," and it can be seen in Figure 15.5 that there are 385 Valid responses and 15 Missing responses. In the frequencies table that follows, SPSS reports the Frequency counts and Percent values, and in both columns, the Missing System or Missing values are counted. (Notice that these are 15 and 3.8%, respectively.)

Then SPSS reports a "Valid Percent" column that does not include the missing values. In other words, in Figure 15.5 the valid percents are based on a total of 385 respondents who did answer the question, and the 15 who did not answer it are disregarded.

Should you use the "Percent" or the "Valid Percent?" It is up to the researcher; however, the vast majority of researchers chose to report the Valid Percent numbers in their reports. When they choose this option, they are explicitly assuming that if the missing data respondents had responded to the question, their answers would be distributed exactly as they are distributed among those respondents who did answer the question.

Finding the Median with SPSS

It is also a simple matter to determine the median using the Analyze—Descriptive Statistics—Frequencies menu sequence. As we indicated, in order for the median to be a sensible measure of central tendency, the values must have some logical order to them. In our 10-respondent example, we used the likelihood of patronizing Hobbit's Choice Restaurant to obtain the median from the full data set. The procedure is very similar to the mode procedure. There are two differences. First, the "likely" variable is selected in the variable selection window; and, second, the median is checked in the statistics window. Refer to Figure 15.4, and just imagine that the likelihood of patronizing is the chosen variable, and that the median is checked instead of the mode.

The resulting SPSS output will have the frequency distribution of our likelihood variable, and it will show that code number 3, pertaining to "neither likely nor unlikely" is the 50/50 location in the scale, or the median.

FIND A MEDIAN WITH SPSS

Active Learning

Use your SPSS Hobbit's Choice data set to find the median likelihood to patronize the upscale restaurant described in the Hobbit's Choice survey questionnaire. Again, use Figure 15.5 as your clickstream guide, but select the likelihood variable for the analysis and place a check mark in the median checkbox. If you do not find that the code number 3, pertaining to "neither likely nor unlikely" is the 50/50 location in the scale, or the median, redo your work carefully to correct any errors you may have made.

Finding the Mean, Range, and Standard Deviation with SPSS

As we have mentioned, computer statistical programs cannot distinguish the level of measurement of various questions. Consequently, it is necessary for the analyst to discern the level of measurement and to select the correct procedure(s). One question in the survey asked, ". . . what would you expect an average evening meal entrée item alone to be priced?" Respondents answered with a specific dollar amount, so we have a ratio scale.

When using SPSS Descriptives, always bear in mind the variables being analyzed should be interval or ratio scaled.

Here we do not want a frequency table for two reasons. First, the average price variable is ratio scaled; and, second, a frequency table will have to be quite large to accommodate all of the different monthly fees. So we will use the Analyze—Descriptive Statistics—Descriptives commands, and click on the Options button after we have selected average price as the variable for analysis. In the Options panel, you can select the mean, standard deviation, range, and so forth. Refer to Figure 15.6 for the SPSS click-stream sequence.

SPSS Student Assistant Element Descriptive Statistics for Scaled Data: Mean, Standard Deviation, Median, Range

Figure 15.7 presents the output generated from this option. In our Hobbit's Choice survey, the output reveals that the average expected entrée price estimate was $18.84, and the standard deviation was $9.83 (both rounded up). You can also see that the lowest estimate (minimum) was $6, and the highest (maximum) was $60, making the range equal to $54.

USING SPSS FOR A MEAN AND RELATED DESCRIPTIVE STATISTICS

In this active learning exercise, you are being asked to stretch your learning a bit, for instead of simply repeating what has just been described for how to obtain the mean, range, and standard deviation with SPSS and comparing it to the SPSS output in this chapter, we want you to find the mean, range, and standard deviation for a different variable. Specifically, use the clickstream shown in Figure 15.6, but select the question that pertains to "How many total dollars do you spend per month in restaurants (for your meals only)?" and direct SPSS to compute these

With SPSS Descriptives, it was found that respondents spend a little less than $19 for an evening dinner.

descriptive statistics. You should find that the mean is $150.02, a standard deviation of $92.71 (rounded), and a range that has a minimum of $5.00 and a maximum of $450.00.

REPORTING DESCRIPTIVE STATISTICS TO CLIENTS

How does a marketing researcher report the findings of the various descriptive statistics used to summarize the findings of a survey? There are at least three possible ways. First, the researcher can build tables that summarize the appropriate statistics. For instance, the researcher may use a table format to show the means, standard deviations, and perhaps the ranges that have been found for a variable or a group of related variables. If percentages are computed, the researcher can develop a percentages table that adds up to 100%, or if an "all that apply" question is involved, the percents of the "yes" answers can be arranged in descending order in a table. Finally, the researcher may opt to construct a format that shows the interpretations of the findings. We have prepared Marketing Research Insight 15.5 that illustrates one such interpretation format. When you read it, you will see that the researchers have opted to use words instead of numbers to summarize the findings of their Internet shopping market segments study.

MARKETING RESEARCH INSIGHT

ONLINE APPLICATION

15.5

Measures of central tendency are extremely useful vehicles for providing a snapshot or quick summary of a survey's findings. Take for example, an online survey recently conducted by researchers[8] interested in looking at various Internet shopper market segments. They sent out e-mail invitations to take part in the online survey to over 20,000 Internet users in the United States. They found four different Internet shopper market segments: Tentative Shoppers who, even though they use the Internet for shopping, do not enjoy the experience, Suspicious Learners who are just learning how to use the Internet for shopping, Shopping Lovers who greatly enjoy Internet shopping in all of its aspects, and Business Users who shop the Internet primarily for business reasons. By comparing means on a scale and using simple interpretations, the researchers found the following profiles for these four Internet shopping segments.

	INTERNET SHOPPING MARKET SEGMENT			
COMPARISON FACTOR	TENTATIVE SHOPPERS	SUSPICIOUS LEARNERS	SHOPPING LOVERS	BUSINESS USERS
Uses the Internet for convenience	Low	Very low	Very high	High
Uses the Internet to - window shop	Low	Very low	Very high	High
Uses the Internet for entertainment	Moderate	Very low	High	High
Believes Internet contributes to his/her life	Low	Low	Very high	High
Amount of Internet literacy	High	Low	Very high	High
Personal income level	High	Low	High	Low

By glancing at the column for any one of the four Internet shopping segments, a reader can quickly gain a mental picture of how the typical user goes about using the Internet, how he/she feels about the Internet, and his/her relative income level. Also, by comparing any two summarization columns, the reader can quickly see the major differences between the two segments involved.

SPSS Student Assistant:
Working with SPSS Output,
Including "What's This?"

SUMMARY

This chapter introduced you to the descriptive statistics researchers use to inspect basic patterns in data sets. These measures help researchers summarize, conceptualize, and generalize their findings. We also previewed the five types of statistical analysis: descriptive, inferential, differences, associative, and predictive. Descriptive analysis is performed with measures of central tendency such as the mean, mode, or median, each of which portrays the typical respondent or the typical answer to the question being analyzed. The chapter contained formulas and examples of how to determine these central tendency measures. Measures of variability, including the frequency distribution, range, and standard deviation, provide bases for envisioning the degree of similarity of all respondents to the typical respondent. The chapter also contained instructions and formulas of key variability measures. Basically, descriptive analysis yields a profile of how respondents in the sample answered the various questions in the survey. The chapter also provides information on how to instruct SPSS to compute descriptive analyses with SPSS using The Hobbit's Choice Restaurant survey data set. Both clickstream sequences for setting up the analyses and the resulting output are shown.

KEY TERMS

Data entry (p. 422)
Data coding (p. 423)
Data code book (p. 423)
Data matrix (p. 424)
Data summarization (p. 424)
Descriptive analysis (p. 424)
Inferential analysis (p. 426)
Differences analysis (p. 426)
Associative analysis (p. 427)
Predictive analysis (p. 427)

Measures of central tendency (p. 429)
Mode (p. 429)
Median (p. 429)
Mean (p. 430)
Measures of variability (p. 430)
Frequency distribution (p. 432)
Percentage distribution (p. 432)
Range (p. 433)
Standard deviation (p. 433)
Variance (p. 434)

REVIEW QUESTIONS/APPLICATIONS

1. Indicate what data summarization is and why it is useful.
2. Define and differentiate each of the following: (a) descriptive analysis, (b) inferential analysis, (c) associative analysis, (d) predictive analysis, and (e) differences analysis.

3. Indicate why a researcher might refrain from reporting the use of highly sophisticated statistical analyses and opt for simpler forms of analysis.

4. What is a data matrix, and how does it appear?

5. What is a measure of central tendency, and what does it describe?

6. Indicate the concept of variability, and relate how it helps in the description of responses to a particular question on a questionnaire.

7. Using examples, illustrate how a frequency distribution (or a percentage distribution) reveals the variability in responses to a Likert-type question in a lifestyle study. Use two extreme examples of much variability and little variability.

8. Indicate what a range is and where it should be used as an indicator of the amount of dispersion in a sample.

9. With explicit reference to the formula for a standard deviation, show how it measures how different respondents are from one another.

10. Why is the mean an inappropriate measure of central tendency in each of the following cases: (a) gender of respondent (male or female); (b) marital status (single, married, divorced, separated, widowed, other); (c) a taste test in which subjects indicate their first, second, and third choices of Miller Lite, Bud Light, and Coors Silver Bullet?

11. For each of the cases in question 10, what is the appropriate central tendency measure?

12. In a survey on magazine subscriptions, respondents write in the number of magazines they subscribe to regularly. What measures of central tendency can be used? Which is the most appropriate and why?

13. If you use the standard deviation as a measure of the variability in a sample, what statistical assumptions have you implicitly adopted?

14. A manager has commissioned research on a special marketing problem. He is scheduled to brief the board of directors on the problem's resolution in a meeting in New York tomorrow morning. Unfortunately, the research has fallen behind schedule, but the research director works late that night in the downtown San Francisco headquarters and completes the basic data analysis, which will be sufficient for the presentation. However, he now has stacks of computer output and less than an hour before the manager calls him for an early-morning briefing on the survey's basic findings. The researcher looks around at the equipment in his office and an idea flashes in his head. He immediately grabs a blank questionnaire. What is he about to do to facilitate the quick communication of the study's basic findings to the manager?

CASE 15.1

THE UPS STORE IMPROVEMENT SURVEY

Mary Smith graduated from college in June 2005. On graduation, she took a job as a marketing research assistant with United Parcel Service, and she was assigned to work in the UPS Stores division. This division conducts the administration of about 3300 UPS Stores that are owned and operated by franchisers, and it is the world's largest franchisor of retail shipping, postal, and business supplies.

When Mary began working, the marketing research department was in the middle of a huge telephone survey of UPS Store customers across the entire United States market area. The objectives of the survey included (1) to determine why people selected the UPS Store, (2) to identify how many and why people use other shipping stores as well as a UPS Store, (3) to investigate satisfaction or dissatisfaction with UPS Stores, (4) to generate suggestions for improved UPS Stores services, and (5) to compare profiles of UPS Stores' "regular" customers with the profiles of customers who are "regulars" at competing shipping stores.

Mary was assigned the responsibility of data analysis because she was fresh out of college. She was informed that UPS Stores headquarters uses a statistical analysis program called "EasyStats" for its data analysis. All of the 5000 respondents' answers have been put into the computer, and all that is left is for someone to use EasyStats to perform the necessary analyses. Of course, someone has to interpret the results, too. It is Mary's responsibility to do the analysis and to interpret it.

The questionnaire designers created a code sheet of the scales used in the survey. This code book is duplicated in the following table:

Variable	Response Scale Used
Age	Actual age in years
Income	Ranges in $10,000 increments
Gender	Male, female
Marital status	Single, married, other
Overall satisfaction with UPS	10-point scale from "poor" to "excellent"
Store service: 10 possible improvements in service	A 5-point, disagree–agree scale for each possible improvement
Preferred shipping store	UPS Store or "some other shipping store"
Usage of various shipping store services	Yes or no for each of 15 different services, such as overnight mail, rental of mail box, company or business account, purchase of shipping box(es), having the shipping store do the packing, etc.
Shipping store loyalty	Total number of different services used at the preferred shipping store (0 to 15)
Exposure to mail advertising	Yes or no to recalling having received mail advertising last month from preferred shipping store

1. What type of descriptive data analysis should Mary instruct EasyStats to perform to determine basic patterns in the factors listed on the code sheet? For each variable, identify the type of descriptive analysis, describe its aspects, and indicate why it is appropriate.

2. Give an example of what each result might "look like" and how it should be interpreted.

AUTO ONLINE WEB SITE USAGE SURVEY (PART I)

Auto Online is a Web site at which prospective automobile buyers can find information about the various makes and models. Individuals can actually purchase a make and model with specific options and features online. Recently, Auto Online posted an online questionnaire on the Internet, and it mailed invitations to the last 5000 automobile buyers who visited Auto Online. Some of these buyers bought their car from Auto Online, whereas the remaining individuals bought their autos from a dealership. However, they did visit Auto Online at least one time prior to that purchase.

The questionniare that was posted online is produced here, and its code numbers are included for your information.

Auto Online Online Survey Questionnaire

Please answer the following questions to the best of your ability. When you have answered all questions, click on the "Submit" button at the end. Please do not respond to this questionnaire more than one time.

1. Have you visited the Auto Online Web site in the past 3 months?
   ___ Yes (1)   ___ No (2)

2. How often do you make purchases through the Internet?

Very Often	Often	Occasionally	Almost Never	Never
5	4	3	2	1

3. Indicate your opinion on each of the following statements. For each one, please indicate if you strongly disagree, somewhat disagree, are neutral, somewhat agree, or strongly agree.

	Strongly Disagree	Neutral			Strongly Agree
I like using the Internet.	1	2	3	4	5
I use the Internet to research purchases I make.	1	2	3	4	5
I think purchasing items from the Internet is safe.	1	2	3	4	5
The Internet is a good tool to use when researching an automobile purchase.	1	2	3	4	5
The Internet should not be used to purchase vehicles.	1	2	3	4	5
Online dealerships are just another way of getting you into the traditional dealership.	1	2	3	4	5
I like the process of buying a new vehicle.	1	2	3	4	5
I don't like to hassle with car salespeople.	1	2	3	4	5

4. About how many times before you bought your automobile did you visit the Auto Online Web site?
   ___ times

5. How did you find out about Auto Online? Indicate all of the ways that you can recall.
   ___ From a friend (0,1)   ___ Web surfing (0,1)   ___ Theater (0,1)
   ___ Billboard (0,1)   ___ Search engine (0,1)   ___ Newspaper (0,1)
   ___ Internet banner ad (0,1)   ___ Television (0,1)   ___ Other (0,1)

6. What is your reaction to the following statements about the Auto Online Web site?

	Strongly Disagree	Strongly Neutral			Agree
The Web site was easy to use.	1	2	3	4	5
I found the Web site was very helpful in my purchase.	1	2	3	4	5
I had a positive experience using the Web site.	1	2	3	4	5
I would use this Web site only for research.	1	2	3	4	5
The Web site influenced me to buy my vehicle.	1	2	3	4	5
I would feel secure in buying from this Web site.	1	2	3	4	5

7. Did you buy your new vehicle on the Auto Online Web site?
___Yes (1)   ___ No (2)
   a. If yes, was it a better experience than buying at a traditional dealership?
     ___Yes (1)   ___ No (2)
   b. If yes, indicate how much better.
     ___ A great deal better (1)   ___ Somewhat better (3)
     ___ Much better (2)   ___ Just a bit better   (4)

8. The next six statements are possible reasons why people may not buy a car from start to finish off the Internet. Please indicate the degree to which you agree or disagree with each statement.

	Strongly Disagree	Strongly Neutral			Agree
People feel that the Internet is not a safe place for personal information.	1	2	3	4	5
People want to test the performance of the vehicle before buying it.	1	2	3	4	5
People feel they can negotiate a better price by talking with a sales representative in person.	1	2	3	4	5
People usually have trade-ins that are too complicated to deal with online.	1	2	3	4	5
People like to have a "hands-on" situation when buying different options for their vehicles.	1	2	3	4	5
People want to see the vehicles before they buy it, to check for imperfections.	1	2	3	4	5

The next few questions pertain to the vehicle you just purchased.

9. For how many weeks were you actively searching for your vehicle? ___ weeks

10. If you traded in a vehicle, approximately how much was it worth? $___

11. What was the approximate sticker price of your new vehicle? $___

12. What was the approximate actual price you paid for it? $___

There are only a few more questions for clarification purposes.

13. What is your age? ___ years

14. What is your marital status?
__ Single (1) __ Married (2) __ Widowed (3) __ Divorced (4) __ Separated (5)

15. How many children under the age of 18 are living with you? _____

16. What is the highest level of education you have completed?
___ Less than high school (1) ___ High school (2) ___ Some college (3)
___ Undergraduate degree (4) ___ Graduate degree (5) ___ Other (Specify:) (6)

17. What is your race?
___ Caucasian (1) ___ Black (2) ___ Asian (3) ___ American Indian (4)
___ Hispanic (5)   ___ Other (6)

18. What range includes your total household income before taxes for last year?
___ Under $35,000 (1) ___ $35,000–$50,000 (2) ___ $50,001–$65,000 (3)
___ $65,001–$80,000 (4) ___ $80,001–95,000 (5) ___ $95,001–$110,000 (6)
___ Over $110,000 (7)

19. Your gender is . . .

___ Male (1) ___ Female (2)

A total of 1400 respondents answered the Auto Online survey, and the SPSS data set is named AutoOnline.sav. To download this data set, find the dataset download area at www.prenhall.com/burnsbush.

Perform the proper descriptive analysis with SPSS Student Version on all of the questions on the questionnaire.

 This is your integrated case, described on pages 38–39. The Hobbit's Choice Restaurant Survey SPSS data set can be downloaded from the text Web site **www.prenhall.com/burnsbush**.

THE HOBBIT'S CHOICE RESTAURANT SURVEY DESCRIPTIVE ANALYSIS

Cory Rogers was happy to call Jeff Dean to inform him that The Hobbit's Choice Restaurant survey data were collected and ready for analysis. Of course, Cory had other marketing research projects and meetings scheduled with present and prospective clients, so he called in his marketing intern, Celeste Brown. Celeste was a senior marketing major at Able State University, and she had taken marketing research in the previous semester. Celeste had "aced" this class, which she enjoyed a great deal. Her professor had invited Cory Rogers to give a talk on "a typical day in the life of a market researcher," and Celeste had approached Cory the next day about a marketing research internship. Like every dedicated marketing major, Celeste had kept her Burns and Bush marketing research textbook for future reference.

Cory called Celeste into his office, and said, "Celeste, it is time to do some analysis on the survey we did for Jeff Dean. For now, let's just get a feel for what the data look like. I'll leave it up to your judgment as to what basic analysis to run. Let's meet tomorrow at 2:30 P.M. and see what you have found."

Your task in Case 15.3 is to take the role of Celeste Brown, marketing intern. As we indicated in this chapter, the file name is HobbitData.sav, and it is in SPSS data file format. We have used this data set in some of the examples of various types of descriptive analysis in this chapter.

1. Determine what variables are categorical (either nominal or ordinal scales), perform the appropriate descriptive analysis, and interpret it.

2. Determine what variables are metric scales (either interval or ratio scales), perform the appropriate descriptive analysis, and interpret it.

16

Generalizing a Sample's Findings to Its Population and Testing Hypotheses about Percents and Means

Nestle's Crunch Annual Mindshare Survey

Nestlé's Crunch competes with a vast variety and huge number of candy bars. Its competitors include Almond Joy, Chunky, Heath Bars, Hershey Bars, M&M's, Milky Way, Rocky Road, Snickers, Tootsie Roll, and Zagnut. The marketing managers of Crunch know that although there are candy bar consumers who tend to be very brand-loyal, such as Milky Way fanatics, a great many candy bar buyers constantly jump from brand to brand. Furthermore, Crunch has found from its research that many of these volatile candy buyers often make up their minds as to what bar to buy as the craving hits them. So, although Crunch knows its Crunch fans will always buy a Crunch, it also knows that it must be prominent in the minds of the other candy bar buyers who are not focused on their favorite brand; a candy bar buyer prospect feels the craving for chocolate or something sweet, and he or she then quickly conjures up a small number of competing candy bar brands in his or her head. The decision as to which candy bar to buy is then made mentally while the person is headed to the store or the closest vending machine. Crunch's challenge then is to have "mindshare." Mindshare is similar to market share, except it exists in the consumer's awareness set and, hopefully, in the consideration set. The awareness set is all the brands of which the consumer is aware in a product category, and the consideration set is those brands in the awareness set that the consumer would consider buying when the purchase urge hits.

■ To distinguish statistics from parameters
■ To understand the concept of statistical inference
■ To learn how to estimate a population mean or percentage
■ To test a hypothesis about a population mean or percentage
■ To learn how to perform and interpret statistical inference with SPSS

Learning
Objectives

To track consumers and, further, to assess the effectiveness of its promotional campaigns aimed at increasing Crunch's mindshare, Crunch commissioned an annual survey. Here is the conversation between Dale, the Crunch marketing manager, and Melissa, the research project director, which took place recently.

Dale: "I see that you have the results of our annual Crunch Mindshare survey."

Melissa: "I certainly do. We do not have the report finished yet, but I have some notes, and I can summarize our major findings."

Dale: "Great. I certainly hope this is good news and not bad."

Melissa: "I bring good news. Should I deliver it?"

Dale: "I can't wait to hear it."

Melissa: "All right, here goes. You probably recall that we found Crunch to have 50% mindshare last year, so we calculated confidence intervals and told you that Crunch had between 42% and 58% mindshare."

Dale: "Yes, I do recall, and it was the basis for our promotional campaign target this year. We are striving for 70% mindshare."

Melissa: "Goals are always good. The movement is in the right direction, so you are doing something right. This year we found 65% mindshare for Crunch. That computes to a 95% confidence interval of 62% to 68%."

Dale: "So we almost made our 70% goal. Wait a minute. Last year, we had 50% ± 8%, and this year we have 65% ± 3%. If we had the 8% from last year, we can say we reached our 70% goal. What gives?"

Melissa: "Two things are different. The 65% means more people are in agreement that Crunch will be considered when they get the craving, and we increased the sample by one-quarter. We have less variability and more sample accuracy, so the plus or minus number is smaller."

Dale: "Oh. Well, you're the expert."[1]

Statistical inference helps Nestle's Crunch study its mindshare and mindshares of competing chocolate bars such as Hersheys.

As you learned in Chapter 15, descriptive measures of central tendency and measures of variability adequately summarize the findings of a survey. However, whenever a probability sample is drawn from a population, it is not enough to simply report the sample's descriptive statistics, for these measures contain a certain degree of error due to the sampling process. Every sample provides some information about its population, but there is always some sample error that must be taken into account. Sample error is what Melissa is communicating to Dale in our opening case. But reading and comprehending the material in this chapter, you should be able to understand Melissa's comments on variability and sample accuracy.

We begin the chapter by noting that the term *statistic* applies to a sample, whereas the term *parameter* pertains to the related population value. Next, we describe the concept of logical inference and show how it relates to statistical inference. There are two basic types of statistical inference, and we discuss both. First, there is parameter estimation, in which a value, such as the population mean, is estimated based on a sample's mean and its size. Second, there is hypothesis testing, in which an assessment is made as to how much of a sample's findings support a manager's or researcher's a priori belief regarding the size of a population value. We provide formulas and numerical examples and also show you examples of SPSS procedures and output using the Hobbit's Choice Restaurant survey data.

SAMPLE STATISTICS AND POPULATION PARAMETERS

Statistics are sample values, whereas parameters are corresponding population values.

We begin the chapter by defining the concepts of statistics and parameters. There is a fundamental distinction you should keep in mind. Values that are computed from information provided by a sample are referred to as the sample's **statistics**, whereas values that are computed from a complete census, which are considered to be precise and valid measures of the population, are referred to as **parameters**. Statisticians use Greek letters (α, β, etc.) when referring to population parameters and Roman letters (a, b, etc.) when referring to statistics. Every sample statistic has a corresponding population parameter. As you can see in Table 16.1, the notation used for a percentage is p for the statistic and π for the parameter, the notations for standard deviation are s (statistic) and σ (parameter), and the notations for the mean are $\bar{x}$ (statistic) and μ (parameter). Because a census is impractical, the sample statistic is used to estimate the population parameter. This chapter describes the procedures used when estimating various population parameters.

THE CONCEPTS OF INFERENCE AND STATISTICAL INFERENCE

Inference is drawing a conclusion based on some evidence.

We will start by defining "inference" because an understanding of this concept will help you understand what statistical inference is all about. **Inference** is a form of logic in which you make a general statement (a generalization) about an entire class based on

TABLE 16.1	Population Parameters and Their Companion Sample Statistics	
Statistical Concept	**Population Parameter (Greek Letters)**	**Sample Statistic (Roman Letters)**
Average	μ (mu)	$\bar{x}$
Standard deviation	σ (sigma)	s
Percentage	π (pi)	p
Slope	β (beta)	b

what you have observed about a small set of members of that class. When you infer, you draw a conclusion from a small amount of evidence. For example, if two of your friends each bought a new Chevrolet and they both complained about their cars' performances, you might infer that *all* new Chevrolets perform poorly. On the other hand, if one of your friends complained about his Chevy, whereas the other friend did not, you might infer that *some* new Chevy's have performance problems.

Inferences are greatly influenced by the amount of evidence in support of the generalization. So, if 20 of your friends bought new Chevrolets, and they all complained about poor performance, your inference would naturally be stronger or more certain than it would be in the case of only two friends complaining.

Statistical inference is a set of procedures in which the sample size and sample statistic is used to make an estimate of the corresponding population parameter; that is, statistical inference has formal steps for estimating the population parameter (the generalization) based on the evidence of the sample statistic and taking into account the sample error based on sample size. For now, let us concentrate on the percentage, p, as the sample statistic we are using to estimate the population percentage, π, and see how sample size enters into statistical inference. Suppose that Chevrolet suspected that there were some dissatisfied customers, and it commissioned two independent marketing research surveys to determine the amount of dissatisfaction that existed in its customer group. (Of course, our Chevrolet example is entirely fictitious. We do not mean to imply that Chevrolets perform in an unsatisfactory way.)

In the first survey, 100 customers who had purchased a Chevy in the past six months were called and asked, "In general, would you say that you are 'satisfied' or 'dissatisfied' with the performance of your Chevrolet since you bought it?" The survey found that 30 respondents (30%) are dissatisfied. This finding could be inferred to be the total population of Chevy owners who had bought one in the past six months, and we would say that there is 30% dissatisfaction. However, we know that our sample, which, by the way, was a probability sample, must contain some sample error, and in order to reflect this you would have to say that there was *about* 30% dissatisfaction in the population. In other words, it might actually be more or less than 30% if we did a census because the sample provided us with only an estimate.

In the second survey, 1000 respondents—that's 10 times more than in the first survey—were called and asked the same question. This survey found that 35% of the respondents are "dissatisfied." Again, we know that the 35% is an estimate containing sampling error, so now we would also say that the population dissatisfaction percentage was *about* 35%. This means that we have two estimates of the degree of dissatisfaction with Chevrolets. One is about 30%, whereas the other is about 35%.

How do we translate our answers (remember they include the word "about") into more accurate numerical representations? Let us say you could translate them into ballpark ranges; that is, you could translate them so we could say "30% ± x%" for the sample of 100 and "35% ± y%" for the sample of 1000. How would x and y compare? To answer this question, think back on how your logical inference was stronger with 20 friends than it was with 2 friends with Chevrolets. With a larger sample (or more evidence), we have agreed that you would be more certain that the sample statistic was accurate with respect to estimating the true population value. In other words, with a larger sample size you should expect the range used to estimate the true population value to be smaller. Intuitively, you should expect the range for y to be smaller than the range for x because you have a large sample and less sampling error.

As these examples reveal, with statistical inference for estimates of population parameters such as the percentage or mean, the sample statistic is used as the beginning point, and then a range is computed in which the population parameter is estimated to

Statistical inference takes into account that large random samples are more accurate than are small ones.

Statistical inference is based on sample size and variability, which then determine the amount of sampling error.

TABLE 16.2	Two Types of Statistical Inference: Results of Online Music Listeners Survey Conducted for RealPlayer	
Type	**Description**	**Example**
Parameter estimation	Estimate the population value (parameter) through the use of confidence intervals	The percent of PC users who listen to music online is 30% ± 10%, or from 20%–40%.
Hypothesis test	Compare the sample statistic with what is believed (hypothesized) to be the population value prior to undertaking the study	Online music listeners listen an average of 45 ± 15 minutes per day, not 90 as believed by RealPlayer managers.

Note: The examples are fictitious.

fall. The size of the sample, or n, plays a crucial role in this computation, as you will see in all of the statistical inference formulas we present in this chapter.

The two types of statistical inference are parameter estimation and hypothesis tests.

Two types of statistical inferences often used by marketing researchers are described in this chapter: parameter estimates and hypothesis tests. Parameter estimation is used to estimate the population value (parameter) through the use of confidence intervals. Hypothesis testing is used to compare the sample statistic with what is believed (hypothesized) to be the population value prior to undertaking the study. Also, for quick reference, we have listed and described these two types of statistical inference in Table 16.2 with examples of findings of an online survey conducted for RealPlayer.

PARAMETER ESTIMATION

To estimate a population parameter you need a sample statistic (mean or percentage), the standard error of the statistic, and the desired level of confidence (95% or 99%).

Estimation of population parameters is a common type of statistical inference used in marketing research survey analysis. As was indicated earlier, inference is largely a reflection of the amount of sampling error believed to exist in the sample statistic. When the *New York Times* conducts a survey and finds that readers spend an average of 45 minutes daily reading the *Times*, or when McDonald's determines through a nationwide sample that 78% of all Egg McMuffin Breakfast buyers buy a cup of coffee, both companies may want to determine more accurately how close these estimates are to what the actual population parameter is.

Parameter estimation is the process of using sample information to compute an interval that describes the range of a parameter such as the population mean (μ) or the population percentage (π). It involves the use of three values: the sample statistic (such as the mean or the percentage), the standard error of the statistic, and the desired level of confidence (usually 95% or 99%). A discussion of how each value is determined follows.

Sample Statistic

In parameter estimation, the sample statistic is usually a mean or a percentage.

The mean, you should recall from the formula provided in Chapter 15, is the average of a set of interval- or ratio-scaled numbers. For example, you might be working with a sample of golfers and researching the average number of golf balls they buy per month. Or you might be investigating how much high-school students spend, on average, on fast foods between meals. For a percentage, you could be examining what percentage of golfers buy only Maxfli Gold balls, or you might be looking at what percentage of high-school students buy from Taco Bell between meals. In either case, the mean or percentage is derived from a sample, so it is the sample statistic.

Standard Error

There usually is some degree of variability in the sample; that is, our golfers do not all buy the same number of golf balls per month and they do not all buy Maxfli. Not all of our high-school students eat fast food between meals and not all of the ones who do go to Taco Bell. In Chapter 15, we introduced you to variability with a mean by describing the standard deviation as a way of describing variability with a mean by describing the normal distribution, and we used the percentage distribution as a way of describing variability when percentages are being used. Also, in Chapter 13, we described how, if you theoretically took many, many samples and plotted the mean or percentage as a frequency distribution, it would approximate a bell-shaped curve called the "sampling distribution." The **standard error** is a measure of the variability in the sampling distribution based on what is theoretically believed to occur were we to take a multitude of independent samples from the same population. We described the standard error formulas in Chapter 13, but we repeat them here because they are vital to statistical inference, since they tie together the sample size and its variability.

The standard error is a measure of the variability in a sampling distribution.

The formula for the **standard error of the mean** is as follows:

Formula for Standard Error of the Mean
$$s_{\bar{x}} = \frac{s}{\sqrt{n}}$$

where

$s_{\bar{x}}$ = standard error of the mean
s = standard deviation
n = sample size

The formula for the **standard error of the percentage** is as follows:

The formula for mean standard error differs from a percentage standard error.

Formula for Standard Error of the Percentage
$$s_p = \sqrt{\frac{p \times q}{n}}$$

where

s_p = standard error of the percentage
p = the sample percentage
$q = (100 - p)$
n = sample size

In both equations, the sample size n is found in the denominator. This means that the standard error will be smaller with larger sample sizes and larger with smaller sample sizes. At the same time, both of these formulas for the standard error reveal the impact of the variation found in the sample. Variation is represented by the standard deviation s for a mean and by $(p \times q)$ for a percentage. In either equation, the variation is in the numerator, so the greater the variability, the greater the standard error. Thus, the standard error simultaneously takes into account both the sample size and the amount of variation found in the sample. The following examples illustrate this fact.

The standard error takes into account sample size and the variability in the sample.

Notice how sample variability affects the standard error in these two examples.

Suppose that the *New York Times* survey on the amount of time spent daily reading the *Times* had determined a standard deviation of 20 minutes and had used a sample size of 100. The resulting standard error of the mean would be as follows:

Calculation of Standard Error of the Mean with Standard Deviation = 20

$$s_{\bar{x}} = \frac{s}{\sqrt{n}}$$

$$s_{\bar{x}} = \frac{20}{\sqrt{100}}$$

$$= \frac{20}{10}$$

$$= 2 \text{ minutes}$$

On the other hand, if the survey had determined a standard deviation of 40 minutes, the standard error would be as follows:

Calculation of Standard Error of the Mean with Standard Deviation = 40

$$s_{\bar{x}} = \frac{s}{\sqrt{n}}$$

$$s_{\bar{x}} = \frac{40}{\sqrt{100}}$$

$$= \frac{40}{10}$$

$$= 4 \text{ minutes}$$

As you can see, the standard error of the mean from a sample with little variability (20 minutes) is smaller than the standard error of the mean from a sample with much variability (40 minutes), as long as both samples have the same size. In fact, you should have noticed that when the variability was doubled from 20 to 40 minutes, the standard error also doubled, given identical sample sizes. Refer to Figure 16.1.

With a 50–50 percent split there is great variability.

The standard error of a percentage mirrors this logic, although the formula looks a bit different. In this case, as we indicated earlier, the degree of variability is inherent in the $(p \times q)$ aspect of the equation. Very little variability is indicated if p and q are very different in

FIGURE 16.1
The Variability found in the Sample Directly Affects the Standard Error (Same Sample Size).

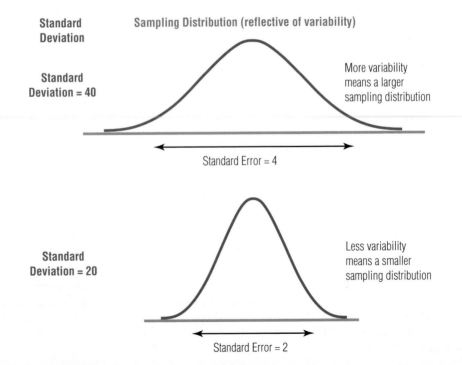

Standard Deviation

Sampling Distribution (reflective of variability)

Standard Deviation = 40

More variability means a larger sampling distribution

Standard Error = 4

Standard Deviation = 20

Less variability means a smaller sampling distribution

Standard Error = 2

McDonald's, or any restaurant for that matter, can use statistical inference to estimate what percent of customers order coffee with their breakfast.

size. For example, if a survey of 100 McDonald's breakfast buyers determined that 90% of the respondents ordered coffee with their Egg McMuffin and 10% of the respondents did not, there would be very little variability because almost everybody orders coffee with breakfast. On the other hand, if the sample determined that there was a 50–50 split between those who had and those who had not ordered coffee, there would be a great deal more variability because any two customers would probably differ in their drink orders.

We can apply these two results to the standard error of percentage for a comparison. Using a 90–10% split, the standard error of percentage is as follows:

Calculation of Standard Error of the Percent with p = 90 and p = 10

$$s_p = \sqrt{\frac{p \times q}{n}}$$
$$= \sqrt{\frac{(90)(10)}{100}}$$
$$= \sqrt{\frac{900}{100}}$$
$$= \sqrt{9}$$
$$= 3\%$$

Using 50–50 percent split, the standard error of the percentage is as follows:

Calculation of Standard Error of the Percent with p = 50 and p = 50

$$s_p = \sqrt{\frac{p \times q}{n}}$$
$$= \sqrt{\frac{(50)(50)}{100}}$$
$$= \sqrt{\frac{2500}{100}}$$
$$= \sqrt{25}$$
$$= 5\%$$

A 50–50% split has a larger standard error than a 90–10 one when the sample size is the same.

Again, these examples show that greater variability in responses results in a larger standard error of the percentage at a given sample size.

Confidence Intervals

Population parameters are estimated with the use of confidence intervals.

Confidence intervals are the degree of accuracy desired by the researcher and stipulated as a level of confidence in the form of a percentage. You may recall that we described sample accuracy in Chapter 13 as a $\pm$ % value, and we are using this concept in the computation of confidence intervals. Because there is always some sampling error when a sample is taken, it is necessary to estimate the population parameter with a range. We did this in the Chevrolet owners' example earlier. One factor affecting the size of the range is how confident the researcher wants to be that the range includes the true population percentage. Normally, the researcher first decides on how confident he or she wants to be; that is, the researcher formally selects a level of confidence. The sample statistic is the beginning of the estimate, but because there is sample error present, a "plus" amount and an identical "minus" amount is added and subtracted from the sample statistic to determine the maximum and minimum, respectively, of the range.

The range of your estimate of the population mean or percentage depends largely on the sample size and the variability found in the sample.

Typically, marketing researchers rely only on the 90%, 95%, or 99% levels of confidence, which correspond to ± 1.64, ± 1.96, and ± 2.58 standard errors, respectively. They are designated z_a, so $z_{0.99}$ is ± 2.58 standard errors. By far, the **most commonly used level of confidence** in marketing research is 95%,[2] corresponding to 1.96 standard errors. In fact, the 95% level of confidence is usually the default level found in statistical analysis programs such as SPSS. Now that the relationship between the standard error and the measure of sample variability—be it the standard deviation or the percentage—is apparent, it is a simple matter to determine the range in which the population parameter will be estimated. We use the sample statistics, $\bar{x}$ or p, compute the standard error, and then apply our desired level of confidence. In notation form these are as follows:

Confidence intervals are estimated using these formulas.

Formula for Population Parameter Estimation (Mean)

$$\bar{x} \pm z_a s_{\bar{x}}$$

where

$\bar{x}$ = sample mean
z_a = z value for 95% or 99% level of confidence
$s_{\bar{x}}$ = standard error of the mean

Formula for Population Parameter Estimation (Percentage)

$$p \pm z_a s_p$$

where

p = sample percentage
z_a = z value for 95% or 99% level of confidence
s_p = standard error of the percentage

If you wanted to be 99% confident that your range included the true population percentage, for instance, you would multiply the standard error of the percentage s_p by 2.58 and add that value to the percentage p to obtain the upper limit, and you would subtract it from the percentage to find the lower limit. Notice that you have now taken into consideration the sample statistic p, the variability that is in the formula for s_p, the sample size n, which is also in the formula for s_p, and the degree of confidence in your estimate.

Marketing researchers typically use only 95% or 99% confidence intervals.

How do these formulas relate to inference? Recall that we are estimating a population parameter; that is, we are indicating a range into which it is believed that the true population parameter falls. The size of the range is determined by those three bits of information we have about the population on hand as a result of our sample. The final ingredient is our level of confidence, or the degree to which we want to be correct in our estimate of the population parameter. If we are conservative and wish to assume the 99% level of confidence, then the range would be more encompassing than if we are less conservative and assume only the 95% level of confidence, because 99% is associated with ± 2.58 standard errors and 95% is associated with ± 1.96 standard errors.

Using these formulas for the sample of 100 *New York Times* readers with a mean reading time of 45 minutes and a standard deviation of 20 minutes, the 95% and the 99% confidence interval estimates would be calculated as follows.

Here are two examples of confidence interval computations with a mean.

Calculation of a 95% Confidence Interval for a Mean

$$\bar{x} \pm 1.96 \times s_{\bar{x}}$$
$$45 \pm 1.96 \times \frac{20}{\sqrt{100}}$$
$$45 \pm 1.96 \times 2$$
$$45 \pm 3.9$$
$$41.1 - 48.9 \text{ minutes}$$

Calculation of a 99% Confidence Interval for a Mean

$$\bar{x} \pm 2.58 \times s_{\bar{x}}$$
$$45 \pm 2.58 \times \frac{20}{\sqrt{100}}$$
$$45 \pm 2.58 \times 2$$
$$45 \pm 5.2$$
$$39.8 - 50.2 \text{ minutes}$$

If 50% of the 100 Egg McMuffin eaters order coffee, the 95% and 99% confidence intervals would be computed using the percentage formula.

Here are two examples of confidence interval computations with a percentage.

Calculation of a 95% Confidence Interval for a Percentage

$$p \pm 1.96 \times s_p$$
$$p \pm 1.96 \times \sqrt{\frac{p \times q}{n}}$$
$$50 \pm 1.96 \times \sqrt{\frac{50 \times 50}{100}}$$
$$50 \pm 1.96 \times 5$$
$$50 \pm 9.8$$
$$40.2\% - 59.8\%$$

Calculation of a 99% Confidence Interval for a Percentage

$$p \pm 2.58 \times s_p$$
$$p \pm 2.58 \times \sqrt{\frac{p \times q}{n}}$$
$$50 \pm 2.58 \times \sqrt{\frac{50 \times 50}{100}}$$
$$50 \pm 2.58 \times 5$$
$$50 \pm 12.9$$
$$37.1\% - 62.9\%$$

Notice that the only thing that differs when you compare the 95% confidence interval computations to the 99% confidence interval computations in each case is Z_a. It is 1.96 for a 95% and 2.58 for a 99% confidence interval. The confidence interval is always wider for 99% than it is for 95% when the sample size is the same and variability is equal.

A 99% confidence interval is always wider than a 95% confidence interval if all other factors are equal.

Active

CALCULATE SOME CONFIDENCE INTERVALS

This Active Learning section will give you some practice in calculating confidence intervals. For this set of exercises, you are working with a survey of 1000 people who responded to questions about satellite radio. The questions, sample statistics, and other pertinent information are listed below. Compute the 95% confidence interval for the population parameter in each case. Be certain to follow the logic of the questions, as it has implications for the sample size pertaining to each question.

Question	Sample Statistic(s)	95% Confidence Interval Lower Boundary	95% Confidence Interval Upper Boundary
Have you heard of satellite radio?	50% responded "yes"	_____	_____
If yes, do you own a satellite radio?	30% responded "yes"	_____	_____
If you own a satellite radio, about how many minutes of satellite radio did you listen to last week?	Average of 100.7 minutes; standard deviation of 25.0 minutes	_____	_____

How to Interpret an Estimated Population Mean or Percentage Range

How are these ranges interpreted? The interpretation is quite simple when you remember that the sampling distribution notion is the underlying theoretical concept. If we were using a 99% level of confidence, and if we repeated the sampling process and computed the sample statistic many times, their frequency distribution (the sampling distribution) would form a bell-shaped curve. A total of 99% of these repeated samples results would produce a range that includes the population parameter.

Obviously, a marketing researcher would take only one sample for a particular marketing research project, and this restriction explains why estimates must be used. Furthermore, it is the conscientious application of probability sampling techniques that allows us to make use of the sampling distribution concept. So, statistical inference procedures are the direct linkages between probability sample design and data analysis. Do you remember that you had to grapple with confidence levels when we determined sample size? Now we are on the other side of the table, so to speak, and we must use the sample size for our inference procedures. Confidence intervals must be used when estimating population parameters, and the size of the random sample used is always reflected in these confidence intervals.

Nevertheless, as you know, a small random sample can be quite accurate. Marketing Research Insight 16.1 has the confidence intervals for various demographic and game-playing characteristics of a sample of 540 players of Sony's online game, Everquest. Despite the fact that there may be over half a million Everquest players, you will find these confidence intervals to be 8% or less in total width.[3]

There are five steps to computing a confidence interval.

There are five steps involved in computing confidence intervals for a mean or a percentage are shown in Table 16.3.

As a final note, we want to remind you that the logic of statistical inference is identical to the reasoning process you go through when you weigh evidence to make a generalization or conclusion of some sort. The more evidence you have, the more precise you will be in your generalization. The only difference is that with statistical inference we must follow certain rules that require the application of formulas so our inferences will be consistent with the assumptions of statistical theory. When you make a

MARKETING
RESEARCH
INSIGHT

ONLINE APPLICATION

16.1

Who Are the *Everquest* Online Gamers?

The following profile of *Everquest* online game players was recently revealed with an online survey.

FACTOR	DESIGNATION	SAMPLE PERCENT	95% CONFIDENCE INTERVAL LOWER BOUNDARY	UPPER BOUNDARY
Gender	Male	81.0%	77.7%	84.3%
	Female	19.0%	15.7%	22.3%
Age	12 to 17	8.0%	5.7%	10.3%
	18 to 30	59.0%	54.9%	63.1%
	31 to 40	22.0%	18.5%	25.5%
Nationality	North America	77.0%	73.5%	80.5%
	United Kingdom	12.0%	9.3%	14.7%
Education	Secondary	20.0%	16.6%	23.4%
	College graduate	30.0%	26.1%	33.9%
Occupation	Information Technology or Computer-related	29.0%	25.2%	32.8%
	Student	20.0%	16.6%	23.4%
How long played online games?	More than 36 months	19.0%	15.7%	22.3%
	31 to 36 months	24.0%	20.4%	27.6%
	25 to 30 months	15.0%	12.0%	18.0%
Play frequency (per week)	Up to 10 hours	16.0%	12.9%	19.1%
	11 to 20 hours	36.0%	32.0%	40.0%
	21 to 30 hours	24.0%	20.4%	27.6%
Play with whom?	Friends	75%	72.4%	79.6%
	Partner	25%	21.3%	28.7%

TABLE 16.3	**How to Compute Confidence Intervals for a Mean or a Percentage**

Step 1. Find the sample statistic, either the mean, $\bar{x}$, or the percentage, p.

Step 2. Determine the amount of variability found in the sample in the form of standard error of the mean, $s_{\bar{x}}$, or standard error of the percentage, s_p.

Step 3. Identify the sample size, n.

Step 4. Decide on the desired level of confidence to determine the value for z: $z_{.95}(1.96)$ or $z_{.99}(2.58)$.

Step 5. Compute your (95%) confidence interval as: $\bar{x} \pm 1.96 s_{\bar{x}}$ or $p \pm 1.96 s_p$.

nonstatistical inference, your judgment can be swayed by subjective factors, so you may not be consistent with others who are making an inference with the same evidence. But in statistical inference, the formulas are completely objective and perfectly consistent. Plus, they are based on accepted statistical concepts.

Y O U R   I N T E G R A T E D   **CASE**

The Hobbit's Choice Restaurant Survey: How to Obtain a Confidence Interval for a Percentage with SPSS

Your Statistical Package for the Social Sciences (SPSS) program will not calculate the confidence intervals for a percentage. This is because with a categorical variable such as the favorite radio format for the Hobbit's Choice survey, there may be many different categories. But, you know now that the computation is fairly easy, and all you need to know is the value of p and the sample size, both of which you can obtain using the "Frequencies" procedure in SPSS.

Here is an example using the Hobbit's Choice data set. We found in our descriptive analysis that "rock" was the most preferred radio show format, and 41.3% of the respondents listened to it. We can calculate the confidence intervals at the 95% level of confidence easily as we know that the sample size was 400. Here are the calculations.

Calculation of a 95% Confidence Interval for the "Rock" Radio Format Percentage in the Hobbit's Choice Population

$$p \pm 1.96 \times s_p$$

$$p \pm 1.96 \times \sqrt{\frac{p \times q}{n}}$$

$$41.3 \pm 1.96 \times \sqrt{\frac{41.3 \times 58.7}{400}}$$

$$41.3 \pm 1.96 \times 2.46$$

$$41.3 \pm 4.8$$

$$36.5\% - 46.1\%$$

Luckily, confidence intervals are easy to calculate for percentages. So all you need to do is a FREQUENCIES analysis to obtain the target percentage and a sample size values to go into the formula to calculate these confidence intervals.

With confidence intervals, Jeff Dean will know what percentage of his target market listens to "rock" radio programming.

The Hobbit's Choice Restaurant Survey: How to Obtain a Confidence Interval for a Mean with SPSS

Fortunately, because the calculations are a bit more complicated and tedious, your SPSS program will calculate the confidence interval for a mean. To illustrate this feature, we will revisit some very critical comments that Cory Rogers, Research Project Manager, made to Jeff Dean.

> In fact, Cory Rogers had already made some estimates of demand using the forecasting model. He told Dean that if only 4% of heads of households in the 12 ZIP code area claimed they were "very likely" to patronize the restaurant and if these same people spent an average of $200 per month in restaurants and were willing to pay an average of $18 for an a là carte entrée, then the model predicted a very successful restaurant operation.

You should have already found via your descriptive analysis (Case 15.3, page 451), that 18% of the respondents indicated "very likely." If you calculate the 95% confidence intervals for the population estimate, you will find the range to be 14.2% to 21.8%, so the first condition is satisfied. The next requirement is an average of $200 per month. We can test this with a 95% confidence interval for the mean dollars spent on restaurants for the "very likely" respondents who represent the "very likely" population.

The requirement says that the "very likely" individuals must spend at average of $200 per month, so we must select only those respondents for this analysis. You learned earlier how to select respondents, and you should recall that it is accomplished with the DATA-SELECT CASES menu sequence. Then, all we need to specify is the selection condition of "if likely to patronize Hobbit's Choice Restaurant" =5. With this operation, SPSS will analyze only these respondents.

Figure 16.2 shows the clickstream sequence to accomplish a 95% confidence interval estimate using SPSS. As you can see, the correct SPSS procedure is a one sample t test, and you use the ANALYZE-COMPARE MEANS-ONE SAMPLE T TEST menu clickstream sequence to open up the proper window. Refer to Figure 16.2 to see that all you need to do is to select the "Dollars spent in restaurants per month" variable into the Test Variables area, and then click "OK."

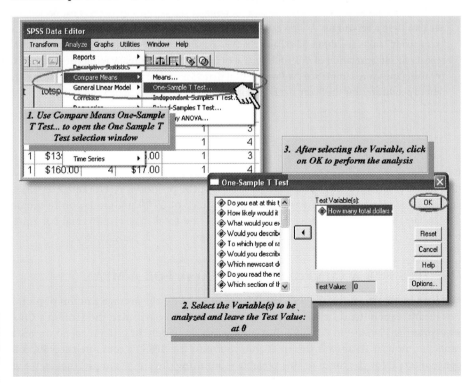

FIGURE 16.2
The SPSS Clickstream to Obtain a 95% Confidence Interval for a Mean

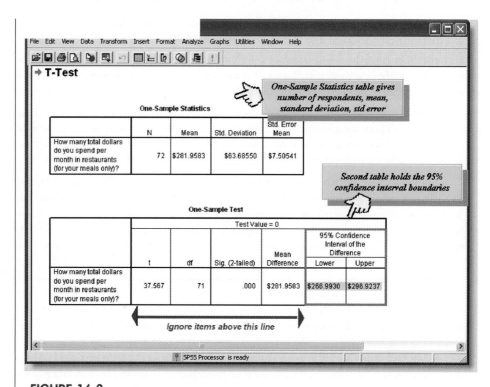

FIGURE 16.3
The SPSS Output for a 95% Confidence Interval for a Mean

SPSS Student Assistant:
Establishing Confidence
Intervals for Means

Figure 16.3 shows the results of ANALYZE–COMPARE MEANS–ONE SAMPLE T TEST for dollars spent per month in a restaurant. As you can see, the average month restaurant expenditures for our "very likely" folks are about $282, and the 95% confidence interval is $266.99 to $296.92. To repeat our interpretation of this finding: if we conducted a great many replications of this survey using the same sample size, we would find that 95% of the sample average monthly restaurant expenditures for the "very likely" respondents fall between about $267 and $297.

This is very good news for our budding restaurateur, Jeff Dean, as we have satisfied two of the three conditions specified by Researcher Cory Rogers: the percent of individuals in the population who are very likely to visit the proposed restaurants exceeds 4%, and these people are spending more than an average of $200 per month on restaurants. In fact, with our findings, we can estimate the total market potential for upscale restaurants in the metropolitan area. See Marketing Research Insight 16.2.

USE SPSS FOR A CONFIDENCE INTERVAL FOR A MEAN

You have just learned that the 95% confidence interval for the average amount of monthly restaurant expenditures that people who are likely to patronize the Hobbit's Choice Restaurant is $266.99 to $296.92. But how much do people in general spend on restaurants per month? To answer this question, you must use SPSS to compute the 95% confidence interval for the mean of this variable—but using the entire sample; that is, we used only respondents who were very likely to patronize the Hobbit's Choice Restaurant in our example in Figures 16.2 and 16.3 because the relevant population is made up of the likely patrons of the Hobbit's Choice. However, to generalize to the entire population, we must

16.2 How to Estimate Market Potential Using a Survey's Findings

A common way to estimate total market potential is to rely on the definition of a market. A market is people with the willingness and ability to pay for a product or a service. This definition can be expressed somewhat like a formula, in the following way.

Market potential = Population base × Percent likely to buy × Amount they are willing to pay

In the Hobbit's Choice Restaurant case, we know that the metropolitan population is about 500,000, which translates to about 167,000 households. We also know that not every household dines out regularly. A recent article in the *City Magazine* reported that 1 out of 10 households eats evening meals at the major restaurants in the city. So there are about 16,700 households comprising the "sit-down" restaurant market population base.

We found the 95% confidence intervals for the individuals (who represent households) who are "very likely" to patronize an upscale restaurant to be 14.2% to 21.8%, and we found that they spend about $282, on average, each month on restaurants. With these facts, findings, and confidence intervals, we can make three estimates of the market potential for an upscale restaurant.

PESSIMISTIC ESTIMATE	BEST ESTIMATE	OPTIMISTIC ESTIMATE
16,700 × 14.2% × $282 = **$668,735**	16,700 × 18.0% × $282 = **$847,692**	16,700 × 21.8% × $282 = **$1,026,649**

Using the 95% confidence intervals and the sample percent, the total market potential is found to be between about $.7 million and $1.0 million dollars per month which amounts to $8.4 million to $12.0 million per year. The best annual estimate is about $850,000. It is "best" because it is based on the sample percent that is the best estimate of the true population percent of "very likely" households. The 95% confidence interval estimates are possible, but if many, many replications of the survey were to take place, most of the percents would fall near 18%.

---

use the entire sample. So, you must "unselect" the SPSS data set by using the SPSS Operation of SELECT CASES and set it to ALL CASES. Once you have performed this operation, use the clickstream identified in Figure 16.2 and use the annotations in Figure 16.3 to find and interpret your 95% confidence interval for the number of dollars people in the metropolitan area spend on restaurants per month, on average. How does this confidence interval compare to the one we found for the likely patrons of the Hobbit's Choice Restaurant?

HYPOTHESIS TESTS

Sometimes, someone, such as the marketing researcher or marketing manager, offers an expectation about the population parameter based on prior knowledge, assumptions, or intuition. This expectation, called a **hypothesis**, most commonly takes the form of an exact specification as to what the population parameter value is.

A **hypothesis test** is a statistical procedure used to "accept" or "reject" the hypothesis based on sample information.[4] With all hypothesis tests, you should keep in mind that the sample is the only source of current information about the population.

> A hypothesis is what the manager or researcher expects the population mean (or percentage) to be.

People test and revise intuitive hypotheses often without thinking about it.

Because our sample is random and representative of the population, the sample results are used to determine if the hypothesis about the population parameter is accepted or rejected.[5]

All of this might sound frightfully technical, but it is a form of inference that you do every day. You just do not use the words *hypothesis* and parameter when you do it. Here is an example to show how hypothesis testing occurs naturally. Your friend, Bill, does not use an automobile seat belt because he thinks only a few drivers actually wear them. But Bill's car breaks down, and he has to ride with his coworkers to and from work while it is being repaired. Over the course of a week, Bill rides with five different coworkers, and he notices that four out of the five buckle up. When Bill begins driving his car the next week, he begins fastening his seat belt.

People engage in intuitive hypothesis testing constantly.

This is intuitive hypothesis testing in action; Bill's initial belief that few people wear seat belts was his hypothesis. **Intuitive hypothesis testing** (as opposed to statistical hypothesis testing) is when someone uses something he or she has observed to see if it agrees with or refutes his or her belief about that topic. Everyone uses intuitive hypothesis testing; in fact, we rely on it constantly. We just do not call it hypothesis testing, but we are constantly gathering evidence that supports or refutes our beliefs, and we reaffirm or change our beliefs based on our findings. Marketing Research Insight 16.3 shows that you perform intuitive hypothesis testing a great deal.

Obviously, if you had asked Bill before his car went into the repair shop, he might have said that only a small percentage, perhaps as low as 10%, of drivers wear seat belts. His week of car rides is analogous to a sample of five observations, and he observes that 4 out of 5 (80%) of his coworkers buckle up. Now his initial hypothesis is not supported by the evidence. So Bill realizes that his hypothesis is in error, and it must be revised. If you asked Bill what percentage of drivers wear seat belts after his week of observations, he undoubtedly would have a much higher percentage in mind than his original estimate. The fact that Bill began to fasten his seat belt suggests he perceives his behavior to be out of the norm, so he has adjusted his belief and his behavior as well. In other words, his hypothesis was not supported, so Bill revised it to be consistent with what is actually the case. The logic of statistical hypothesis testing is very similar to the process Bill has just undergone.

Here are five steps in hypothesis testing.

There are five basic steps involved in hypothesis testing, and we have listed them in Table 16.4. We have also described with each step how Bill's hypothesis that only 10% of drivers buckle their seat belt is tested via intuition.

TABLE 16.4	The Five Basic Steps Involved In Hypothesis Testing (Using Bill's Seat-Belt Hypothesis)
The Steps	**Bill's Intuitive Hypothesis Test**
Step 1. Begin with a statement about what you believe exists in the population; that is, the population mean or percentage.	In our example, Bill believed that only 10% of drivers buckle their seat belts.
Step 2. Draw a random sample and determine the sample statistic.	Bill found that 80% of his friends buckled up.
Step 3. Compare the statistic to the hypothesized parameter	Bill noticed that 80% is different from 10%.
Step 4. Decide whether the sample supports the original hypothesis.	The observed 80% of drivers does not support the hypothesis that 10% buckle up.
Step 5. If the sample does not support the hypothesis, revise the hypothesis to be consistent with the sample's statistic.	The actual incidence of drivers who buckle their seat belts is about 80%. (Bill, *your hypothesis of 10% is not supported; you need to buckle up like just about everyone else.*)

16.3

Intuitive Hypothesis Testing: We Do It All the Time!

People do intuitive hypothesis testing all the time to reaffirm their beliefs or to reform them to be consistent with reality. The following diagram illustrates how you perform intuitive hypothesis testing.

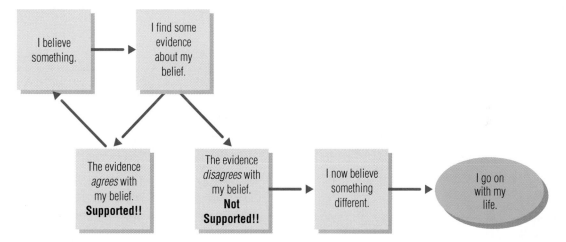

Here is an everyday example. As a student studying marketing research, you believe that you will "ace" the first exam if you study hard the night before the exam. You take the exam, and you score a 70%. Ouch. You now realize that your belief was wrong, and you need to study more for the next exam. So your hypothesis was not supported, and you now have to come up with a new one.

You ask the student beside you who did ace the exam, how much study time he put in. He says he studied for the three nights before the exam. Notice, that he has found evidence (his A grade) that supports his hypothesis, so he will not change his study habits belief. You, on the other hand, must change your hypothesis or suffer the consequences.

Due to the variation that we know will be caused by sampling, it is impossible to be absolutely certain that our assessment of the acceptance or rejection of the hypothesis will be correct if we simply compare our hypothesis arithmetically to the sample finding. Therefore, you must fall back on the sample size concepts discussed in Chapter 13 and rely on the use of probabilities. The statistical concept underlying hypothesis testing permits us to say that if many, many samples were drawn, and a comparison made for each one, a true hypothesis would be accepted, for example, 99% of these times.

Statistical hypothesis testing involves the use of four ingredients: the sample statistic, the standard error of the statistic, the desired level of confidence, and the hypothesized population parameter value. The first three values were discussed in the section on parameter estimation. The final value is simply what the researcher believes the population parameter (π or μ) to be before the research is undertaken.

A hypothesis test gives you the probability of support for your hypothesis based on your sample evidence and sample size.

There is always an alternative hypothesis.

Statisticians often refer to the **alternative hypothesis** when performing statistical tests. This concept is important for you to know about. We have included Marketing Research Insight 16.4 as a way to introduce you to the idea of an alternative hypothesis and to understand how it is used in statistical hypothesis tests.

Test of the Hypothesized Population Parameter Value

The **hypothesized population parameter** value can be determined using either a percentage or a mean. The equation used to test the hypothesis of a population percentage is as follows:

Formula for Test of a Hypothesis about a Percent

$$z = \frac{p - \pi_H}{s_{\bar{x}}}$$

where

p = the sample percentage
π_H = the hypothesized percentage
s_p = the standard error of the percentage

MARKETING RESEARCH INSIGHT

PRACTICAL APPLICATION

16.4

What Is an Alternative Hypothesis?

Whenever you test a stated hypothesis, you always automatically test its alternative. The alternative hypothesis takes in all possible cases that are not treated by the stated hypothesis. For example, if you hypothesize that 50% of all drivers fasten their seat belts, you are saying that the population percentage is equal to 50% (stated hypothesis), and the alternative hypothesis is that the population percent is not equal to 50%. To say this differently, the alternative hypothesis is that the population percentage can be any percentage other than 50%, the stated hypothesis. The alternative hypothesis is always implicit, but sometimes statisticians will state it along with the stated hypothesis.

To avoid confusion, we do not formally provide the alternative hypotheses in this textbook. But here are some stated hypotheses and their alternatives. You may want to refer back to this exhibit if the alternative hypothesis is important to your understanding of the concepts being described.

THE STATED HYPOTHESIS	THE ALTERNATIVE HYPOTHESIS
POPULATION PARAMETER HYPOTHESIS	
The population mean is *equal* to $50.	The population mean is *not equal* to $50.
The population percentage is *equal* to 60%.	The population percentage is *not equal* to 60%.
DIRECTIONAL HYPOTHESIS	
The population mean is *greater than* 100.	The population mean is *less than or equal* to 100.
The population percentage is *less than* 70%.	The population percentage is *greater than or equal* to 70%.

The importance of knowing the alternative hypothesis stems from the fact that it is a certainty that the sample results must support either the stated hypothesis or the alternative hypothesis. There is no other outcome possible. If the findings do not support the stated hypothesis, then they must support the alternative hypothesis because it covers all possible cases not specified in the stated hypothesis. Of course, if the stated hypothesis is supported by the findings, the alternative hypothesis is not supported.

The equation used to test the hypothesis of a mean is identical in logic, except it uses the mean and standard error of the mean.

Formula for Test of a Hypothesis about a Mean

$$z = \frac{\bar{x} - \mu_H}{s_{\bar{x}}}$$

Here are formulas used to test a hypothesized population parameter.

where

$\bar{x}$ = the sample mean
μ_H = the hypothesized mean
$s_{\bar{x}}$ = standard error of the mean

Tracking the logic of the equation for a mean, one can see that the sample mean ($\bar{x}$), is compared to the hypothesized population mean (μ_H). Similarly, the sample percentage (p) is compared to the hypothesized percentage (π_H). In this case, "compared" means "take the difference." This difference is divided by the standard error to determine how many standard errors away from the hypothesized parameter the sample statistic falls. The standard error, you should remember, takes into account the variability found in the sample as well as the sample size. A small sample with much variability yields a large standard error, so our sample statistic could be quite far away from the mean arithmetically but still less than one standard error away in certain circumstances. All the relevant information about the population as found by our sample is included in these computations. Knowledge of areas under the normal curve then come into play to translate this distance into a probability of support for the hypothesis.

To a statistician, "Compare means" amounts to "Take the difference."

Here is a simple illustration using Bill's seat-belt hypothesis. Let us assume that instead of observing his friends buckling up, Bill reads that a Harris Poll finds that 80% of respondents in a national sample of 1000 wear their seat belts. The hypothesis test would be computed as follows (notice we substituted the formula for s_p in the second step):

An example of no support for Bill's seat-belt hypothesis.

Calculation of a Test of Bill's Hypothesis That Only 10% of Drivers "Buckle up" (Sorry, Bill. No support for you.)

$$z = \frac{p - \pi_H}{s_p}$$

$$= \frac{p - \pi_H}{\sqrt{\dfrac{p \times q}{n}}}$$

$$= \frac{80 - 10}{\sqrt{\dfrac{80 \times 20}{1000}}}$$

$$= \frac{70}{\sqrt{\dfrac{1600}{1000}}}$$

$$= \frac{70}{\sqrt{1.6}}$$

$$= 55.3$$

The crux of statistical hypothesis testing is the **sampling distribution concept**. Our actual sample is one of the many, many theoretical samples comprising the assumed bell-shaped curve of possible sample results using the hypothesized value as the center of the bell-shaped distribution. There is a greater probability of finding a sample result close to the hypothesized mean, for example, than of finding one that is far away. But, there is a critical assumption working here. We have conditionally accepted from the outset that the person who stated the hypothesis is correct. So, if our sample mean turns out to be within ± 2.58 standard errors of the hypothesized mean, it supports the

The sampling distribution concept says that our sample is one of many, many theoretical samples that comprise a bell-shaped curve with the hypothesized value as the mean.

hypothesis maker at the 99% level of confidence because it falls within 99% of the area under the curve.

You always assume the sample information to be more accurate than any hypothesis.

But, what if the sample result is found to be outside this range? Which is correct—the hypothesis or the researcher's sample results? The answer to this question is always the same: Sample information is invariably more accurate than a hypothesis. Of course, the sampling procedure must adhere strictly to probability sampling requirements and ensure representativeness. As you can see, Bill was greatly mistaken, because his hypothesis of 10% of drivers wearing seat belts was 55.3 standard errors away from the 80% finding of the national poll.

Does the sample support Rex's hypothesis that student interns make $2750 in the first semester?

The following example serves to describe the hypothesis testing process with a mean. Northwestern Mutual Life Insurance Company has a college student internship program. The program allows college students to participate in an intensive training program and to become field agents in one academic term. Arrangements are made with various universities in the United States whereby students will receive college credit if they qualify for and successfully complete this program. Rex Reigen, district agent for Idaho, believed, based on his knowledge of other programs in the country, that the typical college agent will be able to earn about $2750 in his or her first semester of participation in the program. He hypothesizes that the population parameter, that is, the mean, will be $2750. To check Rex's hypothesis, a survey was taken of current college agents, and 100 of these individuals were contacted through telephone calls. Among the questions posed was an estimate of the amount of money made in their first semester of work in the program. The sample mean is determined to be $2800, and the standard deviation is $350.

How many standard errors is $2800 away from $2750?

In essence, the amount of $2750 is the hypothesized mean of the sampling distribution of all possible samples of the same size that can be taken of the college agents in the country. The unknown factor, of course, is the size of the standard error in dollars. Consequently, although it is assumed that the sampling distribution will be a normal curve with the mean of the entire distribution at $2750, we need a way to determine how many dollars are within ± 1 standard error of the mean, or any other number of standard errors of the mean for that matter. The only information available that would help to determine the size of the standard error is the standard deviation obtained from the sample. This standard deviation can be used to determine a standard error with the application of the standard error formula.

The amount of $2800 found by the sample differs from the hypothesized amount of $2750 by $50. Is this amount sufficiently different to cast doubt on Rex's estimate? In other words, is it far enough from the hypothesized mean to reject the hypothesis? To answer these questions, we compute as follows (note that we have substituted the formula for the standard error of the mean in the second step):

Calculation of a Test of Rex's Hypothesis that Northwestern Mutual Interns Make an Average of $2750 in their First Semester of Work (Rex is right!)

$$
\begin{aligned}
z &= \frac{\bar{x} - \mu_H}{s_{\bar{x}}} \\
&= \frac{\bar{x} - \mu_H}{\dfrac{s}{\sqrt{n}}} \\
&= \frac{2800 - 2750}{\dfrac{350}{\sqrt{100}}} \\
&= \frac{50}{35} \\
&= 1.43
\end{aligned}
$$

The sample variability and the sample size have been used to determine the size of the standard error of the assumed sampling distribution. In this case, one standard error of the mean is equal to $35. When the difference of $50 is divided by $35 to determine the number of standard errors away from which the hypothesized mean the sample statistic lies, the result is 1.43 standard errors. As is illustrated in Figure 16.4, 1.43 standard errors is within ±1.96 standard errors of Rex's hypothesized mean. It also reveals that the hypothesis is supported because it falls in the acceptance region.

Although the exact probability of support for the hypothesized parameter can be determined from the use of a table, it is often handy just to recall the two numbers, 1.96 and 2.58; as we have said, these two are directly associated to the intervals of 95% and 99%, respectively. Anytime that the computed z value falls outside 2.58, the resulting probability of support for the hypothesis is 0.01 or less. Of course, computer statistical programs such as SPSS will provide the exact probability because they are programmed to look up the probability in the z table just as you would have to do if you did the test by hand calculations and you wanted the exact probability.

Directional Hypotheses

It is sometimes appropriate to indicate a directional hypothesis. A **directional hypothesis** is one that indicates the direction in which you believe the population parameter falls relative to some target mean or percentage; that is, the owner of a toy store might not be able to state the exact number of dollars parents spend each time they buy a toy in that store, but the owner might say, "They spend under $100." A directional hypothesis is usually made with a "more than" or "less than" statement. For example, Rex Reigen might have hypothesized that the average college agent working for Northwestern Mutual Life earns *more than* $2750. In both the "more than" case and the "less than" case, identical concepts are brought into play, but one must take into account that only one side (one tail) of the sampling distribution is being used.

There are only two differences to keep in mind for directional hypothesis tests. First, you must be concerned with the sign determined for the z value as well as its size. When you subtract the hypothesized mean from the sample mean, the sign will be positive with "greater than" hypotheses, whereas the sign will be negative for "less than" hypotheses if the hypothesis is true. To use Rex's example again, the hypothesized target of $2750 would be subtracted from the sample mean of $2800, yielding +$50, so the positive sign does support the "greater than" hypothesis. But is the difference statistically significant?

To answer this question requires our second step: to divide the difference by the standard error of the mean to compute the z value. We did this earlier and determined the z value to be 1.43. Because we are working with only one side of the bell-shaped

The z is calculated to be 1.43 standard errors. What does this mean?

A computed z value of 1.43 is less than 1.96, so the hypothesis is supported.

A directional hypothesis is one in which you specify the hypothesized mean (or percentage) to be less than or greater than some amount.

When testing a directional hypothesis, you must look at the sign as well as the size of the computed z value.

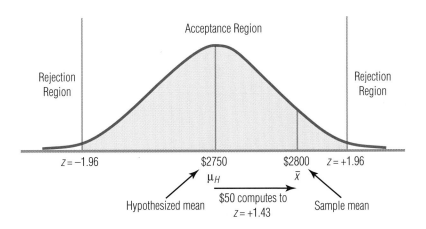

FIGURE 16.4
The Sample Findings Support the Hypothesis in This Example.

TABLE 16.5	With a Directional Hypothesis Test, the Critical Points for z Must Be Adjusted, and the Sign (+ or −) Is Important		
Level of Confidence	**Direction of Hypothesis[a]**		**z Value**
95%	Greater than		+1.64
	Less than		−1.64
99%	Greater than		+2.33
	Less than		−2.33

[a]Subtract the sample statistic (mean or percentage) from the hypothesized parameter (μ or π).

distribution, you need to adjust the critical z value to reflect this fact. As Table 16.5 shows, a z value of ±1.64 standard errors defines the endpoints for 95% of the normal curve, and a z value of ±2.33 standard errors defines the endpoints for 99% confidence levels. Now the directional hypothesis is supported at that level of confidence if the computed z value is larger than the critical cut point, *and*, of course, its sign is consistent with the direction of the hypothesis. Otherwise, the directional hypothesis is not supported at your chosen level of confidence. Although the computed z value is close (1.43), it is not equal to or greater than 1.64, so Rex's directional hypothesis is not supported.

How to Interpret Hypothesis Testing

How do you interpret hypothesis tests? The interpretation of a hypothesis test is again directly linked to the sampling distribution concept. If the hypothesis about the population parameter is correct or true, then a high percentage of sample means must fall close to

Hypothesis testing can be used to see if a restaurant owner's belief that customers desire roast grouse with crispy bacon served with fried bread crumbs is supported.

this value. In fact, if the hypothesis is true, then 99% of the sample results will fall between ±2.58 standard errors of the hypothesized mean. On the other hand, if the hypothesis is incorrect, there is a strong likelihood that the computed *z* value will fall outside ±2.58 standard errors. In other words, you must adjust the "standard" number of standard errors (1.96 or 2.58) for directional hypothesis tests. We have done this for you in Table 16.5.

With the *z* values in the directional hypothesis test, the interpretation remains the same. The further away the hypothesized value is from the actual case, the more likely it is that the computed *z* value will not fall in the critical range. Failure to support the hypothesis essentially tells the hypothesizer that his or her assumptions about the population are in error and that they must be revised in light of the evidence from the sample. This revision is achieved through estimates of the population parameter discussed in the previous section. These estimates can be used to provide the manager or researcher with a new mental picture of the population through confidence interval estimates of the true population value.

> If a hypothesis is not supported by a random sample finding, use the sample statistic and estimate the population parameter.

HOW TO USE SPSS TO TEST A HYPOTHESIS FOR A PERCENT

As you found out earlier, SPSS does not perform statistical tests on percentages, so if you have a hypothesis about a percentage, you are required to do the calculations with your handy calculator. You should use the SPSS FREQUENCIES procedure to have it calculate the sample p value and to determine the sample size if you do not know it precisely. Then apply the percentage hypothesis test formula to calculate the *z* value. If the value is inside the range of ±1.96, the hypothesized percent is supported at the 95% level of confidence, and if it is inside ±2.58, it is supported at the 99% level. You will have an opportunity to use SPSS and do these calculations in Case 16.3 at the end of this chapter.

> SPSS does not perform percentages hypothesis tests, but you can use it to obtain the necessary information to calculate by hand.

HOW TO USE SPSS TO TEST A HYPOTHESIS FOR A MEAN

We can take Cory Rogers' third condition—that the "very likely" customers must be "willing to pay an average of $18 for an a là carte entrée" as a hypothesis, and we can test it with our Hobbit's Choice Restaurant sample findings. Your SPSS software can be easily directed to make a mean estimation or to test a hypothesis for a mean.

To perform a mean hypothesis test, SPSS provides a Test Value box in which the hypothesized mean can be entered. As you can see in Figure 16.5, you get to this box by using the ANALYZE-COMPARE MEANS-ONE SAMPLE T TEST command sequence. You then select the variable, "average price for evening entrée." Next, enter in an "18" as Test Value and click on the OK button. (Remember that we selected only the "very likely" respondent cases earlier, and that selection will remain in place until we direct SPSS to clear it or make a different case selection.)

The resulting output is contained in Figure 16.6. When you look at it, you will notice that the information layout for the output is identical to that in the previous output table. It indicates that 72 respondents were selected, and the mean of their answers was calculated to be $34.06 (rounded up.) The output indicates our test value to be equal to 18, and the bottom contains 95% confidence intervals for the estimated population parameter. (The population parameter is the difference between the hypothesized mean and the sample mean, expected to be 0.) There is a mean difference of $16.0556, which was calculated by subtracting the hypothesized

> To test a hypothesis about a mean with SPSS, use the ANALYZE-COMPARE MEANS-ONE SAMPLE T TEST command sequence.

> **SPSS Student Assistant: Testing a Hypothesis for a Mean**

FIGURE 16.5
The SPSS Clickstream to
Test a Hypothesis about a
Mean

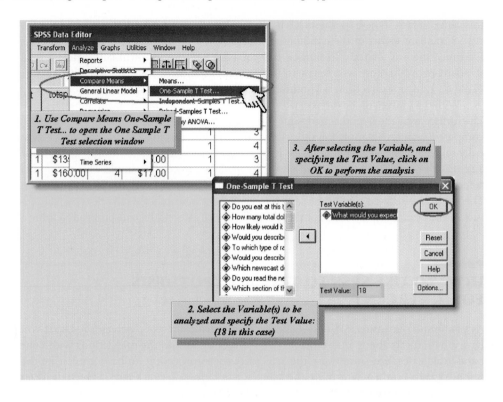

FIGURE 16.6
The SPSS Output for the
Test of a Hypothesis about
a Mean

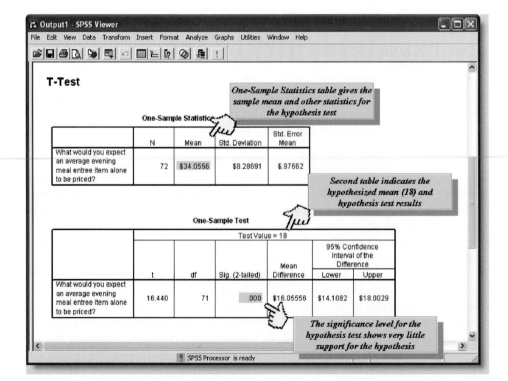

mean value (18) from the sample mean (34.0556), and the standard error is provided in the upper half ($.97662). A t value of 16.440 is determined by dividing 16.0556 by .97662. It is associated with a two-tailed significance level of 0.000. (For now, assume t value is the z value we have used in our formulas and explanations. We describe use of the t value in this Chapter 17.)

In other words, our Hobbit's Choice Restaurant sample finding of a willingness to pay an average of about $34 does not support the hypothesis of $18. The true mean is, in fact, quite a bit greater than $18. The 95% confidence interval for the population mean is $34 to $36, which we obtained by doing a one-sample t test to estimate this range as you learned to do earlier (and we dropped the cents off the amounts when we reported them).

If you were Jeff Dean, and you just learned that the hypothesis of $18 per entrée was not supported, and the true population mean was almost twice as large how would you feel? Surely, you would feel great because this satisfied the third and last condition specified by his researcher's model. Jeff should think seriously about buying a bottle of champagne.

USE SPSS FOR A HYPOTHESIS TEST FOR A MEAN

SPSS Student Assistant: SPSS Statistics Coach and Case Studies

We have just discovered that the likely patrons of Jeff's proposed Hobbit's Choice Restaurant expect to pay a great deal more than $18 per entrée, and this is very good news because the $18 level was Cory Roger's third condition stipulated for success of this new business venture. Let's see if the general population living in the metropolitan area expects to pay $18 per entrée. To perform this hypothesis test, you should unselect the sample so the test will be performed on the entire sample, and not just the very likely patrons of the Hobbit's Choice. That is, use the SELECT CASES-ALL CASES SPSS operation, and then use the clickstream in Figure 16.5 to instruct SPSS to perform this hypothesis test. Use the annotations for the ONE-SAMPLE T TEST output in Figure 16.6 to decipher the SPSS output that is created for the $18 per entrée hypothesis test using the entire sample. What have you found about the support for this hypothesis?

SUMMARY

This chapter began by distinguishing a sample statistic from its associated population parameter. We then introduced you to the concept of statistical inference, which is a set of procedures for generalizing the findings from a sample to the population. A key factor in inference is the sample size, n. It appears in statistical inference formulas because it expresses the amount of sampling error: Large samples have less sampling error than do small samples given the same variability. We illustrated the three inference types commonly used by marketing researchers. First, we described how a population parameter, such as a mean, can be estimated by using confidence intervals computed by application of the standard error formula. Second, we related how a researcher can use the sample findings to test a hypothesis about a mean or a percentage.

We used SPSS and the Hobbit's Choice Restaurant data to illustrate how you can direct SPSS to calculate 95% confidence intervals for the estimation of a mean as well as how to test a hypothesis about a mean. Both are accomplished with the SPSS menu item—ONE-SAMPLE T TEST procedure. For parameter estimation or test of a hypothesis with a percent, you can use SPSS to determine the percent, but you must use the formulas in this chapter to calculate the confidence interval or perform the significance test.

KEY TERMS

Statistics (p. 454)
Parameters (p. 454)
Inference (p. 454)
Statistical inference (p. 455)
Parameter estimation (p. 456)
Standard error (p. 457)
Standard error of the mean
  (p. 457)
Standard error of the percentage
  (p. 457)
Confidence intervals (p. 460)

Most commonly used level of
  confidence (p. 460)
Hypothesis (p. 467)
Hypothesis test (p. 467)
Intuitive hypothesis testing (p. 468)
Alternative hypothesis (p. 470)
Hypothesized population parameter
  (p. 470)
Sampling distribution concept
  (p. 471)
Directional hypothesis (p. 473)

REVIEW QUESTIONS/APPLICATIONS

1. What essential factors are taken into consideration when statistical inference takes place?
2. What is meant by "parameter estimation," and what function does it perform for a researcher?
3. How does parameter estimation for a mean differ from that for a percentage?
4. List the steps in statistical hypothesis testing. List the steps in intuitive hypothesis testing. How are they similar? How are they different?
5. When a researcher's sample evidence disagrees with a manager's hypothesis, which is right?
6. What does it mean when a researcher says that a hypothesis has been supported at the 95% confidence level?
7. Distinguish a directional from a nondirectional hypothesis, and provide an example of each.
8. Here are several computation practice exercises to help you identify which formulas pertain and learn how to perform the necessary calculations. In each case, perform the necessary calculations and write your answers in the last column.

Determine Confidence Intervals for Each of the Following

Sample Statistic	Sample Size	Confidence Level	Your Confidence Intervals?
Mean: 150 Std. dev.: 30	200	95%	_____
Percent: 67%	300	99%	_____
Mean: 5.4	250	99%	_____
Std. dev.: 0.5			
Percent: 25.8%	500	99%	_____

Test the Following Hypothesis and Interpret Your Findings

Hypothesis	Sample Findings	Confidence Level	Your Test Results
Mean = 7.5	Mean: 8.5 Std dev.: 1.2 n = 670	95%	_____
Percent = 86%	p = 95 n = 1000	99%	_____
Mean > 125	Mean: 135 Std dev.: 15 n = 500	95%	_____
Percent < 33%	p = 31 n = 120	99%	_____

9. The manager of the aluminum recycling division of Environmental Services wants a survey that will tell him how many households in the city of Seattle, Washington, will voluntarily wash out, store, and then transport all of their aluminum cans to a central recycling center located in the downtown area and open only on Sunday mornings. A random survey of 500 households determines that 20% of households would do so, and that each participating household expects to recycle about 100 cans monthly, with a standard deviation of 30 cans. What is the value of parameter estimation in this instance?

10. It is reported in the newspaper that a survey, sponsored by *Forbes* magazine, of *Fortune* 500 company executives has found that 75% believe that the United States trails Japan and Germany in automobile engineering. The article notes that executives were interviewed at a recent "Bring the U.S. Back to Competitiveness" symposium held on the campus of the University of Southern California. Why would it be incorrect for the article to report confidence intervals?

11. Alamo Rent-A-Car executives believe that Alamo accounts for about 50% of all Cadillacs that are rented. To test this belief, a researcher randomly identifies 20 major airports with on-site rental car lots. Observers are sent to each location and instructed to record the number of rental company Cadillacs observed in a four-hour period. About 500 are observed, and 30% are observed being returned to Alamo Rent-A-Car. What are the implications of this finding for the Alamo executives' belief?

CASE 16.1

DON'T YOU JUST HATE IT WHEN . . . ? (PART I)

This appears 1:17 A.M. on a laptop screen in an apartment just off campus.

> As can be seen in Exhibit 3, the net present value analysis clearly substantiates that the purchase of the capital equipment is more advantageous than subcontracting the production.
>
> Submitted by
> Marsha Robbins
> Senior, Marketing

Marsha: "Gawd, I hate finance. Now I need to do that econ paper."

This appears at 4:47 A.M. on Marsha's laptop screen.

> So, based on estimated fixed costs, variable costs, and the most likely revenues (refer to Figure 2), Acme will reach breakeven in about 2 years, with a 20% profit margin realized in the fifth year.
>
> Submitted by
> Marsha Robbins
> Senior, Marketing

Marsha thinks: "Gawd, I hate managerial economics."

The sounds of birds chirping come in through Marsha's window.

Marsha thinks: "Gawd, the birds are up, and I need to do that marketing research PowerPoint presentation for our project that we are doing for Pets, Pets, & Pets. Where's that SPSS analysis that Josh e-mailed me?"

Marsha opens the following file.

Statistics

		Times Visited PPP in Past Year	Amount Spent on Last Visit to PPP	How Likely to Buy at PPP Next Time (1–7 Scale)	Number of Pets Owned
N	Valid	162	162	162	162
	Missing	0	0	0	0
Mean		4.4	$18.2	5.3	1.64
Mode		4	15	4	1
Std. dev.		4.98	.85	1.50	.770
Std. error of Mean		.39	.30	.118	.061

Use Pets, Pets, & Pets how often?

		Frequency	Percent	Valid Percent	Cumulative Percent
Valid	Do Not Use Regularly	90	55.6	55.6	55.6
	Use Regularly	72	44.4	44.4	100.0
	Total	162	100.0	100.0	

Recommended PPP to a friend?

		Frequency	Percent	Valid Percent	Cumulative Percent
Valid	No	29	17.9	17.9	17.9
	Yes	133	82.1	82.1	100.0
	Total	162	100.0	100.0	

Recall seeing a PPP newspaper ad in the past month?

		Frequency	Percent	Valid Percent	Cumulative Percent
Valid	Yes	76	46.9	46.9	46.9
	No	86	53.1	53.1	100.0
	Total	162	100.0	100.0	

Marsha: "Oh my Gawd, what is this?" Marsha grabs her cell phone and speed dials.

Josh (sleepily): "Wha . . . Umm. Whassup? Who's calling?"

Marsha: "Wake up Dirtbag! That SPSS analysis you did is crap!"

Josh: "Oh, Marsh! Hey, the birds aren't even up yet, and you're ringing me out of bed."

Marsha: "Wrong. They're up, and so am I. We need to do the statistical inference presentation on the survey we did for Pets, Pets, & Pets in Dr. Z's marketing research class. You need to redo that SPSS analysis right and e-mail it to me PRONTO."

Josh: "No can do for three reasons. Never bought the book, don't have SPSS, and don't own a computer."

Marsha: "Gawd, I really hate this. What is this stuff you sent me?"

Josh: "When DZ turned Dizzy, I just dropped out. It was fun with the taste test, focus groups, and even questionnaire design, but when that SPSS stuff came up on his PowerPoint, I got lost. Besides, the season is in full swing, and I am the conference batting average and RBI leader. Coach Laval says the pro scouts are watching me every time I get up to bat. I could go in the first draft round."

Marsha: "Josh, the only draft I see is the one coming through the hole in your head. What is this stuff that you sent me?"

Josh: "All I could do is the "frequencies" on SPSS, and I clicked on the output items that seemed right. Then I saved it and e-mailed it to you from the computer lab."

Marsha: "Our agreement was that you would do the statistical inferences analysis on your set of questions, and I would present it. Get the book, read Chapter 16, get to the computer lab, and just do it right."

Josh: "No can do, Marsh. Breakfast training table is at 7:30, and Coach Laval wants me in the batting cage at 9. I need to get my ankle taped up by the trainers at 8:30. So I am busy until Dizzy's class at 10:30."

Marsha: "Okay, okay. Just get me the data file, and I'll do it."

Josh: "No can do, Marsh. I left the pin drive thingy you gave me in the computer in the lab, and it was not there when I went back for it the next day. I gotta go. So long." Clicks off.

Marsha thinks: "Gawd, I hate that guy!"

1. Dr. Z's requirement is for each team to present its "statistical inference" findings in class today. What analysis or analyses should have Josh done?

2. It is possible to make the presentation on the variables in output file. Do what Marsha needs to do, now.

AUTO ONLINE SURVEY (PART II)

You will find Case 15.2 (Part I) of the Auto Online survey on pages 448. You will need to refer to the questionnaire on these pages in order to perform the proper analysis with SPSS. You may assume that the respondents to this survey are representative of the population of automobile buyers who visited the Auto Online Web site during their vehicle purchase process.

1. In order to describe this population, estimate the population parameters for the following.
   a. How often they make purchases online.
   b. Number of visits they made to Auto Online.
   c. The percent who actually bought their vehicles from Auto Online.
   d. The percent of those who felt it was a better experience than buying at a traditional dealership.
   e. How do people feel about the Auto Online Web site (question 6 on the questionnaire)?

2. Auto Online principals have the following beliefs. Test these hypotheses.
   a. People will "strongly agree" to all eight statements concerning use of the Internet and purchase (question 3 on the questionnaire).
   b. Prior to buying a vehicle, people will visit the Auto Online Web site approximately 5 times.
   c. Just about everyone will say that buying a vehicle online is "a great deal better" than buying it at a traditional dealership.
   d. Those who buy their vehicles from Auto Online will be adults in their mid-30s.
   e. Those who buy from Auto Online will pay an average of $3500 below the sticker price, while those who buy elsewhere will pay only an average of $2000 less than the vehicle sticker price.

THE HOBBIT'S CHOICE RESTAURANT SURVEY INFERENTIAL ANALYSIS

This is your integrated case, described on pages 38–39.

Cory Rogers was pleased with Celeste Brown's descriptive analysis. Celeste had done all of the proper descriptive analyses, and she had copied the relevant tables and findings into a Word document with notations to which Cory could refer quickly.

Cory says, "Celeste, this is great work. I am going to Jeff Dean's in an hour to show him what we have found. In the meantime, I want you to look a bit deeper into the data. I have jotted down some items that I want you to analyze. This is the next step in understanding how the sample findings generalize to the population of the greater metropolitan area."

Your task here is to again take the role of Celeste Brown, marketing intern. Using the Hobbit's Choice Restaurant survey SPSS data set, perform the proper analysis, and interpret the findings for each of the following questions specified by Cory Rogers.

1. What are the population estimates for each of the following?
   a. Preference for "easy listening" radio programming
   b. Viewing of 10 P.M. local TV news
   c. Subscribe to *City Magazine*
   d. Average age of heads of households
   e. Average price paid for an entrée for an evening meal

2. Because Jeff Dean's restaurant will be upscale, it will appeal to high-income consumers. Jeff hopes that at least 25% of the households have an income level of $100,000 or higher. Test this hypothesis.

3. With respect to those who are "very likely" to patronize the Hobbit's Choice Restaurant, Jeff believes that they will either "very strongly" or "somewhat" prefer each of the following: (a) waitstaff with tuxedos, (b) unusual desserts, (c) large variety of entrees, (d) unusual entrees, (e) elegant décor, and (f) jazz combo music. Does the survey support or refute Jeff's hypotheses? Interpret your findings.

17

Testing for Differences between Two Groups or among More Than Two Groups

Market Segmentation in the New Zealand Wine Market

There are several ways to apply market segmentation, including demographics, benefits, and/or behavior. Recently, marketing researchers sought to detect and profile the market segments found in the New Zealand wine market,[1] where the competition is particularly intense and consumer tastes and behaviors are changing. Using past research on New Zealand wine drinker segments and applying analytical techniques, the researchers identified three distinct wine customer segments based on that amount of wine purchased and consumed per month; that is, the segmentation classification was based on the wine drinkers' behaviors. The three segments were labeled Light, Medium, and Heavy. New Zealand Light wine purchasers bought between 1 and 7 bottles in a typical month (average of 4.0 bottles per month); Medium purchasers bought between 8 and 20 bottles per month (average of 12.7 bottlers per month); and Heavy purchasers bought 21 bottles or more monthly (average of 28.6 bottles per month). In terms of size, the Heavy segment accounts for 57% of New Zealand wine drinkers, the Medium segment amounts to 33%, and the Light segment constitutes the remaining 10%.

The researchers then analyzed these three market segments for differences that might offer insight and/or provide some target marketing implications. For one, they discovered demographic differences between the three wine market segments. These are portrayed in the following graph. This graph shows definite differences

- To learn how differences are used for market segmentation decisions
- To understand when *t* tests or *z* tests are appropriate and why you do not need to worry about this issue
- To be able to test the differences between two percentages or means for two independent groups
- To know what is a pair samples difference test and when to use it
- To comprehend ANOVA and how to interpret ANOVA output
- To learn how to perform differences tests for means using SPSS

between Light and Heavy wine drinkers in New Zealand. The Heavy segment is clearly males who are married, older, and earning the highest income level. One the other hand, the Light segment is males or females, the majority of whom are married, but who are definitely younger and not typically earning the highest income level.

Research identifies market segments within the New Zealand wine market.

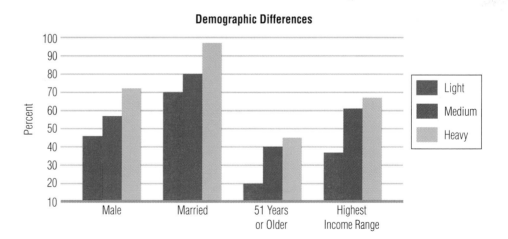

Other differences were found in the purchasing behaviors of the three segments. The following graph identifies the Heavy and Medium wine purchasers as buying their wine at a bottle store and/or directly from a winery by direct mail. The Light purchasers of wine, however, purchase less frequently from the winery and typically not by direct mail. They, too, purchase at bottle stores, but to a somewhat lesser degree than the two other market segments.

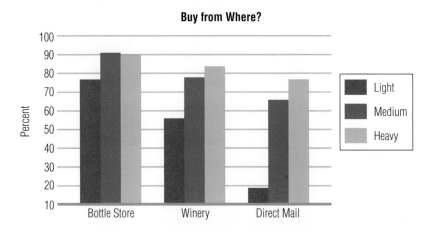

Next, the researchers investigated the types of wine purchased, and they found that about one-half of New Zealand wine drinkers drink at least two types of wine. Across all varieties of wine drinkers, there were segment differences in preferences for white versus red wine. As can be seen in the following graph, the Medium and Light wine segments purchases red and white wine about equally, while the Heavy segment has a slight preference for white wine.

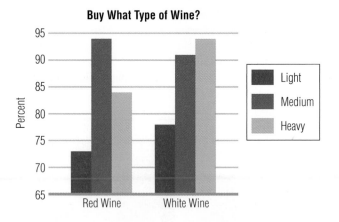

Finally, the researchers looked for differences in the New Zealand wine purchases criteria for buying a particular brand of wine. They found three factors that differed between the wine segments. Specifically, as can be seen in the graph, the market segment of Heavy wine purchasers places greater value on the history of the wine maker and the region in which the wine grapes are grown than do the Medium or Light wine segments. At the same time, while all segments place heavy importance on the wine company (or brand), the Heavy wine drinkers place more importance on this factor than do the other two segments.

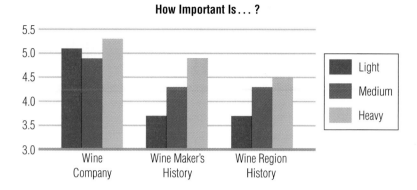

How Important Is...?

As you learned in Chapter 16, it is possible to make inferences about measures of central tendency such as means and percentages found in a random sample survey. These inferences take the form of confidence intervals or tests of hypotheses. A different type of inference concerns differences; that is, as we have described in our New Zealand wine purchasers example, the researcher can ask, "Are there statistically significant differences between two or more groups, and, if so, what are they?" In this chapter, we describe the logic of differences tests, and we show you how to use SPSS to conduct various types of differences tests.[2]

We begin this chapter discussing why differences are important to marketing managers, and we give some guidelines for researchers and managers when interpreting differences tests. Next, we introduce you to differences (percentages or means) between two independent groups, such as a comparison of high-speed cable versus DSL telephone Internet users on how satisfied they are with their Internet connection service. We next show you that it is possible to test the difference between the averages of two similarly scaled questions. For instance, do buyers rate a store higher in "merchandise selection" than they rate its "good values"? Finally, we introduce you to ANOVA, a scary name, but a simple way to compare the means of several groups simultaneously and to quickly spot patterns of significant differences. We provide formulas and numerical examples, and also show you examples of SPSS procedures and output using the Hobbit's Choice Restaurant survey data.

WHY DIFFERENCES ARE IMPORTANT

Perhaps one of the most vital marketing management concepts is market segmentation. In a nutshell, market segmentation holds that different types of consumers have different requirements, and these differences can be the bases of marketing strategies. Our New Zealand example revealed three wine segments with very different demographic, purchasing, and decision-making characteristics. As another example, the Iams Company, which markets pet foods, has approximately 12 different varieties of dry dog food geared to the dog's age (puppy versus adult), weight situation (normal versus overweight), and activity (active versus inactive). Toyota Motors has 17 models, including the two-seat

Market segmentation is based on differences between groups of consumers.

Spyder sports car, the four-door Avalon luxury sedan, the Highlander SUV, and the Tacoma truck. Even Boeing Airlines has seven different types of commercial jets and a separate business jets division for corporate travel. Let's look at differences from the consumer's side. Everyone washes his or her hands, but the kind of soap required differs for weekend gardeners with potting soil under their fingernails, factory workers whose hands are dirty with solvents, preschoolers who have sticky drink residue on their hands and faces, or aspiring beauty princesses who wish their hands to look absolutely flawless. The needs and requirements of each of these market segments differ greatly from the others, and an astute marketer will customize his or her marketing mix to each target market's unique situation.[3]

These differences, of course, are quite obvious, but as competition becomes more intense, with prolific market segmentation and target marketing being the watchword of most companies in an industry, there is a need to investigate differences among consumer groups for consumer marketers and business establishments for business-to-business (B2B) marketers. One commonly used basis for market segmentation is the discovery of statistically significant, meaningful, and stable differences that are actionable. We have dissected this statement into its four contingent requirements with a brief explanation of each. Refer to Table 17.1.

We will discuss each requirement briefly. In our comments, we will assume that we are working with a pharmaceuticals company that markets cold remedies.

To be potentially useful to the marketing researcher or manager, differences must, at minimum, be statistically significant.

The differences must be significant. As you know, the notion of statistical significance underpins marketing research. **Statistical significance of differences** means that the differences found in the sample(s) may be assumed to exist in the population(s) from which the random samples are drawn. So, the differences that are apparent between and among market segments must be subjected to tests that assess the statistical significance of these differences. This is the topic of this chapter, and we will endeavor to

TABLE 17.1	The Four Contingent Requirements of Differences between Groups to Be Useful for Market Segmentation	
Requirement	**Explanation**	**Cold Remedy Example**
First, the differences must be statistically significant.	Statistically significant differences should be demonstrated between the groups.	On a scale of 1 to 10, how important is it to you that your cold medicine relieves your . . . Group / Congestion?* / Muscle Aches?* 1 / 8.2 / 5.3 2 / 5.4 / 9.1 *Average rating
Second, the differences must be meaningful.	The differences between the market segments should be of such a magnitude that the marketer can target them individually.	Group 1 suffers greatly from congestion problems when they have colds, while Group 2 suffers from muscle aches and pains to a great extent. A congestion-relief additive will not reduce aches, nor will a pain relief additive reduce congestion with cold sufferers.
Third, the differences must be stable.	The differences should not be short-term or transitory.	Group 1 sufferers have respiratory weaknesses or situations that are aggravated when they suffer from colds; whereas, Group 2 does not have these preconditions, but they are physically more active, so muscle aches and pains are more of a concern to them.
Fourth, the differences must be actionable.	The market segment groups should be identified and suitable for target marketing.	Group 1's history of respiratory problems makes it identifiable: this group will be vigilant for congestion relief. Group 2's physical activity profile is identifiable, and since they value physical activity, they will be looking for cold remedies that allow them to remain as active as their cold infections permit.

teach you how to perform and interpret tests of the statistical significance of differences in it. With our cold remedy marketer, we could ask cold sufferers "How important is it that your cold remedy relieves your. . . . "The respondents would respond using an scale of 1 = not important and 10 = very important for each cold symptom such as fever, sore throat, congestion, aching muscles, etc. and statistical tests such as those described in this chapter would determine if the responses were significantly different. In Table 17.1, we have noted two groups (1 and 2) that have statistically significant differences. Group 1 greatly desires congestion relief, whereas Group 2 more greatly desires relief from aches and pains associated with their colds.

The differences must be meaningful. A finding of statistical significance in no way guarantees "meaningful" difference. In fact, with the proliferation of data mining analysis due to scanner data with tens of thousands of records, online surveys that garner thousands of respondents, and other ways to capture very large samples, there is a very real danger of finding a great deal of statistical significance that is not meaningful. The reason for this danger is that statistical significance is determined to a very great deal by the sample size.[4] You will see in this chapter by examining the formulas we provide, that the sample size, n, is instrumental in the calculation of z, the determinant of the significance level. Large samples, those in excess of 1000 per sample group, often yield statistically significant results when the absolute differences between the groups are quite small. A **meaningful difference** is one that the marketing manager can potentially use as a basis for marketing decisions. We will offer some guidelines on what might be statistically significant and "meaningful" differences later in the chapter.

With our cold remedy example, we have found meaningful differences because the ingredients to cold remedies are symptom-specific, meaning that some ingredients relieve congestion, while others relieve aches and pains. Granted, the pharmaceutical company could include both ingredients, but the congestion sufferers do not want an ingredient that might make them drowsy from the strong pain relief ingredient and the aches and pains sufferers do not want their throats and nasal passages to feel dry and

To be useful to the marketing researcher or manager, differences must, if statistically significant, be meaningful.

Differences in cold sufferers are used as market segmentation bases by pharmaceutical companies.

uncomfortable from the decongestant ingredient. These differences are meaningful both to the customer groups as well as to the pharmaceutical manufacturer.

The differences must be stable. Stability refers to the requirement that we are not working with a short-term or transitory set of differences. Thus, a **stable difference** is one that will be in place for the foreseeable future. The persistent congestion experienced by Group 1 is most probably due to some respiratory weakness or condition. They may have preconditions such as allergies or breathing problems, or they may be exposed to heavy pollution or some other factor that affects their respiration in general. With Group 2, they may be very active people who do no have respiration weaknesses, but who value active lifestyle practices such as regular exercise, or their occupations may require a good deal of physical activity. In either case, there is a very good possibility that when a cold strikes, the sufferer will experience the same discomfort, either congestion or muscle aches, time and time again; that is, the differences between the two groups are stable. The pharmaceuticals company can develop custom-designed versions of their cold relief product because they know from experience and research that certain consumers will be consistent (stable) in seeking certain types of relief or specific product benefits when they suffer from colds.

The differences must be actionable. Market segmentation requires that standard or innovative market segmentation bases are used, and that these bases uniquely identify the various groups so they can be analyzed and put in the marketer's targeting mechanisms. An **actionable difference** means that the marketer can focus various marketing strategies and tactics, such as advertising, on the market segments to accentuate the differences between the segments. There are a great many segmentation bases that are actionable, such as demographics, lifestyles, and product benefits. In our example, among the many symptoms manifested by cold sufferers, we have identified two meaningful and stable groups, so a cold remedy product line that concentrates on each one of these separately is possible. A quick glance at the cold remedies section of your local drug store will verify the actionability of these market segments of cold symptoms.

You may be confused about meaningful and actionable differences. Recall, that we used the words *potentially use* in our definition of a meaningful difference. With our cold remedies example, a pharmaceutical could potentially develop and market a cold remedy that was specific to every type of cold symptom as experienced by every demographic group and further identified by lifestyle differences. For example, there could be a cold medicine to alleviate the runny noses of teenage girls who participate in high school athletics, and a different one for the sniffles in teenage boys who play high school sports. But, it would be economically unjustifiable to offer so many different cold medicines, so the pharmaceutical companies, and other marketers, must assess actionability based on market segment size and profitability considerations. Nevertheless, the fundamental differences are based on statistical significance, meaningfulness, and stability assessments.

To be sure, the bulk of this chapter deals strictly with statistically significant differences, because it is the beginning point for market segmentation and savvy target marketing. Meaningfulness, stability, and actionability are not statistical issues; rather, they are judgment calls by the marketing manager.

SMALL SAMPLE SIZES: THE USE OF A t TEST OR A z TEST AND HOW SPSS ELIMINATES THE WORRY

Most of the equations related in this chapter will lead to the computation of a z value. But, there are special instances in which the z test is not appropriate. We pointed out in Chapter 16 that computation of the z value makes the assumption that the raw data

---

To be useful to the marketing researcher or manager, differences must, if statistically significant and meaningful, be stable.

To be useful to the marketing researcher or manager, differences must, if statistically significant, meaningful, and stable, be actionable.

for most statistics under scrutiny have normal or bell-shaped distributions. However, statisticians have shown that this normal-curve assumption is invalid when the sample size is 30 observations or less. In this instance, a t value is computed instead of a z value. The **t test** is defined as the statistical inference test to be used with small samples sizes ($n \leq 30$). Instead of a constant normal distribution, the t test relies on Student's t distribution. The t distribution's shape is determined by the number of degrees of freedom defined as being equal to the sample size minus the number of population parameters estimated, which is ($n - 1$) here because the population parameter is the difference between the two population means. The smaller the number of degrees of freedom, the more spread out the curve becomes. It still retains a bell shape, but it flattens out a little bit with each successive loss of a sample unit below 30. Any instance when the sample size is 30 or greater requires the use of a **z test**.

The great advantage to using statistical analysis routines on a computer is that they are programmed to compute the correct statistic. In other words, you do not need to decide whether you want the program to compute a t value, a z value, or some other value. With SPSS, the analyses of differences are referred to as "t tests," but now that you realize that SPSS will always determine the correct significance level whether it is a t or a z, you do not need to worry about which statistic to use. The talent you need to acquire is how to interpret the significance level that is reported by SPSS. We have provided Marketing Research Insight 17.1 to introduce you to a "flag-waving" analogy that students have told us is helpful in this regard.

> The t test should be used when the sample size is 30 or less.

> Most computer statistical programs report only the t value because it is identical to the z value with large samples.

MARKETING RESEARCH INSIGHT

PRACTICAL APPLICATION

17.1 Signal-Flag Waving and Significance in Statistical Analysis

The output from statistical procedures in all software programs can be envisioned as "signal-flag-waving" devices. When the signal flag is waving briskly, statistical significance is present. Then, and only then, is it warranted to look at the findings more closely to determine the pattern of the findings; but if the flag is not waving, your time will be wasted by looking any further. To read statistical flags, you need to know two things. First, where is the flag located? Second, how much does it need to wave for you to pay attention to it and to delve further into the analysis in order to interpret it?

Where Is the Flag?
Virtually every statistical test or procedure involves the computation of some critical statistic, and that statistic is used to determine the statistical significance of the findings. The crit-

ical statistic's name changes depending on the procedure and its underlying assumptions, but usually the statistic is identified as a letter: z, t, F, or something similar. Statistical analysis computer programs will automatically identify and compute the correct statistic, so although it is helpful to know ahead of time what statistic will be computed, it is not essential to know it. Moreover, the statistic is not the flag; rather it is just a computation necessary to raise the flag. You might think of the computed statistic as the flagpole.

The computer program will also raise the flag on the flagpole, but its name changes a bit depending on the procedure. The flags, called p values by statisticians, are identified by the terms "significance" or "probability." Sometimes abbreviations such as "Sig" or "Prob" are used to economize on the output. To find the flag, locate the "Sig" or "Prob" designation in the analysis, and look at the number that is associated with it. The number will be a decimal perhaps as low as 0.000 but ranging to as high as 1.000. When you locate it, you have found the statistical significance flag.

(continued)

How Much Is the Flag Waving?

If the National Hurricane Center announced that there is a 95% chance that a hurricane will make landfall in the location where you are staying, you would definitely know that hurricane force winds are imminent; that is, gentle winds blow all the time, and we are not concerned about them; but when hurricane-force winds build, we become concerned, and we pay a great deal of attention to the weather. For the purposes of this textbook, we have adopted the 95% level of confidence; that is, if you were 95% confident that a hurricane was imminent, you would take significant steps to avoid being in harm's way. In other words, it would definitely get your attention. As we noted above, the significance or probability values reported in statistical analysis output range from .0000 to 1.000, and they indicate the degree of support for the null hypothesis (no differences). If you just take 1 minus the reported significance level—for example if the sig level is .03, you would take 1 − .03 to come up with .97, or 97%—it is the level of confidence for our finding. Any time this value is 95% or greater, we know that the flag is waving frantically to catch your attention.

TESTING FOR SIGNIFICANT DIFFERENCES BETWEEN TWO GROUPS

There are statistical tests for when a researcher wants to compare the means or percentages of two different groups or samples.

Often, as we have done in our pharmaceuticals example, a researcher will want to compare two groups that exist in the same sample; that is, the researcher may have two independent groups such as walk-ins versus loyal customers, and he or she may want to compare their answers to the same question. The question may be either a categorical scale or a metric scale. A categorical scale requires that the researcher compare percentages, while he or she will compare means when a metric scale is involved. As you know by now, the formulas differ depending on whether percentages or means are being tested.

Differences Between Percentages with Two Groups (Independent Samples)

Independent samples are treated as representing two potentially different populations.

When a marketing researcher is interested in making comparisons between two groups of respondents to determine whether or not there are statistically significant differences between them, in concept, he or she is considering them as two potentially different populations. The question to be answered then becomes whether or not their respective population parameters are different. But, as always, a researcher can work only with the sample results. Therefore, the researcher must fall back on statistical significance to determine whether the difference that is found between the two sample statistics is a true population difference. You will shortly discover that the logic of differences tests is very similar to the logic of hypothesis testing that you learned about in Chapter 16.

Again, we refer to the intuitive approach you use every day when comparing two things to make an inference. Let us assume you have read a *Business Week* article about college recruiters that quotes a Louis Harris poll of 100 randomly selected companies, indicating that 65% of them will be visiting college campuses to interview business majors. The article goes on to say that a similar poll taken last year with 300 companies found that only 40% will interview. You cannot be completely confident of a conclusion that more companies will interview this year because of sampling error. If the difference between the percentages was very large, say 80% for this year and 20% for last year, you would be more inclined to believe that a true change had occurred. But if you found that this large difference was based on small sample sizes, you would be less confident with your inference that last year's and this year's college recruiting are different. Intuitively, you have taken into account two critical factors in determining whether statistically significant differences exist between a percentage or a mean compared between two samples: the magnitude of the difference between the compared statistic (65% vs. 40%) and sample sizes (100 vs. 300).

Are your graduating college students' job prospects better this year than last year? Yes, if significantly more companies decide to visit college campuses.

To test whether a true difference exists between two group percentages, we test the **null hypothesis** or the hypothesis that the difference in their population parameters is equal to zero. The alternative hypothesis is that there is a true difference between them. To perform the test of **significance of differences between two percentages**, each representing a separate group (sample) the first step requires a "comparison" of the two percentages. By "comparison," we mean that you find the arithmetic difference between them. The second step requires that this difference be translated into a number of standard errors away from the hypothesized value of zero. Once the number of standard errors is known, knowledge of the area under the normal curve will yield an assessment of the probability of support for the null hypothesis.

We realize that it is confusing to keep in mind the null hypothesis and the alternative hypothesis and to understand all these equations as well. Just as in Chapter 16, where we provided a Marketing Research Insight on what is an alternative hypothesis for a hypothesis test, we have provided one in this chapter that describes what is the alternative hypothesis in the case the differences tests that are described in this chapter.

For a percentage, the equation is as follows:

With a differences test, the null hypothesis states there is no difference between the percents (or means) being compared.

Formula for Significance of the Difference between Two Percentages

$$z = \frac{p_1 - p_2}{s_{p_1 - p_2}}$$

where

p_1 = percentage found in sample 1
p_2 = percentage found in sample 2
$s_{p_1 - p_2}$ = standard error of the difference between two percentages

MARKETING
RESEARCH
INSIGHT

17.2 What Is the Alternative Hypothesis for a Differences Test?

In Chapter 16, Marketing Research Insight 16.4, "What Is an Alternative Hypothesis?" introduced you to the concept of an alternative hypotheses. To refresh your memory, the alternative hypothesis takes in all possible cases that are not treated by the stated hypothesis.

With differences tests, the stated hypothesis, called the "null hypothesis" is that the arithmetic difference between one parameter (e.g., mean) and another one is zero; that is, the statistical test begins with the assumption that the two means (or percentages) are exactly the same value. So, the alternative hypothesis of a differences test is that they are not the same value. In other words, the difference is not equal to zero.

Here are the stated and alternative hypotheses for the two types of differences tests described in this chapter.

STATED HYPOTHESIS	ALTERNATIVE HYPOTHESIS
DIFFERENCES BETWEEN TWO MEANS HYPOTHESIS	
No difference exists between means of two groups (populations).	A difference does exist between the means of two groups (populations).
The mean of one group (population) is greater than the mean of another group (population).	The mean of one group (population) is less than or equal to the mean of another group (population).
DIFFERENCES IN MEANS AMONG MORE THAN TWO GROUPS	
No difference exists between the means of all paired groups (populations).	A difference exists between the means of at least one pair of groups (populations).

The standard error of the difference between two percentages combines the standard error of the percentage for both samples, and it is calculated with the following formula:

With a differences test, you test the null hypothesis that no differences exist between the two group means (or percentages).

Formula for the Standard Error of the Difference between Two Percentages

$$s_{p_1 - p_2} = \sqrt{\frac{p_1 x q_1}{n_1} + \frac{p_2 x q_2}{n_2}}$$ ← i. that haveot/doo것|no

Again, if you compare these formulas to the ones we used in hypothesis testing, you will see two departures, yet the logic is identical. First, in the numerator, we subtract one sample's statistic (p_2) from the other sample's statistic (p_1) just as we subtracted the hypothesized percent from the sample percent in hypotheses testing. You should have noticed that we use the subscripts 1 and 2 to refer to the two different sample statistics. The second difference comes in the form of the sampling distribution that is expressed in the denominator. The sampling distribution under consideration now is the assumed sampling distribution of the differences between the percentage rather than the simple standard error of a percentage used in hypothesis testing; that is, the assumption has been made that the differences have been computed for comparisons of the two sample statistics for many repeated samplings. If the null hypothesis is true, this distribution of differences follows the normal curve with a mean equal to zero and a standard error equal to one. Stated somewhat differently, the procedure requires us, as before, to accept the (null) hypothesis as true until it lacks support from the statistical test. Consequently, the differences of a multitude of comparisons of the two sample percentages generated from many, many samplings would average zero. In other words, our sampling distribution is now the distribution of the difference between one sample and the other, taken many, many times.[5] The following example will walk you through the point we just made.

Here is how you would perform the calculations for the Harris poll on companies coming to campus to hire college seniors. Recall that last year's poll with 300 companies reported that 40% were visiting campuses, while this year's poll with 100 companies reported that 65% were visiting campuses.

Computation of the Significance of the Difference between $p_1 = 65\%$ and $p_2 = 40\%$ ($n_1 = 100$ and $n_2 = 300$)

$$z = \frac{p_1 - p_2}{s_{p_1 - p_2}}$$
$$= \frac{65 - 40}{\sqrt{\dfrac{65 \times 35}{100} + \dfrac{40 \times 60}{300}}}$$
$$= \frac{25}{\sqrt{22.75 + 12.55}}$$
$$= \frac{25}{5.94}$$
$$= 4.21$$

We compare the computed z value with our standard z of 1.96 for a 95% level of confidence, and the computed z of 4.21 is larger than 1.96. A computed z value that is larger than the standard z value of 1.96 amounts to no support for the null hypothesis at the 95% level of confidence. So, there is a statistically significant difference between the two percentages, and we are confident that if we repeated this comparison many, many times with a multitude of independent samples, we would conclude that there is a significant difference in at least 95% of these replications. Of course, we would never do many, many replications, but this is the statistician's basis for the level of significance.

It is a simple matter to apply the formulas to percentages to determine the significance of their differences, for all that is needed is the sample size of each group. We have provided Marketing Research Insight 17.3, which uses the percentage agreement to various life style statements by samples of consumers in each of four different countries. Our Marketing Research Insight highlights the significantly different distinctions of each group.

MARKETING RESEARCH INSIGHT

GLOBAL APPLICATION

17.3 Research Reveals Global Differences in Lifestyles

As was noted in the introduction to this chapter, market segmentation is a vital tool in the marketing manager's neverending quest to stay ahead of the competition. While there are several bases for market segmentation, a particular favorite of those competing in consumer and services markets is lifestyle segmentation. There are a number of proprietary market segmentation

systems, and every marketing researcher has the capability of executing his or her own lifestyle segmentation study.

Recently, researchers applied lifestyle segmentation techniques on a global level.[6] They used members of consumer panels as well as random digit dialing in some areas to survey representative households in four countries: China, Japan, the United Kingdom, and the United States of America. Although market segmentation research can require highly sophisticated and complex analysis techniques, the researchers opted to take a

(continued)

decidedly more basic approach and to work with the percent of agreement expressed by respondents to a number of lifestyle statements. Comparing the percentages across these four countries revealed important differences that provide interesting market segmentation profiles for each country's consumers versus those in the other three countries. Because graphical presentations are often very helpful, we have created the following visual presentations as well as statements that distinguish each country's dominant lifestyle characteristics.

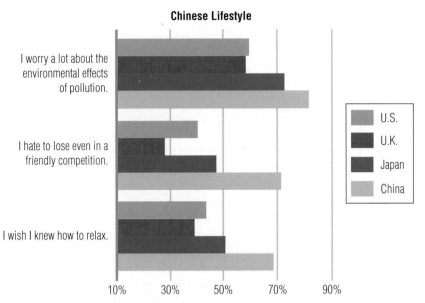

Profile: Chinese consumers worry about pollution; they are highly competitive; and they have trouble relaxing.

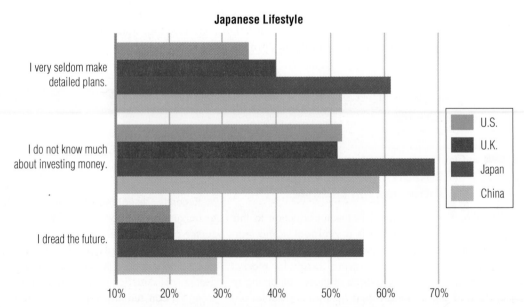

Profile: Japanese consumers dread the future, perhaps because they do not know much about investing money, and they definitely do not plan ahead.

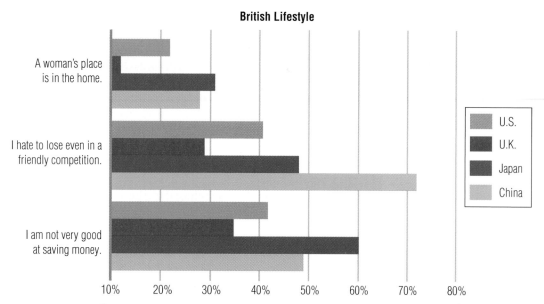

Profile: U.K. residents are the best at saving money; they are not competitive; and they certainly do not expect women to stay at home.

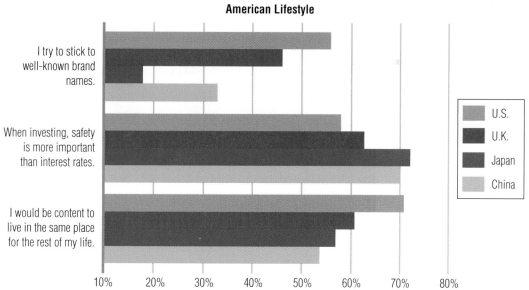

Profile: Americans are loyal to well-known brands, they gravitate to more risky investments, and they are most content to stay where they are currently living.

The statements involved in this study are general lifestyle statements, meaning that they are not specific to a product or service category, or to specific brands, companies, or organizations. Nonetheless, this marketing research insight demonstrates how differences analyses can show important distinctions between the attitudes, opinions, and general concerns of consumers who are living in different regions of the globe.

CALCULATIONS TO DETERMINE SIGNIFICANT DIFFERENCES BETWEEN PERCENTS

You can now perform your own tests of the differences between two percentages using the formulas we have provided and described. A local health club has just finished a media blitz for new memberships. Over the past month, the health club has run advertisements in the newspaper, on the local television news channels, on its Web site, on two different FM radio stations, and in the Yellow Pages. Whenever a prospective new member came to one of the health club's facilities, he or she was asked to fill out a short questionnaire, and one question asked the person to indicate what ads he or she saw in the past month. Some of these prospects joined the health club, while some did not. At the end of the 30 days, a staff member performed the following tabulations.

	Joined the Health Club	Did not Join the Health Club
Total	100	30
Recall newspaper ads	45	15
Recall FM radio station ads	89	20
Recall Yellow Pages ads	16	5
Recall local TV news ads	21	6

Use your knowledge of the test of the significance of the difference between two percents to ascertain if there are any significant differences in this data. What are the implications of your findings with respect to the effectiveness of the various advertising media used during the membership recruitment ad blitz?

Using SPSS for Differences Between Percentages of Two Groups

SPSS does not perform tests of the significance of the difference between the percentages of two groups, but you can use SPSS to generate the relevant information and perform a hand calculation.

As is the case with most statistical analysis programs, SPSS does not perform tests of the significance of the difference between the percentages of two groups. You can, however, use SPSS to determine the sample percentage on your variable of interest along with its sample size. Repeat this descriptive analysis for the other sample, and you will have all the values required (p_1, p_2, n_1, and n_2) to perform the calculations by hand or in a spreadsheet program. (Recall that you can compute q_1 and q_2, based on the "$p + q = 100$" relationship.)

Differences Between Means with Two Groups (Independent Samples)

The procedure for testing **significance of difference between two means**, from two different groups (either two different samples or two different groups in the same sample) is identical to the procedure used in testing two percentages. As you can easily guess, however, the equations differ because a metric scale is involved.

Here is the equation for the test of difference between two sample means:

If the null hypothesis is true, when you subtract one group mean from the other, the result should be about zero.

Formula for Significance of the Difference between Two Means

$$z = \frac{\bar{x}_1 - \bar{x}_2}{s_{\bar{x}_1 - \bar{x}_2}}$$

where

$\bar{x}_1$ = mean found in sample 1
$\bar{x}_2$ = mean found in sample 2
$s_{\bar{x}_1 - \bar{x}_2}$ = standard error of the difference between two means

The standard error of the difference is easy to calculate and again relies on the variability that has been found in the samples and their sizes. Because we are working with means, we use the standard deviations in the formula for the standard error of a difference between two means:

Formula for the Standard Error of the Difference between Two Means

$$s_{\bar{x}_1 - \bar{x}_2} = \sqrt{\frac{s_1^2}{n_1} + \frac{s_2^2}{n_2}}$$

use w/ samples greater than 30.

Here are formulas for the standard errors of the difference between two means and between two percentages.

where

s_1 = standard deviation in sample 1
s_2 = standard deviation in sample 2
n_1 = size of sample 1
n_2 = size of sample 2

To illustrate how significance of difference computations are made, we use the following example that answers the question "Do male teens and female teens drink different amounts of sports drinks?" In a recent survey, teenagers were asked to indicate how many 20-ounce bottles of sports drinks they consume in a typical week. The descriptive statistics revealed that on average males consume 9 bottles and females consume 7.5. The respective standard deviations were found to be 2 and 1.2. Both samples were of size 100. Applying this information to the formula for the test of statistically significant differences, we get the following:

Computation of the Significance of the Difference between $\bar{x} = 9.0$ and $\bar{x}_2 = 7.5$ ($n_1 = 100$ and $n_2 = 100$)

$$z = \frac{\bar{x}_1 - \bar{x}_2}{\sqrt{\frac{s_1^2}{n_1} + \frac{s_2^2}{n_2}}}$$

$$= \frac{9.0 - 7.5}{\sqrt{\frac{2^2}{100} + \frac{1.2^2}{100}}}$$

$$= \frac{1.5}{\sqrt{.04 + 0.144}}$$

$$= \frac{1.5}{0.233}$$

$$= 6.43$$

Here are the calculations for a test of the difference between the means of two groups.

Figure 17.1 indicates how these two samples compare on the sampling distribution assumed to underlie this particular example. In the bottom of the figure, we have provided the standard error of the difference curve, and you know the probability of support for the null hypothesis of no difference between the two means is less than 0.001 because the large number of standard errors (6.43) calculated to exist for this example is much greater than 2.58.

How do you interpret this test for significance of differences? As always, the sampling distribution concept underlies our interpretation. If the hypothesis were true, were we to draw many, many samples and do this explicit comparison each time, then 95% of differences would fall within ± 1.96 standard errors of zero. Of course, only one comparison can be made, and you have to rely on the sampling distribution concept and

FIGURE 17.1

A Significant Difference Exists between the Two Means Because z Is Calculated to Be Greater Than 1.96 (95% Level of Confidence)

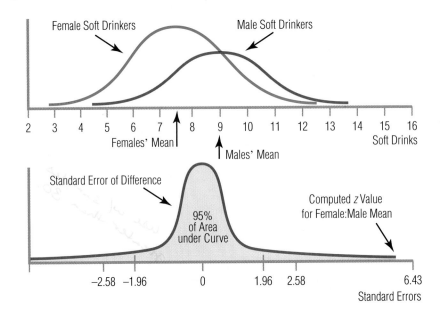

its attendant assumptions to determine whether this one particular instance of information supports or refutes the hypothesis of no significant differences found between the means (or percentages) of your two groups.

Directional hypotheses are also feasible in the case of tests of statistically significant differences. The procedure is identical to directional hypotheses that are stipulated in hypothesis tests; that is, you must first look at the sign of the computed z value to check that it is consistent with your hypothesized direction. Then, you would use a cutoff z value such as 2.33 standard errors for the 99% level of confidence because only one tail of the sampling distribution is being used.

The Hobbit's Choice Restaurant Survey: How to Perform an Independent Samples Significance of Differences between Means Test with SPSS

In the previous chapter on statistical inference, we illustrated the use of SPSS to answer some critical questions on the survival potential of Jeff Dean's The Hobbit's Choice Restaurant. You should recall that we discovered that the survey held good news, as all three criteria specified by Cory Rogers, Research Project Director, were met.

To demonstrate an independent samples significance test, we will take up Jeff's questions on how to promote the Hobbit's Choice Restaurant. One question Jeff voiced during the problem-definition stage was whether or not he should use the *City Magazine* as an advertising vehicle. The questionnaire asked if respondents subscribed or did not subscribe to *City Magazine*, so we have two groups: subscribers and nonsubscribers. We can test the mean of the likelihood of patronizing the Hobbit's Choice Restaurant. This construct was measured on a 5-point scale, where 1 = very likely and 5 = very unlikely.

The clickstream that directs SPSS to perform an independent-samples t test of the significance of the difference between means is displayed in Figure 17.2. As you can see, you begin with the ANALYZE-COMPARE MEANS-INDEPENDENT SAMPLES T-TEST menu sequence. This sequence opens up the selection menu, and the "likelihood of patronizing Hobbit's Choice (likely)" is clicked into the "Test variable" area, while the "Subscribe to City Magazine (citymag)" variable

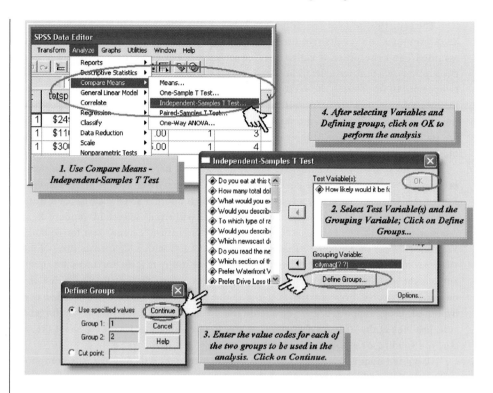

FIGURE 17.2
The SPSS Clickstream to Obtain an Independent-Samples *t* Test

SPSS Student Assistant: Assessing Differences between Means for two Groups (Independent)

To determine the significance of the difference in the means of two groups with SPSS, use the ANALYZE–COMPARE MEANS–INDEPENDENT SAMPLES T-TEST menu sequence.

is clicked into the "Grouping Variable" box. Using the "Define Groups" button, a window opens to let us identify the codes of the two groups (1 = yes and 2 = no). This sets up the t-test, and a click on OK executes it.

The annotated output is found in Figure 17.3. The first table reveals that the mean of the 181 *City Magazine* subscribers is 3.71, while the mean for the 219 nonsubscribers is 2.42.

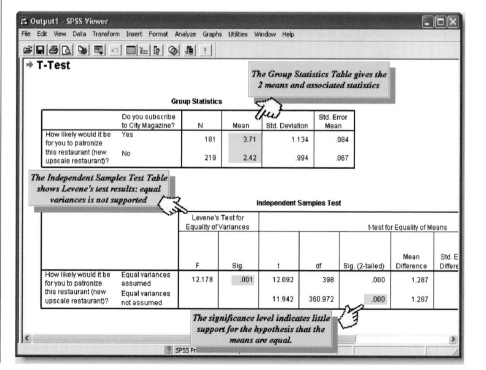

FIGURE 17.3
SPSS Output for an Independent-Samples *t* Test

The statistical test for the difference between the two means is given next. However, SPSS computes the results two different ways. One is identified as the "equal variances assumed," and the other is called the "equal variances not assumed." In our previous descriptions, we omitted a detail involved in tests for the significance of difference between two means. In some cases, the variances (standard deviations) of the two samples are about the same; that is, they are not significantly different. If so, you can use the formula pertaining to the equal variances (same variance for both samples), but if the standard deviations are statistically significant in their differences, you should use the unequal variances line on the output.

How do you know which to use? The null hypothesis here is that there is no difference between the variances (standard deviations), and it is tested with an F value printed in the top row of the independent samples test table. The F test is another statistical test, and it is the proper one here. (Recall that we stated earlier that SPSS will always select and compute the correct statistical test.) The F value is based on a procedure called "Levene's Test for Equality of Variances." In our output, the F value is identified as 12.178 with a Sig (probability) of 0.001 (flag waving). The probability reported here is the probability that the variances are equal, so anytime the probability is greater than, say 0.05, you would use the equal variance line on the output. If the probability associated with the F value is small, say 0.05 or less, the variances null hypothesis is not supported, and you should use the unequal variance line. If you forget this rule, just look at the standard deviations, and try to remember that if they are about the same size, you would use the equal variances t value.

Using the unequal variance estimate information, you will find that the computed t value is 11.942, and the associated probability of support for the null hypothesis of no difference between the *City Magazine* subscribers' mean and the nonsubscribers' mean is .000. In other words, they differ significantly. Subscribers are more likely to patronize the Hobbit's Choice Restaurant. So, the *City Magazine* would definitely be an advertising vehicle that targets potential customers.

Active Learning

PERFORM MEANS DIFFERENCES ANALYSIS WITH SPSS

You have just observed how to perform an independent-samples *t* test with SPSS using your Hobbit's Choice Restaurant survey data. For this active learning exercise, determine if there is a difference in the total monthly restaurant expenditures for the subscribers to City Magazine versus the nonsubscribers. Use the clickstream instruction in Figure 17.2 to direct SPSS to perform this analysis, and use the annotations on the independent-samples *t* test output provided in Figure 17.3 to interpret your findings.

DIFFERENCES BETWEEN TWO MEANS WITHIN THE SAME SAMPLE (PAIRED SAMPLE)

You can test the significance of the difference between two means for two different questions answered by the same respondents using the same scale.

Occasionally, a researcher will want to test for differences between the means for two variables within the same sample. For example, in our pharmaceutical company cold remedy situation described earlier in this chapter, a survey can be used to determine "How important is it that your cold remedy relieves your . . ." using a scale of 1 = not important and 10 = very important for each cold symptom. The question then becomes, "Are any two average importance levels significantly different?" To deter-

17.4

How Do Business Executives Perceive Their Own Business Ethics?

With recent revelations of accounting books "cooking," insider trading, and other unethical business practices, emphasis has been placed on understanding the ethics of senior executives. When one studies ethics, one finds that there are a number of principles or circumstances in which ethical practices are prescribed by a rule. For instance, there is the Golden Rule that stipulates that you should "do unto others as you would have them do unto you." There is the "Professional Ethic" rule that says a businessperson should do only those acts that can be explained by a committee of peers, and there is the Conventionalist Ethic rule that specifies that a person should act only according to those practices that do not violate the law.

In an attempt to better understand the ethical stances of American businesspersons, a researcher surveyed a sample of vice presidents listed in *Standard and Poor's Register*.[7] He found that the ethical standard that most all vice presidents agreed with is the Golden Rule, while the rule they most disagreed with is the "Revelation Ethic,"

which says that businesspersons should pray or otherwise commune with a higher power to have the correct decision or pathway revealed to them. There were eight rules generally agreed with and six generally disagreed with. The six negative agreement rules were all arguably injurious to parties, as for example, the case of the "Means-Ends Ethic," which states that unscrupulous means are acceptable if the ends are sufficiently valuable or desirable.

The businessperson respondents were asked to indicate how strongly they believed other executive to subscribe to these ethical rules, and in every case of the eight "positive" ethical rules, the businessperson had a significantly more positive adherence to the rule than he/she believed was the case for other businesspersons. Plus, for every one of the six negative ethical rules, the businesspersons indicated significantly more disagreement than they believed was the case for other businesspersons. In essence, the researchers demonstrated by use of differences analysis, that the typical businessperson believes he/she is more ethical than others regardless of the ethical rule involved. In a nutshell, American senior executives believe they are "holier than thou" when comparing their ethics to other American business executives.

mine the answer to this question, we must run a **paired samples test for the difference between two means**, which is a test to determine if two means of two different questions using the same scale format, and answered by the same respondents in the sample, are significantly different. Of course, the variables must be measured on the same metric scale; otherwise, the test would be analyzing differences between variables that are logically incomparable, such as the number of dollars spent versus the number of miles driven.

Paired-samples tests are useful when comparing perceptions or preferences that use the same scale across several topics. Marketing Research Insight 17.4 summarizes the use of this difference test by a researcher who investigated the ethical standards of senior executives in American businesses.

But the same respondents answered both questions, so you do not have two independent groups. Instead, you have two independent questions with one group. The logic and equations we have described still apply, but there must be an adjustment factor because there is only one sample involved. We do not provide the equations, but in the following SPSS section we describe how to perform and to interpret a paired samples t test.[8]

The Hobbit's Choice Restaurant Survey: How to Perform a Paired-Samples Significance of Differences between Means Test with SPSS

With the paired-samples test, we can test the significance of the difference between the means of any two questions by the same respondents in our sample. Let's take a critical location decision that Jeff Dean must address, namely, the restaurant décor. In the survey, respondents indicated their preferences on a 5-point scale, where 5 = very strongly prefer and 1 = very strongly not prefer to a "simple decor" and to "elegant decor."

The SPSS clickstream sequence to perform a paired-samples t test of the significance of the difference between means is displayed in Figure 17.4. As you can see, you begin with the ANALYZE-COMPARE MEANS-PAIRED SAMPLES T-TEST menu sequence. This sequence opens up the selection menu, and via cursor clicks, you can select "Prefer Simple Decor" and "Prefer Elegant Decor" as the variable pair to be tested. This sets up the t test, and a click on OK executes it.

The resulting annotated output is found in Figure 17.5. You should notice that the table is similar, but not identical, to the independent-samples output. The relevant information includes: (1) 400 respondents gave answers to each statement and were analyzed; (2) the means for simple décor and elegant décor are 3.58 and 2.33, respectively; (3) the computed t value is 8.564; and (4) the two-tailed significance level is 0.000. In words, the test gives almost no support for the null hypothesis that the means are equal. The simple décor option is definitely preferred over the elegant décor by the general public.

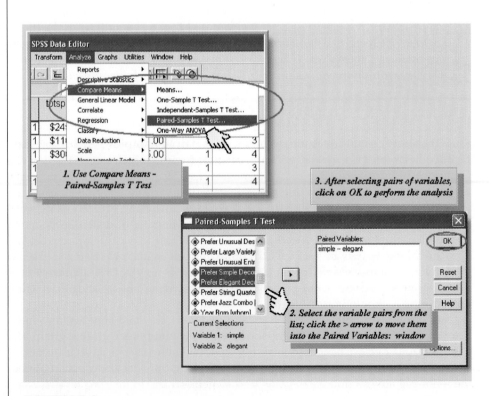

FIGURE 17.4
The Clickstream to Obtain a Paired-Samples t Test

Output1 - SPSS Viewer

File Edit View Data Transform Insert Format Analyze Graphs Utilities Window Help

The Paired Samples Statistics Table gives the 2 means and associated statistics

Paired Samples Statistics

	Mean	N	Std. Deviation	Std. Error Mean
Prefer Simple Decor	3.58	400	1.492	.075
Prefer Elegant Decor	2.33	400	1.510	.076

Paired Samples Correlations

	N	Correlation	Sig.
Prefer Simple Decor & Prefer Elegant Decor	400	-.884	.000

You can ignore items in this table

The significance level indicates little support for the hypothesis that the means are equal.

Paired Samples Test

	Paired Differences							
				95% Confidence Interval of the Difference				
	Mean	Std. Deviation	Std. Error Mean	Lower	Upper	t	df	Sig. (2-tailed)
Prefer Simple Decor - Prefer Elegant Decor	1.248	2.913	.146	.961	1.534	8.564	399	.000

SPSS Processor is ready

FIGURE 17.5
SPSS Output for a Paired-Samples t Test

ONLINE SURVEYS AND DATABASES— A "SIGNIFICANCE" CHALLENGE TO MARKETING RESEARCHERS

You should be aware that sample size has a great deal to do with statistical significance. Sample size, n, appears in every statistical formula we have described in this chapter on differences and in the previous chapter that dealt with confidence intervals and hypothesis tests. As we indicated earlier in this chapter, a statistician considers any sample greater than 30 to be a "large" sample. With the fast, easy, and inexpensive data collection that accompanies online surveys, it is common for market researchers to have samples that are comprised of several thousands of respondents. Further, databases such as those built with the use of a checkout scanner can easily have hundreds of thousands of individuals. With these mega samples, statistical tests are almost always found to be significant. In other words, the significance is determined by the immense sample sizes, and not by the actual differences between the groups being compared.

What is a researcher to do when just about everything is statistically significant? The answer is found in our earlier comments about the importance of differences to marketing managers. Not only should the difference in question be statistically significant, but it must also be meaningful. We have prepared Marketing Insight 17.5, which has some rules of thumb that can be used to judge the meaningfulness of statistically significant differences.

MARKETING RESEARCH INSIGHT

ONLINE APPLICATION

17.5 Statistical Significance and Practical Meaning: How Online Surveys Require a "Difference Percent" to Assess Managerial Meaningfulness

As you learned in Chapter 4, the researcher and the manager are from different worlds, and sometimes in the heat of statistical analysis, the researcher can lose sight of what is relevant to his client-manager.

Researchers are trained to be vigilant to statistical significance. They scour computer output screens looking for p values or "Sig." numbers that are less than .05. They become very excited when they find a value like .01, and they can become downright jubilant when a .000 pops up.

Online surveys are capable of producing thousands of respondents in a short time period. In case you did not notice this fact, the sample size, n, is always in the "denominator of the denominator" of statistical significance tests such as a t test for the significance of the difference between means of two groups. We did not share the ANOVA formulas, but the sample size is, in fact, in the denominator of the term that is the denominator of the computed F statistic formula.

This fact means that as the sample size increases, the denominator decreases, and the t, z, or F value increases. So, with very large sample sizes, any difference can be statistically significant regardless of how small is its arithmetic difference.

Here is how one author characterizes this situation.

For example, suppose that we conduct a study with 1,000,000 people and find that women score an average of 86 on a math test and men score an average of 87. With such a big sample size, we would probably find the difference to be statistically significant. However, what would we conclude about the practical significance of a one-point difference between genders on a 100-point exam? Are men

"superior" to women in math? Will we have adverse impact? Should I discourage my daughter from a career in science? Probably not. The statistical significance allows me to confidently say that there is little difference between men and women on this variable.[9]

With this situation, it is vital that a researcher provide a way for the manager to assess the meaningfulness of the difference between two means or percentages. In a real sense, we must distinguish between the statistical significance of the difference and the practical difference of the difference.[10]

One possibility is to provide a "percent difference" that is calculated by the following formula[11]:

Formula for "Percent Difference"

$$Percent\ difference = \frac{(mean_1 - mean_2)}{Scale\ range}$$

(Note: the sign is irrelevant.)

In our math example, this would compute to be a 1% difference ((absolute (86-87))/100) and hardly worth worrying about. If it was 10% or more, the manager's attention would be warranted.

Here are some guidelines to help the manager assess the meaningfulness of statistically significant differences.[12]

ASSESSING PRACTICAL MEANING AFTER STATISTICAL SIGNIFICANCE	
PERCENT DIFFERENCE	PRACTICAL INTERPRETATION
Less than 10%	Not meaningful
10% to 20%	Probably meaningful
Greater than 20%	Definitely meaningful

TESTING FOR SIGNIFICANT DIFFERENCES IN MEANS AMONG MORE THAN TWO GROUPS: ANALYSIS OF VARIANCE

Sometimes, a researcher will want to compare the means of three, four, five, or more different groups. Analysis of variance, sometimes called ANOVA, should be used to accomplish such multiple comparisons.[13] The use of the word *variance* in the name *analysis of variance* is perhaps misleading—it is not an analysis of the standard deviations of the groups. To be sure, the standard deviations are taken into consideration, and so are the sample sizes, just as you saw in all of our other statistical inference formulas. Fundamentally, **ANOVA (analysis of variance)** is an investigation of the differences between the group means to ascertain whether sampling errors or true population differences explain their failure to be equal[14]; that is, the word *variance* signifies for our purposes differences between two or more groups' means—do they vary from one another significantly? Although a term such as *analysis of variance* or *ANOVA* sounds frightfully technical, it is nothing more than statistical procedures that embody inference when you are comparing the means of several groups. As we noted in our discussion on market segmentations, markets are often comprised of a number of market segments, not just two, so ANOVA is a valuable tool for discovering differences between and among multiple market segments. The following sections explain to you the basic concepts involved with analysis of variance and also how it can be applied to marketing research situations.

> ANOVA is used when comparing the means of three or more groups.

Basic Logic in Analysis of Variance

The basic of analysis of variance is a desire on the part of a researcher to determine whether a statistically significant difference exists between the means for <u>any two groups</u> in his or her sample with a given variable regardless of the number of groups. The end result of analysis of variance is an indication to the marketing researcher as to whether a significant difference at some chosen level of statistical significance exists between *at least* two group means. Significant differences may exist between all of the group means, but analysis of variance results alone will not communicate how many pairs of means are statistically significant in their differences.

To elaborate, ANOVA is a **"signal flag" procedure**, meaning that if at least one pair of means has a statistically significant difference, ANOVA will signal this by indicating significance. (We introduced you to the flag waving notion in Marketing Research Insight 17.1 on page 491.) Then, it is up to the researcher to conduct further tests (called "post hoc" tests) to determine precisely how many statistically significant differences actually exist and which ones they are. Of course, if the signal flag does not pop up, the researcher knows that no significant differences exist.

> ANOVA will "flag" when at least one pair of means has a statistically significant difference, but it does not tell which pair.

Let us elaborate just a bit on how ANOVA works. ANOVA uses some complicated formulas, and we have found from experience that market researchers do not memorize them. Instead, a researcher understands the basic purpose of ANOVA, and he or she is adept at interpreting ANOVA output. Let's assume that we have three groups, A, B, and C. In concept ANOVA performs all possible independent-samples *t* tests for significant differences between the means, comparing, in our A, B, C example, A:B, A:C, and B:C. ANOVA is very efficient as it makes these comparisons simultaneously, not individually as you would need to do if you were running independent-samples *t* tests. ANOVA's null hypothesis is that no single pair of means is significantly different. Because multiple pairs of group means are being tested, ANOVA uses the F-test statistic, and the significance level (sometimes referred to as the *p* value) that appears on the output in this F test, is the probability of support for the null hypothesis.

Here is an example that will help you to understand how ANOVA works and when to use it. A major department store conducts a survey, and one of the questions on the survey is, "In what department did you last make a purchase for over \$250?" There are four departments where significant numbers of respondents made these purchases: (1) electronics, (2) home and garden, (3) sporting goods, and (4) automotive. Another question on the survey is, "How likely are you to purchase another item for over \$250 from that department again?" The respondents indicate how likely they are to do this on a 7-point scale, where 1 = very unlikely and 7 = very likely. It is easy to calculate the

ANOVA is a "flag waving" procedure that signals when at least one pair of means is significantly different.

mean of how likely each group is to return to the department store and purchase another major item from that same department.

The researcher who is doing the analysis decides to compare these means statistically, so five different independent-samples t tests of the significance of the differences are performed. A summary of the findings is found in Table 17.2. It may take a few minutes, but if you examine Table 17.2, you will see that the automotive department's mean is significantly different and lower than the likelihood means of the other three departments. Also, there is no significant difference in the means for the patrons of the other three departments. In other words, there is a good indication that the patrons who

TABLE 17.2	Results of Five Independent-Samples t tests of How Likely Patrons Are to Return to the Same Department to Make their Next Major Purchases	
Groups Compared	**Group Means**	**Significance**
Electronics: Home and Garden	5.1:5.3	.873
Electronics: Sporting Goods	5.1:5.6	.469
Electronics: Automotive	5.1:2.2	.000
Home and Garden: Sporting Goods	5.3:5.6	.656
Home and Garden: Automotive	5.3:2.2	.000
Sporting Goods: Automotive	5.6:2.2	.000

bought an item for more than $250 from the department store's automotive department are not as satisfied with the product as are customers who bought large ticket items from any other department.

Now, look at Table 17.3. It is an abbreviated ANOVA output. Instead of looking at several *p* values, as in Table 17.2, all the researcher needs to do is to look at the significance level (Sig.) for the F test, our signal flag. It is .000, which is less than .05, meaning that there is at least one significant difference, so now it is worth the researcher's time and effort to look at the next table to find the significant difference(s). This table is arranged so the means that are not significantly different fall in the same column, while those that are significantly different fall in separate columns, and each column is identified as a unique subset. The means are arranged in the second table from the lowest mean to the highest mean, and it is immediately apparent that the automotive department has a problem.

ANOVA has two distinct advantages over performing multiple *t* tests of the significance of the difference between means. First, it immediately notifies the researcher if there is any significant difference, because all he or she needs to do is to look at the "Sig." value, our signal flag. Second, in our example, it arranges the means so the significant differences can be located and interpreted easily.

To elaborate, this Sig(nificance) value is the flag that we referred to above left and in Marketing Research Insight 17.1. When the flag is waving, the researcher is then justified at looking at each pair of means to find which one(s) are significantly different. Once you learn how to read SPSS ANOVA output, it is quite easy to identify these cases. Of course, if the F-statistic p-value flag is not waving, meaning that the p-value is greater than .05, it is a waste of time to look at the differences between the pairs of means, as no difference will be statistically significant at the 95% level of confidence.

The Sig. value in the ANOVA table indicates the level of significance.

ANOVA is much more advantageous than running multiple t tests of the significance of the difference between means.

How to Determine Statistically Significant Differences among Group Means

As we mentioned in passing above, there are **"post hoc" tests**, which are options that are available to determine where the pair(s) of statistically significant differences between the means exist(s). As you will soon see in our SPSS example, there are over a dozen of these to chose from, including Scheffé's and Tukey's that you may recognize

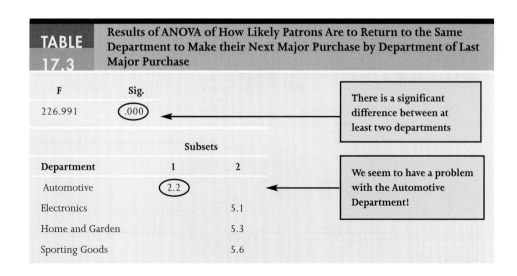

TABLE 17.3	Results of ANOVA of How Likely Patrons Are to Return to the Same Department to Make their Next Major Purchase by Department of Last Major Purchase

F	Sig.
226.991	.000

There is a significant difference between at least two departments

Department	Subsets	
	1	2
Automotive	2.2	
Electronics		5.1
Home and Garden		5.3
Sporting Goods		5.6

We seem to have a problem with the Automotive Department!

from statistics courses. It is beyond the scope of this book to provide a complete delineation of the various types of tests. Consequently, only one test, Duncan's multiple range test, will be shown as an illustration of how the differences may be determined. **Duncan's multiple range test** provides output that is mostly a "picture" of what pair(s) of means are significantly different, and it is much less statistical than most of the other post hoc tests, so we have chosen to use it here for this reason. The picture provided by the Duncan's post hoc test is the arrangement of the means as you saw them in Table 17.3.

The Duncan multiple range test is our preferred post hoc test because its output is easy to interpret.

To run analysis of variance with SPSS, use the ANALYZE-COMPARE MEANS-ONE-WAY ANOVA menu command sequence.

The Hobbit's Choice Restaurant Survey: How to Run Analysis of Variance on SPSS

In the Hobbit's Choice Restaurant survey, there are a number of categorical variables that have more than two groups. Let's take a promotional decision that concerns Jeff Dean: in what section of the newspaper should he place his ads? The questionnaire asked which newspaper section respondents read most frequently, and the options were: editorial, business, local, classifieds, life (health and entertainment), or no preference.

One-way ANOVA in this case is done under the ANALYZE-COMPARE MEANS-ONE-WAY ANOVA menu command sequence illustrated in Figure 17.6. A window opens to set up the ANOVA analysis. The "Dependent list" is where you click in the variable(s) pertaining to the means, while the "Factor" variable is the grouping variable. In our example, the likelihood of patronizing the Hobbit's Choice is our dependent one, and the "Section of Newspaper Read Most Often" is the grouping variable. Figure 17.6 also shows how to select the Duncan's Multiple

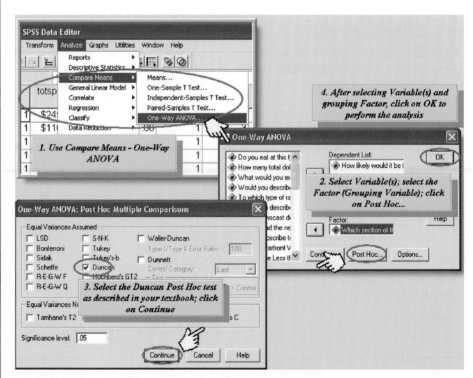

FIGURE 17.6
SPSS Clickstream to Perform Analysis of Variance (ANOVA)

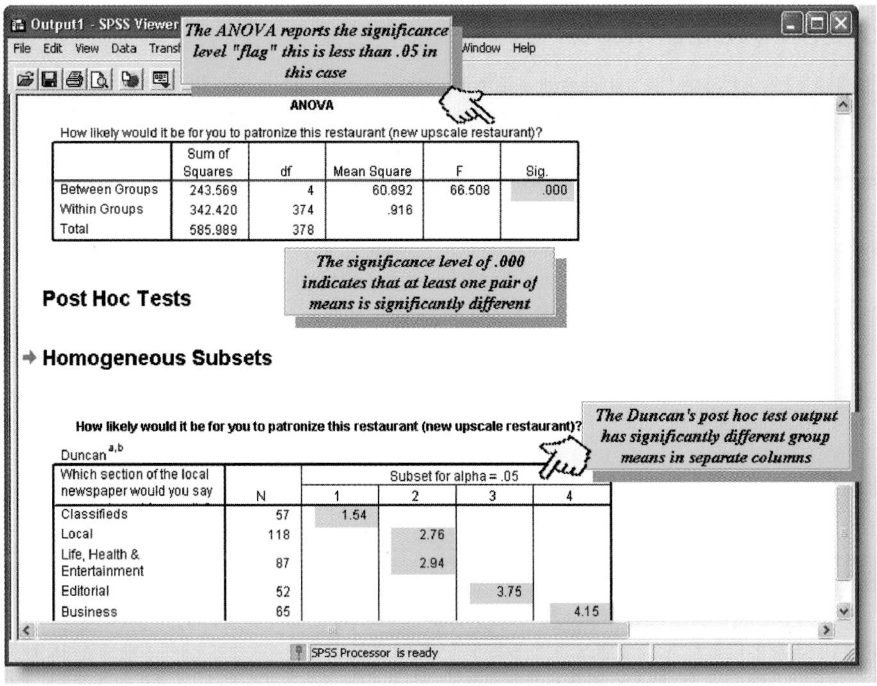

	Sum of Squares	df	Mean Square	F	Sig.
Between Groups	243.569	4	60.892	66.508	.000
Within Groups	342.420	374	.916		
Total	585.989	378			

Which section of the local newspaper would you say	N	Subset for alpha = .05			
		1	2	3	4
Classifieds	57	1.54			
Local	118		2.76		
Life, Health & Entertainment	87		2.94		
Editorial	52			3.75	
Business	65				4.15

FIGURE 17.7
SPSS Output for Analysis of Variance (ANOVA)

Range option under the POST HOC-TESTS menu. Returning to the selection window and clicking on "OK" commences the ANOVA procedure.

Figure 17.7 is an annotated ANOVA output. The first table contains a number of intermediate and additional computational results, but our attention should be focused on the "Sig." column. Here is the support for the null hypothesis that not one pair of means is significantly different. Since, the Sig. value is .000, we are assured that there is at least one significantly different pair. The next table is the Duncan's test output. Specifically, the table is arranged so the means ascend in size from top left to right bottom, and the columns represent subsets of groups that are significantly different from groups in the other columns. You can immediately see that business (4.15), editorial (3.75) life, health and entertainment and local (2.94 and 2.78, but not significantly different from each other), and classifieds (1.54) define four unique groupings of likelihood to patronize the Hobbit's Choice. People who read the Business section are the most likely patrons, so it makes sense for Jeff to place his ads in this section as its readers are more likely to be looking for an upscale restaurant.

Applying ANOVA (Analysis of Variance)

What about the Editorial page? We have a statistically significant difference between the business section frequent readers (4.15) and the editorial page frequent readers (3.75), but is it a *meaningful* difference? If we apply our guideline for meaningfulness, we find that the difference is 8% (i.e., absolute (4.15 − 3.75)/5 = 8%). This is less than 10%, so based on our rule of thumb, it is not definitely meaningful. Instead, it is possibly meaningful, and Jeff may want to experiment by varying his ad placements in these two newspaper sections to see what type of responses are generated.

SPSS Student Assistant: Applying ANOVA (Analysis of Variance)
There are several "post hoc" tests with ANOVA, and we have used Duncan's multiple range test as an illustration with the Hobbit's Choice Restaurant survey data.

PERFORM ANALYSIS OF VARIANCE WITH SPSS

Let's investigate for differences in monthly restaurant expenditures means across the five newspaper sections groups. Use the SPSS Clickstream described in Figure 17.6 to select the factor of newspaper section most read and the dependent variable of how much is typically spent in restaurants per month. In interpreting the SPSS ANOVA output that results, use the annotations provided in Figure 17.7. What did you find about the possible differences in the means of these five groups?

n-Way ANOVA

The Hobbit's Choice Restaurant survey newspaper section reading example illustrates what is normally termed **one-way ANOVA** because there is only one independent factor used to set up the groups. However, it is not unusual to look at two or more grouping factors simultaneously, in which case one would use **n-way ANOVA**. For example, a manager might decide to use age groups and occupation classifications at the same time to test for differences. Or, with a test market experiment, the researcher might want to see the effect of a high versus a low price operating with a newspaper versus billboard advertising. The overlaying of various independent factors permits the marketing researcher to investigate "interaction effects." **Interaction effects** are cases in which the independent factors are operating in concert and simultaneously affecting the means of the groups. Conceptually, n-way ANOVA operates identically to the one-way ANOVA regardless of the number of treatment classification schemes being used. Of course, the formulas and computations are more complicated. We suggest that you refer to more advanced sources if you are interested in using n-way ANOVA.

n-way ANOVA allows you to test multiple grouping variables at the same time.

SUMMARY

The chapter began with a discussion on why differences are important to marketing managers. Basically, market segmentation implications underlie most differences analyses. It is important that differences are statistically significant, but it is also vital that they are meaningful, stable, and a basis of marketing strategy.

We then described how differences between two percentages in two samples can be tested for statistical significance. Then, we described the same test procedure using means. In addition, you were introduced to the t-test procedure in SPSS that is used to test the significance of the difference between two means from two independent samples. We gave an illustration of how to use SPSS for this analysis using the Hobbit's Choice Restaurant data set. In addition, you learned about a paired-samples test and how to perform and interpret it using SPSS.

When a researcher has more than two groups and wishes to compare their various means, the correct procedure involves analysis of variance, or ANOVA. ANOVA is a flagging technique that tests all possible pairs of means for all the groups involved, and indicates via the Sig. (significance) value in the ANOVA table if at least one pair is statistically significant in its difference. If the Sig. value is greater than .05, the researcher will waste his or her time inspecting the means for differences. But if the Sig. value is .05 or less, the researcher can use a post hoc procedure such as Duncan's multiple range test to identify the pair or pairs of groups in which the means are significantly different.

KEY TERMS

Statistical significance of differences
  (p. 488)
Meaningful difference (p. 489)
Stable difference (p. 490)
Actionable difference (p. 490)
t test (p. 491)
z test (p. 491)
Null hypothesis (p. 493)
Significance of differences between two
  percentages (p. 493)
Significance of difference between two
  means (p. 498)

Paired samples test for the difference
  between two means (p. 503)
ANOVA (analysis of variance)
  (p. 507)
"Signal-flag" procedure (p. 507)
Post hoc tests (p. 509)
Duncan's multiple range test
  (p. 510)
One-way ANOVA (p. 512)
n-way ANOVA (p. 512)
Interaction effects (p. 512)

REVIEW QUESTIONS/APPLICATIONS

1. What are differences, and why should market researchers be concerned with them? Why are marketing managers concerned with them?

2. What is considered to be a "small sample," and why is this concept a concern to statisticians? To what extent do market researchers concern themselves with small samples? Why?

3. When a market researcher compares the responses of two identifiable groups with respect to their answers to the same question, what is this called?

4. With regard to differences tests, briefly define and describe each of the following:
   a. Null hypothesis
   b. Sampling distribution
   c. Significant difference

5. Relate the formula and identify each formula's components in the test of significant differences between two groups for when the question involved is:
   a. A "yes/no" type
   b. A metric-scale-type question

6. Are the following two sample results significantly different?

Sample One	Sample Two	Confidence Level	Your Finding?
Mean: 10.6 Std. dev.: 1.5 n = 150	Mean: 11.7 Std. dev.: 2.5 n = 300	95%	_____
Percent: 45% n = 350	Percent: 54% n = 250	99%	_____
Mean: 1500 Std. dev.: 550 n = 1200	Mean: 1250 Std. dev.: 500 n = 500	95%	_____

7. What is a paired-samples test? Specifically how are the samples "paired?"

8. When should one-way ANOVA be used and why?

9. When a researcher finds a significant F value in analysis of variance, why can it be considered a "flagging" device?

10. The circulation manager of the *Daily Advocate* commissions a market research study to determine what factors underlie the circulation attrition. Specifically, the survey is designed to compare current *Daily Advocate* subscribers with those who have dropped their subscriptions in the past year. A telephone survey is conducted with both sets of individuals. Below is a summary of the key findings from the study.

Item	Current Subscribers	Lost Subscribers	Significance
Length of residency in the city	20.1 yr	5.4 yr	.000
Length of time as a subscriber	27.2 yr	1.3 yr	.000
Watch local TV news program (s)	87%	85%	.372
Watch national news program(s)	72%	79%	.540
Obtain news from the Internet	13%	23%	.025
Satisfaction[a] with . . .			
Delivery of newspaper	5.5	4.9	.459
Coverage of local news	6.1	5.8	.248
Coverage of national news	5.5	2.3	.031
Coverage of local sports	6.3	5.9	.462
Coverage of national sports	5.7	3.2	.001
Coverage of local social news	5.8	5.2	.659
Editorial stance of the newspaper	6.1	4.0	.001
Value for subscription price	5.2	4.8	.468

[a]Based on a 7-point scale, where 1 = very dissatisfied and 7 = very satisfied

Interpret these findings for the circulation manager.

11. A researcher is investigating different types of customers for a sporting goods store. In a survey, respondents have indicated approximately how many minutes per week they exercise. These respondents have also rated the performance of the sporting goods store across 12 different characteristics such as good value for the price, convenience of location, helpfulness of the sales clerks, etc. The researcher used a 1–7 rating scale for these 12 characteristics, where 1 = poor performance and 7 = excellent performance. How can the researcher investigate differences in the ratings based on the amount of exercise reported by the respondents?

12. A marketing manager of *Collections, Etc*, a Web-based catalog sales company, uses a segmentation scheme based on the incomes of target customers. The segmentation system has four segments: (1) low income, (2) moderate income, (3) high income, and (4) wealthy. The company database holds information on every customer's purchases over the past several years, and the total dollars spent at *Collections, Etc.* is one of the prominent variables. Using Microsoft Excel on this database, the marketing manager finds that the average total dollar purchases for the four groups are as follows.

Market Segment	Average Total Dollar Purchases
Low income	$101
Moderate income	$120
High income	$231
Wealthy	$595

Construct a table that is based on the Duncan's multiple range test table concept discussed in the chapter that illustrates that the low- and moderate-income groups are not different from each other, but the other groups are significantly different from one another.

13. How would a grocery store chain company go about constructing and validating a market segmentation system? Take the possible segmentation variables of family type (sin-

gle, couple, or with children) and occupation (skilled labor, professional, or retired). Indicate the steps you would take and any considerations you would take into account as a researcher investigating whether there was a useful segmentation system for the grocery store chain company using these two demographic variables as the basis.

DON'T YOU JUST HATE IT WHEN . . . ? (PART II)

Part I (Case 16.1) of this case is on pages 479–480. You do not need to read Part I to answer Part II.

A cell phone chirps at 7:22 P.M. in an apartment just off campus.

Marsha: "Hello."

Josh: "Hi Marsh. How's it going?"

Marsha: "You! What the heck do you care? You skipped Dr. Z's class for our team presentation on statistical inferences, and I haven't seen you for a week and a half. What do you want? My notes for the exam?"

Josh: "Um, Marsh, I realize you don't follow sports, but I blew out my knee running bases on that day, and now I'm scheduled for reconstructive surgery. The docs say I won't play competitively again. So, I'm trying to catch up. I bought the marketing research textbook, and I have been power-reading to catch up. I couldn't make it to class because I had doctor appointments."

Marsha: "Oh? Does this mean you are going to take on your share of the marketing research project we are doing for Pets, Pets, & Pets?"

Josh: "Yeah, that's what I am calling about. I got a laptop computer and installed SPSS. So, I am good to go."

Marsha: "Great, I'll e-mail the SPSS file and a document indicating what we have decided to do for analysis. It is due tomorrow morning with another presentation. You do the analysis, interpret it, and send it back to me to put into the PowerPoint file."

Marsha's file sent to Josh.

Variable Code Book for Pets, Pets, & Pets SPSS File

Variable	Response scale
Times visited PPP in past year	Actual number of times
Amount spent on last visit to PPP	Actual dollar amount rounded to dollars
How likely to buy at PPP next time (1–7 scale)	1–7 scale, where: 1 = unlikely, 7 = very likely
Number of pets owned	Actual number of pets
Use Pets, Pets, & Pets how often?	1 = do not use regularly 2 = use regularly
Recall seeing a PPP newspaper ad in the past month?	1 = yes 2 = no

(continued)

Income level	1 = below $20,000
	2 = between $20,000 and $40,000
	3 = between $40,000 and $60,000
	4 = between $60,000 and $80,000
	5 = between $80,000 and $100,000
	6 = greater than $100,000

Research Questions

1. Do regular PPP patrons differ from those who are not regular patrons, and if so, how?

2. Do regular PPP patrons recall seeing PPP newspaper advertising more or less than those who do not use PPP regularly?

3. Do PPP customers differ by household income level, and if so, how?

Josh: "Great, send it on over."

Ten minutes later, Josh opens up this file.

At 8:26 P.M. Marsha's cell phone chirps.

Marsha: "Hello."

Josh: "Ah, Marsh, I guess I didn't understand the stuff that I read in my marketing research textbook. Can you give me some help?"

Marsha thinks: "Gawd, I hate this guy!"

Indicate the specific differences statistical tests that should be conducted to answer each of the research questions 1, 2, and 3 in the e-mail attachment Marsha sent to Josh. In each of your answers, tell precisely what is the grouping variable, what is the variable being used to compare the groups to each other, and if percentages or means are to be compared.

CASE 17.2

WASHINGTON STREET BISTRO IMPORTANCE-PERFORMANCE SURVEY

Washington Street Bistro is a medium-sized restaurant located very close to a huge medical complex anchored by General Hospital, which is a large regional hospital that employs over 2000 full- and part-time workers, including custodial personnel, nurses, medical technicians, and doctors. There are a great many smaller medical offices and clinics located around General Hospital and close to Washington Street Bistro. As you would expect, the lunch business at Washington Street Bistro is comprised largely of the medical and support personnel for General Hospital and the surrounding medical businesses.

The dinner crowd at Washington Street Bistro appears to be different from the lunch bunch. That is, the dinner patrons do include some medical personnel, but most of them are young professional singles, couples, and groups who work elsewhere in the city, but many of whom live fairly close to Washington Street Bistro. While the lunch patrons are usually dressed in medical attire, the dinner patrons are typically dressed in what might be called "business casual" or simply casual attire.

Emily Wilson, the manager of Washington Street Bistro, is constantly looking for ways to improve her restaurant, so she commissions a marketing survey to be administered to both the lunch and dinner patrons to see what differences, if any, might exist between them. She hires a research company that designs a questionnaire that asks Washington Street Bistro patrons to rate the restaurant on a 7-point satisfaction scale with 1 meaning "very dissatisfied" and 7 meaning "very satisfied." Based on a focus group, 17 different cafeteria attributes are rated. In addition, the importance of each attribute is also rated on an importance scale in which 1 means unimportant and 7 means very important to a respondent's decision to eat at a particular location.

Using systematic sampling over a period of one week, the research company obtains a sample of lunch patrons as well as a sample of dinner patrons. A total of 340 usable questionnaires are gathered by the end of the data-collection phase. The marketing research director prepared the following two tables. In each table, the researcher separated the 240 lunch bunch from the 100 dinner buyers. The mean responses follow.

TABLE A	Importance[a] of Selected Restaurant Attributes by Type of Patron		
Cafeteria Attribute	Lunch	Dinner	Sig.
Courteous employees	5.28	5.18	0.978
Helpful employees	5.20	5.15	0.876
Quality of service	5.07	4.98	0.540
Freshness of salad items	5.07	4.50	0.034
High nutritional value of meals	5.03	4.44	0.045
Overall quality of meals	4.97	4.53	0.035
Comfortable seating	4.96	4.95	0.986
Discounts for frequent patrons	4.89	4.75	0.752
Appetizing look of items	4.88	4.02	0.052
Speed of service	4.83	4.97	0.650
Relaxed atmosphere	4.83	5.23	0.001
Good-tasting dishes	4.80	4.02	0.012
Adequate lighting	4.71	4.80	0.659
Good variety of entrees	4.60	3.53	0.002
Low price of specials	4.52	4.20	0.102
Large portions	4.34	3.87	0.034
Clean surroundings	4.25	4.50	0.286

[a]Based on a scale in which 1 = unimportant and 7 = very important

TABLE B	Evaluation of Washington Street Bistro Performance[a] on Selected Attributes by Type of Patron		
Bistro Attribute	Lunch	Dinner	Sig.
Courteous employees	5.79	5.46	0.182
Helpful employees	5.83	5.51	0.044
Quality of service	5.54	5.60	0.276
Freshness of salad items	5.80	4.46	0.001
High nutritional value of meals	5.29	5.23	0.197
Overall quality of meals	4.48	4.46	0.568
Comfortable seating	4.63	4.53	0.389
Discounts for frequent patrons	5.45	4.56	0.009
Appetizing look of items	5.65	4.64	0.045
Speed of service	5.52	4.22	0.010
Relaxed atmosphere	4.96	5.63	0.061
Good-tasting dishes	5.31	4.37	0.048
Adequate lighting	4.52	4.62	0.369
Good variety of entrees	4.98	3.75	0.019
Low price of specials	5.35	6.86	0.045
Large portions	4.43	5.43	0.038
Clean surroundings	5.56	5.24	0.286

[a]Based on a scale in which 1 = very dissatisfied and 7 = very satisfied

1. Interpret these findings for Ms. Wilson. What do they say about the two subpopulations of lunch and dinner patrons?
2. What implications for a manager are apparent from these findings?

This is your integrated case, described on pages 38–39.

THE HOBBIT'S CHOICE RESTAURANT SURVEY DIFFERENCES ANALYSIS

Cory Rogers called a meeting with Jeff Dean and Celeste Brown. At the beginning of the meeting, Cory's wife called with news that their 5-year-old son was having a stomachache at school, and Cory had to pick him up and take him to the doctor. Cory excused himself, saying, "I am sorry about this, but these things happen when you are a two-career household. Celeste, sit with Jeff for a bit and find out what questions he has about the survey findings. Then run the analysis, and we'll meet about it tomorrow afternoon. I am sure that Cory Junior will be over his stomach ailment by then."

After meeting for about 20 minutes, Celeste had a list of six questions that Jeff Dean was especially interested in. Celeste's notes are below.

Your task here is to take Celeste's role, using the Hobbit's Choice Restaurant survey SPSS data set, perform the proper analysis, and interpret the findings for each of the following questions.

1. Jeff wonders if the Hobbit's Choice Restaurant is more appealing to women than it is to men or vice versa. Perform the proper analysis, interpret it, and answer Jeff's question.

2. With respect to the location of the Hobbit's Choice Restaurant, is a waterfront view preferred more than a drive less than 30 minutes?

3. With respect to the restaurant's atmosphere, is a string quartet preferred over a jazz combo?

4. What about unusual entrees versus unusual desserts?

5. In general, such establishments are appealing to higher-income households, while they are less appealing to lower-income households. Is this pattern the case for the Hobbit's Choice Restaurant?

6. Jeff and Cory speculated that the different geographic areas that they identified by ZIP codes would have different reactions to the prospect of patronizing a new upscale restaurant. Are these anticipated differences substantiated by the survey? Perform the proper analysis and interpret your findings.

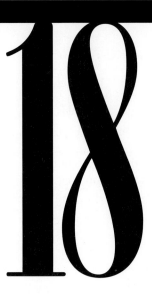

Determining
and Interpreting
Associations
Among Variables

Pet Ownership: A New Market Segmentation Basis?

Marketing managers have a host of bases for segmenting their markets, including demographics, lifestyles, benefits, and product usage, not to mention a number of commercially developed systems that are available. In general, market segmentation holds that if a group of consumers can be identified by some basis, then it will differ from other market segments on key factors such as purchases, beliefs, or some other aspect that is useful to a marketer seeking to target that segment. To state the concept somewhat differently, the members of a market segment will be uniquely associated with predispositions, and when a marketing manager identifies the market segment, he or she can use those predispositons in a marketing strategy.

Seeking to break new ground, researchers investigated the marketing segmentation potential of pet ownership, and, specifically dog versus cat ownership.[1] They surveyed a large number of American adults regarding their attitudes, interests, and opinions across a number of topics, and they compared these respondents' answers to their pet ownership (or nonownership) with a technique called cross-tabulation, which is described in this chapter.

The researchers discovered that pet ownership (cat, dog, or both) was associated or related to a certain lifestyle profile. Namely, relative to nonowners of pets, pet owners were found to:

■ To learn what is meant by an "association" between two variables
■ To examine various relationships that may be construed as associations
■ To understand where and how cross-tabulations with chi-square analysis are applied
■ To become familiar with the use and interpretation of correlations
■ To learn how to obtain and interpret crosstabulations, chi-square findings, and correlations with SPSS

Learning Objectives

Researchers have identified market segments based on dog ownership, cat ownership, or not owning a pet.

■ Be adventurous
■ Be independent
■ Enjoy life

On the other hand, relative to pet owners, nonowners of pets were found to be:

■ Conservative
■ Fatalistic
■ Health-conscious
■ Concerned for the environment

Taking a closer look at the nature of pet ownership, the researchers then investigated possible relationships with cat versus dog owners. The traits and demographic factors associated with owning a dog were found to be:

Traits	Demographics
Conservatism	35–54 years old
Traditionalism	Less educated
	Married

Being a cat owner was associated with the following traits:

Traits	Demographics
Adventurous	More educated
Health-conscious	Metropolitan dweller
Concerned for the environment	

While dog-and-cat segmentation is obvious for a pet food company such as Whiskas (for cats) or Alpo (for dogs), there are more subtle uses of these associations. For example, if an advertiser shows a middle-aged married couple worrying about financial matters, it would lend more credence to the ad if there was a family dog in the ad. On the other hand, if an air purification system was being advertised, it would be appropriate to show the family cat reclining in front of the purification unit.

T his chapter illustrates the usefulness of statistical analyses beyond simple descriptive measures and statistical inference. Often, as we have described in our pet ownership segmentation example, marketers are interested in relationships among variables. For example, Frito-Lay wants to know what kinds of people and under what circumstances these people choose to buy Doritos, Fritos, and any of the other items in the Frito-Lay line. The Pontiac Division of General Motors wants to know what types of individuals would respond favorably to the various style changes proposed for the Firebird. A newspaper wants to understand the lifestyle characteristics of its prospective readers so that it is able to modify or change sections in the newspaper to better suit its audience. Furthermore, the newspaper desires information about various types of subscribers so as to communicate this information to its advertisers, helping them in copy design and advertisement placement within the various newspaper sections. For all of these cases, there are statistical procedures available, termed "associative analyses," which determine answers to these questions. **Associative analyses** determine whether stable relationships exist between two variables; they are the central topic of this chapter.

> **Associative analyses determine whether stable relationships exist between two variables.**

We begin the chapter by describing the four different types of relationships possible between two variables. Then, we describe cross-tabulations and indicate how a cross-tabulation can be used to compute a chi-square value, which in turn, can be assessed to determine whether or not a statistically significant association exists between the two variables. For cross-tabulations, we move to a general discussion of correlation coefficients, and we illustrate the use of Pearson product moment correlations. As in our previous analysis chapters, we show you SPSS steps to perform these analyses and the resulting output.

TYPES OF RELATIONSHIPS BETWEEN TWO VARIABLES

In order to describe a relationship between two variables, we must first remind you of the scale characteristic called "description" that we introduced to you in Chapter 10. Every scale has unique descriptors, sometimes called "labels" or "amounts," that identify the different labels of that scale. The term *levels* implies that the scale is metric, namely interval or ratio; while the term *labels* implies that the scale is not metric, typically nominal. A simple label is a "yes" or "no" one, for instance, if a respondent is labeled as a buyer (yes) or nonbuyer (no) of a particular product or service. Of course, if the researcher measured how many times a respondent bought a product, the amount would be the number of times, and the scale would be metric because this scale would satisfy the assumptions of a ratio scale.

> **A relationship is a consistent and systematic linkage between the labels or amounts for two variables.**

A **relationship** is a consistent and systematic linkage between the labels or amounts for two variables. This linkage is statistical, not necessarily causal. A causal linkage is one in which you are certain one variable affected the other one, but with a statistical linkage you cannot be certain because some other variable might have had some influence. Nonetheless, statistical linkages or relationships often provide us with insights that lead to understanding even though they are not cause-and-effect relationships. For example, if we found a relationship that 9 out of 10 bottled water buyers purchased flavored water, we understand that the flavorings are important to these buyers.

Associative analysis procedures are useful because they determine if there is a consistent and systematic relationship between the presence (label) or amount of one variable and the presence (label) or amount of another variable. There are four basic types of relationships between two variables: nonmonotonic, monotonic, linear, and curvilinear. A discussion of each follows:

Nonmonotonic Relationships

A **nonmonotonic relationship** is one in which the presence (or absence) of one variable is systematically associated with the presence (or absence) of another variable. The term *nonmonotonic* means essentially that there is no discernible direction to the relationship, but a relationship exists. For example, McDonald's knows from experience that morning customers typically purchase coffee, whereas noon customers typically purchase soft drinks. The relationship is in no way exclusive—there is no guarantee that a morning customer will always order a coffee or that an afternoon customer will always order a soft drink. In general, though, this relationship exists, as can be seen in Figure 18.1. The nonmonotonic relationship is simply that the morning customer tends to purchase breakfast foods such as eggs, biscuits, and coffee, and the afternoon customers tend to purchase lunch items such as burgers, fries, and soft drinks.

> A nonmonotonic relationship means two variables are associated, but only in a very general sense.

In other words, with a nonmonotonic relationship, when you find the presence of one label for a variable, you will tend to find the presence of another specific label of another variable: breakfast diners typically order coffee. Here are some other examples of nonmonotonic relationships: (1) People who live in apartments do not buy lawn mowers but homeowners do; (2) tourists in Daytona Beach, Florida, during "bike week" are likely to be motorcycle owners, not college students; and (3) Play Station game players are typically children, not adults. Again each example reports that the presence (absence) of one aspect of some object tends to be joined to the presence (absence) of an aspect of some other object. But the association is very general, and we must state each one by spelling it out verbally. In other words, we know only the general pattern of presence or nonpresence with a nonmonotonic relationship.

Monotonic Relationships

Monotonic relationships are ones in which the researcher can assign a general direction to the association between the two variables. There are two types of monotonic relationships: increasing and decreasing. Monotonic increasing relationships are those in which one variable increases as the other variable increases. As you would guess, monotonic decreasing relationships are those in which one variable increases as the other variable decreases. You should note that in neither case is there any indication of the exact amount of change in one variable as the other changes. "Monotonic" means that the

> A monotonic relationship means you know the general direction of the relationship between two variables.

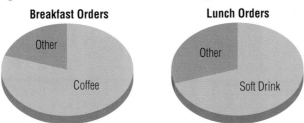

FIGURE 18.1
McDonald's Example of a Nonmonotonic Relationship for the Type of Drink Ordered at Breakfast and at Lunch

Monotonic relationships can be increasing or decreasing.

relationship can be described only in a general directional sense. Beyond this, precision in the description is lacking. The following example should help to explain this concept.

The owner of a shoe store knows that older children tend to require larger shoe sizes than do younger children, but there is no way to equate a child's age with the right shoe size. No universal rule exists as to the rate of growth of a child's foot or to the final shoe size he or she will attain. There is, however, a monotonic increasing relationship between a child's age and shoe size. At the same time, a monotonic decreasing relationship exists between a child's age and the amount of involvement of his or her parents in the purchase of his or her shoes. As Figure 18.2 illustrates, very young children often have virtually no input into the purchase decision, whereas older children tend to gain more and more control over the purchase decision process until they ultimately become adults and have complete control over the decision. Once again, no universal rule operates as to the amount of parental influence or the point in time at which the child becomes independent and gains complete control over the decision-making process. It is simply known that younger children have less influence in the decision-making process, and older children have more influence in the shoe purchase decision. The relationship is therefore monotonic.

Linear Relationships

A linear relationship means the two variables have a "straight-line" relationship.

Now, we will turn to a more precise relationship. Certainly the easiest association to envision between two variables is a linear relationship. A **linear relationship** is a "straight-line association" between two variables. Here, knowledge of the amount of one variable will automatically yield knowledge of the amount of the other variable as a consequence of applying the linear or straight-line formula that is known to exist between them. In its general form, a **straight-line formula** is as follows:

Formula for a Straight Line $y = a + bx$

where:

y = the dependent variable being estimated or predicted
a = the intercept
b = the slope
x = the independent variable used to predict the dependent variable

FIGURE 18.2
A Child's Control of His or Her Shoe Purchases: Monotonic Increasing Relationship

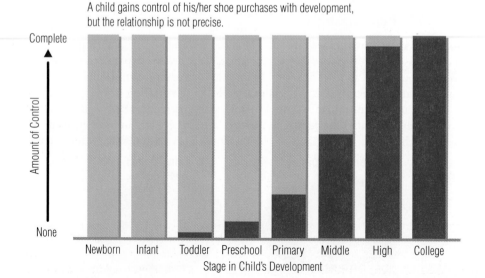

A child gains control of his/her shoe purchases with development, but the relationship is not precise.

Generally, as a child grows, he or she has more influence in his or her shoe purchases, but the relationship is not precise.

The terms *intercept* and *slope* should be familiar to you, but if they are a bit hazy, do not be concerned as we describe the straight-line formula in detail in the next chapter. We also clarify the terms *independent* and *dependent* in Chapter 19.

Linear relationships are quite precise.

It should be apparent to you that a linear relationship is much more precise and contains a great deal more information than does a monotonic relationship. By simply substituting the values of *a* and *b*, an exact amount can be determined for *y* given any value of *x*. For example, if Jack-in-the-Box estimates that every customer will spend about $5 per lunch visit, it is easy to use a linear relationship to estimate how many dollars of revenue will be associated with the number of customers for any given location. The following equation would be used:

Straight-Line Formula Example $y = \$0 + \$5 \times x$

where *x* is the number of customers. So if 100 customers come to a Jack-in-the-Box location, the associated expected total revenues would be $0 plus $5 times 100, or $500 dollars. If 200 customers were expected to visit the location, the expected total revenue would be $0 plus $5 times 200, or $1000. To be sure, the Jack-in-the-Box location would not derive exactly $1000 for 200 customers, but the linear relationship shows what is expected to happen, on average.

Curvilinear Relationships

Now, we turn to the last type of relationship. **Curvilinear relationships** are those in which one variable is associated with another variable, but the relationship is described by a curve rather than a straight line. In other words, the formula for a

A curvilinear relationship means some smooth curve pattern describes the association.

curved relationship is used rather than the formula for a straight line. Many curvilinear patterns are possible. For example, the relationship may be an S-shape, a J-shape, or some other curved-shape pattern. An example of a curvilinear relationship with which you should be familiar is the product life-cycle curve that describes the sales pattern of a new product over time that grows slowly during its introduction and then spurts upward rapidly during its growth stage and finally plateaus or slows down considerably as the market becomes saturated. Curvilinear relationships are beyond the scope of this book; nonetheless, it is important to list them as a type of relationship that can be investigated through the use of special-purpose statistical procedures.

CHARACTERIZING RELATIONSHIPS BETWEEN VARIABLES

Depending on its type, a relationship can usually be characterized in three ways: by its presence, direction, and strength of association. We need to describe these before taking up specific statistical analyses of associations between two variables.

Presence

The presence of a relationship between two variables is determined by a statistical test.

Presence refers to the finding that a systematic relationship exists between the two variables of interest in the population. Presence is a statistical issue. By this statement, we mean that the marketing researcher relies on statistical significance tests to determine whether there is sufficient evidence in the sample to support that a particular association is present in the population. Chapter 17 on statistical inference introduced the concept of a null hypothesis. With associative analysis, the null hypothesis states there is no association present in the population and the appropriate statistical test is applied to test this hypothesis. If the test results reject the null hypothesis, then we can state that an association is present in the population (at a certain level of confidence). We describe the statistical tests used in associative analysis later in this chapter.

Direction (or Pattern)

You have seen that in the cases of monotonic and linear relationships, associations may be described with regard to direction. As we indicated earlier, a monotonic relationship may be increasing or decreasing. For a linear relationship, if b (slope) is positive, then the linear relationship is increasing; and if b is negative, then the linear relationship is decreasing. So the direction of the relationship is straightforward with linear and monotonic relationships.

Direction means that you know if the relationship is positive or negative, while pattern means you know the general nature of the relationship.

For nonmonotonic relationships, positive or negative direction is inappropriate, because we can only describe the pattern verbally.[2] It will soon become clear to you that the scaling assumptions of variables having a nonmonotonic association negate the directional aspects of the relationship. Nevertheless, we can verbally describe the pattern of the association as we have in our examples, and that statement substitutes for direction. Finally, with curvilinear relationships, we can use a formula; however, the formula will define a pattern such as an S-shape that we refer to in characterizing the nature of the relationship.

Strength of Association

Strength means you know how consistent the relationship is.

Finally, when present (that is, statistically significant) the association between two variables can be envisioned as to its strength, commonly using words such as "strong," "moderate," "weak," or some similar characterization; that is, when a consistent and systematic association is found to be present between two variables, it is then up to the marketing researcher to ascertain the strength of the association. Strong associations are those in which there is a high probability of the two variables' exhibiting a dependable relationship, regardless of the type of relationship being analyzed. A low degree of association, on the other hand, is one in which there is a low probability of the two variables' exhibiting a dependable relationship. The relationship exists between the variables, but it is less evident.

There is an orderly procedure for determining presence, direction, and strength of a relationship. First, you must decide what type of relationship can exist between the two variables of interest. The answer to this question depends on the scaling assumptions of the variables; as we illustrated earlier, low-level (nominal) scales can embody only imprecise, pattern-like, relationships, but high-level (interval or ratio) scales can incorporate very precise and linear relationships. Once you identify the appropriate relationship type as either nonmonotonic, monotonic, or linear, the next step is to determine whether that relationship actually exists in the population you are analyzing. This step requires a statistical test, and, again, we describe the proper test for each of these three relationship types beginning with the next section of this chapter.

When you determine that a true relationship does exist in the population by means of the correct statistical test, you then establish its direction or pattern. Again, the type of relationship dictates how you describe its direction. You might have to inspect the relationship in a table or graph, or you might need only to look for a positive or negative sign before the computed statistic. Finally, the strength of the relationship remains to be judged. Some associative analysis statistics indicate the strength in a very straightforward manner—that is, just by their absolute size. With nominal-scaled variables, however, you must inspect the pattern to judge the strength. We describe this procedure next.

> **Based on scaling assumptions, first determine the type of relationship, and then perform the appropriate statistical test.**

CROSS-TABULATIONS *(Nominal data)*
95% CL

Cross-tabulation and the associated chi-square value that we are about to explain are used to assess if a nonmonotonic relationship exists between two nominal-scaled variables. Remember that nonmonotonic relationships are those in which the presence of one variable coincides with the presence of another variable, such as lunch buyers ordering soft drinks with their meals.

Inspecting the Relationship with a Bar Chart

A handy graphical tool that illustrates a nonmonotonic relationship is a stacked bar chart. With a stacked bar chart, two variables are accommodated simultaneously in the same bar graph. Each bar in the stacked bar chart stands for 100%, and it is divided proportionately by the amount of relationship that one variable shares with the other variables. For instance, you can see in Figure 18.3 that there are two variables: buyer type and occupational category. The two bars are made up of two types of individuals: buyers of Michelob Beer and nonbuyers of Michelob. There are two types of occupations: professional workers, who might be called "white collar" employees, and manual workers, who are sometimes referred to as "blue collar" workers. With the buyers stacked bar, you can see that a large percent of the white collar stacked bar is accounted for by the Michelob buyers, while a smaller percent of Michelob buyers is apparent on the blue collar workers bar graph.

> **Bar charts can be used to "see" a nonmonotonic relationship.**

FIGURE 18.3
Michelob Light Purchases
and Occupational Status

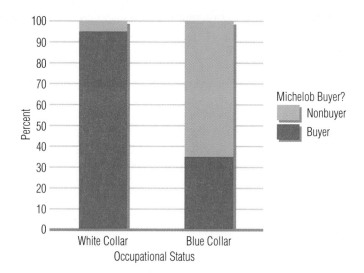

You should remember that we described a nonmonotonic relationship as an identifiable association in which the presence of one variable is paired with the presence (or absence) of another. This pattern is apparent in the stacked bar chart in Figure 18.3: buyers tend to be professional workers, while nonbuyers tend to be manual workers. Alternatively, nonbuyers tend not to be white collar workers, while buyers tend not to have blue collar occupations.

Cross-Tabulation Table

A cross-tabulation consists of rows and columns defined by the categories classifying each variable.

While a stacked bar chart provides a way of visualizing nonmonotonic relationships, the most common method of presentation for these situations is through the use of a **cross-tabulation table**, defined as a table in which data are compared using a row-and-column format. A cross-tabulation table is sometimes referred to as an "r × c" (r-by-c) table because it comprises rows and columns. The intersection of a row and a column is called a **cross-tabulation cell**. A cross-tabulation table for the stacked bar chart that we have been working with is presented in Table 18.1. Notice that we have identified the four cells with lines for the rows and columns. The columns are in vertical alignment and are indicated in this table as either "Buyer" or "Nonbuyer" of Michelob Light, whereas the rows are indicated as "White Collar" or "Blue Collar" for occupation.

Types of Frequencies and Percentages in a Cross-Tabulation Table

Look at the Frequencies Table section in Table 18.1. The upper left-hand cell number identifies people in the sample who are both white-collar workers and buyers of Michelob Light (152), and the cell to its right identifies the number of individuals who are white-collar workers who do not buy Michelob Light (8). These cell numbers represent frequencies; that is, the number of respondents who possess the quality indicated by the row label as well as the quality indicated by the column label.

A cross-classification table can have four types of numbers in each cell: frequency, raw percentage, column percentage, and row percentage.

Table 18.1 illustrates how at least four different sets of numbers can be computed for cells in the table. These four sets are the frequencies table, the raw percentages table, the column percentages table, and the row percentages table. The **frequencies table** contains the raw numbers determined from the preliminary tabulation.[3] The lower right-hand number of 200 refers to the total sample size, sometimes called the

TABLE 18.1	Cross-Tabulation Tables for a Michelob Light Survey

Frequencies Table

$$152 + 8 = 160$$
$$14 + 26 = 40$$

		Buyer	Nonbuyer	Totals
	White Collar	152	8	160
Occupational status	Blue Collar	14	26	40
$152 + 14 = 166$ $8 + 26 = 34$	Totals	166	34	200

Raw Percentages Table

		Buyer	Nonbuyer	Totals
$152/200 = 76\%$	White Collar	76% (152)	4% (8)	80% (160)
Occupational status	Blue Collar	7% (14)	13% (26)	20% (40)
	Totals	83% (166)	18% (34)	100% (200)

Column Percentages Table

		Buyer	Nonbuyer	Totals
$152/166 = 92\%$	White Collar	92% (152)	24% (8)	80% (160)
Occupational status	Blue Collar	8% (14)	76% (26)	20% (40)
	Totals	100% (166)	100% (34)	100% (200)

Row Percentages Table

		Buyer	Nonbuyer	Totals
$152/160 = 95\%$	White Collar	95% (152)	5% (8)	100% (160)
Occupational status	Blue Collar	35% (14)	65% (26)	100% (40)
	Totals	83% (166)	18% (34)	100% (200)

"grand total." Just above it are the totals for the number of white-collar (160) and blue-collar (40) occupation respondents in the sample. Going to the left of the grand total are the totals for Michelob Light nonbuyers (34) and buyers (166) in the sample. The four cells are the totals for the intersection points: 152 white-collar Michelob Light buyers, 8 white-collar nonbuyers, 14 blue-collar Michelob Light buyers, and 26 blue-collar nonbuyers.

Raw percentages are cell frequencies divided by the grand total.

These raw frequencies can be converted to raw percentages by dividing each by the grand total. The second cross-tabulation table, the **raw percentages table**, contains the percentages of the raw frequency numbers just discussed. The grand total location now has 100 percent (or 200/200) of the grand total. Above it are 80% and 20% for the raw percentages of white-collar occupational respondents and blue-collar occupational respondents, respectively, in the sample. Divide a couple of the cells just to verify that you understand how they are derived. For instance $152 \div 200 = 76$ percent.

Two additional cross-tabulation tables can be presented, and these are more valuable in revealing underlying relationships. The **column percentages table** divides the raw frequency by its column total raw frequency. The formula is as follows:

Formula for a Column Cell Percent

$$\text{Column cell percent} = \frac{\text{Cell frequency}}{\text{Total of cells in that column}}$$

For instance, it is apparent that of the nonbuyers, 24% were white-collar and 76% were blue-collar respondents. Note the reverse pattern for the buyers group: 92% of white-collar respondents were Michelob Light buyers and 8% were blue-collar buyers. You are beginning to see the nonmonotonic relationship.

Associations between product and brand preferences and demographic characteristics help marketers identify their target markets.

The **row percentages table** presents the data with the row totals as the 100 percent base for each. That is, a row cell percentage is computed as follows:

Formula for a Row Cell Percent

$$\text{Row cell percent} = \frac{\text{Cell frequency}}{\text{Total of cells in that row}}$$

Now, it is possible to see that, of the white-collar respondents, 95% were buyers and 5% were nonbuyers. As you compare the Row Percentages Table to the Column Percentages Table, you should detect the relationship between Occupational Status and Michelob Light beer preference. Can you state it at this time?

Unequal percentage concentrations of individuals in a few cells, as we have in this example, illustrates the possible presence of a nonmonotonic association. If we had found that approximately 25% of the sample had fallen in each of the four cells, no relationship would be found to exist—it would be equally probable for any person to be a Michelob Light buyer or nonbuyer and a white- or a blue-collar worker. However, the large concentrations of individuals in two particular cells here suggests that there is a high probability that a buyer of Michelob Light beer is also a white-collar worker, and there is also a tendency for nonbuyers to work in blue-collar occupations. In other words, there is probably an association between occupational status and the beer-buying behavior of individuals in population represented by this sample. We must test the statistical significance of the apparent relationship before we can say anything more about it.

Row (column) percentages are row (column) cell frequencies divided by the row (column) total.

CHI–SQUARE ANALYSIS

Chi-square (χ^2) analysis is the examination of frequencies for two nominal-scaled variables in a cross-tabulation table to determine whether the variables have a nonmonotonic relationship.[4] The formal procedure for chi-square analysis begins when the researcher formulates a statistical null hypothesis that the two variables under investigation are *not* associated in the population. Actually, it is not necessary for the researcher to state this hypothesis in a formal sense, for chi-square analysis always explicitly takes this hypothesis into account. In other words, whenever we use chi-square analysis with a cross-tabulation, we always begin with the assumption that no association exists between the two nominal-scaled variables under analysis.[5]

Chi-square analysis assesses nonmonotonic associations in cross-tabulation tables.

Observed and Expected Frequencies

The statistical procedure is as follows. The first cross-tabulation table in Table 18.1 contains **observed frequencies**, which are the actual cell counts in the cross-tabulation table. These observed frequencies are compared to **expected frequencies**, which are defined as the theoretical frequencies that are derived from this hypothesis of no association between the two variables. The degree to which the observed frequencies depart from the expected frequencies is expressed in a single number called the "chi-square statistic." The computed chi-square statistic is then compared to a table chi-square value (at a chosen level of significance) to determine whether the computed value is significantly different from zero.

Observed frequencies are the counts for each cell found in the sample.

Expected frequencies are calculated based on the null hypothesis of no association between the two variables under investigation.

Here's a simple example to help you understand what we just stated. Suppose you perform a blind taste test with 10 of your friends. First, you pour Diet Pepsi in 10 paper cups with no identification on the cup. Next, you assemble your 10 friends, and you let each one try a taste from his or her paper cup. Then, you ask each friend to guess whether it is Diet Pepsi or Diet Coke. If your friends guessed randomly, you would expect five to guess Diet Pepsi and five to guess Diet Coke. This is your null hypothesis: There is no relationship between the Diet Coke being tested and the guess. But you find that 9 of your friends correctly guess "Diet Pepsi," and 1 incorrectly guesses "Diet

Coke." In other words, you have found a departure in your observed frequencies from the expected frequencies. It looks like your friends can correctly identify Diet Pepsi about 90% of the time. There *seems* to be a relationship, but we are not certain of its statistical significance, because we have not done any significance tests. The chi-square statistic is used to perform such a test. We will describe the chi-square test and then apply it to your blind taste test using Diet Pepsi.

The expected frequencies are those that would be found if there were no association between the two variables. Remember, this is the null hypothesis. About the only "difficult" part of chi-square analysis is in the computation of the expected frequencies. The computation is accomplished using the following equation:

Formula for an Expected Cell Frequency

$$\text{Expected cell frequency} = \frac{\text{Cell column total} \times \text{Cell row total}}{\text{Grand total}}$$

The application of this equation generates a number for each cell that would have occurred if the study had taken place and no associations existed. Returning to our Michelob Light beer example, you were told that 160 white-collar and 40 blue-collar consumers had been sampled, and it was found that there were 166 buyers and 34 nonbuyers of Michelob Light. The expected frequency for each cell, assuming no association, calculated with the expected cell frequency is as follows:

Calculations of Expected Cell Frequencies Using the Michelob Beer Example

$$\text{White-collar buyer} = \frac{160 \times 166}{200} = 132.8$$

$$\text{White-collar nonbuyer} = \frac{160 \times 34}{200} = 27.2$$

$$\text{Blue-collar buyer} = \frac{40 \times 166}{200} = 33.2$$

$$\text{Blue-collar nonbuyer} = \frac{40 \times 34}{200} = 6.8$$

The Computed χ^2 Value

The computed chi-square value compares observed to expected frequencies.

Next, compare the observed frequencies to these expected frequencies. The **chi-square formula** is as follows:

Chi-Square Formula

$$\chi^2 = \sum_{i-1}^{n} \frac{(\text{Observed}_i - \text{Expected}_i)^2}{\text{Expected}_i}$$

where

Observed_i = observed frequency in cell i
Expected_i = expected frequency in cell i
n = number of cells

Applied to our Michelob beer example,

Calculation of Chi-Square Value (Michelob Example)

The chi-square statistic summarizes how far away from the expected frequencies the observed cell frequencies are found to be.

$$\chi^2 = \frac{(152 - 132.8)^2}{132.8} + \frac{(8 - 27.2)^2}{27.2} + \frac{(14 - 33.2)^2}{33.2} + \frac{(26 - 6.8)^2}{6.8} = 81.64$$

You can see from the equation that each expected frequency is compared to the observed frequency and squared to adjust for any negative values and to avoid the cancellation effect. This value is divided by the expected frequency to adjust for cell size differences, and these amounts are summed across all of the cells. If there are many large deviations of observed frequencies from the expected frequencies, the computed chi-square value will increase; but if there are only a few slight deviations from the expected frequencies, the computed chi-square number will be small. In other words, the computed chi-square value is really a summary indication of how far away from the expected frequencies the observed frequencies are found to be. As such, it expresses the departure of the sample findings from the null hypothesis of no association.

Some researchers think of an expected-to-observed comparison analysis as a "goodness of fit" test. It assesses how closely the actual frequencies fit the pattern of expected frequencies. We have provided Marketing Research Insight 18.1 as an illustration of the goodness-of-fit notion.[6]

Chi-square analysis is sometimes referred to as a "goodness-of-fit" test.

Let us apply this equation to the example of your 10 friends guessing about Diet Pepsi or Diet Coke. We already agreed that if they guessed randomly, you would find five guessing for each brand, or a 50–50 split. But if we found an 90–10 vote for Diet Pepsi, you would be inclined to conclude that they could recognize Diet Pepsi; that is, most recognized the cola taste, so they gave the name, Diet Pepsi, that is related to it. Let's use the chi-square formula with observed and expected frequencies to see if the relationship is statistically significant.

MARKETING RESEARCH INSIGHT

PRACTICAL APPLICATION

18.1 "Zeroing in" on Goodness-of-Fit

Can you guess the next number based on the apparent pattern of 1, 3, 5? Okay, what about this series: 1, 6, 11, 16?

In the first series, you realize that 2 was added to determine the next number (1, 3, 5, 7, 9, and so on). You looked at the series and noticed the equal intervals of 2. You then created a mental expectation of the series based on your suspected pattern.

Let us take the second series because it is a bit more difficult. Suppose your first intuition was to add a 3 to the previous number. Here is your expected series and the actual one compared:

Expected	1	4	7	10
Actual	1	6	11	16
Difference	0	2	4	6

Oops, not much of a match here. So let's try a 4.

Expected	1	5	9	13
Actual	1	6	11	16
Difference	0	1	2	3

Getting closer, but still not there. Now try a 5.

Expected	1	6	11	16
Actual	1	6	11	16
Difference	0	0	0	0

You have been performing "goodness-of-fit" tests. Notice that the differences became smaller as you zeroed in on the true pattern. (Catch the pun?) In other words, when the actual numbers are equal to the expected numbers, there is no difference, and the fit is perfect. This is the concept used in chi-square analysis. When the differences are small, you have a good fit to the expected values. When the differences are larger, you have a poor fit, and your hypothesis (the expected number sequence) is incorrect.

To determine the chi-square value, we calculate as follows:

Calculation of Chi-Square Value Using Diet Pepsi Taste Test

$$\chi^2 = \sum_{i-1}^{n} \frac{(\text{Observed}_i - \text{Expected}_i)^2}{\text{Expected}_i}$$

$$= \frac{(9-5)^2}{5} + \frac{(1-5)^2}{5}$$

$$= 6.4$$

Remember, you need to use the frequencies, not the percentages.

The Chi-Square Distribution

Now that you've learned how to calculate a chi-square value, you need to know if it is statistically significant. In Chapter 17, we described how the normal curve, or z distribution, the F distribution and Student's t distribution, all of which exist in tables, are used by a computer statistical program to determine level of significance. Chi-square analysis requires the use of a different distribution. The **chi-square distribution** is skewed to the right and the rejection region is always at the right-hand tail of the distribution. It differs from the normal and t distributions in that it changes its shape depending on the situation at hand, but it does not have negative values. Figure 18.4 shows examples of two chi-square distributions.

The chi-square distribution's shape changes depending on the number of degrees of freedom.

The chi-square distribution's shape is determined by the number of degrees of freedom. The figure shows that the more the degrees of freedom, the more the curve's tail is pulled to the right. In other words, the more the degrees of freedom, the larger the chi-square value must be to fall in the rejection region for the null hypothesis.

It is a simple matter to determine the number of degrees of freedom. In a cross-tabulation table, the degrees of freedom are found through the formula below:

Formula for Chi-Square Degrees of Freedom

$$\text{Degrees of freedom} = (r - 1)(c - 1)$$

where

r is the number of rows and
c is the number of columns.

FIGURE 18.4
The Chi-Square Curve's Shape Depends on Its Degrees of Freedom

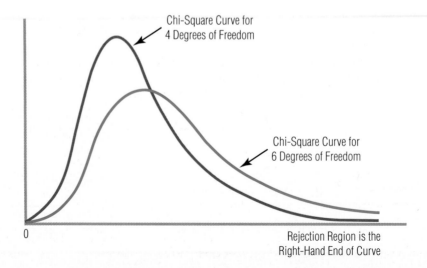

Chi-Square Curve for 4 Degrees of Freedom

Chi-Square Curve for 6 Degrees of Freedom

0

Rejection Region is the Right-Hand End of Curve

A table of chi-square values contains critical points that determine the break between acceptance and rejection regions at various levels of significance. It also takes into account the numbers of degrees of freedom associated with each curve; that is, a computed chi-square value says nothing by itself—you must consider the number of degrees of freedom in the cross-tabulation table because more degrees of freedom are indicative of higher critical chi-square table values for the same level of significance. The logic of this situation stems from the number of cells. With more cells, there is more opportunity for departure from the expected values. The higher table values adjust for potential inflation due to chance alone. After all, we want to detect real nonmonotonic relationships, not phantom ones.

> **The computed chi-square value is compared to a table value to determine statistical significance.**

SPSS and virtually all computer statistical analysis programs have chi-square tables in memory and print out the probability of the null hypothesis. Let us repeat this point: The program itself will take into account the number of degrees of freedom and determine the probability of support for the null hypothesis. This probability is the percentage of the area under the chi-square curve that lies to the right of the computed chi-square value. When rejection of the null hypothesis occurs, we have found that a statistically significant nonmonotonic association exists between the two variables.

> **Computer statistical programs look up table chi-square values and print out the probability of support for the null hypothesis.**

As an example of the use of cross-tabulations and chi-square, we have prepared Marketing Research Insight 18.2, which illustrates how cross-tabulation can be used with qualitative data. In this case, the researchers judged the models and the wording of *Seventeen* magazine advertisements and use a nominal classification system. Thus, the only way to analyze the data is with cross-tabulations.

COMPUTE CHI-SQUARE VALUES

Active Learning

We have described the concepts of observed frequencies, expected frequencies, and computed chi-square value. Plus, we have provided formulas for the latter two concepts. Your task in this Active Learning exercise will be to compute the expected frequencies and chi-square values for two different cross-tabulation tables. Marketing Research Insight 18.2 has a cross-tabulation for Visual and a cross-tabulation for Verbal judged "girlish" advertisements in *Seventeen* magazine. Compute the expected frequencies and chi-square values for each.

How to Interpret a Chi-Square Result

How does one interpret a chi-square result? Chi-square analysis yields the amount of support for the null hypothesis if the researcher repeated the study many, many times with independent samples. By now, you should be well acquainted with the concept of many, many independent samples. For example, if the chi-square analysis yielded a 0.02 significance level for the null hypothesis, the researcher would conclude that only 2% of the time he or she would find evidence to support the null hypothesis. Since the null hypothesis is not supported, this means there is a significant association.

It must be pointed out that chi-square analysis is simply a method to determine whether a nonmonotonic association exists between two variables. Chi-square does not indicate the nature of the association, and it indicates only roughly the strength of association by its size. It is best interpreted as a prerequisite to looking more closely at the two variables to discern the nature of the association that exists between them. That is, the chi-square test is another one of our "flags" that tell us whether or not it is worthwhile to inspect all those row and column percentages.

18.2 Cross-Tabulations Reveal Cultural Differences between Japanese and American *Seventeen* Magazine Ads

Occasionally a researcher must work with purely qualitative data, and this Marketing Research Insight describes this situation. Researchers were interested in comparing the way *Seventeen* magazine portrayed teen-age girls in different cultures.[7] Specifically, the Japanese culture emphasizes shared identity and deemphasizes individuality while the American culture emphasizes individuality and even rebellion. Since consumers' self-identities are shaped in part by mass media and advertising, researchers examined all of the relevant ads in four successive issues of the English (American) version and the Japanese version of *Seventeen* magazine. They used a judging system to classify the visual or pictured models and another judging system to classify the words (verbal) in the ads. In classifying the visual and verbal aspects of the advertisements, the judges decided whether or not the advertisement's components were "girlish" meaning that they were indicative of child-like norms. The cross-tabulation tables that resulted follow.

	VISUAL (PICTURES)			VERBAL (WORDS)	
	JAPANESE *SEVENTEEN*	U.S. *SEVENTEEN*		JAPANESE *SEVENTEEN*	U.S. *SEVENTEEN*
Girlish	73	64	Girlish	45	39
Not girlish	31	95	Not girlish	59	120

In both cases, the computed chi-square values were large and statistically significant, meaning that there was a relationship between the country's culture and the portrayal of teenaged females in the *Seventeen* magazine advertisements. The following column percentage tables vividly depict the nature of how the advertisements in *Seventeen* magazine communicate Japanese cultural norms to Japanese teenaged females, while the American version of *Seventeen* strongly communicates American cultural norms to American teenaged female readers.

	VISUAL (PICTURES)			VERBAL (WORDS)	
	JAPANESE *SEVENTEEN*	U.S. *SEVENTEEN*		JAPANESE *SEVENTEEN*	U.S. *SEVENTEEN*
Girlish	70%	40%	Girlish	43%	25%
Not girlish	30%	60%	Not girlish	57%	75%
	100%	100%		100%	100%

A significant chi-square means the researcher should look at the cross-tabulation row and column percentages to "see" the association pattern.

When the computed chi-square value is small, the null hypothesis or the hypothesis of independence between the two variables is generally assumed to be true. It is not worth the marketing researcher's time to focus on associations, because they are more a function of sampling error than they are of meaningful relationships between the two variables. However, when chi-square analysis identifies a relationship with a significance level of .05 or less (the flag is waving), the researcher can be assured that he or she is not wasting time and is actually pursuing a real association, a relationship that truly exists between the two variables in the population. In our Diet Pepsi blind taste test, the chi-square table value for the 95% level of significance was 3.8, and the computed value was 6.4, so the computed value is larger than the critical value. If we used SPSS, the significance level would be reported as .0001, indicating that the relationship is statistically significant.

YOUR INTEGRATED CASE   SPSS

The Hobbit's Choice Restaurant Survey: Analyzing Cross-Tabulations for Significant Associations by Performing Chi-Square Analysis with SPSS

We are going to use our the Hobbit's Choice Restaurant survey data to demonstrate how to perform and interpret cross-tabulation analysis with SPSS. You may recall that we used subscription to *City Magazine* as a grouping variable and performed an independent-samples *t* test in Chapter 16. We found that *City Magazine* subscribers were more likely to intend to patronize the Hobbit's Choice Restaurant. We can use cross-tabulation analysis to get a better picture of the effectiveness of *City Magazine* as an advertising medium. Subscription to *City Magazine* is a nominal variable because respondents indicated "yes" or "no." We can categorize the respondents based on how likely they are to patronize the Hobbit's Choice. By taking those who are "very likely" or are "somewhat likely" and creating a "probable patron of the Hobbit's Choice Restaurant" variable in which respondents are either "probable patron," or "not probable patron."

The clickstream command sequence to perform a chi-square test with SPSS is ANALYZE-DESCRIPTIVE STATISTICS-CROSSTABS, which leads to a dialog box in which you can select the variables for chi-square analysis. In our example in Figure 18.5, we have selected Subscribe to *City Magazine* as the row variable, and Probable patron of the Hobbit's Choice Restaurant as the column variable. There are three options buttons at the bottom of the box. The Cells . . . option leads to the specification of observed frequencies, expected frequencies, row percentages, column percentages, and so forth. We have opted for just the observed frequencies (raw counts) and the column percents. The Statistics . . . button opens up a menu of statistics that can be computed from cross-tabulation tables. Of course, the only one we want is the chi-square option.

The resulting output is found in Figure 18.6. In the first table, you can see that we have variable and value labels, and the table contains the raw frequency as the first entry in each cell. Also, the row percentages are reported along with each row and column total. In the second table, there is information on the chi-square analysis result. For our purposes, the only relevant statistic is the Pearson chi-square, which has been computed to be 112.878. The df column pertains to the number of degrees of freedom, which is 1; and the Asymp. Sig. corresponds to the probability of support for the null hypothesis. Significance in this example is .000, which means that there is practically no support for the hypothesis that subscription to *City Magazine* and Probably patronage of the Hobbit's Choice Restaurant are not associated. In other words, they are related. (Actually, the probability is not exactly equal to zero because SPSS reports only three decimal places. If it reported, say, 10 places, you would see a number somewhere past the third decimal place.)

So, SPSS has effected the first step in determining a nonmonotonic association. Through chi-square analysis it has signaled that a statistically significant association

With SPSS, chi-square is an option under the "Crosstabs" analysis routine.

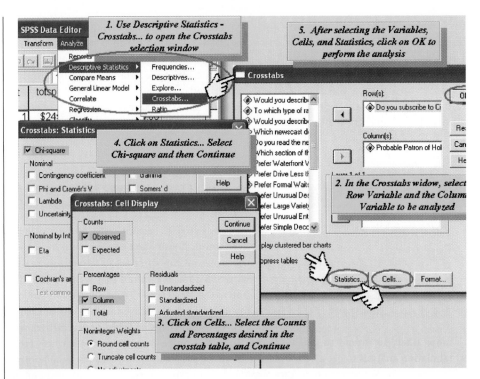

With chi-square analysis, interpret the SPSS significance level as the amount of support for no association between the two variables being analyzed.

FIGURE 18.5
The SPSS Clickstream to Create Cross-Tabulation with Chi-Square Analysis

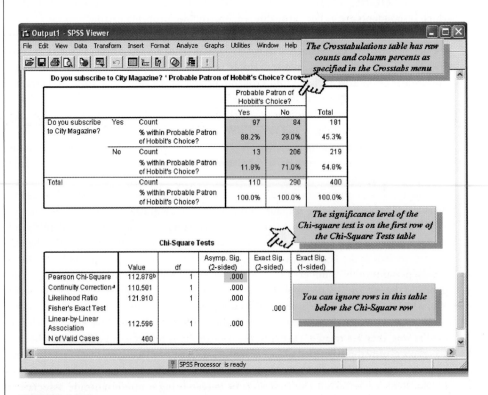

FIGURE 18.6
SPSS Output for Cross-Tabulations with Chi-Square Analysis

actually exists. The next step is to fathom the nature of the association. Remember that with a nonmonotonic relationship, you must inspect the pattern and describe it verbally. When we looked for the pattern in our example, we converted the frequencies into row and column percentages. Now, you have a cross-tabulation table with row percentages in their respective cells. The row percentages show that about 88% of Probable patrons are *City Magazine* subscribers. At the same time, 71% of the Not probable patrons are nonsubscribers to *City Magazine* . You can interpret this finding in the following way. If Jeff places an ad in *City Magazine* for the Hobbit's Choice Restaurant, almost 90% of the readers of the magazine will be members of his target market.

In other words, because the significance was less than .05, it was worthwhile to inspect and interpret the percentages in the cross-tabulation table. By doing this, we can discern the pattern or nature of the association, and the percentages indicate its relative strength. More importantly, because the relationship was determined to be statistically significant, you can be assured that this association and the relationship you have observed will hold for the population that this sample represents.

SPSS Student Assistant Online
The Integrated Case
Setting up and Analyzing
Cross-Tabulations

Presentation of Cross-Tabulation Findings

When we introduced the notion of relationship or association analysis, we noted that characterizing the direction and strength of nonmonotonic relationships that are detected in crosstabulations with chi-square analysis are not possible because nominal scales are involved. Nominal scales do not have order or magnitude: they are simply categories or labels that uniquely identify the data. To reveal the nonmonotonic relationships found significant in cross-tabulation tables, researchers often turn to graphical presentations, as pictures will show the relationships very adequately. Read Marketing Research Insight 18.3 for an example of how graphical presentations can effectively summarize and communicate these relationships.

MARKETING
RESEARCH
INSIGHT

ONLINE APPLICATION

18.3

Use of Cross-Tabulations to Test and Graphical Presentations to Show Cross-Tabulation Relationships for Online versus Nononline Shoppers

The frequencies found in cross-tabulations, when converted to percentage tables, are quite amenable to graphical presentations that are very useful in depicting the nature of the relationships found in a survey. With this Marketing Research Insight, we are using the cross-tabulations reported in a Web-based survey that compared online shoppers with individuals who had never made an online purchase.[8] In the survey, these two types of purchasers were measured by a number of demographic characteristics such as gender, age, education, ethnicity, marital status, and income. They were also measured on self-reports of computer competency and how they prefer to search for information about marketplace alternatives. The following three relationships were found to be statistically significant, meaning that the relationships exist in the population. The finding of significance with a cross-tabulation allows the researcher to examine and describe the relationship, as it is a nonmontonic pattern and not one that can be characterized by direction or strength from the chi-square results alone. We have included a statement of the apparent relationships in each graph. This graphical approach is an appropriate one for nonmontonic relationships.

(continued)

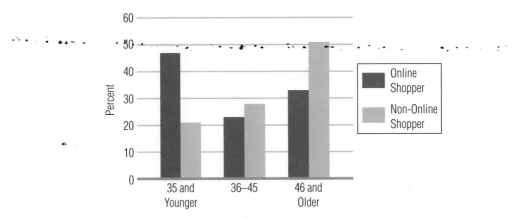

Online Shopping and Age. Relationship: Online shoppers are younger than Non–online shoppers.

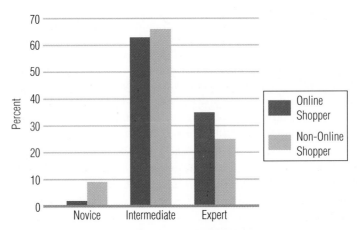

Online Shopping and Computer Competence. Relationship: Online shoppers have more computer competence than do Non–online shoppers.

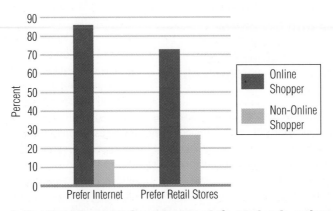

Online Shopping and Information Search for Marketplace Alternatives. Relationship: Online shoppers prefer to use the Internet to search about marketplace alternatives more than do Non–online shoppers.

CORRELATION COEFFICIENTS AND COVARIATION

PPMCC(r) Pearson Product Moment Correlation Coefficients (r) p.544

The **correlation coefficient** is an index number, constrained to fall between the range of −1.0 and +1.0, that communicates both the strength and the direction of a linear relationship between two variables. The strength of association between two variables is communicated by the absolute size of the correlation coefficient, whereas its sign communicates the direction of the association. Stated in a slightly different manner, a correlation coefficient indicates the degree of "covariation" between two variables. *(interval + ratio)* **Covariation** is defined as the amount of change in one variable systematically associated with a change in another variable. The greater the absolute size of the correlation coefficient, the greater is the covariation between the two variables, or the stronger is their relationship.[9]

> A correlation coefficient standardizes the covariation between two variables into a number ranging from −1.0 to +1.0.

Let us take up the statistical significance of a correlation coefficient first. Regardless of its absolute value, a correlation that is not statistically significant has no meaning at all. This is because of the null hypothesis, which states that the population correlation coefficient is equal to zero. If this null hypothesis is rejected (statistically significant correlation), then you can be assured that a correlation other than zero will be found in the population. But if the sample correlation is found to be not significant, the population correlation will be zero. Here is a question. If you can answer it correctly, you understand the statistical significance of a correlation. If you repeated a correlational survey many, many times and computed the average for a correlation that was not significant across all of these surveys, what would be the result? (The answer is zero because if the correlation is not significant, the null hypothesis is true, and the population correlation is zero.)

> To use a correlation, you must first establish that it is statistically significantly different from zero.

How do you determine the statistical significance of a correlation coefficient? Tables exist that give the lowest value of the significant correlation coefficients for given sample sizes. However, most computer statistical programs will indicate the statistical significance level of the computed correlation coefficient. Your SPSS program provides the significance in the form of the probability that the null hypothesis is supported. In SPSS, this is a "Sig." value that we will identify for you when we show you SPSS correlation output. In addition, it will also allow you to indicate a directional hypothesis about the size of the expected correlation just as with a directional means hypothesis test.

Rules of Thumb for Correlation Strength

After we have established that a correlation coefficient is statistically significant, we can talk about some general rules of thumb concerning the strength of association. Correlation coefficients that fall between +1.00 and +.81 or between −1.00 and −.81 are generally considered to be "strong." Correlations that fall between +.80 and +.61 or −.80 and −.61 generally indicate a "moderate" association. Those that fall between +.60 and +.41 or −.60 and −.41 are typically considered to be "low," and they denote a weak association. Finally, any correlation that falls between the range of ±.21 and ±.40 is usually considered indicative of a very weak association between the variables. Next, any correlation that is equal to or less than ±.20 is typically uninteresting to marketing researchers because it rarely identifies a meaningful association between two variables. We have provided Table 18.2 as a reference on these rules of thumb. As you use these guidelines, remember two things: First, we are assuming that the statistical significance of the correlation has been established. Second, researchers make up their own rules of thumb, so you may encounter someone whose guidelines differ slightly from those in the table.[10]

> Rules of thumb exist concerning the strength of a correlation based on its absolute size.

In any case, it is helpful to think in terms of the closeness of the correlation coefficient to zero or to ±1.00. Statistically significant correlation coefficients that are close to

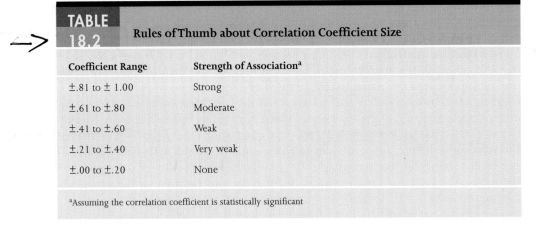

TABLE 18.2	Rules of Thumb about Correlation Coefficient Size
Coefficient Range	**Strength of Association[a]**
±.81 to ±1.00	Strong
±.61 to ±.80	Moderate
±.41 to ±.60	Weak
±.21 to ±.40	Very weak
±.00 to ±.20	None

[a]Assuming the correlation coefficient is statistically significant

zero show that there is no systematic association between the two variables, whereas those that are closer to +1.00 or −1.00 express that there is some systematic association between the variables.

The Correlation Sign

A correlation indicates the strength of association between two variables by its size. The sign indicates the direction of the association.

But what about the sign of the correlation coefficient? The sign indicates the direction of the association. A positive sign indicates a positive direction; a negative sign indicates a negative direction. For instance, if you found a significant correlation of 0.83 between years of education and hours spent reading *National Geographic*, it would mean that people with more education spend more hours reading this magazine. But if you found a significant negative correlation between education and cigarette smoking, it would mean that more educated people smoke less.

Graphing Covariation Using Scatter Diagrams

We addressed the concept of covariation between two variables in our introductory comments on correlations. It is now time to present covariation in a slightly different manner. Here is an example: A marketing researcher is investigating the possible relationship between total company sales for Novartis, a leading pharmaceutical company, in a particular territory and the number of salespeople assigned to that territory. At the researcher's fingertips are the sales figures and number of salespeople assigned for each of 20 different Novartis territories in the United States.

Covariation can be examined with the use of a scatter diagram.

It is possible to depict the raw data for these two variables on a scatter diagram such as the one in Figure 18.7. A **scatter diagram** plots the points corresponding to each matched pair of x and y variables. In this figure, the vertical axis is Novartis sales for the territory and the horizontal axis contains the number of salespeople in that territory. The arrangement or scatter of points appears to fall in a long ellipse. Any two variables that exhibit systematic covariation will form an ellipse-like pattern on a scatter diagram. Of course, this particular scatter diagram portrays the information gathered by the marketing researcher on sales and the number of salespeople in each territory and only that information. In actuality, the scatter diagram could have taken any shape, depending on the relationship between the points plotted for the two variables concerned.[11]

A number of different types of scatter diagram results are portrayed in Figure 18.8. Each of these scatter diagram results is indicative of a different degree of covariation. For instance, you can see that the scatter diagram depicted in Figure 18.8(a) is one in which

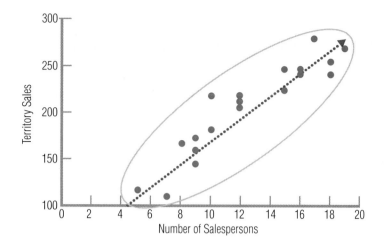

FIGURE 18.7
A Scatter Diagram Showing Covariation: Novartis Sales Data

there is no apparent association or relationship between the two variables; the points fail to create any identifiable pattern. Instead, they are clumped into a large, formless shape. The points in Figure 18.8(b) indicate a negative relationship between variable x and variable y; higher values of x tend to be associated with lower values of y. The points in Figure 18.8(c) are fairly similar to those in Figure 18.8(b), but the angle or the slope of the ellipse is different. This slope indicates a positive relationship between x and y, because larger values of x tend to be associated with larger values of y.

What is the connection between scatter diagrams and correlation coefficients? The answer to these questions lies in the linear relationship described earlier in this chapter. Look at Figures 18.7 and 18.8(b) and 18.8(c). All form ellipses. Imagine taking an ellipse and pulling on both ends. It would stretch out and become thinner until all of its points fall on a straight line. If you happened to find some data that formed an ellipse with all of its points falling on the axis line and you computed a correlation, you would find it to be exactly 1.0 (+1.0 if the ellipse went up to the right and −1.0 if it went down to the right). Now imagine pushing the ends of the ellipse until it became the pattern in Figure 18.8(a). There would be no identifiable straight line. Similarly, there would be no systematic covariation. The correlation for a bell-shaped scatter diagram is zero because there is no discernible linear relationship. In other words, a correlation coefficient indicates the degree of covariation between two variables, and you can envision this relationship as a scatter diagram. The form and angle of the scatter pattern is revealed by the size and sign, respectively, of the correlation coefficient.

Two highly correlated variables will yield a scatter diagram pattern of a tight ellipse.

Your Student Assistant movie shows graphical representations of covariation.

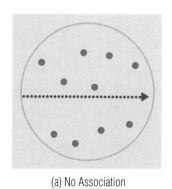
(a) No Association

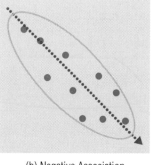
(b) Negative Association

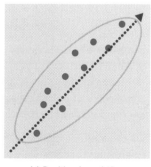
(c) Positive Association

FIGURE 18.8
Scatter Diagrams Illustrating Various Relationships

THE PEARSON PRODUCT MOMENT CORRELATION COEFFICIENT

The Pearson product moment correlation coefficient measures the degree of linear association between two variables.

The **Pearson product moment correlation** measures the linear relationship between two interval- and/or ratio-scaled variables such as those depicted conceptually by scatter diagrams. The correlation coefficient that can be computed between the two variables is a measure of the "tightness" of the scatter points to the straight line. You already know that in a case in which all of the points fall exactly on the straight line, the correlation coefficient indicates this as a +1 or a −1. In the case in which it was impossible to discern an ellipse such as in scatter diagram Figure 18.8(a), the correlation coefficient approximates zero. Of course, it is extremely unlikely that you will find perfect 1.0 or 0.0 correlations. Usually, you will find some value in between that could be interpreted as "high," "moderate," or "weak" correlation using the rules of thumb given earlier.

MARKETING RESEARCH INSIGHT

PRACTICAL APPLICATION

18.4 How to Compute a Pearson Product Moment Correlation Coefficient

Marketing researchers almost never compute statistics such as chi-square or correlation, but it is useful to learn about this computation.

The computational formula for Pearson product moment correlations is as follows:

Formula for Pearson Product Moment Correlation

$$r_{xy} = \frac{\sum_{n}^{i=1} (x_i - \bar{x})(y_i - \bar{y})}{n s_x s_y}$$

where

x_i = each x value
$\bar{x}$ = mean of the x values
y_i = each y value
$\bar{y}$ = mean of the y values
n = number of paired cases
s_x, s_y = standard deviations of x and y, respectively

We briefly describe the components of this formula to help you see how the concepts we just discussed fit in. In the statistician's terminology, the numerator represents the cross-products sum and indicates the covariation or

"covariance" between x and y. The cross-products sum is divided by n to scale it down to an average per pair of x and y values. This average covariation is then divided by both standard deviations to adjust for differences in units. The result constrains r_{xy} to fall between −1.0 and +1.0.

Here is a simple computational example. You have some data on population and retail sales by county for 10 counties in your state. Is there a relationship between population and retail sales? You do a quick calculation and find that the average number of people per county is 690,000, and the average retail sales if $9.54 million. The standard deviations are 384.3 and 7.8, respectively, and the cross-products sum is 25,154. The computations to find the correlation are:

Calculation of a Correlation Coefficient

$$r_{xy} = \frac{\sum_{i=1}^{n} (x_i - \bar{x})(y_i - \bar{y})}{n s_x s_y}$$
$$= \frac{25,154}{10 \times 7.8 \times 384.4}$$
$$= \frac{25,154}{29,975.4}$$
$$= .84$$

A correlation of 0.84 is a high positive correlation coefficient for the relationship. This value reveals that the greater the number of citizens living in a county, the greater the county's retail sales.

The formula for calculating a Pearson product moment correlation is complicated, and researchers never compute it by hand, as they invariably find these on computer output. However, some instructors believe that students should understand the workings of the correlation coefficient formula. We have described this formula and provided an example in Marketing Research Insight 18.4.

Pearson product moment correlation and other linear association correlation coefficients indicate not only the degree of association but the direction as well, because as we described in our introductory comments on correlations, the sign of the correlation coefficient indicates the direction of the relationship. Negative correlation coefficients reveal that the relationship is opposite: As one variable increases, the other variable decreases. Positive correlation coefficients reveal that the relationship is increasing: Larger quantities of one variable are associated with larger quantities of another variable. It is important to note that the angle or the slope of the ellipse has nothing to do with the size of correlation coefficient. Everything hinges on the width of the ellipse. (The slope will be considered in Chapter 19 on regression analysis.)

> **A positive correlation signals an increasing linear relationship, whereas a negative correlation signals a decreasing one.**

DATE.NET: MALE USERS CHAT-ROOM PHOBIA

Date.net is an online meeting service. Its purpose is to operate a virtual meeting place for men seeking women and women seeking men. Internal analysis has revealed that female chat-room users greatly outnumber male chat-room users. This is frustrating to Date.net principals, as they know that the number of "men seeking women" is about the same as "women seeking men." Men seem to have a chat-room phobia.

They commissioned an online marketing research company to design a questionnaire that was posted on the date.net Web site for 15 days. The survey is a success, as over 5000 date.net users fill it out in this time period. Date.net executives request a separate analysis of "men seeking women" user respondents to look into the chat-room-related questions. The research company decided to report all correlations that are significant at the 0.01 level. Here is a summary of the correlation analysis findings

Factor		Correlation with Amount of date.net Chat-Room Use
Demographics:	Age	−.68
	Income	−.76
	Education	−.78
	Number of years divorced	+.57
	Number of children	+.68
	Years at present address	−.90
	Years at present job	−.85
Satisfaction with:	Relationships	−.76
	Job/career	−.86
	Personal appearance	−.72
	Life in general	−.50
Online behavior:	Minutes online daily	+.90
	Online purchases	−.65
	Other chatting time/month	+.86
	Number of e-mail accounts	+.77
Use of date.net (1 = not important and 5 = very important)		
	Meet new people	+.38
	Only way to talk to women	+.68
	Looking for a life partner	−.72
	Not much else to do	+.59

For each factor, use your knowledge of correlations and provide a statement of how it characterizes the typical date.net male chat room user. Given your findings, what tactics do you recommend to Date.net to combat the male chat phobia problem?

The Hobbit's Choice Restaurant Survey: How to Obtain Pearson Product Moment Correlation(s) with SPSS

With SPSS, it takes only a few clicks to compute correlation coefficients. Once again, we will use the Hobbit's Choice Restaurant survey case study because you are familiar with it. If you recall, we have determined from previous analysis, that a waterfront view is generally preferred. Remembering this, you would probably feel very confident about recommending this location to Jeff. But let's take a closer look using correlation analysis. Correlation analysis can be used to find out what people want with the waterfront view; that is, high positive correlations would indicate that they wanted the waterfront location and the items that are highly correlated with this location preferences. Conversely, high negative correlations would signal that they did not want those items with the waterfront location. Recall that there were several menu, décor, and atmosphere questions being mulled over by Jeff Dean. Correlation analysis is very powerful, as it can reveal to what extent people prefer (or do not prefer) these items as they prefer the waterfront view. We'll only do a few of the items here, and you can do the rest in your SPSS integrated case analysis work specified at the end of the chapter.

So, we need to perform correlation analysis with the waterfront location preference variable and the other factors that will determine the Hobbit's Choice Restaurant's "personality." The clickstream sequence is ANALYZE-CORRELATE-BIVARIATE, which leads, as can be seen in Figure 18.9, to a selection box to specify which variables are to be correlated. Note that we have selected the waterfront location and several other items related to décor, atmosphere, and menu. Different types of correlations are optional, so we have selected Pearson's, and the two-tailed test of significance is the default.

The output generated by this command is provided in Figure 18.10. Whenever you instruct SPSS to compute correlations, its output is a symmetric correlation matrix composed of rows and columns that pertain to each of the variables. Each cell in the matrix contains three items: (1) the correlation coefficient, (2) the significance level, and (3) the sample size. As you can see in Figure 18.10, the computed correlations between "prefer waterfront location" and three of Jeff's questions—Simple décor? Prefer unusual entrees? Prefer unusual desserts?—are +.780, −.782, and −.810, respectively. They all have a "Sig" value of .000, which translates into a .001 or less probability that the null hypothesis of zero correlation is supported. If you look at our correlation printout, you will also notice that a correlation of 1.000 is reported, in which a variable is correlated with itself. This reporting may seem strange, but it serves the purpose of reminding you that the correlation matrix that is generated with this procedure is symmetric. In other words, the correlations in the matrix above the diagonal 1s are identical to those correlations below the diagonal. With only a few variables, this fact is obvious; however, sometimes several variables are compared in a single run, and the 1s on the diagonal are handy reference points.

Since we now know that the correlations are statistically significant, or significantly different from zero, we can assess their strengths. They hover around .80 which, according to our rules of thumb on correlation size indicates a moderately strong association. In other words, we have some relationships that are stable and fairly strong. Last, we can use the signs to interpret the associations. What is your interpretation?

With SPSS, correlations are computed with the CORRELATE-BIVARIATE feature.

With correlation analysis, each correlation will have a unique significance level.

SPSS Student Assistant: The Integrated Case: Working with Correlations

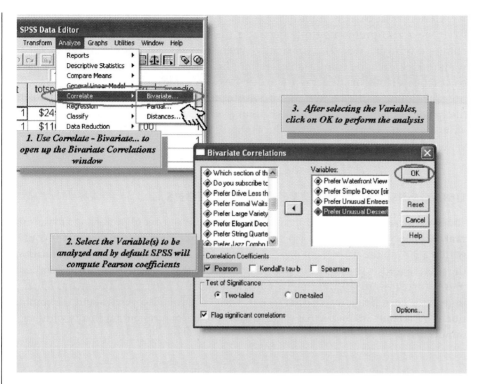

FIGURE 18.9
The SPSS Clickstream to Obtain Correlations

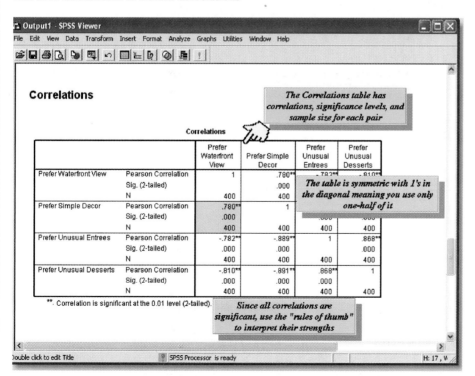

FIGURE 18.10
SPSS Output for Correlations

A correlation matrix is symmetric with 1s on the diagonal.

Here is what we have found. People who prefer to eat at a restaurant with a waterfront view also prefer a simple décor. At the same time, they do not want unusual entrees or unusual desserts. Apparently, when folks go to a waterfront restaurant they want to kick back, be comfortable, and not be bothered with choosing from a variety of curious dishes or an array of exotic desserts. They probably want seafood. An upscale Hobbit's Choice Restaurant with unusual entrees and desserts would definitely not fit the preferences of these people. So, now how do you feel about your previous recommendation to locate the Hobbit's Choice Restaurant on some expensive waterfront property?

Active **Learning**

USING SPSS TO COMPUTE CORRELATIONS

You have just seen the correlation analysis findings for one set of preferences for a restaurant. Now let's take a specific aspect of the restaurant, namely, the fact that it could be within a 30-minute drive from patron's homes. Use SPSS to determine the correlation of the preference for this location with preferences for string quartet music, jazz combo music, formal waitstaff wearing tuxedos, and unusual entrees on the menu. When you inspect the correlation matrix that results, what have you discovered about the combination of restaurant attributes that these patrons prefer for a restaurant that is within a 30-minute drive?

Special Considerations in Linear Correlation Procedures

We have prepared Table 18.3 to summarize and remind you of four considerations to keep in mind when working with correlations. We will discuss each of these in turn. To begin, the scaling assumptions underlying linear correlation should be apparent to you,

When dining on seafood, restaurant patrons often like to keep it simple.

TABLE 18.3	Four Caveats of Correlation

1. Use correlations only for metric variables (interval or ratio scaling).

2. Correlation assumes that only the two variables involved are relevant: all other variables and factors are considered to be constant.

3. Correlation does not indicate cause-and-effect, only covariance between the two variables is being analyzed.

4. Correlation expresses only the linear relationship between two variables.

but it does not hurt to reiterate that the correlation coefficient discussed in this section assumes that both variables share interval-scaling assumptions at minimum. If the two variables have nominal scaling assumptions, the researcher would use cross-tabulation analysis, and if the two variables have ordinal scaling assumptions, the researcher would opt to use a rank order correlation procedure. (We do not discuss rank order correlation in this chapter, as its use is relatively rare.)

Next, the correlation coefficient takes into consideration only the relationship between two variables. It does not take into consideration interactions with any other variables. In fact, it explicitly assumes that they do not have any bearing on the relationship with the two variables of interest. All other factors are considered to be constant or "frozen" in their bearing on the two variables under analysis.

Second, the correlation coefficient explicity does not assume a **cause–and–effect relationship**, which is a condition of one variable bringing about the other variable. Although you might be tempted to believe that more company salespeople cause more company sales or that an increase in the competitor's sales force in a territory takes away sales, correlation should not be interpreted to demonstrate such cause-and-effect relationships. Just think of all of the other factors that affect sales: price, product quality, service policies, population, advertising, and more. It would be a mistake to assume that just one factor causes sales. Instead, a correlation coefficient merely investigates the presence, strength, and direction of a linear relationship between two variables.

Correlation does not demonstrate cause and effect.

Third, the Pearson product moment correlation expresses only linear relationships. Consequently, a correlation coefficient result of approximately zero does not necessarily mean that the scatter diagram that could be drawn from the two variables defines a formless ball of points. Instead, it means that the points do not fall in a well-defined elliptical pattern. Any number of alternative, curvilinear patterns such as an S-shaped or a J-shaped pattern are possible, and the linear correlation coefficient would not be able to communicate the existence of these patterns to the marketing researcher. Any one of several other systematic but nonlinear patterns is entirely possible and would not be indicated by a linear correlation statistic. Only those cases of linear or straight-line relationships between two variables are identified by the Pearson product moment correlation. In fact, when a researcher does not find a significant or strong correlation, but still believes some relationship exists between two variables, he or she may resort to running a scatter plot. This procedure allows the researcher to visually inspect the plotted points and possibly to spot a systematic nonlinear relationship. You already know that your SPSS program has a scatter plot option that will provide a scatter diagram that you can use to obtain a sense of the relationship, if any, between two variables.

Correlation will not detect nonlinear relationships between variables.

CONCLUDING COMMENTS ON ASSOCIATIVE ANALYSES

Researchers always test the null hypothesis of no association or no correlation, even though they hope to find a significant association or correlation to yield useful managerial implications.

The scaling assumptions of the data being analyzed are the key to understanding associative analysis.[12] Sometimes a marketing researcher must use categorical measurements (nominal scale). As you know, nominal measurement provides the least amount of information about an object, whereas ratio measures provide the greatest amount of information. The amount of information in scales directly impacts the amount of information yielded by their appropriate associative test. So the chi-square statistic, which uses two nominal-scaled variables cannot have as much information as the Pearson product moment correlation, which may be used for two interval or ratio-scaled variables. Similarly, the underlying relationships reflect the differences in information. Chi-square describes a nonmonotonic relationship, a Pearson product moment correlation describes a linear relationship, and a rank order correlation's relationship falls between these two with a monotonic relationship.

Finally, throughout our descriptions of various statistical tests, we have referred to the "null hypothesis." For example, with chi-square analysis, there is the null hypothesis of no association between the two nominal-scaled variables, and with correlation analysis there is the null hypothesis of no correlation. But marketing managers really want to find strong evidence of an association that exists and can be used to their advantage; that is, they really want to find support for the "alternative hypothesis" that an association does exist. So why do we always test the null hypothesis? Here is an example that answers this question.

The Tree-Free Company of Medford, Massachusetts, makes paper products from 100 percent recycled paper. As a strategy to entice Kleenex to buy its tissue boxes, Tree-Free might conduct a survey asking, "If you learned that a company used recycled paper boxes, would that fact influence your decision to purchase a particular brand of tissue?" and "Do you typically buy Kleenex, or do you buy some other brand of facial tissue?" Of course, what Tree-Free management would love to discover is that buyers of some brand other than Kleenex are sensitive to the recycled paper issue. Then, they could make a persuasive argument that Kleenex should use Tree-Free tissue boxes, advertise how it is helping the environment, and increase its market share over tissue brands that do not use recycled paper boxes. The "hypothesis of interest" is a strong association between a "yes" answer to the first question and a "some other brand" answer to the second question.

When the null hypothesis is rejected, the researcher may have a managerially important relationship to share with the manager.

In truth, marketing managers and researchers typically have hypotheses of interest in mind. But statistical tests do not exist that can assess these hypotheses conveniently. Instead, the researcher must use the two-step process we have described. First, the existence of an association must be demonstrated. If there is no association, there is no sense in looking for evidence of the hypothesis of interest. However, when the null hypothesis is rejected, an association does exist in the population, and the researcher is then justified in looking at the direction of the association. When the second step takes place, the researcher is in pursuit of the hypothesis of interest. Now, the strength and direction aspects of the relationship are assessed to see if they correspond with the suspicions held by the marketing manager who wants to turn this association into managerial action.

Just think of the millions of boxes used by the facial tissue industry for packaging. Now do you see why Tree-Free has such a strong interest in a hypothesis other than the null? To do competent work, a researcher must ferret out all of the hypotheses of interest during the problem definition stage.

SPSS Student Assistant Online: Your Integrated Case Genie in the Bottle: SPSS Statistics Coach

SUMMARY

This chapter dealt with instances in which a marketing researcher wants to see if there is a relationship between the responses to one question and the responses to another question in the same survey. Four different types of relationship are possible. First, there is a nonmonotonic relationship, in which the presence (or absence) of one variable is systematically associated with the presence (or absence) of another. Second, a monotonic relationship indicates the direction of one variable relative to the direction of the other variable. Third, a linear relationship is characterized by a straight-line appearance if the variables are plotted against one another on a graph. Fourth, curvilinear relationship means the pattern has a definite curved shape. Associative analyses are used to assess these relationships statistically.

Associations can be characterized by presence, direction, and strength, depending on the scaling assumptions of the questions being compared. With chi-square analysis, a cross-tabulation table is prepared for two nominal-scaled questions, and the chi-square statistic is computed to determine whether the observed frequencies (those found in the survey) differ significantly from what would be expected if there were no nonmonotonic relationship between the two. If the null hypothesis of no relationship is rejected, the researcher then looks at the cell percentages to identify the underlying pattern of association.

A correlation coefficient is an index number, constrained to fall in the range of $+1.0$ to -1.0, that communicates both the strength and the direction of association between two variables. The sign indicates the direction of the relationship and the absolute size indicates the strength of the association. Normally, correlations in excess of $\pm.8$ are considered high. With two questions that are interval and/or ratio in their scaling assumptions, the Pearson product moment correlation coefficient is appropriate as the means of determining the underlying linear relationship. A scatter diagram can be used to inspect the pattern.

KEY TERMS

Associative analyses (p. 522)
Relationship (p. 522)
Nonmonotonic relationship (p. 523)
Monotonic relationships (p. 523)
Linear relationship (p. 524)
Straight-line formula (p. 524)
Curvilinear relationship (p. 525)
Cross-tabulation table (p. 528)
Cross-tabulation cell (p. 528)
Frequencies table (p. 528)
Raw percentages table (p. 530)
Column percentages table (p. 530)

Row percentages table (p. 531)
Chi-square χ^2 analysis (p. 531)
Observed frequencies (p. 531)
Expected frequencies (p. 531)
Chi-square formula (p. 532)
Chi-square distribution (p. 534)
Correlation coefficient (p. 541)
Covariation (p. 541)
Scatter diagram (p. 542)
Pearson product moment correlation (p. 544)
Cause-and-effect relationship (p. 549)

REVIEW QUESTIONS/APPLICATIONS

1. Explain the distinction between a statistical relationship and a causal relationship.
2. Define and provide an example for each of the following types of relationship: (a) nonmonotonic, (b) monotonic, (c) linear, and (d) curvilinear

3. Relate the three different aspects of a relationship between two variables.

4. What is a cross-tabulation? Give an example.

5. With respect to chi-square analysis, describe or identify each of the following: (a) r-by-c table, (b) frequencies table, (c) observed frequencies, (d) expected frequencies, (e) chi-square distribution, (f) significant association, (g) scaling assumptions, (h) row percentages versus column percentages, and (i) degrees of freedom.

6. What is meant by the term *significant correlation*?

7. Briefly describe the connections among the following: covariation, scatter diagram, correlation, and linear relationship.

8. Indicate, with the use of a scatter diagram, the general shape of the scatter of data points in each of the following cases: (a) a strong positive correlation, (b) a weak negative correlation, (c) no correlation, (d) a correlation of −.98.

9. What are the scaling assumptions assumed by Pearson product moment correlation?

10. Listed below are various factors that may have relationships that are interesting to marketing managers. With each one, (1) identify the type of relationship, (2) indicate its nature or direction, and (3) specify how knowledge of the relationship could help a marketing manager in designing marketing strategy.
    a. Readership of certain sections of the Sunday newspaper and age of the reader for a sporting goods retail store.
    b. Ownership of a telephone answering machine and household income for a tele-marketing service being used by a public television broadcasting station soliciting funds.
    c. Number of miles driven in company cars and need for service such as oil changes, tune-ups, or filter changes for a quick auto service chain attempting to market fleet discounts to companies.
    d. Plans to take a five-day vacation to Jamaica and the exchange rate of the Jamaican dollar to that of other countries for Sandals, an all-inclusive resort located in Montego Bay.
    e. Amount of do-it-yourself home repairs and declining state of the economy (for example, a recession) for Ace Hardware stores.

11. Indicate the presence, nature, and strength of the relationship involving purchases of intermediate size automobiles and each of the following factors: (a) price, (b) fabric versus leather interior, (c) exterior color, and (d) size of rebate.

12. With each of the following examples, compose a reasonable statement of an association you would expect to find existing between the factors involved, and construct a stacked bar chart expressing that association.
    a. Wearing of braces to straighten teeth by children attending expensive private schools versus those attending public schools.
    b. Having a Doberman pinscher as a guard dog, use of a home security alarm system, and ownership of rare pieces of art.
    c. Adherence to the "diet pyramid" recommended by the Surgeon General of the United States for healthful living and family history of heart disease.
    d. Purchases of toys as gifts during the Christmas buying season versus other seasons of the year by parents of preschool-aged children.

13. Below is some information about 10 respondents to a mail survey concerning candy purchasing. Use SPSS to construct the four different types of cross-tabulation tables that are possible. Label each table, and indicate what you perceive to be the general relationship apparent in the data.

Respondent	Buy Plain M&Ms	Buy Peanut M&Ms
1	Yes	No
2	Yes	No
3	No	Yes
4	Yes	No
5	No	No
6	No	Yes
7	No	No
8	Yes	No
9	Yes	No
10	No	Yes

14. Morton O'Dell is the owner of Mort's Diner, which is located in downtown Atlanta, Georgia. Mort's opened up about 12 months ago, and it has experienced success, but Mort is always worried about what food items to order as inventory on a weekly basis. Mort's daughter, Mary, is an engineering student at Georgia Tech, and she offers to help her father. She asks him to provide sales data for the past 10 weeks in terms of pounds of food bought by customers. With some difficulty, Mort comes up with the following list.

Week	Meat	Fish	Fowl	Vegetables	Desserts
1	100	50	150	195	50
2	91	55	182	200	64
3	82	60	194	209	70
4	75	68	211	215	82
5	66	53	235	225	73
6	53	61	253	234	53
7	64	57	237	230	68
8	76	64	208	221	58
9	94	68	193	229	62
10	105	58	181	214	62

Mary uses these sales figures to construct scatter diagrams that illustrate the basic relationships among the various types of food items purchased at Mort's Diner over the past 10 weeks. She tells her father that the diagrams provide some help in his weekly inventory ordering problem. Construct Mary's scatter diagrams with your SPSS to indicate what assistance they are to Mort. Perform the appropriate associate analysis with SPSS and interpret your findings.

DON'T YOU JUST HATE IT WHEN . . . ? (PART III)

Part I (Case 16.1) of this case is on pages 479–480, and Part II (Case 17.1) of this case is on pages 515–516.

At 10:01 P.M., in an apartment north of campus, a cell phone suddenly blasts out the school's fight song. After checking the incoming number, Josh answers.

Josh: "Hey, Marsh. What's up?"
Marsha: "It is after 10 P.M. and I am looking for our Pets, Pets & Pets marketing research data analysis that you said you would have completed and e-mailed to me by 10 tonight."

Josh: "Jeeze, Marsh, I am studying for that big finance test that we both have tomorrow. Finance has, like numbers and equations, and I am really spooked about it."

Marsha: "I am done studying finance, and I need to prepare the association analysis presentation that we, or should I say "I," have to give in Dr. Z's marketing research tomorrow morning. I need that analysis now!"

Josh: "Okay, okay, I will do it right away and e-mail you the file. Just keep checking for it. Bye."

At 12:13 A.M. an e-mail from Josh arrives at Marsha's computer. She opens up the file and finds the following

Correlations

		Times Used PPP in the Past Year	Dollar Amount Spent at PPP on Last Visit	How Likely to Revisit PPP	Number of Pets	Use PPP Regularly or Not?	Recall Seeing PPP in Newspaper in the Past Month	Income Level
Times used	Pearson Correlation	1	.403**	.382**	.778**	.702**	.310**	−.067
PPP in the	Sig. (2-tailed)		.000	.000	.000	.000	.000	.412
past year	N	152	99	150	152	152	152	152
Dollar amount	Pearson Correlation	.403**	1	.604**	−.226*	.398**	.165	.228*
spent at PPP	Sig. (2-tailed)	.000		.000	.024	.000	.102	.023
on last visit	N	99	99	99	99	99	99	99
How likely	Pearson Correlation	.382**	.604**	1	.009	.490**	.011	.115
to revisit PPP	Sig. (2-tailed)	.000	.000		.910	.000	.890	.163
	N	150	99	150	150	150	150	150
Number of	Pearson Correlation	.778**	−.226*	.009	1	.490**	.271**	−.331**
pets	Sig. (2-tailed)	.000	.024	.910		.000	.001	.000
	N	152	99	150	152	152	152	152
Use PPP	Pearson Correlation	.702**	.398**	.490**	.490**	1	.241**	−.126
regularly or	Sig. (2-tailed)	.000	.000	.000	.000		.003	.123
not?	N	152	99	150	152	152	152	152
Recall seeing PPP	Pearson Correlation	.310**	.165	.011	.271**	.241**	1	.173*
newspaper in	Sig. (2-tailed)	.000	.102	.890	.001	.003		.033
the past month	N	152	99	150	152	152	152	152
Income level	Pearson Correlation	−.067	.228*	.115	−.331**	−.126	.173**	1
	Sig. (2-tailed)	.412	.023	.163	.000	.123	.033	
	N	152	99	150	152	152	152	152

**Correlation is significant at the 0.01 level (2-tailed).

*Correlation is significant at the 0.05 level (2-tailed).

At 12:14 A.M. Josh's cell phone blasts out the school fight song.

Josh answers: "Hey Marsh, I know it took a while, but I did it and there are some big correlations and so now you can do your thing for the presentation."

Marsha thinks: "Gawd, I really hate this guy!" and says "Were you like completely unconscious when Dr. Z went over cross-tabulations and the data scaling assumptions for crosstabs versus correlations?"

Josh: "Oh, you mean the matrix stuff with the formulas for types of frequencies and the chi-square value? Hey, I told you that I don't do numbers and formulas well. But the correlations with the cool rules of thumb made a lot sense to me, so I did them."

Marsha thinks: "Gawd, no, no, no!"

Josh: "Um, so maybe I did some of it not quite right? Look, I am coming right over to your apartment and will do it right if you tell me what to do. Besides, I need some help with studying for our finance test. I will pick up a pizza and be there in 30 minutes. What type of cold drink do you want me to pick up for you?"

Marsha sighs loudly and says: "Never mind the cold drink, I will be drinking a lot of coffee for sure."

Marsha clicks off her cell phone, looks up at the ceiling of her apartment, and thinks, "Gawd, I hate it when this happens."

Here is the code book and variable definitions for the Pets, Pets & Pets marketing research study that Josh and Marsha are working on.

Variable Code Book for Pets, Pets, & Pets SPSS File

Variable	Response Scale
Times visited PPP in past year	Actual number of times
Amount spent on last visit to PPP	Actual dollar amount rounded to dollars
How likely to buy at PPP next time (1–7 scale)	1–7 scale, where: 1 = unlikely, 7 = very likely
Number of pets owned	Actual number of pets
Use Pets, Pets, & Pets how often?	1 = do not use regularly 2 = use regularly
Recall seeing a PPP newspaper ad in the past month?	1 = yes 2 = no
Income level	1 = below $20,000 2 = between $20,000 and $40,000 3 = between $40,000 and $60,000 4 = between $60,000 and $80,000 5 = between $80,000 and $100,000 6 = greater than $100,000

What associative analysis is appropriate, and why is it appropriate to answer each of the following questions?

1. Is the number of visits to Pets, Pets & Pets in the past year related to the dollar amount that buyers spent there for their last purchase?

2. Is the number of visits related to being likely to buy at Pets, Pets & Pets next time?

3. Is recall of Pets, Pets & Pets newspaper advertisings related to shoppers being regular users of Pets, Pets & Pets?

4. Do higher-income buyers spend more at Pet, Pets & Pets?

5. Are specific income groups more or less likely to be regular users of Pets, Pets & Pets, and if so, which one(s)?

FRIENDLY MARKET VERSUS CIRCLE K

Friendly Market is a convenience store located directly across the street from a Circle K convenience store. Circle K is a national chain, and its stores enjoy the benefits of national advertising campaigns, particularly the high visibility these campaigns bring. All Circle K stores have large red-and-white store signs, identical merchandise assortments, standardized floor plans, and they are open around the clock. Friendly Market, in contrast, is a one-of-a-kind "mom-and-pop" variety convenience store owned and managed by Bobby Jones. Bobby's parents came to the United States from Palestine when Bobby was 15 years old. The family members became American citizens and adopted the last name of Jones. Bobby had difficulty making the transition to U.S. schools, and he dropped out without finishing high school. For the next 10 years of his life, Bobby worked in a variety of jobs, both full- and part-time, and for most of the past 10 years, Bobby has been a Circle K store employee.

Three years ago, Bobby made a bold move to open his own convenience store. Don's Market, a mom-and-pop convenience store across the street from the Circle K where Bobby was working at the time, had closed six months before, and Bobby watched it month after month as it remained boarded up with a for sale sign on the front door with no apparent interested parties. Bobby gathered up his life savings and borrowed as much money as he could from friends, relatives, and banks. He bought the old Don's Market building and equipment, renamed it Friendly Market, and opened its doors for business. Bobby's core business philosophy was to greet everyone who came in and to get to know all his customers on a first-name basis. He also watched Circle K's prices closely and sought to have lower prices on at least 50% of merchandise sold by both stores.

To the surprise of the manager of the Circle K across the street, Friendly Market prospered. Recently, Bobby's younger sister, who had gone on to college and earned an MBA degree at Indiana University, conducted a survey of Bobby's target market to gain a better understanding of why Friendly Market was successful. She drafted a simple questionnaire and did the telephone interviewing herself. She used the local telephone book and called a random sample of over 150 respondents whose residences were listed within three miles of Friendly Market. She then created an SPSS data set with the following variables name and values.

Variable Name	Value Labels
Friendly	0 = Do not use Friendly Market regularly; 1 = Use Friendly Market regularly
Circle K	0 = Do not use Circle K regularly; 1 = Use Circle K regularly
Dwelling	1 = Own home; 2 = Rent
Sex	1 = Male; 2 = Female
Work	1 = Work full-time; 2 = Work part-time; 3 = Retired or Do not work
Commute	0 = Do not pass by Friendly Market/Circle K corner on way to work; 1 = Do pass by Friendly Market/Circle K corner on way to work

In addition to these demographic questions, respondents were asked if they agreed (coded 3), disagreed (coded 1), or neither agreed nor disagreed (coded 2) with each of five lifestyle statements. The variable names and questions are listed below:

Variable Name	Lifestyle Statement
Bargain	I often shop for bargains.
Cash	I always pay cash.
Quick	I like quick, easy shopping.
Know me	I shop where they know my name.
Hurry	I am always in a hurry.

The data set is available to you at your textbook Web site (**www.prenhall.com/ burnsbush**). It is named **"friendly.sav."** Use SPSS to perform the associative analyses necessary to answer the following questions.

1. Do Friendly Market and Circle K have the same customers?

2. What is the demographic profile associated with Friendly Market's customers?

3. What is the demographic profile associated with Circle K's customers?

4. What is the lifestyle profile associated with Friendly Market's customers?

 This is your integrated case, described on page 38–39.

THE HOBBIT'S CHOICE RESTAURANT SURVEY ASSOCIATIVE ANALYSIS

Cory Junior's stomach ailment turned out to be much worse than Cory Rogers expected, and Cory Senior, called in to inform Celeste that it would probably be several days before he would be able to get back in to the office. Cory says to Celeste, "I know you are a bit lost with the Hobbit's Choice Restaurant project, but why don't you take a look at the proposal, and see if there is any further analysis that you can do while I am out. Have Tonya pull the proposal from the file."

Celeste looks at the research proposal, and she jots down some notes with respect to research questions that need to be addressed. Her notes are below.

Your task here is to use the Hobbit's Choice Restaurant SPSS data set and perform the proper analysis. You will also need to interpret the findings.

1. Perform the correct analysis and interpret your findings with regard to the Hobbit's Choice Restaurant menu, décor, and atmosphere for those people who prefer to drive less than 30 minutes to get to the restaurant.

2. Do older or younger people want unusual desserts and/or unusual entrees?

3. Use the variable that distinguishes the "Probable patrons" (somewhat and very likely to patronize Hobbit's Choice) from the "Not probable patrons" (neither, somewhat, and very likely to patronize Hobbit's Choice =3, =4, or =5). If the probable patrons constitute the Hobbit's Choice Restaurant target market, what is the demographic makeup of this target market? Use the demographics of household income, education level, gender, and ZIP code.

Celeste knows (from the analysis described in this chapter) that the *City Magazine* is a viable advertising medium for Jeff Dean to use. Are there other viable promotion vehicles that Jeff should know about?

19

Regression Analysis in Marketing Research

Internet Shopper Segments Identified and Described with Marketing Research

The Internet is a global marketing phenomenon, at least in the great many countries where Internet access is common. Nonetheless, Internet usage varies across countries for a number of reasons. For instance, Internet penetration may vary in households, schools, and businesses across global regions. At the same time, Internet purchasing opportunities and experiences may differ because of language, cultural norms, or the retail environment to which people are accustomed. Investigating differences in Internet usage across the globe is a challenge, but some researchers have succeeded in focusing on specific regions and making comparisons on region-to-region basis. A study that accomplished this goal recently took place in the United States, a representative Western country, and Belgium, a representative European country.[1] Researchers used samples of over 2000 U.S. and Belgian Internet users, each to identify Internet shopper market segments. They found four Internet shopper segments existing in both countries, and they then sought to identify what characteristics distinguished U.S. from Belgian Internet shoppers within each market segments.

The following presentation summarizes the findings of comparisons for two segments. The "shopping lovers" market segment is one that uses the Internet frequently and extensively to make purchases of all types, while the "business shoppers" is a

- To understand the basic concept of prediction
- To learn how marketing researchers use regression analysis
- To learn how marketing researchers use bivariate regression analysis
- To see how multiple regression differs from bivariate regression
- To appreciate various types of stepwise regression, how they are applied, and the interpretation of their findings
- To learn how to obtain and interpret regression analyses with SPSS

Learning
Objectives

market segment that uses the Internet similarly although business shoppers, as the name indicates, tend to make purchases that are related to their professional lives or otherwise for business purposes.

Marketing research reveals similarities and dissimilarities between Internet shoppers across countries.

	Internet Shopping Lovers		Internet Business Users	
Factor	**U.S.**	**Belgium**	**U.S.**	**Belgium**
Internet convenience	Very high		High	Low
Internet trust	Very high		Low	
Internet window-shopping	Very high		High	
Internet use: Shopping	Very high		Low	Moderate
Internet use: Fun	High	Very high	High	
Internet use: Information	High	Very high	Moderate	Low
Internet use: Business	Very high		High	Very high
Computer literacy	High		High	
Internet literacy	High		High	
Age	Not related	Younger	Not related	Younger
Education	Moderate	Not related	High	Not related
Income	High	Lower	Low	Moderate
Like to explore Web sites	Very high	High	High	Very high
Like to shop on Internet	Very high		Moderate	
Web contributes to my life	Very high		High	

The comparisons of U.S. and Belgian shopping lovers and business users Internet market segments may seem complicated to decipher, but they would be incomprehensible to you if we had included the statistical values that were generated by the use of multiple regression analysis. In our presentation, we have used words such as "high" or "low" that describe the market segment relative to other market segments on the factor being measured. For instance, Belgian business users rate their Internet convenience "low," while U.S. business users rate their Internet convenience as "high." Where the U.S. and Belgian market segment users agree, we have merged the two columns, as for example, both U.S. and Belgian shopping lovers rate their Internet convenience as "very high."

With this presentation, you can quickly see how U.S. and Belgian Internet shoppers in a given market segment are similar or how they differ, and you can see how "Internet business users" differ from or are similar to "Internet shopping lovers" on a global level. To be certain, a great deal of information is summarized in this presentation, and, again, it is the result of the use of regression analysis, which is the topic of this chapter. Researchers often rely on this technique when they are faced with a great abundance of variables that they need to somehow narrow down or when they want to precisely describe the relationship between two variables.

Thishis chapter is the last one in which we discuss statistical procedures frequently used by marketing researchers. A researcher sometimes wishes to predict what might result if the manager were to implement a certain alternative. Or the researcher may be seeking a parsimonious way to describe market segments or the differences between various types of consumers such as was the case in our Internet segment comparisons vignette. In this chapter, we will describe regression analysis. Although it may seem like an intimidating procedure, we will show you how regression relates directly to the scatter diagrams and linear relationship you learned about in Chapter 18. Three types of regression analysis are described in this chapter. The first, bivariate regression, simply takes correlation analysis between two variables into the realm of prediction. Next, multiple regression analysis introduces the concept of simultaneously using two or more variables to make the prediction of a target variable such as sales. Finally, we will briefly introduce you to stepwise regression. This is a technique used by a researcher when faced with a large number of candidate predictors, and he or she is looking for the subset of these that best predicts or describes the phenomenon under study, just as was the situation in the vignette.

UNDERSTANDING PREDICTION

Prediction is a statement of what is believed will happen in the future made on the basis of past experience or prior observation.

A **prediction** is a statement of what is believed will happen in the future made on the basis of past experience or prior observation. We are confronted with the need to make predictions on a daily basis. For example, you must predict whether it will rain to decide whether to carry an umbrella. You must predict how difficult an examination will be in order to study properly. You must predict how heavy the traffic will be in order to decide what time to start driving to make it to your dentist appointment on time.

Marketing managers are also constantly faced with the need to make predictions, and the stakes are much higher than in the three examples just cited; that is, instead of getting caught in a downpour, receiving a disappointingly low grade, or missing a dentist appointment, the marketing manager has to worry about competitors' reactions, changes in sales, wasted resources, and whether profitability objectives will be achieved. Making accurate predictions is a vital part of the marketing manager's workaday world.

Two Approaches to Prediction

There are two ways of making a prediction: extrapolation and predictive modeling. In **extrapolation**, you can use past experience as a means of predicting the future. This process identifies a pattern over time and forecasts that pattern into the future. For example, if the weather forecaster had predicted an 80% chance of rain every day for the past week and it had rained every day, you would expect it to rain if he or she predicted an 80% chance of rain today. Similarly, if the last two exams you took for a professor were quite easy, you would predict the next one would be easy as well. Of course, it might not rain or the professor might administer a hard exam, but the observed patterns argue for rain today and an easy next exam. In both cases, you have detected a consistent pattern over time and based your predictions on this pattern.

In the other case, prediction relies on an observed relationship believed to exist between the factor you are predicting and some condition you judge to influence the factor. For example, how does the weather forecaster make his or her predictions? He or she inspects several pieces of evidence such as wind direction and velocity, barometric pressure changes, humidity, jet stream configuration, and temperature; that is, he or she goes far beyond taking what happened yesterday and forecasting that it will happen today. To make a prediction he or she builds a predictive model, using the relationships believed to exist among variables. A **predictive model** relates the condition or conditions expected to be in place and influencing the factor you are predicting. It is not an extrapolation of a consistent pattern over time; rather, it is an observed relationship that exists across time.

> The two approaches to prediction are extrapolation and predictive modeling.

> Extrapolation detects a pattern in the past and projects it into the future. Predictive modeling uses relationships found among variables to make a prediction.

How to Determine the "Goodness" of Your Predictions

Regardless of the method of prediction, you will always want to judge the "goodness" of your predictions, which is how good your method is at making those predictions. The acid test for a predictive model is to compare its predictions to what actually happened and to decide on the accuracy or "goodness" of its predictions. Here is a simple example that will explain the basic approach. Imagine that you are away at college. Your younger brother, who is a high school sophomore, works part-time at the movie theater in your hometown. He is rather conceited, and this irks you a bit. When you come home for a school vacation, he claims that he can predict the theater's popcorn sales for each day in the week. It turns out that you also worked at the theater while in high school, and you know the theater manager very well. She agrees to keep a record of popcorn sales and to provide the daily amount to you for the next week. So you challenge your little brother to write down the sales for the next seven days. After the week passes, how would you determine the accuracy of your brother's prediction?

The easiest way would be to compare the predictions for each day's popcorn sales to the actual amount sold. We have done this in Table 19.1. When you look at the table, you will see that we have calculated the difference between your brother's prediction and the actual sales for each evening. Notice that for some days, the predictions were high, whereas for others, the predictions were low. When you compare how far the predicted

> All predictions should be judged as to their "goodness" (accuracy).

TABLE 19.1	Weekly Popcorn Sales: Using Residuals to Assess the Goodness of a Forecast			
Day of Week	Your Brother's Forecast	Actual Sales	Residual (Difference)	Type of Error
Monday	$100	$125	−25	Very low
Tuesday	$110	$130	−20	Low
Wednesday	$120	$135	−15	Low
Thursday	$125	$125	0	Exact
Friday	$260	$225	+35	Very high
Saturday	$300	$250	+50	Very high
Sunday	$275	$235	+40	Very high
Averages	**$185**	**$175**	**+10**	**High**

The goodness of a prediction is based on examination of the residuals.

Residuals are the errors: comparisons of predictions to actual values.

values are from the actual or observed values, you are performing **analysis of residuals**. Stated differently, assessment of the goodness of a prediction requires you to compare the pattern of errors in the predictions to the actual data. Analysis of residuals underlies all assessments of the accuracy of a forecasting method, and because researchers cannot wait a month, a quarter, or a year to compare a prediction with what actually happens, they fall back on past data. In other words, they select a predictive model and apply it to the past data. Then, they examine the residuals to assess the model's predictive accuracy.

There are many ways to examine residuals. For example, in the case of your brother's forecast, you could judge it either on a total basis or an individual basis. On a total basis, you might compute the average as we have done in the table, or you could sum all of the daily residuals. Of course, you would need to square the daily residuals or use the absolute values to avoid cancellation of the positive differences by the negative differences. (You have seen the necessary squaring operation before, for instance, in the formula for a standard deviation or the sums of squares formula we described in Chapter 18 for chi-square analysis.) For the individual error, you might look for some pattern.[2] On an individual basis, you might notice a pattern: Your brother tends to underestimate how much popcorn will be bought on weekdays, which are low-sales days; whereas he overestimates it for Friday through Sunday, which are high-sales days. As you can see, the goodness of a prediction approach depends on how closely it predicts a set of representative values judged by examining the residuals (or errors).

Now that you have a basic understanding of prediction and how you determine the goodness of your predictions, we turn our attention to regression analysis.

BIVARIATE LINEAR REGRESSION ANALYSIS

In this chapter on predictive analysis, we will deal exclusively with linear regression analysis, a prediction technique often used by marketing researchers. However, regression analysis, particularly "multiple" regression, which is described later, is a complex statistical technique with a large number of requirements and nuances. Consequently, we will begin with a very simple form of regression to introduce you to basic concepts, and after you have completed this introduction, we will move to complicated notions. Still, our chapter is basically an introduction to this area, and as we will warn you toward the end of the material, there are a great many aspects of regression analysis that are beyond the scope of this textbook.

We first define **bivariate regression analysis** as a predictive analysis technique in which one variable is used to predict the level of another by use of the straight-line formula. We review the equation for a straight line and introduce basic terms used in regression. We also describe basic computations and significance with bivariate regression. We show how a regression prediction is made and we illustrate how to perform this analysis on SPSS.

With bivariate regression, one variable is used to predict another variable using the formula for a straight line.

A straight-line relationship underlies regression, and it is a powerful predictive model. Figure 19.1 illustrates a straight-line relationship, and you should refer to it as we describe the elements in a general straight-line formula. The formula for a straight line is:

Formula for a Straight Line Relationship

$$y = a + bx$$

The straight-line equation is the basis of regression analysis.

where

y = the predicted variable
x = the variable used to predict y
a = the **intercept**, or point where the line cuts the y axis when $x = 0$
b = the **slope** or the change in y for any 1 unit change in x

You should recall the straight-line relationship we described underlying the correlation coefficient: When the scatter diagram for two variables appears as a thin ellipse, there is a high correlation between them. Regression is directly related to correlation. In fact, we use one of our correlation examples to illustrate the application of bivariate regression below.

Regression is directly related to correlation by the underlying straight-line relationship.

Basic Procedure in Bivariate Regression Analysis

We now describe independent and dependent variables and show how the intercept and slope are computed. Then we use SPSS output to show how tests of significance are interpreted.

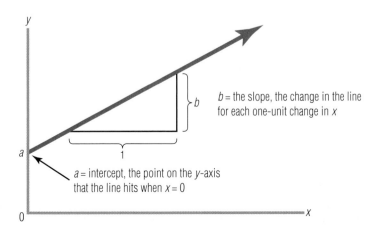

FIGURE 19.1
The General Equation for a Straight Line in Graph Form

b = the slope, the change in the line for each one-unit change in x

a = intercept, the point on the y-axis that the line hits when $x = 0$

In regression, the independent variable is used to predict the dependent variable.

▶ **Independent and Dependent Variables** As we indicated, bivariate regression analysis is a case in which only two variables are involved in the predictive model. When we use only two variables, one is termed "dependent" and the other is termed "independent." The **dependent variable** is that which is predicted, and it is customarily termed *y* in the regression straight-line equation. The **independent variable** is that which is used to predict the dependent variable, and it is the *x* in the regression formula. We must point out that the terms *dependent* and *independent* are arbitrary designations and are customary to regression analysis. There is no cause-and-effect relationship or true dependence between the dependent and the independent variable. It is strictly a statistical relationship, not causal, that may be found between these two variables.

▶ **Computing the Slope and the Intercept** To compute *a* (intercept) and *b* (slope), you must work with a number of observations of the various levels of the dependent variable paired with different levels of the independent variable, identical to the ones we illustrated previously when we were demonstrating how to perform correlation analysis.

The formulas for calculating the slope (*b*) and the intercept (*a*) are rather complicated, but some instructors would like their students to learn these formulas, so we have included them in Marketing Research Insight 19.1.

The least squares criterion used in regression analysis guarantees that the "best" straight-line slope and intercept will be calculated.

When SPSS or any other statistical analysis program computes the intercept and the slope in a regression analysis, it does so on the basis of the "least squares criterion." The **least squares criterion** is a way of guaranteeing that the straight line that runs through the points on the scatter diagram is positioned so as to minimize the vertical distances away from the line of the various points. In other words, if you draw a line for which the regression line is calculated and measure the vertical distances of all the points away from that line, it would be impossible to draw any other line that would result in a lower total of all of those vertical distances. Or, to state the least squares criterion using residuals analysis, the line is the one with the lowest total squared residuals.

The Two-Step Method for Evaluating Regression Findings

By now, you realize that every statistical analysis beyond simple descriptive ones involves some sort of statistical test, and the complexity of regression analysis requires multiple tests. The formulas for these tests are quite complicated, so rather than detailing the formulas, we will describe the tests and then use SPSS Hobbit's Choice Restaurant survey data output to identify where to look and how to interpret them.

In bivariate regression, the researcher identifies the dependent and independent variable pair and instructs SPSS or some other statistical analysis program to perform a regression analysis. When inspecting the regression output, there are two steps. First, the researcher must find out whether or not a linear relationship exists in the population. This step is analogous to determining the statistical significance of the correlation between the two variables. You should recall that if a relationship coefficient is not statistically significant, then the population correlation is zero. In other words, there is no intercept and no slope for the population correlation scatter diagram. This first step is one of our "flag" notions, for if there is no significant correlation, then there is no reason to continue and examine the intercept or slope on the computer output.

However, when the overall relationship is statistically significant, the researcher can move to the second step. Step 2 involves determining the statistical significance of the intercept (*a*), and the slope (*b*). Here, as will be described using the Hobbit's Choice Restaurant survey data, the researcher must assess individually whether or not the intercept and the slope are statistically significant from zero.

PRACTICAL APPLICATION

19.1

How to Calculate the Intercept
and Slope of a Bivariate
Regression

In the example below, we are using the Novartis pharmaceutical company sales territory and number of salespersons data found in Table 19.2. Intermediate regression calculations are included in Table 19.2.

TABLE 19.2	Bivariate Regression Analysis Data and Intermediate Calculations			
Territory (I)	Sales ($ millions) (y)	Number of Salespersons (x)	xy	x^2
1	102	7	714	49
2	125	5	625	25
3	150	9	1350	81
4	155	9	1395	81
5	160	9	1440	81
6	168	8	1344	64
7	180	10	1800	100
8	220	10	2200	100
9	210	12	2520	144
10	205	12	2460	144
11	230	12	2760	144
12	255	15	3825	225
13	250	14	3500	196
14	260	15	3900	225
15	250	16	4320	256
16	275	16	4400	256
17	280	17	4760	289
18	240	18	4320	324
19	300	18	5400	324
20	310	19	5890	361
Sums	**4325**	**251**	**58603**	**3469**
	(Average = 216.25)	(Average = 12.55)		

(continued)

The formula for computing the regression parameter b is:

**Formula for b,
the Slope, in
Bivariate Regression**

$$b = \frac{n\sum_{i=1}^{n} x_i y_i - \left(\sum_{i=1}^{n} x_i\right)\left(\sum_{i=1}^{n} y_i\right)}{n\sum_{i=1}^{n} x_i^2 - \left(\sum_{i=1}^{n} x_i\right)^2}$$

where

x_i = an x variable value
y_i = a y value paired with each x_i value
n = the number of pairs

The calculations for b, the slope, are as follows:

**Calculation of b,
the Slope, in
Bivariate Regression
Using Novartis Sales
Territory Data**

$$b = \frac{n\sum_{i=1}^{n} x_i y_i - \left(\sum_{i=1}^{n} x_i\right)\left(\sum_{i=1}^{n} y_i\right)}{n\sum_{i=1}^{n} x_i^2 - \left(\sum_{i=1}^{n} x_i\right)^2}$$

$$= \frac{20 \times 58603 - 251 \times 4325}{20 \times 3469 - 251^2}$$

$$= \frac{1172060 - 1085575}{69380 - 63001}$$

$$= \frac{86485}{6379}$$

$$= 13.56$$

The formula for computing the intercept is:

**Formula for a,
the Intercept, in
Bivariate Regression**

$$a = \bar{y} - b\bar{x}$$

The computations for a, the intercept, are as follows:

**Calculation of a, the Intercept,
in Bivariate Regression Using
Novartis Sales Territory Data**

$$a = \bar{y} - b\bar{x}$$
$$= 216.25 - 13.56 \times 12.55$$
$$= 216.25 - 170.15$$
$$= 46.10$$

In other words, the bivariate regression equation has been found to be:

Novartis Sales Regression Equation $y = 46.10 + 13.56 \, x$

The interpretation of this equation is as follows. Annual sales in the average Novartis sales territory are $46.10 million, and they increase $13.56 million annually with each additional salesperson.

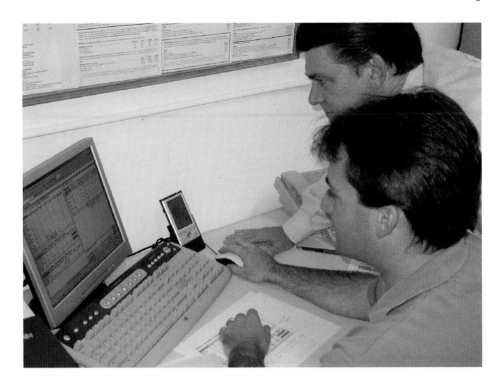

Al Muller, CEO of MMTInfo, oversees an associate conducting data analysis for a marketing research project. By permission MMTInfo.

YOUR INTEGRATED **CASE**

The Hobbit's Choice Restaurant Survey: How to Run and Interpret Bivariate Regression Analysis on SPSS

Now let us illustrate bivariate regression with SPSS using the Hobbit's Choice Restaurant survey data with which you are well acquainted. Our purpose is to help you learn the basic SPSS commands for bivariate regression and to familiarize you with the SPSS output and various regression statistics found on it.

The first step in bivariate regression analysis is to identify the dependent and independent variables. For our example, we will use the amount spent in restaurants per month as our dependent variable. Logically, we would expect expenditures to be related to income, so the before-tax household income level is a logical independent variable. However, we have used a code system for income level: the code numbers are not in dollars or dollar units (such as thousands). In any regression, it is best to use realistic values because realistic values are easiest to interpret. Consequently, we will recode the income values to represent the midpoints of the income ranges on the questionnaire. For example, we will recode the "less than $15,000" to 7.5 meaning $7500, so our recode units are in tens of thousands of dollars. The recoded income values are $7.5, $20.0, $37.5, $62.5, $87.5, $125, and $175. Notice that the highest income level of "$150,000 or higher" did not have an upper limit, so we arbitrarily use the range of the income level just below it.

As you can see in Figure 19.2, the SPSS menu commands clickstream to run bivariate regression is ANALYZE-REGRESSION-LINEAR. This opens up the linear regression selection window, in which you would indicate which variable is the dependent variable and which is the independent variable. In our example, we are investigating what you would expect to be a linear relationship between the amount spent per month in restaurants (dependent variable) and household income (independent variable). When these variables are entered into their respective locations on the SPSS Linear Regression setup window, clicking on OK will generate the SPSS output we are about to describe.

When working with ranges of a metric variable (such as income) in regression analysis, we recommend using the midpoints.

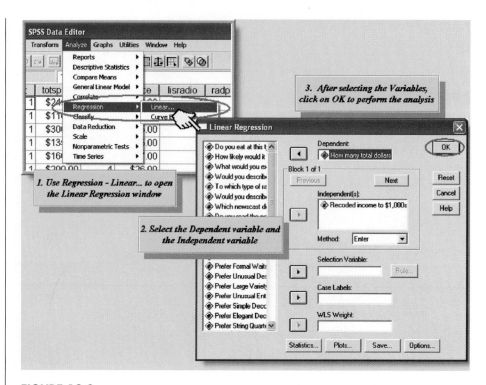

FIGURE 19.2
The SPSS Clickstream for Bivariate Regression Analysis

SPSS Student Assistant:
The Integrated Case:
Running and Interpreting
Bivariate Regression

The annotated SPSS linear regression output is shown in Figure 19.3. There are several pieces of information provided with a regression analysis such as this. In the Model Summary table, three types of "Rs" are indicated. For bivariate regression, R Square (.738 on the output) is the square of the correlation coefficient of 0.859. The Adjusted R Square (.737) reduces the R^2 by taking into account the sample size and number of parameters estimated. This R Square value is very important, because it reveals how well the straight-line model fits the scatter of points. Because a correlation coefficient ranges from -1.0 to $+1.0$, its square will range from 0 to $+1.0$. The higher the R Square value, the better is the straight line's fit to the elliptical scatter of points. A standard error value is reported, and we explain its use later.

Next, an analysis of variance (ANOVA) section is provided, and this information is necessary for the first step in our two-step process described above. As you can see, regression is related to analysis of variance.[3] We must first determine whether the straight-line model we are attempting to apply to describe these two variables is appropriate. The F value is significant (.000), so we reject the null hypothesis that a straight-line model does *not* fit the data we are analyzing. Just as in ANOVA as we described above, this test is a flag, and the flag has now been raised, making it justifiable to continue inspecting the output for more significant results. If the ANOVA F test is not significant, we would have to abandon our regression analysis attempts with these two variables. That is, we should not continue to the second step.

Since the ANOVA significance is less than .05, we can move to the second step. This step involves the next table in the SPSS output. In the Coefficients Table that the values of *b* and *a* are listed under "Unstandardized Coefficients." The constant (*a*) is 35.462 whereas *b*, identified as

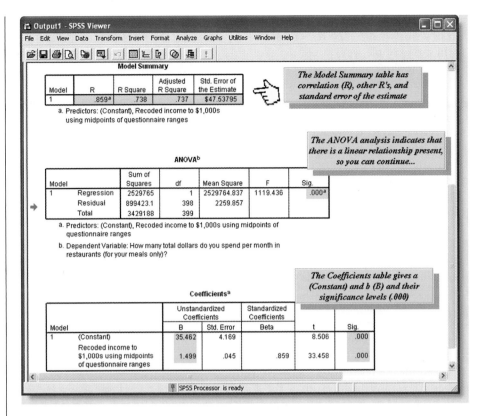

FIGURE 19.3
SPSS Output for Bivariate Regression Analysis

"B," is 1.499. In other words, rounding to hundredths, the regression equation has been found to be identical to the one we calculated before:

Bivariate Regression Equation Determined by SPSS Using the Hobbit's Choice Data	Dollars spent in restaurants per month = \$35.46 + \$1.50 × Income in \$10,000s

To relate this finding to our regression line in Figure 19.1, it says that the regression line will intercept the dollars spent in restaurants per month (the y axis) at \$35.46, and the line will increase \$1.5 per month for each \$10,000 unit increase in the income level (the x axis).

▶ **Testing for Statistical Significance of the Intercept and the Slope** Because the determination of the significance of the intercept and the slope are so vital to bivariate regression analysis, we will elaborate on the second step in this section. Simply computing the values for a and b is not sufficient for regression analysis, because the two values must be tested for statistical significance. The intercept and slope that are computed are sample estimates of population parameters of the true intercept, α (alpha), and the true slope, β (beta). The tests for statistical significance are tests as to whether the computed intercept and computed slope are significantly different from zero (the null hypothesis). To determine statistical significance, regression analysis requires that a t test be undertaken for each parameter estimate. The

You must always test the regression model, intercept, and slope for statistical significance.

interpretation of these t tests is identical to other significance tests you have seen. We next describe what these t tests mean.

In our example, you would look at the "Sig." column in the Coefficients table. This is where the slope and intercept t test results are reported. Both of our tests have significance levels of .000, which are below our standard significance level cutoff of .05, so our computed intercept and slope are valid estimates of the population intercept and slope. If x and y do not share a linear relationship, the population regression slope will equal zero and the t test result will support the null hypothesis. However, if a systematic linear relationship exists, the t test result will force rejection of the null hypothesis, and the researcher can be confident that the calculated slope estimates the true one that exists in the population. Remember, we are dealing with a statistical concept, and you must be assured that the straight-line parameters α and β really exist in the population before you can use your regression analysis findings as a prediction device.

Regression analysis predictions are estimates that have some amount of error in them.

▶ **Making a Prediction and Accounting for Error** Now, there is one more step to relate, and it is the most important one. How do you make a prediction? The fact that the line is a best approximation representation of all the points means we must account for a certain amount of error when we use the line for our predictions. The true advantage of a significant bivariate regression analysis result lies in the ability of the marketing researcher to use that information gained about the regression line through the points on the scatter diagram and to estimate the value or amount of the dependent variable based on some level of the independent variable. For example, with our regression result calculated for the relationship between total monthly restaurant purchases and income level, it is now possible to estimate the dollar amount of restaurant purchases predicted to be associated with households at specific income levels. However, we know that the scatter of points does not describe a perfectly straight line because the correlation is .859, not 1.0. So our regression prediction can only be an estimate.

Generating a regression prediction is conceptually identical to estimating a population mean; that is, it is necessary to express the amount of error by estimating a range rather than stipulating an exact estimate for your prediction. Regression analysis provides for a **standard error of the estimate**, which is a measure of the accuracy of the predictions of the regression equation. This standard error value is listed in the top half of the SPSS output and just beside the Adjusted R Square in Figure 19.3. It is analogous to the standard error of the mean you used in estimating a population mean from a sample, but it is based on the residuals, or how far away each predicted value is from the actual value. Do you recall the popcorn sales example of residuals we described earlier in this chapter? SPSS does the same comparison by using the regression equation it computed to predict the dollar amount of monthly restaurant purchases for each respondent, and this predicted value is compared with the actual amount given by the respondent. The differences, or residuals, are translated into a standard error of estimate value. In our Hobbit's Choice Restaurant survey example, the standard error of the estimate was found to be $47.54 (rounded to the nearest cent).

The standard error of the estimate is used to calculate a range of the prediction made with a regression equation.

The use of a 95% or a 99% confidence interval is standard.

One of the assumptions of regression analysis is that the plots on the scatter diagram will be spread uniformly and in accordance with the normal curve assumptions over the regression line. Figure 19.4 illustrates how this assumption might be depicted graphically. The points are congregated close to the line and then become more diffuse as they move away from the line. In other words, a greater percentage of the points is found on or close to the line than is found further away. The great advantage of this assumption is that is allows the marketing researcher to use his or her knowledge of the normal curve to specify the range in which the dependent variable is predicted to fall. For example, if the researcher used the predicted dependent value result ±1.96 times the standard error of the estimate, he or she would be stipulating a range with a 95%

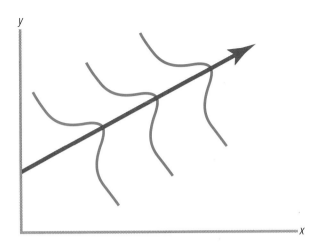

FIGURE 19.4
**Regression Assumes That
Data Points Form a Bell-
Shaped Curve around the
Regression Line**

level of confidence; whereas if he or she uses ±2.58 times the standard error of the estimate, he or she would be stipulating a range with a 99% level of confidence. The interpretation of these confidence intervals is identical to interpretations for previous confidence intervals: Were the prediction made many times and an actual result determined each time, the actual results would fall within the range of the predicted value 95% or 99% of these times.

Figure 19.5 illustrates how you can envision a regression prediction. Let's use the regression equation to make a prediction about the dollar amount of monthly restaurant purchases that would be associated with and income level of $75,000. Applying the regression formula, we have the following:

$$y = a + bx$$

**Calculation of Monthly
Restaurant Purchases
Predicted with an Income
Level of $75,000**

Dollars spent in restaurants per month

= $35.46 + $1.50 × Income in $10,000s
= $35.46 + $1.50 × 75
= $35.46 + $112.5
= $147.96

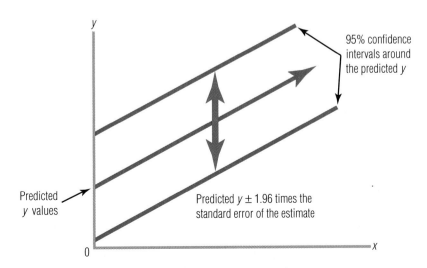

95% confidence
intervals around
the predicted *y*

Predicted
y values

Predicted *y* ± 1.96 times the
standard error of the estimate

FIGURE 19.5
**To Predict with Regression,
Apply Levels of Confidence
around the Regression Line.**

Regression predictions are made with confidence intervals.

Next, to reflect the imperfect aspects of the predictive tool being used, we must apply confidence intervals. If the 95% level of confidence were applied, the computations would be:

Calculation of 95% Confidence Intervals for the Predicted Monthly Restaurant Purchases

Predicted $y \pm z_a$ (Standard error of the estimate)
$147.96 \pm 1.96 \times \$47.54$
147.96 ± 93.18
54.78 to 241.14

As you can see, the predicted y is the monthly dollar amount of restaurant purchases we just computed for an income level of $75,000, the 1.96 pertains to a 95% level of confidence, and the standard error of the estimate is the value indicated in the regression analysis output. The interpretation of these three numbers is as follows: For a typical individual in the Hobbit's Choice Restaurant survey population, if that person's household income before taxes was $75,000, the expected amount of monthly restaurant purchases would be about $148 but because there are differences between income ranges and monthly restaurant purchases, the restaurant purchases would not be exactly that amount. Consequently, the 95% confidence interval reveals that the sales figure should fall between $55 and $241. Finally, the prediction is valid only if conditions remain the same as they were for the time period from which the original data were collected.[4]

The precision of a prediction based on a regression analysis finding depends on the size of the standard error of the estimate.

You may be troubled by the large range of our confidence intervals, and well you should be. If you recall our popcorn sales estimation example in the beginning of the chapter, you should remember that it is important to assess the precision of the predictions generated by a predictive model. How precisely a regression analysis finding predicts is determined by the size of the standard error of the estimate, a measure of the variability of the predicted dependent variable. In our Hobbit's Choice survey case, the average dollars spent on restaurants per month may be predicted by our bivariate regression findings; however, if we repeated the survey many, many times, and made our $75,000 income prediction of the average dollars spent every time, 95% of these predictions would fall between $55 and $241. There is no way to make this prediction more exact because its precision is dictated by the variability in the data.

PERFORM A BIVARIATE REGRESSION WITH SPSS

You have just observed how to perform a bivariate regression using the average dollars spent on restaurants per month as the dependent variable and income, recoded using midpoints of the ranges as the independent variable. Now, you have an opportunity to apply your knowledge. Using the clickstream and annotated SPSS output in Figures 19.2 and 19.3, respectively, and the Hobbit's Choice Restaurant survey data set provided to you, perform bivariate regression analysis using the amount respondents expect to pay, on average, for an evening-meal entree in the new restaurant. When you have determined the results, make a prediction of how much a person who earns an income of $100,000 per year expects to pay for this entree.

How to Improve a Regression Analysis Finding

There are two situations in which a researcher would want to improve a regression analysis. In the first step of our two-step method, the researcher may find that the overall test (the flag) is not significant, while in the second step, the researcher may find that the correlation (R square) between the independent and dependent variables is lower than desired. In either case, the researcher can use a scatter diagram to identify outlier pairs of points. An **outlier**[5] is a data point that is substantially outside the normal range of the data points being analyzed. As one author has noted, outliers "stick out like sore thumbs."[6] When using a scatter diagram to identify outliers,[7] draw an ellipse that encompasses most of the points that appear to be in an elliptical pattern.[8] As noted in Figure 19.6, there are

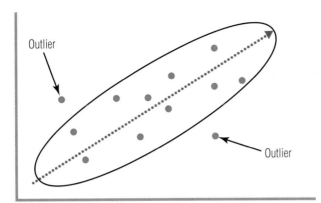

FIGURE 19.6
How to Identify Outliers in
Regression Analysis

two outlier points, so the researcher would eliminate them from the regression analysis and rerun it. Generally, this approach will improve the regression analysis results, meaning that the R square value will increase and the standard error of the estimate will decrease, so the predictions will have narrower confidence intervals.

MULTIPLE REGRESSION ANALYSIS

Now that you are familiar with bivariate regression analysis, you are ready to step up to a higher level. In this section, we will introduce you to multiple regression analysis. You will find that all of the concepts in bivariate regression apply to multiple regression, except you will be working with more than one independent variable.

An Underlying Conceptual Model

In Chapter 4, where you learned about problem definition in marketing research, we referred to a model as a structure that ties together various constructs and their relationships. In that chapter, we indicated that it is beneficial for the marketing manager and the market researcher to have some sort of model in mind when designing the research plan. The bivariate regression equation that you just learned about is a model that ties together an independent variable and its dependent variable. The dependent variables that market researchers are interested in are typically sales, potential sales, or some attitude held by those who make up the market. For example, in the Novartis example, the dependent variable was territory sales. If Dell computers commissioned a survey, it might want information on those who intend to purchase a Dell computer, or it might want information on those who intend to buy a competing brand as a means of understanding these consumers and perhaps persuading them to buy a Dell computer. The dependent variable would be purchase intentions for Dell computers. If Maxwell House Coffee was considering a line of gourmet iced coffee, it would want to know how coffee drinkers feel about gourmet iced coffee, that is, their attitudes toward buying, preparing, and drinking it would be the dependent variables.

Figure 19.7 provides a general conceptual model that fits many marketing research situations, particularly those that are investigating consumer behavior. A **general conceptual model** identifies independent and dependent variables and shows their expected basic relationships to one another. In Figure 19.7, you can see that purchases, intentions to purchase, and preferences are in the center, meaning they are dependent. The surrounding concepts are possible independent variables; that is, any one could be used to predict any dependent variable. For example, one's intentions to purchase an expensive automobile like a Lexus could depend on one's income. It could also depend

There is an underlying general conceptual model in multiple regression analysis.

FIGURE 19.7
A Conceptual Model for
Multiple Regression
Analysis

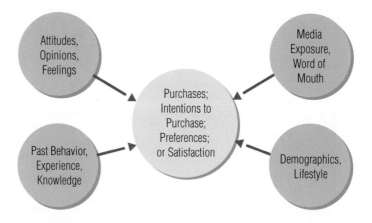

The researcher and the manager identify, measure, and analyze specific variables that pertain to the general conceptual model in mind.

on friends' recommendations (word of mouth), one's opinions about how a Lexus would enhance one's self-image, or experiences riding in or driving a Lexus.

In truth, consumers' preferences, intentions, and actions are potentially influenced by a great number of factors, as would be very evident if you listed all of the subconcepts that make up each concept in Figure 19.7. For example, there are probably a dozen different demographic variables; there could be dozens of lifestyle dimensions, and a person is exposed to a great many types of advertising media every day. Of course, in the problem-definition stage, the researcher and manager slice the myriad independent variables down to a manageable number to be included on the questionnaire; that is, they have the general model structure in Figure 19.7 in mind, but they identify and measure specific variables that pertain to the problem at hand. Because bivariate regression analysis treats only dependent–independent pairs, it would take a great many bivariate regression analyses to account for all possible relevant dependent–independent pairs of variables in a general model such as Figure 19.7. Fortunately, there is no need to perform a great many bivariate regressions, as there is a much better tool, called "multiple regression analysis," a technique we are about to describe in some detail.

Our underlying conceptual model example is one of many different conceptual models that researchers have available to them. In truth, every research project has a unique conceptual model that depends entirely on the research objectives. As an example of how regression analysis can be applied to possible explanations, that is, a conceptual model, of how business executives view various unethical business practices, read Marketing Research Insight 19.2.

Active Learning

THE GENERAL CONCEPTUAL MODEL FOR INTENTIONS TO PATRONIZE THE HOBBIT'S CHOICE RESTAURANT

Understandably, Jeff Dean wants everyone to intend to patronize his new restaurant; however, this will not be the case because of different restaurant dining preferences in the population. Regression analysis will assist Jeff by revealing what variables are good predictors of intentions to patronize his new restaurant. What is the general conceptual model apparent in the Hobbit's Choice Restaurant survey data set?

In order to answer this question and to portray the general conceptual model in the format of Figure 19.7, you must inspect the several variables in this SPSS data set or otherwise come up with a list of the variables in the survey. Using the variable labeled "How likely would it be for you to patronize this restaurant (new upscale restaurant)?" as the dependent variable, diagram the general types of independent or predictor variables that are apparent in this study. Comment on the usefulness of this general conceptual model to Jeff Dean; that is, assuming that the regression results are significant, what marketing strategy implications will become apparent?

ETHICAL ISSUES

19.2

Regression Analysis Shows Predictors of Businesspersons' Tendencies toward Unethical Practices across Nine Countries

In negotiating with other business entities, businesspersons may opt for strategies that are deemed by some as unethical. A study identified five such unethical business negotiation strategies:

- Misrepresenting the facts
- Exaggerating or hiding information
- Obtaining inside information by bribe or false friendship
- Discrediting or threatening the other party
- Making false promises

A researcher was able to access samples of businesspersons in nine different countries: Brazil, Chile, Great Britain, India, Mexico, the Netherlands, Norway, Spain,

and the United States to question them in a survey about their attitudes toward these five unethical business practices.[9] One question on the survey asked about how likely these businesspersons would be to use each of the five unethical strategies if they were in a negotiation situation. The researcher identified several possible predictor variables in his conceptual model with the likelihood of using the unethical negotiation strategy as the dependent variable, and he ran a number of regression analyses to find what predictors tended to persist in significance across the five unethical strategies. He found that male businesspersons were more likely than female businesspersons to use four out of five of the unethical practices, and younger businesspersons were more likely than older ones to use every one of the five unethical business practices. Remember, the study used respondents from nine different countries, so the findings strongly suggest that these relationships exist in a great majority of businesspersons across the globe.

Multiple Regression Analysis Described

Multiple regression analysis is an expansion of bivariate regression analysis in that more than one independent variable is used in the regression equation. The addition of independent variables complicates the conceptualization by adding more dimensions or axes to the regression situation. But it makes the regression model more realistic because, as we have just explained with our general model discussion, predictions normally depend on multiple factors, not just one.

Multiple regression means that you have more than one independent variable to predict a single dependent variable.

▶ **Basic Assumptions in Multiple Regression** Consider our example with the number of salespeople as the independent variable and territory sales as the dependent variable. A second independent variable such as advertising levels can be added to the equation. The addition of a second variable turns the regression line into a regression plane because there are three dimensions if we were to try to graph it: territory sales (Y), number of sales people (X_1), and advertising level (X_2). A **regression plane** is the shape of the dependent variable in multiple regression analysis. If other independent variables are added to the regression analysis, it would be necessary to envision each as a new and separate axis existing at right angles to all other axes. Obviously, it is impossible to draw more than three dimensions at right angles. In fact, it is difficult to even conceive of a multiple dimension diagram, but the assumptions of multiple regression analysis require this conceptualization.

With multiple regression, you work with a regression plane rather than a line.

Everything about multiple regression is essentially equivalent to bivariate regression except you are working with more than one independent variable. The terminology is slightly different in places, and some statistics are modified to take into account the multiple aspects, but for the most part, concepts in multiple regressions are analogous to those in the simple bivariate case. We note these similarities in our description of multiple regressions.

The equation in multiple regressions has the following form:

A multiple regression equation has two or more independent variables (x's).

Multiple Regression Equation $y = a + b_1x_1 + b_2x_2 + b_3x_3 + \ldots + b_mx_m$

where

> y = the dependent, or predicted, variable
> x_i = independent variable i
> a = the intercept
> b_i = the slope for independent variable i
> m = the number of independent variables in the equation

As you can see, the addition of other independent variables has done nothing more than to add b_ix_is to the equation. We still have retained the basic $y = a + bx$ straight-line formula, except now we have multiple x variables, and each one is added to the equation, changing y by its individual slope. The inclusion of each independent variable in this manner preserves the straight-line assumptions of multiple regression analysis. This is sometimes known as **additivity** because each new independent variable is added on to the regression equation.

Let's look at a multiple regression analysis result so you can better understand the multiple regression equation. Here is a possible result using our Lexus example.

Lexus Purchase Intention Multiple Regression Equation Example

> Intention
> to Purchase
> a Lexus = 2
> + 1.0 × Attitude toward Lexus (1–5 scale)
> − .5 × Attitude toward current auto (1–5 scale)
> + 1.0 × Income level (1–10 scale)

This multiple regression equation says that you can predict a consumer's intention to buy a Lexus level if you know three variables: (1) attitude toward Lexus, (2) attitude toward the automobile he/she owns now, and (3) income level using a scale with 10 income grades. Further, we can see the impact of each of these variables on Lexus purchase intentions. Here is how to interpret the equation. First, the average person has a "2" intention level, or some small propensity to want to buy a Lexus. Attitude toward Lexus is measured on a 1–5 scale, and with each attitude scale point, intention goes up 1 point; that is, an individual with a strong positive attitude of 5 will have a greater intention than one with a strong negative attitude of 1. With attitude toward the current automobile he/she owns (for example, a potential Lexus buyer may currently own a Cadillac or a BMW), the intention decreases by .5 for each level on the 5-point scale. Of course, we are assuming that these potential buyers own automobile makes other than a Lexus. Finally, the intention increases by 1 with each increasing income grade.

Here is a numerical example for a potential Lexus buyer whose Lexus attitude is 4, current automobile make attitude is 3, and income is 5.

Calculation of Lexus Purchase Intention Using the Multiple Regression Equation

> Intention
> to Purchase
> a Lexus = 2
> + 1.0 × 4
> − .5 × 3
> + 1.0 × 5
> = 9.5

Multiple regression is a very powerful tool, because it tells us what factors predict the dependent variable, which way (the sign) each factor influences the dependent variable, and how much (the size of b_i) each factor influences it.

Just as was the case in bivariate regression analysis in which we used the correlation between y and x, it is possible to inspect the strength of the linear relationship between the independent variables and the dependent variable with multiple regression. Multiple R, also called the **coefficient of determination**, is a handy measure of the strength of the overall linear relationship. Just as was the case in bivariate regression analysis, the multiple regression analysis model assumes that a straight-line (plane) relationship exists among the variables. Multiple R ranges from 0 to $+1.0$ and represents the amount of the dependent variable "explained," or accounted for, by the combined independent variables. High multiple-R values indicate that the regression plane applies well to the scatter of points, whereas low values signal that the straight-line model does not apply well. At the same time, a multiple regression result is an estimate of the population multiple regression equation, and, just as was the case with other estimated population parameters, it is necessary to test for statistical significance.

> **Multiple R indicates how well the independent variables can predict the dependent variable in multiple regression.**

Multiple R is like a lead indicator of the multiple regression analysis findings. As you will see soon, it is one of the first pieces of information provided in a multiple regression output. Many researchers mentally convert the multiple R into a percentage. For example a multiple R of .75 means that the regression findings will explain 75% of the dependent variable. The greater the explanatory power of the multiple regression finding, the better and more useful it is for the researcher.

Let us issue a caution before we show you how to run a multiple regression analysis using SPSS. The **independence assumption** stipulates that the independent variables must be statistically independent and uncorrelated with one another. The independence assumption is very important because if it is violated, the multiple regression findings are untrue. The presence of moderate or stronger correlations among the independent variables is termed **multicollinearity** and will violate the independence assumption of multiple regression analysis results when it occurs.[10] It is up to the researcher to test for and remove multicollinearity if it is present.

> **With multiple regression, the independent variables should have low correlations with one another.**
>
> **Multicollinearity can be assessed and eliminated in multiple regression with the VIF statistic.**

The way to avoid this problem is to use warnings statistics issued by most statistical analysis programs to identify this problem. One commonly used method is the **variance inflation factor**, sometimes referred to as **VIF**. The VIF is a single number, and a rule of thumb is that as long as VIF is less than 10, multicollinearity is not a concern. With a VIF of greater than 10 associated with any independent variable in the multiple regression equation, it is prudent to remove that variable from consideration or to otherwise reconstitute the set of independent variables.[11] In other words, when examining the output of any multiple regression, the researcher should inspect the VIF number associated with each independent variable that is retained in the final multiple regression equation by the procedure. If the VIF is greater than 10, the researcher should remove that variable from the independent variable set and rerun the multiple regression.[12] This iterative process is used until only independent variables that are statistically significant and that have acceptable VIFs are in the final multiple regression equation.

The Hobbit's Choice Restaurant Survey: How to Run and Interpret Multiple Regression Analysis on SPSS

Running multiple regression is almost identical to performing simple bivariate regression with SPSS. The only difference is that you will select more than one independent variable for the analysis. Let's think about a general conceptual model that might predict how much people spend on restaurants per month. We already know from our bivariate regression analysis work with the Hobbit's Choice Restaurant data set that income predicts this dependent variable. Another predictor could be family size, as larger families will order more entrees because there are more family members. So, we will add this independent variable. A third independent variable could be preferences. People who prefer an elegant décor surely will pay for this atmosphere, as elegant décors are typically found in the most expensive restaurants. To summarize, we have determined our conceptual model: the average amount paid at restaurants per month may be predicted by: (1) household income level, (2) family size, and (3) preference for restaurants with elegant décors.

Just as with bivariate regression, the ANALYZE-REGRESSION-LINEAR command sequence is used to run a multiple regression analysis, and the variable, dollars spent in restaurants per month, is selected as the dependent variable, while the other three are specified as the independent variables. You will find this annotated SPSS clickstream in Figure 19.8.

As the computer output in Figure 19.9 shows, the Multiple R value (Adjusted R Square in the Model Summary table) indicating the strength of relationship between the independent variables and the dependent variable is .749, signifying that there is some linear relationship present. Next, the printout reveals that the ANOVA F is significant, signaling that the null hypothesis of no linear relationship is rejected, and it is justifiable to use a straight-line relationship to model the variables in this case.

Just as we did with bivariate regression, it is necessary in multiple regression analysis to test for statistical significance of the b_is (betas) determined for the independent variables. Once again, you must determine whether sampling error is influencing the results and giving a false reading. You should recall that this is a test for significance from zero (the null hypothesis) and is achieved through the use of separate t tests for each b_i. The SPSS out-

The SPSS ANALYZE-REGRESSION-LINEAR command is used to run multiple regression.

With multiple regression, look at the significance level of each calculated beta.

SPSS Student Assistant:
The Integrated Case:
Running and Interpreting
Multiple Regression

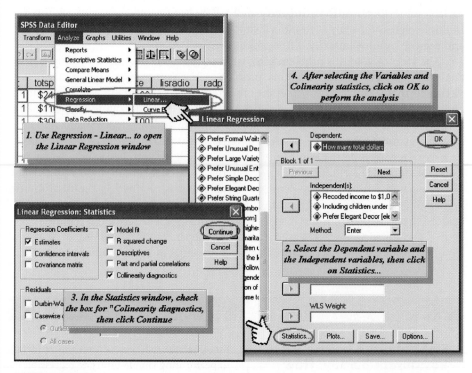

FIGURE 19.8
SPSS Clickstream for Multiple Regression Analysis

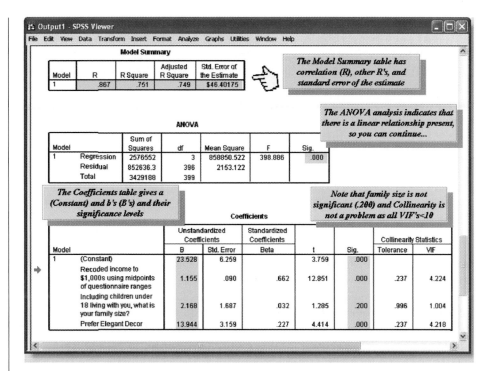

FIGURE 19.9
SPSS Output for Multiple Regression Analysis

put in Figure 19.9 indicates the levels of statistical significance. In this particular example, it is apparent that the recoded income level and the preference for an elegant dining décor are significant, as both have significance levels of .000. The constant (a) also is significant as it, too, has a significance level of .000. However, the independent variable size of family is not significant, as its significance level is .200 and above our standard cutoff value of .05.

In the Hobbit's Choice Restaurant survey, family size was not found to be related to the amount spent on restaurants per month.

A trimmed regression means that you eliminate the non-significant independent variables and rerun the regression.

▶ **"Trimming" the Regression for Significant Findings** What do you do with the mixed significance results we have just found in our dollars spent on restaurants per month multiple regression example? Before we answer this question, you should be aware that this mixed result is very likely, so how to handle it is vital to your understanding of how to perform multiple regression analysis successfully. Here is the answer: it is standard practice in multiple regression analysis to systematically eliminate independent variables that are shown to be insignificant through a process called "trimming." You then rerun the trimmed model and inspect the significance levels again. This series of eliminations or iterations helps to achieve the simplest model by eliminating the nonsignificant independent variables. The trimmed multiple regression model with all significant independent variables is found in Figure 19.10. Notice that the VIF diagnostics were not selected, as they were examined on the untrimmed SPSS output and found to be acceptable.

Run trimmed regressions iteratively until all betas are significant.

This additional run enables the marketing researcher to think in terms of fewer dimensions within which the dependent variable relationship operates. Generally, successive iterations sometimes cause the Multiple R to decrease somewhat, and it is advisable to scrutinize this value after each run. You can see that the new multiple R is still .749, so in our example, there has been no decrease. Iterations will also cause the beta values and the intercept value to shift slightly; consequently, it is necessary to inspect all significance levels of the betas once again. Through a series of iterations, the marketing researcher finally arrives at the final regression equation expressing the salient independent variables and their linear relationships with the dependent variable. A concise predictive model has been found.

Once the multiple regression equation coefficients are determined, one can make a prediction of the dependent variable using independent variable values.

▶ **Using Results to Make a Prediction** The use of a multiple regression result is identical in concept to the application of a bivariate regression result—that is, it relies on an analysis of residuals that reflect the amount of error in its predictions. Remember,

FIGURE 19.10
SPSS Output for Trimmed Multiple Regression Analysis

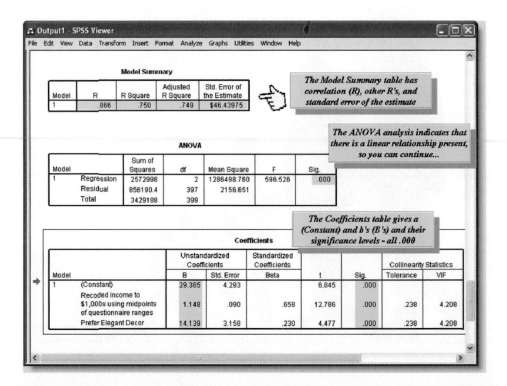

we began this chapter with a description of residuals and indicated that residuals analysis is a way to determine the goodness of a prediction. Ultimately, the marketing researcher wishes to predict the dependent variable based on assumed or known values of the independent variables that are found to have significant relationships within the multiple regression equation. The standard error of the estimate is provided on all regression analysis programs, and it is possible to apply this value to forecast the ranges in which the dependent variable will fall, given levels of the independent variables.

Making a prediction with multiple regression is simple: all you need to do is to apply the final (significant) multiple regression intercept and various coefficients. For a numerical example, let us assume that we are interested in upscale restaurant patrons so we can give Jeff Dean an estimate of how much they spend monthly on restaurants. We will specify an upscale restaurant patron as someone with a household income of $100,000 and who very strongly prefers an elegant décor. To "very strongly prefer" means a 5 on the 5-point scale of preferences for various restaurant features.

Using our SPSS trimmed multiple regression findings, we can predict the amount of dollars spent on restaurants each month by upscale consumers. The calculations follow. Remember the constant and betas are from the trimmed multiple regression output in Figure 19.10.

Calculation of Monthly Restaurant Purchases Predicted with an Income Level of $100,000 and Preference for Elegant Décor of 5

$$y = a + b_1 x_1 + b_2 x_2 + b_3 x_3$$
$$= \$29.39 + \$1.15 \times 100 + \$14.14 \times 5$$
$$= \$29.39 + \$132.25 + \$70.0$$
$$= \$231.64$$

Here is an example of a prediction using multiple regression.

The calculated prediction is about $232; however, we must take into consideration the sample error and variability of the data with a confidence interval—that is, the predicted dollars spent on restaurants per month ± 1.96 times the standard error of the estimate.

Calculation of 95% Confidence Interval for a Prediction Based on Multiple Regression Findings with the Hobbit's Choice Restaurant Survey

Predicted y ± 1.96 × Standard error of the estimate
$231.64 ± 1.96 × $46.44
$231.64 ± 91.02
$140.62 to $322.66

The interpretation would be that individuals with a household income before taxes of $100,000 and who very strongly prefer an elegant décor when they dine can be expected to spend between about $141 and $323 monthly on restaurants, averaging about $232. Again, the confidence interval range is quite large, but it is perfectly reflective of the variability in the data and in no way a flaw in the multiple regression analysis.

Special Uses of Multiple Regression Analysis

There are a number of special uses and considerations to keep in mind when running multiple regression analysis. These include using a "dummy" independent variable, using standardized betas to compare the importance of independent variables, and using multiple regression as a screening device.

▶ **Using a "Dummy" Independent Variable** A **dummy independent variable** is defined as one that is scaled with a nominal 0-versus-1 coding scheme. The 0-versus-1 code is traditional, but any two adjacent numbers could be used, such as 1-versus-2. The

The interval-at-minimum scaling assumption requirement of multiple regression may be relaxed by use of a dummy variable.

scaling assumptions that underlie multiple regression analysis require that the independent and dependent variables both be at least interval-scaled. However, there are instances in which a marketing researcher may want to use an independent variable that does not embody interval-scaling assumptions. It is not unusual, for instance, for the marketing researcher to wish to use a dichotomous or two-level variable, such as gender, as an independent variable in a multiple regression problem. For instance, a researcher may want to use gender coded as 0 for male and 1 for female as an independent variable. Or you might have a buyer–nonbuyer dummy variable that you want to use as an independent variable. In these instances, it is usually permissible to go ahead and slightly violate the assumption of metric scaling for the independent variable to come up with a result that is in some degree interpretable.

▶ **Using Standardized Betas to Compare the Importance of Independent Variables** Regardless of the application intentions of the marketing researcher, it is usually of interest to the marketing researcher to determine the relative importance of the independent variables in the multiple regression result. Because independent variables are often measured with different units, it is erroneous to make direct comparisons between the calculated betas. For example, it is improper to directly compare the regression coefficient for family size to another for money spent per month on personal grooming because the units of measurement are so different (people versus dollars). The most common approach is to standardize the independent variables through a quick operation that involves dividing the difference between each independent variable value and its mean by the standard deviation of that independent variable. This results in what is called the **standardized beta coefficient**. In other words, standardization translates each independent value into the number of standard deviations away from its own mean. Essentially, this procedure transforms these variables into a set of values with a mean of zero and a standard deviation equal to 1.0.

> The researcher can compare the sizes of standardized beta coefficients directly, but comparing unstandardized betas is like comparing apples and oranges.

> Standardized betas indicate the relative importance of alternative predictor variables.

When they are standardized, direct comparisons may be made between the resulting betas. The larger the absolute value of a standardized beta coefficient, the more relative importance it assumes in predicting the dependent variable. SPSS and most other statistical programs provide the standardized betas automatically. If you review the SPSS output in Figure 19.10, you will find the standardized values under the column designated "Standardized Coefficients." It is important to note that this operation has no effect on the final multiple regression result. Its only function is to allow direct comparisons of the relative impact of the significant independent variables on the dependent variable. As an example, if you look at the "Standardized Coefficients" reported in our Hobbit's Choice Restaurant regression printout (Figure 19.10), you will see that the income level is the most important variable (.658), whereas preference for an elegant restaurant décor is much less important (.230).

Active **Learning**

SEGMENTATION ASSOCIATES, INC.

Segmentation Associates, Inc. is a marketing research company that specializes in market segmentation studies. It has access to large and detailed databases on demographics, lifestyles, asset ownership, consumer values, and a number of other consumer descriptors. It has developed a reputation for reducing these large databases into findings that are managerially relevant to its clients; that is, Segmentation Associates is known for its ability to translate its findings into market segmentation variables for its clients to use in their marketing strategies.

In the past year, Segmentation Associates has conducted a great many market segmentation studies for a number of automobile manufacturers. The company has agreed to provide disguised findings of some of its work. In the following table segmentation variables

are identified, and each of three different types of automobile buyer types is identified. For each segmentation variable, Segmentation Associates has provided the results of its multiple regression findings. The values are the standardized beta coefficients of the segmentation variables found to be statistically significant. Where no value appears, that regression coefficient was not statistically significant.

Segmentation Variable	Compact Automobile Buyer	Sports Car Buyer	Luxury Automobile Buyer
Demographics			
Age	−.28	−.15	+.59
Education	−.12	+.38	
Family size	+.39	−.35	
Income	−.15	+.25	+.68
Lifestyle/values			
Active		+.59	−.39
American pride	+.30		+.24
Bargain hunter	+.45	−.33	
Conservative		−.38	+.54
Cosmopolitan	−.40	+.68	
Embraces change	−.30	+.65	
Family values	+.69		+.21
Financially secure	−.28	+.21	+.52
Optimistic		+.71	+.37

Here are some questions to answer.

1. What is the underlying conceptual model used by Segmentation Associates that is apparent in these three sets of findings?

2. What are the segmentation variables that distinguish compact automobile buyers, and in what ways?

3. What are the segmentation variables that distinguish sports car buyers, and in what ways?

4. What are the segmentation variables that distinguish luxury automobile buyers, and in what ways?

▶ **Using Multiple Regression Analysis as a Screening Device** Another application of multiple regression analysis is as a screening or identifying device; that is, the marketing researcher may be faced with a large number and variety of prospective independent variables, and he or she may use multiple regression as a **screening device** or a way of spotting the salient (statistically significant) independent variables for the dependent variable at hand. In this instance, the intent is not to determine some sort of a prediction of the dependent variable; rather, it may be to search for clues as to what factors help the researcher understand the behavior of this particular variable. For instance, the researcher might be seeking market segmentation bases, and could use regression to spot which demographic variables are related to the consumer behavior variable under study. While the use of multiple regression is prevalent in marketing research, and particularly for segmentation analysis, you are now well aware of the many requirements and pitfalls of using this tool. There has emerged in the past decade a new analysis technique that accomplishes what multiple regression analysis accomplishes, and then some, and it does not work under the severe restrictions on multiple regression. This technique is called "neural network analysis," and we have prepared Marketing Research Insight 19.3 to describe the advantages of this technique.

Multiple regression analysis can be used to identify the characteristics of buyers of different types of automobiles.

19.3 Will Neural Network Analysis Replace Multiple Regression Analysis?

As noted in this chapter, multiple regression analysis is used extensively by marketing researchers who are testing or otherwise investigating a general conceptual model that has a large number of independent variables—demographics, lifestyles, product experiences, attitudes, values, etc.—competing to predict one or more critical dependent variables such as product usage or satisfaction. The critical assumptions of restrictions of multiple regression analysis include:

- A general conceptual model should be specified
- Linear relationships are assumed
- Outlier variables are identified and eliminated
- Multicollinearity is low
- Interactions among the independent variables are minimal

Neural network analysis is, in a nutshell, a system that "learns" the relationships among variables and finds the best possible combination of independent variables to predict a given dependent variable such as customer satisfaction. Although it is far too complicated to describe here, the advantages of neural networks over multiple regression are:[13]

- A conceptual model is unnecessary
- Linear and nonlinear (such as curvilinear) relationships are accommodated
- Outliers are less of a problem
- Multicollinearity can be present without detrimental effects
- Interactions among independent variables are taken into account

In other words, this technique does not labor under the critical assumptions of multiple regression. Perhaps in future editions of this textbook, you will be learning about how to perform neural network analysis instead of reading about the strict requirements of multiple regression analysis.

STEPWISE MULTIPLE REGRESSION ANALYSIS

When the researcher is using multiple regression analysis as a screening tool or he/she is otherwise faced with a large number of independent variables in the conceptual model that are to be tested by multiple regression, it can become tedious to narrow down the independent variables by manual trimming. Fortunately, there is a type of multiple regression that does the trimming operation automatically: it is called "stepwise multiple regression."

Here is a simple explanation. With **stepwise multiple regression**, the one independent variable that is statistically significant and explains the most variance in the dependent variable is determined, and it is entered into the multiple regression equation. Then the statistically significant independent variable that contributes most to explaining the remaining unexplained variance in the dependent variable is determined and entered. This process is continued until all statistically significant independent variables have been entered into the multiple regression equation.[14] In other words, all of the insignificant independent variables are eliminated from the final multiple regression equation based on the level of significance stipulated by the researcher in the multiple regression options. The final output contains only statistically significant independent variables. Stepwise regression is used by researchers when they are confronted with a large number of competing independent variables and they do want to narrow down the analysis to a set of statistically significant independent variables in a single regression analysis. With stepwise multiple regression, there is no need to trim and rerun the regression analysis because SPSS does the trimming automatically based on the stepwise method selected by the researcher. A researcher recently used stepwise multiple regression in an attempt to understand the factors that predict television viewing of the Summer Olympic Games. When you read Marketing Research Insight 19.4, you will find that this technique effectively reduced a large number of possible explanatory (independent) variables to a very small set.

Stepwise regression is useful if a researcher has many independent variables and wants to narrow the set to a smaller number of statistically significant variables.

How to Do Stepwise Multiple Regression Analysis with SPSS

A researcher executes stepwise multiple regression by using the ANALYZE-REGRESSION-LINEAR command sequence precisely as was described for multiple regression. The dependent variable and many independent variables are selected into their respective windows as before. To direct SPSS to perform stepwise multiple regression, use the "Method" menu to select "Stepwise." The findings will be the same as those arrived at by a researcher who uses iterative trimmed multiple regressions. Of course, with stepwise multiple regression output, there will be information on the independent variables that are taken out of the multiple regression equation based on nonsignificance, and, if the researcher wishes, SPSS stepwise multiple regression will also take into account the VIF statistic to ensure that multicollinearity is not an issue.

We do not have screenshots of stepwise multiple regression, as this technique is quite advanced. In fact, we do not recommend that you use stepwise multiple regression unless you gain a good deal more background on multiple regression, as you may encounter findings that are difficult to understand or are even counter intuitive.[15]

19.4 Who Watches the Summer Olympic Games? Stepwise Regression Gives the Answer

Every four years, the Summer Olympic Games offer sports enthusiasts hours and hours of prime time—as well as non-prime time—television viewing. But, who are the viewers of the Summer Olympic Games? To answer this question, a researcher studied the Summer Olympic Games and surveyed American adults regarding the amount of time they spent watching the games during the first week. The researcher hypothesized that a number of factors were related to watching the Olympic Games, including a variety of demographics such as gender, education, race, a host of lifestyle dimensions, personal interests, and core beliefs and values. Patriotism, religiousness, attitudes toward advertising, and personal relevance of the Olympic Games were also considered as possible predictor variables, as was the person's typical television sports viewing habits (not during the Olympics).

Faced with a large number of competing independent variables in his general conceptual model, the researcher turned to stepwise multiple regression (after being assured there were no outliers and that multicollinearity was not a problem) to identify the statistically significant ones. This approach worked effectively and determined the three primary factors related to Summer Olympics television viewing:

- Gender: males watch more than females
- Patriotism: people who are more patriotic watch more
- Typical television sports TV viewing: those who watch more sports in general watch more Olympic Game coverage

When the researcher repeated his analysis using only the males in the sample, he found that patriotism was replaced by a different variable: involvement with the Summer Olympic Games. Thus, watching sports on television in general and patriotism explain why women watch the Summer Olympic Games, and watching sports on television in general and a keen interest in the Summer Olympic Games explain why American men watch these broadcasts.

THREE WARNINGS REGARDING MULTIPLE REGRESSION ANALYSIS

Regression is a statistical tool, not a cause-and-effect statement.

Before leaving our description of multiple regression analysis, we must issue a warning about your interpretation of regression. We all have a natural tendency to think in terms of causes and effects, and regression analysis invites us to think in terms of a dependent variable's resulting or being caused by an independent variable's actions. This line of thinking is absolutely incorrect: Regression analysis is nothing more than a statistical tool that assumes a linear relationship between two variables. It springs from correlation analysis, which is a measure of the linear association and not the causal relationship between two variables. Consequently, even though two variables, such as sales and advertising, are logically connected, a regression analysis does not permit the marketing researcher to make cause-and-effect statements because other independent variables are not controlled.

The second warning we have is that you should not apply regression analysis to predict outside of the boundaries of the data used to develop your regression model; that is, you may use the regression model to interpolate within the boundaries set by the range (lowest value to highest value) of your independent variable(s), but if you use it to predict for independent values outside those limits, you have moved into an area that is not accounted for by the raw data used to compute your regression line. For this reason, you are not assured that the regression equation findings are valid. For example, it would not be correct to use our restaurants regression equation findings on income-dollars spent on individuals who are wealthy and have annual incomes in the millions of dollars because these individuals were not represented in the Hobbit's Choice Restaurant survey.

Our last warning is about the small amount of knowledge you have gained about multiple regression analysis in this chapter. You may be surprised that you have learned so little, but there is a great deal more to multiple regression analysis that is beyond the scope of this textbook. Our coverage in this chapter introduces you to regression analysis, and it provides you with enough information about it to run uncomplicated regression analyses on SPSS, identify the relevant aspects of the SPSS output, and to interpret the findings. As you will see when you work with the SPSS regression analysis procedures, we have only scratched the surface of this topic. There are many more options, statistics, and considerations involved.[16] In fact, there is so much material that whole textbooks on regression exist. Our purpose has been to teach you the basic concepts and to help you interpret the statistics associated with these concepts as you encounter them as statistical analysis program output. Our descriptions are merely an introduction to multiple regression analysis to help you comprehend the basic notions, common uses, and interpretations involved with this predictive technique.[17]

Despite our simple treatment of it, we fully realize that even simplified regression analysis is very complicated and difficult to learn, and that we have showered you with a great many regression statistical terms and concepts in this chapter. Seasoned researchers are intimately knowledgeable about them and very comfortable in using them. However, as a student encountering them for the first time, you undoubtedly feel very intimidated. While we may not be able to reduce your anxiety, we have created Table 19.3, which lists all of the regression analysis concepts we have described in this chapter, and it provides an explanation of each one. At least, you will not need to search through the chapter to find these concepts when you are trying to learn or use them.

TABLE 19.3	Regression Analysis Concepts
Concept	**Explanation**
Regression analysis	A predictive model using the straight line relationship of $y = a + bx$
Intercept	The constant, or a, in the straight line relationship that is the value of y when $x = 0$
Slope	The b, or the amount of change in y for a 1 unit change in x
Dependent variable	y, the variable that is being predicted by the x(s) or independent variable(s)
Independent variable(s)	The x variable or variables that are used in the straight line equation to predict y
Least squares criterion	A statistical procedure that ensures that the computed regression equation is the best one possible
R square	A number ranging from 0 to 1.0 that reveals how well the straight-line model fits the scatter of points, the higher, the better
Standard error of the estimate	A value that is used to make a prediction at the (e.g.) 95% level of confidence with the formula $y \pm z$ times s_e

(continued)

TABLE 19.3	Regression Analysis Concepts (Continued)
Concept	**Explanation**
Multiple regression analysis	A powerful form of regression where more than one x variable is in the regression equation
Additivity	A statistical assumption that allows the use of more than one x variable in a multiple regression equation: $y = a + b_1x_1 + b_2x_2 \ldots + b_mx_m$
Independence assumption	A statistical requirement that when more than one x variable is used, no pair of x variables has a high correlation
Multiple R	Also called the coefficient of determination, a number that ranges from 0 to 1.0 that indicates the strength of the overall linear relationship in a multiple regression, the higher the better
Multicollinearity	The term used to denote a violation of the independence assumption that causes regression results to be in error
Variance inflation factor (VIF)	A statistical value that identifies what x variable(s) contribute to multicollinearity and should be removed from the analysis to eliminate multicollinearity. Any variable with a VIF of 10 or greater should be removed
Trimming	Removing an x variable in multiple regression because it is not statistically significant, rerunning the regression, and repeating until all remaining x variables are significant
Standardized beta coefficients	Slopes (β values) that are normalized so they can be compared directly to determine their relative importance in y's prediction
Dummy independent variable	Use of an x variable that has a 0,1 or similar coding, used sparing when nominal variables must be in the independent variables set
Stepwise multiple regression	A specialized multiple regression that is appropriate when there is a large number of x variables that need to be trimmed down to a small, significant set and the researcher wishes the statistical program to do this automatically

SUMMARY

Predictive analyses are methods used to forecast the levels of a variable such as sales. Model building and extrapolation are two general options available to market researchers. In either case, it is important to assess the goodness of the prediction. This assessment is typically performed by comparing the predictions against the actual data with procedures called "residuals analyses."

Market researchers use regression analysis to make predictions. The basis of this technique is an assumed straight-line relationship existing between the variables. With bivariate regression, one independent variable, x, is used to predict the dependent variable, y, using the straight-line formula of $y = a + bx$. A high R square and a statistically significant slope indicate that the linear model is a good fit. With multiple regression, the underlying conceptual model specifics that several independent variables are to be used, and it is necessary to determine which ones are significant. By systematically eliminating the nonsignificant independent variables in an iterative manner, a process called "trimming," a researcher will ultimately derive a set of significant independent variables that yield a significant predictive model. The standard error of the estimate is used to compute a confidence interval range for a regression prediction.

Seasoned researchers may opt to use stepwise multiple regression if faced with a large number of candidate independent variables such as several demographic, lifestyle, and buyer behavior characteristics. With stepwise multiple regression, independent variables are entered into the multiple regression equation containing only statistically significant independent variables.

KEY TERMS

Prediction (p. 560)
Extrapolation (p. 561)
Predictive model (p. 561)
Analysis of residuals (p. 562)
Bivariate regression analysis (p. 563)
Intercept (p. 563)
Slope (p. 563)
Dependent variable (p. 564)
Independent variable (p. 564)
Least squares criterion (p. 564)
Standard error of the estimate (p. 570)
Outlier (p. 572)

General conceptual model (p. 573)
Multiple regression analysis (p. 575)
Regression plane (p. 575)
Additivity (p. 576)
Coefficient of determination (p. 577)
Independence assumption (p. 577)
Multicollinearity (p. 577)
Variance inflation factor (VIF) (p. 577)
Dummy independent variable (p. 581)
Standardized beta coefficient (p. 582)
Screening device (p. 583)
Stepwise multiple regression (p. 585)

REVIEW QUESTIONS/APPLICATIONS

1. Construct and explain a reasonably simple predictive model for each of the following cases:
   a. What is the relationship between gasoline prices and distance traveled for family automobile touring vacations?
   b. How do hurricane warnings relate to purchases of flashlight batteries in the expected landfall area?
   c. What do florists do with regard to their inventory of flowers for the week prior to and the week following Mother's Day?
2. Indicate what the scatter diagram and probable regression line would look like for two variables that are correlated in each of the following ways (in each instance, assume a negative intercept): (a) −0.89, (b) +0.48, and (c) −0.10
3. Circle K runs a contest, inviting customers to fill out a registration card. In exchange, they are eligible for a grand prize drawing of a trip to Alaska. The card asks for the customer's age, education, gender, estimated weekly purchases (in dollars) at that Circle K, and approximate distance the Circle K is from his or her home. Identify each of the following if a multiple regression analysis were to be performed: (a) independent variable, (b) dependent variable, and (c) dummy variable.
4. Explain what is meant by the independence assumption in multiple regression. How can you examine your data for independence, and what statistic is issued by most statistical analysis programs? How is this statistic interpreted? In other words, what would indicate the presence of multicollinearity, and what would you do to eliminate it?

5. What is multiple regression? Specifically, what is "multiple" about it, and how does the formula for multiple regression appear? In your indication of the formula, identify the various terms and also indicate the signs (positive or negative) that they may take on.

6. If one uses the "enter" method for multiple regression analysis, what statistics on an SPSS output should be examined to assess the result? Indicate how you would determine each of the following:
   a. Variance explained in the dependent variable by the independent variables
   b. Statistical significance of each of the independent variables.
   c. Relative importance of the independent variables in predicting the dependent variable

7. Explain what is meant by the notion of "trimming" a multiple regression result. Use the following example to illustrate your understanding of this concept.

   A bicycle manufacturer maintains records over 20 years of the following retail price in dollars, cooperative advertising amount in dollars, competitors' average retail price in dollars, number of retail locations selling the bicycle manufacturer's brand, and whether or not the winner of the *Tour de France* was riding the manufacturer's brand (coded as a dummy variable where $0 =$ no, and $1 =$ yes).

   The initial multiple regression result determines the following:

Variable	Significance Level
Average retail price in dollars	.001
Cooperative advertising amount in dollars	.202
Competitors' average retail price in dollars	.028
Number of retail locations	.591
Tour de France	.032

   Using the "enter" method, what would be the trimming steps you would expect to undertake to identify the significant multiple regression result? Explain your reasoning.

8. Using the bicycle example in question 7, what do you expect would be the elimination of variables sequence using stepwise multiple regression? Explain your reasoning with respect to the operation of each of this technique.

9. Using SPSS graphical capabilities, diagram the regression plane for the following variables.

Number of Gallons of Gasoline Used per week	Miles Computed for Work per Week	Number of Riders in Carpool
5	50	4
10	125	3
15	175	2
20	250	0
25	300	0

10. The Maximum Amount is a company that specializes in making fashionable clothes in large sizes for large people. Among its customers are Sinbad and Shaquille O'Neal. A survey was performed for the Maximum Amount, and a regression analysis was run on some of the data. Of interest in this analysis was the possible relationship between self-esteem (dependent variable) and number of Maximum Amount articles purchased last year (independent variables). Self-esteem was mea-

sured on a 7-point scale in which 1 signifies very low and 7 indicates very high self-esteem. Below are some items that have been taken from the output.

Pearson product moment correlation = +0.63
Intercept = 3.5
Slope = +0.2
Standard error = 1.5

All statistical tests are significant at the 0.01 level or less. What is the correct interpretation of these findings?

11. For most of his life, Wayne LaTorte has been fascinated by UFOs. He has kept records of UFO sightings in the desert areas of Arizona, California, and New Mexico over the past 15 years and he has correlated them with earthquake tremors. A fellow engineer suggests that Wayne use regression analysis as a means of determining the relationship. Wayne does this and finds a "constant" of 30 separate earth tremor events and a slope of 5 events per UFO sighting. Wayne then writes an article for the *UFO Observer*, claiming that earthquakes are largely caused by the subsonic vibrations emitted by UFOs as they enter the Earth's atmosphere. What is your reaction to Wayne's article?

CASE 19.1

DON'T YOU JUST HATE IT WHEN . . . ? (PART IV)

Part I (Case 16.1) of this case is on pages 479–480, Part II (Case 17.1) of this case is on pages 515–516, and Part III (Case 18.1) is on pages 553–554.

A cell phone chirps at 9:13 P.M. in an apartment just off campus. Marsha checks the caller identification, presses the On button and says, "Josh! What a surprise. Are you calling to say that you can't do that regression analysis for our Pets, Pets & Pets marketing research project that you promised to send me by 7 P.M. tonight?"

Josh: "Boy, are you heartless, and after I brought pizza to your place last week."

Marsha: "Yeah, right, and you kept me up all night going over that present value finance stuff that was in our finance class test the next day. Then, you said you couldn't stay awake and crashed on my couch at 3 A.M. I could hardly finish our marketing research presentation on crosstabs and correlations for Dr. Z's class because of your loud snoring."

Josh: "Well, anyway, I did pass that test, and I did the regression analysis just like we agreed. It is a good thing that Dr. Z let us have a wildcard construct or two in our project. Otherwise we would not have gotten much at all. I used the evaluations of Pets, Pets & Pets that we added plus some of the lifestyle statements that we added in the regressions. Plus, I even summarized them into tables."

Marsha thinks, "Oh oh, this sounds like a disaster. He summarized them . . . ?" and says, "So where are they?"

Josh: "I just e-mailed them. Too bad you are on the phone, Marsh, or you could look at them. The ball is in your court. Bye."

Marsha: "Hey, wait! I can look at them right now because I have DSL and I can use the phone and my high-speed computer connection at the same time."

Marsha checks her e-mail and opens up Josh's document. The document is below.

Table 1
Times visited PPP in past year

Independent Variable(s)	Standardized
I usually purchase pet supplies form from the same company.[a]	0.31
Pets, Pets & Pets helps me stretch my wallet.[a]	−0.25
Buying pet supplies at Pets, Pets & Pets gives me time to do more important things.[a]	0.25
My pet is a large part of my life.[a]	0.30
I am pleased with my pet right now.[a]	0.13
I enjoy taking care of my pet.[a]	0.15
How many miles do you live from Pets, Pets & pets?	−0.19
Indicate your gender (1 = male, 2 = female)	−0.18

Table 2
How likely to buy at PPP next time (1–7 scale)

Independent Variable(s)	Standardized
Wide variety of pet supplies at Pets, Pets & Pets[a]	−0.25
Good values at Pets, Pets & Pets[a]	0.49
Helpful employees at Pets, Pets & Pets[a]	0.33

Table 3
Amount Spent at PPP Last Time

Independent Variable(s)	Standardized
Number of pets owned	−0.17
Recall seeing a PPP newspaper ad in the past month? (1 = yes, 2 = no)	−0.21
Family income level	0.38

[a]Based on a scale where 1 = strongly disagree and 5 = strongly agree

Marsha: "All right, I see three tables with the multiple regression findings. You did separate ones for how many times they visited PPP in the past year, how likely they are to use PPP the next time, and the amount they spent the last time they visited PPP. Your tables have the standardized beta coefficients for the statistically significant independent variables, right?"

Josh: "Um, I didn't follow all of that. If you say so, yeah."

Marsha: "What I mean is that you used the two-step method described in Chapter 19, and you trimmed out all of the nonsignificant independent variables like you were supposed to. Right?"

Josh: "Actually, I ran the analyses and picked out the results that seemed useful and that kinda made sense to me. Didn't Dr. Z stress that with multiple regression, you should get results that help you to understand the relationships? Well, the ones I put in the tables kinda helped me to understand. You are doing the presentation in class tomorrow, so you should have an easy time of it."

Marsha thinks, "Gawd, I can't believe this is happening to me over and over again," and says, "Josh, don't speak to me again until your grandchildren are in college! I will rerun the analysis myself and do it right. Good bye!"

1. Describe the two-step process and trimming approach that Josh should have used in running his three multiple regression analyses with the Pets, Pets, & Pets data.

2. Assume that the independent variables reported in each of Josh's three tables are the result of correctly using the two-step process and trimming the nonsiginficant independent variables. Describe the relationships revealed in each table, and indicate the implications of these relationships for Pets, Pets & Pets marketing strategy.

SPSS

SALES TRAINING ASSOCIATES, INC.

Sales Training Associates, Inc. (STA) is a training company headquartered in Atlanta, Georgia. It specializes in training courses for sales, sales management, and marketing management. STA was founded by Harold "Bud" Simmons, who began his sales career selling vacuum cleaners door-to-door in 1970. Bud Simmons never attended college, and, in fact, he barely graduated from high school, but he demonstrated a strong aptitude for sales, and he took a job as a sales rep immediately following graduation.

Bud was very successful from the start, and he moved through a succession of sales jobs in the 1970s and 1980s. In 1991, Bud joined the Equitable Life Insurance Company, and in two short years he was a member of the coveted million dollar round table. By the mid-1990s, Bud's annual sales were averaging over $5 million. Equitable realized that Bud had special selling talent, and it gradually shifted Bud's activities from selling to training of Equitable sales personnel. Bud developed a series of in-house training programs and special-purpose seminars that received high acclaim from all Equitable salespersons who participated in them. In 1996, Bud left Equitable to found Sales Training Associates, Inc., beginning at first with sales training in insurance sales only, but soon STA training programs covered practically all types of sales.

Bud's son, Harold Jr., joined STA in 1999 after struggling for six years to earn his undergraduate degree in marketing at the University of Alabama-Birmingham. Harold, or Hal, as he prefers to be called, took the position of administrative director, and his duties included home office management, human resources management, advertising, and long-range planning. One of Hal's early projects involved developing a predictive model of sales performance. Hal and Bud reasoned that if they could prove that STA training is a key success factor, it would be very valuable in future STA advertising and probably in long-range planning as well. From STA files, Hal selected 30 salespeople who had been enrolled in STA education, and he pulled selected demographic factors from their files as well. Finally, to gauge sales success, he devised a 20-point overall sales performance index, and he called each salesperson, and asked him or her to rate last year's performance on that scale. These self-ratings and the other factors are listed in the following table:

Selected Factors and Self-Evaluated Sales Performance for Last Year

Sales Performance Rating	Total STA Training Hours	Number of STA Certificates Earned	Salesperson's Age	Salesperson's Gender	Number of Years with Present Company
20	300	12	45	Male	25
2	60	2	22	Female	1
4	75	3	25	Male	5
12	200	7	37	Female	4
6	180	6	36	Male	12
3	30	5	23	Female	4
15	150	7	46	Male	2
18	200	8	59	Male	30
7	85	2	33	Male	7
10	100	3	43	Male	17
12	120	2	53	Female	18
7	90	3	35	Female	8
19	200	7	45	Male	15
13	150	5	25	Male	5
17	100	4	35	Female	4
12	100	4	45	Male	15
16	125	3	50	Female	10
20	175	7	65	Male	35
9	60	1	24	Male	4
16	150	5	48	Male	10

1. Using SPSS, perform a series of bivariate regressions using the sales performance measure as the dependent variable, and each of the other factors in the table as independent measures. What did you find, and how do you interpret these findings?

2. Use multiple regression to determine the relationship of the various factors to self-evaluated sales performance for last year. What did you find, and what are the implications of the findings for STA?

This is your integrated case, described on pages 38–39.

THE HOBBIT'S CHOICE RESTAURANT SURVEY PREDICTIVE ANALYSIS

Jeff Dean was a very happy camper. He has learned that his dream of The Hobbit's Choice Restaurant could be a reality. Through the research conducted under Cory Rogers' expert supervision and Celeste Brown's SPSS analysis, Jeff knows the approximate size of the upscale restaurant market, he has a good idea of what features are desired, where it should be located, and even what advertising media to use to promote it. He has all the information he needs to return to his friend, Walter Stripling, the banker, to obtain the financing necessary to design and build the Hobbit's Choice Restaurant.

Jeff calls Cory on Friday morning, and says, "Cory, I am very excited about everything that your work has found about the good prospects of the Hobbit's Choice. I want to set up a meeting with Walter Stripling next week to pitch it to him for the funding. Can you get me the final report by then?"

Cory is silent for a moment, and then he says, "Celeste is doing the final figures and dressing up the tables so we can paste them into the report document. But, I think you have forgotten about the last research objective. We still need to address the target market definition with a final set of analyses. I know that Celeste just finished some exams at school, and she has been asking if there is any work she can do over the weekend. I'll give her this task. Why don't you plan on coming over at 11:00 A.M. on Monday? Celeste and I will show you what we have found, and then we can take Celeste to lunch for giving up her weekend."

Your task in Case 19.3 is to take Celeste's role, use the Hobbit's Choice Restaurant SPSS data set, and perform the proper analysis. You will also need to interpret the findings.

1. What is the demographic target market definition for the Hobbit's Choice Restaurant?

2. What is the restaurant spending behavior target market definition for the Hobbit's Choice Restaurant?

3. Develop a general conceptual model of market segmentation for the Hobbit's Choice Restaurant. (You may have already done this with one of the active learning exercises in this chapter.) Test it using multiple regression analysis and interpret your findings for Jeff Dean.

The Marketing Research Report: Preparation and Presentation

The Final Report

Data analysis for Jeff Dean's project is finished. Cory Rogers and his CMG Research team have worked diligently to investigate the market potential for the Hobbit's Choice Restaurant, and they are ready to prepare their findings and recommendations for presentation to Jeff Dean and his banker, Walker Stripling. You might think the bulk of their work is finished, but that is not the case. Now begins the task of sifting through the hundreds of pages of printouts and other information to determine what to present and then how to present it clearly and effectively. When the members of the team have prepared the written report, they will also need to decide which elements are critical to include in the oral presentation to the client.

Compiling a market research report is a challenging (and sometimes daunting) task. Cory and his team meet to discuss what parts need to be in the report, what content needs to be in each part, what kinds of visuals to include, and what format to follow for headings and subheadings. Then they assign responsibilities to the members of the team and agree on a timetable. When they have a common understanding of what their objectives are and what each team member will do, they are ready to strike out on their individual tasks, meeting frequently to ensure that all tasks will be completed on time and to maintain consistency in their ideas and understandings.

■ To appreciate the importance of the marketing research report
■ To know what material should be included in each part of the marketing research report
■ To learn the basic guidelines for writing effective marketing research reports
■ To know how to use visuals such as figures, tables, charts, and graphs
■ To learn how to make visuals such as tables and figures such as pie charts and bar charts using SPSS
■ To learn the basic principles for presenting your report orally

Learning
Objectives

Cory Rogers and his team at CMG Research work on preparing the final report for their client.

I t is very likely that you have worked on a team project and you have been required to assemble a report representing your teams' work. Determining objectives and organizing the team members to carry out specific responsibilities is a key to team management, and marketing researchers use these same techniques to assemble final reports for their clients. Though report writing is our final chapter this does not indicate that it is less important than our other topics have been.[1] On the contrary, it means that communicating the results of your research is the culmination of the entire process. Being able to do so effectively and efficiently is critical to your success. In fact, all of your outstanding data and significant findings and recommendations are meaningless if you cannot communicate them in such a way that the client knows what you have said, understands your meaning, and responds appropriately. Michael A. Lotti, marketing researcher at Eastman Kodak Company has stated that even the best research will not drive the appropriate action unless the audience understands the outcomes and implications.[2] It is important that you be able to transfer exactly what is in your mind to the mind of the receiver of your message. The ultimate result of your hard labor is communication with your client.

Communicating the results of your research is the culmination of the entire process.

The marketing research report is a factual message that transmits research results, vital recommendations, conclusions, and other important information to the client, who in turn bases his or her decision making on the contents of the report.

The **marketing research report** is a factual message that transmits research results, vital recommendations, conclusions, and other important information to the client, who in turn bases his or her decision making on the contents of the report. This chapter deals with the essentials of writing and presenting the marketing research report.

THE IMPORTANCE OF THE MARKETING RESEARCH REPORT

The time and effort expended in the research process are wasted if the report does not communicate effectively.

Researchers must provide client value in the research report. The marketing research report is the product that represents the efforts of the marketing research team, and it may be the only part of the project that the client will see. If the report is poorly written, riddled with grammatical errors, sloppy, or inferior in any way, the quality of the research (including its analysis and information) becomes suspect and its credibility is reduced. If organization and presentation are faulty, the reader may never reach the intended conclusions. The time and effort expended in the research process are wasted if the report does not communicate effectively.

If, on the other hand, all aspects of the report are done well, the report will not only communicate properly, but it will also serve to build credibility. Marketing research users,[3] as well as marketing research suppliers,[4] agree that reporting the research results is one of the most important aspects of the marketing research process. Many managers will not be involved in any aspect of the research process but will use the report to make business decisions. Effective reporting is essential, and all of the principles of organization, formatting, good writing, and good grammar must be used.

IMPROVING THE EFFICIENCY OF REPORT WRITING

Report writing can be complex, involved and time-consuming. However, if you read this chapter closely you will take a great step toward being a more effective and efficient report writer!

There are several software tools now available to help researchers gain efficiency in report writing.

Online reporting software electronically distributes marketing research reports to selected managers in an interactive format that allows each user to conduct his/her own analyses.

So far we have tried to explain to you just how important the report is to the success of the research project. You are probably thinking, based on your report writing (term papers!) you have done thus far in your college career, that writing a marketing research report is a formidable task. You are right. It is complex and involved and very time-consuming. However, in recent years several technological advances have greatly improved report writing. There are several software tools now available to help researchers gain efficiency in report writing. Burke, Inc. provides its clients with access to its online reporting tool, Digital Dashboard. This service allows clients to watch data come in as they are being collected and organizes data into presentation-quality tables. Readers can examine total results or conduct their own subgroup analysis even down to examining the results of individual respondents. Because the reports are available online, different client users can access the reports and conduct analyses that are important to their unit or division of the company. **Online reporting software** electronically distributes marketing research reports to selected managers in an interactive format that allows each user to conduct his/her own analyses.

E-Tabs has an award-winning software product that allows users to create standard tables and headings for repetitive reports, such as is the case with tracking studies. Once banners, titles, and table formats are created, the report-writing task is made efficient by avoiding these steps for future reports. Of course online reporting not only aids in the dissemination and use of reports but they also avoid the expensive process of producing and storing paper reports. Read more about E-Tabs in Marketing Research Insight 20.1.

ONLINE APPLICATION

20.1

E-Tab's Automated Reporting Software Helps Marketing Research Efficiency

New marketing researchers are often in for a big surprise after the data are collected—after they think their research work is complete. Preparing reports and presentations is a detailed undertaking that requires much planning and effort. But now there is help for the researcher in the form of E-Tabs.

E-Tabs Enterprise is a software system designed specifically for reporting on continuous, tracking, or syndicated studies and ad hoc projects with multilevel reporting. It automates the production of charts, graphs, diagrams, summary tables, maps, and reports directly from the research data. It then facilitates the process of updating or extending them automatically for every wave, region or subcategory.

The user can extract data from any source—tables, spreadsheets or databases; perform searches, calculations, and statistical tests, while E-Tabs Enterprise automatically gathers the relevant data for each report and populates data in PowerPoint charts, Word reports, Excel spreadsheets, etc.

Anyone working with continuous tracking or ad hoc projects spanning several segments (e.g., multidepartmental or multiregional) will be aware of the time it takes to generate executive summaries and reports. It takes a huge effort to extract data from multiple sets of tables and to collate, summarize, and analyze the figures before inserting them into PowerPoint charts, Excel spreadsheets or Word reports.

Having then to reproduce many decks of similar (but not identical) slides for each market, region, brand or

wave is time-consuming and error-prone. It diverts researchers from professional to administrative tasks, and restricts their creativity in report writing or chart styles. All this amounts to significant delays in report delivery; long after the data have been collected and analyzed.

With E-Tabs Enterprise, researchers can automate all these reporting processes. After some simple setup procedures, the system is ready to run. There is no need to sacrifice any special chart types, as E-Tabs Enterprise can use existing templates without any modification, and generate entire reports and presentations in seconds—even packaging them up for automatic e-mailing to the client.

And when the next wave, brand, or region is ready for reporting, E-Tabs Enterprise will facilitate the dynamic updating of previous or existing charts or summary tables, checking for data consistency, updating calculations, highlighting key findings, and adjusting charts or graphs to accommodate the rolling data entries.

E-Tabs Enterprise won the 2004 MRS/ASC Award for Technology Effectiveness in London, England in October 2004. See **www.e-tabs.com/enterprise** for more information. By permission, E-Tabs.

TAKE A TOUR OF AN ONLINE MARKETING RESEARCH REPORT SERVICE

Active Learning

For our active learning exercise we will take a closer look at Burke, Inc.'s online reporting writing software, Digital Dashboard. Go to **www.digitaldashboard.com**. Click on "About Digital Dashboard." Read about the features and take a look at the example output pages. (Don't run the demonstration yet!) Note the feature of "In the Customer's Words," "Individual Reports," and "Data Collection Status Report." When you have read all the features, it is time to take the tour, noted at the bottom of the screen. (The program will run automatically—just give it a few seconds.) Watch for features such as the data filter, executive summary, trends over time, comparing the results of significant subgroups, the ability to filter to examine any subgroup results desired, the ability to search for verbatim comments, the ability to conduct statistical testing using the report

software, and the ability to create your own charts and titles and transfer data to spreadsheets. Can you see how such tools can make the reporting process more efficient and the report more usable for clients?

ORGANIZING THE WRITTEN REPORT

Marketing research reports are tailored to specific audiences and purposes, and you must consider both in all phases of the research process, including planning the report. Before you begin writing, then, you must answer some questions:

- What message do you want to communicate?
- What is your purpose?
- Who is the audience?
- If there are multiple audiences, who is your primary audience? Your secondary audience?
- What does your audience know?
- What does your audience need to know?
- Are there cultural differences you need to consider?
- What biases or preconceived notions of the audience might serve as barriers to your message?
- What strategies can you use to overcome these negative attitudes?
- Do demographic and lifestyle variables of your audience affect their perspective of your research?
- What are your audience's interests, values, and concerns?

These and other questions must be addressed before you know how to structure your report.

When you are preparing the final report, it is often helpful "to get on the other side of the desk." Assume you are the reader instead of the sender. Doing so will help you see things through the eyes of your audience and increase the success of your communication. This is your opportunity to ask that basic (and very critical) question from the reader's point of view: "What's in it for me?"

Once you have answered these questions, you need to determine the format of your document. If the organization for which you are conducting the research has specific guidelines for preparing the document, you should follow them. However, if no specific guidelines are provided, there are certain elements that must be considered when you are preparing the report. These elements can be grouped in three sections: front matter, body, and end matter. Table 20.1 depicts these three sections as well as elements covered in each section.

When you are preparing the final report, it is often helpful "to get on the other side of the desk." Assume you are the reader instead of the sender.

TABLE 20.1	The Elements of a Marketing Research Report

A. Front Matter
1. Title Page
2. Letter of Authorization
3. Letter/Memo of Transmittal
4. Table of Contents
5. List of Illustrations
6. Abstract/Executive Summary

B. Body
1. Introduction
2. Research Objectives
3. Method
4. Results
5. Limitations
6. Conclusions or Conclusions and Recommendations

C. End Matter
1. Appendices
2. Endnotes

Front Matter

The **front matter** consists of all pages that precede the first page of the report—the title page, letter of authorization (optional), letter/memo of transmittal, table of contents, list of illustrations, and abstract/executive summary.

Front matter consists of all pages that precede the first page of the report.

Title Page

The **title page** (Figure 20.1) contains four major items of information: (1) the title of the document, (2) the organization/person(s) for whom the report was prepared, (3) the organization/person(s) who prepared the report, and (4) the date of submission. If names of individuals appear on the title page, they may be in either alphabetical order or some other agreed-upon order; each individual should also be given a designation or descriptive title.

The document title should be as informative as possible. It should include the purpose and content of the report, such as "An Analysis of the Demand for a Branch Office of the CPA Firm of Saltmarsh, Cleaveland & Gund" or "Alternative Advertising Copy to Introduce the New M&M/Mars Low-Fat Candy Bar." The title should be centered and printed in all uppercase (capital) letters. Other items of information on the title page should be centered and printed in uppercase and lowercase letters. The title page is counted as page i of the front matter; however, no page number is printed on it. See Figure 20.1. On the next page, the printed page number will be ii.

Some experts recommend that you change the title to be brief and understandable if you are making a presentation on the survey results.[5] For example, "An Analysis of the Demand for a Branch Office of the CPA Firm of Saltmarsh, Cleaveland & Gund" would be simply changed to "Demand for a Branch Office of Saltmarsh, Cleaveland & Gund." We provide you with some additional insights on preparing for an oral presentation later in the chapter.

FIGURE 20.1
A Title Page

THE HOBBIT'S CHOICE:
A MARKETING RESEARCH STUDY
TO DETERMINE INTENTION TO PATRONIZE,
PREFERENCES FOR OPERATING/DESIGN
CHARACTERISTICS, LOCATION,
AND MEDIA HABITS

Prepared for
Mr. Jeff Dean

Prepared by
CMG Research, Inc.

May, 2006

Letter of Authorization

The **letter of authorization** is the marketing research firm's certification to do the project, and it is optional. It includes the name and title of the persons authorizing the research to be performed, and it may also include a general description of the nature of the research project, completion date, terms of payment, and any special conditions of the research project requested by the client or research user. If you allude to the conditions of your authorization in the letter/memo of transmittal, the letter of authorization is not necessary in the report. However, if your reader may not know the conditions of authorization, inclusion of this document is helpful.

Letter/Memo of Transmittal

Use a **letter of transmittal** to release or deliver the document to an organization for which you are not a regular employee. Use a **memo of transmittal** to deliver the document within your own organization. The letter/memo of transmittal describes the general nature of the research in a sentence or two and identifies the individual who is releasing the report. The primary purpose of the letter/memo of transmittal is to orient the reader to the report and to build a positive image of the report. It should establish rapport between the writer and receiver. It gives the receiver a person to contact if questions arise.

Writing style in the letter/memo of transmittal should be personal and slightly informal. Some general elements that may appear in the letter/memo of transmittal are a brief identification of the nature of the research, a review of the conditions of the authorization to do the research (if no letter or authorization is included), comments on findings, suggestions for further research, and an expression of interest in the project and further research. It should end with an expression of appreciation for the assignment, acknowledgment of assistance from others, and suggestions for following up. Personal observations, unsupported by the data, are appropriate. Figure 20.2 presents an example of a letter of transmittal.

Table of Contents

The **table of contents** helps the reader locate information in the research report. The table of contents (Figure 20.3) should list all sections of the report that follow; each heading should read exactly as it appears in the text and should identify the number of the page on which it appears. If a section is longer than one page, list the page on which it begins. Indent subheadings under headings. All items except the title page and the table of contents are listed with page numbers in the table of contents. Front-matter pages are numbered with lowercase Roman numerals: i, ii, iii, iv, and so on. Arabic numerals (1, 2, 3) begin with the introduction section of the body of the report.

List of Illustrations

If the report contains tables and/or figures, include in the table of contents a **list of illustrations** with page numbers on which they appear (Figure 20.4). All tables and figures should be included in this list, which helps the reader find specific illustrations that graphically portray the information. **Tables** are words or numbers that are arranged in rows and columns; **figures** are graphs, charts, maps, pictures, and so on. Because tables and figures are numbered independently, you may have both a Figure 1 and a Table 1 in your list of illustrations. Give each a name, and list each in the order in which it appears in the report.

Abstract/Executive Summary

Your report may have many readers. Some of them will need to know the details of your report, such as the supporting data on which you base your conclusions and recommendations. Others will not need as many details but will want to read the conclusions and recommendations. Still others with a general need to know may read only the executive summary. Therefore, the **abstract or executive summary** is a "skeleton" of your report. It serves as a summary for the busy executive or a preview for the in-depth reader. It provides an overview of the most useful information, including the conclusions and recommendations. The abstract or executive summary should be very carefully written, conveying the information as concisely as possible. It should be single-spaced and should briefly cover the general subject of the research, the scope of the research (what the research covers/does not cover), identification of the methods used (i.e., a mail survey of 1000 homeowners), conclusions, and recommendations.

FIGURE 20.2
A Letter of Transmittal

CMG Research, Inc.
1100 St. Louis Place
St. Louis, MO

May 21, 2006

Mr. Jeff Dean
2010 Main St.
Anytown, USA 00000

Dear Mr. Dean:

As you requested in your letter of authorization dated February 25, 2006, I have completed the marketing research analysis for The Hobbit's Choice. The results are contained in the report entitled "The Hobbit's Choice: A Marketing Research Study to Determine Intention to Patronize, Preferences for Operating/Design Characteristics, Location, and Media Habits." The report is based on interviews with 400 households in Anytown.

The complete methodology is described in the report. Standard marketing research practices were used throughout the research project. You will find that the results of the report provide the information necessary to achieve the research objectives we set out for this project. These results represent "the voice of your future consumers" and we trust you will be able to use these results to make the best decisions for The Hobbit's Choice.

Should you need further assistance please do not hesitate to call me at (877) 492-2891. I enjoyed working with you on this project and I look forward to working with you again in the future.

Sincerely,

Cory Rogers

Cory Rogers

ii

Body

The **body** is the bulk of the report. It contains an introduction to the report, an explanation of your methods, a discussion of your results, a statement of limitations, and a list of conclusions and recommendations. Do not be alarmed by the repetition that may appear in your report. Only a few people will read it in its entirety. Most will read the executive summary, conclusions, and recommendations. Therefore, formal reports are repetitious. For example, you may specify the research objectives in the executive summary and refer to them again in the findings section as well as in the conclusions section. Also, do not be concerned that you use the same terminology to introduce the tables and/or figures. In many lengthy reports, repetition actually enhances reader comprehension.

FIGURE 20.3
A Table of Contents

Contents

iii

The first page of the body contains the title, centered on the top of the page; this page is counted as page 1, but no page number is printed on it. All other pages throughout the document are numbered consecutively.

Introduction

The **introduction** to the marketing research report orients the reader to the contents of the report. It may contain a statement of the background situation leading to the problem, the statement of the problem, and a summary description of how the research process was initiated. It should contain a statement of the general purpose of the report and also the specific objectives for the research.

FIGURE 20.4
A List of Illustrations

List of Illustrations

vi

Listing of research objectives should follow the statement of the problem.

Research objectives may be listed either as a separate section (see Table 20.1) or within the introduction section. The listing of research objectives should follow the statement of the problem, since the two concepts are closely related. The list of specific research objectives often serves as a good framework for organizing the results section of the report.

The method describes in detail how the research was conducted, who (or what) the subjects were, and what tools or methods were used to achieve the objectives.

Method

The **method** describes, in as much detail as necessary, how you conducted the research, who (or what) your subjects were, and what tools or methods were used to achieve your objectives. Supplementary information should be placed in the appendix. If you used secondary information, you will need to document your sources (provide enough information so that your sources can be located).[6] You do not need to document facts that are common knowledge or can be easily verified. But if you are in doubt, document! **Plagiarism** refers to representing the work of others as your own. Plagiarism is a serious offense; it can cost you your job. Make certain you read Marketing Research Insight 20.2 carefully.

> Make sure you understand what *plagiarism* means. If in doubt, provide a reference to the source and put the citation in the proper format.

MARKETING RESEARCH INSIGHT

ETHICAL ISSUES

20.2

Do You Feel Like This About Documentation?

"It's just a few words."
"It's just a document for my office."
"I'm not making money off it."
"The information is from the Web; everyone can find it and use it."
"I could never say it better."
"The words are perfect; who cares who wrote it?"
"A bunch of citations just makes the report more difficult to read."
"Nobody expects me to reinvent the wheel."

Plagiarism is derived from a Latin word for kidnapping a Roman citizen's slave.[7] Words can be thought of as property. Avoiding plagiarism involves respect for the original author's work and respect for your audience's needs or desire to trace data and learn more from the source.

Just as all printed sources must be documented, so must information found online. In a letter to the *New York Times*, Marilyn Bergman, the president of the American Society of Composers, Authors, and Publishers, expressed a disturbing trend of online theft of words when she said that Americans are prompted by a "free for the taking" feeling of information on the Web.[8] The Internet is not public domain. Proper documentation of all sources helps a writer avoid public humiliation and maintain professional integrity.

Documentation of Online Sources: Why and How?

Copyright laws provide four general types of rights for an author:

1 Right to produce copies of the document
2 Right to sell or distribute document
3 Right to create new works based on the copyrighted work
4 Right to perform work in public

APA (American Psychological Association) and MLA (Modern Language Association) are two styles that offer formats for citation. Generally APA is used in business fields, and MLA is used in the humanities. Style books and university Web sites offer examples on documentation for a range of sources, including electronic formats.

For example, the preceding information was found on the library services Web site of the University of Maryland University College (UMUC). The source citation and format follow.

> University of Maryland University College (1998). "Citing Internet Resources: APA Style," [On-line]. Available: **http://www.umuc.edu/library/apa.html** [2/4/99].

Format:

> Author, I., Author, I., & Author, I. (Year, month date). Title, [Type of medium]. Available: Site/Path/File [Access date].

UMUC library services explains each field below.

Author—The creator or compiler of the information on the Web page. This can be the Web master or the name of the organization that is responsible for the page.

Year, month date—The date that the Web page was put online; it should be the same as the "last updated" date if available.

Title—The title of the document. Often, this can be found at the top of the Web page.

Type of medium—The way the document was accessed. If the document was found on the Web or through another Internet service, this field should read "Online."

Site/Path/File—The address or URL of the Web site.

Access date—The date that you viewed the Web page or accessed the information.

In most cases, the method section does not need to be long. It should, however, provide the essential information your reader needs to understand how the data were collected and how the results were achieved. It should be detailed enough that the data collection could be replicated by others for purposes of reliability. In other words, the method section should be clear enough that other researchers could conduct a similar study.

In some cases, the needs of the research user may dictate a very extensive method section. A client may, for example, want the researcher to not only thoroughly describe the method that was used but also discuss why other methods were not selected. For example, in situations in which research information will be provided in litigation, where there is certain to be an adversary, a researcher may be asked to provide an exhaustive description of the methods used in conducting the study and the methods that were not chosen.

Method or Methodology?

For the section of the report in which you describe the details of the procedures and tools used in the research project you should call this section the "method" section. Do not call this section the "methodology."

You will note that we have named the section of the research report that describes the details of the procedures and tools used as the 'method' section. However, in many cases, you will see the word 'methodology' being used as the title for this section of the report. You should use the word 'method.' Why? The two terms have different meaning. Because so many people use them interchangeably does not mean that such usage is correct. **Methodology** refers to the science of determining appropriate methods to conduct research. Webster's defines it as the theoretical analysis of the methods appropriate to a field of study or to the body of methods and principles particular to a branch of knowledge.[9] Therefore, it would be appropriate to say that there are *objections to the methodology of a consumer survey* (that is, objections dealing with the appropriateness of the methods used in the survey) or to say the *methodology of modern marketing research* (that is, the principles and practices that underlie research in the field of marketing research).[10] Consequently, there is an important conceptual distinction between methodology and method. "Method" refers to the tools of scientific investigation (and the tools used in a marketing research project are described in detail in the method section of the report). "Methodology" refers to the principles that *determine how* such tools are deployed and interpreted. Marketing research *methodology* prescribes, for example, that we must use probability samples if we desire to have a sample that is representative of some population. Researchers would describe their use of their probability sample for a particular study in the *method* section of their paper. Use "method" not "methodology."

Results

The results section is the major portion of your report and should logically present the findings of the research.

The **results** section is the most important portion of your report. Some researchers prefer the use of the term *findings*. This section should logically present the findings of your research and be organized around your objectives for the study. The results should be presented in narrative form and accompanied by tables, charts, figures, and other appropriate visuals that support and enhance the explanation of results. Tables and figures are supportive material; they should not be overused or used as filler. Each should contain a number and title and should be referred to in the narrative.

Outline your results section before you write the report. The survey questionnaire itself can serve as a useful aid in organizing your results because the questions are often grouped in a logical order or in purposeful sections. Another useful method for organizing your results is to individually print all tables and figures and arrange them in a logical sequence. Once you have the results outlined properly, you are ready to write the introductory sentences, definitions (if necessary), review of the findings (often referring to tables and figures), and transition sentences to lead into the next topic.

Limitations

Do not attempt to hide or disguise problems in your research; no research is faultless. Always be above board and open regarding all aspects of your research. To avoid discussion of limitations often is to render suspect your integrity and your research. Suggest what the limitations are or may be and what impact they have on the results. You might also suggest opportunities for further study based on the limitations. Typical **limitations** in research reports often focus on but are not limited to factors such as time, money, size of sample, and personnel. Consider the following example: "the reader should note that this study was based on a survey of graduating students at a midsized public university in the Southeast United States. Budget constraints limited the sample to this university and this region of the country. Care should be exercised in generalizing these findings to other populations."

> Do not attempt to hide or disguise problems in your research. Suggest the possible limitations and what impact they have on the results.

Conclusions and Recommendations

Conclusions and recommendations may be listed together or in separate sections, depending on the amount of material you have to report. In any case, you should note that conclusions are not the same as recommendations. **Conclusions** are the outcomes and decisions you have reached based on your research results. **Recommendations** are suggestions for how to proceed based on the conclusions. Unlike conclusions, recommendations may require knowledge beyond the scope of the research findings themselves, that is, information on conditions within the company, the industry, and so on. Therefore, researchers should exercise caution in making recommendations. The researcher and the client should determine prior to the study whether the report is to contain recommendations. A clear understanding of the researcher's role will result in a smoother process and will help avoid conflict. Although a research user may desire the researcher to provide specific recommendations, both parties must realize that the researcher's recommendations are based solely on the knowledge gained from the research report, not familiarity with the client. Other information, if made known to the researcher, could totally change the researcher's recommendations.

> Conclusions are outcomes or decisions based on results. Recommendations are suggestions for how to proceed based on conclusions.

If recommendations are required and if a report is intended to initiate further action, however, recommendations are the important map to the next step. Writing recommendations in a bulleted list and beginning each with an action verb help to direct the reader to the logical next step.

End Matter

The **end matter** comprises the **appendices**, which contain additional information to which the reader may refer for further reading but that is not essential to reporting the data. Appendices contain the "nice to know" information, not the "need to know." Therefore, that information should not clutter the body of the report but should instead be inserted at the end for the reader who desires or requires additional information. Tables, figures, additional reading, technical descriptions, data-collection forms, and appropriate computer printouts are some elements that may appear in an appendix. (If they are critical to the reader, however, they may be included in the report itself.) Each appendix should be labeled with both a letter and a title, and each should appear in the table of contents. A reference page or endnotes (if appropriate) should precede the appendix.

> End matter contains additional information to which the reader may refer for further reading but that is not essential to reporting the data.

GUIDELINES AND PRINCIPLES FOR THE WRITTEN REPORT

The parts of the research report have been described. However, you should also consider their form and format and their style.

Form and Format

Form and format concerns include headings and subheadings and visuals.

Headings and subheadings act as signals and signposts to serve as a road map for a long report.

▶ **Headings and Subheadings** In a long report, your reader needs signals and signposts that serve as a road map. Headings and subheadings perform this function. **Headings** indicate the topic of each section. All information under a specific heading should relate to that heading, and **subheadings** should divide that information into segments. A new heading should introduce a change of topic. Choose the kind of heading that fits your purpose—single word, phrase, sentence, question—and consistently use that form throughout the report. If you use subheadings within the divisions, the subheadings must be parallel to one another but not to the main headings. Learn how to use headings and subheadings and you will improve your writing skills. Marketing Research Insight 20.3 will give you the information you need to learn how to create headings and subheadings.

Visuals

Visuals can dramatically and concisely present information that might otherwise be difficult to comprehend.

Visuals are tables, figures, charts, diagrams, graphs, and other graphic aids. Used properly, they can dramatically and concisely present information that might otherwise be difficult to comprehend. Tables systematically present numerical data or words in columns and rows. Figures translate numbers into visual displays so that relationships and trends become comprehensible. Examples of figures are graphs, pie charts, and bar charts.

Visuals should tell a story; they should be uncluttered and self-explanatory. Even though they are self-explanatory, the key points of all visuals should be explained in the text. Refer to visuals by number: ". . . as shown in Figure 1." Each visual should be titled and numbered. If possible, place the visual immediately below the paragraph in which its first reference appears. Or, if sufficient space is not available, continue the text and place the visual on the next page. Visuals can also be placed in an appendix. Additional information on preparing visuals is presented later in this chapter.

Style

Stylistic devices can make the difference in whether or not your reader gets the message as you intended it.

Consider stylistic devices when you are actually writing the sentences and paragraphs in your report. These can make the difference in whether or not your reader gets the message as you intended it. Therefore, consider the following "tips" for the writer.

(1) A good paragraph has one main idea, and a topic sentence should state that main idea. As a general rule, begin paragraphs with topic sentences. However, topic sentences can appear in the middle or at the end of a paragraph. See Marketing Research Insight 20.4 to help you become a better paragraph writer.

(2) Avoid long paragraphs (usually those with more than nine printed lines). Long paragraphs are a strategy for burying a message because most readers do not read the middle contents of long paragraphs.

20.3

How Headings Can Help You Write a Professional Report

Most students have difficulty organizing their reports. Yet, rarely will they take the time to outline their report as they were taught to do in grade school. There are few more effective methods to improving your writing skills than properly outlining before you begin writing. Below we provide you with a few key thoughts that will help you improve your writing skills through the proper use of headings.

First, before you can outline, you must do some basic planning. Go back to your research objectives. Make certain that your report addresses the research objectives that were identified at the beginning of the research project.

Second, read the information you have! Many students just start writing without reading over the information they have generated either from secondary data or even from analysis of the results in primary data collection.

Third, what information has been gathered for each of the research objectives? Organize your information into separate areas based on how it addresses a particular research objective. For example, if one objective is to gather information on likelihood to subscribe to a new service, find that information and file it under the research objective. Was any other information gathered that addresses this objective?

Fourth, now that you are familiar with your research objectives and the information gathered for each, start outlining the information gathered by using headings. Headings are the *most useful* way a writer can organize a paper. Headings are very useful to readers in that they serve as guideposts telling the reader where they are, where they've been, and where they are headed.

Fifth, understand your format for headings before you begin to write. We provide the following to help you with your headings. Read this and use it!

TITLE

Titles are centered at the top of the page and are either boldfaced or underlined. Titles are normally in a larger font than the rest of the paper.

FIRST-LEVEL HEADING

First-level headings indicate what the following section, usually consisting of several subdivisions, is about. First-level headings are centered, bold, and all caps and are usually in larger font sizes than the other material but smaller than the title.

Second-Level Heading

Second-level headings are centered, bold, with capitals used only on the first letter of each word. Font size may be the same as that of the rest of the report. Try to always use more than one second-level heading if you are going to use them following a first-level heading.

Third-Level Heading

Left-justified, third-level headings should be bold and in the same font size as the rest of the report.

Fourth-Level Heading. These are left-justified and on the same line as the first sentence in the paragraph. Use bold and the same-sized font as remainder of report.

Fifth-level headings are in bold and are part of sentences. While this is generally the lowest level of outline you use, you can go further by indenting and numbering ideas or italicizing the first word in each item of the list.

Source: Portions of the above adapted from Bovée, C., and Thill, J. (2000). *Business Communication Today*, 6th ed. Upper Saddle River, NJ: Prentice Hall, 499.

MARKETING RESEARCH INSIGHT

PRACTICAL APPLICATION

20.4

Developing Logical Paragraphs

"A **paragraph** is a group of related sentences that focus on one main idea."[a] The first sentence should include a **topic sentence**, which identifies the main idea of the paragraph. For example: "To assess whether residents would patronize an upscale restaurant, respondents were asked their likelihood of patronizing an upscale restaurant." Next, the **body of the paragraph** provides the main idea of the topic sentence by giving more information, analysis, or examples. For example, continuing from the topic sentence example given above: "A description of an upscale restaurant was read to all respondents. The description was as follows: . . . The respondents were then asked to indicate their likelihood of patronizing an upscale restaurant by selecting a choice on a 5-point response rating scale ranging from 'Very likely to patronize' to 'Very unlikely to patronize.' The actual scale was as follows: . . . "

Paragraphs should close with a sentence that signals the end of the topic and indicates where the reader is headed.

For example: "How respondents answered the likelihood-to-patronize scale is discussed in the following two paragraphs." Note this last sentence contains a **transitional expression**. A transitional expression is a word, or group of words, that tells the reader where they are heading. Some examples include *following, next, second, third, at last, finally, in conclusion, to summarize, for example, to illustrate, in addition, so, therefore,* and so on.[b]

Controlling for the **length of paragraphs** should encourage good communication. As a rule, paragraphs should be short. Business communication experts believe most paragraphs should be under or around the 100-word range.[c] This is long enough for the topic sentence and three or four sentences in the body of the paragraph. The paragraph should never cover more than one main topic. Complex topics should be broken into several paragraphs.

[a] Ober, S. (1998). *Contemporary Business Communication*, 3rd ed. Boston Houghton Mifflin, 121.
[b] Ober, S. (1998). *Contemporary Business Communication*, 3rd ed. Boston Houghton Mifflin, 123.
[c] Bovee, C. and Thill, J. (2000) *Business Communication Today*, 6th ed. Upper Saddle River, NJ: Prentice Hall, 153.

(3) Capitalize on white space. Immediately before and immediately after white space (the beginning and the end of a paragraph) are points of emphasis. So are the beginning and the end of a page. Therefore, place more important information at these strategic points.

(4) Use jargon sparingly. Some of your audience may understand technical terms; others may not. When in doubt, properly define the terms for your readers. If many technical terms are required in the report, consider including a glossary of terms in an appendix to assist the less-informed members of your audience.

(5) Use strong verbs to carry the meaning of your sentences. Instead of "making a recommendation," "recommend." Instead of "performing an investigation," "investigate."

(6) As a general rule, use the active voice. Voice indicates whether the subject of the verb is doing the action (active voice) or receiving the action (passive voice). For example, "The marketing research was conducted by Judith" uses the passive voice. "Judith conducted the marketing research" uses the active voice. Active voice is direct and forceful, and the active voice uses fewer words.

(7) Eliminate extra words. Write your message clearly and concisely. Combine and reword sentences to eliminate unnecessary words. Remove opening fillers and eliminate unnecessary redundancies. For example, instead of writing, "There are 22 marketing research firms in Newark," remove the opening filler by writing, "Twenty-two marketing research firms are located in Newark." Instead of saying, "the end results," say, "the results."

(8) Avoid unnecessary changes in tense. Tense tells if the action of the verb occurred in the past (past tense—*were*), is happening right now (present tense—*are*), or will happen in the future (future tense—*will be*). Changing tenses within a document is an error writers frequently make.

(9) In sentences, keep the subject and verb close together. The farther apart they become, the more difficulty the reader has understanding the message and the greater the chance for errors in subject/verb agreement.

(10) Vary the length and structure of sentences and paragraphs.

(11) Use faultless grammar. If your grammar is in any way below par, you need to take responsibility for finding ways to improve. Poor grammar can result in costly errors and loss of your job. It can jeopardize your credibility and the credibility of your research. There is no acceptable excuse for poor grammar.

(12) Maintain 1-inch side margins. If your report will be bound, use a 1 1/2-inch left margin.

(13) Use the organization's preference for double- or single-spacing.

(14) Edit carefully. Your first draft is not a finished product; neither is your second. Edit your work carefully, rearranging and rewriting until you communicate the intent of your research as efficiently and effectively as possible. Some authors suggest that as much as 50% of your production time should be devoted to improving, editing, correcting, and evaluating an already written document.[11]

(15) Proofread! Proofread! Proofread! After you have finished a product, check it carefully to make sure everything is correct. Double-check names and numbers, grammar, spelling, and punctuation. Although spell-checkers and grammar-checkers are useful, you cannot rely on them to catch all errors. One of the best ways to proofread is to read a document aloud, preferably with a reader following along on the original. An alternative is to read the document twice—once for content and meaning and once for mechanical errors. The more important the document is, the more time and readers you need to use for proofreading.

USING VISUALS: TABLES AND FIGURES

Visuals assist in the effective presentation of numerical data. The key to a successful visual is a clear and concise presentation that conveys the message of the report. The selection of the visual should match the presentation purpose for the data. Common visuals include the following[12]:

> *Tables*, which identify exact values (see Marketing Research Insight 20.5).
> *Graphs* and *charts*, which illustrate relationships among items.
>> *Pie charts*, which compare a specific part of the whole to the whole (see Marketing Research Insight 20.6).
>> *Bar charts* (see Marketing Research Insight 20.7) and *line graphs*, which compare items over time or show correlations among items.
>> *Flow diagrams*, which introduce a set of topics and illustrate their relationships (Figure 20.5).

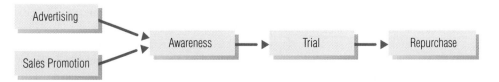

FIGURE 20.5
A Flow Diagram Introduces Topics and Shows How They Are Related

Maps, which define locations.

Photographs, which present an aura of legitimacy because they are not "created" in the sense that other visuals are created. Photos depict factual content.

Drawings, which focus on visual details.

A discussion of some of these visuals follows.

Tables

Tables allow the reader to compare numerical data.

Tables allow the reader to compare numerical data. Effective table guidelines are as follows:

(1) Do not allow computer analysis to imply a level of accuracy that is not achieved. Limit your use of decimal places (12% or 12.2% instead of 12.223%).

(2) Place items you want the reader to compare in the same column, not the same row.

(3) If you have many rows, darken alternating entries or double-space after every five entries to assist the reader in accurately lining up items.

(4) Total columns and rows when relevant.

Marketing Research Insight 20.5 gives you the necessary keystroke instructions to create tables using SPSS.

MARKETING RESEARCH INSIGHT

ONLINE APPLICATION

20.5 How to Create a Table Using SPSS

We will use the Hobbit's Choice data set (HobbitData.sav) that you are familiar with, as we have been using it for all of the statistical analysis examples in previous chapters. Let's say we wish to find out the likelihood that our respondents will patronize the Hobbit's Choice. To do this, we create a simple frequency table for responses to the question on the questionnaire: "How likely would it be for you to patronize this restaurant?"

1 The first step is to create a frequency table for responses to the question on the questionnaire: "How likely would it be for you to patronize this restaurant?" After opening the data file, use the ANALYZE-DESCRIPTIVE STATISTICS-FREQUENCIES and select the variable corresponding to likelihood of patronizing the Hobbit's Choice. The resulting frequency table is displayed in the SPSS output Viewer.

2 To edit the table, put the cursor anywhere on the table and double-click. This activates the table editor, which is indicated by a shaded highlight box appearing around the table, and a red arrow pointing to the selected table. A toolbar will also appear on your screen.

3 Figure 20.6 illustrates how to change the format of the table (after you have double-clicked on it). Select FORMAT-TABLELOOKS.

4 To select a particular table format, browse through the directory and select one that suits your need. In this case, we used Boxed (VGA) format. However, because we want to change the fonts, we have to edit the format we had selected.

5 To edit an already available format, click EDIT LOOK while in TABLELOOKS. To change the fonts, alignment, margins, and so on, click on CELL FORMATS. Change the fonts, size, style, and so on to suit your needs. To change borders, click on BORDERS and select appropriate borders. An example of a finished table is in Figure 20.6. You can hide categories by shading all the data in a column, right clicking and select CLEAR. You can also do this by moving your cursor to the right side of the border of a column and dragging the border to close the column.

6 After adjusting the table properties for the attributes you want, save your customized table format by clicking on SAVE AS within the TABLELOOKS dialog box and saving the table under a new file name. Keep reading. We show you how to recall this new table format for all the tables you make without having to reedit each new table. You can use this customized table look for any future tables you create. After you click SAVE AS and name the table format to be saved, click SAVE-OK.

7 You are now back in the table edit mode. The next step is to change the text in specific cells. To do this, double-click on the cell in which you want to change the text. The selected text will be highlighted. Simply type over and press Enter when you are done.

FIGURE 20.6

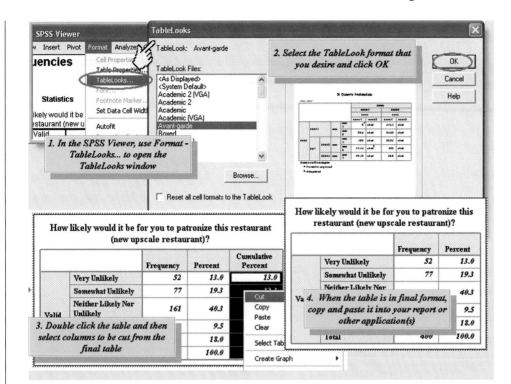

Pie Charts

When you want to illustrate the *relative* sizes or *proportions* of one component versus others, pie charts are useful. For example, if you wanted to illustrate to your reader the proportions of consumers that preferred different types of radio programming, a pie chart would be an excellent tool for showing the relative sizes of each type of programming preference. The **pie chart** is a circle divided into sections. Each section represents a percentage of the total area of the circle associated with one component. Today's data analysis programs easily and quickly make pie charts. Your SPSS 13.0 program, for example, allows you to build customized pie charts.

Most experts agree that the pie chart should have a limited number of segments (four to eight, at most). If your data have many small segments, consider combining the smallest or the least important into an "other" or "miscellaneous" category. Because internal labels are difficult to read for small sections, labels for the sections should be placed outside the circle.

Marketing Research Insight 20.6 gives you the keystroke instructions for creating pie charts using SPSS 13.0.

When you want to illustrate the *relative* sizes or *proportions* of one component versus others, pie charts are useful.

The pie chart is a circle divided into sections. Each section represents a percentage of the total area of the circle associated with one component.

Bar Charts

Bar charts are used often in reporting survey data because they are easy to interpret. They are useful to report the magnitude of response or to show magnitude or response comparisons between groups. They are also useful for illustrating change over time. Several types of **bar charts** can be used. See Figure 20.10 for a simple bar chart created by SPSS 13.0. Marketing Research Insight 20.7 gives you the keystroke instructions for creating

Bar charts are used often in reporting survey data because they are easy to interpret. They are useful to report the magnitude of response or to show magnitude or response comparisons between groups. They are also useful for illustrating change over time.

20.6 How to Create a Pie Chart Using SPSS

We again use data from the Hobbit's Choice survey (HobbitData.sav) to demonstrate the creation of a simple pie graph using SPSS. Let's say we want to show responses to the question, "To which type of radio programming do you most often listen?" in the form of a pie chart.

1 Create a pie chart for responses to the question on the questionnaire: "To which type of radio programming do you most often listen?"

Figure 20.7 shows that you use the Command sequence of GRAPHS and PIE. Click Summaries for Groups of Cases and then Define.

The next screen allows you to choose the variable that you want to graph. Select the variable corresponding to the question on the questionnaire, click the button for Define Slices By, and the variable will be entered.

You can choose what you want your slices to represent. In this case, we selected the slices to represent % of cases.

2 At this stage, you can also enter the titles and footnotes for the chart by clicking on TITLES and entering the appropriate labels.

Using the command OPTIONS, you can decide how you want missing values to be treated. Here we have not included missing values in the chart by clicking *off* the check mark (3) on the Display Groups Defined by Missing Values.

Click OK and the resulting pie chart will appear in the SPSS Viewer. SPSS 13.0 displays a legend with the pie chart. You are now ready to edit the chart.

(If you have an existing template of a pie graph, you can request the output to be formatted according to template specifications by double-clicking anywhere on the chart; go to FILE-APPY TEMPLATE and select the saved file name.)

3 Scroll down to the pie chart. To edit the chart, double-click anywhere on the chart. This takes you to the SPSS Chart Editor screen. You will do all your editing in this screen.

FIGURE 20.7

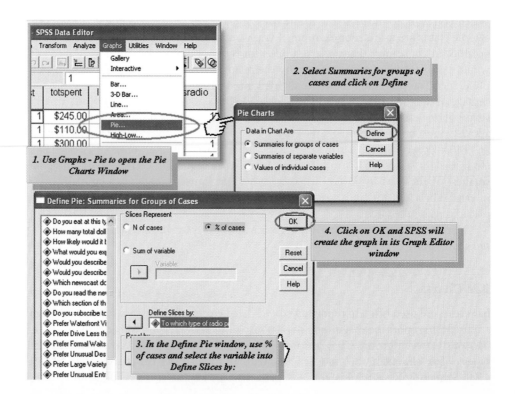

4 In the Chart Editor screen, click on the area you wish to edit. This puts a border around the area to be edited. It also changes the editing tools available to you in Chart Editor. Click once on the title. You can now edit the font. Click once on the pie. Go to CHART-SHOW DATA LABELS. This places values within each slice. Click once on the C&W slice such that *only* the C&W slice is highlighted with a border. Go to CHART-EXPLODE SLICE.

5 Still in Chart Editor, click on pie slice. Go to EDIT-PROPERTIES. Select DEPTH & ANGLE-3-D for EFFECT, –60 for ANGLE, 3 for DISTANCE. APPLY & CLOSE.

6 You can add text *anywhere* on the chart in SPSS 13.0. Click the TEXT icon in Chart Editor (or go CHART-ADD CHART ELEMENT-TEXT BOX).

7 After making all the changes, you can save your customized chart by using command options FILE-SAVE CHART TEMPLATE. For future charts, you can call up the customized template, saving the need for you to edit every pie chart you create.

8 The chart is now ready to be transferred to a word processing document. The chart that we have created is shown in Figure 20.8.

FIGURE 20.8

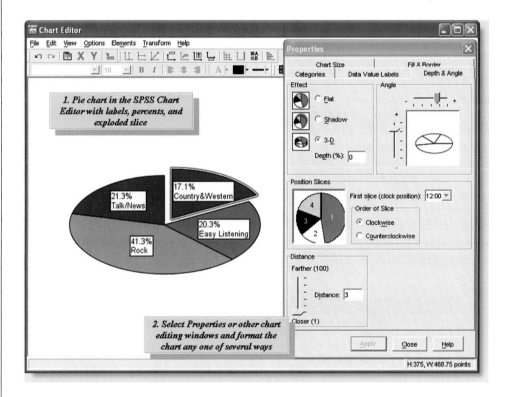

bar charts of various types using SPSS. Study the types of bar charts available to you in SPSS. Your selection of the type of bar chart will depend on what you are trying to communicate to your reader.

Line Graphs

Line graphs are easy to interpret if they are designed properly. Line graphs may be drawn in SPSS using the GRAPHS option. You will notice there are several options in types of line graphs.

   Flow diagrams introduce a set of topics and illustrate their relationships. Flow diagrams are particularly useful to illustrate topics that are sequential, for example, step 1, step 2, and so on. (See Figure 20.5.)

Flow diagrams introduce a set of topics and illustrate their relationships.

20.7 How to Create a Bar Chart Using SPSS

We use data from the Hobbit's Choice (HobbitData.sav) to demonstrate the creation of a simple bar graph using SPSS. Let's say we want to show graphically the frequency distribution of the likelihood of respondents patronizing the Hobbit's Choice.

1 Create a bar chart for responses to question 4 on the questionnaire: "How likely would it be for you to patronize this restaurant?"

As you can see in Figure 20.9, after opening the data file, use the Command GRAPHS-BAR. You have the option of choosing from three different styles of bar charts. In this case, we used the Simple chart. Click Summaries for Groups of Cases and then Define.

The next screen allows you to choose the variable that you want to graph. Select the variable "likely," highlight the variable, and click on the Category Axis button.

You can choose what you want your bars to represent. In this case, we selected the bars to represent %

of cases because we want to know the percentages of respondents citing likelihood to patronize the Hobbit's Choice. Click OK.

2 At this stage, you can also enter the titles and footnotes for the chart by clicking on TITLES. Also, by selecting OPTIONS, you can decide how you want missing values to be treated. Here, we have not included missing values in the chart by clicking *off* the check mark (3) on the Display Groups Defined by Missing Values.

Click OK and the bar chart will appear in the SPSS Viewer. You are now ready to edit the chart.

(If you have an existing template of a bar graph while in the Define Simple Bar Summaries for Groups of Cases box, you can request the output to be formatted according to template specifications by clicking on Use Chart Specifications From, and selecting the saved file name.)

3 To edit the chart, double-click anywhere on the chart. This opens the SPSS Chart Editor screen. You will do all your editing in this screen. Figure 20.10 shows the operation of the SPSS Chart Editor screen with our bar chart.

4 In the Chart Editor screen, click on the area you wish to edit. This puts a border on the area to be edited. It

FIGURE 20.9

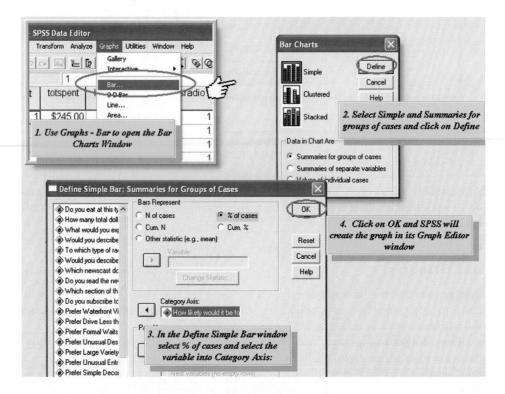

FIGURE 20.10

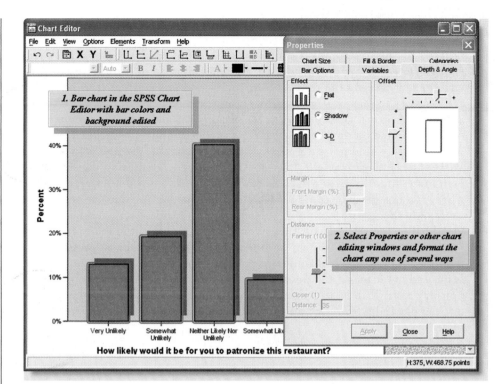

also changes the editing tools available to you in Chart Editor. Click once on the title. You can now edit the title in several ways by using the tools in the menu bar. You can change fonts, font size, color, fill, alignment, and so on.

5 Click once on one of the bars. All the bars should now be highlighted with a border around them. Notice the tools available to you on the menu bar. Go to the PROPERTIES icon (or go EDIT-PROPERTIES). Select DEPTH & ANGLE-SHADOW (for EFFECT) and set OFFSET to +15. APPLY and CLOSE. Again, click on a bar and then the PROPERTIES icon. Select FILL & BORDER and select a pattern and fill color for your bars. *Note:* Click the fill button to change the color of the bars. The border button allows you to change the color of the border line of the bars.

6 Still in Chart Editor, click anywhere other than a bar. Select PROPERTIES-FILL & BORDER. Change the color of the background.

7 To edit the textual content of the chart, select the TEXT icon in Chart Editor (or go to OPTIONS-TEXT BOX). A box and a set of markers will appear. Insert your text and then drag the box where you want the text to appear.

8 After making all the changes, you can save your customized chart by using the command FILE-SAVE CHART TEMPLATE. For future charts, you can call up the customized template, saving the need for you to edit every bar chart you create.

9 The chart is now ready to be transferred to a word-processing document. The chart that we have created is shown in Figure 20.10.

PRODUCING AN ACCURATE AND ETHICAL VISUAL

A marketing researcher should always follow the doctrine of full disclosure. An **ethical visual** is one that is totally objective in terms of how information is presented in the research report. Sometimes misrepresenting information is intentional (as when a client asks a researcher to misrepresent the data in order to promote his or her "pet project") or it may be unintentional. In the latter case, those preparing a visual are sometimes so familiar with the material being presented that they falsely assume that the graphic message is apparent to all who view it.

> An ethical visual is one that is totally objective in terms of how information is presented in the research report.

To illustrate how one can be unethical in preparing a visual, let's assume that the entrepreneur in the Hobbit's Choice Restaurant case, Jeff Dean, is seeking financial backing for his restaurant. He must convince potential investors that there are enough potential patrons in the local area to support an upscale restaurant. Our entrepreneur receives the results of the survey and prepares the visuals that he feels are necessary to make his presentation. Using SPSS he generates the bar chart shown in Figure 20.11(a), labeled "An Ethical Visual." SPSS automatically assigns the range of values located on the y axis. Although it is expected that the majority of people in the local area would not patronize an upscale restaurant, the results look extremely skewed to the negative, with the "neutral" respondents making the situation look even more dire. However, this is an ethical presentation of the research data. If our manager is unethical, he could use SPSS to eliminate the "no opinion" respondents to show only those with opinions. Furthermore, he could eliminate the percentages identified on the vertical axis. These alterations, which result in the bar chart labeled "An Unethical Visual," shown in Figure 20.11(b), gives the impression that the results are more positive than they actually are. This bar chart is unethical because it is misleading; it makes the possibility of patronizing the restaurant appear proportionally greater than it is. As a result, potential investors may be duped into believing that the possibility of restaurant patronization is greater than what is ethically supported by the data.

To ensure that you have objectively and ethically prepared your visuals you should do the following:

(1) Double- and triple-check all labels, numbers, and visual shapes. A faulty or misleading visual discredits your report and work.
(2) Exercise caution if you use three-dimensional figures. They may distort the data by multiplying the value by the width and the height.
(3) Make sure all parts of the scales are presented. Truncated graphs (having breaks in the scaled values on either axis) are acceptable only if the audience is familiar with the data.

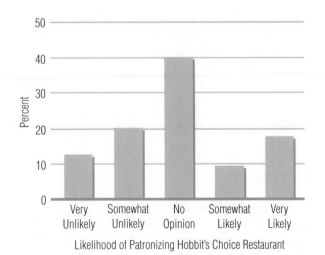

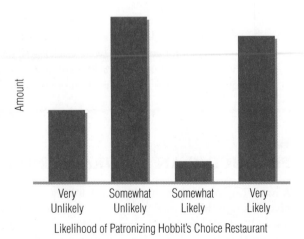

FIGURE 20.11
Comparison of an Ethical Visual with an Unethical Visual

PRESENTING YOUR RESEARCH ORALLY

You may be asked to present an oral summary of the recommendations and conclusions of your research. The purpose of the **oral presentation** is to succinctly present the information and to provide an opportunity for questions and discussion. The presentation may be accomplished through a simple conference with the client, or it may be a formal presentation to a roomful of people. In any case, says Jerry W. Thomas, CEO of Decision Analyst, research reports should "be presented orally to all key people in the same room at the same time." He believes this is important because many people do not read the research report, and others may not understand all the details of the report. "An oral presentation ensures that everyone can ask questions to allow the researchers to clear up any confusion."[13] It also ensures that everyone hears the same thing.

The purpose of the oral presentation is to succinctly present the research information and to provide an opportunity for questions and discussion.

To be adequately prepared when you present your research orally, follow these steps:

(1) Identify and analyze your audience. Consider the same questions you addressed at the beginning of the research process and at the beginning of this chapter.
(2) Find out the expectations your audience has for your presentation. Is the presentation formal or informal? Does your audience expect a graphical presentation?
(3) Determine the key points your audience needs to hear.
(4) Outline the key points, preferably on 3-by-5 cards to which you can easily refer.
(5) Present your points succinctly and clearly. The written report will serve as a reference for further reading.
(6) Make sure your visuals graphically and ethically portray your key points.
(7) Practice your presentation. Be comfortable with what you are going to say and how you look. The more prepared you are and the better you feel about yourself, the less you will need to worry about jitters.
(8) Check out the room and media equipment prior to the presentation.
(9) Arrive early.

A researcher uses WebSurveyor to create a pie chart to be shown in a presentation.

(10) Be positive and confident. You are the authority; you know more about your subject than anyone else.

(11) Speak loudly enough for all in the room to hear. Enunciate clearly. Maintain eye contact and good posture. Dress professionally.

SUMMARY

The preparation and presentation of the marketing research report is the final stage of the marketing research process. This stage is as important as, if not more important than, any other stage in the research process. This importance is attributed to the fact that, regardless of the care in the design and execution of the research project itself, if the report does not adequately communicate the project to the client, all is lost.

While preparing and writing the report may be time-consuming, advances are being made to make report writing more efficient. Online reporting software is an efficient tool that assists marketing researchers in monitoring data collection and disseminating research results. It also allows data users to interact with the reports and to massage data.

Marketing research reports should be tailored to their audiences. They are typically organized into the categories of front matter, body, and end matter. Each of these categories has subparts, with each subpart having a different purpose. Conclusions are based on the results of the research, and recommendations are suggestions based on conclusions. Guidelines for writing the marketing research report include proper use of headings and subheadings, which serve as signposts and signals to the reader, and proper use of visuals such as tables and figures. Style considerations include beginning paragraphs with topic sentences, spare use of jargon, strong verbs, active voice, consistent tense, conciseness, and varied sentence structure and length. Editing and proofreading, preferably by reading the report aloud, are important steps in writing the research report. Care should be taken to ensure that all presentations are clear and objective to the reader. Many visual aids may be distorted so that they have a different meaning to the reader. This means that ethical considerations must be made in the preparation of the research report. Reports rely on tables, figures, and graphical displays of various types. SPSS includes routines for creating report tables and graphs. We describe step-by-step commands on how to use SPSS to make professional-appearing tables and graphs.

In some cases, marketing researchers are required to present the findings of their research project to the client orally. Guidelines for making an oral presentation include knowing the audience and their expectations and the key points you wish to make; correctly preparing visuals; practicing; checking out presentation facilities and equipment prior to the presentation; and being positive.

KEY TERMS

Marketing research report (p. 598)
Online reporting software (p. 598)
Front matter (p. 601)
Title page (p. 601)
Letter of authorization (p. 602)
Letter of transmittal (p. 603)
Memo of transmittal (p. 603)
Table of contents (p. 603)

List of illustrations (p. 603)
Tables (p. 603)
Figures (p. 603)
Abstract/executive summary (p. 603)
Body (p. 604)
Introduction (p. 605)
Research objectives (p. 606)
Method (p. 606)

REVIEW QUESTIONS/APPLICATIONS

1. Discuss the relative importance of the marketing research report to the other stages in the marketing research process.
2. What are the components of the marketing research report?
3. When should you include or omit a letter of authorization?
4. Distinguish among results, conclusions, and recommendations.
5. When should you use a subheading?
6. What is the most important consideration in determining the style in which you will report your findings?
7. When should you use a letter and when should you use a memo?
8. How does online reporting software assist market researchers and report users?
9. What visual would be the best at displaying the relative changes in spending between four promotion mix variables over time?
10. What kind of visual would you create if you wanted to use images of people to illustrate the differences in employment levels among three industries?
11. Why do you think we included a discussion of ethics in preparing visuals? Can you illustrate how a visual could present data in an unethical fashion?
12. Visit your library and ask your reference librarian if he or she is aware of any marketing research reports that have been placed in the library. Chances are good that you will be able to find several reports of various kinds. Examine the reports. What commonalities do they have in terms of the sections that the authors have created? Look at the sections carefully. What types of issues were addressed in the introduction section? The method section? How did the authors organize all of the information reported in the results section? Are recommendations different from conclusions?

CASE 20.1

DON'T YOU HATE IT WHEN . . . ? (PART V)

Part I (Case 16.1) of this case is on pages 479–480, Part II (Case 17.1) of this case is on pages 515–516, Part III (Case 18.1) is on pages 553–554, and Part IV (Case 19.1) is on pages 591–593.

At 11:23 P.M. in an apartment just off campus, Marsha speed dials Josh's cell phone number, and in an apartment just north of campus, Josh's cell phone blasts out the university's fight song.

Josh: "Uh, oh, hi Marsh. What's up?"

Marsha: "Josh, it is almost midnight on Wednesday of the last week of classes, and our team marketing research project is due by noon on Friday. I distinctly recall that you promised to have your part of the report finished and in my hands by noon today. In case you don't have a watch with a calendar function or you can't read one that was about 12 hours ago."

Josh: "Yeah, but I promised it before the team got into the playoffs. I can't play anymore because of my knee blow-out, but I do follow them on the radio, and they played a doubleheader out of the losers' bracket today. Unfortunately, they lost the second game. It just ended a couple of hours ago."

Marsha thinks, "Speaking of losers . . . ," and says, "Does this mean you will send me the graphs you agreed to do for the report? I have written just about everything else, and I need them for the Findings section."

Josh: "Yeah, I will get right on it and e-mail you the graphs. Look for them in, say 20 minutes. Bye."

At 1:37 A.M. an e-mail from Josh arrives at Marsha's inbox.

Marsha immediately thinks, "Oh Gawd, I am very afraid to open up this document and look at whatever horror show Josh sent me. Okay, Girl, take a deep gulp of air and click on it."

Following are the three graphs that Josh sent to Marsha.

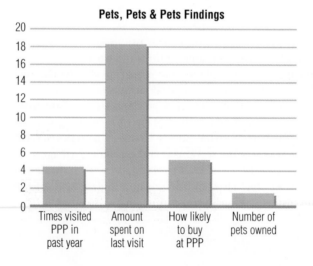

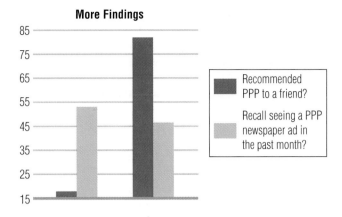

More Findings

Recommended PPP to a friend?

Recall seeing a PPP newspaper ad in the past month?

Marsha thinks, "Oh, my Gawd, is this man totally dense or just brain dead?"

Marsha speed dials Josh's number; the fight song ringer blasts out.

Josh answers: "Hey, pretty cool, huh? I thought about it for a while, and I went the extra mile to make the graphs impressive. I put in the numbers and everything. I figure that I saved you a lot of work. Say, now that we are done with our marketing research team project, there is that new Vin Diesel movie coming out this weekend. What about going to the movie together?"

Marsha thinks, "Gawd, he is clueless that he did it all wrong, and now he is hitting on me!"

Josh continues: "Oh, and Marsh, I know that you have to give Dr. Z a confidential team member evaluation for my performance on our team. I am giving you 100% for sure on mine, and I know that I have not done 100%, but my grades are going take a big hit from that finance class, and I need all the help I can get from my marketing research class. So, what do you say about the movie on Friday?"

Marsha thinks, "I really, really hate it when this happens. . . ."

What errors did Josh commit in preparing his graphs? Identify the error(s) and recommend proper ways to present the findings in the case of each graph.

YOUR INTEGRATED **CASE**

CASE **20.2**

THE HOBBIT'S CHOICE: MAKING A POWERPOINT PRESENTATION

Cory Rogers completed the report for the Hobbit's Choice Restaurant. He decided he wanted to make some PowerPoint slides to use in his presentation of the findings. Working in Word, he wrote a title to his presentation: The Hobbit's Choice Restaurant: Research Findings. Then he wrote out several other comments that he wanted to include in the beginning of his presentation, including the following: Survey of 400 randomly selected residents; Sample screened to include only those who eat at restaurants at least every two weeks; Findings of those Very Likely to patronize the Hobbit's Choice, and so on. When Cory wrote out a number of the statements that he thought would help him communicate the purpose and method of the study, he turned his attention to presenting the findings.

Cory thought he would begin his presentation of the findings with a frequency distribution of the question that asked for the likelihood of patronizing an "upscale" restaurant. He prepared a frequency distribution of the responses to this question using SPSS. He continued by making several key analyses of the data using SPSS.

1. Using a word-processing program, write out several of the statements that you think would be appropriate to present to the client, Jeff Dean, for an oral presentation.

2. Import the statements you prepared in question 1 into PowerPoint using copy and paste. Experiment with different color text and font sizes and styles.

3. Using SPSS, run several frequency distributions. Using TABLELOOKS, select an output format you like and import that output into PowerPoint.

4. Using SPSS, make a bar chart of the answers to the question regarding the likelihood of patronizing an "upscale" restaurant. Experiment with the different options of bar charts available to you in SPSS. Select a bar chart and import that chart into PowerPoint using copy and paste. Experiment with making edits on your slide.

Chapter 1

1. The certification program represents a significant event in the research industry. You may find additional information at the MRA website at **www.mra–net.org**.
2. Keefe, L. M. (2004, September 15). What is the meaning of "marketing"? In: *Marketing News*. Chicago: American Marketing Association, 17–18.
3. Schultz, D. E. (2005, January 15). New definition of marketing reinforces idea of integration. *Marketing News*. Chicago: American Marketing Association, 8.
4. Drucker, Peter (1973). *Management: Tasks, Responsibilities, Practices.* New York: Harper & Row, 64–65.
5. Students will recognize these philosophies as the product concept and the selling concept. See Kotler, Philip, and Armstrong, Gary (2001). *Principles of Marketing*, 9th ed. Upper Saddle River, NJ: Prentice Hall, 18.
6. Kotler, P. (2003). *Marketing Management*, 11th ed. Upper Saddle River, NJ: Prentice Hall, 19.
7. For additional reading on this topic see: Kotler, P. and Keller, K. L. (2006). *Marketing Management*, 12th ed. Upper Saddle River, NJ: Prentice Hall, 15–23.
8. Bennett, P. D. (Ed.) (1995). *Dictionary of Marketing Terms*, 2nd ed. Chicago: American Marketing Association, 169.
9. Bennett, P. D. (Ed.) (1995). *Dictionary of Marketing Terms*, 2nd ed. Chicago: American Marketing Association, 165.
10. Without insights we cannot keep customers loyal. (2004, February 26). *Marketing*, p. 20.
11. Clancy, K., and Krieg, P. C. (2000). *Counterintuitive Marketing: Achieve Great Results Using Uncommon Sense.* New York: The Free Press.
12. Merritt, N. J., and Redmond, W. H. (1990). Defining marketing research: perceptions vs. practice. *Proceedings: American Marketing Association*, 146–150.
13. Market research: pre-testing helps ad effectiveness. (2003, May 8). *Marketing*, 27.
14. Tracy, K. (1998). *Jerry Seinfeld: The Entire Domain.* Secaucus, NJ: Carol Publishing, 64–65.
15. Marconi, J. (1998, June 8). What marketing aces do when marketing research tells them, "don't do it!" *Marketing News*, and Zangwill, W. (1993, March 8). When customer research is a lousy idea. *Wall Street Journal*, A12.
16. Market research: pre-testing helps ad effectiveness. (2003, May 8). *Marketing*, 27.
17. Hise, P. (1998). Grandma got run over by bad research. *Inc.*, 20: 1, 27.
18. Heilbrunn, J. (1989, August). Legal lessons from the Delicare affair—1. United States. *Marketing and Research Today*, 17(3):156–160. Also see Frederickson, P., and Totten, J. W. (1990). Marketing Research Projects in the Academic Setting: Legal Liability after Beecham vs. Yankelovich." In: Capello, L. M.,

et al., eds., Progress in Marketing Thought, *Proceedings of the Southern Marketing Association*, 250–253.
19. See **www.Mintel.com**.
20. Scientific research pumps up new products: the benefits of health and wellness ingredients. (2003, March). *Stagnito's New Products Magazine*, 3(3): 30.
21. Communication to the authors from Kimberly-Clark Worldwide on March 15, 2005. Visit the Kotex Web site at: **www.kotex.com**.
22. Business Ignorance (2004, August). *Industrial Engineer*, 36(8):12.
23. The description of the MIS is adapted from Kotler, P., and Keller, K. L., *Marketing Management*, 12th ed. Upper Saddle River, NJ: Prentice Hall.
24. Fine, Brian (2000). Internet research: the brave new world. In: Chakrapani, C. (Ed.) *Marketing Research: State of the Art Perspectives.* Chicago: American Marketing Association, 143.
25. Grossnickle, J., and Raskin, O. (2001). *Online Marketing Research; Knowing Your Customer Using the Net.* New York: McGraw Hill, xix.
26. Berkowitz, D. (2003, October 24). Harsh realities for marketing research. Retrieved from eMarketer.com on October 27, 2003.
27. Seeber, C., Harap, S. V., and Miller, T. W. *SIRCS Report.* (2001, Fall). Retrieved from IMRO.com on April 10, 2005.
28. Berkowitz, D. (2003, October 24). Harsh realities for marketing research. Retrieved from eMarketer.com on October 27, 2003.
29. Honomichl, J. (2004, June 15). Gradual gains: Growth in U.S. revenues inches higher over '02. *Marketing News*, H3.
30. Honomichl, J. (2004, August 15). Despite acquisitions, firms' revenue dip. Marketing News, H3.
31. *Marketing News* (2003, June 9), H16.
32. Information for this case was obtained from: Ahrens, F. (2003 April 29). Different tune: Jobs sells web music service as solution to piracy. *The Washington Post*. Financial section, E01; Apple Computer Inc. (2003). iTunes music store sells over one million songs in first week. Accessed May 5, 2003 at **www.apple.com/pr/library/2003/may/05musicstore. html**; Evangelista, B. (2003, April 23) Apple kicks off online music store. *The San Francisco Chronicle*. Business Section, B1; Gaither, C. (2003, April 29). Apple unveils service to sell 200,000 digital music titles online. *The Boston Globe*. Business section, D1; Leonard, D. (2003 May 12). Songs in the key of Steve. *Fortune*, 147(9); Moody, G. (2003, January 23). MP3 wins the ear of the public. *Computer Weekly*. 28.
33. Yin, S. (2001). Grandpa gets fit: Older Americans are going to the gym—for emotional as well as health reasons. *American Demographics*, 23(11):13–14.

Chapter 2

1. Others have broken the marketing research process down into different numbers of steps. Regardless, there is widespread agreement that using a step-process approach is a useful tool for learning marketing research.
2. Adapted from Adler, L. (1979, September 17). Secrets of when, and when not to embark on a marketing research project, *Sales & Marketing Management Magazine*, 123:108.
3. Adapted from Adler, L. (1979, September 17). Secrets of when, and when not to embark on a marketing research project, *Sales & Marketing Management Magazine*, 123:108.
4. Wellner, A. S. (2001, April). Research on a shoestring. *American Demographics*, 38–39.
5. Lohse, G. L., and Rosen, D. L. (2001, Summer). Signaling quality and credibility in Yellow Pages advertising: the influence of color and graphics on choice. *Journal of Advertising*, 73–85.
6. Clancy, K. J., and Shulman, R. S. (1994). *Marketing Myths That Are Killing Business*. New York: McGraw Hill, 63.
7. This case was prepared expressly for this chapter by Heather Donofrio, Ph.D.

Chapter 3

1. Jack J. Honomichl received a B.S. degree from Northwestern University and a master's degree from the University of Chicago; Mr. Honomichl has spent a good part of his life in the research industry. He has held executive positions with the Marketing Information Center, a subsidiary of Dun & Bradstreet; Audits & Surveys, Inc.; MRCA; and the *Chicago Tribune*. He frequently contributes to *Advertising Age* and the American Marketing Association's *Marketing News*. His book on the industry, entitled *Honomichl on Marketing Research*, is published by National Textbook Company, Lincolnwood, IL. He has published nearly 400 articles in the trade and the academic press. He was inducted into the Market Research Council's Hall of Fame at the Yale Club in New York in 2002. Other members of the Hall of Fame include such notables as Arthur C. Nielsen, Sr., George Gallup, Sr., David Ogilvy, Marion Harper, Daniel Yankelovich, Daniel Starch, Ernest Dicter, Alfred Politz, and Elmo Roper.
2. Bartels, R. (1976). *The history of marketing thought*, 2nd ed. Columbus, OH: Grid, 124–125.
3. Hardy, H. (1990). *The politz papers: Science and truth in marketing research*. Chicago: American Marketing Association.
4. Bartels, *The history of marketing thought*, 125.
5. Honomichl, J. (2004, August 15). Despite acquisitions, firms' revenue dips. *Marketing News*, H3.
6. Honomichl, J. (2004, August 15). Despite acquisitions, firms' revenue dips. *Marketing News*, H3.
7. Personal communication with J. Honomichl, April 27, 2005; and Honomichl, J. (2004, June 15). Gradual gains: growth in U.S. revenues inches higher over '02. *Marketing News*, H3.
8. Personal communication with J. Honomichl, April 27, 2005.
9. Personal communication with J. Honomichl, April 27, 2005.
10. Honomichl, J. (2003, June 9). Honomichl top 50, company profiles, Synovate. *Marketing News*, H19.

11. Malhotra, N. K. (1999). *Marketing Research*, 3rd ed. Upper Saddle River, NJ: Prentice Hall, 16–19.
12. Kinnear, T. C., and Root, A. R. (1994). *Survey of marketing research: Organization function, budget, and compensation*. Chicago: American Marketing Association, 38.
13. Kinnear and Root, *Survey of marketing research*, 12.
14. Opinion Research Corporation (2001, August 27). *Marketing News*, 5.
15. Honomichl, J. (2004, August 15). Despite acquisitions, firms' revenue dips. *Marketing News*, H6.
16. Honomichl, J. (2004, August 15). Despite acquisitions, firms' revenue dips. *Marketing News*, H8.
17. Honomichl, J. (2004, August 15). Despite acquisitions, firms' revenue dips. *Marketing News*, H10–H12.
18. Honomichl, J. (2004, August 15). Despite acquisitions, firms' revenue dips. *Marketing News*, H8–H9.
19. Honomichl, J. (2004, August 15). Despite acquisitions, firms' revenue dips. *Marketing News*, H19.
20. Personal communication with Creative & Response Research Service, Inc., August 12, 2003.
21. Krum, J. R. (1978, October). B for marketing research departments. *Journal of Marketing*, 42:8–12; Krum, J. R., Rau, P. A., and Keiser, S. K. (1987–1988, December–January). The marketing research process: role perceptions of researchers and users. *Journal of Advertising Research*, 27:9–21; Dawson, S., Bush, R. F., and Stern, B. (1994, October). An evaluation of services provided by the marketing research industry. *Service Industries Journal*, 14(4):515–526; Austin, J. R. (1991). An exploratory examination of the development of marketing research service relationships: an assessment of exchange evaluation dimensions. In: M. C. Gilly, et al. (Eds.), *Enhancing Knowledge Development in Marketing*, 1991 AMA Educators' Conference Proceedings Chicago, IL: American Marketing Associations, 133–141; Swan, J. E., Trawick, I. F., and Carroll, M. G. (1981, August). Effect of participation in marketing research on consumer attitudes toward research and satisfaction with a service. *Journal of Marketing Research*, 356–363; also see Malholtra, N. K., Peterson, M., and Kleiser, S. B. (1999, Spring). Marketing research: a state-of-the-art review and directions for the 21st century. *Journal of the Academy of Marketing Science*, 27(2):160–183.
22. See Neal, W. D. (2002, September 16). Shortcomings plague the industry. *Marketing Research*, 36(19):37ff.
23. See, for example: McManus, J. (2004, April 1). Stumbling into intelligence: market research organizations are trying to grab a bigger piece of the pie. *American Demographics*, 26:3.
24. The following paragraphs are based on: Mahajan, V. & Wind, J. (1999, Fall). Rx for marketing research: a diagnosis of and prescriptions for recovery of an ailing discipline in the business world. *Marketing Research*, 7–13.
25. Baker, S., and Mouncey, P. (2003). The market researcher's manifesto. International Journal of Market Research, 45(4):415ff.
26. Blackwell, R. D. (1998). Why the new market research? An interview appearing in Inc., 20(10):86.
27. Clancy, K., and Krieg, P. C. (2000). *Counterintuitive marketing: Achieve great results using uncommon sense*. New York: The Free Press.
28. Witt, L. (2004). Inside intent. *American Demographics*, 26:2.

29. Honomichl, J. (2003). *The marketing research industry: As old order crumbles a new vision takes shape.* Marketing Aid Center, Barrington, IL.

30. Honomichl, J. (2003). *The marketing research industry: as old order crumbles a new vision takes shape.* Marketing Aid Center; Krum, J. R. (1978, October). B for marketing research departments. *Journal of Marketing,* 42:8–12; Krum, J. R.,Rau, P. A., and Keiser, S. K. (1987–1988, December–January). The marketing research process: role perceptions of researchers and users. *Journal of Advertising Research,* 27:9–21; Dawson, S., Bush, R. F., and Stern, B. (1994, October). An evaluation of services provided by the marketing research industry. *Service Industries Journal,* 14(4):515–526; also see Austin, J. R. (1991). An exploratory examination of the development of marketing research service relationships: An assessment of exchange evaluation dimensions. In M. C. Gilly, et al.(eds.), *Enhancing Knowledge Development in Marketing,* (p. 133–141). 1991 AMA Educators' Conference Proceedings; also see Swan, J. E., Trawick, I. F., and Carroll, M. G. (1981, August). Effect of participation in marketing research on consumer attitudes toward research and satisfaction with a service. *Journal of Marketing Research,* p. 356–363; also see Malholtra, N. K., Peterson, M., and Kleiser, S. B. (1999, Spring). Marketing research: a state-of-the-art review and directions for the 21st century. *Journal of the Academy of Marketing Science,* 27(2):160–183.

31. Quoted in Chakrapani, C. (2001, Winter). From the editor. *Marketing Research,* 13(4):2.

32. What's wrong with marketing research? (2001, Winter). *Marketing Research,* 13:4.

33. Dawson, S., Bush, R. F., and Stern, B. (1994, October). An evaluation of services provided by the market research industry. *Service Industries Journal,* 144:515–526.

34. Consensus eludes certification issue. (1989, September 11). *Marketing News,* 125, 127; Stern, B., and Crawford, T. (1986, September 12). It's time to consider certification of researchers. *Marketing News,* 20–21; Stern, B. L., and Grubb, E. L. (1991). Alternative solutions to the marketing research industry's "quality control" problem. In: R. L. King (Ed.), *Marketing: Toward the twenty-first century.* Proceedings of the Southern Marketing Association, 225–229; Jones, M. A., and McKinney, R. (1993). The need for certification in marketing research. In: D. Thompson (Ed.), *Marketing and education: Partners in progress* Proceedings of the Atlantis Marketing Association, 224–229. Also, for an excellent review of the pros and cons of certification, see Rittenburg, T. L., and Murdock, G. W. (1994, Spring). Highly sensitive issue still sparks controversy within the industry. *Marketing Research,* 6(2):5–10. Also see Giacobbe, R. W., and Segel, M. N. (1994). Credentialing of marketing research professionals: An industry perspective. In: R. Archoll and A. Mitchell (Eds.), *Enhancing knowledge development in marketing.* A.M.A Educators' Conference Proceedings, 229–301.

35. Achenbaum, A. A. (1985, June–July). Can we tolerate a double standard in marketing research? *Journal of Advertising Research,* 25:RC3–RC7.

36. Murphy, P. E., and Laczniack, G. R. (1992, June). Emerging ethical issues facing marketing researchers. *Marketing Research,* 4(2):6–11.

37. See Steinberg, M. S. (1992, June). The "profesionalization" of marketing. *Marketing Research,* 4(2):56. Also see McDaniel, S. W., and Solano-Mendez, R. (1993). Should marketing researchers be certified? *Journal of Advertising Research,* 33(4):20–31.

38. Bernstein, S. (1990, September). A call to audit market research providers. *Marketing Research,* 2(3):11–16.

39. McDaniel, S., Verille, P., and Madden, C. S. (1985, February). The threats to marketing research: an empirical reappraisal. *Journal of Marketing Research,* 74–80; Akaah, I. P., and Riordan, E. A. (1989, February). Judgements of marketing professionals about ethical issues in marketing research. *Journal of Marketing Research,* 112–120; Laczniak, G. R., and Murphy, P. E. *Marketing Ethics.* Lexington, MA: Lexington Books; Ferrell, O. C., and Gresham, L. G. (1985, Summer). A contingency framework for understanding ethical decision making in marketing. *Journal of Marketing Research,* 87–96; Reidenbach, R. E., and Robin, D. P. (1990). A partial testing of the contingency framework for ethical decision making: a path analytical approach. In: L. M. Capella, H. W. Nash, J. M. Starling, and R. D.Taylor (Eds.), *Progress in Marketing Thought.* Proceedings of the Southern Marketing Association, 121–128; LaFleur, E. K., and Reidenbach, R. E. (1993). A taxonomic construction of ethics decision rules: an agenda for research. In: T. K. Massey, Jr. (Ed.), *Marketing: Satisfying a diverse customerplace.* Proceedings of the Southern Marketing Association, 158–161; Reidenbach, R. E., LaFleur, E. K., Robin, D. P., and Forest, P. J. (1993). Exploring the dimensionality of ethical judgements made by advertising professionals concerning selected child-oriented television advertising practices. In:T. K. Massey, Jr. (Ed.), *Marketing: Satisfying a diverse customerplace.* Proceedings of the Southern Marketing Association, 166–170; Klein, J. G., and Smith, N. C. (1994). Teaching marketing research ethics in business school classroom. In: R. Achrol and A. Mitchell (Eds.), *Enhancing knowledge development in marketing.* A.M.A Educators' Conference Proceedings, 92–99.

40. Dolliver, M. (2000, July 10). Keeping honest company. *Adweek,* 41:28, 29.

41. See Kelley, S., Ferrell, O. C., and Skinner, S. J. (1990). Ethical behavior among marketing researchers: an assessment. *Journal of Business Ethics,* 9(8):681ff.

42. See Whetstone, J. T. (2001, September). How virtue fits within business ethics. *Journal of Business Ethics,* 33(2):101–114; and Pallister, J., Nancarrow, C., and Brace, I. (1999, July). Navigating the righteous course: a quality issue. *Journal of the Market Research Society,* 41(3):327–342.

43. Hunt, S. D., Chonko, L. B. & Wilcox, J. B. (1984, August). Ethical problems of marketing researcher. *Journal of Marketing Research,* 21:309–324.

44. For an excellent article on ethics see: Hunt, S. D., and Vitell, S. (1986). A general theory of marketing ethics. *Journal of Macromarketing,* 5–16.

45. Hunt, S. D., Chonko, L. B., and Wilcox, J. B. (1984). Ethical problems of marketing researcher. *Journal of Marketing Research,* 21:309–324.

46. For an excellent discussion of these two philosophies relative to marketing research see: Kimmel, A. J., and Smith, N. C.

(2001, July). Deception in marketing research: ethical, methodological, and disciplinary implications. *Psychology & Marketing*, 18(7):672–680.

47. Full code of ethics/in the area of marketing research. Retrieved from **www.marketingpower.com** on February 16, 2002.

48. Bowers, D. K. (1995, Summer). Confidentiality challenges. *Marketing Research*, 7(3):34–35.

49. Hunt, S. D., Chonko, L. B., and Wilcox, J. B., Ethical problems of marketing researcher. *Journal of Marketing Research*, 21:309–324.

50. Hoffman, T. (2003). Market research providers confront credibility concerns; IT chiefs say they want ethics policies and disclosures stated more clearly. *Computerworld*, 37(41):4ff.

51. Kiecker, P. L., and Nelson, J. E. (1989). Cheating behavior by telephone interviewers: a view from the trenches. In: P. Bloom, et al. (Eds.), *Enhancing knowledge development in marketing* A.M.A. Educators' Conference Proceedings, Chicago, IL 182–188.

52. Hunt, S. D., Chonko, L. B., and Wilcox, J. B., Ethical problems of marketing researcher. *Journal of Marketing Research*, 21:309–324.

53. Ibid.

54. Jarvis, S. (2002, February 4). CMOR finds survey refusal rate still rising. *Marketing News*, 36(3):4. Also see: D. K. Bowers (1997). CMOR's first four years. *Marketing Research*, 9:44–45; Shea, C. Z., and LeBourveau C. (2000, Fall). Jumping the "hurdles" of marketing research. *Marketing Research*, 12(3):22–30.

55. Jarvis, S. (2002, February 4). CMOR finds survey refusal rate still rising. *Marketing News*, 36(3):4.

56. 2003 Respondent Cooperation and Industry Image Study. Retrieved on April 9, 2005, from **www.cmor.org**.

57. Kimmel, A. J., and Smith, N. C. (2001, July). Deception in marketing research: ethical, methodological, and disciplinary implications. *Psychology & Marketing*, 18(7):663–689.

58. Shing, M., and Spence, L. (2002). Investigating the limits of competitive intelligence gathering: is mystery shopping ethical? *Business Ethics: A European Review*, 11(4):343ff.

59. Chavez, J. (2003, October 19). Do-not-call registry contains loopholes for some businesses. Knight Ridder/Tribune Business News. Retrieved on December 7, 2003, from BusinessFile ASAP.

60. Mail abuse prevention system definition of spam. Retrieved March 1, 2002, from **www.mailabuse.org/standard.html**.

61. "New law: Is Spam on the lam? *Managing Technology*. Retrieved on December 6, 2003, from **knowledge.wharton.upenn.edu**; Galgano, M. (2004, August 16). Spam wars. *The Edge: IMRO's Quarterly Newsletter for the Online Research Industry*.

62. Galgano, M. (2004, August 16). Spam wars. *The Edge: IMRO's Quarterly Newsletter for the Online Research Industry*.

63. *National do not email registry: A report to Congress* (2004, June). Washington, DC: Federal Trade Commission; and FTC declines to create do not spam registry. Retrieved from **www.cmor.org** on April 10, 2005.

64. Baldinger, A., and Perterson, B. (1993, August 16). CMOR concentrates on six key areas to improve cooperation. *Marketing News*, 27(17):A15.

65. Go to **www.cmor.org** and go to "Respondent Cooperation."

66. The author makes no pretense that this is an original case. Rather, this case has been adapted from Sparks, J. R., and

67. Hunt, S. D. (1998). Marketing researcher ethical sensitivity; conceptualization, measurement, and exploratory investigation. *Journal of Marketing*, 62(2):92–109.

67. Ramasastry, A. (2003, December 5). Why the new federal 'Can Spam' law probably will not work. Find Law. Retrieved on December 7, 2003, from **www.cnn.com**.

68. Ramasastry, A. (2003, December 5). Why the new federal 'Can Spam' law probably will not work. *Find Law*. Retrieved on December 7, 2003 from CNN.com.

69. Gillin, Donna (2001, Summer). Opt in or opt out? *Marketing Research*, 6–7.

70. The following statements are taken from the CASRO Code of Ethics, Responsibilities to Respondents; Privacy and the Avoidance of Harassment, Section 3. Internet Research. See **www.casro.org**.

71. See **www.bls.gov/oco/home.htm**. Retrieved on April 10, 2005.

72. See **www.bls.gov/oco/home.htm**. Retrieved on March 3, 2002.

73. Jarvis, S. (2001, August 14). Compensation prize. *Marketing News*. Retrieved from **www.marketingpower.com** on December 19, 2001.

Chapter 4

1. The Operative Product Word: Ambitiousness *Advertising Age*, December 21, 1996, p. 14; Murtaugh, P. Consumer Research: The Big Lie. *Food & Beverage Marketing*, May, 1998, p. 16; and Parasuraman, A., Grewal, D., and Krishnan, R. (2004). *Marketing Research*. Boston: Houghton Mifflin, 41–42.

2. Koten, J., and Kilman, S. (1985, July 15). Marketing classic; how Coke's decision to offer 2 colas undid $4\frac{1}{2}$ years of planning—after successful introduction of New Coke, firm began to see market slip away—which one will be flagship? *Wall Street Journal*, 1.

3. Gibson, L. D. (1998, Spring). Defining marketing problems: don't spin your wheels solving the wrong puzzle. *Marketing Research*, 10(4):7.

4. Retrieved from **www.dictionary.com** on November 13, 2003.

5. Kotler, P. (2003). *Marketing management: Analysis, planning, implementing, and control*, 11th ed. Upper Saddle River, NJ: Prentice Hall, 102.

6. For example, see: Gordon, G. L., Schoenbachler, D. D., Kaminski, P. F., and Brouchous, K. A. (1997). New product development: using the salesforce to identify opportunities. *Business and Industrial Marketing*, 12(1):33; and Ardjchvilj, A., Cardozo, R., and Ray, S. (2003, January). A theory of entrepreneurial opportunity identification and development. *Journal of Business Venturing*, 18(1):105.

7. Personal communication with Lawrence D. Gibson. Also see: Gibson, Defining marketing problems.

8. Kane, C. (1994, November 28). New product killer: the research gap. *Brandweek*, 35(46):12.

9. Gibson, Defining marketing problems: don't spin your wheels solving the wrong puzzle.

10. For example, see: Tomas, S. (1999, May). Creative problem-solving: an approach to generating ideas. *Hospital Material Management Quarterly*, 20(4):33–45.

11. Kotler, *Marketing Management*, 103.

12. Semon, T. (1999, June 7). Make sure the research will answer the right question. *Marketing News*, 33(12):H30.

13. Dictionary. American Marketing Association. Retrieved on December 10, 2003 from **www. marketingpower.com**.

14. Adapted from Dictionary.com. Retrieved on November 15, 2003. Also see Bagozzi, R. P., Phillips, L. W. (1982, September). Representing and testing organizational theories: a holistic construal. *Administrative Science Quarterly*, 27(3):459.

15. For more information on proposals and reports, see Carroll, N., Mohn, M., and Land, T. H. (1989, January/February/March). A guide to quality marketing research proposals and reports. *Business*, 39(1):38–40.

Chapter 5

1. Singleton, D. (2003, November 24). Basics of good research involve understanding six simple rules. *Marketing News*, 22–23.

2. For an excellent in-depth treatment of research design issues see: Creswell, J. (2003). *Research design; Qualitative, quantitative, and mixed methods approaches*. Thousand Oaks, CA: Sage.

3. Burns, A. C., and Bush, R. F. (2005). *Basic marketing research using Microsoft Excel Data Analysis*. Upper Saddle River, NJ: Prentice Hall, 100–102.

4. Personal communication with Holly McLennan, Marketing Director, 1-800-GOT-JUNK? on April 27, 2005; and Martin, J. (2003, October 27). Cash from trash: 1-800-Got Junk? *Fortune*, 148:196.

5. For one example, see Parasuraman, A., Berry, L. L. and Zeithaml, V. A. (1991, Winter). Refinement and reassessment of the SERVQUAL scale. *Journal of Retailing*, 67(4):420ff. A small effort of exploratory research on this topic will find many references on measuring service quality.

6. Stewart, D. W. (1984). *Secondary research: Information sources and methods*. Newbury Park, CA: Sage; Davidson, J. P. (1985, April). Low cost research sources. *Journal of Small Business Management*, 23:73–77.

7. Knox, N. (2003, December 16). Volvo teams up to build what women want. *USA Today*, 1B.

8. Bonoma, T. V. (1984). Case research in marketing: Opportunities, problems, and a process. *Journal of Marketing Research*, 21:199–208.

9. Myers, J. Wireless for the 21st century. *Telephony*, 231(6):24–26.

10. Greenbaum, T. I. (1988). *The Practical Handbook and Guide in Focus Group Research*. Lexington, MA: D.C. Heath.

11. Stoltman, J. J., and Gentry, J. W. (1992). Using focus groups to study household decision processes and choices. In: R. P. Leone and V. Kumar (Eds.). *AMA Educator's Conference Proceedings*: Vol. 3: *Enhancing knowledge development in marketing*. Chicago: American Marketing Association, 257–263.

12. Miller, C. (1991, May 27). Respondents project let psyches go crazy. *Marketing News*, 25(11):1, 3.

13. See Churchill, G. A., Jr., and Iacobucci, D. (2005). *Marketing research: Methodological foundations*. Mason, OH: Thomson/South-Western, 679.

14. Kinnear, T. C., and Taylor, J. R. (1991). *Marketing research: An applied approach*. New York: McGraw-Hill, 142.

15. Sudman, S., and Wansink, B. (2002). *Consumer Panels*, 2nd ed. Chicago: American Marketing Association. This book is recognized as an authoritative source on panels.

16. Personal communication with Allison Groom, American Heart Association, March 12, 2002.

17. Lohse, G. L., and Rosen, D. L. (2002, Summer). Signaling quality and credibility in Yellow Pages advertising: the influence of color and graphics on choice. *Journal of Advertising*, 30(2):73–85.

18. Wyner, G. (2000, Fall). Learn and earn through testing on the Internet: the Web provides new opportunities for experimentation. *Marketing Research*, 12(3):37–38.

19. For example, see Montgomery, D. (2001). *Design and analysis of experiments*. New York: Wiley; and Kerlinger, F. N. (1986). *Foundation of behavioral research*, 3rd ed. New York: Holt, Rinehart, and Winston.

20. Campbell, D. T., and Stanley, J. C. (1963). *Experimental and quasi-experimental designs for research*. Chicago: Rand McNally.

21. Calder, B. J., Phillips, L. W., and Tybour, A. M. (1992, December). The concept of external validity. *Journal of Consumer Research*, 9:240–244.

22. Gray, L. R., and Diehl, P. L. (1992). *Research Methods for Business and Management*. New York: Macmillan, 387–390.

23. Doyle, J. (1994, October). In with the new, out with the old. *Beverage World*, 113(1576):204–205.

24. Brennan, L. (1988, March). Test marketing. *Sales Marketing Management Magazine*, 140:50–62.

25. Miles, S. (2001). MyTurn is cutting back in unusual way. *Wall Street Journal*, Eastern Edition.

26. A root beer float in a bottle? (2003, June 19). *The Columbus Dispatch*. Retrieved on December 19, 2003, from Lexis-Nexis.

27. Kaushik, N. (2003, July 23). Thai co introduces children's furniture. *Businessline*, 1.

28. Liddle, A. (2002, May 20). DQ field tests irradiated burgers as farm bill relaxes labeling law. *Nation's Restaurant News*, 36(20):3ff.

29. Keep jellyfish at bay. (2003, April 1). *Community Pharmacy*, 26.

30. Thompson, S. (2003, November 11). Snacks take flight. *Advertising Age*, 73(45):6.

31. Churchill, G. A., Jr. (2001). *Basic Marketing Research*, 4th ed. Fort Worth, TX: The Dryden Press, 144–145.

32. Spethmann, B. (1985, May 8). Test market USA. *Brandweek*, 36:40–43.

33. Clancy, K. J., and Shulman, R. S. (1995, October). Test for success. *Sales & Marketing Management Magazine*, 147(10):111–115.

34. Melvin, P. (1992, September). Choosing simulated test marketing systems. *Marketing Research*, 4(3):14–16.

35. *Ibid*. Also see Turner, J., and Brandt, J. (1978, Winter). Development and validation of a simulated market to test children for selected consumer skills. *Journal of Consumer Affairs*, 266–276.

36. Blount, S. (1992, March). It's just a matter of time. *Sales & Marketing Management*, 144(3):32–43.

37. Power, C. (1992, August 10). Will it sell in Podunk? Hard to say. *Business Week*, 46–47.

38. Nelson, E. (2001, February 2). Colgate's net rose 10 percent in period, new products helped boost sales. *Wall Street Journal*, Eastern edition, p. B6.

39. Ihlwan, M. (2002, February 4). A nation of digital guinea pigs: Korea is a hotbed of such experiments as a cash-free city. *Business Week*, 50.

40. Greene, S. (1996, May 4). Chattanooga chosen as test market for smokeless cigarette. *Knight-Ridder/Tribune Business News*, 5040084.

41. Hayes, J. (1995, January 3). McD extends breakfast buffet test in south-east markets. *National Restaurant News*, 29(4):3.
42. Kotler, P. (1991). *Marketing management: Analysis, planning, implementation, and control*. Upper Saddle River, NJ: Prentice Hall, 335.
43. Power, C. (1992, August 10). Will it sell in Podunk? Hard to say. *Business Week*, 46–47.
44. Murphy, P., and Laczniak, G. (1992, June). Emerging ethical issues facing marketing researchers. *Marketing Research*, 6.

Chapter 6

1. For an example of using secondary data for a marketing research project, see Castleberry, S. B. (2001, December). Using secondary data in marketing research: a project that melds Web and off-Web sources. *Journal of Marketing Education*, 23(3):195–203.
2. Wagner, C. G. (2001, July–August). Technology: the promise of Internet2. *The Futurist*, 35(4):12–13.
3. Kotler, P. (2003). *Marketing management*, 11th ed. Upper Saddle River, NJ: Prentice Hall, 53.
4. Senn, J. A. (1988). *Information technology in business: Principles, practice, and opportunities*. Upper Saddle River, NJ: Prentice Hall, 66.
5. Grisaffe, D. (2002, January 21). See about linking CRM and MR systems. *Marketing News*, 36(2):13.
6. Drozdenko, R. G., and Drake, P. D. (2002). *Optimal database marketing*. Thousand Oaks, CA: Sage.
7. Lewis, L. (1996, November). Retailers begin tracking consumer purchases and recording consumer preferences and demographic data. *Progressive Grocer*, 75(11):18.
8. McKim, R. (2001, September). Privacy notices: what they mean and how marketers can prepare for them. *Journal of Database Marketing*, 9(1):79–84.
9. See, for example, U.S. Industrial Outlook 1999. (1999). Washington, DC: International Trade Administration, U.S. Department of Commerce.
10. Gordon, L. P. (1995). *Using secondary data in marketing research: United States and Worldwide*. Westport, CT: Quorum Books, 24.
11. Market Statistics is a division of Bill Communications, Corporate Headquarters: 355 Park Ave. S., New York, NY 10010.
12. These questions and much of the following discussion is taken from Stewart, D. W. (1984). *Secondary research: information sources and methods*. Newbury Park, CA: Sage.
13. Murray, D., Schwartz, J., & Lichter, S. R. (2001). *It ain't necessarily so: How media make and unmake the scientific picture of reality*. Lanham, MD: Rowman & Littlefield.
14. Ibid., 71–76.
15. Ibid., vii–ix.
16. Crossen, C. (1994). *Tainted truth: The manipulation of fact in America*. New York: Simon & Schuster, 140.
17. See Goldberg, B. (2002). *Bias*. Washington, DC: Regnery Publishing; and Best, J. (2001). *Damned lies and statistics*. Berkeley, CA: University of California Press.
18. Chapman, J. (1987, February). Cast a critical eye: small area estimates and projections sometimes can be dramatically different. *American Demographics*, 9:30.
19. These steps are updated and adapted from Stewart, D. W. *Secondary Research*, 20–22, by Ms. Peggy Toifel, MSLS, MBA, University Librarian, University of West Florida, 2004.
20. America's experience with Census 2000. (2000, August). *Direct Marketing*, 63(4):46–51.
21. Researchers wishing to use SIC codes should refer to the *Standard Industrial Classification Manual 1987*, rev. ed. (1987). Executive office of the President, Office of Management and Budget, Washington, DC: Government Printing Office.
22. Winchester, J. (1998, February). Marketers prepare for switch from SIC codes. *Business Marketing*, 1:34.
23. Boettcher, J. (1996, April–May). NAFTA prompts a new code system for industry—the death of SIC and birth of NAICS. *Database*, 42–45.
24. Information found in this section may be referenced in *Demographics USA* (2002). Chicago: Bill Communications.

Chapter 7

1. Actually, virtually all these firms offer some customization of data analysis, and many offer varying methods of collecting data. Still, while customization is possible, these same companies provide standardized processes and data.
2. See *Rocking the ages: The Yankelovich perspective on generational marketing*. (1997). New York: Harper Business.
3. Solutions & Services/consumer trends research/monitor annually. Retrieved from **www.yankelovich.com** on September 6, 2002.
4. Retrieved from **www.yankelovich.com/monitor** on May 10, 2005.
5. Retrieved from **www.yankelovich.com** on May 10, 2005.
6. Harris poll. Retrieved from **www.HarrisInteractive.com** on May 10, 2005.
7. What does America think about? (undated publication). Wilmington, DE: Scholarly Resources.
8. Fish, D. (2000, November). Untangling psychographics and lifestyle. *Quirk's Marketing Research Review*, 138ff.
9. SRI Consulting Business Intelligence. Retrieved from **www.sric-bi.com/VALS/** on May 10, 2002; and by personal communications on May 11, 2005.
10. Stolzenberg, M. (2000, February). 10 tips on tracking research. *Quirk's Marketing Research Review*, 20–24.
11. For an example of analysis of supermarket data using Scantrack, see Heller, W. (2000, July). Surfing retail channels. *Progressive Grocer*, 79(7):48–58.
12. Retail Measurement (2005). Retrieved from **www.acnielsen. com** on May 7, 2005.
13. Custom Store Tracking (2004). Retrieved on January 10, 2004 from **www.infores.com**.
14. Retrieved from **www.infores.com/** on May 10, 2005.
15. Consumer Panel: Understanding your customers. (2005). Retrieved from **www.acnielsen.com** on May 7, 2005.
16. Bachman, K. (2003, May 5). Arbitron unveils initiatives to boost response rates. *Mediaweek.com*, 13(18):6ff.
17. NPD group, food and beverages worldwide. (2002). Retrieved from **www.npd.com** on May 16, 2002.
18. Category Business Planner. (2004). Retrieved from **www.ACNielsen.com** on January 10, 2004.
19. Nielsen SoundScan now tracking more online music (2003, November 18). Retrieved online from Total Telecom on December 21, 2004.
20. VNU names Connors to head new media group. (2001, June 13). Retrieved from **www.ACNielsen.com** on January 10, 2004.

21. Retrieved on May 13, 2005 from Nielsen Media Research website at **www.nielsenmedia.com**.

22. Repeat-viewing with people meters. *Journal of Advertising Research*, 9–13; Stoddard, L. R., Jr. (1987, October). The history of people meters. *Journal of Advertising Research*, 10–12.

23. See Arbitron.com.

24. See NOP World website at **www.nopworld.com**.

25. Adnorms (2002). RoperASW, p. iv. Additional material retrieved from NOPWorld at **www.nopworld.com** on May 13, 2005.

26. Patchen, R. H., and Kolessar, R. S. (1999, August). Out of the lab and into the field: a pilot test of the Personal Portable Meter. *Journal of Advertising Research*, 39(4):55–68. Also see Moss, L. (2002, February 11). A constant companion. *Broadcasting & Cable*, 132(6):17.

27. Hughes, L. Q. (2001, June 18). Buyers demand more data. *Advertising Age*, 72(25):T2.

28. Reid, A. (2000, January 28). Is ITV's tvSPAN the holy grail adland has been waiting for? *Campaign*, 20.

29. For a review of these discussions, see Peters, B. (1990, December). The brave new world of single-source information. *Marketing Research*, 2(4):16; Churchill, V. B. (1990, December). The role of ad hoc survey research in a single source world. *Marketing Research*, 2(4):22–26; and Metzger, G. D. (1990, December). Single source: yes and no (the backward view). *Marketing Research*, 2(4):29.

Chapter 8

1. Ezzy, D. (2001, August). Are qualitative methods misunderstood? *Australian and New Zealand Journal of Public Health*, 25(4):294–297.

2. Clark, A. (2001, September 13). Research takes an inventive approach, *Marketing*, 25–26.

3. DeNicola, N. (2002, March 4). Casting finer net not necessary. *Marketing News*, 36(5):46.

4. Griffen, D. S., and Duley, R. (2000, July/August). Read all about it. *Quirks Marketing Research Review*, 14(7):20–21, 104–106.

5. For some guidelines to direct observation, see Becker, B. (1999, September 27). Take direct route when data-gathering. *Marketing News*, 33(20):29, 31.

6. Smith, S. M., and Whitlark, D. B. (2001, Summer). Men and women online: what makes them click? *Marketing Research*, 13(2):20–25.

7. Piirto, R. (1991, September). Socks, ties and videotape. *American Demographics*, 6.

8. Fellman, M. W. (1999, Fall). Breaking tradition. *Marketing Research*, 11(3):20–34.

9. Modified from Tull, D. S., and Hawkins, D. I. (1987). *Marketing Research*, 4th ed. New York: Macmillan, 331.

10. Rust, L. (1993, November/December). How to reach children in stores: Marketing tactics grounded in observational research. *Journal of Advertising Research*, 33(6):67–72, and Rust, L. (1993, July/August). Parents and children shopping together: A new approach to the qualitative analysis of observational data. *Journal of Advertising Research*, 33(4):65–70.

11. Thomas, J. (1999, February). Motivational research. *Quirks Marketing Research Review*, 12(2):40–43.

12. Viles, P. (1992, August 24). Company measures listenership in cars. *Broadcasting*, 122(35):28.

13. Kephart, P. (1996, May). The spy in aisle 3. *American Demographics Marketing Tools*, **www.marketingtools.com/Publications/ MT/96_mt/9605MD04.htm**.

14. Del Vecchio, E. (1988, Spring). Generating marketing ideas when formal research is not available. *Journal of Services Marketing*, 2(2):71–74.

15. Mariampolski, H. (1988, January 4). Ethnography makes comeback as research tool. *Marketing News*, 22(1):32, 44.

16. Hellebursch, S. J. (2000, September 11). Don't read research by the numbers. *Marketing News*, 34(19):25.

17. Greenbaum, T. I.. (1988). *The practical handbook and guide in focus group research*. Lexington, MA: D. C. Heath.

18. Stoltman, J. J., and Gentry, J. W. (1992). Using focus groups to study household decision processes and choices. In R. P. Leone and V. Kumar (Eds.), *AMA Educator's Conference Proceedings*, Vol. 3. Enhancing knowledge development in marketing (Chicago: American Marketing Association, 257–263).

19. Last, J. and Langer, J. (2003, December). Still a valuable tool. *Quirk's Marketing Research Review*, 17(11):30.

20. Kahn, A. (1996, September 6). Focus groups alter decisions made in business, politics. *Knight-Ridder/Tribune Business News*, 916.

21. Wellner, A. (2003, March). The new science of focus groups. *American Demographics*, 25(2):29ff.

22. Langer, J. (2001). *The mirrored window: Focus groups from a moderator's viewpoint*. New York: Paramount Market Publishing, 4.

23. Greenbaum, T. L. (1993, March 1). Focus group research is not a commodity business. *Marketing News*, 27(5):4.

24. Greenbaum, T. L. (1991, May 27). Answer to moderator problems starts with asking right questions. *Marketing News*, 25(11):8–9; and Fern, E. F. (1982, February). The use of focus groups for idea generation: The effects of group size, acquaintanceship, and moderator on response quantity and quality. *Journal of Marketing Research*, 1–13.

25. Greenbaum, T. L. (1991). Do you have the right moderator for your focus groups? Here are 10 questions to ask yourself. *Bank Marketing*, 23(1):43.

26. Based on Henderson, N. R. (2000, December). Secrets of our success: insights from a panel of moderators. *Quirk's Marketing Research Review*, 14(11):62–65.

27. For guidelines for "backroom observers," see Langer, J. (2001, September 24). Get more out of focus group research. *Marketing News*, 35(20):19–20.

28. Grinchunas, R., and Siciliano, T. (1993, January 4). Focus groups produce verbatims, not facts. *Marketing News*, 27(1):FG-19.

29. Zinchiak, M. (2001, July/August). Online focus groups FAQs, *Quirk's Marketing Research Review*, 15(7):38–46.

30. Adapted from Zinchiak, Online focus group FAQs.

31. Lonnie, K. (2001, November 19). Combine phone, Web for focus groups. *Marketing News*, 35(24):15–16.

32. For interesting comments, see DeNicola, N., and Kennedy, S. (2001, November 19). Quality Inter(net)action. *Marketing News*, 35(24):14.

33. Jarvis, S., and Szynal, D. (2001, November 19). Show and tell. *Marketing News*, 35(24):1, 13.

34. Langer, J. (2001). The mirrored window: Focus groups from a moderator's viewpoint. New York: Paramount Market Publishing, 11.

35. Quinlan, P. (2000, December). Insights on a new site. *Quirk's Marketing Research Review*, 15(11):36–39.

36. Hines, T. (2000). An evaluation of two qualitative methods (focus group interviews and cognitive maps) for conducting research into entrepreneurial decision making. *Qualitative Market Research*, 3(1):7–16.

37. Berlamino, C. (1989, December/January). Designing the qualitative research project: addressing the process issues. *Journal of Advertising Research*, 29(6):S7–S9.

38. Flores Letelier, M., Spinosa, C., and Calder, B. (2000, Winter). Taking an expanded view of customers' needs: qualitative research for aiding innovation. *Marketing Research*, 12(4):4–11.

39. Kahan, H. (1990, September 3). One-on-ones should sparkle like the gems they are. *Marketing News*, 24(18):8–9.

40. Roller, M. R. (1987, August 28). A real in-depth interview wades into the stream of consciousness. *Marketing News*, 21(18):14.

41. Kahan, One-on-ones should sparkle like the gems they are.

42. An interesting article on recent developments in depth interviewing is Wansink, B. (2000, Summer). New techniques to generate key marketing insights. *Marketing Research*, 12(2):28–36.

43. Kates, B. (2000, April). Go in-depth with depth interviews. *Quirk's Marketing Research Review*, 14(4):36–40.

44. Mitchell, V. (1993, First Quarter). Getting the most from in-depth interviews. *Business Marketing Digest*, 18(1):63–70.

45. Reynolds, T. J. and Gutman, J. (1988). Laddering, method, analysis, and interpretation. *Journal of Advertising Research*, 28(1):11–21.

46. Berstell, G., and Nitterhouse, D. (2001, Fall). Asking all the right questions. *Marketing Research*, 13(3):14–20.

47. Qualitative Research Services, Word Association Tests. Retrieved from **www.decisionanalyst.com** on May 20, 2005.

48. Qualitative Research Services, Sentence Completion Tests. Retrieved from **www.decisionanalyst.com** on May 20, 2005.

49. An example is Piirto, R. (1990, December). Measuring minds in the 1990s. *American Demographics*, 12(12):30–35.

50. Dictionary. American Marketing Association. Retrieved on December 16, 2003 from **www.marketingpower.com**.

51. Taylor, C. (2003, December). Whats all the fuss about? *Quirk's Marketing Research Review*, 17(11):40–45.

52. Miles, L. (2003, December 11). Market research: living their lives. *Marketing. Market Research Bulletin*. Retrieved online from **www.brandrepublic.com** on May 20, 2005.

53. Marshall, S., Drapeau, T., and DiSciullo, M. (2001, July/August). An eye on usability. *Quirk's Marketing Research Review*, 15(7):20–21, 90–92.

54. Allmon, D. E. (1988). Voice stress and likert scales: a paired comparison. In: David L. Moore (Ed.), "Marketing: Forward Motion," *Proceedings of the Atlantic Marketing Association* (1988), 710–714.

55. Green, P., Wind, Y., Krieger, A., and Saatsoglou, P. (2000, Spring). Applying qualitative data. *Marketing Research*, 12(1):17–25.

56. Clarke, A. (2001, September 13). Research takes an inventive approach. *Marketing*, 2–26.

57. Wellner, A. S. (2001, April). Research on a shoestring. *American Demographics*, 23(4):38–39.

Chapter 9

1. Musa, G., Hall, C. M., Higham, J. E. S (2004). Tourism sustainability and health impacts in high altitude adventure, cultural and ecotourism destinations: a case study of Nepal's Sagarmatha National Park. *Journal of Sustainable Tourism*, 12(4):306–331. The description was provided by Dr. Ghazall Musa via personal communication.

2. Malhotra, N. (1999). *Marketing research: An applied orientation*, 3rd ed. Upper Saddle River, NJ: Prentice Hall, 125.

3. Tourangeau, R. (2004). Survey research and societal change. *Annual Review of Psychology*, 55(1):775–802.

4. Cuneo, A. Z., and Bulik, B. S. (2003, February), Unified voice at risk as HP CEO departs. *Advertising Age*, 76(7):3–5.

5. See Oishi, S. M. (2003). *How to conduct in-person interviews for surveys*. Thousand Oaks, CA: Sage, 6.

6. Tourangeau, R. (2004), Survey research and societal change. *Annual Review of Psychology*, 55(1):775–802.

7. Tourangeau, R. Survey research and societal change. *Annual Review of Psychology*, 55(1):775–802.

8. Cleland, K. (1996, May). Online research costs about one-half that of traditional methods. *Business Marketing*, 81(4):B8–B9.

9. See, for example, Dudley, D. (2001, January). The name collector. *New Media Age*, 18–20, Kent, R., and Brandal, H. (2003), Improving email response in a permission marketing context. *International Journal of Market Research*, 45(4):489–540, or Agrawal, A., Basak, J., Jain, V., Kothari, R., Kumar, M., Mittal, P. A., Modani, N., Ravikumar, K., Sabharwal, Y., and Sureka, R. (2004, September/October). Online marketing research. *IBM Journal of Research & Development*, 48(5/6):671–677.

10. See Macer, T. (2002, December). CAVI from OpinionOne. *Quirk's Marketing Research Review*. Electronic archive, **www.quirks.com**.

11. Bourque, L., and Fielder, E. (2003). *How to conduct self-administered and mail surveys*, 2nd ed. Thousand Oaks, CA: Sage.

12. Jang, H., Lee, B., Park, M., and Stokowski, P. A. (2000, February). Measuring underlying meanings of gambling from the perspective of enduring involvement. *Journal of Travel Research*, 38(3):230–238.

13. Ericson, P. I., and Kaplan, C. P. (2000, November). Maximizing qualitative responses about smoking in structured interviews. *Qualitative Health Research*, 10(6):829–840.

14. Some authors restrict the definition to only cases in which two or more data-collection methods are used in the same phase of the study. See: Hogg, A. (2002, July), Multi-mode research dos and don'ts. *Quirk's Marketing Research Review*, electronic archive. Electronic archive, **www.quirks.com**, May 1, 2005.

15. Cuneo, A. Z. (2004, November), Researchers flail as public cuts the cord. *Advertising Age*, 75:46–48.

16. See, for example: **www.uwf.edu/panel**.

17. Green, K., Medlin, B., and Whitten, D. (2001, July). A comparison of Internet and mail survey methodology. *Quirk's Marketing Research Review*. Electronic archive, **www.quirks.com**.

18. See Roy, A. (2003). Further issues and factors affecting the response rates of e-mail and mixed-mode studies. In: Barone, M., et. al. (Eds.) *Enhancing Knowledge Development in Marketing*. Proceedings: AMA Educator's Conference. Chicago, IL: American Marketing Association, 338–339; and Bachmann, D., Elfrink, J., and Vazzana, G. (1999). E-mail and snail mail face off in rematch. *Marketing Research*, 11(4):11–15.

19. Hogg, A. (2002, July), Multi-mode research dos and don'ts. *Quirk's Marketing Research Review*. Electronic archive, **www.quirks.com**.

20. Roy, S. (3004, July), The littlest consumers. *Display & Design Ideas*, 16(7):18–21.

21. See Jacobs, H. (1989, Second Quarter). Entering the 1990s—the state of data collection—from a mall perspective. *Applied Marketing Research*, 30(2):24–26; Lysaker, R. L. (1989, October). Data collection methods in the U.S. *Journal of the Market Research Society*, 31(4):477–488; Gates, R., and Solomon, P. J. (1982, August/September). Research using the mall intercept: state of the art. *Journal of Advertising Research*, 43–50; Bush, A. J., Bush, R. F., and Chen, H. C. (1991). Method of administration effects in mall intercept interviews. *Journal of the Market Research Society*, 33(4):309–319.

22. Hornik, J., and Ellis, S. (1989, Winter). Strategies to secure compliance for a mall intercept interview. *Public Opinion Quarterly*, 52(4):539–551.

23. At least one study refutes the concern about shopping frequency. See DuPont, T. D. (1987, August/September). Do frequent mall shoppers distort mall-intercept results? *Journal of Advertising Research*, 27(4):45–51.

24. Bush, A. J., and Grant, E. S. (1995, Fall). The potential impact of recreational shoppers on mall intercept interviewing: An exploratory study. *The Journal of Marketing Theory and Practice*, 3(4):73–83.

25. Bourque, L., and Fielder, E. (2003). *How to conduct telephone interviews*, 2nd ed. Thousand Oaks, CA: Sage.

26. Bush, A. J., and Hair, J. F. (1983, May). An assessment of the mall intercept as a data collection method. *Journal of Marketing Research*, 22:158–167.

27. Holbrook, A. L., Green, M. C., Krosnick, J. A. (2003, Spring), Telephone versus face-to-face interviewing of national probability samples with long questionnaires. *Public Opinion Quarterly*, 67(1):79–126.

28. Sheppard. J. (2000, April). Half-empty or half-full? *Quirk's Marketing Research Review*, 14(4):42–45.

29. See, for example, Xu, M., Bates, B. J., and Schweitzer, J. C. (1993). The impact of messages on survey participation in answering machine households. *Public Opinion Quarterly*, 57(2):232–237; Meinert, D. B., Festervand, T. A., and Lumpkin, J. R. (1992). Computerized questionnaires: pros and cons. In: R. L. King (Ed.), *Marketing: Perspectives for the 1990s*. Proceedings of the Southern Marketing Association, 201–206.

30. Remington, T. D. (1993). Telemarketing and declining survey response rates. *Journal of Advertising Research*, 32(3):RC-6–RC-7.

31. Brennan, M., Benson, S., Kearns, Z. The effect of introductions on telephone survey participation rates. (2005). *International Journal of Market Research*, 47(1):65.

32. Fielding, M. (2004, November), Recent converts. *Marketing News*, 38(19):21–22.

33. Bos, R. (1999, November). A new era in data collection, *Quirk's Marketing Research Review*, 12(10):32–40; and Fletcher, K. (1995, June 15). Jump on the omnibus. *Marketing*, 25–28.

34. Gates, R. H., and Jarboe, G. R. (Spring). Changing trends in data acquisition for marketing research. *Journal of Data Collection*, 27(1):25–29; also see Synodinos, N. E., and Brennan, J. M. (1998, Summer). Computer interactive interviewing in survey research. *Psychology and Marketing*, 117–138.

35. DePaulo, P. J., and Weitzer, R. (1994, January 3). Interactive phone technology delivers survey data quickly. *Marketing News*, 28(1):15.

36. Jones, P., and Palk, J. (1993). Computer-based personal interviewing: state-of-the-art and future prospects. *Journal of the Market Research Society*, 35(3):221–233.

37. Heun, C. T. (2001, October 15). Procter & Gamble readies online market-research push. *Informationweek*, 859:26.

38. For a "speed" comparison, see Cobanoglu, C., Warde, B., and Moeo, P. J. (2001, Fourth Quarter). A comparison of mail, fax and Web-based survey methods. *International Journal of Market Research*, 43(3):441–452.

39. Bruzzone, D., and Shellenberg, P. (2000, July/August). Track the effect of advertising better, faster, and cheaper online. *Quirk's Marketing Research Review*, 14(7):22–35.

40. Sudman, S., and Blair, E. (1999, Spring). Sampling in the twenty-first century. *Academy of Marketing Science Journal*, 27(2):269–277.

41. Miles, Louiella (2004, June 16), Online market research panels offer clients high response rates at low prices. *Marketing*, 39.

42. Grecco, C. (2000, July/August). Research non-stop. *Quirk's Marketing Research Review*, 14(7):70–73.

43. Greenberg, D. (2000, July/August). Internet economy gives rise to real-time research. *Quirk's Marketing Research Review*, 14(7):88–90.

44. Aster, A. Z. (2001, June), Consumer research goes online. *Marketing Magazine*, 109(20):13–14.

45. See, for example, Coderre, F., St-Laurent, N., and Mathieu, A. (2004). Comparison of the quality of qualitative data obtained through telephone, postal and email surveys, *International Journal of Market Research*, 46(3):347–357; Kaplowitz, M. D., Hadlock, T. D., Levine, R. X. (2004, Spring), A comparison of web and mail survey response rates. *Public Opinion Quarterly*, 68(1):94–1–1; and Sparrow, N., and Curtice, J. (2004), Measuring the attitudes of the general public via Internet polls: an evaluation. *International Journal of Market Research*, 46(1):23–44.

46. Brown, J. (2003, November), Survey metrics ward off problems. *Marketing News*, 37(24):17–18.

47. Fielding, M. (2004, November). Recent converts. *Marketing News*, 38(19):21–22.

48. Brown, S. (1987). Drop and collect surveys: a neglected research technique? *Journal of the Market Research Society*, 5(1):19–23.

49. See Ibeh, K. I. N., Brock, J. K. U. (2004). Conducting survey research among organisational populations in developing countries, *International Journal of Market Research*, 46(3):375–383; and Ibeh, K., Brock, J. K. U., Zhou, Y. J. (2004, February). The drop and collect survey among industrial populations: theory and empirical evidence, *Industrial Marketing Management*, 33(2):155–165.

50. See Bourque and Fielder, *How to conduct self-administered and mail surveys*, 2nd edition. Thousand Oaks, CA: Sage Publications.

51. American Statistical Association (1997). More about mail surveys, ASA Series: What is a survey? Electronic archive, **www.amstat.org/sections/srms/brochures/mail.pdf**

52. Nonresponse is a concern with any survey, and our understanding of refusals is minimal. See, for example, Groves, R. M., Cialdini, R. B., and Couper, M. P. (1992). Understanding the decision to participate in a survey. *Public Opinion Quarterly*, 56:475–495.

53. Anderson, R. C., Fell, D., Smith, R. L., Hansen, E. N., Gomon, S. (2005, January). Current consumer behavior research in forest products. *Forest Products Journal*, 55(1):21–27.

54. Grandcolas, U., Rettie, R., and Marusenko, K. (2003), Web survey bias: Sample or mode effect? *Journal of Marketing Management,* 19:541–561.

55. See, for example, McDaniel, S. W., and Verille, P. (1987, January). Do topic differences affect survey nonresponse? *Journal of the Market Research Society,* 29(1):55–66; and Whitehead, J. C. (1991, Winter). Environmental interest group behavior and self-selection bias in contingent valuation mail surveys. *Growth & Change,* 22(1):10–21.

56. A large number of studies have sought to determine response rates for a wide variety of inducement strategies. See, for example, Fox, R. J., Crask, M., and Kim, J. (Winter). Mail questionnaires in survey research: a review of response inducement techniques. *Public Opinion Quarterly,* 52(4):467–491.

57. Yammarino, F., Skinner, S., and Childers, T. (1991). Understanding mail survey response behavior. *Public Opinion Quarterly,* 55:613–639.

58. See Conant, J., Smart, D., and Walker, B. (1990). Mail survey facilitation techniques: an assessment and proposal regarding reporting practices. *Journal of the Market Research Society,* 32(4):369–380; Kaplowitz, M. D., Lupi, F. (2004, Summer). Color photographs and mail survey response rates. *Journal of Public Opinion Research,* 16(2):199–206; and Trussell, N., Lavrakas, P. I. (2004, Fall). The influence of incremental increases in token cash incentives on mail survey response. *Public Opinion Quarterly,* 68(3):349–367.

59. Jassaume, R. A., Jr., and Yamada, Y. (1990, Summer). A comparison of the viability of mail surveys in Japan and the United States. *Public Opinion Quarterly,* 54(2):219–228.

60. Newby, R., Watson, J., Woodliff, D. (2003, Winter). SME survey methodology: response rates, data quality, and cost effectiveness. *Entrepreneurship:Theory & Practice,* 28(2):163–172.

61. Arnett, R. (1990, Second Quarter). Mail panel research in the 1990s. *Applied Marketing Research,* 30(2):8–10.

62. A recent industry study identified effectiveness, demand for a specific method, cost, speed of data collection, and available resources as the top five selection criteria when selecting a data-collection method. Source: Research Industry Trends: 2004 Report (2004, April). Prepared by Pioneer Marketing Research for Dialtek L. P. (available at **www.dialtek.com**).

63. For an example of a new data-collection method, see Wentz, L. (2004, April 12). Mindshare to read 20,000 media minds. *Advertising Age,* 75(15):1.

64. Philpott, G. (2005, February). Get the most from Net-based panel research, *Marketing News,* 39(2):58.

65. Gerlotto, C. (2003, November). Learning on the go: tips on getting international research right. *Quirk's Marketing Research Review,* 44.

66. Weiss, L. (2002, November). Research in Canada. *Quirk's Marketing Research Review,* 40.

67. Ilieva, J., Baron, S., Healey, N. M. (2002). Online surveys in marketing research: pros and cons, *International Journal of Market Research,* 44(3):361–376.

68. De Rada, V. D. (2005, Quarter 1), Response effects in a survey about consumer behaviour, *International Journal of Market Research,* 47(1):45–64.

Chapter 10

1. Chrzan, K., and Michaud, J. (2004, October). Response scales for customer satisfaction research. *Quirk's Marketing Research Review,* 18(9):50–55.

2. Sometimes open-ended questions are used to develop closed-ended questions that are used later. See, for example, Erffmeyer, R. C., and Johnson, D. A. (2001, Spring). An exploratory study of sales force automation practices: expectations and realities. *The Journal of Personal Selling & Sales Management,* 21(2):167–175.

3. Fox, S. (2001, May). Market research 101. *Pharmaceutical Executive,* Supplement: Successful Product Management: A Primer, 34.

4. Honomichl, J. (1994). Satisfaction measurement jump-starts survey research. *Marketing News,* 25:14–15.

5. See, for example, Leigh, J. H., and Martin, C. R., Jr. (1987). Don't know item nonresponse in a telephone survey: effects of question form and respondent characteristics. *Journal of Marketing Research,* 29(3):317–339.

6. See, for example, Yoon, S, and Kim, J. (2001, November/December). Is the Internet more effective than traditional media? Factors affecting the choice of media, *Journal of Advertising Research,* 41(6):53–60; Donthu, N. (2001, November/December). Does your web site measure up? *Marketing Management,* 10(4):29–32; and Finn, A., McFadyen, S., Hoskins, C., and Hupfer, M. (2001, Fall). Quantifying the sources of value of a public service. *Journal of Public Policy & Marketing,* 20(2):225–239.

7. See, for example, Wellner, A. S. (2002, February) The female persuasion. *American Demographics,* 24(2):24–29; Wasserman, T. (2002, January 7). Color me bad. *Brandweek,* 43(1):2; and Wilke, M., and Applebaum, M. (2001, November 5). Peering out of the closet. *Brandweek,* 42(41):26–32.

8. Statements are taken from Wells, W. D., and Tigert, D. J. (1971). Activities, interests, and opinions. *Journal of the Advertising Research,* reported in Kassarjain, H. H., and Robertson, T. S. *Perspectives in Consumer Behavior* (Glenview, IL: Scott Foresman, 1973), 175–176.

9. Another way to avoid the halo effect is to have subjects rate each stimulus on the same attribute and then move to the next attribute. See Wu, B. T. W., and Petroshius, S. (1987).The halo effect in store image management. *Journal of the Academy of Marketing Science,* 15(1):44–51.

10. The halo effect is real and used by companies to good advantage. See, for example, Moukheiber, Z., and Langreth, R. (2001, December 10).The halo effect, *Forbes,* 168(15):66; and Anonymous (2002, March 11). Sites seeking advertising (the paid kind). *Advertising Age,* 73(10):38.

11. Garg, R. K. (1996, July). The Influence of positive and negative wording and issue involvement on responses to Likert scales in marketing research. *Journal of the Marketing Research Society,* 38(3):235–246.

12. Yu, J. H., Albaum, G., and Swenson, M. (2003). Is a central tendency error inherent in the use of semantic differential scales in different cultures? *International Journal of Market Research,* 45(2):213–228.

13. Scale development requires rigorous research. See, for example, Churchill, G. A. (1979, February). A paradigm for developing better measures of marketing constructs. *Journal of Marketing Research,*

16:64–73, for method; or Ram, S., and Jung, H. S. (1990). The conceptualization and measurement of product usage. *Journal of the Academy of Marketing Science*, 18(1):67–76, for an example.

14. See, for example, Bishop, G. F. (1985, Summer). Experiments with the middle response alternative in survey questions. *Public Opinion Quarterly*, 51:220–232; and Schertizer, C. B., and Kernan, J. B. (1985, October). More on the robustness of response scales. *Journal of the Marketing Research Society*, 27:262–282.

15. See also Duncan, O. D., and Stenbeck, M. (1988, Winter). No opinion or not sure? *Public Opinion Quarterly*, 52:513–525; and Durand, R. M., and Lambert, Z. V. (1988, March). Don't know responses in survey: analyses and interpretational consequences. *Journal of Business Research*, 16:533–543.

16. Semon, T. T. (2001, October 8). Symmetry shouldn't be goal for scales. *Marketing News*, 35(21):9.

17. Elms. P. (2000, April). Using decision criteria anchors to measure importance among Hispanics. *Quirk's Marketing Research Review*, 15(4):44–51.

18. Ashley, D. (2003, February). The questionnaire that launched a thousand responses. *Quirk's Marketing Research Review*. Electronic archive, **www.quirks.com**, May 1, 2005.

19. Grapentine, T. (2003, Winter). Scales: still problematic 10 years later. *Marketing Research*, 15(4):45–46; and Grapentine, T. (2003, Fall). Problematic scales. *Marketing Research*, 15(3):16–19.

20. Developed from Hiscock, J. (2002, February 14). Most trusted brands 2002. *Marketing*, 20–21.

21. Devlin, S. J., Dong, H. K., Brown, M. (2003, Fall). Selecting a scale for measuring quality, *Marketing Research*, 15(3):13–16.

22. Wittink, D. R., Bayer, L. R. (2003, Fall). The measurement imperative. *Marketing Research*, 15(3):19–23.

23. Schmalensee, D. H. (Fall, 2003). The "perfect" scale. *Marketing Research*, 15(3):23–25; and Agarwal, S. (2003, Fall). The art of scale development. *Marketing Research*, 15(3):10–12.

24. For example, bogus recall was found to be negatively related to education, income, and age, but positively related to "yea-saying" and attitude toward a slogan. See Glassman, G., and Ford, J. B. (1988, Fall). "An empirical investigation of bogus recall." *Journal of the Academy of Marketing Science*, 16(3, 4):38–41; Singh, R. (1991). "Reliability and validity of survey research in marketing: the state of the art." In: Robert L. King (Ed.). *Marketing: Toward the twenty-first century*. Proceedings of the Southern Marketing Association, 210–213; Pressley, M. M., Strutton, H. D., and Dunn, M. G. (1991). Demographic sample reliability among selected telephone sampling replacement techniques. In: Robert L. King (Ed.). *Marketing: Toward the twenty-first century*. Proceedings of the Southern Marketing Association, 214–219; Babin, B. J., Darden, W. R., and Griffin, M. (1992). A note on demand artifacts in marketing research." In: Robert L. King (Ed.). *Marketing: Perspectives for the 1990s*. Proceedings of the Southern Marketing Association, 227–230; Dunipace, R. A., Mix, R. A., and Poole, R. R. Overcoming the failure to replicate research in marketing: a chaotic explanation." In: Tom K. Massey Jr. (Ed.). *Marketing: Satisfying a Diverse Customerplace*. Proceedings of the Southern Marketing Association, 194–197; Malawian, K. P., and Butler, D. D. (1994). The semantic differential: is it being misused in marketing research? In: Ravi Achrol and Andrew Mitchell (Eds.). *Enhancing Knowledge Development in Marketing*. A.M.A. Educators' Conference Proceedings, 19.

25. Statistical analysis can sometimes be used to assist in estabishing face validity. See, for example, Wolburg, J. M., and Pokrywczynski, J. (2002, September/October). A psychographic analysis of Generation Y college students. *Journal of Advertising Research*, 41(5):33–52.

26. For an example, see Russell, C., Norman, A., and Heckler, S. (2004, June). The consumption of television programming: development and validation of the connectedness scale. *Journal of Consumer Research*, 31(1):150–161.

Chapter 11

1. This example was provided by Michelle McCann of WebSurveyor.

2. Carroll, S. (1994). Questionnaire design affects response rate. *Marketing News*, 28:H25; and Sancher, M. E. (1992). Effects of questionnaire design on the quality of survey data. *Public Opinion Quarterly*, 56:206–217.

3. For more comprehensive coverage of this topic, see Baker, M. J. (2003, Summer). Data collection—questionnaire design. *Marketing Review*, 3(3):343–370.

4. Babble, E. (1990). *Survey research methods*, 2nd ed. Belmont, CA: Wadsworth, 131–132.

5. Hunt, S. D., Sparkman, R. D., and Wilcox, J. (1982, May). The pretest in survey research: issues and preliminary findings. *Journal of Marketing Research*, 26(4):269–273.

6. Dillman, D. A. (1978). *Mail telephone surveys: The total design method.* New York: Wiley.

7. Loftus, E., and Zanni, G. (1975). Eyewitness testimony: the influence of the wording of a question. *Bulletin of the Psychonomic Society*, 5:86–88.

8. Other marketing researchers advocate question focus. See Baker, M. J. (2003, Summer). Data collection—questionnaire design. *Marketing Review*, 3(3):343–370.

9. Webb, J. (2000, Winter). Questionnaires and their design. *Marketing Review*, 1(2):197–218.

10. *Ibid.*

11. Question clarity must be achieved for respondents of different education levels, ages, socioeconomic strata, and even intelligence: Noelle-Neumann, E. (1970, Summer). Wanted: rules for wording structured questionnaires. *Public Opinion Quarterly*, 34(2):191–201.

12. Webb, J. (2000, Winter). Questionnaires and their design. *Marketing Review*, 1(2):197–218.

13. For memory questions, it is advisable to have respondents recontruct specific events. See, for example, Cook, W A. (1987, February–March). Telescoping and memory's other tricks. *Journal of Advertising Research*, 27(1):RC5–RC8.

14. Baker, M. (2003, Summer), Data collection—Questionnaire Design, *Marketing Review*, 3(3):343–370.

15. Connell, S. (2002, Winter). Travel broadens the mind: the case for international research. *International Journal of Marketing Research*, 44(1):97–108.

16. Sinickas, A. (2005, December/January). Cultural differences and research. *Strategic Communication Management*, 9(1):12.

17. Baker, M. (2003, Summer), Data collection—Questionnaire Design, *Marketing Review*, 3(3):343–370.

18. Peterson, R. A. (2000). Constructing effective questionnaires, 58.

19. Webb, J. (2000, Winter). Questionnaires and their design. *Marketing Review*, 1(2):197–218.

20. Baker, M. (2003, Summer). Data collection—Questionnaire design, *Marketing Review*, 3(3):343–370.

21. Webb, J. (2000, Winter). Questionnaires and their design. *Marketing Review*, 1(2):197–218.

22. Patten, M. (2001). Questionnaire research. Los Angeles: Pyrczak Publishing, 9.

23. There is some evidence that mention of confidentiality has a negative effect on response rates, so the researcher should consider not mentioning it in the introduction even if confidentiality is in place. See Brennan, M., Benson, S., Kearns, Z. (2005). The effect of introductions on telephone survey participation rates. *International Journal of Market Research*, 47(1):65–74.

24. Screens can be used to quickly identify respondents who will not answer honestly. See Waters, K. M. (1991, Spring–Summer). Designing screening questionnaires to minimize dishonest answers. *Applied Marketing Research*, 31(1):51–53.

25. Glassman, N. A., Glassman, M. (1998, Fall). Screening questions. *Marketing Research*, 10(3):26–31.

26. The Marketing Research Association offers recommendations and model introduction, closing, and validation scripts on its Web site (**http://cmor.org/resp_coop_tools.htm**).

27. For recommended guidelines for introductions in "b-to-b" surveys, see Durkee, A. (2005, March). First impressions are everything in b-to-b telephone surveys. *Quirk's Marketing Research Review*, 19(3):30–32.

28. Smith, R., Olah, D., Hansen, B., Cumbo, D. (2003, November/December). The effect of questionnaire length on participant response rate: a case study in the U.S. cabinet industry. *Forest Products Journal*, 53(11/12):33–36.

29. Webb, J. (2000, Winter). Questionnaires and their design. *Marketing Review*, 1(2):197–218.

30. Bethlehem, J. (1999/2000, Winter). The routing structure of questionnaires, *International Journal of Market Research*, 42(1):95–110.

31. Baker, M. (2003, Summer). Data collection—Questionnaire Design, *Marketing Review*, 3(3):343–370.

32. At least one group-administered survey found that question sequence had no effect on cooperation rate. See: Roose, H., De Lange, D., Agneessens, F., and Waege, H. (2002, May). Theatre audience on stage: three experiments analysing the effects of survey design features on survey response in audience research. *Marketing Bulletin*, 13:1–10.

33. Based on Sudman, S., and Bradhurn, N. (1982). *Asking Questions*. San Francisco: Jossey-Bass, 219–221.

34. Webb, J. (2000, Winter), Questionnaires and their design. *Marketing Review*, 1(2):197–218.

35. Patten, M. (2001). *Questionnaire research* , p. 19.

36. Blunch, N. J. (1984, November). Position bias in multiple choice questions. *Journal of Marketing Research*, 21:216–220; Welch, J. L., and Swift, C. O. (1992, Summer). Question order effects in taste testing of beverages. *Journal of Academy of Marketing Science* , 265–268; Bickatt, B. A. (1993, February). Carryover and backfire effects in marketing research. *Journal of Marketing Research*, 52–62.

37. Dillman, D. A., Sinclair, M. D., and Clark, J. R. (1993). Effects of questionnaire length, respondent-friendly design, and a difficult question on response rates for occupant-addressed census mail surveys. *Public Opinion Quarterly*, 57:289–304.

38. Question order may also affect responses. See, for example, Ayidiya, S. A., and McClendon, M. J. (1990, Summer). Response effects in mail surveys. *Public Opinion Quarterly*, 54(2):229–247.

39. Carroll, S. (1994). Questionnaire design affects response rate. *Marketing News*, 25(14):23.

40. Highly sophisticated questionnaire design systems have a great many question formats and types in their libraries, and they sometimes have algorithms built into them to arrange the questions into a logical format. See Jenkins, S., and Solomonides, T. (1999/2000, Winter). Automating questionnaire design and construction. *International Journal of Market Research*, 42(1):79–95.

41. Smith, L. (2003, December), Proven ways to generate reliable online survey results. *Direct Marketing*, 1–7.

42. At least one author says that not to pretest is foolhardy: Webb, J. (2000, Winter). Questionnaires and their design. *Marketing Review*, 1(2):197–218.

43. Some authors refer to "pretesting" as "piloting" the questionnaire, meaning "pilot testing" the questionnaire. See: Baker, M. (2003, Summer). Data collection—Questionnaire Design. *Marketing Review*, 3(3):343–370.

44. Normally pretests are done individually, but a focus group could be used. See Long, S. A. (1991, May 27). Pretesting questionnaires minimizes measurement error. *Marketing News*, 25(11):12.

45. For a detailed description of the goals and procedures used in preteing, see Czaja, R. (1998, May), Questionnaire pretesting comes of age, *Marketing Bulletin*, 9:52–64.

46. For a comprehensive article on pretesting, see Presser, S., Couper, M. P., Lessler, J. T., Martin, E., Martin, J., Rothgeb, J. M., and Singer, E. (2004, Spring). Methods for testing and evaluating survey questions. *Public Opinion Quarterly*, 68(1):109–130.

Chapter 12

1. Frey, S., Schegg, R., and Murphy, J. (2003, March), E-mail customer service in the Swiss hotel industry. *Tourism & Hospitality Research*, 4(3):197–212.

2. Wyner, G. A. (2001, Fall). Representation, randomization, and realism. *Marketing Research*, 13(3):4–5.

3. Garland, S. (1990, September 19). Money, power and numbers: A firestorm over the census. *Business Week*, 45.

4. Sample frame error is especially a concern in business samples. See, for example, Macfarlene, P. (2002). Structuring and measuring the size of business markets. *International Journal of Market Research*, 44(1):7–30.

5. See, for example, Stephen, E. H., and Soldo, B. J. (1990, April). How to judge the quality of a survey. *American Demographics*, 12(4):42–43.

6. Bradley, N. (1999, October). Sampling for Internet surveys. An examination of respondent selection for internet research. *Journal of the Market Research Society*, 41(4):387.

7. The Excel cell entry is =ROUND(RAND()*30,1) meaning a random number from 0 to .9999 times 30, rounded to no decimal, generating random numbers from 0 to 30.

8. Foreman, J., and Collins, M. (1991, July). The viability of random digit dialing in the UK. *Journal of the Market Research*

Society, 33(3):219–227; Hekmat, F., and Segal, M. (1984). Random digit dialing: some additional empirical observations. In: David M. Klein and Allen E. Smith (Eds.). *Marketing Comes of Age.* Proceedings of the Southern Marketing Association, 176–180.

9. A recent change in the British telephone system has greatly increased the ability of RDD to access a representative sample. See: Nicolaas, G., and Lynn, P. (2002, August). Random-digit dialing in the UK: viability revisited, *Journal of the Royal Statistical Society:* Series A (Statistics in Society), 165(2):297–316.

10. Random digit dialing is used by the major Web traffic monitoring companies. See Fatth, H. (2000, November 13). The metrics system, *Adweek,* 41(46):98–102.

11. Tucker, C., Lepkowski, J. M., and Piekarski, L. (2002). The current efficiency of list-assisted telephone sampling designs, *Public Opinion Quarterly,* 66(3):321–338.

12. See also Sudman, S. (1985, February). Efficient screening methods for the sampling of geographically clustered special populations. *Journal of Marketing Research,* 22:20–29.

13. Cronish, P. (1989, January). Geodemographic sampling in readership surveys. *Journal of the Market Research Society,* 31(1):45–51.

14. For a somewhat more technical description of cluster sampling, see Carlin, J. B., and Hocking, J. (1999, October). Design of cross-sectional surveys using cluster sampling: An overview with Australian case studies. *Australian and New Zealand Journal of Public Health,* 23(5):546–551.

15. Thomas, J. S., Reinartz, W., and Kumar, V. (2004, July/August), Getting the most out of all your customers. *Harvard Business Review,* 82(7/8):116–124.

16. Academic marketing researchers often use convenience samples of college students. See Peterson, R. A. (2001, December). On the use of college students in social science research: insights from a second-order meta-analysis. *Journal of Consumer Research,* 28(3):450–461.

17. Wyner, G. A. (2001, Fall). Representation, randomization, and realism. *Marketing Research,* 13(3):4–5.

18. A variation of the snowball sample is found in Eaton, J., and Struthers, C. W. (2002, August), Using the Internet for organizational research: a study of cynicism in the workplace. *CyberPsychology & Behavior,* 5(4):305–313, where university students were required to return surveys completed by family, friends, or coworkers.

19. For an application of referral sampling, see Moriarity, R. T., Jr., and Spekman, R. E. (1984, May). An empirical investigation of the information sources used during the industrial buying process. *Journal of Marketing Research,* 21:137–147.

20. Tinsley, H. E. A., Tinsley, D. J., and Croskeys, C. E. (2002, April), Park usage, social milieu, and psychosocial benefits of park use reported by older urban park users from four ethnic groups. *Leisure Sciences,* 24(2):199–218.

21. Chan, K. (2000, March). Hong Kong children's understanding of television advertising, *Journal of Marketing Communications,* 6(1):37–52.

22. Personal communication with Jerry W. Thomas, President/CEO, Decision Analyst, Inc.

23. For a historical perspective and prediction about online sampling, see Sudman, S., and Blair, E. (1999, Spring). Sampling in the twenty-first century. *Academy of Marketing Science,* 27(2):269–277.

24. Internet surveys can access hard-to-reach groups. See Anonymous (1999, Summer). Pro and con: Internet interviewing. *Marketing Research,* 11(2):33–36.

25. Sudhaman, A. (2005, February 11). TNS creates first regional online panel with launch in HK. *Media Asia,* 4.

26. See as an example, Dahlen, M. (2001, July/August). Banner advertisements through a new lens. *Journal of Advertising Research,* 41(4):23–30.

27. For a comparison of online sampling to telephone sampling, see Couper, M. P. (2000, Winter). Web surveys: a review of issues and approaches. *Public Opinion Quarterly,* 64(4):464–494.

28. For a comparison on invitation online sample to a RDD sample for a low incidence population, see Mathy, R. M., Schillace, M., Coleman, S. M., and Berquist, B. E. (2002, June), Methodological rigor with internet samples: new ways to reach underrepresented populations. *CyberPsychology & Behavior,* 5(3):253–266.

29. Provided by DMS, by permission.

30. For recommendations about online panel management, see Miles, L. (2004, June 16). Online on tap. *Marketing,* 39–40.

31. Grossnickle, J., and Raskin, O. (2001, Summer). What's ahead on the Internet. *Marketing Research,* 13(2):8–13.

32. Miller, T. W. (2001, Summer). Can we trust the data of online research? *Marketing Research,* 13(2):26–32.

33. Lewis, J. (2004, January). Painting a truer picture. *Quirk's Marketing Research Review.* Electronic archive, **www.quirks.com**.

34. Personal communication from David Stanton, Director, Marketing Communications, Knowledge Networks.

35. Sample plans are useful wherever someone desires to draw a representative group from a population. For an auditing example, see Martin, J. (2004, August). Sampling made simple. *The Internal Auditor,* 61(4):21–23.

36. Rothman, J., and Mitchell, D. (1989, October). Statisticians can be creative too. *Journal of the Market Research Society,* 31(4):456–466.

37. The need for substitutions can be affected by the respondent selection procedure. See, for example, Hagen, D. E., and Collier, C. M. (1982, Winter). Must respondent selection procedures for telephone surveys be so invasive? *Public Opinion Quarterly,* 47:547–556.

38. Cooperation is known to vary across demographic groups. See Guggenheim, B. (1989, February/March). All research is not created equal! *Journal of Advertising Research,* 29(1):RC7–RC11.

Chapter 13

1. Lenth, R. (2001, August), some practical guidelines for effective sample size determination, *The American Statistician,* 55(3):187–193; Williams, G. (1999, April). What size sample do I need? *Australian and New Zealand Journal of Public Health,* 23(2):215–217; and Cesana, B. M., Reina, G., and Marubini, E. (2001, November). Sample size for testing a proportion in clinical trials: a "two-step" procedure combining power and confidence interval expected width. *The American Statistician,* 55(4):288–292.

2. Our chapter simplifies a complex area. See, for example, Williams, G. (1999, April). What size sample do I need? *Australian and New Zealand Journal of Public Health,* 21(2):215–217.

3. This chapter pertains to quantitative marketing research samples. For qualitative research situations, see, for example, Christy, R., and Wood, M. (1999). Researching possibilities in marketing. *Qualitative Market Research*, 2(3):189–196.

4. Frendberg, N. (1992, June), Increasing survey accuracy. *Quirk's Marketing Research Review*, electronic archive: **www.quirks.com**.

5. One author has simply said, "sampling error has the unique distinction of being a measurable source of error in survey research . . . ", Frendberg, N. (1992, June). Increasing survey accuracy. *Quirk's Marketing Research Review*, electronic archive: **www.quirks.com**.

6. Xu, G. (1999, June), Estimating sample size for a descriptive study in quantitative research, *Quirk's Marketing Research Review*, electronic archive: **www.quirks.com**.

7. For a similar, but slightly different treatment, see Sangren, S. (1999, January), A simple solution to nagging questions about survey, sample size and validity, *Quirk's Marketing Research Review*, electronic archive: **www.quirks.com**.

8. See Shiffler, R. E., and Adams, A. J. (1987, August). A correction for biasing effects of pilot sample size on sample size determination. *Journal of Marketing Research*, 24(3):319–321. For more information see, Lenth. R. V. (2001, August). Some practical guidelines for effective sample size determination. *The American Statistician*, 55(3):187–193.

9. For a different formula that uses the difference between two means, see Minchow, D. (2000, June). How large did you say the sample has to be? *Quirk's Marketing Research Review*, electronic archive: **www.quirks.com**

10. For a caution on this approach, see Browne, R. H. (2001, November). Using the sample range as a basis for calculating sample size in power calculations. *The American Statistician*, 55(4):293–298.

11. There are, of course, other factors that affect the final sample size, see for example, Sangren, S. (2000, April). Survey and sampling in an imperfect world, *Quirk's Marketing Research Review*, electronic archive: **www.quirks.com**.

12. For information on Survey Samping, Inc. and SurveySpot, visit their Web sites at **www.surveysampling.com** and **www.surveyspot.com**, respectively.

13. See, for example, Cesana, B. M., Reina, G., and Marubini, E. (2001, November). Sample size for testing a proportion in clinical trials: a "two-step" procedure combining power and confidence interval expected width. *The American Statistician*, 55(4):288–192.

14. To see how simple cross tabulations can increase the required sample size, see Sangren, S. (2000, April). Survey and sampling in an imperfect world, *Quirk's Marketing Research Review*, electronic archive: **www.quirks.com**.

15. Kupper, L. L., Hafner, K. B. (1989, May). How appropriate are popular sample size formulas? *American Statistician*, 43(2): 101–195.

16. Barlet, J., Kotrlik, J., and Higgins, C. (2001, Spring), Organizational research: determining appropriate sample size in survey research. *Information Technology, Learning, and Performance Journal*, 19(1):43–50.

17. Hunter, J. E. (2001, June). The desperate need for replications. *Journal of Consumer Research*, 28(1):149–158.

18. A different statistical analysis determination of sample size is through use of estimated effect sizes. See, for example, Semon, T. T. (1994). Save a few bucks on sample size, risk millions in opportunity cost. *Marketing News*, 28(1):19.

19. Ball, J. (2004, February 1). A numbers game: simple rules shape proper sample size. *Marketing News* (Special Report), 38.

20. See, for example, Hall, T. W., Herron, T. L., Pierce, B. J, and Witt, T. J. (2001, March). The effectiveness of increasing sample size to mitigate the influence of population characteristics in haphazard sampling. *Auditing*, 20(1):169–185.

Chapter 14

1. This introductory vignette is based on: de Leeuw, E. D., and Hox, J. J. (2004, Winter). I am not selling anything: 29 experiments in telephone introductions. *International Journal of Public Opinion Research*, 16(4):464–473.

2. In Chapter 13 you learned to control sampling error by using a sample-size formula that allowed you to determine the sample size required in order to control for the amount of sample error (e) you are willing to accept.

3. For a breakdown of the types of nonsampling errors encountered in business-to-business marketing research studies, see Lilien, G., Brown, R., and Searls, K. (1991, January 7). Cut errors, improve estimates to bridge biz-to-biz info gap. *Marketing News*, 25(1):20–22.

4. Interviewer errors have been around for a very long time. See Snead, R. (1942). Problems of field interviewers. *Journal of Marketing*, 7(2):139–145.

5. Intentional errors are especially likely when data are supplied by competitors. See Croft, R. (1992). How to minimize the problem of untruthful response. *Business Marketing Digest*, 17(3):17–23.

6. To better understand this area, see Barker, R. A. (1987, July). A demographic profile of marketing research interviewers. *Journal of the Market Research Society*, 29:279–292.

7. For some interesting theories on interviewer cheating, see: Harrison, D. E., Krauss, S. I (2002, October). Interviewer cheating: implications for research on entrepreneurship in Africa. *Journal of Developmental Entrepreneurship*, 7(3):319–330.

8. Peterson, B. (1994, Fall). Insight into consumer cooperation, *Marketing Research*, 6(4):52–53.

9. These problems are international in scope. See Kreitzman, L. (1990, February 22). Market research: virgins and groupies. *Marketing*, 35–38.

10. The items are based on items developed and the research reported by: Chapman, K. J., Davis, R., Toy, D., and Wright, L. (2004, December). Academic integrity in the business school environment: I'll get by with a little help from my friends. *Journal of Marketing Education*, 26(3):236–249.

11. Collins, M. (1997, January). Interviewer variability: a review of the problem, *Journal of the Market Research Society*, 39(1):67–84.

12. Oksenberg, L., Coleman, L., and Cannell, C. F. (1986, Spring). Interviewers' voices and refusal rates in telephone surveys. *Public Opinion Quarterly*, 50(1):97–111.

13. Pol, L. G., and Ponzurick, T. G. (1989, Spring). Gender of interviewer/gender of respondent bias in telephone surveys. *Applied Marketing Research*, 29(2):9–13.

14. Based on: Muller, G. D., and Miller, J. (1996, Spring). Interviewers make the difference. *Marketing Research*, 8(1):8–9.

15. Sanchez, M. E. (1992, Summer). Effects of questionnaire design on the quality of survey data. *Public Opinion Quarterly*, 56(2):206–217.

16. Kiecker, P., and Nelson, J. E. (1996, April). Do interviewers follow telephone survey instructions? *Journal of the Market Research Society*, 38(2):161–173.

17. Loosveldt, G., Carton, A., and Billiet, J. (2004). Assessment of survey data quality: a pragmatic approach focused on interviewer tasks. *International Journal of Market Research*, 46(1):65–82.

18. Roster, C.A., Rogers, R. D., Albaum, G., and Klein, D. (2004). A comparison of response characteristics from web and telephone surveys. *International Journal of Market Research*, 46(3):359–373.

19. Honomichl, J. (1991, June 24). Legislation threatens research by phone. *Marketing News*, 25(13):4; Webster, C. (1991). Consumers' attitudes toward data collection methods, In: R. L. King (Ed.). *Marketing: Toward the Twenty-First Century*. Proceedings of the Southern Marketing Association, 220–224.

20. Jarvis, S. (2002, February 4). CMOR finds survey refusal rate still rising. *Marketing News*, 36(3):4.

21. See, for example, Honomichl, J. (1991, May 27). Making a point—again—for an "industry identifier." *Marketing News*, 25(11): H35; or Spethmann, B. (1991, June 10). Cautious consumers have surveyors wary. *Advertising Age*, 62(24):34.

22. Arnett, R. (1990). Mail panel research in the 1990s. *Applied Marketing Research*, 30(2):8–10.

23. Schlossberg, H. (1991, January 7). Research's image better than many think. *Marketing News*, 25(1):24–25.

24. This item is based on: Lynn, P., and Clarke, P. (2002). Separating refusal bias and non-contact bias: evidence from UK national surveys. *The Statistician*, 51(3):319–333.

25. One author refers to responses to questions on a survey as "hearsay," which includes potential for misunderstanding: Semon, T. (2003). Settle for personal truth vs. facts in surveys. *Marketing News*, 37(2):17.

26. Of course, eliminating the interviewer entirely may be an option. See Horton, K. (1990, February). Disk-based surveys: new way to pick your brain. *Software Magazine*, 10(2):76–77.

27. For early articles on interviewers and supervision, see Clarkson, E. P. (1949, January). Some suggestions for field research supervisors, *Journal of Marketing*, 13(3):321–329; and Reed, V. D., Parker, K. G., and Vitriol, H. A. (1948, January). Selection, training, and supervision of field interviewers in marketing research. *Journal of Marketing*, 12(3):365–378.

28. For a book on interviewer error reduction, see Fowler, F., and Mangione, T. (1990). *Standardized Survey Interviewing: Minimizing Interviewer-Related Error*. Newburry Park, CA: Sage.

29. There is a move in the United Kingdom for interviewer certification. See Hemsley, S. (2000, August 17). Acting the part. *Marketing Week*, 23(28):37–40.

30. Tucker, C. (1983, Spring). Interviewer effects in telephone surveys. *Public Opinion Quarterly*, 47(1):84–95.

31. See: Childers, T., and Skinner, S. (1985, January). Theoretical and empirical issues in the identification survey respondents. *Journal of the Market Research Society*, 27:39–53; and Finlay, J. L., and Seyyet, F. J. (1988). The impact of sponsorship and respondent attitudes on response rate to telephone surveys: an exploratory investigation. In: D. L. Moore (Ed.). *Marketing:*

Forward Motion. Proceedings of the Atlantic Marketing Association, 715–721; Goldsmith, R. E. Spurious response error in a new product survey. In: J. Joseph Cronin Jr. and Melvin T. Stith, (Eds.). *Marketing: Meeting the Challenges of the 1990s*. Proceedings of the Southern Marketing Association (1987), 172–175; Downs, P. E., and Kerr, J. R. (1982). Recent evidence on the relationship between anonymity and response variables. In: J. H. Summey, B. J. Bergiel, and C. H. Anderson (Eds.). *A Spectrum of Contemporary Marketing Ideas*. Proceedings of the Southern Marketing Association, 258–264; Glisan, G., and Grimm, J. L. (1982). Improving response rates in an industrial setting: will traditional variables work?" In: J. H. Summey, B. J. Bergiel, and C. H. Anderson (Eds.). A spectrum of contemporary marketing ideas. Proceedings of the Southern Marketing Association, 265–268; Taylor, R. D., Beisel, J., and Blakney, V. (1984). The effect of advanced notification by mail of a forthcoming mail survey on the response rates, item omission rates, and response speed. In: D. M. Klein and A. E. Smith (Eds.). *Marketing Comes of Age*. Proceedings of the Southern Marketing Association, 184–187; Friedman, H. H. (1979, Spring). The effects of a monetary incentive and the ethnicity of the sponsor's signature on the rate and quality of response to a mall survey. *Journal of the Academy of Marketing Science*, 95–100; Goldstein, L., and Friedman, H. H. (1975, April). A case for double postcards in surveys. *Journal of Advertising Research*, 43–49; Hubbard, R., and Little, E. L. (1988, Fall). Cash prizes and mail response rates: a threshold analysis. *Journal of the Academy of Marketing Science*, 42–44; Childers, T. L., and Ferrell, O. C. (1979, August). Response rates and perceived questionnaire length in mail surveys. *Journal of Marketing Research*, 429–431; Childers, T. L., Pride, W. M., and Ferrell, O. C. (1980, August). A reassessment of the effects of appeals on response to mail surveys. *Journal of Marketing Research*, 365–370; Steele, T., Schwendig, W., and Kilpatrick, J. (1992, March/April). Duplicate responses to multiple survey mailings: a problem? *Journal of Advertising Research*, 26–33; Wilcox, J. B. (1977, November). The interaction of refusal and not-at-home sources of nonresponse bias. *Journal of Marketing Research*, 592–597.

32. An opposite view is expressed by Pruden and Vavra who believe it is important to identify participants and provide some sort of follow-up acknowledgment of their participation in the survey: Pruden, D. R., and Vavra, T. G. (2000, Summer), Customer research, not marketing research, *Marketing Research*, 12(2):14–19.

33. See, for example, Lynn, P. (2002, Autumn). The impact of incentives on response rates to personal interview surveys: role and perceptions of interviewers. *International Journal of Public Opinion Research*, 13(3):326–336.

34. A comparison on nonresponse errors under different incentives appears in Barsky, J. K., and Huxley, S. J. (1992, December). A customer-survey tool: using the "quality sample." *The Cornell Hotel and Restaurant Administration Quarterly*, 33(6):18–25.

35. Screening questionnaires can also be used. See Waters, K. M. (1991, Spring/Summer). Designing screening questionnaires to minimize dishonest answers. *Applied Marketing Research*, 31(1):51–53.

36. For examples, see Prete, D. D. (1991, September 2). Clients want more specific research—and faster. *Marketing News*, 25(18):18; Hawk, K. (1992, November 12). More marketers going online for decision support. *Marketing News*, 24(23):14;

Riche, M. F. (1990). Look before leaping. *American Demographics,* 12(2):18–20; or Wolfe, M. J. (1989, September 11). New way to use scanner data and demographics aids local marketers. *Marketing News,* 23(19):8–9.

37. Miller, T. W. (2001, September 24). Make the call: online results are mixed bag. *Marketing News,* 35(20):30–35.

38. Curtin, R., Presser, S., and Singer, E. (2005, Spring). Changes in telephone survey nonresponse over the past quarter century. *Public Opinion Quarterly,* 69(1):87–108.

39. Coleman, L. G. (1991, January 7). Researchers say nonresponse is single biggest problem. *Marketing News,* 25(1):32–33; and Landler, M. (1991, February 11). The "bloodbath" in market research. *Business Week,* 72:74.

40. Baim, J. (1991, June). Response rates: a multinational perspective. *Marketing & Research Today,* 19(2):114–119.

41. Vogt, C. A.; Stewart, S. I. (2001). Response problems in a vacation panel study. *Journal of Leisure Research,* 33(1):91–105.

42. Groves, R. M., Presser, S., and Dipko, S. (2004, Spring). The role of topic interest in survey participation decisions, *Public Opinion Quarterly,* 68(1):2–31.

43. Farrell, B., and Elken, T. (1994, August 29). Adjust five variables for better mail surveys. *Marketing News,* 20.

44. Tyagi, P. K. (1989, Summer). The effects of appeals, anonymity, and feedback on mail survey response patterns from salespeople. *Journal of the Academy of Marketing Science,* 17(3):235–241.

45. Anonymous (1993, August 16). The researchers' response: four industry leaders tell how to improve cooperation. *Marketing News,* A12.

46. Some authors use the term "unit nonresponse" to refer to item omissions. See, for example, Hudson, D., Seah, L.-H., Hite, D., and Haab, T. (2004). Telephone presurveys, self-selection, and non-response bias to mail and Internet surveys in economic research. *Applied Economics Letters,* 11(4):237–240.

47. Shoemaker, P. J., Eichholz, M., and Skewes, E. A. (2002, Summer). Item nonresponse: distinguishing between don't know and refuse, *International Journal of Public Opinion Research,* 14(2):193–201.

48. A different approach is to measure nonresponse and make adjustments with weights. See Colombo, R. (2000, January/April). A model for diagnosing and reducing nonresponse bias, *Journal of Advertising Research,* 40(1/2):85–93.

49. Monetary incentives have been used successfully with consumer and organizational respondents. See Jobber, D., Saunders, J., and Mitchell, V.-W. (2004, April). Prepaid monetary incentive effects on mail survey response. *Journal of Business Research,* 57(4):347–350.

50. For a comparison of response rates by mail versus fax, see Dickson, J. P., and MacLachlan, D. L. (1996, February). Fax surveys: return patterns and comparison with mail surveys. *Journal of Marketing Research,* 33(1):108–113.

51. Frankel, L. R. *On the Definition of Response Rates. A Special Task Force Report Published by the Council of American Survey Research Organizations,* Port Jefferson, NY.

52. There are more complex methods. See, for example, Bollinger, C. R., and H. D. Martin, (2001, April). Estimation with response error and nonresponse: food-stamp participation in the SIPP. *Journal of Business & Economic Statistics,* 19(2):129–141.

53. For more complex procedures see Armstrong, J. S., and Overton, T. S. (1977, August). Estimating nonresponse bias in mail surveys. *Journal of Marketing Research,* 14:396–402; Pearl, D. K., and Fairley, D. (1985, Winter). Testing for the potential of nonresponse bias in sample surveys. *Public Opinion Quarterly,* 49:553–560; or Sharlot, T. (1986, July). Weighting the survey results. *Journal of the Market Research Society,* 28:363–366.

54. For yea-saying and nay-saying, see Bachman, J. G., and O'Malley, P. M. (1985, Summer). Yea-saying, nay-saying, and going to extremes: black–white differences in response styles. *Public Opinion Quarterly,* 48:491–509; and Greenleaf, E. A. (1992, May). Improving rating scale measures by detecting and correcting bias components in some response styles. *Journal of Marketing Research,* 29(2):176–188.

Chapter 15

1. The information in the opening case is based on Dolliver, M. (2004). Many years in which to have many ailments. *Adweek* 45(46): 27.

2. It is important for the researcher and client to have a partnership during data analysis. See, for example, Fitxpatrick, M. (2001, August). Statistical analysis for direct marketers—in plain English. *Direct Marketing,* 64(4): 54–56.

3. For an alternative presentation, see Ehrnberg, A. (2001, Winter). Data, but no information. *Marketing Research,* 13(4): 36–39.

4. The use of descriptive statistics is sometimes called "data reduction," although some authors term any appropriate analysis that makes sense of data, "data reduction." See: Vondruska, Richard (1995, April), The fine art of data reduction, *Quirk's Marketing Research Review,* online archive www.quirks.com, May 9, 2005.

5. Some authors argue that central tendency measures are too sterile. See, for example, Pruden, D. R., and Vavra, T. G. (2000, Summer). Customer research, not marketing research. *Marketing Research,* 12(2): 14–19.

6. Shoham, A., Dalakas, V. (2003). Family consumer decision making in Israel: the role of teens and parents. *Journal of Consumer Marketing,* 20(3): p 238.

7. Gutsche, A. (2001, September 24). Visuals make the case. *Marketing News,* 35(20): 21–23.

8. This element is based on certain findings reported in: Brengman, M., Geuens, M., Weijters, B., Smith, S. M., Swinyard, W. R. (2005). Segmenting Internet shoppers based on their Web-usage-related lifestyle: a cross-cultural validation. *Journal of Business Research,* 58(1): 79.

Chapter 16

1. This case is for pedagogical purposes only.

2. The 95% level is standard in academic research and commonly adopted by practitioners; however, some authors prefer to use the "probability" or 1 minus the discovered significance level of a finding being true. See: Zucker, H. (1994). What is significance? *Quirk's Marketing Research Review,* electronic archive: **www.quirks.com**.

3. The confidence intervals were calculated by us based on information and percentages reported in Griffiths, M. D., Davies, M. N. O., and Chappell, D. (2004, August). Demographic factors and playing variables in online computer gaming, *CyberPsychology & Behavior,* 7(4):479–487.

4. It has been well documented that tests of statistical significance are often misused in the social sciences, including the field of marketing research. Critics note that researchers endow the tests with more capabilities than they actually have and rely on them as the sole approach for analyzing data (Sawyer & Peter, 1983). Other critics note that combining p values with α levels in the often used model $p \leq \alpha$ =significance, is inappropriate since the two concepts arise from incompatible philosophies (Hubbard & Bayarri, 2003). Users of statistical tests should be familiar with these arguments and other writings noting misinterpretations of statistical significance testing (Carver, 1978). See Sawyer, A. G., and Peter, J. P. (1983, May). The significance of statistical significance tests in marketing research. *Journal of Marketing Research*, 20:122–133; Hubbard, R., and Bayarri, M. J. (2003, August). Confusion over measures of evidence (p's) versus errors (α's) in classical statistical testing (with comments). *The American Statistician*, 57:171–182; and Carver, R. P. (1978, August). The case against statistical significance testing. *Harvard Educational Review*, 48:278–399.

5. Some disciplines, such as psychology and medicine, encourage their researchers to refrain from hypothesizing and to report confidence intervals instead. See: Fidler, F., Cumming, G., Burgman, M., and Thomason, N. (2004, November). Statistical reform in medicine, psychology and ecology. *Journal of Socio-Economics*, 33(5):615–630; or Fidler, F., Thomason, N., Cumming, G., Finch, S., and Leeman, J. (2004, February). Research article editors can lead researchers to confidence intervals, but can't make them think: statistical reform lessons from medicine. *Psychological Science*, 15(2):119–126.

Chapter 17

1. Thomas, A., and Pickering, G. (2002, August/December), Behavioural segmentation: a New Zealand wine market application. *Journal of Wine Research*, 14(2/3):127–138.

2. One author considers t tests (differences tests) to be one of the most important statistical procedures used by marketing researchers. See: Migliore, V. T. (1996). If you hate statistics. . . . *Quirk's Marketing Research Review*, electronic archive: **www.quirks.com**.

3. For a contrary view, see Mazur, L. (2000, June 8). The only truism in marketing is they don't exist.*Marketing*, 20.

4. Meaningful difference is sometimes called "practical significance." See Thompson, B. (2002, Winter)."Statistical," "practical," and "clinical": how many kinds of significance do counselors need to consider? *Journal of Counseling and Development*, 30(1):64–71.

5. For some cautions about differences tests, see Helgeson, N. (1999). The insignificance of significance testing. *Quirk's Marketing Research Review*, electronic archive: **www.quirks.com**.

6. Based on: Sun, T., Horn, M., and Merritt, D. (2004). Values and lifestyles of individualists and collectivists: a study on Chinese, Japanese, British and US consumers, *Journal of Consumer Marketing*, 21(5):318–334.

7. Das, T. K. (2005, January). How strong are the ethical preferences of senior business executives? *Journal of Business Ethics*, 56(1):69–80.

8. For an example of the use of paired-samples t tests, see Ryan, C., and Mo, X. (2001, December). Chinese visitors to New Zealand: demographics and perceptions. *Journal of Vacation Marketing*, 8(1):13–27.

9. Aamodt, M. (1999, Spring). Why are there five million types of statistics? *Public Personnel Management*, 28(1):157–160.

10. For elaboration, see Baldasare, P., and Mittel, V. (1994). The use, misuse and abuse of significance. *Quirk's Marketing Research Review*, electronic archive: **www.quirks.com**.

11. A more complicated approach is Bobko, P., Roth P. L., and Bobko, C. (2001, January). Correcting the effect size of d for range restriction and unreliability. *Organizational Research Methods*, 4(1):46–61.

12. For a criticism of the use of difference scores in consumer research, see Paul, J. P., Churchill, Jr. G. A., and Brown, T. J. (1993, March). Caution in the use of difference scores in consumer research. *Journal of Consumer Research*, 19(4):655–662.

13. Hellebusch, S. J. (2001, June 4). One chi-square beats two Z tests. *Marketing News*, 35(12):11, 13.

14. For illumination, see Burdick, R. K. (1983, August). Statement of hypotheses in the analysis of variance. *Journal of Marketing Research*, 20:320–324.

Chapter 18

1. James, W., McMellon, C. A., and Torres-Baumgarten, G. (2004, October). Dogs and cats rule: a new insight into segmentation. *Journal of Targeting, Measurement & Analysis for Marketing*, 13(1):70–77.

2. For elaboration and an example, see Semon, T. (1999, August). Use your brain when using a chi-square. *Marketing News*, 33(16):6.

3. It is not advisable to use cross-tabulations analysis with chi-square when there are cases of cell frequencies of less than five cases. See Migliore, V. (1998). Ten research industry secrets and how to handle them. *Quirk's Marketing Research Review*, electronic archive: **www.quirks.com**

4. For advice on when to use chi-square analysis, see Hellebush, S. J. (2001, June 4). One chi-square beats two Z tests. *Marketing News*, 35(12):11, 13.

5. An alternative view is that the researcher is testing multiple cases of percentage differences (analogous to multiple independent group means tests), in a cross-tabulation table, and use of the chi-square test compensates for type I error that reduces the confidence level. See Neal, W. (1989, March). The problem with multiple paired comparisons in crosstabs. *Marketing Research*, 1(1):52–54.

6. Some articles that use cross-tabulation analysis are: Burton, S., and Zinkhan, G. M. (1987, Fall). Changes in consumer choice: further investigation of similarity and attraction effects. *Psychology in Marketing*, 4:255–266; Bush, A. J., and Leigh, J. H. (1984, April/May). Advertising on cable versus traditional television networks. *Journal of Advertising Research*, 24:33–38; and Langrehr, F. W. (1985, Summer). Consumer images of two types of competing financial institutions. *Journal of the Academy of Marketing Science*, 13:248–264.

7. Maynard, M. L., and Taylor, C. R. (1999, Spring). Girlish images across cultures: analyzing Japanese versus U.S. *Seventeen* magazine ads. *Journal of Advertising*, 28(1):39–48.

8. Lokken, S. L., Cross. G. W., Halbert, L. K., Lindsey, G., Derby, C., and Stanford, C. (2003, March). Comparing online and non-online shoppers. *Journal of Consumer Studies*, 27(2):126–133.

9. Garee, M. (1997, September). Statistics don't lie if you know what they're really saying. *Marketing News*, 31(9):11.

10. Correlation is sensitive to the number of scale points, especially in instances when variables have less than 10 scale points. See Martin, W. (1878, May). Effects of scaling on the correlation coefficient: additional considerations. *Journal of Marketing Research*, 15(2):304–308.

11. For a more advanced treatment of scatter diagrams, see Goddard, B. L. (2000, April). The power of computer graphics for comparative analysis. *The Appraisal Journal*, 68(2):134–141.

12. Refer, also, to Babakus, E., and Ferguson, C. E., Jr. (1988, Spring). On choosing the appropriate measure of association when analyzing rating scale data. *Journal of the Academy of Marketing Science*, 16:95–102.

Chapter 19

1. Brengman, M., Geuens, M., Weijters, B., Smith, S., and Swinyard, W. (2005, January). Segmenting Internet shoppers based on their Web-usage-related life style: a cross-cultural validation. *Journal of Business Research*, 58(1):79–88.

2. Residual analysis can take many forms. See, for example, Dempster, A. P., and Gasko-Green, M. (1981). New tools for residual analysis. *Annals of Statistics*, 9:945–959.

3. See Melnick, E. L., and Shoaf, F. R. (1977, June). Regression equals analysis of variance. *Journal of Advertising Research*, 17:27–31.

4. We admit that our description of regression is introductory. Two books that expand our description are Lewis-Beck, M. S. (1980). *Applied Regression: An Introduction*. Newbury Park, CA: Sage; and Schroeder, L. D., Sjoffquist, D. L., and Stephan, P. E. (1986). *Understanding Regression Analysis: An Introductory Guide*, Newbury Park, CA: Sage.

5. There are, of course, other and more acceptable ways of identifying outliers. However, our approach relates to the graphical presentation we have used for visualizing linear relationships existing in correlations and regression. At best, our approach simply introduces students to outlier analysis and helps them identify the most obvious cases.

6. Semon, T. (1999, June 23). Outlier problem has no practical solution. *Marketing News*, 31(16):2.

7. A well-known marketing academic has recommended graphing to researchers: Zinkhan, G. (1993). Statistical inference in advertising research, *Journal of Advertising*, 22(3):1.

8. For more sophisticated handling of outliers, see Clark, T. (1989, June). Managing outliers: qualitative issues in the handling of extreme observations in marketing research. *Marketing Research*, 2(2):31–48.

9. Volkema, R. (2004, January). Demographic, cultural, and economic predictors of perceived ethicality of negotiation behavior: a nine-country analysis. *Journal of Business Research*, 57(1):69–78.

10. For more information, see, for example, Grapentine, T. (1997, Fall). Managing multicollinearity. *Marketing Research*, 9(3):11–21, and Mason, R. L., Gunst, R. F., and Webster, J. T.

(1986). Regression analysis and problems of multicollinearity in marketing models: diagnostics and remedial measures. *International Journal of Research in Marketing*, 3(3):181–205.

11. For a graphical presentation, see Stine, R. (1995, February). Graphical interpretation of variance inflation factors. *The American Statistician*, 49(1):53–56.

12. For alternatives see Wang, G. (1996, Spring). How to handle multicollinearity in regression modeling. *The Journal of Business Forecasting*, 14(4):23–27.

13. Based on Gronholdt, L. and Nartnesen, A. (2005). Analysing customer satisfaction data: a comparison of regression and artificial neural networks. *International Journal of Marketing Research*, 24(2):121–130.

14. Our description pertains to "forward" stepwise regression. We admit that this is a simplification of stepwise multiple regression.

15. See, for example, Kennedy, P. (2005, Winter). Oh no! I got the wrong sign! What should I do? *Journal of Economic Education*, 36(1):77–92.

16. For readable treatments of problems encountered in multiple regression applied to marketing research, see Mullet, G. (1994, October). Regression, regression, *Quirk's Marketing Research Review*, electronic archive: **www.quirks.com**: Mullet, G. (1998, June). Have you ever wondered. . . . , *Quirk's Marketing Research Review*, electronic archive; and Mullet, G. (2003, February). Data abuse. *Quirk's Marketing Research Review*, electronic archive.

17. Regression analysis is commonly used in academic marketing research. Here are some examples: Callahan, F. X. (1982, April/May). Advertising and profits 1969–1978. *Journal of Advertising Research*, 22:17–22; Dubinsky, A. J., and Levy, M. (1989, Summer). Influence of organizational fairness on work outcomes of retail salespeople. *Journal of Retailing*, 65:221–252; Frieden, J. B., and Downs, P. E. (1986, Fall). Testing the social involvement model in an energy conservation context. *Journal of the Academy of Marketing Science*, 14:13–20; and Tellis, G. J., and Fornell, C. (1988, February). The relationship between advertising and product quality over the product life cycle: a contingency theory. *Journal of Marketing Research*, 25:64–71. For an alternative to regression analysis, see Quaintance, B. S., and Franke, G. R. (1991). Neural networks for marketing research. In Robert L. King (ed.). *Marketing: Toward the Twenty-First Century*. Proceedings of the Southern Marketing Association, 230–235.

Chapter 20

1. We wish to acknowledge that this chapter was originally written by M. Howard, Ph.D., and H. Donofrio, Ph.D., assisted us in updating the chapter. Both Dr. Howard and Dr. Donofrio are experts in business communications.

2. Burns, A., and Bush, R. (2005). *Marketing Research: Online Research Applications*, 4th ed. Upper Saddle River, NJ: Prentice Hall, 580.

3. Deshpande, R., and Zaltman, G. (February 1982). Factors affecting the use of market research information: a path analysis. *Journal of Marketing Research*, 19:14–31.

4. Deshpande, R., and Zaltman, G. (February 1984). A comparison of factors affecting researcher and manager

perceptions of market research use. *Journal of Marketing Research*, 21:32–38.

5. Fink, A. (2003). *How to report on surveys*, 2nd ed. Thousand Oaks, CA: Sage, 35.

6. To properly cite your sources see *MLA Handbook for Writers of Research Papers*, 5th ed. (2001). New York: The Modern Language Association of America; or *Publication Manual of the American Psychological Association*, 5th ed. Washington, DC: The American Psychological Association.

7. Jameson, D. A. (June 1993). The ethics of plagiarism: how genre affects writers' use of source materials. *The Bulletin*, 2:18–27.

8. Imperiled copywrights, *New York Times* (April 15, 1998), A24.

9. *The American Heritage Dictionary of the English Language*, 4th ed. (2000). Boston: Houghton-Mifflin. Retrieved from **www.dictionary.com** on May 24, 2005.

10. *The American Heritage Dictionary of the English Language*, 4th ed. (2000). Boston: Houghton-Mifflin. Retrieved from **www.dictionary.com** on May 24, 2005. See "methodology."

11. Guffey, M. E. (2000). *Business communication: Process and product*, 3rd ed. Cincinnati: South-Western College Publishing, 103.

12. Tufte, E. R. (1983). *The Visual Display of Quantitative Information*. Cheshire, CT: Graphics Press.

13. Thomas, J. (2001, November). Executive excellence. *Marketing research*, 13:11–12.

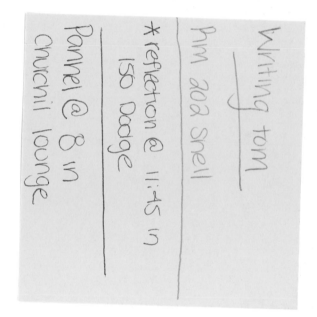

Credits

Chapter 1
Page 2 (Logo): Courtesy of Marketing Research Association.
Page 3 (Photo): Courtesy of Marketing Research Association.
Page 4: Courtesy of Marketing Research Association. Page 6 (Photo, left): Courtesy NewProductWorks, a division of the Arbor Strategy Group. Page 6 (Photo, right): Courtesy NewProductWorks, a division of the Arbor Strategy Group. Page 9 (Photo, top): By permission, Kimberly-Clark Worldwide Inc. Page 9 (Photo, bottom): By permission, Kimberly-Clark Worldwide Inc. Page 9 (Photo, bottom): By permission, Kimberly-Clark Worldwide Inc. Page 9 (Photo, bottom): By permission, Kimberly-Clark Worldwide Inc. Page 9 (Photo, bottom): By permission, Kimberly-Clark Worldwide Inc. Page 11 (Logo, top): By permission, MRSI. Page 11 (Ad, bottom): Courtesy of WebSurveyor Corporation. Page 12 (Logo): Courtesy of Burke, Inc.

Chapter 2
Page 22 (Logo): Courtesy of Carroll College. Page 23 (Photo): Courtesy of Carroll College. Page 26 (Photo): Courtesy of Carroll College. Page 30 (Photo): Courtesy of TLG Marketing Research. Page 31 (Logo): Courtesy of AC Nielsen. Page 32 (Logo): Courtesy of WebSurveyor Corporation. Page 34 (Logo, left): Courtesy of Survey Sampling International. Page 34 (Photo, right): Courtesy of Survey Sampling International. Page 35 (Photo): By permission, Mktg. Inc.

Chapter 3
Page 40 (Logo): Courtesy of Inside Research. Page 41 (Photo): Marketing Aid Center, Inc. Page 51 (Logo): Courtesy of InsightExpress®. Page 52 (Logo, top): Courtesy of Knowledge Networks. Page 52 (Logo, bottom): Courtesy of The PreTesting Company. Page 53 (Photo): Courtesy of Don E. Schultz, Professor; Page 57 (Photo): Courtesy of SDR Consulting. Page 57 (Logo): Courtesy of SDR Consulting. Page 59 (Photo): Courtesy of Stephen W. McDaniel, Professor. Page 60 (Ad): Courtesy of Marketing Research Association. Page 61 (Photo): Courtesy of Marketing Research Association. Page 62 (Logo): Courtesy of Burke Institute. Page 65 (Photo): Courtesy of Brian Dautch. Page 67 (Ad): Courtesy of ABACO Marketing Research – Brazil.

Chapter 4
Page 85 (Ad): Courtesy of Golf Digest Companies Research Resource Center. Page 88 (Photo): Courtesy of Lawrence D. Gibson. Page 93 (Photo): Courtesy of Burke, Inc. Page 101 (Photo): Courtesy of ABACO Marketing Research – Brazil. Page 102 (Ad): Courtesy of ABACO Marketing Research – Brazil.

Chapter 5
Page 115 (Photo): Eric Marder Associates/by permission, Lawrence D. Gibson. Page 118 (Photo): Courtesy of Holly McLennan. Page 119 (Photo): Courtesy of Holly McLennan. Page 121 (Photo): Courtesy of Opinion Suites. Page 122 (Ad, left): Courtesy of InsightExpress®. Page 122 (Ad, right): Courtesy of InsightExpress®. Page 124 (Ad, top): Courtesy of C&R Research/KidzEyes. Page 124 (Screen, bottom): By permission, University of West Florida and The Listener Group®. Page 131 (Ad, left): Courtesy of AC Nielsen. Page 131 (Line art, right): Courtesy of AC Nielsen. Page 138: Dave King © Dorling Kindersley.

Chapter 6
Page 145 (Screen): By permission, MarketResearch.com. Page 146 (Ad): Courtesy of Decision Analyst. Page 147 (Logo): Courtesy of Decision Analyst. Page 148 (Photo): Peter Jordan, REUTERS/Landov. Page 152 (Logo): By permission, MarketResearch.com. Page 156 (Photo): Dave King © Dorling Kindersley. Page 159 (Screen): Courtesy of ProQuest ABI Inform. Page 160 (Screen, top): Courtesy of ProQuest ABI Inform. Page 160 (Screen, bottom): Courtesy of ProQuest ABI Inform.

Chapter 7
Page 176 (Logo): By permission, ESRI Business Information Solutions (ESRI BIS). Page 177 (Map): By permission, ESRI Business Information Solutions (ESRI BIS). Page 182 (Line art, top): Courtesy of SRI Consulting Business Intelligence (SRI-BI). Page 182 (Line art, bottom): Courtesy of SRI Consulting Business Intelligence (SRI-BI). Page 183 (Ad): Courtesy of Claritas Inc. Page 184 (Logo): Courtesy of Claritas Inc. Page 187 (Maps): By permission, ESRI Business Information Solutions (ESRI BIS). Page 188 (Logo): By permission, SPINS.

SUBJECT INDEX